Technological Development and Impact on Economic and Environmental Sustainability

Yilmaz Bayar
Bandirma Onyedi Eylul University, Turkey

Mahmut Unsal Sasmaz
Usak University, Turkey

Omer Faruk Ozturk
Usak University, Turkey

IGI Global
PUBLISHER of TIMELY KNOWLEDGE

A volume in the Practice, Progress, and Proficiency in Sustainability (PPPS) Book Series

Published in the United States of America by
IGI Global
Engineering Science Reference (an imprint of IGI Global)
701 E. Chocolate Avenue
Hershey PA, USA 17033
Tel: 717-533-8845
Fax: 717-533-8661
E-mail: cust@igi-global.com
Web site: http://www.igi-global.com

Library of Congress Cataloging-in-Publication Data

Names: Bayar, Yilmaz, 1977- editor. | Sasmaz, Mahmut, 1986- editor. | Öztürk, Ömer, 1981- editor.
Title: Technological development and impact on economic and environmental sustainability / Yilmaz Bayar, Mahmut Sasmaz, and Ömer Öztürk, editors.
Description: Hershey PA : Engineering Science Reference, [2022] | Includes bibliographical references and index. | Summary: "The book investigates the technological development and its impact on economic and environmental sustainability in the world from an interdisciplinary perspective"-- Provided by publisher.
Identifiers: LCCN 2021058145 (print) | LCCN 2021058146 (ebook) | ISBN 9781799896487 (hardcover) | ISBN 9781799896494 (paperback) | ISBN 9781799896500 (ebook)
Subjects: LCSH: Technological innovations--Economic aspects. | Technological innovations--Environmental aspects. | Sustainable development--Technological innovations.
Classification: LCC HC79.T4 .T43112 2022 (print) | LCC HC79.T4 (ebook) | DDC 338/.064--dc23/eng/20220107
LC record available at https://lccn.loc.gov/2021058145
LC ebook record available at https://lccn.loc.gov/2021058146

This book is published in the IGI Global book series Practice, Progress, and Proficiency in Sustainability (PPPS) (ISSN: 2330-3271; eISSN: 2330-328X)

British Cataloguing in Publication Data
A Cataloguing in Publication record for this book is available from the British Library.

Practice, Progress, and Proficiency in Sustainability (PPPS) Book Series

Ayman Batisha
International Sustainability Institute, Egypt

ISSN:2330-3271
EISSN:2330-328X

Mission

In a world where traditional business practices are reconsidered and economic activity is performed in a global context, new areas of economic developments are recognized as the key enablers of wealth and income production. This knowledge of information technologies provides infrastructures, systems, and services towards sustainable development.

The **Practices, Progress, and Proficiency in Sustainability (PPPS) Book Series** focuses on the local and global challenges, business opportunities, and societal needs surrounding international collaboration and sustainable development of technology. This series brings together academics, researchers, entrepreneurs, policy makers and government officers aiming to contribute to the progress and proficiency in sustainability.

Coverage

- Technological learning
- Eco-Innovation
- Innovation Networks
- Global Content and Knowledge Repositories
- Intellectual Capital
- Socio-Economic
- Environmental informatics
- Sustainable Development
- Green Technology
- Knowledge clusters

IGI Global is currently accepting manuscripts for publication within this series. To submit a proposal for a volume in this series, please contact our Acquisition Editors at Acquisitions@igi-global.com or visit: http://www.igi-global.com/publish/.

The Practice, Progress, and Proficiency in Sustainability (PPPS) Book Series (ISSN 2330-3271) is published by IGI Global, 701 E. Chocolate Avenue, Hershey, PA 17033-1240, USA, www.igi-global.com. This series is composed of titles available for purchase individually; each title is edited to be contextually exclusive from any other title within the series. For pricing and ordering information please visit http://www.igi-global.com/book-series/practice-progress-proficiency-sustainability/73810. Postmaster: Send all address changes to above address.

Titles in this Series

For a list of additional titles in this series, please visit: www.igi-global.com/book-series/practice-progress-proficiency-sustainability/73810

Handbook of Research on Monitoring and Evaluating the Ecological Health of Wetlands
Ashok K. Rathoure (Akone Services, India)
Engineering Science Reference • © 2022 • 370pp • H/C (ISBN: 9781799894988) • US $295.00

Blockchain Technologies for Sustainable Development in Smart Cities
P. Swarnalatha (Vellore Institute of Technology, India) and S. Prabu (Vellore Institute of Technology, India)
Engineering Science Reference • © 2022 • 285pp • H/C (ISBN: 9781799892748) • US $215.00

Impacts of Climate Change and Economic and Health Crises on the Agriculture and Food Sectors
Vítor João Pereira Domingues Martinho (Polytechnic Institute of Viseu, Portugal)
Engineering Science Reference • © 2022 • 420pp • H/C (ISBN: 9781799895572) • US $195.00

Handbook of Research on Resource Management and the Struggle for Water Sustainability in Africa
Innocent Simphiwe Nojiyeza (University of Zululand, South Africa) Oliver Mtapuri (University of KwaZulu-Natal, South Africa) Prosper Bazaanah (University of Johannesburg, South Africa) and Edzisani Ellen Netshiozwi (Office of the Chief Justice, South Africa)
Engineering Science Reference • © 2022 • 437pp • H/C (ISBN: 9781799888093) • US $295.00

Innovative Strategic Planning and International Collaboration for the Mitigation of Global Crises
Gabriela Antošová (University College of Business in Prague, Czech Republic)
Information Science Reference • © 2022 • 327pp • H/C (ISBN: 9781799883395) • US $195.00

Handbook of Research on Changing Dynamics in Responsible and Sustainable Business in the Post-COVID-19 Era
Cristina Raluca Gh. Popescu (University of Bucharest, Romania & The Bucharest University of Economic Studies, Romania & The National Institute for Research and Development in Environmental Protection (INCDPM), Romania & National Research and Development Institute for Gas Turbines (COMOTI), Romania)
Business Science Reference • © 2022 • 512pp • H/C (ISBN: 9781668425237) • US $315.00

Achieving Sustainability Using Creativity, Innovation, and Education A Multidisciplinary Approach
Ziska Fields (University of Johannesburg, South Africa)
Information Science Reference • © 2022 • 260pp • H/C (ISBN: 9781799879633) • US $215.00

IGI Global
PUBLISHER of TIMELY KNOWLEDGE

701 East Chocolate Avenue, Hershey, PA 17033, USA
Tel: 717-533-8845 x100 • Fax: 717-533-8661
E-Mail: cust@igi-global.com • www.igi-global.com

EDITORIAL ADVISORY BOARD

Table of Contents

Detailed Table of Contents

The significant improvements have been achieved in information and communication technologies. Furthermore, use of information and communication technologies have been spread swiftly in the world with the contribution of globalization. The raising ICT penetration has led many social, economic, and environmental impacts for the countries. In this study, the interaction between ICT indicators and CO2 emissions was analyzed in sample of EU transition countries over the 1996-2018 period through causality analysis with cross-sectional dependency. The causality analysis revealed a unilateral causality from internet usage to CO2 emissions in Croatia, Czech Republic; a unilateral causality from mobile cellular subscriptions to CO2 emissions in panel and in Croatia, Estonia, Romania and Slovak Republic, and a unilateral causality from CO2 emissions to internet usage in Romania. In other words, the ICT had a significant impact on CO2 emissions.

Numerous studies on climate change have been conducted in different parts of the world, and many studies have examined the effect of changes in meteorological parameters on the performance of the energy sector. In this study, using the results of climate change calculations in the provinces of Iran, which are obtained from the microscale exponential method with a neural network, its effect on the performance of the energy production sector in the country's power plants in the next decade has been investigated. Calculations show that, on average, the efficiency of gas power plants decreases by about 0.6% for every 1oC increase in temperature. Also, the efficiency of heating and combined power plants decreases by about 0.5 and 0.4% on average. This chapter is aimed to use the P-index reliability index to study the climate change impacts on the thermal power plant performance.

Today, climate change due to global warming, extraordinary deterioration in the natural environment, and the melting of glaciers seriously threaten human health and existence. Cases such as forest fires and flood disasters, which have been seen frequently in the summer months, and the COVID-19 pandemic due to the melting of glaciers, seriously threaten humanity. Within the scope of this study, the measures taken by the enterprises for the relationship between environmental responsibility and environmental sustainability were examined. In this direction, the 2020 environmental sustainability reports of 15 companies operating in different sectors in Turkey and listed on the Istanbul Stock Exchange were examined. The absence of a similar study in the literature increases the originality of the study. It is expected that the studies planned for the future will contribute positively to the literature by deepening it further (for example, in different countries, comparisons in different cultures, practical studies).

Productiveness present in soil, productive weather conditions, plant growth information, rainfall in regional areas, and information on seed planting, among other things are significant parameters to consider for the development and improvement of Indian agriculture. All parameters can be gathered via IoT sensors and digital devices and stored in real-time database environments for sharing with digital machines. It aids farmers in obtaining information on all aspects of agriculture. Modern farming may be recorded using different sensors, smart digital cameras, and gadgets such as micro-chips thanks to the internet technology era. The automated technology provided by the internet of things (IoT) assists farmers in a variety of ways, including the most efficient use of resources (resources are finite) and agricultural problems.

As the environmental consequences of climate change continue to expand across international boundaries, many nations in the industrialized and developing world are struggling to find ways to cope with the onslaught of adverse social effects caused by this unprecedented phenomenon. Research spearheaded by environmental organizations such as the United Nations and other government-backed climate monitoring agencies suggests that the ecological disruptions caused by the dramatic shift in global weather patterns is one of the primary factors driving the escalation of mass migration and human population displacement in many parts of the civilized world. This chapter will examine the social, economic, and political issues associated with climate-induced migration in the United States and abroad. It will analyze how this phenomenon influences the development of climate policy capable of assisting vulnerable nations worldwide to implement strategic measures that will enable them to resolve the complex national security and border immigration issues associated with the climate crisis.

Economic growth is one of the goals of economic policy. The study analyzes the determinants of output for the BRICS-T country group during the period 1992-2019. The results of the analysis show that the inflation variable has no effect on output in the long run. Looking at the effects of other variables shows that all variables are statistically significant both in the short and long term. According to the results of the analysis, the most effective variable in the short run is the patent applications variable. In the study, openness variable and inflation variable were taken as explanatory variables to see the effect of macroeconomic policy intervention. The results of the analysis made with the pooled mean group method show that the variable that affects most the output is trade openness. Furthermore, it has been observed that the inflation variable included in the model as a macroeconomic policy variable has an effect on output in the short run but not in the long run.

The research and development (R&D) activities are some of the crucial factors affecting the economic growth through raising the technological development, resource base enlargement, and promotion in the capability of resource utilization. This study analyzed the mutual interplay between R&D investments and economic growth in a sample of the EU transition states by means of causality test. The consequences of causality analysis pointed out a unidirectional causality from R&D expenditures to economic growth in Slovenia and a unidirectional causality from economic growth to R&D expenditures at panel level and in Bulgaria, Croatia, Estonia, and Slovakia.

Technology creates a difference in production factors, methods, and products, and as a result of these differences increasing production and efficiency, it creates an increase in profit and competitive advantage. Technology is of great importance not only on the basis of companies or sectors, but also on the basis of countries. It also has an important role in determining the development and development levels of countries. For this reason, the use of appropriate technologies at appropriate times is also important in terms of national policies. In the globalizing world economy, technology is decisive for the competition among countries. Technological developments are of great importance as the driving force of growth, especially for emerging economies. The aim of this study is to determine the effect of technological developments on growth in emerging economies with the help of panel causality analysis. As a result of the analysis, one-way causality from technological development to economic growth was determined.

Due to the opportunities and conveniences it provides to human life, the use of new technologies is becoming more and more common in daily life, becoming indispensable. With the spread of technology, the increase in the number of people using technology has made it possible to produce new information that creates added value, thanks to the ability to easily access information all over the world to combine and analyze big data. The development of technology and the circulation of knowledge have become important elements of economic and social change. The aim of this study is to determine the effects of attitudes and behaviors towards new technologies on the performance for 450 academicians working in four research universities in Istanbul, for academics who are expected to have high compliance with innovative approaches. As a result of the structural equation model, a positive 38.4% increasing relationship was determined between the attitudes and behaviors towards new technologies and performance.

Innovation activities, which have been on a rapid increase, impact countries' degrees of development. Countries that are able to produce and export advanced technology are one step ahead of other countries in terms of international competition. For this reason, exports of high-tech products and related determining factors have become an issue that needs to be addressed. The aim of this study is to examine the determinants of high technology product exports between 2010-2020 for the BRICS-T developing country group using panel regression analysis. As a result of the analysis, GDP and R&D were specified as the most influential variables on exports of high-tech products. A GDP variable of 29.1%, R&D variable 28.9%, FDI variable 16.5%, EMP variable 13.5%, and finally, an ICT variable of 12.8% positively affect high technology product exports in terms of statistics. For developing countries, it is important to improve policies that increase income as well as achieve higher levels of R&D.

The relationship between economic growth, technological change, and institutions has been the subject of various theoretical evaluations. In this chapter, the relationship in question will be examined in the context of the systematics of thought of two great thinkers, J. A. Schumpeter and T. Veblen. In this study, evaluations are made by theoretically putting Schumpeter, who examines the effects of economic growth and institutional structure as the dominant factor of the change brought about by technological development, at one end of the spectrum and Veblen, who states that the structure of institutions and society is more dominant in technological change, on the other side.

This study aims to examine the impact of the COVID-19 pandemic on various agricultural commodity futures (cocoa, coffee, corn, cotton, soybean meal, soybeans, sugar, and wheat) in the United States for the period from January 24, 2020, to July 6, 2021, considering oil prices as a control variable. Specifically, the study employs a novel Fourier quantile causality test and its time-varying form. The results show that the causal relationships between COVID-19 cases and agricultural commodity futures are highly time-varying. The empirical findings also demonstrate that COVID-19 has the strongest causal effect on coffee futures, followed by sugar, soybeans, and corn. In contrast, the impact of COVID-19 on cocoa and cotton futures is relatively limited. The causal effect of COVID-19 on agricultural futures is more pronounced at lower quantiles and in the spring and summer months. In general, COVID-19 has significant predictive power for the six agricultural commodity futures over 100 days in the analysis period, with the exception of cocoa and cotton.

Chapter 16
Secure Smart Grid Management Maturity Within Big Data 221
Zühre Aydın Yenioğlu, Energy Market Regulatory Authority, Turkey
Vildan Ateş, Ankara Yıldırım Beyazıt University, Turkey

Smart energy systems of smart energy grid and meters are effective on operational processes and regulations in terms of security, continuity, and remote effective management. For a better development of smart grid, in which the data volume and complexity increases rapidly, smart energy management security plans should be implemented for efficiency and reliability of the network. Big data in energy systems plays an important role both in assessing the capacity needed and in making smarter investments to manage energy demand and supply. In this chapter, a novel secure smart energy management maturity model is presented in the context of capacity planning, demand forecasting, predictive maintenance, software optimization, network optimization, detecting and preventing threats, disaster recovery, and business intelligence and data visualization on which security criterias should be considered, planned, and managed for smart grids including big data. Relevant international big data and smart grid standards have been proposed for security, continuity, and performance in smart networks.

Chapter 17
The Transformation Framework: The Role of Artificial Intelligence for Military Strategies (RAI4MS) 245
Antoine Trad, IBISTM, France

It is known that geopolitical knowledge, conflicts, wars, and military investments are the backbone for flourishing global economies' evolution, stagnation, or failure. Military and defence organizations are those who drive major intelligence-based technology transformation and innovation trends. Countries, military environments, and organizations (or simply entities) are increasingly using complex and intelligent technologies, like artificial intelligence (AI). One of the most complex military tasks and geopolitical risks is using AI to balance and coordinate in real-time the following military technology artefacts: autonomous and fixed objects, financial and resources capabilities, combative and morale statuses, mass management, information technology and data, developing military scenarios, evolution of demography, and others. Therefore, the stability and evolution of an entity depends on the role of artificial intelligence for military strategies (RAI4MS).

Preface

The global population, production and consumption has considerably increased in the world and in turn led a significant environmental degradation mainly resulting from non-renewable energy use. Furthermore, high dependence on non-renewable energy poses a serious risk for sustainable economic growth. In this context, technological development, one of the key factors underlying the economic growth and the added value of the products, may be a remedy to the concerns about economic and environmental sustainability through increasing the labor productivity and energy efficiency, and environmentally friendly technologies. Therefore, countries attach a great importance to technology development for sustainable economic growth and environment sustainability. This investigates the impact of economic and environmental impacts of technological development from a multidisciplinary perspective.

Chapter 1 investigates the mutual interaction between indicators of information and communication technologies and CO_2 emissions in sample of the European Union transition members through causality analysis and uncovers that information and communication technologies are significant determinants of CO_2 emissions. On the other hand, Chapter 2 analyzes the effect of climate change on performance of the thermal power plants in the provinces of Iran and reveals that temperature increases negatively affects the power plants.

Chapter 3 examines the relationship between environmental responsibility and environmental sustainability in 15 Turkish companies operating in different sectors and listed on the Borsa Istanbul Stock Exchange and discovers that environmental responsibility is important factor for the environmental sustainability. On the other hand, Chapter 4 focuses on use of Internet of Things in agriculture in modernization of farming. In Chapter 5, the author explores the social, economic, and political issues associated with climate-induced migration in the United States and abroad and analyzes how this phenomenon influences the development of climate policy capable of assisting vulnerable nations worldwide to implement strategic measures that will enable them to resolve the complex national security and border immigration issues associated with the climate crisis.

Chapter 6 investigates the determinants of output in BRICS-T economies through pooled mean group estimator and reveals that economic growth, gross capital fixed formation, labor, trade openness, and patent applications are signigificant determinants of output in short and long run and the patent applications variable is found to be the most effective factor of ouput in the short run. Chapter 7 examines the causality between research and development expenditures and economic growth in sample of the EU transition economies and finds that economic growth has a significant effect on research and development expenditures. In Chapter 8, the author examines the interaction between technological development and economic growth in sample of emerging market economies and reveals the technological development as a significant determinant of economic growth.

Chapter 9 explores the effects of attitudes and behaviors towards new technologies on performance for 450 academicians studying in four research universities in Istanbul by means of structural equation model and discovers a positive relationship between attitudes and behaviors towards new technologies and performance. In Chapter 10, the author investigates the determinants of high-tech product export in BRICS-T countries through regression analysis and gross domestic product, qualified employment, foreign direct investment, research and development expenditures, and information and communication technologies are found to be significant factors underlying exports of high-tech products.

Chapter 11 examines the relationship between technological change and economic growth from the perspective of institutional economics. The research is conducted in the context of the thoughts by Thorstein Veblen and Joseph Alois Schumpeter. In Chapter 12, the authors examined the relationship between R&D incentives and innovation in 81 provinces of Turkey and reveal that 81 provinces are divided into five clusters. Chapter 13 explores the augmented reality technology and use of augmented reality technology in marketing strategies. On the other hand, Chapter 14 researches the possible tactics and strategies for sustainable tourism in crisis periods such as Covid-19.

In Chapter 15, the authors investigate the impact of the COVID-19 pandemic on various agricultural commodity futures cocoa, coffee, corn, cotton, soybean meal, soybeans, sugar, and wheat) by means of Fourier quantile causality test and its time-varying form and reveal that the causal relationships between COVID-19 cases and agricultural commodity futures are highly time-varying. Chapter 16 presents a novel secure smart energy management maturity model in the context of, capacity planning, demand forecasting, predictive maintenance, software optimization, network optimization, detecting and preventing threats, disaster recovery and business intelligence and data visualization on which security criteria should be considered, planned and managed for smart grids including big data. Chapters 17 and 18 respectively examine the role of artificial intelligence for military strategies and enterprise holistic security risk management

Yilmaz Bayar
Bandirma Onyedi Eylül University, Turkey

Chapter 1
Impact of Information and Communication Technology on CO2 Emissions:
Evidence From EU Transition Economies

Aysun Karamikli
https://orcid.org/0000-0002-8744-7977
Bandirma Onyedi Eylul University, Turkey

Yilmaz Bayar
https://orcid.org/0000-0002-6776-6524
Bandirma Onyedi Eylul University, Turkey

ABSTRACT

The significant improvements have been achieved in information and communication technologies. Furthermore, use of information and communication technologies have been spread swiftly in the world with the contribution of globalization. The raising ICT penetration has led many social, economic, and environmental impacts for the countries. In this study, the interaction between ICT indicators and CO_2 emissions was analyzed in sample of EU transition countries over the 1996-2018 period through causality analysis with cross-sectional dependency. The causality analysis revealed a unilateral causality from internet usage to CO_2 emissions in Croatia, Czech Republic; a unilateral causality from mobile cellular subscriptions to CO_2 emissions in panel and in Croatia, Estonia, Romania and Slovak Republic, and a unilateral causality from CO_2 emissions to internet usage in Romania. In other words, the ICT had a significant impact on CO_2 emissions.

INTRODUCTION

The information is accepted as a main production factor in context of the new growth theories and has become a significant determinant of economic growth. The information and communications technolo-

DOI: 10.4018/978-1-7998-9648-7.ch001

gies (ICT) include all the technologies which allow the individuals, firms and institutions to interact in the digital world. Therefore, ICT includes telecommunications, media broadcasts, intelligent building management systems, audiovisual activities, communication systems, and all technologies employed to process network-based control and monitoring functions (EuropeYou Asociación, 2020). All the technologies including computers and communication technologies for data collection, storage and processing, data transcription to the users are called as the information technology (Tonta, 1999). The ICT enables us to easily access to the information anywhere in the world without waste of time through communication instruments and in turn the information may spread quickly in the world. The aforementioned positive externality of the ICT can also make a contribution to human and physical capital and in turn economic growth. The considerable improvements at ICT and the raising role of the ICT in the world increased the development in every part of societies (Gries et al., 2017).

The change in production structure in the world together with the industrialization, energy dependence in production and considerable increases in fossil fuel consumption accompanied the environmental problems (Li et al., 2019). Many countries, especially the developed countries, have given priority to the decreasing the negative environmental effects of the human beings, resource conservation, and green energy. In this context, the ICT has become an important factor for environmental protection and sustainable development towards a low carbon economy as of 2000s (Klimova et al., 2016). The carbon emissions can be reduced by expanding the use of energy-saving or energy-efficient technologies such as ICT (Shahnazi and Shabani, 2019). The development of ICT for remote detection, measurement and observation of the factors polluting the environment can decrease the carbon emissions through raising the environment quality (Asongu et al., 2018: Berkhout and Hertin, 2001). Therefore, e-commerce, e-government, e-shopping, e-banking, virtual learning, and virtual meetings are generally expected to decrease the CO_2 emissions (Jorgenson, 2001; Toffel and Horvath, 2004; Schmidt and Kløverpris, 2009).

The ICT industry has a significant role in the productive and low carbon development. The use of smart ICT systems is suggested to develop the environmental monitoring and decrease the environmental pollution and carbon emissions. Furthermore, the ICT has a significant role in reducing the greenhouse gas emissions and modern ICT can be used to transit the high productive and low carbon markets (GeSI, 2008).

Transition from the industrial society to the information society occurred together with the rapid developments in technology and the diffusion of advanced technologies in human life. The information society is a social phenomenon which reflects the use of information in all economic, socio-cultural, political, and technological dimensions of the society (Yeşilorman and Koç, 2014). Therefore, the developments in scientific and technological fields can lead the changes in manufacturing type and environment. This study aims to analyze the causality between ICT indicators and CO_2 emissions in EU transition members over the 1996-2018 periodn. The study targets to make a contribution to the relevant literature considering the limited related literature. Furthermore, the study will be the one of the first studies analyzing the interaction between ICT and CO_2 emissions in sample of EU transition economies. The next section presents a literature summary, and then data and method are described. Then empirical analysis is conducted and findings are discussed. The study is concluded with Conclusions.

LITERATURE REVIEW

The considerable improvements in ICT development and penetration have caused the scholars to empirically analyze the economic and environmental effects of ICT development and penetration. The studies analyzing the interaction between ICT and CO_2 emissions can be classified under two groups. The first group studies suggest that the ICT makes a positive contribution to the environmental quality through decreasing the CO_2 emissions via improvements in the energy efficiency (e.g. see Al-Mulali et al., 2015; Zang and Liu, 2015; Asongu, 2018; Lu, 2018; Haseeb et al., 2019; Nguyen et al., 2020; Ulucak and Khan, 2020). On the other side, the second group studies suggest that the ICT harms the environment through raising the CO_2 emissions (Lee and Brahmasren, 2014; Salahuddin et al., 2016; Park et al., 2018; Tsaurai and Chimbo, 2019; Zhou et al., 2019; Raheem et al., 2020). Furthermore, some scholars have revealed an inverted U interaction between ICT and CO_2 emissions (Higon et al., 2017). Lastly, some scholars have revealed that the ICT development did not have a significant impact on the CO_2 emissions (Al-Mulali et al., 2015; Amri et al., 2019)

In the studies reaching a negative effect of the ICT on the CO_2 emissions, Al-Mulali et al. (2015) explored the impact of internet retailing on CO_2 emissions in 77 developed and developing economies over the 2000-2013 period through regression analysis and revealed a negative effect of internet retailing on CO_2 emissions. However, internet retailing had a negative impact on CO_2 emissions in the developed economies, but did not have a significant impact in the developing economies. On the other side, Zhang and Liu (2015) researched the impact of ICT on CO_2 emissions in 29 Chinese provinces over the 2000-2010 period and revealed a negative effect of ICT on CO_2 emissions, but the impact was greater in the central region than that in the eastern region and insignificant in the western region of China.

Asongu (2018) analyzed the effect of ICT on the CO_2 emissions in 44 countries from Sub-Saharan Africa over the 2000-2012 period through dynamic regression analysis and disclosed a negative impact of ICT development on the CO_2 emissions. Lu (2018) also analyzed the effect of ICT on CO_2 emissions in 12 Asian economies (Australia, China, Hong Kong, Japan, India, Indonesia, South Korea, Malaysia, Philippines, Singapore, Thailand and Turkey) over the 1993-2013 duration through cointegration analysis and discovered a significant decreasing effect of ICT on CO_2 emissions. Haseeb et al. (2019) explored the effect of internet usage and mobile cellular subscriptions on environmental quality in BRICS economies over the 1994-2014 period through Westerlund cointegration and Granger causality tests and reached that both internet usage and mobile cellular subscriptions made a significant contribution to the environmental quality.

Nguyen et al. (2020) researched the interaction among ICT, economic growth, and CO_2 emissions in selected 13 economies from G-20 countries over the 2000-2014 period through FMOLS and panel quantile regression and found a negative effect of ICT on CO_2 emissions. Ulucak and Khan (2020) also researched the effect of ICT on CO_2 emissions in BRICS economies over the 1990-2015 duration through Westerlund-Durbin-Hausman (2008) cointegration test and Dumitrescu and Hurlin (2012) causality test and revealed that ICT decreased the CO_2 emissions.

In the studies revealing a positive effect of ICT on CO_2 emissions, Lee and Brahmasren (2014) explored the effect of ICT on CO_2 emissions in 9 ASEAN (Association of Southeast Asian Nations) economies during the 1991-2009 period through cointegration analysis and revealed that ICT development raised the CO_2 emissions. On the other side, Salahuddin et al. (2016) explored the effect of internet usage and economic growth on CO_2 emissions in OECD states over the 1991-2012 duration through Pedroni cointegration analysis and revealed a positive interaction between ICT and CO_2 emissions. Park et al.

(2018) explored the effect of ICT, financial development, economic growth, and trade openness on CO_2 emissions in selected EU members over the 2001-2014 duration through cointegration and causality analysis and disclosed a unilateral causality from internet usage to CO_2 emissions and positive effect of ICT on CO_2 emissions.

Tsaurai and Chimbo (2019) investigated the relationship between ICT and CO_2 emissions in developing countries over the 1994-2014 period through regression analysis and discovered that ICT raised the CO_2 emissions. Zhou et al. (2019) researched the relationship between ICT and CO_2 emissions in China over the 2002-2012 duration through input-output analysis and reached that ICT raised the CO_2 emissions. Raheem et al. (2020) explored the effect of ICT and financial development on CO_2 emissions in G7 economies over the 1990-2014 period through cointegration analysis and revealed a positive impact of ICT on CO_2 emissions.

In another study, Higon et al. (2017) researched the relationship between ICT and CO_2 emissions in 26 developed and 116 developing economies over the 1995-2010 duration and revealed an inverse U interaction between ICT and CO_2 emissions. On the other side, Amri et al. (2019) explored the relationship between ICT and CO_2 emissions in Tunisia over the 1975-2014 period through ARDL approach and revealed an insignificant relationship between ICT and CO_2 emissions. Shabani (2019) researched the relationship between ICT and CO_2 emissions in Iran over the 2002-2013 duration and revealed a positive effect of ICT on CO_2 emissions in industrial sector and a negative effect of ICT on CO_2 emissions in transportation and service sectors. Furthermore, a bilateral causality between ICT and CO_2 emissions in industrial and transportation sectors and a unilateral causality from ICT to CO_2 emissions in service sector was discovered.

Altinoz et al. (2020) explored the effect of internet usage, fixed broadband subscriptions, and mobile cellular subscriptions on CO_2 emissions in China, India, Mexico, Brazil, Turkey, Thailand, South Africa, Malaysia, Russia and Indonesia over the 1995-2014 duration through PVAR model and revealed that mobile cellular subscriptions decreased the CO_2 emissions, but internet usage and fixed broadband subscriptions raised the CO_2 emissions. Furthermore, their causality analysis also revealed a bilateral causality between ICT indicators and CO_2 emissions.

DATA AND ECONOMETRIC METHODOLOGY

In the study, the causal interaction between CO_2 emissions and ICT indicators in EU transition members over the 1996-2018 duration was explored through Emirmahmutoglu and Kose (2011) causality test. The CO_2 emissions was proxied by CO_2 emissions in terms of metric tons per capita and ICT was represented by individuals using the internet and mobile cellular subscriptions. All the series are annual and obtained from World Bank databases.

The study sample includes 11 EU states (Bulgaria, Croatia, Czech Republic, Estonia, Hungary, Latvia, Lithuania, Poland, Romania, Slovakia, and Slovenia). The study covered the 1996-2018 duration, because CO_2 emissions existed for the 1996-2018 duration. The empirical analyses were conducted by means of Stata 14.0 and EViews 10.0

The causality between CO_2 emissions and ICT indicators was checked by Emirmahmutoglu and Kose (2011) causality test in view of cross-sectional and heterogeneity's presence among the variables. The Emirmahmutoglu and Kose (2011) causality test is the developed version of Toda-Yamamoto (1995) causality test for the heterogeneous panels and regards the existence of cross-sectional dependence and

Table 1. Dataset description

Variables	Variable Description	Data Source
CO	CO_2 emissions (metric tons per capita)	World Bank (2021a)
INTERNET	Individuals using the Internet (% of population)	World Bank (2021b)
MOBILE	Mobile cellular subscriptions (per 100 people)	World Bank (2021c)

Table 2. Cross-sectional dependence tests' results

Test	Test Statistic	Prob.
LM	294.6	0.0000
LM CD*	14.12	0.0000
LM adj*	55.03	0.0000

*two-sided test

heterogeneity. Therefore, the series should not be required to be stationary (Emirmahmutoglu and Kose, 2011). Furthermore, Emirmahmutoglu and Kose (2011) causality test allows the lag length to differentiate for each cross-section and decreases the long-term information loss because it models the series with level values (Emirmahmutoglu and Kose, 2011; Toda and Yamamato, 1995).

EMPIRICAL ANALYSIS

In the empirical analysis section, first heterogeneity and cross-sectional dependency of the series were examined. Breusch and Pagan (1980) LM test, Pesaran (2004) LM CD test, and Pesaran et al. (2008) LM adj. test were employed to check the existence of cross-sectional dependency. The findings of the aforementioned cross-sectional dependency tests were displayed in Table 2. The test findings indicated that there existed a cross-sectional dependency among the series.

Then, Pesaran and Yamagata (2008) homogeneity tests were employed to test the slope homogeneity of the panel. The findings of the tests displayed in Table 3 revealed that there existed heterogeneity in the panel dataset. The results of both heterogeneity and cross-sectional dependency tests directed us to use a panel causality test considering cross-sectional dependency and heterogeneity.

The stationarity of the series employed in the empirical analysis was checked by Pesaran (2007) CIPS (Cross-sectionally augmented IPS (Im- Pesaran-Shin, 2003) unit root test regarding the existence

Table 3. Homogeneity tests' results

Test	Test Statistic	Prob.
$\tilde{\Delta}_{adj.}$	12.091	0.000
$\tilde{\Delta}$	10.989	0.000

Table 4. Results of CIPS panel unit root test

Variables	Level		1. level	
	Constant	Constant + Trend	Constant	Constant + Trend
LNCO	2.061	-1.277	-7.158***	-5.889***
LNINTERNET	-4.403***	-3.708***	-8.247***	-6.921***
LNMOBILE	-6.588***	-4.511***	-6.399***	-5.335***

*** indicated that it is significant at 1% significance level.

of cross-sectional dependence among three variables. The unit root test results were displayed in Table 4. The unit root analysis indicated that LNCO was I (1), but LNINTERNET and LNMOBILE was I(0).

The causal relationship between ICT indicators and CO_2 emissions was investigated through Emirmahmutoglu and Kose (2011) causality test regarding the presence of heterogeneity and cross-sectional dependency and causality test findings were presented in Table 5 and 6. The causality analysis revealed a one-way significant causality from internet usage to CO_2 emissions in Croatia, Czech Republic and a one-way causality from CO_2 emissions to internet usage in Romania.

On the other side, the causality analysis between LNCO and LNMOBILE revealed a unilateral causality from mobile cellular subscriptions to CO_2 emissions in panel and in Croatia, Estonia, Romania and Slovak Republic.

The causality analysis revealed a unilateral causality from internet usage to the CO_2 emissions in Croatia and Czech Republic and a unilateral causality from mobile cellular subscription to the CO_2 emissions in Croatia, Estonia, Romania, and Slovak Republic. So, the causality analysis revealed a significant effect of ICT indicators on CO_2 emissions in compatible with the theoretical considerations and empirical findings by Park et al. (2018) and Shahnazi and Shabani (2019).

Table 5. Results of causality analysis between LNCO and LNINTERNET

Countries	LNINTERNET ↛ LNCO		LNCO↛ LNINTERNET	
	Test statistic	P value	Test statistic	P value
Bulgaria	0.357	0.550	0.004	0.948
Croatia	**2.730**	**0.098**	0.005	0.944
Czech Republic	**6.421**	**0.011**	0.005	0.944
Estonia	3.769	0.152	0.175	0.916
Hungary	0.154	0.926	1.881	0.391
Latvia	1.604	0.448	2.551	0.279
Lithuania	1.401	0.496	1.061	0.588
Poland	2.763	0.251	1.468	0.480
Romania	3.059	0.217	**9.376**	**0.009**
Slovak Republic	0.360	0.835	1.154	0.562
Slovenia	0.225	0.635	0.182	0.670
Panel	28.818	0.150	18.805	0.657

Table 6. Results of causality analysis between LNCO and LNMOBILE

Countries	LNMOBILE ↛ LNCO		LNCO↛ LNMOBILE	
	Test statistic	P value	Test statistic	P value
Bulgaria	0.469	0.493	0.002	0.964
Croatia	**11.377**	**0.003**	0.632	0.729
Czech Republic	1.392	0.238	0.303	0.582
Estonia	**3.795**	**0.051**	0.023	0.878
Hungary	0.881	0.644	0.907	0.635
Latvia	0.215	0.643	0.560	0.454
Lithuania	2.008	0.366	2.239	0.326
Poland	4.292	0.117	1.779	0.411
Romania	**8.203**	**0.017**	3.015	0.222
Slovak Republic	**4.851**	**0.088**	1.222	0.543
Slovenia	0.010	0.922	0.504	0.478
Panel	**42.877**	**0.005**	14.266	0.892

CONCLUSION

In the present information age, all communication devices such as the internet, television, mobile phone and computers which help us to easily access, store and transmit information are the information and communication technologies. The rapid technological developments and the fast penetration of the advanced technologies to human life with the help of globalization led the transition from the industrial society to the information society in the world. The scientific and technological developments can cause the changes in the social structure, production style and environmental changes in the world. Therefore, the information and communication technologies can lead economic and environmental impacts.

The industrialization, urbanization, and global population growth have led the environmental problems and the countries overcome the environmental problems through use of renewable energy and advanced green information technologies producing less CO_2 emissions. In this study, we explored the interaction between ICT indicators and CO_2 emissions in the EU transition economies over the 1996-2018 period through Emirmahmutoğlu and Köse (2011) causality test with cross-sectional dependence. The causality analysis revealed a unidirectional causality from internet usage to CO_2 emissions in Croatia and Czech Republic, and a unidirectional causality from CO_2 emissions to internet usage in Romania. On the other hand, a unilateral causality from mobile cellular subscriptions to CO_2 emissions in Croatia, Estonia, Romania and the Slovak Republic was reached.

The information and communication technologies can make a contribution to environmental quality through increasing the energy efficiency. The services such as e-signature, e-invoice, and e-banking facilitating the production processes, e-books to printed books, e-mail to mail, and electronic paper to newspaper provided by ICT can minimize the waste and save the energy. Furthermore, the development of smart transportation systems and smart home can help us to increase the energy efficiency and in turn reduce the carbon emissions. However, the continuous increases in expectations for technological development can direct the firms to develop the new products and it can cause the technological pollution and environmental destruction. In this context, green information technologies and technologies with clean energy sources are important in combat with environmental problems.

REFERENCES

Al-Mulali, U., Sheau-Ting, L., & Ozturk, I. (2015). The global move toward internet shopping and it's influence on pollution: An empirical analysis. *Environmental Science and Pollution Research International*, *22*(13), 9717–9727. doi:10.100711356-015-4142-2 PMID:25631741

Altinoz, B., Vasbieva, D., & Kalugina, O. (2020). The effect of information and communication technologies and total factor productivity on co2 emissions in top 10 emerging market economies. *Environmental Science and Pollution Research International*. Advance online publication. doi:10.100711356-020-11630-1 PMID:33201509

Amri, F., Zaied, Y. B., & Lahouel, B. B. (2019). ICT, total factor productivity, and carbon dioxide emissions in Tunisia. *Technological Forecasting and Social Change*, *146*, 212–217. doi:10.1016/j.techfore.2019.05.028

Asongu, S. A. (2018). ICT, openness and CO2 emissions in Africa. *Environmental Science and Pollution Research International*, *25*(10), 9351–9359. doi:10.100711356-018-1239-4 PMID:29349735

Berkhout, F., & Hertin, J. (2001). *Impacts of ınformation and communication technologies on environmental sustainability: Speculations and evidence*. Report to the OECD. https://www.oecd.org/sti/inno/1897156.pdf

Breusch, T. S., & Pagan, A. R. (1980). The lagrange multiplier test and its applications to model specification in econometrics. *The Review of Economic Studies*, *47*(1), 239–253. doi:10.2307/2297111

Dehghan Shabani, Z., & Shahnazi, R. (2019). Energy consumption, carbon dioxide emissions, information and communications technology, and gross domestic product in Iranian economic sectors: A panel causality analysis. *Energy*, *169*, 1064–1078. doi:10.1016/j.energy.2018.11.062

Emirmahmutoglu, F., & Kose, N. (2011). Testing for granger causality in heterogeneous mixed panels. *Economic Modelling*, *28*(3), 870–876. doi:10.1016/j.econmod.2010.10.018

EuropeYou Asociación. (2020). *What is Information and Communication Technology?* https://europeyou.eu/es/what-is-informationand-communication-technology

GeSI. (2008). SMART 2020: Enabling The Low Carbon Economy In *The İnformation Age*. The Climate Group on behalf of the Global eSustainability Initiative (GeSI). https://gesi.org/research/download/7

Gries, T., Grundmann, R., Palnau, I., & Redlin, M. (2017). Innovations, growth and participation in advanced economies-a review of major concepts and findings. *International Economics and Economic Policy*, *14*(2), 293–351. doi:10.100710368-016-0371-1

Haseeb, A., Xia, E., Saud, S., Ahmad, A., & Khurshid, H. (2019). Does information and communication technologies improve environmental quality in the era of globalization? an empirical analysis. *Environmental Science and Pollution Research International*, *26*(9), 8594–8608. doi:10.100711356-019-04296-x PMID:30710332

Higon, D. A., Gholami, R., & Shirazi, F. (2017). ICT and environmental sustainability: A global perspective. *Telematics and Informatics*, *34*(4), 85–95. doi:10.1016/j.tele.2017.01.001

Im, K. S., Pesaran, M. H., & Shin, Y. (2003). Testing for unit roots in heterogeneous panels. *Journal of Econometrics*, *115*(1), 53–74. doi:10.1016/S0304-4076(03)00092-7

Jorgenson, D. W. (2001). Information technology and the US economy. *The American Economic Review*, *91*(1), 1–32. doi:10.1257/aer.91.1.1

Klimova, A., Rondeau, E., Andersson, K., Porras, J., Rybin, A., & Zaslavsky, A. (2016). An international Master's program in green ICT as a contribution to sustainable development. *Journal of Cleaner Production*, *135*, 223–239. doi:10.1016/j.jclepro.2016.06.032

Lee, J. W., & Brahmasrene, T. (2014). ICT, CO2 emissions and economic growth: Evidence from a panel of ASEAN. *Global Economic Review*, *43*(2), 93–109. doi:10.1080/1226508X.2014.917803

Li, S., Deng, H., & Zhang, K. (2019). The İmpact Of Economy On Carbon Emissions: An Empirical Study Based On The Synergistic Effect Of Gender Factors. *International Journal of Environmental Research and Public Health*, *16*(19), 2–16. doi:10.3390/ijerph16193723 PMID:31581715

Lu, W. C. (2018). The impacts of information and communication technology, energy consumption, financial development, and economic growth on carbon dioxide emissions in 12 Asian countries. *Mitigation and Adaptation Strategies for Global Change*, *23*(1), 1351–1365. doi:10.100711027-018-9787-y

Nguyen, T. T., Pham, T. A. T., & Tram, H. T. X. (2020). Role of information and communication technologies and innovation in driving carbon emissions and economic growth in selected G-20 countries. *Journal of Environmental Management*, *1*(261), 110162. doi:10.1016/j.jenvman.2020.110162 PMID:32148259

Park, Y., Meng, F., & Baloch, M. A. (2018). The effect of ICT, financial development, growth, and trade openness on CO 2 emissions: An empirical analysis. *Environmental Science and Pollution Research International*, *25*(30), 30708–30719. doi:10.100711356-018-3108-6 PMID:30178410

Pesaran, M. H. (2004). *General diagnostic tests for cross section dependence in panels* (CESifo Working Paper No. 1229). Academic Press.

Pesaran, M. H. (2007). A simple panel unit root test in the presence of cross-section dependence. *Journal of Applied Econometrics*, *22*(2), 265–312. doi:10.1002/jae.951

Pesaran, M. H., Ullah, A., & Yamagata, T. (2008). A bias-adjusted LM test of error cross-section independence. *The Econometrics Journal*, *11*(1), 105–127. doi:10.1111/j.1368-423X.2007.00227.x

Pesaran, M. H., & Yamagata, T. (2008). Testing slope homogeneity in large panels. *Journal of Econometrics*, *142*(1), 50–93. doi:10.1016/j.jeconom.2007.05.010

Raheem, I. D., Tiwari, A. K., & Balsalobre-Lorente, D. (2020). The role of ICT and financial development in CO 2 emissions and economic growth. *Environmental Science and Pollution Research International, 27*(2), 1912–1922. doi:10.100711356-019-06590-0 PMID:31760620

Salahuddin, M., Alam, K., & Ozturk, I. (2016). The effects of Internet usage and economic growth on CO2 emissions in OECD countries: A panel investigation. *Renewable & Sustainable Energy Reviews, 62*, 1226–1235. doi:10.1016/j.rser.2016.04.018

Schmidt, A., & Kløverpris, N. H. (2009). *Environmental impacts from digital solutions as an alternative to conventional paper-based solutions final report*. FORCE Technology, Applied Environmental Assessment. http://seeds4green.net/sites/default/files/e-Boks_LCA.pdf

Toda, H. Y., & Yamamoto, T. (1995). Statistical inference in vector autoregressions with possibly integrated processes. *Journal of Econometrics*, *66*(1-2), 225–250. doi:10.1016/0304-4076(94)01616-8

Toffel, M. W., & Horvath, A. (2004). Environmental Implications Of Wireless Technologies: News Delivery and Business Meetings. *Environmental Science & Technology*, *38*(11), 2961–2970. doi:10.1021/es035035o PMID:15224723

Tonta, Y. (1999). Bilgi Toplumu ve Bilgi Teknolojisi. *Türk Kütüphaneciliği*, *13*(4), 363-375. http://www.tk.org.tr/index.php/TK/article/view/910/904

Tsaurai, K., & Chimbo, B. (2019). The impact of information and communication technology on carbon emissions in emerging markets. *International Journal of Energy Economics and Policy*, *9*(4), 320–326. doi:10.32479/ijeep.7677

Ulucak, R., & Khan, S. U. D. (2020). Does information and communication technology affect CO2 mitigation under the pathway of sustainable development during the mode of globalization? *Sustainable Development*, *28*(4), 857–867. doi:10.1002d.2041

World Bank. (2021a). *CO2 emissions (metric tons per capita)*. https://data.worldbank.org/indicator/EN.ATM.CO2E.PC

World Bank. (2021b). *Individuals using the Internet (% of population)*. https://data.worldbank.org/indicator/IT.NET.USER.ZS

World Bank. (2021c). *Mobile cellular subscriptions (per 100 people)*. https://data.worldbank.org/indicator/IT.CEL.SETS.P2

Yeşilorman, M., & Firdevs, K. O. Ç. (2014). Bilgi toplumunun teknolojik temelleri üzerine eleştirel bir bakış. *Fırat Üniversitesi Sosyal Bilimler Dergisi*, *24*(1), 117–133. doi:10.18069/fusbed.72486

Zhang, C., & Liu, C. (2015). The impact of ICT industry on CO_2 emissions: A regional analysis in China. *Renewable & Sustainable Energy Reviews*, *44*, 12–19. doi:10.1016/j.rser.2014.12.011

Zhou, X., Zhou, D., Wang, Q., & Su, B. (2019). How information and communication technology drives carbon emissions: a sector-level analysis for China. *Energy Economics, 81*(C), 380-392. doi:10.1016/j.eneco.2019.04.014

ADDITIONAL READING

Mirza, F. M., Ansar, S., Ullah, K., & Maqsood, F. (2020). The impact of information and communication technologies, CO 2 emissions, and energy consumption on inclusive development in developing countries. *Environmental Science and Pollution Research International*, *27*(3), 3143–3155. doi:10.100711356-019-07131-5 PMID:31836991

Moyer, J. D., & Hughes, B. B. (2012). ICTs: Do they contribute to increased carbon emissions? *Technological Forecasting and Social Change*, *79*(5), 919–931. doi:10.1016/j.techfore.2011.12.005

Stewart, K. (2015). Assessing the carbon impact of ICT measures: A case study investigation using Latis model. *International Journal of Transportation Science and Technology*, *4*(3), 277–294. doi:10.1260/2046-0430.4.3.277

Ullah, S., Ozturk, I., Majeed, M. T., & Ahmad, W. (2021). Do technological innovations have symmetric or asymmetric effects on environmental quality? Evidence from Pakistan. *Journal of Cleaner Production*, *316*, 128239. doi:10.1016/j.jclepro.2021.128239

Usman, A., Ozturk, I., Ullah, S., & Hassan, A. (2021). Does ICT have symmetric or asymmetric effects on CO2 emissions? Evidence from selected Asian economies. *Technology in Society*, *67*, 101692. doi:10.1016/j.techsoc.2021.101692

Chapter 2
Assessing Climate Change and Predicting Its Effect on Efficiency and Heat Rate of Thermal Power Plants in 2050

Nima Norouzi
https://orcid.org/0000-0002-2546-4288
Bournemouth University, UK

ABSTRACT

Numerous studies on climate change have been conducted in different parts of the world, and many studies have examined the effect of changes in meteorological parameters on the performance of the energy sector. In this study, using the results of climate change calculations in the provinces of Iran, which are obtained from the microscale exponential method with a neural network, its effect on the performance of the energy production sector in the country's power plants in the next decade has been investigated. Calculations show that, on average, the efficiency of gas power plants decreases by about 0.6% for every 1°C increase in temperature. Also, the efficiency of heating and combined power plants decreases by about 0.5 and 0.4% on average. This chapter is aimed to use the P-index reliability index to study the climate change impacts on the thermal power plant performance.

INTRODUCTION

Energy and environmental issues have become one of the major issues today, to which many countries pay special attention. Since the protection of the environment is essential for the continuation of a healthier life and survival requires continuous energy consumption, it is necessary always to study energy production and its adverse effects on the environment to find better solutions for degradation as little as possible. Presented the environment as a result of dynamic earth processes or external factors such as changes in the intensity of sunlight or human activities that lead to increased concentrations of greenhouse gases, climate change occurs globally and has significant effects on countries(Arnell, 1998).

DOI: 10.4018/978-1-7998-9648-7.ch002

Climate change causes changes in temperature and rainfall time patterns and changes in rainfall (Boadi & Owusu, 2019). To study climate systems globally, models called general circulation models (GCM) are used. These models mathematically simulate the physical behavior of the Earth, atmosphere, and ocean systems (Berger et al., 2014). Crook et al. (2011) used a leading artificial neural network model and an error propagation algorithm with a sigmoid transfer function to predict future wind speeds for three regions in the United States (Texas, California, and Carolina). The results show a decrease in wind speed of 0.4 and 0.8% in the two study points and an increase of 2.6% in one of the study points on an annual scale. Chuang & Sue (2005) also compared the performance of the SDSM model and the artificial neural network (TLFN) for exponential microscale temperature and large-scale precipitation of the HadCM3 model in the Karkheh catchment in western Iran.

On the other hand, temperature changes have a direct effect on energy production performance. The output of the gas turbine and its efficiency are a function of ambient air temperature (Durmayaz & Sogut, 2006). In the studies that have been done, almost similar results have been obtained. For example, it has been reported that in the gas turbine type, the output power decreases by 5 to 10% for every 10 degrees increase in temperature above 15 °C. Fant et al. (2016) studied the impacts of increasing the ambient temperature by 1°C, which caused a 1% reduction in the gas turbine capacity. In a steam power plant, the boiler is the main cause of exergy destruction in the power plant, and in return for increasing the ambient temperature up to 5 °C at constant relative humidity, the thermal efficiency decreases by 2.35%, and the exergy efficiency of the power plant decreases by 8.2% (Fant, 2016). For every 1-degree increase in temperature, the efficiency of the steam power plant decreases by about 0.45%.

Some researchers have concluded that with increasing ambient temperature per 1°C in a 50 MW combined cycle power plant, the capacity of the combined cycle power plant decreases by about 0.5%. (Gaetani et al., 2014). Also, Ibrahim et al. (2014), in their study on a 16.6 MW gas turbine, showed that with decreasing the temperature from 34.2 to 15 °C, the average output of the power plant increases by more than 11.3%. For each degree of increase in ambient temperature, the gas turbine power output will decrease by 0.64%. By studying a gas turbine and its combined cycle with a capacity of about 110 MW and reducing the temperature from 35 to 20 ° C, it was shown that the output power of the gas turbine is about 10.6%, and the output power of the combined cycle is increased about 6.24%(Kaygusuz, 2003). For every 1 degree of temperature decrease, the efficiency of the gas turbine increases by about 0.61% and the combined cycle efficiency by about 0.41% in a 110 MW power plant. Also, another study showed that the average power output of the power plant per 1°C increase in inlet temperature decreases by 0.56%, and output power increases by 10% in cold humidity and 18% in hot humidity (Fant, 2016). This study aims to determine the effect of climate change (specifical temperature) on the performance of Iran's thermal power plants in 2050.

In this research, these gaps are filled with an exergy-climate change model to relate and formulate global warming to the energy performance or the energy efficiency of the power generating technologies and introduce a new index to describe the quantitative reliability of each power source toward climate change impacts. The main aims of this paper are as modeling power-generating technologies; studying climate change impacts on these models; using the results of this analysis to estimate the vulnerability of each technology to the climate change effects; using the estimated quantities of vulnerability to define a reliability index for each power generating technology, and prioritizing main power generating technologies in term of their reliability toward climate change impacts.

Figure 1. Overview of feed-forward neural networks

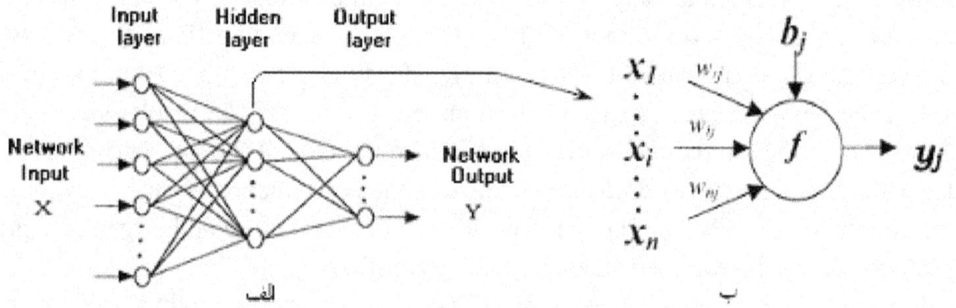

METHODS AND MATERIAL

Study Area and Required Information

Because of the studies in the provincial section, a meteorological station with a suitable statistical period is selected in each province, and the inputs, which are the large-scale variables of the NCEP databases, are given to the neural network model. On the other hand, each province's power plants should be studied, and the type of power plant cycle, capacity, efficiency, utilization coefficient, production capacity, amount, and type of fuels consumed to be determined using detailed statistics of Iran's electricity industry. In this study, in 30 provinces of Iran, all cases are identified separately and considered basic data.

Artificial Neural Network Model

With the help of various artificial neural networks and performance evaluation, the best network for each province has been determined, and since 90% of the networks used in various issues are leading networks, in the present study, the leading neural network with backward algorithm Error propagation is used (Chang & Liao, 2012). An overview of the leading neural network is presented in Figure 1.

The output of the model is the daily temperature, daily rainfall, and daily wind speed. Each daily variable is examined separately, and the most appropriate networks are selected by changing the number of neurons in the middle layer, changing the latency at the input, and using a different transmission and training function. Once the network is ready, how it works should be evaluated. For this purpose, the criteria of correlation coefficient (ρ) and squared mean squared error (RMSE) are used. After evaluation and calculations, the model outputs, the same as daily temperature, precipitation, and wind speed, are determined.

Mathematics

When all parameters remain constant in a combined cycle, and only the ambient temperature is considered variable, the power plant's performance will strongly depend on the ambient air temperature (Sarabpreet & Rajesh, 2012). In Equation 1, W_{GT} is the work of a gas turbine, calculated according to various

Figure 2. Schematic of a combined cycle power plant

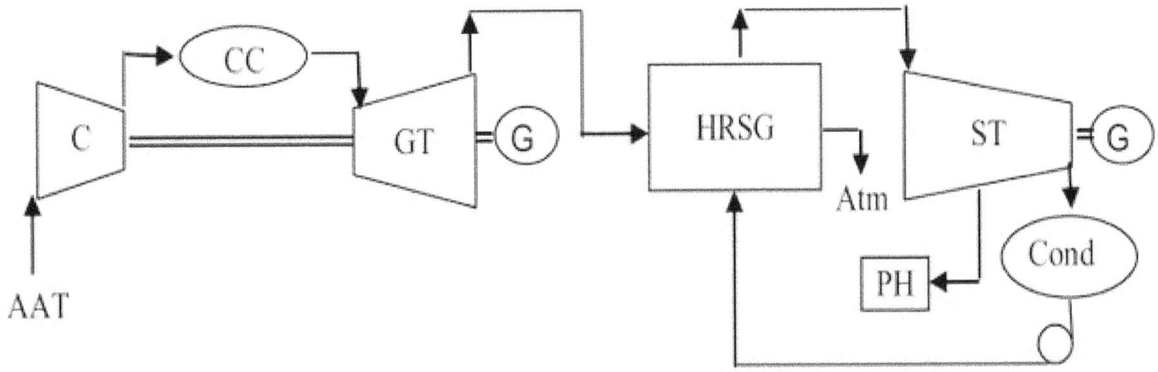

parameters such as initial temperature, initial pressure and volume, compressor efficiency, compressor and combustion chamber outlet temperatures, and other factors(see figure 2).

$$W_{GT} = \frac{P_1 V_1}{R T_1} C_{pg} \left(T_3 - T_4\right) \left[1 + \left\{ \frac{C_{pg} T_3 - C_{pa} T_1 \left(1 + \frac{r\left(1 - \frac{1}{\gamma}\right) - 1}{\eta_c} \right)}{CV \eta_{comp} - C_{pg} T_3} \right\} \right] \tag{1}$$

Where the W_{GT} is gas turbine work, T_3 is inlet temperature to the gas turbine, $m_a = P_1 V_1 / RT_1$ is the air mass flow, C_{pg} is the heat capacity at gas pressure, T_1 is the Ambient temperature, C_{pa} is the heat capacity at the air pressure, ϒ is the combustion efficiency, and r is the compaction rate.

Assuming that all the above parameters are constant and the gas turbine outlet temperature, the operation of the gas turbine will be inversely related to the ambient temperature (Khajehpour, 2021). In Equation 2, the efficiency of the gas turbine can be calculated according to the mentioned parameters in the whole process.

$$\eta_{GTP} = \frac{C_{pg}\left(T_3 - T_4\right)\eta_{gen}}{CV\eta_{comp}}\left[1 + \left\{\frac{\left(\frac{1}{T_1} + \frac{RW_C}{P_1V_1}\right)\left(CV\eta_{comp} - C_{pg}T_3\right)}{\frac{C_{pg}T_3}{T_1}C_{pa}\left(1 + \frac{r\left(1 - \frac{1}{\gamma}\right) - 1}{\eta_c}\right)}\right\}\right] \tag{2}$$

Where the η_{GTP} is the gas turbine efficiency, and η_{comp} is the compressor efficiency. Given that compressor efficiency, gas turbine efficiency, generator efficiency, inlet temperature (T_3) to gas turbine and combustion ratio are constant, and gas turbine power and energy consumption are inversely related to ambient temperature, gas turbine efficiency is also inversely related to ambient temperature (Khajehpour, 2021). If the exhaust gases of the gas turbine are sent to the steam cycle, the mass flow rate of the fuel with a constant inlet temperature (T_5) is obtained from the following equation:

$$m_{f2} = \frac{P_1V_1C_{pg}\left(T_5 - T_4\right)}{RCV\eta_{comp} - C_{pg}T_5}\left[1 + \left\{\frac{C_{pg}\left(\frac{T_3}{T1}\right) - C_{pa}T_1\left(1 + \frac{r\left(1 - \frac{1}{\gamma}\right) - 1}{\eta_c}\right)}{CV\eta_{comp} - C_{pg}T_3}\right\}\right] \tag{3}$$

Where the m_{f2} is the fuel mass flow rate with constant inlet temperature, the fuel's mass flow rate is inversely related to the ambient temperature (Khajehpour, 2021). The mass flow rate of steam is equal to:

$$m_s = \frac{\left(m_a + m_{f1} + m_{f2}\right)C_{pg}\left(T_5 - T_{10}\right)\eta_{HRSG}}{h_{23} - \left(x' + y'\right)h_{f12} - z'h_{24a}} \tag{4}$$

The m_s is the vapor mass flow rate, assuming that all parameters are constant, m_a, $m_{f1,}$ and m_{f2} are inversely related to ambient temperature, so m_s is also inversely related to ambient temperature (Coulibaly et al., 2000). Steam turbine output:

$$W_{st} = \eta_{st}\left(m_s\left(h_{23} - h_{24a}\right) + \left(m_s - m_{24b}\right)\left(h_{24b} - h_{24a}\right) + \left(m_s - m_{24b} - m_{24a}\right)\left(h_{24a} - h_{24}\right)\right) \tag{5}$$

Figure 3. The algorithm of the methodology and modeling process

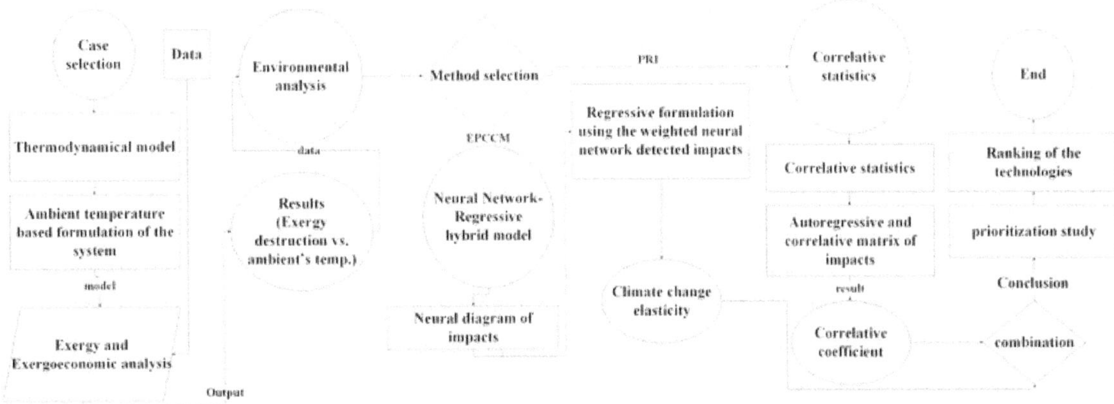

Where W_{ST} is the steam turbine work, assuming that all the enthalpy parameters and efficiency of the steam turbine are constant, m_{24a}, $m_{24b,}$ and m_{24} are directly related to m_s, so the power of the steam turbine is inversely proportional to the ambient temperature (Khajehpour, 2021). The efficiency of a combined cycle power plant is obtained from equation 6.

$$\eta_{CC} = \frac{W_{NGT} + W_{NST}}{\left(m_{f1} + m_{f2}\right) CV \eta_{comb}} \tag{6}$$

Where the η_{CC} is the combined Cycle Efficiency, W_{NGT} is the net power of the gas turbine, W_{NST} is the net power of the steam turbine, and m_{f1}, m_{f2} are inlet fuel flow rates compressor and steam turbine. Since the net power of gas turbine and steam turbines and the rate of inlet fuel flow to the compressor and steam turbine are inversely related to ambient temperature, the combined cycle efficiency is also inversely related to ambient temperature (Khajehpour, 2021). In this study, having the characteristics of each cycle studied and the ambient temperature of each region with the ambient temperature in the future obtained using the artificial neural network model, the new efficiencies of each power plant are recalculated and then using energy and environment software. The bio-amount of fuel consumed in the future will be determined. Also, this software provides the number of emissions and the social costs caused by each power plant. The method to investigate this variable is shown in figure 3.

RESULTS AND DISCUSSION

Impacts on the Fuel Consumption, Carbon Emissions, and Social Costs

In this study, by examining the studies performed in the field of exponential microscopy with the help of an artificial neural network, the networks were determined for each province, and from the leading network with the exponential error propagation algorithm, the exponential meteorological parameters of meteorological parameters in each province were determined. Having the temperature changes in each province and having statistics and information of thermal power plants in each province (Sailor et al., 2000), temperature change on efficiencies was investigated. In most provinces, except the Hormozgan, Khuzestan, and Qazvin provinces, where the temperature affecting the performance of power plants has not changed significantly, temperature changes have often increased up to 3 degrees. However, the effective temperature change in most of them is less. In the whole country, about 69 existing heating, gas, and hybrid power plants were studied. On average, the efficiency of gas power plants has decreased between 0.7-1% due to each degree of temperature increase, and the efficiency of steam and combined cycle power plants due to unit temperature increase has been between 0.5-3% and -0.7%, respectively. It decreases by 0.3%. With the new efficiencies calculated from the above equations, the percentage of fuels consumed in each power plant, and their access coefficient with the help of energy and environmental software, the amount of fuels consumed in each power plant is obtained in the new state. Each power plant's current and future modes determine the amount of carbon produced and social costs using this software. Table 1 presents the results of these calculations by province.

Power plant performance calculations due to climate change in Iran in 2050 show that the performance of Khorramshahr, Zargan gas and heating plants, Abadan combined, Ramin heater, Persian Gulf, and Bandar Abbas gas and heating plants will remain unchanged, and the rest of the power plants will have lower performance. According to the table above, about 313912 cubic meters of diesel consumption and about 316072 cubic meters of fuel oil consumption in power plants will increase per year. Also, the consumption of natural gas will increase by about 1261202 thousand cubic meters per year. Considering that each cubic meter of diesel is equal to 6.6176 barrels of crude oil, about 1975287 barrels of crude oil due to the increase in diesel consumption will increase consumption in power plants. On the other hand, every thousand cubic meters of gas is equal to 6.07 barrels of crude oil, so about 7811731 barrels of crude oil due to increased gas consumption, we will have an increase in consumption in power plants, and finally, each cubic meter of furnace oil is equal to 7.06 barrels of crude oil. An increase of about 2277008 barrels of crude oil consumption is estimated due to increased fuel oil consumption. In general, due to climate change in 2050, we will have about 12067027 barrels of crude oil per year or 33060 barrels of crude oil per day increase in consumption in the country's power sector, in other words, in 2050, based on studies and calculations of fuel consumption in the power sector will increase by about 2.49%. The software can also estimate the number of pollutants produced by the plant, including NOx, CO, SO_2, SO_3, CH, CO_2 and SPM. In each power plant, the amount of emissions is calculated, and all the values obtained are summarized in Table 3 in Appendix. At present, 165184877 tons of carbon dioxide, 634884 tons of NO_x, 709408 tons of SO_2, 5130 tons of SO_3, 148500 tons of CO, 30724 tons of SPM, and 4087 tons of CH are emitted. According to climate change studies, emissions in 2050 reach 167341831 tons of carbon dioxide, 638585 tons of NO_x, 719577 tons of SO_2, 52669 tons of SO_3 148504 tons of CO, 31177 tons of SPM, and 4046 tons of CH.

It should be noted that the total social costs due to the emission of pollutants in the thermal power plant sector increased from 6.8 billion USD to 7 billion USD, which is a total increase of 150 million USD to the annual costs. All of the power-generating technologies have an environmental effect. These effects are caused in every

The indexing process results are illustrated in a table called Pahlev's table (table 2 below).

According to Table 2, the P-index or PRI is determined for each power technology, which is -0.43, -0.74, and -0.57 for Steam, Gas, and combined power plants, respectively.

Table 1. Forecast of changes in fuel consumption, social costs, and carbon production in Iranian power plants due to climate change by province by 2050

State	Cost, M$/a	Carbon, 10^6kg	Fuel Consumption		
			Diesel,m3	Fuel oil,m^3	Gas, 10^3m^3
Yazd	8.5	17199	2119	0	28590
Fars	12.2	64203	12175	0	117925
E.Azarbaijan	1.6	7846	704	190952	10364
Esfahan	8.8	52801	4343	28165	35359
W.Azarbaijan	3.6	18827	23859	0	3245
Zanjan	3.8	22716	2475	0	38467
Qom	2.2	12871	4324	0	18286
Gilan	8.5	56217	13038	0	74639
Hamedan	0.8	299900	0	2870	3558
Markazi	3.7	7734	37	12690	21238
Luristan	0.2	1006	4	0	1689
N. Khorasan	2.1	11235	2110	0	19708
Kermanshah	6.3	37758	9570	16423	22473
Kurdistan	3.2	14774	7873	0	23435
Gulistan	1.2	9874	1474	0	11830
Tehran	17.2	96514	61905	27434	75266
Sistan	6.1	30056	31192	9625	0
S. Khorasan	3.5	23329	3815	0	33717
Kerman	6.0	31952	15782	3121	36328
Bushehr	3.0	16578	3018	0	29628
Khuzistan	0.0	0	0	0	0
R. Khorasan	8.0	41262	22653	10671	37888
Hormozghan	0.0	0	0	0	0
Mazandaran	3.6	24549	3510	14121	5724
Semnan	20.7	188556	87931	0	611847
Total	134.7	1087757	313912	316072	1261202

Table 2. Results of the climate change impact on the power technologies analysis (Pahlev's table) (for the IPCC baseline scenario) adopted from Norouzi (2021)

Technology	PRI	EPCCM formula	RMSE	SSE	MSA
Steam plant	-0.43	-2.0E-05T+30.557	0.92	0.87	0.85
Gas turbine	-0.74	-3.0E-04T+40.706	0.90	0.86	0.84
Combined cycle	-0.57	-8.0E-05T+44.094	0.95	0.91	0.89

DISCUSSION

In recent years, climate change has affected most parts of the world in weather and climate crises. Energy is one of the areas sensitive to climate change, and its consumption and prospects in the coming decades are important indicators in the planning and macro-policies of the country. Increases environmental pollution and greenhouse gases on the planet and ›Increases its temperature. Following the implementation of the targeted subsidy scheme in the country, a relatively significant share of the cost of goods and services has been allocated to energy. Fluctuations in electricity consumption in the country show that various factors affect the amount of electricity consumption; On the other hand, the geographical extent of Iran, despite the different climatic zones, has caused different provinces to have different needs for electricity consumption.

Given that the amount of electricity consumption in Iran has been reported to be three times equal to global consumption, and since its amount fluctuates in different seasons, attention to temperature, the most important climatic element, which has increased in recent years due to global warming, the new approach creates a connection between global warming and the amount of electricity consumed. In its fourth report in 2007, the International Committee on Climate Change attributed global warming to human activity and predicted that global warming would rise by 1 to 4 degrees by 2100. This amount will vary based on different greenhouse gas emission scenarios, especially carbon dioxide. In addition, according to the First Working Group of the Fifth International Climate Change Assessment Report, global average temperatures have been steadily rising over the last three decades, with the 1983-83 period being the warmest in 1400 years. Studies conducted in the country show that the average temperature in the period 2039-2011 increases by about 0.5 degrees Celsius compared to the average of the statistical period. Temperature events are maximum, and hot days are more likely to increase.

The current concentrations of carbon dioxide, methane and nitrous oxide have been unprecedented for 800,000 years. The concentration of carbon dioxide has increased by 40% compared to the period before the Industrial Revolution, mainly due to the release of fossil fuels and later changes in land use. The cumulative concentration of carbon dioxide determines the increase in surface temperature in the 21st century and beyond. Even if carbon dioxide emissions are stopped, many of the consequences and aspects of climate change will last for centuries. The current increase in carbon dioxide (CO2) in the Earth's atmosphere is mainly due to the combustion of fossil fuels for electricity generation and transmission. The United States, for example, accounts for 34 percent of the total greenhouse gas emissions in the United States. In addition, it is one of the largest producers of sulfur dioxide (SO2), nitrogen oxide (NOx), and mercury. Norouzi (2021) and Khajehpour et al. (2021) state that thermal power plants are greatly affected by climate change. In these papers, some quantitative amounts are being estimated, and they state that thermal power plants lose 0.3-0.7% of their energy performance per degree of the mean global temperature change. The results of this paper also show that a similar amount of the exergy and energy efficiencies decrease per each one-degree global mean temperature rise (0.465% for combined cycle, 0.332% for the Nuclear cycle, and 0.732% for the gas turbine power plants). Also, there will be more thermal power plants issues in the severe climate change stages. Reduced water resources for cooling systems are expected for the coming decades, causing load reduction or shutdown of the power plants (Panagea, 2017).

SOLUTIONS AND RECOMMENDATIONS

Using the combination of the steam and gas cycles because of its higher energy and exergy efficiency emits lesser greenhouse gas to the atmosphere and uses a smaller amount of fuel and also considering the results of the climate change impact analysis, this kind of technology is not as sensitive to the climate change as the other thermal technologies (Khajehpour, 2021).

FUTURE RESEARCH DIRECTIONS

This is a novel method published in 2021 as the PRI method, which determines the cross impacts of climate change and economics. It is recommended to researchers consider this method to get results with greater accuracy during their environmental assessments of processes and projects. Also, it is recommended to link this concept to economics and the concept of social cost.

CONCLUSION

In this study, using the results of climate change, using an artificial neural network in the exponential temperature scale, the performance of thermal power plants in each province in 2050 has been investigated. In most provinces of the country, an increase in average temperature can be seen. 2050 was considered as the year under study. This year, the provinces of Khuzestan, Hormozgan, and Qazvin will not experience a significant temperature change compared to the current temperature in the average state. On average, the temperature of the country will increase by about 1.36 degrees Celsius. Then, the temperature change affecting the performance (due to the effect of temperatures above 15 degrees on the power plant's performance and no change in the efficiency of the power plant at temperatures below 15°C) was determined for power plants in each province. It was lower, and its average in the whole country was about 1.1°C. Using the obtained results, fuel consumption in the energy sector of thermal power plants was investigated due to the inverse effect of ambient temperature on the efficiency and performance of power plants. After studying climate change, it was concluded that all power plants, except for eight power plants in the mentioned provinces, will have declining efficiency. The results show that in general, due to climate change in 2050, it will be equivalent to about 12067020 barrels of crude oil per year or 33060 barrels of crude oil per day, or a 2.49% increase in fuel consumption in the country's power sector. Due to the increase in fuel consumption, carbon dioxide emissions per kilowatt-hour will increase from 616 grams to 629 grams. In total, about 2509696 tons or 1.3% of carbon dioxide emissions will increase. The increase in sulfur dioxide and NOx emissions is also significant and is about 10169 and 3701 tons, respectively. CO will have the lowest increase (about 5.4 tons). The total social costs from the emission of pollutants in the thermal power plant sector will increase by $ 135 million or 2%.

ACKNOWLEDGMENT

This research received no specific grant from any funding agency in the public, commercial, or not-for-profit sectors.

REFERENCES

Arnell, N. W. (1998). Climate change and water resources in Britain. *Climatic Change*, *39*(1), 83–110. doi:10.1023/A:1005339412565

Berger, T., Amann, C., Formayer, H., Korjenic, A., Pospichal, B., Neururer, C., & Smutny, R. (2014). Impacts of urban location and climate change upon energy demand of office buildings in Vienna, Austria. *Building and Environment*, *81*, 258–269. doi:10.1016/j.buildenv.2014.07.007

Boadi, S. A., & Owusu, K. (2019). Impact of climate change and variability on hydropower in Ghana. *African Geographical Review*, *38*(1), 19–31. doi:10.1080/19376812.2017.1284598

Chang, C. L., & Liao, C. S. (2012). Parameter sensitivity analysis of artificial neural network for predicting water turbidity. *International Journal of Geological and Environmental Engineering*, *6*(10), 657–660.

Chuang, C. C., & Sue, D. C. (2005). Performance effects of combined cycle power plant with variable condenser pressure and loading. *Energy*, *30*(10), 1793–1801. doi:10.1016/j.energy.2004.10.003

Coulibaly, P., Anctil, F., & Bobée, B. (2000). Daily reservoir inflow forecasting using artificial neural networks with stopped training approach. *Journal of Hydrology (Amsterdam)*, *230*(3-4), 244–257. doi:10.1016/S0022-1694(00)00214-6

Crook, J. A., Jones, L. A., Forster, P. M., & Crook, R. (2011). Climate change impacts on future photovoltaic and concentrated solar power energy output. *Energy & Environmental Science*, *4*(9), 3101–3109. doi:10.1039/c1ee01495a

Durmayaz, A., & Sogut, O. S. (2006). Influence of cooling water temperature on the efficiency of a pressurized-water reactor nuclear-power plant. *International Journal of Energy Research*, *30*(10), 799–810. doi:10.1002/er.1186

Fant, C., Schlosser, C. A., & Strzepek, K. (2016). The impact of climate change on wind and solar resources in southern Africa. *Applied Energy*, *161*, 556–564. doi:10.1016/j.apenergy.2015.03.042

Gaetani, M., Huld, T., Vignati, E., Monforti-Ferrario, F., Dosio, A., & Raes, F. (2014). The near future availability of photovoltaic energy in Europe and Africa in climate-aerosol modeling experiments. *Renewable & Sustainable Energy Reviews*, *38*, 706–716. doi:10.1016/j.rser.2014.07.041

Ibrahim, S., Ibrahim, M., & Attia, S. (2014). The impact of climate changes on the thermal performance of a proposed pressurized water reactor: nuclear-power plant. *International Journal of Nuclear Energy*.

Kaygusuz, K. (2003). Energy policy and climate change in Turkey. *Energy Conversion and Management*, *44*(10), 1671–1688. doi:10.1016/S0196-8904(02)00170-X

Khajehpour, H., Norouzi, N., & Fani, M. (2021). An exergetic model for the ambient air temperature impacts on the combined power plants and its management using the genetic algorithm. *International Journal of Air-Conditioning and Refrigeration*, *29*(1), 2150008. doi:10.1142/S2010132521500085

Kim, K. (2019). Elasticity of substitution of renewable energy for nuclear power: Evidence from the Korean electricity industry. *Nuclear Engineering and Technology*, *51*(6), 1689–1695. doi:10.1016/j.net.2019.04.005

Koch, H., Vögele, S., Hattermann, F., & Huang, S. (2014). Hydro-climatic conditions and thermoelectric electricity generation–Part II: Model application to 17 nuclear power plants in Germany. *Energy*, *69*, 700–707. doi:10.1016/j.energy.2014.03.071

Linnerud, K., Mideksa, T. K., & Eskeland, G. S. (2011). The impact of climate change on nuclear power supply. *Energy Journal*, *32*(1). Advance online publication. doi:10.5547/ISSN0195-6574-EJ-Vol32-No1-6

Mahmood, N., Wang, Z., & Zhang, B. (2020). The role of nuclear energy in the correction of environmental pollution: Evidence from Pakistan. *Nuclear Engineering and Technology*, *52*(6), 1327–1333. doi:10.1016/j.net.2019.11.027

Norouzi, N. (2020). 4E Analysis and design of a combined cycle with a geothermal condensing system in Iranian Moghan diesel power Plant. *International Journal of Air-Conditioning and Refrigeration*, *28*(03), 2050022. doi:10.1142/S2010132520500224

Norouzi, N. (2021). The Pahlev Reliability Index: A measurement for the resilience of power generation technologies versus climate change. *Nuclear Engineering and Technology*, *53*(5), 1658–1663. doi:10.1016/j.net.2020.10.013

Norouzi, N., & Fani, M. (2020). Exergetic design and analysis of an SMR reactor nuclear tetrageneration (combined water, heat, power, and chemicals generation) with designed PCM energy storage and a CO2 gas turbine inner cycle. *Nuclear Engineering and Technology*.

Panagea, I. S., Tsanis, I. K., & Koutroulis, A. G. (2017). Climate change impact on photovoltaic energy output: the case of Greece. In *Climate Change and the Future of Sustainability* (pp. 85–106). Apple Academic Press.

Patt, A., Pfenninger, S., & Lilliestam, J. (2013). Vulnerability of solar energy infrastructure and output to climate change. *Climatic Change*, *121*(1), 93–102. doi:10.100710584-013-0887-0

Sailor, D. J., Hu, T., Li, X., & Rosen, J. N. (2000). A neural network approach to local downscaling of GCM output for assessing wind power implications of climate change. *Renewable Energy*, *19*(3), 359–378. doi:10.1016/S0960-1481(99)00056-7

Sarabpreet, S., & Rajesh, K. (2012). Ambient Air Temperature Effect on Power Plant Performance. *International Journal of Engineering Science and Technology*, *4*(8).

Talebi, S., & Norouzi, N. (2020). Entropy and exergy analysis and optimization of the VVER nuclear power plant with a capacity of 1000 MW using the firefly optimization algorithm. *Nuclear Engineering and Technology*, *52*(12), 2928–2938. doi:10.1016/j.net.2020.05.011

ADDITIONAL READING

Bauer, N., Brecha, R. J., & Luderer, G. (2012). Economics of nuclear power and climate change mitigation policies. *Proceedings of the National Academy of Sciences of the United States of America*, *109*(42), 16805–16810. doi:10.1073/pnas.1201264109 PMID:23027963

Cradden, L. C., Harrison, G. P., & Chick, J. P. (2012). Will climate change impact on wind power development in the UK? *Climatic Change*, *115*(3), 837–852. doi:10.100710584-012-0486-5

Jerez, S., Tobin, I., Vautard, R., Montávez, J. P., López-Romero, J. M., Thais, F., Bartok, B., Christensen, O. B., Colette, A., Déqué, M., Nikulin, G., Kotlarski, S., van Meijgaard, E., Teichmann, C., & Wild, M. (2015). The impact of climate change on photovoltaic power generation in Europe. *Nature Communications*, *6*(1), 1–8. doi:10.1038/ncomms10014 PMID:26658608

Khan, I., Alam, F., & Alam, Q. (2013). The global climate change and its effect on power generation in Bangladesh. *Energy Policy*, *61*, 1460–1470. doi:10.1016/j.enpol.2013.05.005

Linnerud, K., Mideksa, T. K., & Eskeland, G. S. (2011). The impact of climate change on nuclear power supply. *Energy Journal*, *32*(1). Advance online publication. doi:10.5547/ISSN0195-6574-EJ-Vol32-No1-6

Mideksa, T. K., & Kallbekken, S. (2010). The impact of climate change on the electricity market: A review. *Energy Policy*, *38*(7), 3579–3585. doi:10.1016/j.enpol.2010.02.035

Panteli, M., & Mancarella, P. (2015). Influence of extreme weather and climate change on the resilience of power systems: Impacts and possible mitigation strategies. *Electric Power Systems Research*, *127*, 259–270. doi:10.1016/j.epsr.2015.06.012

Sailor, D. J., Smith, M., & Hart, M. (2008). Climate change implications for wind power resources in the Northwest United States. *Renewable Energy*, *33*(11), 2393–2406. doi:10.1016/j.renene.2008.01.007

KEY TERMS AND DEFINITIONS

Climate Change: Climate change refers to any change in climate that lasts longer than individual climatic events, while climate change refers only to those changes that last for longer periods, typically decades or longer. In addition to the general meaning that "climate change" may have in any period, the use of the term is more common about the current climate change that is taking place. Since the Industrial Revolution, the climate has been increasingly influenced by human activities that have caused global warming and climate change.

Globalization: Globalization is the interaction and integration of people, companies, and governments around the world. Globalization has grown due to the advancement of communication and transportation technology. Increasing global interaction leads to the growth of international trade, ideas, and culture. Globalization is primarily an economic process in the form of economic interaction that is associated with cultural and social aspects. Nevertheless, conflict and diplomacy have always been part of the history of globalization (especially modern globalization).

Green Economy: A green economy emerges in the shadow of advanced human life and social justice while minimizing environmental hazards and damage. A green economy is an economy or economic development based on sustainable development and knowledge of the local economy.

Marxian Economics: The school of economics is based on the work of Karl Marx, in which labor creates and grows capital in the process of capital accumulation. The theory holds that the value of goods and services includes not only the cost of labor (wages) and the cost of capital (machinery, tools, and materials), but that there is also surplus labor in the value of a commodity, and that labor is the source of labor. Profit becomes capitalist. This school takes a critical look at the classical approach based on Adam Smith's theory of productivity and wages.

Sustainable Architecture: Green Architecture or sustainable architecture is one of the new trends and approaches to architecture that has attracted the attention of many contemporary designers and architects around the world in recent years. This architecture, which arises from the concepts of sustainable development, seeks to adapt and harmonize with the environment is one of the basic human needs in today's world. Creating green buildings aims to improve the climate, prevent the loss of energy used for cooling and heating, and prevent the negative effects of construction on the environment.

Waste Management: It is a set of activities and measures necessary for waste management from production to its final disposal. These activities include collecting, transferring, and disposal of waste and monitoring the implementation of waste management laws.

Water Resources Management: Water resources management is an activity in planning, development, distribution, and management of optimal use of water resources. Water resources management is a sub-set of water cycle management.

APPENDIX 1

Table 3. Predicting the decrease/increase of pollutants and carbon dioxide emissions from the country's power plants due to climate change in 2050 (in tons per year)

NOx	SO2	CO2	SO3	CO	CH	SPM	Power plant name
205	703	118389	6	0	8	29	Rudshor gas
108	787	65748	11	0	8	17	Montazer ghaem steam
108	91	69553	0	0	4	11	Montazer ghaem comb.
57	23	37119	0	0	1	5	Rey Gas
9	0	6961	0	0	0	1	Tarasht Steam
74	462	45049	8	0	6	11	Besat
93	876	55603	13	1	8	19	Iranshahr Steam
26	78	13197	1	0	1	5	Kanarak Gas
54	163	27579	2	0	3	10	Zahedan Gas
77	233	60651	3	0	5	15	Chabahar Gas
4	4	1694	0	0	0	1	Ghaen Gas
118	54	77815	1	1	3	11	Kaveh Combined
81	114	6804	1	0	4	12	Shirvan Gas
25	142	9011	2	0	1	3	Zarand Steam
175	196	108144	3	0	10	22	Kerman combined
15	45	7481	-1	0	1	3	Kahnoj
29	0	20217	0	0	0	3	Kangan
7	0	4778	0	0	0	0	Bushehr Gas
62	29	40976	1	0	1	7	Assaluyeh
6	18	3039	0	0	0	1	Ghenave
0	0	0	0	0	0	0	Ramin Steam
0	0	0	0	0	0	0	Abadan combined
0	0	0	0	0	0	0	Zargan Steam
0	0	0	0	0	0	0	Zargani gas
0	0	0	0	0	0	0	Khoramshahr
2	0	1550	0	0	0	0	Shariati Gas
85	240	44390	4	0	5	16	Ferdowsi combined
25	16	15837	0	0	0	2	Shariati combined
55	38	35495	0	0	2	6	Neishabour combined
14	0	9670	0	0	0	1	Mashhad Steam
14	0	9820	0	0	0	1	Mashhad gas
68	485	41673	8	0	5	11	Tus Steam
67	52	43350	0	0	2	8	Gilan gas
0	0	0	0	0	0	0	Persian gulf
0	0	0	0	0	0	0	Bandar Abbas Gas
0	0	0	0	0	0	0	Bandar Abbas Steam
85	642	51862	10	0	-5	14	Neka Steam
17	54	9011	1	0	1	3	Neka combined

continued on following page

Table 3. Continued

NOx	SO2	CO2	SO3	CO	CH	SPM	Power plant name
1	0	719	0	0	0	1	Nevshahr
NOx	**SO2**	**CO2**	**SO3**	**CO**	**CH**	**SPM**	**Power plant name**
34	17	14695	0	0	1	3	Kashan
26	26	10346	0	0	1	3	Zavareh Combined
66	402	40870	7	0	4	10	Isfahan Steam
137	881	85176	13	0	8	23	Montazeri
42	23	28244	0	0	1	4	Golestan
22	8	729	0	0	2	6	Shahroud
66	23	43342	1	0	2	7	Jahrom
48	7	31759	0	0	1	3	Hafiz
3	10	2986	0	0	0	0	Shirkuh Yazd
8	1	5886	0	0	1	1	Tabriz Gas
15	68	9932	1	0	1	2	Tabriz Steam
84	10	7000	0	0	1	2	Sufi Gas
15	71	9329	1	0	1	3	Sahand Steam
8	10	4691	0	0	0	1	Khoy combined
115	347	58530	6	0	7	7	New Urmia Gas
8	7	4732	0	0	1	1	Urmia Gas
129	38	85893	0	0	3	12	Soltanieh
77	66	48909	1	0	3	8	Qom Combined
67	52	43350	0	0	2	8	Gilan combined
70	33	46750	0	0	2	6	Lushan combined
38	56	22305	1	0	1	4	Paresar
33	131	15645	2	1	1	4	Mofateh Steam
8	2	3042	6	1	0	3	Shazand Arak
6	0	3501	0	0	0	0	Dorud
114	747	66211	11	0	8	17	Biston Steam
89	145	52233	2	0	4	12	Zagros Gas
110	120	68671	2	0	3	12	Sanandaj Combined
115	713	63642	1	0	2	11	Semnan
67	51	41071	1	0	1	8	Damavand combined
133	54	86452	4	0	1	3	Parand
3516	9661	2049107	133	4	134	430	Total

Chapter 3
Effects of Environmental Corporate Social Responsibility Practices on Environmental Sustainability:
A Study on Industrial Companies in Turkey

Bekir Değirmenci
https://orcid.org/0000-0001-5236-5245
Adiyaman University, Turkey

ABSTRACT

Today, climate change due to global warming, extraordinary deterioration in the natural environment, and the melting of glaciers seriously threaten human health and existence. Cases such as forest fires and flood disasters, which have been seen frequently in the summer months, and the COVID-19 pandemic due to the melting of glaciers, seriously threaten humanity. Within the scope of this study, the measures taken by the enterprises for the relationship between environmental responsibility and environmental sustainability were examined. In this direction, the 2020 environmental sustainability reports of 15 companies operating in different sectors in Turkey and listed on the Istanbul Stock Exchange were examined. The absence of a similar study in the literature increases the originality of the study. It is expected that the studies planned for the future will contribute positively to the literature by deepening it further (for example, in different countries, comparisons in different cultures, practical studies).

INTRODUCTION

Today, climate change due to global warming, extraordinary deterioration in the natural environment and the melting of glaciers seriously threaten human health and existence. Cases such as forest fires and flood disasters, which have been seen frequently in the summer months, and the covid-19 epidemic due to the melting of glaciers, seriously threaten humanity. Public institutions and businesses have important

DOI: 10.4018/978-1-7998-9648-7.ch003

duties in the construction of a more livable and healthy natural environment. It is seen that many studies have been carried out in the literature on environmental sustainability (Önce at al., 2015; Solomon and Marun, 2012; Surty at al., 2018; Ebner at al., 2006; Finnveden at al., 2009; Gatimbu at al., 2018).

Within the scope of this study, the measures taken by the enterprises for the relationship between environmental responsibility and environmental sustainability were examined. When the issue of environmental sustainability is examined in the literature, it is seen that there are many studies on this subject (Menteşe, 2017; Şenocak and Mohan, 2018; Gedik, 2020; Sun et al., 2020; Van Huis et al., 2017; Oláh et al., 2020). However, none of the previous studies have examined publicly traded companies. It is thought that this study provides new contributions to the literature compared to its counterparts. When the reason for this is examined, first of all, the environmental sustainability reports for 15 companies from the 30 largest publicly traded companies operating in different business lines in Turkey were examined. The reports cover environmental management activities in 2020. In this respect, it is thought that the study will contribute positively to the literature.

Yücel (2021), in his study, "The environment, which is defined as the mechanism of a balanced / dynamic functioning in the relations of living things among themselves and with other living things, constitutes the whole of life support systems consisting of living and non-living beings that are used to sustain the lives of living things living in air / water / soil" (Yücel, 2001). 2021: 54) has made the definition of the environment. Değirmenci and Aytekin (2021), in their study, stated that "In order to protect the natural environment, enterprises should prioritize recycling activities, benefit from environmentally protective technologies during production, and encourage environmentally sensitive behaviors of employees" (Değirmenci and Aytekin, 2021: 28). Süklüm (2020) stated in his study that "Especially with the industrial revolution, the technological developments in the production processes, the rapid increase in the population, the profit-oriented thinking of the enterprises in the production processes and not paying attention to the issues such as waste management and environmental pollution, the environment suffers. However, the level of damage to the environment, both on an individual basis and on a business basis, has reached dangerous levels and this has led to social reactions and non-governmental organizations have started to engage in activities that draw attention to the issue. As a result, legal measures have been taken at the national and international level. Businesses inevitably take measures on environmental issues such as preventing environmental pollution, reducing waste management, greenhouse gas and carbon emissions, and develop strategies and policies in this direction" (Süklüm, 2020: 157).

In the study of Yücel (2021), "pollution control" approaches, which are defined as "the elimination of pollution after it occurs within the scope of waste reduction, recycling and designing products/ services in a more environmentally friendly manner, leave their place to "eco-efficiency" approaches. Reducing the pollution that arises as a result of the design-production processes with pollution control can create costs for the economies.In this context, it advocates a negative relationship between product / service production and energy / resource consumption, prioritizes environmental efficiency and states that environmental effects should be resolved before they occur co-efficiency approach, It is important for the sustainable development goals of the economies to be achieved" (Yücel, 2021: 57-58).

In their study, Değirmenci and Aytekin (2021) stated, "Businesses should use limited natural resources more carefully to protect the natural environment and comply with the measures to be taken in the axis of using tools and equipment to protect nature with optimum capacity and environmentally friendly behaviors of employees. environmental sustainability; flexibility can be explained as a condition of balance and interdependence. In the axis of environmental sustainability, businesses should fulfill their environmental responsibilities by preventing the reduction of biological diversity that may result from their activities, while helping the society to provide goods and services. While fulfilling their environmental responsibilities, businesses can benefit from the 3R strategy in rebuilding the nature that has suffered human-induced destruction in today's world. In other words, institutional policies can be developed through reduction, reuse and recycling. Today, due to the rapid development of industrialization, excessive urbanization has had some negative effects on the environment" (Değirmenci and Aytekin: 2021: 28). "While it provides tangible benefits such as improved social and environmental performance, cost reduction and risk management, and intangible benefits such as improved reputation and increased competitiveness, it forms the basis of the emergence of the concept of corporate social responsibility (CSR)" (Gedik, 2020: 266-267).

Within the scope of the study, it is claimed that corporate social responsibility policies implemented in businesses have positive contributions to environmental sustainability. In the next part of this study, the reports published by 15 companies, which are among the 30 largest publicly traded companies in Turkey, in 2020 and related to the environmental sustainability part are mentioned. Finally, the conclusion part of the study is mentioned. It is thought that this study will make important contributions to the environmental sustainability studies planned to be carried out in the future.

BACKGROUND

Environmental Sustainability

Today, environmental sustainability plays an important role in the management policies of businesses. Considering the sensitivity of societies and legislators on this issue, businesses need to act more carefully about environmental sustainability. "While the emergence of easily accessible market structures as a result of globalization and technological and industrial developments creates an increase in the competition process; It creates a decrease in natural resources and environmental values. Since the negative impact of human-industrial activities on the environment causes concerns about the future, Brundtland (1987) reported in his report, taking into account environmental concerns, considering ecological balance and economic growth as a whole, making efficient use of scarce resources, and meeting current needs while meeting future needs. The concept of sustainable development, which expresses the ability to meet Sustainable development includes consumption models and policy practices to raise awareness of consumers as well as production processes, and consists of three different dimensions that support each other: human-economy-environment" (Yücel, 2021: 55).

Tüpraş Environmental Sustainability Report (Year 2020)

Tüpraş, one of Turkey's leading industrial companies and operating in the field of energy production, carries out its activities within the scope of environmental sustainability. In this section, the activities carried out by Tüpraş in the environmental sustainability report (2020) are included.

Environmental Management

"Management of environmental impacts is considered as a priority area within Tüpraş's risk management activities. With these studies, the potential risks that the company's activities may pose on natural areas and living things are identified and precautionary mechanisms are established. In line with these decisions, specialized units operate throughout the operation. In this context, environmental issues throughout Tüpraş operations are managed by the Environment Directorate. In the management of these issues, internal and international standards are followed. In this direction, all activities are implemented through processes that comply with the ISO 14001 Environmental Management System Standard. While the management of environment, climate and energy issues is evaluated in a wide scope, the basic principle is primarily to protect compliance with the relevant legal regulations and legislation. The main fields of study of environmental management are climate change, water efficiency, waste reduction, monitoring and reduction of greenhouse gas and air emissions, minimizing all other environmental effects, increasing environmental awareness among employees and society, protecting and improving natural life. Another important aspect of environmental management is raising environmental awareness among Tüpraş and its business partners, and throughout society. In this direction, Tüpraş continues its training activities uninterruptedly. In this context, in 2020, 2,502 personxhours were provided to 1251 Tüpraş employees, 4,518 personxhours to 6,503 contractor employees, and 200 personxhours to children on environment day. On the other hand, 238 million TL of environmental investment was made during the year. Tüpraş refinery facilities are located in areas reserved for industrial activities. Therefore, there are no 1st degree natural protected areas, environmental protection areas, RAMSAR or similar wetlands with high biodiversity value within the physical impact area. When deciding on physical investment locations, it is a criterion that is taken into account that they are far from such special status areas. Environmental management studies are audited throughout Tüpraş's operations, and the performance achieved is constantly monitored. Environmental performance is subject to the Ministry of Environment and Urbanization audit, external audits carried out by authorized independent institutions, and Koç Group Environmental Audit practices, in addition to internal audit studies. In 2020, there were no lawsuits or significant fines against the company due to non-compliance with environmental laws and regulations. In the reporting period, efforts to manage the environmental impacts arising from operations and planned investments with a holistic approach within the scope of Life Cycle Analysis (YDA) in line with the Sustainable Development Goals continued. In this context, the environmental effects of emissions created by different fuel scenarios used in production, taking into account operational conditions, are reported with the LDA approach. The energy, steam, cooling water, auxiliary facilities and the amount of catalyst that will be needed in the case of the application of the innovative catalyst developed within the scope of the "CO2 -to-fuels" R&D project for the production of methanol and dimethyl ether (DME) from carbon dioxide, are modeled and all inputs and outputs are modeled on climate change. The impact of the product has been calculated and reported from a life-cycle perspective. Also; A road map was created to evaluate the YDA results of important projects within the scope of the investment program, together with the economic indicators that emerged as a result of the feasibility studies. In the study called Environmental Sustainable Investment Support Mechanism; It is aimed to use various environmental impact measurement methods (YDA, input/output analysis, etc.) for the projects that are in the investment program and to identify the environmental impacts that will occur and integrate them with economic indicators. With this project, which is the basis of the impact valuation approach, sustainable ones among Tüpraş investment scenarios will be brought to the fore. At the same time, since the environmental impacts originating from the investment will be known with a proactive approach, it will be ensured that the technically and economically possible measures are taken. A working group, in which the environmental impacts of the Izmit Refinery processes are determined from a life-cycle perspective, was established and started its work. With the study, the existing environmental effects and categories are determined and the points that need improvement are determined. In the reporting period, the current situation has been evaluated within the scope of "Best Reference Document for Refining of Mineral Oil and Gas" and "BAT Conclusions" published by the EU Commission, and points for improvement have been determined" (Tüpraş Sustainability Report, 2020: 34).

Eregli Environmental Sustainability Report (2020)

The 2020 environmental sustainability report on Ereğli, one of the leading industrial organizations in the iron and steel sector of Turkey, has been accessed from the company's website. In this part of the study, the Ereğli environmental sustainability report was cited. In the related report, environmental sustainability activities are explained as follows (Erdemir, n.d.):

Environmental Performance: "Production in the steel sector, including our Mining Metallurgical Companies, is dependent on natural resources such as iron ore and water and includes energy-intensive processes. Industry-induced carbon dioxide emissions directly affect global climate change. Climate change, limited natural resources and rapidly decreasing biodiversity pose serious risks to the steel sector with a high environmental impact. Our Mining and Metallurgical Companies; in order to fulfill its environmental responsibility, Jul has determined that its main focus is to use the available resources effectively, efficiently and correctly, to use communication channels for the development and awareness of all stakeholders, and to continuously improve its environmental performance to leave a cleaner and livable world to future generations as a legacy. The environmental policy of our Mining and Metallurgical Companies, which follow a proactive approach to environmental management, consists of the following elements:

- Applying environmentally friendly technologies as a result of technical, economic and commercial assessments from the point of view of the life cycle and sustainable development, using natural resources effectively and efficiently, and protecting biodiversity.
- Reduce residues at their source, improve recovery methods and promote recovery.
- Employees, customers, suppliers, society and all stakeholders in the Mining Metallurgical Company our perspective on the state of the environment, practices and open communication about the results, inform and raise awareness.

In line with the Environmental Policy Metallurgy Mining Companies the potential environmental risks while carrying out its activities in production facilities, those risks identified in advance, and is taking measures to monitor and minimize the environmental impact and keeps it under control with continuous measurements of improvement and implementing investment projects. The technologies used in these projects contribute to the development of the economy through the efficient use of vital reserves. Policies and processes designed by our Mining Metallurgical Companies; it aims to reduce the environmental footprint and energy use in the entire value chain, to use effective resources, to reduce waste, to act in accordance with recycling, especially at each stage of the operating cycle, to protect and develop human capital. International standards and certifications are applied in environmental management. Erdemir, Isdemir and Erdemir Romania have ISO 14001:2015 (Environmental Management System Standard) and ISO 50001 (Energy Management System Standard) certifications. Mining Metallurgical Companies; it follows the process of monitoring environmental performance and targets as well as national standards and certifications with an original model developed by it, the Environmental Performance Index (EPE).

The Environmental Performance Index identifies the environmental impacts of production, products and services, monitors the sustainability of environmental management systems, evaluates the impacts of facilities in the regions and is prepared by observing data at local, national or international levels. Index; the permit and license certificate are calculated by the realization rate of the goals collected under 3 parameters, namely compliance with the legislation and success criteria. After the evaluations, the environmental performance is reported to the senior management. After the review of senior management, environmental factors that the sector prioritizes, taking into account legislation and international developments, are included in the management strategies of our Mining and Metallurgical Companies. Also Mining Metallurgical Companies; By providing data to the Environmental Performance Index, it also makes it possible for environmental goals to be adopted, internalized and considered as a goal by employees by including environmental criteria in the individual target report cards of many units and employees" (Ereğli Environmental Sustainability Report, 2020: 75).

Vakıfbank Environmental Sustainability Report (2020)

Vakıfbank's activities in the field of social responsibility are analyzed under three headings: "education, culture and sports". The company's subsidiaries and subsidiaries support sports culture and broadcasts continuously. Breakthroughs in the field of education T.C. It is based on a project developed with the Ministry of National Education. In this direction, since 2017, 54 mechatronics, mind games and artificial intelligence workshops and more than 170 information technologies have been undertaken within the body of "Science and Art Education Centers". The company's support in the field of culture brought 85 books to their readers. "Vakıfbank Sports Club" is one of the projects supported in the field of sports. Vakıfbank Volleyball team stands out with the support given to sports for girls from an early age (Vakıfbank, https://www.vakifbank.com.tr/sosyal-sorumluluk.aspx?pageID=128).

Kardemir

Kardemir company was established in 1937 as Turkey's first integrated iron and steel factory.

Environment and Climate (Kardemir Sustainability Report 2020)

In order to reduce the negative activities of the company on the environment and climate; It carries out studies for the protection of water resources and the protection of water consumption, the management of solid wastes, the management of greenhouse gas and flue gas emissions, and the development of environmental awareness. It adopts the "Kardemir Environmental Policy" as the basic guide on the environment and climate. The company, which develops policies in line with the ISO 14001 Environmental Management Standard, carries out its activities within this framework. In 2020, the company provided 1899 hours of environmental training to its employees. The company also takes some precautions regarding the use of water in integration with the production area. "The amount of water recovered through the company's water efficiency studies has reached the level of 585 million m3 in 2020." 381 thousand tons of raw materials used by the company in 2020 were recycled. "Within the scope of the Zero Waste Regulation, 162 sets of indoor recycling bins and 32 indoor direction boards and 95 sets of outdoor recycling bins and 19 outdoor signage boards were distributed in 2020, in order to ensure that the wastes are separated according to their class at the source within the facility. In order to fulfill the obligations within the scope of the Continuous Emission Measurement Systems (CEÖS) communiqué, systems were installed in the process chimneys, where combustion gas, dust and flow parameters are measured and continuously monitored. In order to transmit the emission data of 11 chimneys to the system of the Ministry of Environment and Urbanization, feasibility reports were approved in the previous periods, their tests were completed and the data connection to the SEÖS system was completed (Kardemir, 2020).

Dogan Holding Environment and Climate (Sustainability Report 2020)

The company took its first steps into the business world by registering with the Mecidiyeköy Tax Office in 1959 by Aydın DOĞAN and establishing the first company in the automotive sector in 1961. Today, the company; operates in the energy, fuel, finance, internet, entertainment, industry, automotive, tourism and real estate sectors.

Within the scope of environmental sustainability, Doğan Holding uses new generation cooling devices and environmentally friendly R 410 and R 132 gases in these devices. Equipped with state-of-the-art environmentally friendly fire extinguishing systems, the weight of the fire extinguisher tubes in the system has been reduced, and instead of them, systems that comply with EU standards, contain FM 200 and Novac 1230 gas, are more compatible with the environment and human health. The company has also started recycling garden waste. The precious soil obtained from the wastes with the compost machine placed in the existing gardens is used in the company's own gardens. In a short time, with the works to be started for the composting of the food wastes in the Holding, all organic waste from the building will be recycled and reintroduced into the soil as fertilizer. Within the scope of carbon emission reduction studies at Şah WPP, the Gold Standard registration process has been completed. As a result of the second verification process, 901.912 tons of CO2 emission reductions were confirmed between 2011 and 2018. Şah WPP, which has planted approximately 1,000 trees within the scope of its environmental studies, has also provided vehicles, personnel and various devices to Bursa National Parks Wildlife Protection Directorate. During the winter months, studies are carried out to leave food for wild birds and roe deer at suitable points. Since the power plant site remains in the forest and wildlife protection zone, maximum sensitivity is shown to the protection of the environment. Activities are carried out in harmony with nature, in constant contact with the relevant institutions. The company also engages in activities listed below on environmental sustainability:

- Treatment sludge, which is classified as non-hazardous waste, is sent to licensed companies under appropriate conditions.
- Studies on packaging waste are carried out in cooperation with the 'ÇEVKO Foundation'.
- Hazardous wastes are temporarily stored in the area with a 'Temporary Waste Storage Permit' within the facility and in containers created for hazardous wastes and sent to licensed institutions.
- There are collection units for waste batteries in offices and certain areas in the production area. The collected batteries are delivered to organizations that have been authorized by the Portable Battery Manufacturers and Importers Association (TAP).
- Waste oils that are evaluated in the hazardous waste class and that are released after the expiry of their usage period are referred to as '1. It is in the category 'Waste Oil' category. It is reused in the system and/or sent to 'Licensed Recovery Facilities'.
- There are collection units for contaminated materials formed in the production area. The materials collected in these areas are sent to licensed organizations (Doğan Holding, n.d.).

Akbank Environment And Climate (Sustainability Report 2020)

The company has made reports to the Climate Change Program of the Carbon Transparency Project (CDP) and shared information with its stakeholders. It is also included in the BIST Sustainability Index. The company aims to conduct reporting in accordance with the recommendations of the Task Force on Climate Related Financial Disclosures (TCFD) by 2030. The Headquarters building strives for the conscious consumption of natural resources by saving energy, water and paper in branches and ATMs. It has turned to paperless banking and is carrying out its activities. in 2021, work has been started on international environmental management standards and Energy Management System, and the necessary arrangements are underway. Recycling activities are carried out in order to make recycling activities a part of the corporate culture. After sorting the wastes from the operations at their source, these wastes are delivered to the relevant recycling organizations or the municipality in accordance with the legislation. The company's milestones related to the fight against climate change are listed as follows:

- It is the first Turkish bank to sign the 2007 United Nations Global Compact.
- It is the first Turkish Bank to publish the 2010 United Nations Global Compact Progress Statement. In support of the implementation of the Carbon Disclosure Project (CDP) in Turkey, attention was drawn to the issue of environmental transparency. As the first and only company included from Turkey in the Global 500 Report of the Carbon Transparency Project for 2010, it was included in the category of World Sector Leaders with a high score. As a result of the importance given to environmental sustainability, an Energy-Friendly Loan has been implemented. In cooperation with the Regional Environment Center (REC), support was given to the "Without Extinction" project to draw attention to the regions at risk due to climate change in Turkey. The Regional Environment Center (Regional Climate Change Summit) was the sponsor of the Cancun and Durban papers prepared in advance.
- It is one of the first companies in the world to sign the "Carbon Price Statement" prepared by the Principality of Wales Climate Change Leaders Group in 2012, which draws attention to the need to develop a clear and transparent pricing policy for carbon emissions.
- To create a new roadmap for combating global climate change in Paris 2015 COP21 conference of the Parties (Conference of the parties, COP) to the calling statement, signed by the parties and to combat climate change was signed.
- In 2018, the UN Global Compact working group participated in the updating of the Declaration on Sustainable Finance signed in 2017.
- The Environmental and Social Impact Assessment limit has been reduced to US$20 million in accordance with the UN Global Compact Turkey sustainable financing statement, to which we are a signatory in 2019.
- In 2020, the Environmental and Social Impact Assessment limit was reduced to US$10 million in order to better manage the impacts of the projects it is financing (Akbank Integrated Report, 2020).

Tekfen

Different steps are being taken to manage water risks and seize opportunities in the environmental sustainability climate of Tekfen Holding. In this context, the following items are included in the company's policies:

- Toros Agriculture is increasing its production and sales of special water decoluble fertilizers through R & D studies. Special fertilizers, drops and sprinklers are preferred in irrigation systems and require less water.
- Tekfen Agriculture reduces water consumption by using intelligent irrigation systems (Metos) and digital farm management applications (Doktar).
- Toros Agriculture is working on a Water and Wastewater Treatment and Recovery Project at the Mersin Enterprise. Upon completion of the project, wastewater treatment, recovery of ammonia and nitrate from wastewater as products and rehabilitation of the existing demineralization system at the plant will be provided.
- Toros Agriculture strives to prevent nitrate pollution by ensuring that the right fertilizer is used by farmers at the right time, in the right place and in the right amount. For this purpose, tools such as training videos, Smart Farmer Application and face-to-face farmer trainings are used.
- Tekf Dec Agriculture and Taurus Agriculture R & D Centers carry out product and seed development studies in accordance with changing climatic conditions.

Tekfen Inşaat has also carried out various studies on restoring dormant areas to nature upon requests received so far. in 2020, after obtaining the necessary permits for the rehabilitation of an old quarry located in Vize, upon request from the local population within the scope of the Kırklareli Kıyıköy TurkStream Project, the area was restored to nature by cooperating with the relevant institutions. January 2020. Thus, the region was given a completely new look in terms of the landscape, while the risks such as slips, falls and traffic accidents that pose a danger to humans and animals were also eliminated. Over time, the area was made suitable for livestock activities, and the surrounding woodland began to be used by the local community for recreational purposes (Tekfen Holding, 2020).

Ford Otosan

As Ford Otosan, Yesildirim has signed the "Declaration on the Transition to Zero Emission Freight Transportation" of the European Automotive Association (ACEA), which is also in line with the Green Consensus strategy of the European Union. With the declaration, it is aimed to reduce the carbon footprint of the heavy commercial fleet to zero starting from 2040. it aims to reduce carbon emissions per vehicle by 50-55% compared to 2017 in 2030 and to become carbon-neutral in 2050 (Ford otosan, 2020).

Garanti Bank

Garanti Bank, founded in 1946 in Ankara, is the second largest private bank in Turkey with a consolidated asset size exceeding 423 billion Turkish Liras as of March 31, 2019.

2020 Integrated Annual Report

The Bank has developed innovative financial instruments and solutions in Turkey, such as yesil kredi and gender equality loan structure. in 2020, Garanti BBVA set a target of reducing carbon emissions by 29% by 2025 and 71% by 2035 within the framework of Science-Based Targets in line with the target of a maximum temperature increase of 1.5 °C envisaged by the Paris Treaty. The bank became the first company in Turkey to announce such a goal. in 2020, by purchasing carbon credits for emissions from its activities, it became a carbon neutral Bank. Thus, it has reached much more than the 71% reduction target it has given for 2035 at the end of 2020, that is, 15 years ago (Garanti Bank, 2020)).

Koza Mining

"Koza Anadolu Metal Madencilik", one of the Koza-İpek Holding companies, produces copper, lead-zinc, iron etc. is a corporate mining company that aims to develop continuously with the research, development and production of metallic mineral deposits. The company's environmental policies are listed below (Koza Mining, n.d.):

- Adhering to all legal requirements applied in line with the Environmental Legislation,
- To establish and implement an environmental management system that identifies, evaluates and effectively controls commercial and social environmental risks,
- Establishing environmental procedures and implementing these procedures in an auditable manner by an independent organization.
- To save energy, water and natural resources by increasing efficiency and encouraging the use of new technology,
- Initiating regular inspection and evaluation programs and accepting suggestions for improvement by taking appropriate follow-up measures. Ensuring that the accepted improvements are implemented,
- Establishing an open communication for environmental risks, incidents, emergencies and improvement of views in order to take effective decisions and measures,
- To evaluate the environmental impacts of the activities it carries out, to implement appropriate measures and monitoring procedures to eliminate or minimize the negative environmental impact, to design and operate the infrastructure related to these, and to minimize the long-term financial responsibilities related to them,
- To ensure / maintain the original conditions and productivity of the land during and after the activities it carries out,
- Besides its employees; To raise awareness of Sub-Contractors, Contractors, Suppliers and their employees about environmental policy and to provide necessary trainings so that they can continue their activities within the scope of Environmental Policy,
- To carry out studies for the reduction, reuse and recycling of wastes.

Arcelik White Goods

The company, which started its activities in the white goods sector in 1955, has more than 40,000 employees globally, 12 brands (Arçelik, Beko, Grundig, Blomberg, ElektraBregenz, Arctic, Leisure, Flavel,

Defy, Altus, Dawlance, Voltas Beko), sales and marketing services in 48 countries. With its marketing offices and 28 production facilities in 9 countries, it provides products and services to many different points of the world. For environmental sustainability, the company has taken the following steps with the "Healing the Planet Project" Arçelik, 2020):

1. **Climate Change**
    - To reduce the average energy consumption per product by 45% in production
    - The targets for reducing greenhouse gas emissions, which were determined in parallel with the aim of keeping global warming "well below 2 degrees" within the framework of the Paris Agreement, were approved by the Science-Based Targets Initiative.
    - Our global production facilities13 (Scope 1 and Scope 2) were carbon neutral in 2019 and 2020 with our own carbon credit, which we produced with the Energy Efficient Refrigerators Carbon Financing Project.
    - A total of 5,217 tons of CO2 emission reduction was achieved.
    - 100% green electricity was purchased at production facilities in Turkey and Romania, which account for more than 75% of the total electricity consumption in our global production facilities.
    - Scope 1 and Scope 2 greenhouse gas emissions in Turkey operations were reduced by 73% compared to 2010.
    - With the photovoltaic solar panels with an installed power of 930 kWp at the Washing Machine Plant in Romania, 3,171 GJ of electricity was produced, and 238 tons of CO2 e greenhouse gas emissions were prevented.
2. **Energy Efficiency in Production: The company could not reach the targets it set.**
3. **Water Management**
    - Total financial savings from waste reduction and water efficiency projects: EUR 1,593.000
    - Total water savings achieved through efficiency projects: 352,844 m3
    - Reduction in water withdrawal thanks to water efficiency projects in our production facilities: - 18% in Turkey - 13% in Romania - 9% in Russia - 29% in Thailand - 13% in South Africa
4. **Waste Management**
    - Total financial savings achieved through waste reduction and water efficiency projects: 1.593.000 Euro • Total waste recycling and recovery rate in production facilities included in the reporting scope was 96%.
    - Waste recycling rate in Turkey operations increased to 98%.
    - The average amount of hazardous waste per product at production facilities in Turkey, Romania, Gaeşti, Russia, China and South Africa was reduced by 30% compared to 2012.
    - Between 2014 and 2020, approximately 1.3 million AEEEs were recycled, resulting in a total energy saving of 326 GWh, approximately 160,000 tons of CO2 emissions were prevented and approximately 6.5 million tons of water was saved.
5. **Packaging**
    - Approximately 88% recycled cardboard was used in 29,537 tons of boxes used in packaging in all our businesses around the world, and 314.5 tons of 100% recycled and recyclable cardboard boxes were used in small household appliances produced in Turkey.

- Expanded polystyrene (EPS) in ventilation hoods and Turkish coffee machines was replaced with 39.6 tons of 100% recycled and recyclable cardboard.
- Approximately 3.84 million recycled PET bottles were used in packaging strips of white goods.
- The annual packaging waste generated in the production facilities was reduced by 366 tons, thanks to the packaging improvement studies carried out in the supply chain.

6. **Circular Economy**
    - PET Boiler: With the use of 28.2 million recycled PET bottles, the total number has reached 58 million since 2017. 2,200 tons of CO2 emissions were prevented and 19,000 GJ of energy was saved.
    - EcoSustain: The rate of EcoSustain, a recycled plastic raw material, reached 31% in Atak vacuum cleaners, 17% in Jaguar vacuum cleaners, and 64%-73% in toasters and grills. A total of 190.4 tons of recycled plastic was used in these product categories.
    - Eight tons of recycled fishing net and 111.7 tons of industrial yarn waste were converted into high-performance recycled polyamide compounds used in oven, washer, dryer and dishwasher parts.
    - Bio Refrigerator: The version produced with bio-based fan cover and eggshell-containing biocomposite was launched. Studies on the use of bioplastics in small household appliances were accelerated, and coffee grounds were used in coffee machines and tea fiber was used in tea machines.

Sasa

Established in 1966, the company; is one of the world's leading manufacturers of polyester, fiber, filament yarn, polyester-based polymers, special polymers and intermediates.

Environmental Management (Sasa, n.d.):

The company, which prioritizes the evaluation of environmental impacts in its past and future investments, has "Environmental Permit and License Certificate" and "Environmental Management Unit" certificates obtained from the Ministry of Environment and Urbanization. A total of 5 environmental engineers work in the Environmental Management Unit, and the monitoring and implementation of legal processes, as well as our declaration and reporting obligations in environmental processes are carefully managed. The company also has ISO 14001 Environmental Management System certificate.

In all investments of our facility; It has "Environmental Impact Assessment" reports within the scope of local legislation and "Environmental and Social Impact Assessment" reports within the scope of international legislation and is monitored within this framework. In our new investments, Environmental and Social Management Plans for our investments have been prepared, taking into account both the national environmental legislation and the IFC Environmental, Social and Security Directives. In addition, our facility has successfully completed the audits carried out by third party auditors in this context.

In the process of harmonization with the European Green Agreement (AYM), studies are carried out in all our enterprises for waste reduction, efficient use of resources, and the recovery of chemicals and energy, and 6 sigma methodology is applied in the projects carried out within this scope.

Waste Water Management

In the facility owned by the company, there is a wastewater treatment plant where industrial wastewater, process washing water and domestic wastewater are treated. The capacity of the wastewater treatment plant, which was first established in 1998, was increased in 2011 and 2019 and additional units were added to the plant. Physical, biological, chemical and advanced treatment processes are used in our facility, which has the "Wastewater Treatment Plant Identity Certificate". In addition, both anaerobic and aerobic treatment methods are applied in our biological treatment system. There are 1 operating specialist and 13 operators in the treatment plant, the plant works continuously in 3 shifts and the whole process can be monitored from the control room. Apart from the inspections carried out by the Ministry, daily sample analyzes are carried out in the environmental laboratory within our waste water treatment plant and the plant performance is constantly monitored.

For a sustainable environment, water is discharged to the receiving environment in accordance with both the discharge limits we are subject to in the Water Pollution Control Regulation and international legislation and standards. The quality of the effluent we discharge is monitored by the Ministry with the Continuous Waste Monitoring System (SAİS). Suspended Solid Matter, Conductivity, Dissolved Oxygen, pH and Chemical Oxygen Demand parameters of the discharge water are monitored online via SAIS.

For the purpose of Waste-to-Energy Recovery, high pressure steam is produced by burning the biogas formed in the anaerobic treatment process and used in the enterprises within the factory. It is aimed to reduce the greenhouse gas effect and reduce our carbon footprint by preventing the release of methane gas into the atmosphere.

The feasibility and engineering studies for our new wastewater treatment plant, which will be commissioned in 2023 within the scope of the PTA Production Facility Project, have been completed. The water treated in our new wastewater treatment plant will be recovered by using advanced treatment technologies, and the water obtained will be reused in the processes.

Waste Management

Our facility has a Zero Waste Certificate within the scope of the Zero Waste Project. Considering the product life cycle in our processes, policies of reduction at source, separation at source and reuse of waste produced in our facility are implemented. Industrial and domestic wastes from our facility are collected in temporary waste storage areas authorized by the Provincial Directorate of Environment and Urbanization and transferred to licensed facilities. 1 business expert and 5 operators take part in the management of these processes. Almost 100% of the waste generated in our factory is recycled. The leftovers from the cafeterias are sent to the feeding points for stray animals in order to prevent waste.

One of the subjects included in our environmental permit and license document is co-incineration. In our co-incineration facility, energy is obtained from process wastes with energy recovery technology. Thus, a reduction is achieved in the use of fossil fuels.

Management of Emissions:

Emissions are monitored online in 5 of the emission sources in our facility, and Continuous Emission Measurement Systems (SEÖS) are available at these points. It provides instant data transfer to the Ministry of Environment and Urbanization via SEÖS about the emissions from these chimneys. In addition, air quality modeling for the emissions of our facility is made and cumulative effects are taken into account.

İşbank

İşbank, the first national bank of the Republican era, was established on August 26, 1924, in line with the decisions taken at the Izmir First Economics Congress, with Atatürk's directives. İşbank started its operations with two branches and 37 personnel under the leadership of its first General Manager, Celal Bayar. Its nominal capital was 1 million TL. The actual paid portion of 250 thousand TL of this capital was paid by Atatürk himself (İşbankası, 2020).

Combating Climate Change Restrictions applied in many countries in the world due to the coronavirus (COVID-19) pandemic caused a decrease in global greenhouse gas emissions in 2020. However, as the 2008-2009 financial crisis showed, emissions are expected to return to pre-pandemic values in a short time after the end of the restrictions. Although the pandemic seems to have created an opportunity for the transition to a green economy, the cost of inaction continues to increase day by day. In 2021, the World Economic Forum identified the risk of "failure in climate action" as the most impactful and second most likely long-term risk. İşbank supports the transition to a low carbon economy. The Bank analyzes the risks and opportunities created by the transition economy and increases the number of products and services that support the green economy day by day. At the corporate level, İşbank takes all risks arising from climate change into account. These risks are prioritized based on a qualitative and quantitative assessment. Most of the climate change risk that the Bank is exposed to arises from its customers in its commercial loan portfolio. For the measurement of this risk, the commercial loan portfolio covering all sectors is taken into account and analyzed. A two-stage approach is followed to assess the exposure of the loan portfolio to climate change risks (İşbank, 2020):

1. Scenario: Sectoral climate change heat map is used to identify the sectors that need to be considered as a priority when assessing climate change risk. A 5-level risk scale is used to determine the extent to which each sector is exposed to climate change risks.
2. Scenario: With the help of this analysis, impact analysis is performed for risk events in sectors with high and medium-high risk of climate change as a result of the heat map. The approach adopted within the scenario analysis has been prepared in line with the climate change methodology followed by the United Nations Environment Program Finance Initiative (UNEP-FI). In terms of the management of climate change risk; The impact of a possible carbon tax or carbon trading system implementation on the Bank is measured within the scope of scenario analysis. With this method, the financial data of loan customers operating in sectors that are exposed to high transition risks and are expected to be most affected by these regulations are stressed by taking into account additional liabilities and the possible effects of changes in customers' creditworthiness on the Bank's balance sheet are analyzed. Within the scope of the Climate Change Risk Management Project carried out in 2020, the actions that are foreseen to be implemented by the end of 2022 regarding the opportunities arising from climate change have been defined. Studies are underway to determine the responsibilities and roadmaps to be followed for these initiatives, which include actions such as enriching the product and financing opportunities that will support the transition to a low carbon economy, and increasing access to sustainable funding sources. In addition to the work carried out by the Risk Management Department for the measurement of climate change risks, all new investment projects financed by İşbank with an investment amount of more than USD 10 million are subject to the Environmental and Social Risk Evaluation Tool (ERET). evaluated using A reputable independent Environmental Consultant is appointed to work on behalf of the Bank

in all projects deemed appropriate as a result of the evaluations of İşbank Sustainable Finance Team. Field visits supported by literature studies are carried out by the Independent Environmental Consultant in order to determine the current situation and possible environmental and social effects of the investment within the scope of the project. As a result of this study, an Environmental and Social Due Diligence (ESDD) including the current status, suitability and consultant comments of any permit/approval process regarding environmental obligations and an Environmental and Social Action Plan (ESAP) for limiting, eliminating and managing the process of these effects. prepared and submitted to the Bank. In high-risk projects, apart from the EIA application file prepared in line with legal requirements, international standards (I) containing more detailed current situation analyzes.

Aselsan

Aselsan was established in 1975 to meet the communication needs of the Turkish Armed Forces with national means. It is a joint stock company affiliated to the Turkish Armed Forces Foundation (TSKGV). 74.20% of ASELSAN shares are owned by TAFF, 25.80% of shares are traded on Borsa Istanbul (BIST) (Aselsan, n.d.).

Aselsan carries out the Energy Systems Program with the aim of being the leading domestic technology supplier among companies that produce energy system solutions by using its deep-rooted engineering experience with innovative approaches. It is aimed to develop efficient, reliable and economical products and services that will reduce Turkey's dependence on foreign sources and meet the needs of stakeholders in the global market, in all energy systems sub-headings covering the fields of electricity generation, transmission, distribution, consumption and management. For this purpose (Aselsan, n.d.);

- With Energy Management and Smart Grid Systems
- Renewable Energy Systems

Studies are carried out to provide system solutions covering R&D, design, production, integration and after-sales support.

The company carries out its activities under 3 headings related to environmental sustainability. These:

- Energy Management and Smart Grid Systems
- Power Converters
- It is examined under 3 headings, namely hybrid energy systems.

PETKIM

The Idea of Establishing a Petrochemical Industry in Turkey Was Adopted In 1962, The Beginning of The First Five-Year Plan Period, And as A Result of The Studies and Researches, Petkim Petrokimya A.C. It Was Established On 03.04.1965 Under the Leadership of Tpao (Petkim, n.d.).

Petkim Added the Value Of "Taking Responsibility for A Sustainable Future" To Its Corporate Values In 2010, Once Again Demonstrating the Sensitivity It Has Shown Over the Years in This Regard. Our Company, Which Uses Many Tools to Realize Its Values at Every Stage of Its Corporate Structure, Has

Created a Platform Called the Sustainability Board in Order to Carry Out Its Sustainability Efforts in A More Coordinated Manner. The Sustainability Board Reports to The General Manager of The Company, And Its Activities Are Supported and Monitored by The General Manager. The Work of The Sustainability Board Can Be Reported to The Board Of Directors Through The General Manager. The Main Focus of The Sustainability Board Is Establishing Environmental Policies and Managing the Environment. In This Context; An Institutional Structure Has Been Established in Order to Monitor Environmental Impacts and Climate Change Issues and The Risks Within This Scope with A Wide Participation and At the Highest Level. All Relevant Units of Our Company Contribute to This Committee by Expressing Their Opinions, And the Decisions Taken Are Supported and Instructions of The General Manager, Who Is the Highest Executive of The Company, Are Implemented.

Environmental Permit and License Certificate: Petkim Carries Out Its Activities Within the Scope Of Environmental Legislation And Documented The Compliance Of Its Activities With The Legislation With The Environmental Permit And License Certificate Numbered 114, Which It Received From The Ministry Of Environment And Urbanization On 09.10.2014. This Environmental Permit and License Certificate, Valid Until 09.10.2019, Has Been Issued on The Subjects Of "Air Emission, Wastewater Discharge, Waste Incineration and Co-Incineration, Waste Acceptance Facility", And Internal Monitoring and Reporting On The Subject Are Carried Out In Different Periods.

Waste Management: Preventing Pollution at Its Source Is One of The Most Important Environmental Principles. In This Context, Petkim Acts Jointly with All Its Employees to Prevent Waste Generation And Reduce Waste By Increasing Reuse, And Disposes Of Combustible Wastes In The Central Treatment Facilities It Has Established. The Wastes Generated by Our Activities Are Collected Separately As Recyclable, Combustible And Storable According To Their Disposal Methods, Are Temporarily Stored In Licensed Areas, And Are Subject To Recycling/Disposal Processes By Determining The Waste Code According To The Legislation. Petkim Has Become The First And Only Industrial Enterprise Of Our Country To Establish A Licensed Waste Incineration Facility Within Its Own Structure By Making An Important And Large Environmental Investment. It Has Been A Great Advantage That We Have A Solid-Liquid Waste Incineration Facility Since 2006 In Order To Ensure Efficient And Effective Waste Management In Our Company. In This Facility, It Has Been Designed According To The Regulation On The Control Of Hazardous Wastes, And Combustible Wastes Are Disposed Of By Burning At A High Temperature (1100°C), And The Environmental Effects Of These Gases Are Prevented By Passing The Waste Gases Through Activated Carbon Filters.

Water Management: Petkim Has A Very Serious Knowledge In Water Supply And Wastewater Treatment Since 1984, And This Experience Turns Into A Great Advantage In Water Management. It Includes Petkim, Other Industrial Facilities And The Güzelhisar Dam Operated By Dsi, Which Was Established By Petkim To Meet The Water Needs Of The People Of Aliağa, With A Total Storage Volume Of 150 Million M3. In Addition, There Is A Water Pre-Treatment Unit Where The Water Coming From The Dam Is Processed Into Raw Water, Fire Water, Process Water, Cooling Water And Drinking Water, There Is A Demineralized Water Unit Where Demineralized Water Is Produced By Using Process Water, And All Wastewater Generated In The Facility And Lodgings Is Physical, Chemical And Chemical. The Fact That It Has A Wastewater Treatment Plant, Where It Is Treated In Biological Treatment Systems, Shows That Petkim Provides A Serious Integrated Water And Wastewater Management. Waste Water Is Treated In Our Industrial Wastewater Treatment Plant And Discharged To The Sea In Accordance With The Water-Related Legislation.

Marine Pollution Control: Our Company, Which Operates On The Coast Of Nemrut Bay, Is Considered As A Coastal Facility According To The Current Environmental Legislation Due To Its Port Activities. In This Context, An Emergency Response Plan Was Prepared By An Authorized Institution Having A Risk Assessment Done For Our Port Activities. According To The Emergency Response Plan Approved By The Ministry, Petkim has The Capacity To Respond To A Level 1 Incident With Its Own Means.

Another field of activity carried out within the scope of port activities is the management of ship waste. According to marpol and the environmental legislation that came into force in parallel with this issue, petkim port (petkim, n.d.).

CONCLUSION

In today's world, developments in the industrial and technological fields and human and business activities harmful to the environment have made the attention of the world's nations focus on environmental issues. Our world is aging day by day and human-induced harmful activities cause dangerous destruction in our world. The rapid migration (from the village to the city) in parallel with the developments in the industry has brought along important problems. In a scientific research that mentions the importance of the subject, the negative effects of industrialization and the concentration of its population in industrial cities are listed as follows (Değirmenci, 2019: 29):

- "Decrease in green areas as a result of excessive migration from rural areas to big cities due to industrialization,
- Decreases in living species as a result of the decrease in green areas,
- Conversion of fertile agricultural lands into residential areas as a result of rapid urbanization,
- Visual and noise pollution as a result of rapid immigration in industrial cities,
- Excessive air pollution as a result of the use of harmful fuels,
- An increase in noise and gas emissions due to developments in aircraft technology "Değirmenci and Aytekin, 2021: 29).

There have been many studies in the literature on corporate social responsibility. In addition, a common definition of corporate social responsibility has not been developed in the literature. In some of the studies, the legal aspect of the concept, the ethical aspect of the concept, and the economic aspect of the concept were mentioned in some. In this study, corporate social responsibility is shaped on the axis of environmental sustainability. In a study, corporate social responsibility "It is seen that corporate social responsibility programs generally have a positive relationship with perceived reputation, corporate customer satisfaction and environmental management practices" (Tran and Nguyen, 2020: cited in Gedik, 2020: 270).

FUTURE RESEARCH DIRECTIONS

Within the scope of the study, the environmental sustainability reports of 15 publicly traded corporate companies were examined. In this context, it is understood from the 2020 sustainable reports that these companies make significant contributions to environmental sustainability.In this study, the leading companies of energy production, iron and steel production and automobile production were examined. It is thought that the information conveyed within the scope of the study will mirror the future studies. In addition, it is envisaged that future research will be conducted on companies operating in different fields such as "glass, plastic, furniture, food, yarn" production.

REFERENCES

Arçelik. (2020). Retrieved from https://www.arcelikglobal.com/media/6365/arcelik_2020surdurulebilirlikraporu_yoneticiozeti.pdf

Aselsan. (n.d.). Retrieved from https://www.aselsan.com.tr/tr/cozumlerimiz/enerji-sistemleri

Brundtland, G. (1987). *Ortak Geleceğimiz Dünya Çevre ve Kalkınma Komisyonu*. Raporu, Türkiye Çevre Sorunları Vakfı.

Değirmenci, B., & Aytekin, M. (2021). Çalışanların Çevreci Davranışları Merinos A.Ş. Uygulaması. Gazi Kitabevi.

Ebner, D., & Baumgartner, R. (2006). The Relationship Between Sustainable Development and Corporate Social Responsibility. *Corporate Responsibility Research Conference, 4*(5-9), 1-17.

Erdemir Çevresel Sürdürülebilirlik Raporu. (n.d.). *Kurumsal*. Retrieved from https://www.erdemir.com.tr/kurumsal/

Finnveden, G., Hauschild, M., Ekvall, T., Guinee, J., Heijungs, R., Hellweg, S., Koehler, A., Pennington, D., & Suh, S. (2009). Recent Developments In Life Cycle Assessment. *Journal of Environmental Management, 91*(1), 1–21. doi:10.1016/j.jenvman.2009.06.018 PMID:19716647

Fordotosan. (2020). Retrieved from https://www.fordotosan.com.tr/documents/Documents/Surd_Raporlari/2020_surduruleklilik_raporuv1.pdf

Garanti Bank. (2020). Retrieved from https://surdurulebilirlik.garantibbva.com.tr/surdurulebilirlik-yaklasimimiz/

Gatimbu, K., & Ogada, M., Budambula, N., & Kariuk, S. (2018). *Environmental Sustainability And Financial Performance Of The Small-Scale Tea Processors in Kenya. Business Strategy & the Environment, 27*(8), 1765-1771.

Gedik, Y. (2020). Kurumsal Sosyal Sorumluluk: Tanımları, Tarihi, Teorileri, Boyutları ve Avantajları Üzerine Kuramsal Bir Çerçeve. *Haliç Üniversitesi Sosyal Bilimleri Dergisi, 3*(2), 265-304. Retrieved from https://dergipark.org.tr/en/pub/husbd/issue/58132/776380

Gedik, Y. (2020). Sosyal, Ekonomik Ve Çevresel Boyutlarla Sürdürülebilirlik Ve Sürdürülebilir Kalkınma. *Uluslararası Ekonomi Siyaset İnsan ve Toplum Bilimleri Dergisi, 3*(3), 196–215.

HoldingD. (n.d.). Retrieved from https://www.doganholding.com.tr/surdurulebilirlik/cevre-ile-ilgili-projeler/

Holding, T. (2020). *Surdurulebilirlik Raporu.* Retrieved from https://www.tekfen.com.tr/Uploads/pdfs/318202191845964surdurulebilirlik-raporu-2020-web.pdf

İşbank. (2020). Retrieved from https://www.isbank.com.tr/contentmanagement/IsbankSurdurulebilirlik/pdf/2020EntegreRaporu.pdf

Kardemir 2020 Sustainability Report. (2020). Retrieved from https://www.kardemir.com/dosyalar/Sayfalar/1338/05082021/2021080508550667_Sayfalar_1338_05082021.pdf?v=eb7ea1d2_a131_7764_d20d_1028a70f35c0

Menteşe, S. (2017). Çevresel Sürdürülebilirlik Açısından Toprak, Su Ve Hava Kirliliği: Teorik Bir İnceleme. *Journal of International Social Research, 10*(53), 381–389. doi:10.17719/jisr.20175334127

MiningK. (n.d.). *Çevre Politikasi.* Retrieved from https://www.kozametal.com.tr/sorumluluklarimiz/cevre-politikasi /

Mosca, F., & Civera, C. (2017). The Evolution of CSR: An Integrated Approach, Symphonya. *Emerging Issues in Management,* (1), 16–35.

Oláh, J., Aburumman, N., Popp, J., Khan, M. A., Haddad, H., & Kitukutha, N. (2020). Impact of Industry 4.0 on environmental sustainability. *Sustainability, 12*(11), 4674. doi:10.3390u12114674

Önce, S., Onay, A., & Yeşilçelebi, G. (2015). Kurumsal Sürdürülebilirlik Raporlaması ve Türkiye'deki Durum. *Journal of Economics, Finance and Accounting, 2*(2), 230-252.

Petkim. (n.d.). *Çevre.* Retrieved from https://www.petkim.com.tr/Sayfa/1/12/KURUMSAL-SURDU-RULEBILIRLIK-CEVRE.aspx

ReportA. I. (2020). Retrieved from https://www.akbankinvestorrelations.com/tr/images/pdf/2020-akbank-entegre-raporu.pdf

Sasa. (n.d.). Retrieved from https://www.sasa.com.tr/kurumsal/surdurulebilirlik/cevre-yonetimi

Şenocak, B., & Mohan, Y. B. (2018). İşletmelerde Çevresel Sürdürülebilirlik Bilinci Ve Yeşil İşletmecilik Uygulamalari İle İşletme Başarisi Arasindaki İlişki. *Süleyman Demirel Üniversitesi İktisadi ve İdari Bilimler Fakültesi Dergisi, 23*(1), 161–183.

Solomon, J., & Maroun, W. (2012). *Integrated Reporting: The Influence of King III on Social, Ethical and Environmental Reporting*. The Association of Chartered Certified Accountants (ACCA).

Süklüm, N. (2020). Kurumsal Sosyal Sorumluluk, Yeşil Muhasebe Ve Yeşil Denetim İlişkisine Kavramsal Bir Bakış. *Bilecik Şeyh Edebali Üniversitesi Sosyal Bilimler Dergisi, 100*, 151-163. doi:10.33905/bseusbed.752576

Sun, H., Mohsin, M., Alharthi, M., & Abbas, Q. (2020). Measuring environmental sustainability performance of South Asia. *Journal of Cleaner Production, 251*, 119519. doi:10.1016/j.jclepro.2019.119519

Surty, M., Yasseen, Y., & And Padia, N. (2018). Trends in integrated reporting: A stateowned company analysis. *Southern African Business Review, 22*(1), 1–22. doi:10.25159/1998-8125/3841

Tran, K., & Nguyen, P. V. (2020). Corporate Social Responsibility: Findings from the Vietnamese Paint Industry. *Sustainability*, *12*(3), 1044. doi:10.3390u12031044

Tüpraş Çevresel Sürdürülebilirlik Raporu. (n.d.). https://www.tupras.com.tr/

Van Huis, A., & Oonincx, D. G. (2017). The environmental sustainability of insects as food and feed. A review. *Agronomy for Sustainable Development*, *37*(5), 1–14. doi:10.100713593-017-0452-8

Yücel, M. A. (2021). Çevresel Sürdürülebilirliğin Değerlendirilmesi: Dinamik Mekânsal Panel Veri Yaklaşımı. *Bilgi Sosyal Bilimler Dergisi, 23*(1), 53-90. Retrieved from https://dergipark.org.tr/en/pub/bilgisosyal/issue/60370/908722

KEY TERMS AND DEFINITIONS

Concept of Waste Management: It is defined as a set of processes covering the collection, control, accumulation, removal, and waste processing procedures within the scope of human and nature protection related to waste.

Corporate Sustainability: It is a concept that includes only a part of sustainable development - especially the economic decision units responsible for production - expressing the continuity of commercial enterprises.

Environment: The sum of the economic, social, legal, technological, and natural conditions in which one lives and interacts.

Environmental Sustainability: It means ensuring the continuity of natural resources.

Recycling: It is called the re-production of waste that has the possibility of being re-evaluated by being converted into raw materials or by-products by undergoing various processes.

Sustainability: Development that meets today's requirements without compromising the ability of future generations to meet their own requirements.

Sustainable Development: Development that meets the needs of the present without compromising the ability of future generations to meet their needs.

Chapter 4
Cooperative Approach for Intelligent and Smart Agriculture System

Jay Prakash Maurya
https://orcid.org/0000-0002-5574-5822
Lakshmi Narain College of Technology, India

Bhupesh Gour
Lakshmi Narain College of Technology, India

ABSTRACT

Productiveness present in soil, productive weather conditions, plant growth information, rainfall in regional areas, and information on seed planting, among other things are significant parameters to consider for the development and improvement of Indian agriculture. All parameters can be gathered via IoT sensors and digital devices and stored in real-time database environments for sharing with digital machines. It aids farmers in obtaining information on all aspects of agriculture. Modern farming may be recorded using different sensors, smart digital cameras, and gadgets such as micro-chips thanks to the internet technology era. The automated technology provided by the internet of things (IoT) assists farmers in a variety of ways, including the most efficient use of resources (resources are finite) and agricultural problems.

INTRODUCTION

The populace has quadrivial in the last century. There were approximate 1.8 billion human beings on the globe in year 1915. There are approximate 7.3 billion human being on the globe today, with a potential of 9.7 billion by 2050 as per UN report. Global food demand is rising as a result of this growth, as well as improving financial conditions in developing countries. At this point, no one can prevent a major increase in death rate on the globe (Verónica Saiz-Rubio, 2020). Furthermore, numerous sceptics trust

DOI: 10.4018/978-1-7998-9648-7.ch004

Figure 1. World population growth from 1800 to 2100
(Partha, 2007)

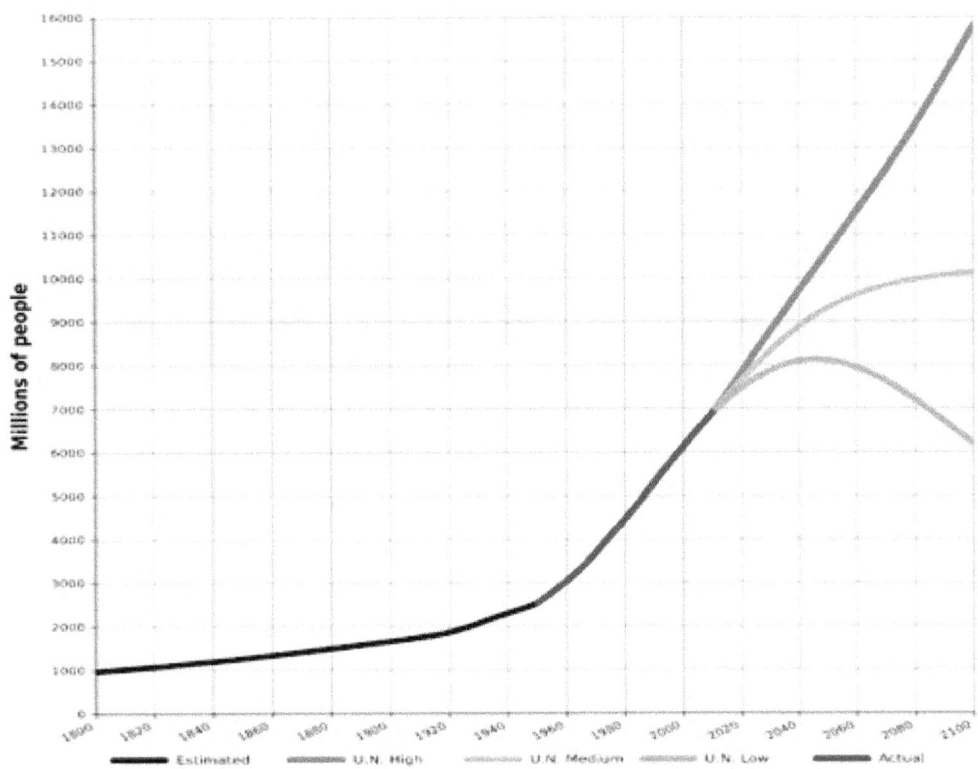

Ehrlich's claim is overemphasized, claiming that human population growth follows an exponential pattern. However, according to the principles of nature; exponential growth cannot be approached indefinitely.

Aside from food shortages, population growth is doing havoc on the ecosystem in a variety of ways that are irreversible. Many scientists agree that global climate change is caused by CO2 (CO2) emissions and is a substantial result of human activity (Partha, 2007). Throughout the late twentieth century, a succession of accords was signed for committed to reducing their CO2 emissions to stop rise in global warming; however, not every government has ratified these treaties, owing to economic and political considerations. In some circles, the role of act in global climate change is strongly contested. For limiting human population growth and conserving the ecosystem in the long run, there is a lot of uncertainty.

Food demand is predicted to extend from 59 – 98 percentages till 2050 (Muhammad, 2019). It is a demand of farming market to be structure in such a type that hasn't taken earlier. Common village farmers must participate in raising crop production, either by expanding their farm for more production or by strengthen the farms using organic compost, irrigation, & the use of recent technologies or techniques such as precision farming. The expected gain in demands of farming products on global are depicted in Figure 2. Meat, fish, roots, and tubers demand is expanding at around 50% decrease as compared to last decade, and hardly as fast as the increase in population, one percent a year. The downfall in much more pronounced for oils refined from vegetables, and experienced rapid expansion from last ten years. The

Figure 2. Percentage increase in demand of farming products, 2007-16 and 2017-26
(Vinayak, 2016)

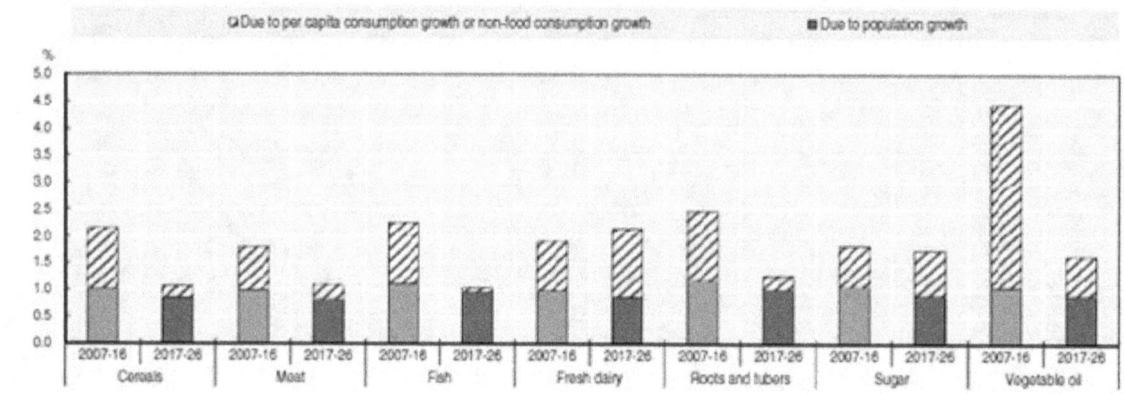

other options are dairy, which is seeing an increase in demand, and sugar, which is expected to expand at a similar percentage (Zhang, 2019).

However, particularly in tropic regions, the ecological and socioeconomic costs of opening land for farming are typically considerable. Crop yield, per unit of farming area, is now increasing steadily in order to satisfy projected food demand.

More issues, like global change in weather, change of rural areas in urban, and a decrease in investment, will cause meeting food urging difficult. Change in weather cause water level decrease, increase the temperatures, and other unfortunate weather will cause serious long-term effects on farming pro-

Figure 3. Temperature change growth
(Accenture, 2019)

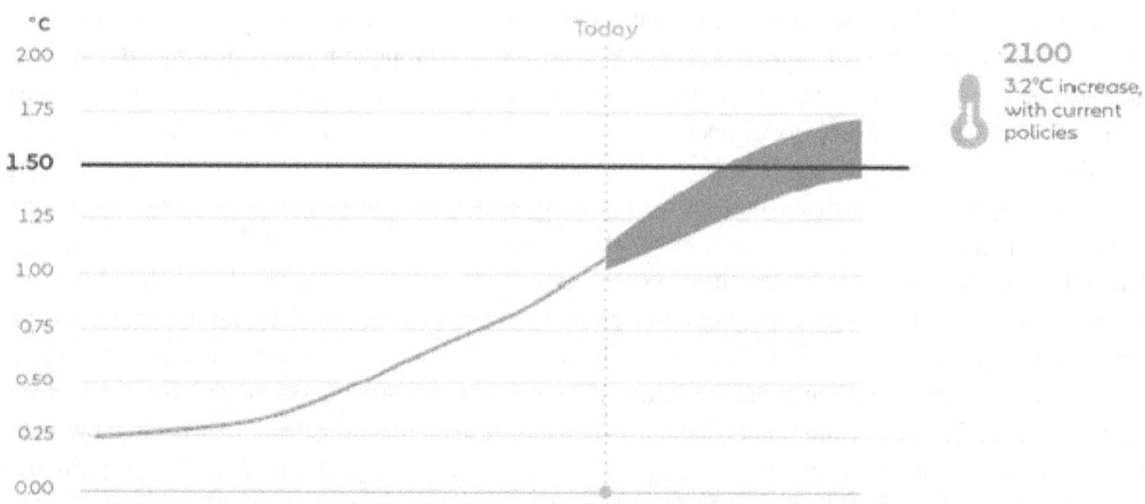

duction yields, according to academic agreement. Majority of farming regions, particularly those are near to Equator, may be affected (voxeu org, 2018). The change in global climate, MatoGrosso, which is most important region for agricultural, analyzed an 18 – 23 percentage decrease in soy & corn output till next 30 years (Accenture, 2019).

Extreme heat can also cause significant reductions in agricultural productivity in the Midwest of the United States and Australia (east) are 2 additional interested regions. Despite the fact that certain places will initially interest from global change in climate, China, Canada, and Russia (northern countries) are expected that they have more time for summer and temperature growth in certain areas. Due to substantial crop yield gaps and broad ditched agriculture land (40 million hectares and greater in comparison with Germany) giving the fall in Soviet Nation in 1991, Russia already have significant policies to export grains with large untapped potential of production (Zhang, 2019). This country offers the best agricultural opportunity on the planet, but to take advantage of it, some institution have policies to work with huge investment policies in agriculture and rural in structure development but more it require in this field. Some soft agriculture product trading organizations, like Cargill, Louis Dreyfus, or COFCO, usually demanded in modern era (Ritika, 2020). Big food processing corporations such as Trade Mills and Unilever impact on global market due to what population eat, this food require security because these needed distributor of prepared foods like bread and others used as huge Food product, such as rice, wheat, corn, and sugar, as well as soybeans (CEMA, 2019). These corporation store oilseeds as well as grain produced throughout the year for consumption, and they prepare soft commodities for decrease in value chain.

Despite the fact that certain places produce greater production and trade decrease the demand chain imbalance, it hope two times food production demand by next 30 years will be a significant problem. To achieve a sustainable global food balance, choose government and private business organization must need to collaborate to increase production, innovation in same, and optimization in supply chain. Farmers, riding firms, and other processing industries (especially Big Food) must first prepare for deforestation-free supply chains. Deforestation not only causes quick and irreparable ecological losses, but also the second biggest CO2 emission source compared to fossil, and global warming is a result—it add negative attributes for farming as well as our forest. “Sustainable intensification” refers to the requirement for farmers to grow on the land area where they are currently operating. This suggests the use of precision instruments like GPS sensors for fertilizer information and moisture sensors, and a crop rotation schedule that is environmentally friendly. The strategies listed above aid in the production of other agriculture yields, in particular areas of Africa state, America, and Europe where production gaps is substantial. These will help mitigate the opposite weather impact of exaggerate resources by reducing water level depletion in ground, as a result, the degradation of productive areas due to fertilizer overuse. A good long-term investment from commercial companies, as well as public spending, is required in the agriculture sector.

Because money investments in land have traditionally give good return values in money, enhanced diversity, and surpassed escalation, top investors such as pension companies and sovereign wealth companies, made large devotion to help global agricultural work and commerce in today era. Nonetheless, compared to rich countries, developing countries’ agricultural investment plans have dropped over the previous 30 years, and significantly less money is spent on research and development (Abhijit Pathaka, 2019). This leads to decrease in productiveness and sluggish yield, and because financial firms in developing nations provide fewer financial help as loans to the farmer, both farmers and large enterprises are still constrained in their investment opportunities (Vinayak, 2016). Governments must lower risks in order to attract greater funding and investment in agriculture. Regulators must modify laws that impede the financial inclusion of small, rural farmers. Quick loans and interest rate limitations. Furthermore, policies, rule and laws, and infrastructure investments aids in the development of a future investment or agriculture (Muthunoori Naresh, 2019). The food balance on globe must be prioritized by policymakers, corporations, and consumers. International business people involved in demand-supply chain must commit the need for policy change, as well as for developed countries to promote financial expenditure in regions with the greatest growth aspect.

BACKGROUND

Precision agriculture is a term that is currently being used a lot in the business. It assists growers in better responding to variations within one land area in order to improve quality of crop and production. Digital farming framework is a collection of technology, tools and software to import data for precision farming decisions and, when utilized correctly, can help minimize waste, enhance revenues (Md Ashifuddin, 2019). Market retails man and suppliers are now using agricultural tools into their modern agriculture strategy, including field applications such as devices and sensor collection that regulate goods, and may give real-time data. Platforms for software application development are likewise getting more popular, expanding the number of possibilities accessible. These digital agricultural solutions frequently gather data and analyze it for market vendors in making a variety of crop production decisions. Some digital agriculture solutions can assist in increasing field output (VerónicaSaiz, 2020).

Soil and Plant Data Collection

Growers can use modern digital tools to assess maximum plant growth conditions and nutrients the crops received to check and meet maximum production targets on a farm to farm basis. Today's technology offers a wide range of alternatives. Placement of sensors around the agriculture farm to measure moisture and soil attributes in these various places is one technique. This will aid in the reduction of VRT and the improvement of yields in major issue regions. These sensors work in conjunction with software tools that help producers take advantage of modern tools and equipments. Computer applications, and related software along with other digital component that can be used in conjunction for farming manually to record data based on soil sample, fertilizer given, rainfall happened, and other factors. Agronomists can use new technologies to better understand and improve their farming decisions for individual areas. Many electronic smart instruments are available that can be programmed to figure out how to operate a grower's equipment or customized & programmed with field data (Ritika, 2020).

Automate Field Management

If a producer uses technology systems along with sensors, soil and plant are frequently optimized through sensors & delivered from a choice network, which may decide the most efficient watering and fertilization schedules for the actual crops. If a producer uses a tool like Field View, they may track growth throughout the season using a range of resources available on the platform. Field health photography, for example, allows producer to view and check the status of the crop and crop looking and agriculture farm management decisions as the season advances, allowing them to maintain the highest yield potential (MdAshifuddin, 2019).

Real-Time Data Collection

If a producer installs sensing equipments across the agriculture farm, it will be monitored using selected attributes as well as real-time scenarios to provide producer good decisions during all over the crop period. Producer / farmer can use real- statistical data at important point of time to make them help and decisions with digital agriculture solutions. If a farmer has uploaded data of plat statistics or utilized the Field View during planting, for example, Google maps will be created in their private account. These virtual maps subsequently be used during harvesting, or they can be paired with current harvest crop data to provide specific production results by farming land, and its variety (Partha, 2017).

Excellent Policies for Results from Labor and Resources

Farmers and market retailers are ready to adopt technology so that they can maximize and take benefits of crop nutrients, protection, and minimize expenses of irrigation by deploying autonomous system through sensors so that it can notify growers when it's time to irrigation and giving fertilizer for their crops. Farmers can develop a type of seeding and prescriptions for fertility (scripts) using digital agriculture tools like Climate Field View, incorporating nitrogen, potassium, phosphorus, and other important nutrients. It is calculated that about 50 percent of all farmers use agricultural technology, and other remaining is expected to continue to increase the agronomists and producer see the benefits of digital farming technologies and how farmer can plan to enhance their production results as a broader accurate agriculture plans (MUHAMMAD, 2019) . There are also dealer choices for a few digital programs, allowing the farmer to check results and analyze how crops plant performed in greater areas or under all of growing conditions. Different Technologies used in Intelligent Agriculture System (IAS) are:

1. Sensing Technology
2. Software Applications
3. Communication Systems
4. Positioning Technologies
5. Advanced Information Technology Hardware
6. Data Analytics

PROPOSED MODEL

Smart farming is a new term for agriculture farming with additional technologies (ICT) to increase quality while reducing human effort required. Following listed technology and devices can be used by farmers:

- Soil, water, light, humidity, temperature Sensors.
- IoT platforms.
- Cellular, Zigbee communication technology.
- GPS, Satellite services.

Figure 4. Smart farming technology stack

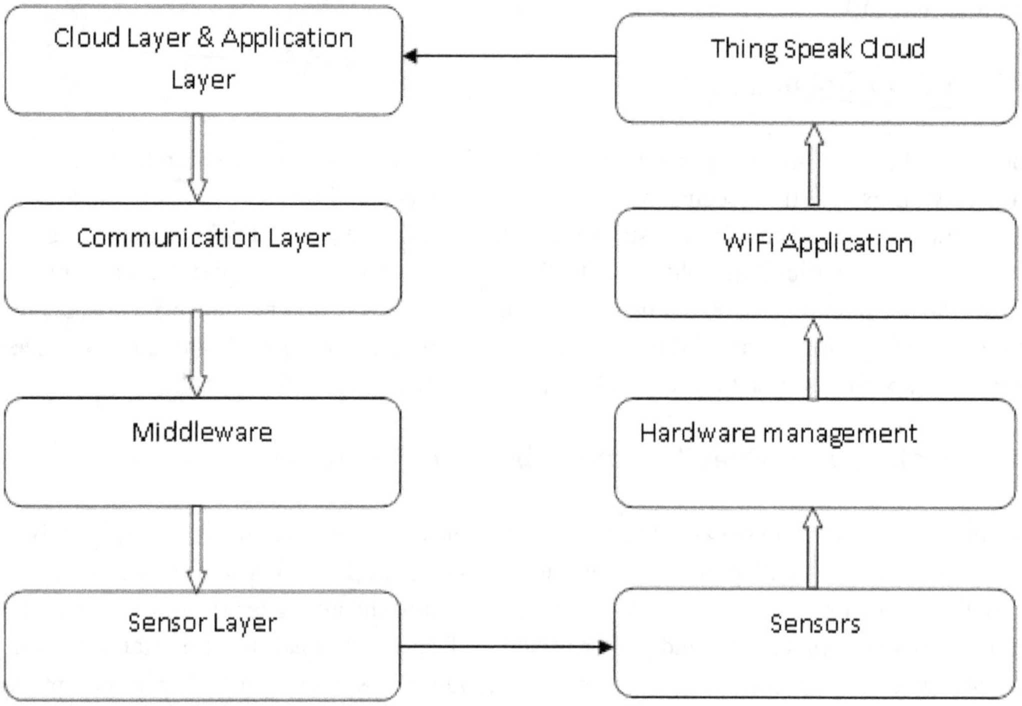

- Robotics, Autonomous tractors, processing facilities.
- Data analytics solutions etc.

System Design

To achieve the goals of the smart farming model, it will be necessary to develop an IoT-based smart farming system that will regulate electrical devices such as pumps, house flaps, and other similar devices without requiring human intervention in environmental parameters like soil moisture and agriculture farm temperature. Future data analysis on these attributes can be saved on the internet cloud Environment. A more regulated environment, farming is done in playhouses. The suggested system will be made up of several levels, as shown in Figure 4. Cloud & Application Layer, Communication Layer, Middleware, and Sensor layer, are the four modules.

Sensor's Layer: -This is first layer of proposed framework. It is in charge of recording and monitoring various environmental factors. This layer continuously senses or collects parameters from many types of sensors placed throughout the agricultural field. Two types of sensors were employed in this study: the moisture sensor SEN-13322, for humidity data and a temperature sensor ERC8973 for temperature information within poly homes. All of these sensors must be communicated with an Arduino-based microcontroller, and is connected to sensors to construct basic IoT objects that are used in agriculture.

Middleware:-The second layer in suggested systems is needed for automotive processing of the farming work and in control manner. It will be made for a microcontroller. The microcontroller receives the sensed values as input and acts accordingly based on the measured values of several monitoring field parameters. This layer keeps a close eye on the soil temperature and moisture level, as these two factors have a direct impact on crop output and subsequent actions.

- If the moisture level in the soil does not reach the saturation level, the microcontroller will engage the pump machine to water the sector, as insufficient moisture content in the soil reduces crop output. The soil moisture content threshold varies depending on the kind of soil (Zhang, 2019). According to, the appropriate moisture content threshold values for all types of soil where irrigation needed are mentioned in given Table 1. A threshold of 15% soil moisture content is used in the proposed method. When the moisture level hits the limit, the pump will shut down automatically, saving you money on electricity.
- If the temperature level exceeds the edge value, the IOT arduino will open the poly house flap. The suggested system uses a threshold of temperature around 40° C. Temperature rises shorten crop life and disrupts the delicate balance between crops and menace. It also increases crop respiration while decreasing fertilizer rate. Aside from operating the driving microcontroller it also communicates the detected information from the sector with the Thing Speak cloud via a gateway.

Communication Layer: -Because Wi-Fi has an advantage over Bluetooth, the microcontroller connects with the gateway wirelessly in this layer. Bluetooth offers a shorter range of connection than Wireless, and the gateway can be located outside of the vigilance area. Because of the extensive wiring, Ethernet-based communication is avoided. Here, a microcontroller is equipped with sensors that are placed across the monitoring field, delivering the measured moisture in the soil, reported humidity and temp data to the cloud through gateway. On the gateway, a hardware-based protocol may be in use. The arduino may send a HTTP request on Thing Speak cloud, requesting that the sensed information be sent to the appropriate channel.

- Cloud computing is a new computer based technology that has the potential to be useful in smart farming. This approach proposes using a cloud computing platform to record several aspects of agricultural farm information. All types of channels are formed throughout the same layer, each of them associated with specific field within Think Speak cloud to store real agriculture farm data. Through a communication protocol, the arduino sends real-time data on appropriate channel on a regular period. This real-time data is graphed over period and can help for further investigation. Agricultural area conditions are frequently checked from remote area using the Thing Speak online service's graph.

Farming-related applications are frequently developed and deployed on the cloud, where they can be used by farmers.

Various equipments are being employed to realize the envisioned system. All sensors are connected to the Arduino, which may be often used in place of microcontroller. The LM35 is frequently used to record temperature, whereas the VL95 is frequently used to record moisture content in soil. To regulate high voltage devices, stepper motors and fans are frequently linked to Arduino UNO boards using 6 pin relay. The detected data is supplied into the arduino board's middleware, which supports recorded values and controls the equipments like Controlling Pump, Fan. Apart from operating actuators automatically, the Arduino IDE is used to create middleware and sends gathered parameters to the Cloud. For storing environmental parameters, Arduino boards communicate wirelessly with the Thing Speak cloud

Figure 5. IoT based smart farming development

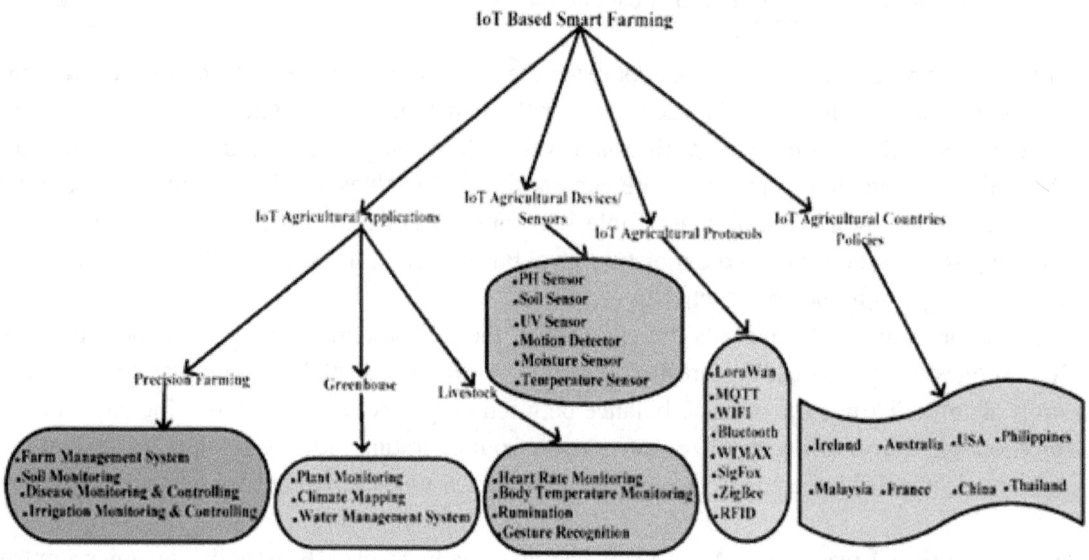

through a router. During proposed agriculture model, Wi-Fi (ESP8266)- is used for communication. To communicate with the Cloud, the ESP8266 connects with gateway device having internet access. These observed data are then plotted in the cloud-based Thing Speak web service every 15 seconds, as Thing Speak requires a 15-second delay between periodic updates. Different levels of moisture and temperature information of farm and supported predetermined threshold values, and the Arduino manages the farming equipments those work on high voltage without farmer interaction, based on the above-mentioned system design. This technology helps in continuous monitoring and triggers the appropriate occurrences corresponding with the need in the absence of a human in the agriculture field. It reduces the amount of work and the farming cost at some level. In order to test the proposed technology in the various soil

Table 1. Soil type and moisture content

Type of Soil	Texture& Moisture Content in soil (%)
Simple	7.0
Loamy	12.0
Loam (Sandy)	15.0
Silt	20.0
Simple Clay (Sandy)	22.0
Loam	23.0
Sandy Clay Loam	24.0
Clay	27.0
Silty Clay	28.0
Clay	31.0

Figure 6. Sensors and device distribution

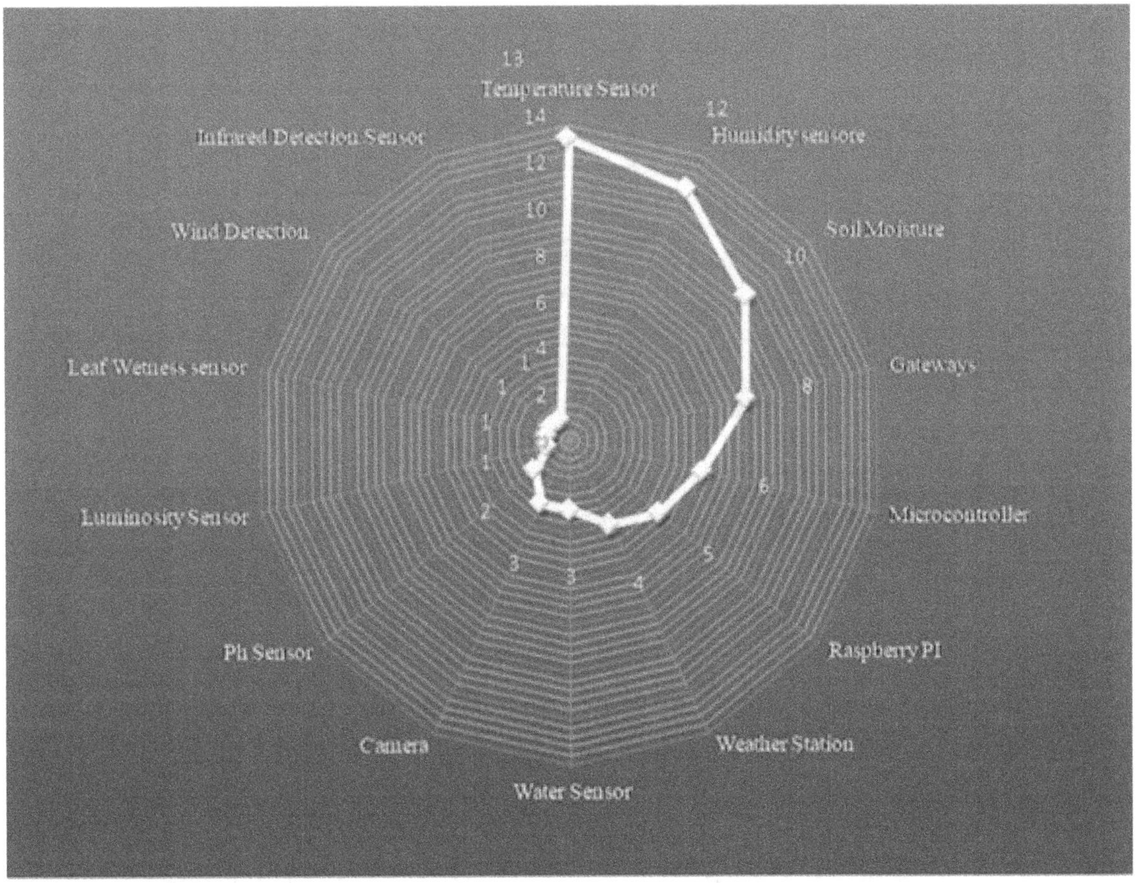

texture environments listed in Table 1, the edge soil moisture and temperature must fluctuate, and incorporated into the middleware without change in physical structure.

Proposed model may need above all sensors and devices fig -6 that are to be used in real time environment for framework design. The sensors and devices can be attached and integrated with other module also like data analyses, process, visualization and prediction fig-7. The analysis and prediction module of framework will use some cloud application to manage the data generated by sensors as well as it can help to predict the weather and other parameter so that resources can be saved by the farmer as well as government authority involved like electricity Distribution Company.

RESULTS

The proposed IoT framework for agriculture is sort of interesting and a recent developing area and therefore the results of given system often compared with previous system with IOT automated agriculture works. This proposed model has been worked with issues and challenges related to the implementation of IoT applications of previous works like security, cost, reliability, scalability, localization and interoperability.

Figure 7. Smart farming modern design and application

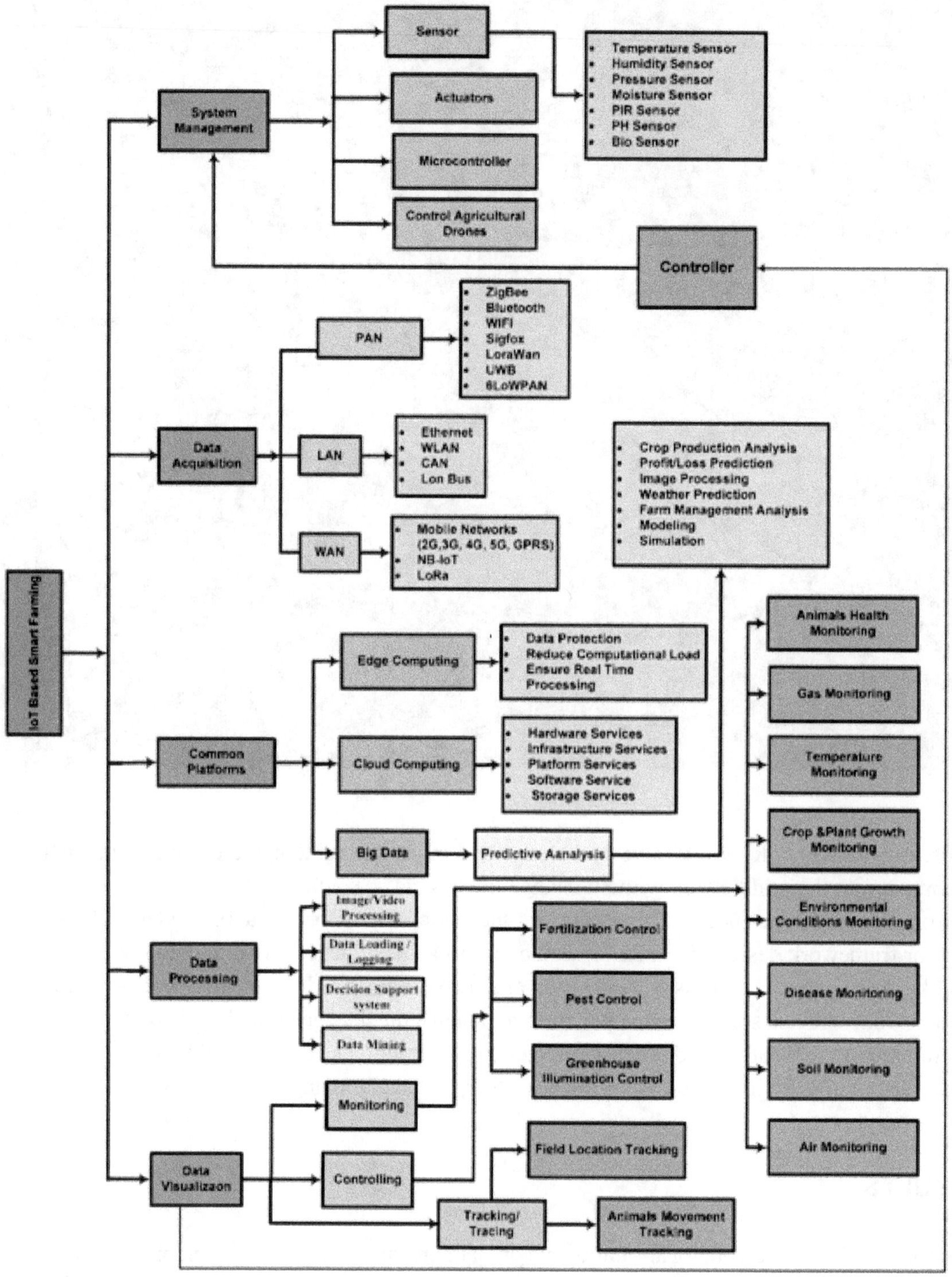

Users encounter numerous issues as a result of insufficient security, including knowledge loss and other on-field parameters. The presence of unwanted one on agriculture farm, such as attacks by animals, puts IoT devices in the agriculture field in jeopardy. Furthermore, sophisticated and complicated algorithms are difficult to implement due to energy and memory constraint. Hijacking assaults, session hijacking, database difficulties, and denial of service attacks are all major security threats to cloud infrastructure. Several cost-related challenges exist when using IoT in agriculture, such as setup and running costs. Apart from cost of hardware, the ongoing costs include a continuous subscription for IoT device administration, data sharing, and other services, as well as centralized services that provide information/data collecting. The major challenge for farmers living in rural areas is a lack of understanding of technology. This is a prevalent problem in underdeveloped countries, since the majority of farmers are illiterate.

The adoption of IoT in agriculture could be difficult due to the significant expenditure necessary in farmer training prior to the deployment of IoT infrastructure. In this regard the modern agriculture system must be in safe environments so that it can be resisted from physical damage. But, it's very critical to make ensure the safety of used IoT devices/sensors from harsh weather conditions. Moreover in agricultural sector, a lot of IoT sensors and devices are used, as intelligent IoT system to control of every equipment in system. When it comes to deploying devices/sensors, there are numerous variables to consider. Without deploying new devices with extra configuration; such devices should be able to give support to the globe. Furthermore, the simplest deployment position should be chosen so that equipments can exchange data without any difficulty. To work with, IoT equipments, it requires standards, and communication protocols in proper mode. Semantic, syntactic, technical, and organizational policies all play a role in interoperability.

Semantic interoperability refers to the ability to alter the understanding of content communicated among humans. For data and its syntactical interoperability: javascript object notation (JSON), and extensible terminology (XML), and variables separated by a comma are considered. The technical interoperability deals with infra, communication protocols, and hardware/software and connection of IoT devices. Interoperability policies are for properly working of communication and data transfer in multiple geo- regions. In contrast, 3 strategies are offered in for achieving interoperability: (i) open and closed standards, (ii) services and merchandise partnership for providers, (iii) middle one and adaptor services. More work is required in this filed in order to achieve high interoperability among multiple IoT devices.

CONCLUSION

The chapter recommends combining the most recent innovation in the field of autonomous agriculture with current tactics to indicate on/off for water systems, resulting towards profit and decrease in temperate. The interesting technology can be taken, that can transform proposed methods of an agricultural land into a product that manages sensor data via cloud administrations. Many points of interest have been started to use sensors that employment consequently improving. This concept of modernization of farming is cheap and operable for farmers and a requirement of today life. The thought of modernization is even developing and continuously growing as change in digital circuit improvements also as technology to handle the system cannot stop this research. The predictive model of the framework, which involves data analysis, can improves the functionality of model and with the assistance of this we will save lot of resources like electricity, manual human resources & can make strategies for disaster and may be functional for farmers. If all the parameters for the irrigation with smart IOT devices are set for machine learning model these system can improve the agriculture system of a rustic which is productive and effective.

ACKNOWLEDGMENT

I take the opportunity to express my cordial gratitude to Dr. Anupam Chouksey, Executive Secretary, Lakshmi Narain College of Technology, Bhopal for the valuable guidance and inspiration throughout the work I feel thankful for his innovative ideas, which led to successful completion of this work. I give special thanks to Dr. Dr. V.K Sahu, Principal, Lakshmi Narain College of Technology, Bhopal, to always being willing to help find solutions to any problems I had with my work I extend my deepest gratitude to, Lakshmi Narain College of Technology, and Bhopal for providing all the necessary facilities and true encouraging environment to bring out the best of my endeavors. I also want to acknowledge Dr. Ashok Rai, Dean of Administration & OSD, Lakshmi Narain College of Technology, Bhopal, for giving me the opportunity to present my work successfully and giving me the assistance for my article works. I express my gratitude and thanks to all the staff members of Department of Computer Science & Engineering for supporting my work and providing me the proper guidance during my work. I would like to thank my family & friends.

REFERENCES

Abdurrahman, Gebru, & Bezabih. (2015, May). Sensor Based Automatic Irrigation Management System. *International Journal of Computer and Information Technology, 4*(3). https://www.ijcit.com/archives/volume4/issue3.

Agrawal, S., & Das, M. L. (2011, December). *Internet of Things — A Paradigm Shift Of Future Internet Applications.* https://ieeexplore.ieee.org/document/6153246

Ayaz, Ammad-Uddin, Sharif, Mansour, & Aggoune. (2019). Internet-of-Things (IoT)-Based Smart Agriculture: Toward Making the Fields Talk. In *New Technologies For Smart Farming 4.0: Research Challenges And Opportunities.* https://ieeexplore.ieee.org/document/8784034

CEMA. (2019, September). *Digital Farming: What Does It Really Mean?* https://www.cema-agri.org/publication/digital-farming-what-does-it-really-mean

Chikankar, Mehetre, & Das. (2015, April). *An Automatic Irrigation System Using ZigBee In Wireless Sensor Network.* https://ieeexplore.ieee.org/document/7086997

Chikankar, P. B., Mehetre, D., & Das, S. (2015). An automatic irrigation system using ZigBee in wireless sensor network. *International Conference on Pervasive Computing (ICPC)*, 1-5. 10.1109/PERVASIVE.2015.7086997

European Commission. (2012). *Generational Renewal in EU Agriculture: Statistical Background.* https://www.europeansources.info/record/rural-development-in-the-eu-statistical-and-economic-information/

Farooq, M. S., Riaz, S., Abid, A., Umer, T., & Zikria, Y. B. (2020, February 12). Electronics | Free Full-Text | Role Of IoT Technology In Agriculture: A Systematic Literature Review. *MDPI.* https://www.mdpi.com/2079-9292/9/2/319

Himesh, S. (2018, September). *Digital Revolution And Big Data: a New Revolution In Agriculture.* Research Gate. https://www.researchgate.net/publication/327572166

Hossain, M. S., Rahaman, S., Kor, A.-L., Andersson, K., & Pattison, C. (2017). A Belief Rule Based Expert System for Datacenter PUE Prediction under Uncertainty. *IEEE Transactions on Sustainable Computing*, *2*(2), 140–153. doi:10.1109/TSUSC.2017.2697768

Hridoy, M. S., Islam, R. U., Hossain, M. S., & Andersson, K. (2017, December). *A Web Based Belief Rule Based Expert System for Assessing Flood Risk*. ACM. https://dl.acm.org/doi/10.1145/3151759.3151807

John, Palaparthy, Sarik, Baghini, & Kasbekar. (2015, March). *Design And Implementation of a Soil Moisture Wireless Sensor Network*. https://ieeexplore.ieee.org/abstract/document/7084901/.

Khadam, U., Iqbal, M. M., Alruily, M., Al Ghamdi, M. A., Ramzan, M., & Almotiri, S. H. (2020). Text Data Security And Privacy In the Internet Of Things: Threats, Challenges, And Future Directions. *Wireless Communications and Mobile Computing*, *2020*, 1–15. doi:10.1155/2020/7105625

Malavade & Akulwar. (2016). *Role of IoT in Agriculture*. https://www.iosrjournals.org/iosr-jce/papers/Conf.16051/Volume-1/

Mondal & Rehena. (2019). IoT Based Intelligent Agriculture Field Monitoring System. *Second International Conference on Advanced Computational and Communication Paradigms (ICACCP-2019)*. https://zdocs.pub/doc/contoh-artikel-d6w2xzyw9w68

Naresh & Munaswamy. (2019, January). Smart Agriculture System using IoT Technology. *International Journal of Recent Technology and Engineering, 7*(5). https://www.ijrte.org/wp-content/uploads/papers/v7i5/E1987017519.pdf

Pathaka, Uddina, Abedina, Anderssonb, Mustafac, & Shahad. (2019, September 13). *IoT Based Smart System To Support Agricultural Parameters: A Case Study*. ScienceDirect. https://www.sciencedirect.com/science/article/pii/S1877050919310087

Ray, P. P. (2017). Internet of things for smart agriculture: Technologies, practices and future direction. *Journal of Ambient Intelligence and Smart Environments*, *9*(4), 395–420. doi:10.3233/AIS-170440

Saiz-Rubio, V., & Rovira-Más, F. (2020, February 3). From Smart Farming Towards Agriculture 5.0: A Review On Crop Data Management. *MDPI*. https://www.mdpi.com/2073-4395/10/2/207/

Schimmelp Fennig, D. (2017, November). *Farm Profits and Adoption of Precision Agriculture*. https://www.ers.usda.gov/webdocs/publications/80326/

ScienceDirect. (2003, August 28). *A real-time grading method of apples based on features extracted from defects*. https://www.sciencedirect.com/science/article/abs/pii/S0260877403001894?via%3Dihub

Shahin, M. A., Tollner, E. W., McClendon, R. W., & Arabnia, H. R. (2002). *Apple Classification Based On Surface Bruises Using Image Processing And Neural Networks - PubAg*. https://pubag.nal.usda.gov/catalog/815360

Srivastava, Sharma, Jaiswal, & Raj. (2020, July). A Research Paper On Smart Agriculture Using IoT. *International Research Journal of Engineering and Technology, 7*(7). https://www.irjet.net/archives/V7/i7/IRJET-V7I7479.pdf

Zhang, Y. (2019, September). The Role of Precision Agriculture. Resource. *Resource Magazine, 26*(6), 9-9. https://elibrary.asabe.org/abstract.asp?aid=50990

KEY TERMS AND DEFINITIONS

Agriculture: It is the practice of cultivating plants and livestock.

Digital Devices: A digital device processes electronic signals that represent either a one ("on") or a zero ("off").

Digital Machines: The digital machines are CPU oriented and the intermediate software layers convert the user commands to binary level operations as bit, nibble, byte, word, word-groups, arrays, and matrices dimensioned and partitioned in the declaration statements in the higher level programs.

Internet of Things (IoT): The internet of things, or IoT, is a system of interrelated computing devices, mechanical and digital machines.

Microchip: A microchip (sometimes just called a "chip") is a unit of packaged computer circuitry (usually called an integrated circuit).

Sensors: A sensor is a device that produces an output signal for the purpose of sensing of a physical phenomenon.

Soil: Soil is the loose surface material that covers most land. It consists of inorganic particles and organic matter.

Chapter 5
The Socioeconomic and Political Ramifications of Climate Migration in the 21st Century

Mitchell Alan Kaplan
Independent Researcher, USA

ABSTRACT

As the environmental consequences of climate change continue to expand across international boundaries, many nations in the industrialized and developing world are struggling to find ways to cope with the onslaught of adverse social effects caused by this unprecedented phenomenon. Research spearheaded by environmental organizations such as the United Nations and other government-backed climate monitoring agencies suggests that the ecological disruptions caused by the dramatic shift in global weather patterns is one of the primary factors driving the escalation of mass migration and human population displacement in many parts of the civilized world. This chapter will examine the social, economic, and political issues associated with climate-induced migration in the United States and abroad. It will analyze how this phenomenon influences the development of climate policy capable of assisting vulnerable nations worldwide to implement strategic measures that will enable them to resolve the complex national security and border immigration issues associated with the climate crisis.

BASIC FACTS ABOUT CLIMATE MIGRATION

Throughout humanity's history, environmental factors have played a critical role in influencing human migration and displacement patterns worldwide. Scientists analyzing the interconnection between climate change, migration, and displacement have noted that the professional literature on the environment utilizes different terminology interchangeably to describe the strength of the association between the mass movement of human populations within and across international borders and a host of environment-related factors (Bustos et al., 2021). According to a definition cited in a recent White House report issued by the Biden Harris administration in October 2021, climate-induced migration is the permanent or temporary displacement of human populations across international borders in regional locations impacted by

DOI: 10.4018/978-1-7998-9648-7.ch005

the adverse social conditions precipitated by climate change. Unlike planned relocation, which usually involves a cooperative agreement between residents in global communities and government officials occurring in an atmosphere of mutual consent that is voluntary, in contrast, climate-induced migration generally occurs under less favorable environmental and social conditions linked to involuntary population displacement (White House report, 2021).

In recent decades, the results of scientific inquiry into the emerging secondary effects of ecological disruption have taken center stage on the legislative agenda of political officials in many nations of the global community currently experiencing the most severe social and political fallout of climate vulnerability. Results of a host of environmental studies documented in the scientific literature on climate change have sought to broaden understanding of the adverse effects of this expanding global phenomenon, whose consequential impact on human populations shows no indication of slowing down in the near future. A landmark study by researchers at the Institute on the Environment University of Minnesota published in the *Journal of Sustainability* in 2017 draws a strong connection between human migratory behavior and the degree of population vulnerability to the secondary effects of climate change. The research examines the link between climate vulnerability and international patterns of global migration in 179 countries. To make definitive determinations about the degree of correlation between these two phenomena, the investigators utilized climate vulnerability scores and national forced migration rates to measure country-specific differences over time. Results indicated that forced migration is an adaptive social response to climate variability's disruptive impact. Data analysis suggests that as the consequential effects of climate change continue to worsen globally, increasing the destructive power of cyclonic storms and magnum force hurricanes that destroy property, disrupt essential services, and cause large scale human displacement, the mass movement of asylum-seeking refugees across international borders will become a transitional phenomenon that is increasingly more commonplace. Analysis of the data revealed that differences in climate vulnerability scores are essential determinants of the degree of impact the rising flow of cross-border migrants will have on a spectrum of nations. Findings indicated that countries with the highest climate vulnerability scores had the lowest flow of asylum-seeking refugees. In contrast, those with the lowest climate vulnerability scores had the most increased flow of refugees seeking asylum.

Based on these findings, the researchers posit that global communities that adopt an adaptive approach to responding to climate change's impact will reap the most favorable outcomes of forced migration. The researchers argue that this type of migratory behavior stimulates a decrease in population vulnerability to environmental change's most significant risk factors. They conjecture that even though the harmful effects of climate change vary from country to country, those with the most considerable susceptibility are usually the ones that require the highest degree of targeted intervention to avoid humanitarian crises that exacerbate the burden of existing social and economic inequalities such as food insecurity, homelessness, and acute poverty all of which represent social concerns that policymakers in the most affected nations have yet to find sustainable solutions (Grecequet et al., 2017).

Research by other scholars of a similar mindset provides scientific evidence supporting the direct connection between climate change and the detrimental consequences of forced migration, such as political unrest, civil war, and violent regional conflict in many developing nations worldwide. For decades, journalists in the mainstream media have suggested a direct link between these two phenomena, despite the lack of definitive evidence in the literature that justifies this contention. However, this situation has changed in recent years as an increasing number of academicians have turned their professional attention to the scholarly exploration of the secondary effects of the climate crisis on vulnerable populations. A recent study by investigators at the International Institute for Applied Systems Analysis in 2019 attempts to provide empirical evidence that supports the premise that climate change is responsible for creating adverse social conditions in developing nations of the third world that is subsequently fueling the uptick in the forced migration of asylum-seeking refugees in the United States and across Europe.

The research team used three data sets to determine the connection between patterns of forced migration and climate change. The first data set contained applications for asylum filed by refugees seeking to migrate from 157 countries between 2006 and 2015, processed by the United Nations High Commission on Human Rights. The second set contained assessment data on climate vulnerability from the countries of origin that refugees sought asylum obtained via the Standardized Precipitation Evapotranspiration Index (S.P.E.I.). The research team used the S.P.E.I. data as an assessment tool to discern the impact of extreme differences in regional rainfall patterns on transitional expansion of international migrant populations. The third set contained data collected from military death records from the Uppsala Conflict Data Program (U.C.D.P.). The research team used the information to identify social and political factors that confirm the resilience of the relationship between climate change and the risk of global conflict.

Additionally, the team utilized socioeconomic and geographic data from a variety of related sources to develop a framework for an analytic model with the capacity to assess environmental factors driving the rise in geopolitical conflict associated with the expansion of international patterns of migration. Data from these two additional sources incorporated into the model focused on demographic information about the distance between migrants country of origin and their intended destination, size of international populations forced to undergo climate-induced migration, availability of global networks to assist displaced migrants and their families, and the impact of climate conditions on the political status of countries that immigrant populations are leaving along with additional data about the ethnic and religious composition of migrant groups entering the new homeland. The data analysis revealed a significant causal connection between climate change and population migration patterns in the developing world. The data indicate that countries with the most severe drought conditions had the highest social and political unrest incidence. The research team found that the disruptive effects of climate change on the proliferation of regional conflict were most evident in the developing nations of western Asia and the middle east, such as Syria, Yemen, Tunisia, and Libya, between 2010 and 2012, when national water shortages precipitated by sustained periods of seasonal drought caused consistent crop failures resulting in a rise in climate-induced migration from agriculture-dependent rural areas to urban environments in cities. This led to a significant increase in social conditions of overcrowding, unemployment, and political unrest, which escalated into civil war in many of these countries. Results of the data analysis caused the research team to conclude that there is a significant connection between climate change, conflict, and forced migration patterns linked to increased competition for scarce natural resources in vulnerable global societies (Abel et al., 2019).

Further evidence of the relationship between climate change and demographic transition resulting from population migration is revealed in research by the World Bank in 2018. The study focused on transitional international migration patterns in three geographic regions, Sub-Saharan Africa, South Asia, and Latin America. These global locations comprise 55 percent of the total population of the developing world. Researchers collected primary demographic, socioeconomic, and climate impact data associated with population migration from selected geographic locations and secondary data of the exact nature for contrast from three subregions Mexico, Central America, and East Africa. To determine the extent of the adverse consequences of slow-onset environmental events, such as water stress, frequent agricultural downturns, and rising global sea levels on patterns of international migration, the investigators developed a cross-regional model that combines the three types of data into a matrix grid to make predictions about the amount of internal shift in population dynamics that is projected to occur in developing nations by mid-century.

Analysis of results predicts that unless government officials take significant action to implement effective methods of intervention capable of addressing the escalating consequences of environmental disruption,143 million people representing 3 percent of the total population of the three primary regions cited, will be subject to forced migration to escape the detrimental effects of air pollution, food and water shortages, agricultural degradation, and rainfall instability which are all directly related to climate change. Data analysis projects that developing countries with the most limited access to clean water and the poorest agricultural productivity in combination with the desertification of sea levels will witness the most significant expansion of internal migration of regional populations. The analysis further projects that the most climate-vulnerable nations with the lowest socioeconomic status resulting in extreme poverty will see the most significant surge in internal patterns of population migration in the foreseeable future. Results also predict that internal patterns of population migration in the developing world will see dramatic acceleration after 2050 unless adequate measures are untaken by the United States in partnership with other nations to reduce greenhouse gas production in the earth's atmosphere. Based on this outcome, the researchers conclude the emergence of regional hotspots of internal and external migration has important socioeconomic and geopolitical implications for the infrastructure and social support systems of the most climate-sensitive countries in the developing world (Rigaud et al., 2018).

A meta-analysis of ecological studies by the Center for American Progress released by the Brookings Institute in 2019 provide scientific evidence that documents the severity of the humanitarian challenges global societies will face in future decades resulting from the unprecedented expansion of migrating populations associated with the consequences of the climate crisis (Podesta, 2019). Recent statistics on global migration patterns compiled by the United Nations High Commissioner for Refugees (U.N.H.C.R.) at the end of 2020 indicate 82 million refugees worldwide are currently displaced by the escalation of dangerous social and political conditions in their homeland linked to climate change. Analysis of U.N.H.C.R. data suggests that conflict, violence, human rights violations, and related events mitigated by weather instability are the key factors driving the current wave of displacement forcing thousands of refugees to migrate. The analysis identified three subgroups of internally displaced refugees forced to migrate under different climate-linked social and geopolitical circumstances. The distribution of global refugee populations forced to migrate internally is shown in Table 1.

A similar set of circumstances exist for refugees involuntarily displaced abroad by climate conditions in their homeland. Table 2 and Table 3 show the distribution of climate refugee populations displaced externally by national origin, host country of residence, and percent.

Based on this data, researchers at the United Nations predict that one out of every ninety-five people in the world is expected to undergo forced migration shortly to escape the escalating geopolitical conflict, violence, and persecution associated with the climate crisis. Environmental impact data from empirical research supports a growing consensus of opinion within the scientific community that global displacement of refugee populations will cause substantial social and economic hardship in many of the most climate-vulnerable nations of the third world. Scientists posit that the sustained worsening of worldwide environmental conditions such as global warming is destined to increase ecological pressures that will significantly influence the demographic trajectory of patterns of mass migration that affect geopolitical instability in regions of the developing world that have the most vulnerable social and political structures and the highest economic disadvantage. Evidence supporting this position is presented in an analysis of published findings from environmental impact studies by Dr. Marram Ahmed, a research fellow in the

Table 1. Distribution of refugees internally displaced by cause and subpopulation

Primary Cause of Displacement	Number of Refugees Displaced Internally	Categories of Refugees Displaced Internally	Size of Subpopulation Displaced Internally
U.N.R.W.A. Palestine Mandate	6 million	Venezuelans	4 million
U.N. H.C.R. Public Mandate	21 million	Asylum Seekers	4 million
Climate Conditions	48 million	Children under 18	26 million
Combined Total	75 million	Combined Total	34 million

Source: United Nations High Commissioner of Refugees 2020

Note: All figures shown above are rounded to the nearest whole number.

Note: Public mandates issued by the United Nations High Commissioner of Refugees (U.N.H.C.R.) and the United Nations Relief and Works Agency in Palestine (U.N.R.W.A.) are responsible for the combined internal displacement of 27 million refugees globally.

Note: Of the 48 million refugees internally displaced worldwide by climate conditions, 4 million are asylum-seekers from poverty-stricken countries in the developing world, and 4 million are displaced Venezuelans from Latin America.

Note: U.N.H.C.R. global trend data indicates that 26 million children under 18 have been internally displaced because of rapidly deteriorating social, economic, and political conditions in their native country linked to climate change.

Table 2. Distribution of climate refugee populations externally displaced by country

Country of Origin	Population Size	Host Country	Number of Refugees
Syria/Arab Republic	7 million	Turkey	4 million
Venezuela	4 million	Columbia	2 million
Afghanistan	3 million	Pakistan	1 million
South Sudan	2 million	Uganda	1 million
Myanmar	1 million	Germany	1 million
Combined Total	17 million	Combined Total	9 million

Source: United Nations High Commissioner of Refugees 2020

Note: All figures shown above are rounded to the nearest whole number.

Note: Climate change is responsible for the external displacement of 17 million people in five developing countries in East Africa, The Middle East, India, South America, and South Central Asia. Of that population, 9 million climate refugees have resettled in host nations located in Western and Southern Asia, South America, East Africa, and Europe, many of which are close to their homeland.

Table 3. Distribution of climate refugees displaced by external location and percent

Regional Location	Percent	Location of Host Country	Percent
Developing Countries	86	Adjacent	73
Developed Countries	14	Non-Adjacent	27
Combined Percent	100	Combined Percent	100

Source: United Nations High Commissioner of Refugees 2020

Note: Over 80 percent of refugees experiencing climate-related external displacement abroad live in developing nations, compared to less than 20 percent who reside in developed industrialized countries of the western world.

Note: More than 70 percent of displaced climate refugees live in host countries that border their country of origin. In comparison, less than 30 percent live in host countries not adjacent to their homeland.

Department of Oriental and African Studies University of London, which suggests that climate change's ecological consequences are already responsible for the disproportionate displacement of 16.1 million people worldwide. The vast majority of these climate refugees reside in Africa and the Middle East, two of the most economically fragile and agriculturally insecure regions of the developing world.

Ahmed's analysis makes a dire prediction about the future consequences of global migration's expansion. He posits that as environmental conditions decline in many regions, approximately 150 to 200 million people will be displaced involuntarily by escalating socioeconomic and political events connected to climate-induced change within the next three decades. This evolving crisis will subsequently intensify the need for humanitarian aid in the form of enhanced economic resources and social services in the most climate-vulnerable nations, something the current network of international relief agencies around the world is not well equipped to provide under the current system of humanitarian funding requirements. Dr. Ahmed argues that the United Nations established sustainable development goals committed to *leaving no one behind* fall short of prioritizing climate-induced humanitarian concerns such as global migration, and do not allocate the full range of financial resources necessary to address these emerging problems effectively. He contends that the current system of humanitarian finance needs substantial reform for the present network of global relief organizations to keep pace with the growing demand for funding to assist international societies struggling with the economic impact of the climate crisis. Empirical evidence that substantiates the economic shortfall in global funding to combat climate vulnerability is documented in a review of financial tracking data summarized in a joint report by the United Nations Office for the Coordination of Humanitarian Affairs and its partners. Analysis of data associated with global humanitarian funding requirements for 2019 indicates that relief organizations allocated 22 billion dollars in humanitarian assistance to finance projects focused on reducing the impact of climate change in the world's most vulnerable nations, a need whose economic cost Dr. Ahmed estimates is expected to grow to 50 billion dollars by 2030. He posits that at the present rate of global expansion of population displacement the need to develop a reliable source of multi-year funding to finance projects and resources with the capacity to address the complex humanitarian issues posed by climate change is expected to grow. He argues that implementing a stable multi-year funding source would contribute to establishing a solid economic foundation for developing financial solutions that will help international communities become more resilient to the impact of population displacement connected to the climate crisis (Ahmed, 2019).

Although studies have shown that finding an effective method of building a reliable source of funding constitutes an essential first step in the process of assisting climate-vulnerable nations in the developing world to finance global projects that help them to become more resilient to the humanitarian impact of climate change, getting the collaborative cooperation of banks in partnership with non-government organizations to commit to economic investment in community-based healthcare and social programs that prioritize climate-friendly goals is challenging in many developing nations, where a substantial proportion of the general population lives in poverty. The essential role that banking institutions play in the social investment of economic capital in innovative projects designed to help developing nations in the third world deal with the humanitarian problems created by the climate crisis is highlighted in an article by Peter Maurer, President of the International Committee of the Red Cross posted online in 2017. In his analysis, Maurer describes how banking systems operating in some of the poorest countries of the developing world, such as Nigeria, Mali, and the Democratic Republic of the Congo, are using green bonds as an economic tool for financing humanitarian programs and innovative projects that help their citizens to cope more effectively with the impact of climate change. In addition, these nations have also created collaborative partnership agreements between social investors, institutional funders, government officials, and the International Committee of the Red Cross to issue humanitarian impact bonds as a strategic approach to securing monetary investment in ground-breaking projects such as the building of rehabilitation centers that provide access to treatment services to migrants with disabilities and their families which they otherwise might not be able to afford because of their impoverished social status. Based on the economic principle of *payment for results,* humanitarian impact bonds have become the centerpiece of a five-year sustainable funding model developed by ICRC to implement global strategies that promote the active involvement of all stakeholders in social issues such as population migration, displacement, and relocation mitigated by the environmental impact of the climate crises. It has been demonstrated that building public and private partnerships between the business community and government, such as those generated by the ICRC financial model and others, constitute the surest and most influential strategy for eliminating budgetary constraints and increasing investor confidence in supporting the funding of humanitarian projects focused on the improvement of the social and economic conditions in the most fragile nations of the third world impacted by international migration and displacement caused by climate vulnerability. This is particularly evident in war-torn regional locations like Syria, Iraq, Yemen, South Sudan, the Central African Republic, and the Horn of Africa, where periods of violence and political conflict associated with climate-induced migration are becoming increasingly frequent and complex, heightening the need for humanitarian assistance. A review of the results of demographic studies by the World Bank indicates that an estimated 2 billion people live in countries affected by conditions of economic fragility, social conflict, and political violence exacerbated by the effects of climate-induced migration. Results also show that 17 percent of refugee populations forced to migrate to countries in the developing world because of worsening social and economic conditions linked to the climate crisis are poor, a figure expected to reach close to 50 percent by 2030, subsequently increasing the financial cost of humanitarian programs such as those focused on resettlement to more than 15 billion dollars a year. The rising cost of financing targeted assistance to relief organizations focused on addressing the social and economic issues related to the environment is fast becoming the driving force behind the growing utilization of collaborative partnerships as a means of funding humanitarian projects that can provide practical solutions to the global problems caused by climate change (Maurer, 2017).

IMPLICATIONS OF CLIMATE MIGRATION FOR NATIONAL SECURITY

The economic costs and social consequences of climate change will define the path of population migration internationally throughout the 21st Century. Scholars studying the rising tide of global conflict and persecution driven by food insecurity and the dwindling availability of natural resources like clean drinking water have made dire predictions about the impact that these events will have on the national security and immigration policy of the United States as well as the nations of the European Union over time. According to an analysis by the United Nations, Intergovernmental Panel on Climate Change documented in the organization's fifth assessment report released by the Center for American Progress in 2012, the cumulative effects of the climate crisis are destined to have long-term environmental consequences so severe that they compromise national security in the United States and send shockwaves that will have a destabilizing ripple effect on the fragile nations in the developing world where the volume of social unrest, violence, and political conflict have increased to the point that will require military intervention to restore order. The I.P.C.C. panel predicts that as the ecological pressures precipitated by global patterns of weather instability build worldwide, this will have significant consequences for the lives of hundreds of millions of people, both directly and indirectly. Increased competition for the declining availability of natural resources will trigger more frequent geopolitical conflict in many fragile regions in the developing world already experiencing the after-effects of environmental disruption (Werz & Conley,2012). The premise that climate-induced migration will have a significant transformative effect on the national security policies of the European Union in future decades is further documented in an analysis of projected demographic shifts in population flow by the International Organization for Migration. I.O.M. estimates that between 25 million and one billion refugees from climate-vulnerable countries in the developing world are expected to migrate to E.U. nations within the next 40 years (I.O.M., 2009).

In a statement cited in a joint report to the European Council in 2008, Javier Solana, the European Union's High Representative for Common, Foreign, and Security Policy, in collaboration with the European Commission, argues that the climate-induced migration of refugee populations from countries in the developing world is a threat multiplier that exacerbates existing political tensions and regional instability that impact national security interests throughout Europe. Solana and his colleagues believe the unpredictable nature of the social repercussions of climate-related migration is the catalyst that will drive the acceleration of geopolitical conflict in some of the most overburdened states and fragile regions of the European Union. For this reason, they argue that it is essential for government officials and policymakers to recognize that the social and economic risks posed by environmental disruption are not just humanitarian in scope; they also encompass geopolitical security factors that are interconnected to the impact of climate change. They contend that the critical connection between risk factors will require a comprehensive policy approach to address these issues effectively. Solana's report makes the following projections about the national security outcomes for nations of the European Union affected by climate challenges. He predicts that:

- Climate change will cause a significant reduction in the availability of natural resources such as arable land for food production, along with irregular rainfall patterns that will cause a twenty to thirty percent decline in fresh water supplies in many third world countries;
- Declines in agricultural production combined with water shortages will increase food insecurity in the most poverty-stricken third world countries resulting in an uptick in hunger, food-related illness, and economic hardship associated with rising prices that decrease access to the essentials of sustainable nutrition on a global level. Water shortages will also increase the potential for social unrest and economic loss in climate-affected regions. Two factors that raise the potential for geopolitical conflict as natural resources are depleted;
- Climate change will cause substantial damage to the economies of developing countries like India, China, Central America, and the Caribbean, countries where a significant proportion of the general population live in coastal cities with a high climate vulnerability to infrastructure damage that accelerates the need for humanitarian assistance from other nations;
- Climate change will play a critical role in the redistribution of global landmass, subsequently increasing the potential for territorial disruption and border disputes related to rising competition for energy resources, particularly in polar regions like the Antarctic, where natural resource exploitation is already taking a considerable toll on the integrity of the environment;
- Climate change will also exacerbate regional border disputes over territory in developing nations causing international populations to migrate to the United States and host countries in Europe to escape political tyranny and violence (European Council, 2008).

In environmentally challenged regions of the developing world, the effects of climate change have already begun to take root in the most politically fragile nations, where adverse social and economic conditions heighten the risk of conflict. Many climate-affected countries, such as those in Africa, the Middle East, and Asia, are currently experiencing a significant surge in migration to E.U. nations precipitated by a rise in social unrest and depletion of natural resources caused by the climate crisis.

In Africa, a continent with a high climate vulnerability and low adaptive capacity, water scarcity caused by irregular rainfall and frequent drought combined with soil degradation tied to overuse has led to a 75 percent reduction n arable land for agricultural production. Erratic weather patterns on the ground combined with a significant increase in the frequency and intensity of harmful weather events such as tropical storms, magnum force hurricanes, and undersea volcanic eruptions serve to limit access to sustainable water sources used by millions of African citizens for drinking and bathing purposes. In addition, compromised water resources also result in an increase in vector-borne disease and food shortages that pose a risk to the health and welfare of the general population in the northern and southern regions of nation. The intensification of such environmental conditions within the next few decades is expected to increase the number of African refugees forced to migrate to the nation-states of the European Union, exacerbating social and political tensions in host countries that increase the likelihood of geopolitical conflict which enhances the risk of destabilization of national security across international borders of the western world.

Similar disastrous circumstances are cropping up in climate-vulnerable regions of the Middle East, South, and Central Asia, Latin America, the Caribbean, and the Antarctic, where the steady rise in temperature on land and in the oceans is contributing to a dramatic increase in trans-regional shortages of food and fresh water, unsustainable levels of natural resources, maritime conflict over territory, and economic downturn connected to the loss of seasonal employment in the agricultural industry. The disruptive effects of the climate crisis have become a primary source of geopolitical stress in these unstable regions where the institutional foundations of government are at their weakest point. The potential for the rise of the destabilizing impact of conflict has become a paramount issue of international focus, primarily as these concerns affect the national security interests of the European Union. As the climate-induced debate over territory and access to trade routes continues to expand globally, the challenge to Europe's ability to find effective methods of protecting the security of national borders from the environmental pressures of forced migration is gaining momentum among political leaders. Climate-induced migration has become the focal point of E.U.'s efforts to introduce more stringent border containment policies that place tighter regional restrictions on immigration.

Solana concludes his analysis with a series of practical suggestions for proactive measures that he believes could significantly improve the European Union's capacity to resolve national security problems at its borders caused by the growth of population migration influenced by climate change. These recommendations identify several concrete steps that E.U. nations can put into motion to develop an early warning response that will enable them to circumvent the impending threat to national security that comes with the onset of geopolitical conflict that accompanies global events associated with climate-induced migration. Suggested recommendations for resolving this crisis include:

- The intensification of the E.U.'s capacity to develop an international network of government-backed security agencies focused on research, analysis, and monitoring to detect the early warning signs of a rise in detrimental conditions which constitute circumstances made worse by the transitional pressures of climate-induced migration from the third world;

- Provide E. U. nations with the capacity to plan for the building of capabilities in civil protection, crisis management, and disaster relief that would enable them to improve their response to the national security risks posed by social and environmental consequences of climate change;
- Invest in the commissioning and implementation of practical long-term surveillance programs designed to identify the social and economic implications of trans-regional national security risks influenced by climate change that can potentially harm the global interests of the European Union;
- Focus multilateral attention on the national security risks associated with climate change that need to be addressed through the collaborative efforts of specialized organizational bodies such as the U.N. Security Council and the G8 intergovernmental political forum agencies with authority to amend rules that strengthen international laws which pertain to the current migration crisis;
- Enhance the level of international cooperation among nations to detect national security threats around the world mitigated by climate change;
- Consider environmental disruption as a cause of migratory stress in the development and implementation of comprehensive European migration policy;
- Integrate adaptive resilience to climate change as part of the E.U.'s ongoing strategic approach to developing solid global alliances with other countries that will reduce national security risks in the most vulnerable parts of the developing world;
- Develop a comprehensive E.U. policy based on the evolving geo-strategy for dealing with the impact of climate change on the Arctic region, taking into account environmental concerns associated with access to resources and opening up new trade routes that could resolve shortages fueling forced migration in many regional locations in the developing world;
- Begin a constructive dialog between E.U. nations and climate-affected nations in the third world, so essential information about the security implications of the environmental crisis is shared for collaborative analysis (Ibid, 2008).

The national security impact of climate-induced migration is not just a phenomenon of significant concern to the nations of the European Union. The problem has also become a focal point of national interest in the United States. The impending risk to our nation's national security posed by the detrimental effects of the climate crisis has become the main priority of both the U.S. military establishment and the U.S. intelligence community. In a report released by the CATO Institute, an American Libertarian think tank headquartered in Washington D.C. in June of 2020, Professor of Civil Engineering Mark G. Stewart of the University of Newcastle in Australia posits that the effects of climate change will have a significant adverse impact on U.S. military operations that will present a considerable challenge to the national security of the United States in the years ahead. He conjectures that the infrastructure damage caused by the unpredictable weather-related effects of climate change will cause severe interruption of military services at more than 200 bases across the country. This will drive the economic cost of rebuilding and relocating these facilities to new levels of financial expenditure for the U.S. government because of the enhanced need to invest in implementing new technology capable of adapting them to the pitfalls of the climate crisis. He points out that climate change will cause a significant shift in the primary mission of several branches of the armed forces that will affect the integrity of our national security. The United States will be forced to commit more military resources and personnel to assist those affected by natural disasters and humanitarian crises at home and abroad, making the rapid deployment of armed forces in times of a national security emergency more time-consuming and less efficient. Professor Stewart documents several fine examples in his analysis of recent climate-related natural disasters that have resulted in military personnel and resources being deployed for nonconventional humanitarian purposes. For instance, in 2010, the U.S.S. aircraft carrier Carl Vinson operated as a sea base for the deployment of military personnel and supplies to assist the people of Haiti whose island home had been devastated by the after-shock of a powerful earthquake that caused massive infrastructure damage and a considerable loss of human life. When Hurricane Katrina hit the city of New Orleans in August of 2005, the storm caused 80 billion dollars in property damage, killed more than 1800 people, and displaced 270,000 others. The devastating impact of this catastrophic event caused the mobilization of 70,000 soldiers, including 22,000 active-duty troops and 50,000 plus members of the national guard deployed in the relief effort to assist those who lost their homes and family members in the aftermath of this tragedy. In addition to the loss of life and personal property, Katrina also caused significant infrastructure damage taking crude oil production and refinery capacity offline, which disrupted the delivery of essential energy supplies to homes and business establishments, further enhancing the need for military intervention to save lives. These are just two of the many examples of what some experts would argue are necessary diversions of military operations and resources to assist in domestic emergencies. In contrast, Professor Stewart and his esteemed colleague Professor Joshua W. Busby of the University of Texas Department of Public Affairs and distinguished scholar at the Robert S Strauss Center for International Security and Law present compelling arguments that paint a more realistic picture of the magnitude of harm to our country's national security military deployment of this type can cause, especially during times of national emergency abroad such as the military action in Iraq and Afghanistan to protect the nation from the threat of terrorist attack by foreign governments.

Both Stewart and Busby conjecture that while some military experts in the U.S. Defense Department believe that a reduction in rapid deployment response can be adequately compensated for by the operational readiness of military staff stationed at other facilities across the country, they argue that the diversion of human resources and staffing of this kind from their principal mission of defending the nation from national security threats places an undue burden on our country in terms of increased vulnerability to regional instability caused by climate-related events such as the mass migration of refugees.

The two scholars conclude their analysis by pointing out that climate change's concentrated socioeconomic and political impacts are slated to have significant national security implications domestically and internationally that will adversely affect U.S. interests in strategically essential countries worldwide. As previously noted earlier in this analysis, extreme weather events precipitated by environmental disruption are expected to cause substantial damage to critical components of the U.S. infrastructure, leaving millions of people without access to essential resources such as food, clean water, and housing services. A catastrophic situation that will require intervention by the military to stave off the global threat of domestic crisis. Climate change is also expected to lead to the refugee crisis's expanded growth, which will immerse a substantial proportion of the world's population in humanitarian turmoil exacerbating regional instability, further contributing to the risk to national security on the international and domestic level (Busby, 2007 & Stewart, 2020).

CLIMATE MIGRATION AND BORDER IMMIGRATION POLICY

The emerging threat to the United States' national security has an intricate connection to the deteriorating socioeconomic, political, and environmental conditions generated by climate change worldwide. As I have noted throughout the context of the discussion presented in this paper, the ecological consequences of climate change have significantly impacted the regional stability of the most environmentally vulnerable nations in the global community. For more than two decades, these consequences have become the primary focus of the efforts of scientists and government monitoring agencies to unravel the dynamic that is driving the present increase in involuntary cross-border movement by refugee populations seeking asylum and resettlement in the United States. Research has shown that the sustained uptick in geopolitical conflict associated with the expansion of organized criminal activities such as gang violence and drug smuggling in developing countries such as Guatemala, El Salvador, and Honduras, combined with the recent surge of natural disasters that have taken their toll on countries like Haiti, are two fine examples of climate-induced events advancing the current upswing in international cross border migration by refugee populations from these regions involuntarily displaced by these events

Border containment measures such as involuntary family separation, detainment of adults and children in cages at border facilities, and government-backed construction of a border wall all constitute strategic efforts by Trump officials to protect the safety and security of American citizens by closing the U.S. Mexico border to those they consider a national security risk to the nation. Although border patrol officials have implemented such methods under former President Trump's administration as a means of discouraging undocumented migrants from attempting to cross the border illegally, three studies by border researchers, Dr. Antonio N. Zavaleta, Professor Emeritus of Anthropology at the University of Texas, and Dr. Mitchell A. Kaplan, a clinical sociologist in private practice in New York City, have produced empirical results that have primarily disproven the effectiveness of such methods of deterrence. Findings reveal that despite the former Trump administration's best efforts to promote draconian policies of border containment designed to have a dissuasive effect on migration, the massive flow of displaced climate refugees approaching border entry points seeking asylum in the United States has continued to grow in recent decades. Statistics from the U.S. Customs and Border Protection Agency reveal that agents apprehended a total of 91,786 asylum-seeking migrant families attempting to make border crossings into the United States illegally in 2018, representing an average increase of close to 2000 percent over the previous decade.

Recent data cited in a news article by journalist Anna Giaritelli published on Yahoo.com in July of 2021 indicates that the composition of refugee populations seeking asylum at America's borders is undergoing a significant transformation with substantial national security implications for our country. Analysis of cross-border apprehension data collected by border patrol agents in October 2020 shows a considerable shift in the number of undocumented migrants from countries other than Central America apprehended at border checkpoints. A change that has prompted border patrol agents to invest significant time and resources into implementing deterrence and containments strategies that can reverse the current trend in migration at our nation's southern border effectively.

A public statement by Theresa Cardinal Brown, managing director of immigration and cross border policy at the Bipartisan Policy Center in Washington D.C., acknowledges that the U.S. southern border is fast becoming a primary route of entry for refugees from all over the world, not just Central America a forced migration phenomenon that represents new challenges to our overburdened border containment system in terms of undocumented immigration that impacts the nation's national security interests. Evidence of this impact is noted in recent border patrol data reported by agents in the twelve months between June of 2020 and June of 2021, which reveals a marked increase of 26,000 asylum-seeking Venezuelans approaching border entry points in hopes of escaping the political repression and dire economic conditions in their native country. In addition, border authorities also apprehended 14,000 refugees from Cuba, 34,000 from the Philippines, 4,369 from Romania, and 37,000 migrants from countries that could not be categorized. More recent data from January of 2022 documented in an article on Immigration Reform.com by Mathew Tragesser, communications and media affairs assistant at the Federation for American Immigration Reform (FAIR) in Washington, D.C., support the contention that the present stream of illegal immigration at the U.S-Mexico border continues to expand unabated. Preliminary findings show a 321 percent increase in migrant encounters with border patrol officials over the same period last year. Border agents reported 153,941 migrant encounters at the U.S-Mexico border during the first month of this year, a figure four times higher than the final year of the Trump administration, which averaged 36,585 border encounters with migrants during January of 2020. Such figures represent a more than 96 percent uptick in border crossings by undocumented migrants in the first twelve months of President Biden's administration.

Tragesser points out that despite the increase in encounters between migrants and border patrol officials during the past year, the Biden Harris administration has taken some significant steps toward the reformation of the U.S. immigration system that are of potential benefit to undocumented migrants who want to make border crossings. These include the suspension of exclusionary border security measures implemented by former President Trump, such as constructing a border wall and the asylum cooperation agreements with the Northern Triangle countries of Central America. The administration has also offered guidance that places strict limitations upon the circumstances under which migrants can be unlawfully apprehended and detained at border crossings as a prelude to being forcibly removed from the country, rendering the Remain in Mexico program put in place by the prior administration nonexistent in defiance of a federal court order that requested reimplementation of the program. However, despite these progressive measures, many experts believe that Biden policies will do little to reform an immigration system whose operations are already fragmented and overwhelmed by the ramifications of the current border crisis tied to the secondary effects of a global assault on the environment. They conjecture that the continued surge of international refugees from developing countries in Central America and elsewhere is symptomatic of the fact that deterrence policies at border crossings implemented by the U.S. government during former presidential administrations have yet to foster a practical solution that can resolve the migration crisis effectively (Zavaleta & Kaplan, 2015, 2018, Kaplan, 2020, Giaritelli, 2021, Tragesser, 2022).

RECOMMENDATIONS FOR REFORM OF CLIMATE MIGRATION POLICY

The analysis of findings from the studies cited provides considerable evidence to indicate that the deteriorating effects of the climate situation are expected to culminate in the displacement of millions of refugees across a spectrum of countries in the developing world over the next two decades. To address the significant public concern with the continued acceleration of border migration caused by the climate crisis, the Biden Harris administration, in consultation with several non-government organizations (N.G.O.'s) and the United Nations High Commissioner for Refugees, has put forward a series of recommendations for the inclusion of climate displacement as a critical component of the reform of U.S. immigration policy. These measures include the following:

- Development of a complete understanding of the impact of rapid and slow-moving weather events on climate-induced migration and displacement;

- Expansion of temporary emergency relief programs designed to protect the fundamental human rights of displaced migrants from outside the United States that have fallen victim to the effects of climate change;
- Incorporation of government-issued renewable climate visas that would allow for an extension of the period that climate refugees from Central America would be able to remain in the United States legally and subsequently apply for permanent citizenship;
- Expansion of the definition of national interest to include a framework that encompasses the interrelationship between climate change and global patterns of migration in conjunction with a broad understanding of U.S. policies and laws that provide oversight of the distribution of humanitarian aid to nations in need of assistance;
- Incorporation of climate change into the present framework of asylum and international government operations;
- Adoption of specific measures of immigration reform that strengthen the restoration of the U.S asylum system;
- Incorporate research findings on climate migration into government policy decisions associated with environmental sustainability and safety (Ibid, 2021).

SUMMARY OF CLIMATE POLICY INITIATIVES AND CONCLUSIONS

The research findings reviewed in this chapter suggest a growing consensus among scientists and public policy professionals that climate change constitutes one of the most influential global forces directing the path of essential environmental policy in the United States and across Europe. Scholars studying the impact of erratic weather patterns on population migration worldwide present convincing arguments for developing climate policy of sufficient scope to handle the fundamental socioeconomic and political problems associated with this escalating phenomenon. They argue that federal legislation with the capacity to resolve social issues related to the climate crisis must contain built-in provisions that foster protective measures that ensure sufficient access to essential supplies of natural resources while simultaneously supporting the reduction of risk factors that impact national security in the United States and other countries. Climate policy must incorporate specific initiatives to make existing environmental problems less severe. Policies must include adaptive methods that emphasize the following ecological initiatives:

- Implement early warning systems to reduce the impact of natural disasters on the general population of the United States;
- Incorporate climate-friendly building codes in all existing and future structures:
- Set up emergency response backup systems that utilize specially trained civilian and military personnel able to activate appropriate population evacuation and relocation procedures;
- Strengthen U.S. coastal defenses to lower the risk of conflict with foreign nations related to climate change;

Experts agree that while risk reduction programs constitute a critical component of utilizing climate policy as a tool to address national security concerns in the United States and overseas, it is just a starting point for a meaningful dialogue between nations with the potential to change the course of this advancing crisis. Countries still need to join forces in a global alliance committed to taking proactive steps to decarbonize energy sources before the end of the century by adopting climate-friendly technologies designed to lower greenhouse gas emissions, a significant source of rising global temperatures. The scientific community believes that a collaborative agreement to transfer clean energy technology to countries like China and India will reduce dangerous carbon emissions, set the stage for increasing regional stability, and enhance the potential for conflict resolution in areas of the developing world with the highest climate vulnerability.

Recommendations for the reform of climate policy will have a transformative effect on the ideological thinking of international government institutions by giving a new voice to the ongoing debate over national security and environmental issues associated with climate change. Professionals in the public policy arena and those in the scientific community contend that implementing proposals that can radically change the course of policy decisions related to the environment represents one of the surest methods of strengthening national security in ways that ensure the reduction of U.S. vulnerabilities to the effects of climate change at home and abroad, secure the stabilization of the national interests of our European allies, and make a significant contribution to other related goals such as energy security and industrial revitalization. In a world where the challenges presented by threats to the environment continue to increase the risk to our global security, many observers believe in the foregone conclusion that forging sound evidence-based climate policy per the proposed guidelines cited needs to become the number one priority of the government administrations around the world in the decades to come (Ibid, 2007).

REFERENCES

Abel, G. J., Brottrager, M., Crespo Cuaresma, J., & Muttarak, R. (2019). Climate, conflict, and Forced Migration. *Journal of Global Environmental Change, 54*, 239–249. doi:10.1016/j.gloenvcha.2018.12.003

Ahmed, M. (2019). *How climate change exacerbates the refugee crisis and what can be done about it*. World Economic Forum. Retrieved from https://www.weforum.org/agenda/2019/06/how-climate-change-exacerbates-the-refugee-crisis-and-what-can-be-done-about-it/

Busby, J. W. (2007). *Climate Change and National Security: An Agenda for Action*. Report to the Council on Foreign Relations, C.S.R. No. 32. Retrieved from https://cdn.cfr.org/sites/default/files/report_pdf/ClimateChange_CSR32%20%281%29.pdf

Bustos, C., Willshire, J., Carrera, D. A., Becker, T., & Chase, J. C. (2021). *Shelter from the Storm: Policy Options to Address Climate-Induced Migration from the Northern Triangle*. Harvard Immigration and Refugee Clinical Program, H.L.S. Immigration Project, the University Network for Human Rights, Yale Immigrant Justice Project, and Yale Environmental Law Association. Retrieved from https://static1.squarespace.com/static/5b3538249d5abb21360e858f/t/6092e7854c5e4362887c0197/1620240265281/Shelter_Final_5May21.pdf

Climate Refugee. (n.d.). *Cambridge English Dictionary*. Retrieved January 30, 2022, from https://dictionary.cambridge.org/us/dictionary/english/climate-refugee

European Council. (2008). *Climate change and international security*. Joint Paper from the High Representative and the European Commission to the European Council, S113/08. Retrieved from https://www.consilium.europa.eu/uedocs/cms_data/docs/pressdata/en/reports/99387.pdf

Food Insecurity. (n.d.). *Merriam-Webster Dictionary.* Retrieved January 31, 2022, from https://www.merriam-webster.com/dictionary/food%20insecurity

Forced Migration. (n.d.). *Definitions.net.* Retrieved January 31, 2022, from https://www.definitions.net/definition/forced+migration

Geopolitics. (n.d.). *Merriam-Webster Dictionary.* Retrieved January 31, 2022, from https://www.merriam-webster.com/dictionary/geopolitics

Giaritelli, A. (2021, July). *Migrants arrive to the U.S. border from all over the world: We are seeing a permanent change.* Retrieved from https://news.yahoo.com/migrants-arrive-us-border-over-100100416.html?fr=sycsrp_catchall

Grecequet, M., Dewaard, J., Hellmann, J. J., & Abel, G. J. (2017). Climate Vulnerability and Human Migration in Global Perspective. *Journal of Sustainability, 9*(5). Retrieved from https://www.mdpi.com/2071-105/9/5/720/htm

Humanitarian Crisis. (2013, May). *Complex Humanitarian Emergency Program, Education and Training.* Retrieved January 31, 2022, from https://globalhealthsciences.ucsf.edu/education-training/complex-humanitarian-emergency-program

Kaplan, M. A. (2020). *The Social Political and Environmental Forces Contributing to the Immigration Crisis at the Texas-Mexico Border.* In M. Kearney, A. Knopp, A. N. Zavaleta, & T. D. Knight (Eds.), *Fresh Studies in Rio Grande Valley History* (Vol. 17, pp. 233–254). The U.T.B. Regional History Series, The University of Texas Rio Grande Valley. Retrieved from https://drtonyzavaleta.com/the-social-political-and-environmental-forces-contributing-to-the-immigration-crisis-at-the-texas-mexico-border-fresh/

Laczko, F., & Aghazarm, C. (2009). *Migration, Environment, and Climate Change: Assessing the evidence.* International Organization for Migration. Retrieved from https://publications.iom.int/system/files/pdf/migration_and_environment.pdf

Maurer, P. (2017). *It's not just N.G.O.s tackling humanitarian crises: Banks have a role to.* World Economic Forum. Retrieved from https://www.weforum.org/agenda/2017/05/humanitarian-impact-bonds-icrc-red-cross/

Mcmahon, S., Tintori, G., Perez Fernandez, M., Alessandrini, A., Goujon, A., Ghio, D., Petroliagkis, T., Conte, A., Minora, U., & Kalantaryan, S. (2021). Population exposure and migrations linked to climate change in Africa. EUR 30881 EN, Publications Office of the European Union. doi:,JRC126594 doi:10.2760/4151

National Security. (2021, September). *Thoughtco.com.* Retrieved January 31, 2022, from https://www.thoughtco.com/national-security-definition-and-examples-5197450

Podesta, J. (2019). *The Climate Crisis Migration and Refugees.* Policy brief commissioned for the 16th annual Brookings Blum Roundtable 2020 and beyond: Maintaining a bipartisan narrative on U.S. global development. Retrieved from https://www.brookings.edu/research/the-climate-crisis-migration-and-refugees/

Rigaud, K. K., de Sherbinin, A., Jones, B., Bergmann, J., Clement, V., Ober, K., Schewe, J., Adamo, S., McCusker, B., Heuser, S., & Midgley, A. (2018). *Groundswell: Preparing for Internal Climate Migration.* World Bank. Retrieved from https://openknowledge.worldbank.org/handle/10986/29461

Stewart, M. G. (2020). *Climate Change and National Security: Balancing the Costs and Benefits.* CATO Institute. Retrieved from https://www.cato.org/publications/climate-change-national-security-balancing-costs-benefits

Tragesser, M. (2022). *January Southern Border Encounters Increased by 321 Percent from Trump's Final Full Year.* Retrieved from https://www.immigrationreform.com/2022/02/17/border-data-hardly-good-news-immigrationreform-com/

UNHCR Global Trends. (2020). *Figures at a Glance.* Retrieved from https://www.unhcr.org/figures-at-a-glance.html

United Nations Office for the Coordination of Humanitarian Affairs. (2019). *Global Humanitarian Overview 2019.* Retrieved from https://www.unocha.org/sites/unocha/files/GHO2019.pdf

Water Scarcity. (n.d.). *Definitions.net.* Retrieved January 31, 2022, from https://www.definitions.net/definition/Water+scarcity

Werz, M., & Conley, L. (2012). *Climate Change Migration and Conflict: Addressing complex crisis scenarios in the 21st Century.* Center for American Progress Climate Migration Series. Retrieved from https://cdn.americanprogress.org/wp-ent/uploads/issues/2012/01/pdf/climate_migration.pdf?_ga=2.85303775.772595288.1641935207-813556300.1641595164

White House. (2021, October). *Report on the Impact of Climate Change on Migration.* Retrieved from https://www.whitehouse.gov/wp-content/uploads/2021/10/Report-on-the-Impact-of-Climate-Change-on-Migration.pdf

Zavaleta, A., & Kaplan, M. A. (2015). The Tragedy of Unaccompanied Child Immigrants to the U.S.-Mexico Border 2014. In Yet More Studies in Rio Grande Valley History (Vol. 13, pp. 249-271). The U.T.B. Regional History Series, The University of Texas at Brownsville. Retrieved from file:///C:/Users/drmka/Desktop/Mitchell%20Kaplan%20PhD%20journal%20articles%20and%20textbook%20chapters%202021)/The%20Tragedy%20of%20Unaccompanied%20Child%20Immigrants%20to%20the%20U.S.-Mexico%20Border%202014.pdf

Zavaleta, A., & Kaplan, M. A. (2018). Immigrant Caging on the Texas-Mexico Border. In *New Studies in Rio Grande Valley History* (Vol. 16, pp. 341-400). The U.T.B. Regional History Series, The University of Texas Rio Grande Valley. Retrieved from https://riograndeguardian.com/zavaleta-kaplan-immigrant-caging-on-the-texas-mexico-border/

ADDITIONAL READING

Cantat, C., Thiollet, H., & Pécoud, A. (2020). *Migration as crisis. A framework paper.* Retrieved from https://www.magyc.uliege.be/wp-content/uploads/2020/04/D3.1-v2-April-2020-1.pdf

Tempus, A. (2020, March). *Are We Thinking About Climate Migration All Wrong?* Rolling Stone. Retrieved from https://www.rollingstone.com/politics/politics-features/climate-migration-predicted-number-climate-refugees-962251/

KEY TERMS AND DEFINITIONS

Climate Refugee: The term climate refugee refers to an individual or group of individuals forced to migrate both within their country of origin or externally because environmental conditions caused by climate change make it impossible for them to continue living and working there (Cambridge English Dictionary online, 2022).

Food Insecurity: The United States Department of Agriculture defines food insecurity as a household's inability to provide enough food to keep each member healthy and active. The term has also been applied to low-income households where the primary source of nutrition is processed calorie-dense prepackaged food with inadequate nutritional value (Merriam-Webster Dictionary, 2022).

Forced Migration: The term forced migration refers to the physical removal of a population of individuals and families from their native country because of deteriorating social, economic, and political conditions resulting from environmental pressures that cause food insecurity, threats of violence, and geopolitical conflict (Definitions.net, 2022).

Geopolitics: The term geopolitics refers to the study of how geographic, economic, and social factors influence political environments that contribute to the onset of conflict in climate-vulnerable nations around the world (Merriam-Webster Dictionary, 2022).

Humanitarian Crisis: The term humanitarian crisis refers to a singular or series of events that threaten to disrupt the health, safety, and overall well-being of a large group of people or an entire community (Complex Humanitarian Emergency Program online, 2013).

National Security: National security refers to the ability of the government to utilize military force to protect its citizen's safety, economic welfare, and social institutions from the threat of attack by foreign or domestic invaders (Thoughtco.com, 2021).

Water Scarcity: Water scarcity refers to the inability of fresh water supplies to meet the resource demands of individuals and families living in a specific regional location of the developing world (Definitions.net, 2022).

Chapter 6
Applying a Panel Data Analysis to Determinants of Output in BRICS-T Countries

Murat Gündüz
Usak University, Turkey

Naib Alakbarov
Usak University, Turkey

Mehmet Hilmi Özkaya
Usak University, Turkey

ABSTRACT

Economic growth is one of the goals of economic policy. The study analyzes the determinants of output for the BRICS-T country group during the period 1992-2019. The results of the analysis show that the inflation variable has no effect on output in the long run. Looking at the effects of other variables shows that all variables are statistically significant both in the short and long term. According to the results of the analysis, the most effective variable in the short run is the patent applications variable. In the study, openness variable and inflation variable were taken as explanatory variables to see the effect of macroeconomic policy intervention. The results of the analysis made with the pooled mean group method show that the variable that affects most the output is trade openness. Furthermore, it has been observed that the inflation variable included in the model as a macroeconomic policy variable has an effect on output in the short run but not in the long run.

INTRODUCTION

In neo-classical growth models, the share of growth created by capital and labor in production is subtracted from the national income growth. The remainder is a growth driven by technology. This remainder is called total factor productivity. Solow, on the other hand, defined the part of the change in production

DOI: 10.4018/978-1-7998-9648-7.ch006

that cannot be explained by input factors as 'Solow residual'. Under the assumption that technological development is considered an exogenous factor or constant, the production function is shown as follows:

$Y = A. f(K, L)$

Considering the production function $Y = A f(K, L)$, it can be expressed in the following equation in which the increase in production is explained by the increase in the amount of capital and labor.

$\Delta Y = (MPK. \Delta K) + (MPL. \Delta L)$

While (MPK. ΔK) expresses the share that the change in production is caused by the change in the amount of capital, (MPL. ΔL) indicates the share that the change in production is caused by the change in the amount of labor (Kılıç & Dilber, 2019).

According to Goel's study (2011) on economic growth in BRICS-countries, since BRIC- countries show higher economic growth, there are significant differences within the group. It is revealed that China and Russia mostly have higher growth, India's growth process is varied and Brazil is not outperforming others.

According to Streltsov et al. (2021), the main factors that lead to the economic expansion of the BRICS-country group are predominantly labor and large economic resources. For example, Brazil and Russia mainly have large mineral reserves, while China and India have the advantage of cheap labor as well as resources at low prices. Finally, all BRICS-countries, except Brazil, exhibit very high investment rates.

As Shayanewako's study (2018) shows BRICS-countries have attached importance to strengthening and expanding foreign trade since their establishment in 2006. The study conducted by Shayanewako (2018) on BRICS countries investigates the relationship between trade openness and economic growth for the period 1990-2017 using the Autoregressive Distributed Latency (ARDL) bounds test, Cointegration and Granger causality tests (1969). According to this study, a long-term relationship between trade openness and economic growth is revealed. The evidence obtained from the analysis shows that, with exception to China where there is a unidirectional causality between trade openness and output growth, there is bidirectional causality from trade openness to economic growth in BRICS-countries. Similar results are also shown by Mercan et al. (2013) study results. According to this study, there is a positive relationship between openness and economic growth in Brazil, Russia, India, China, and Turkey (BRIC-T) country group.

Kurt and Kurt (2015) in their study on innovation and labor productivity in BRICS-countries concluded that there is a positive causality relationship between the two variables, innovation and labor productivity.

Yapraklı (2007) analyzes the relationship between commercial and financial openness and economic growth in Turkey during the period 1990-2006. As the results show, trade openness has a positive effect on economic growth, whereas financial openness has a negative effect.

Erkişi (2018) analyzing the factors affecting economic growth in BRICS countries for both the long run and the short run for the period 1996-2016, concludes that the Morgan Stanley Capital International Index is statistically significant and is the only variable that positively affects GDP in both the long and short run. Money supply and foreign trade variables are statistically significant in the short run, but not in the long run. In the short run, foreign trade affects GDP positively, while money supply affects growth negatively. Credits are not statistically significant either in the short or in the long term.

An article by Burange, Ranadive and Karnik (2018) analyzes the causal relationship between trade openness and economic growth in BRICS-member countries with the help of an econometric time series analysis. From the late 1980s, the BRICS-countries adopted a series of liberalization reforms almost simultaneously. The results of the analysis show that the relationship between the structural composition of GDP and the four aspects of trade openness, namely exports and imports (including exports of

Table 1. Variables and definitions

Variable	Symbol	Source
GDP (US$)	LNGDPCO	World Development Indicators
Gross Capital Fixed Formation (USD$)	LNGROSS	World Development Indicators
Labor force, total	LNLABO	World Development Indicators
Trade Openness	LNTROP	World Development Indicators
Consumer price index (2010 = 100)	LNENF	World Development Indicators
Patent applications, residents	LNPAT	World Development Indicators

services and imports of services). The study found that the hypothesis of growth-led trade in services is valid in India. The article presents the positive impact of exports and imports on growth in China and South Africa. However, according to the results of the study, no causal relationship is observed in Brazil and Russia.

Asongu, Akpan, and Isihak (2018) study analyzing the determinants of economic growth in the BRICS (Brazil, Russia, India, China, and South Africa) and MINT (Mexico, Indonesia, Nigeria, and Turkey) country group saw that the inflation variable is statistically insignificant. One possible reason for this is that BRICS and MINT countries with higher inflation rates tend to attract more FDI. Another interpretation of the subject is that the macro-economic stability in BRICS and MINT countries tends to play a lesser role in the investment decisions of multinational companies in these countries. The trade coefficient was found to be positive and significant as expected. The reason for this situation shows that countries that are more open to foreign trade are more likely to attract more FDI.

This study consists of four parts, the first part includes this introduction. The second part of the study presents an analysis of data and method. The third part presents an empirical analysis. The last part shows the results.

DATA AND METHOD

The study investigates the determinants of economic output in 6 BRICS-T countries between 1992 and 2019. In determining the variables used in the study, theoretical and empirical explanations as well as the supply side in determining the economic output were taken into account. All variables used in the study were obtained from the World Bank database and World Development Indicators. Table (1) includes the variables and definitions used in the study;

The model was estimated by using the Pooled Mean Group (PMG) estimator in the study. First of all, it was tested to know whether there was a cross-section dependency relationship between the series. Afterwards, the homogeneity and stationarity of the series were examined. The model used in the study is functioning as follows (Fatima et al., 2020; Raghutla, 2020):

$$Y = (AL)^{\alpha} K^{\beta} \pi^{\sigma}$$

Y – Gross Domestic Product; A - the technological level; K-capital formation; L- labor participation; and π shows inflation as an indicator of the government's macroeconomic policies. In the model, technological development is included as a patent application. Whereas, inflation variable is included in the

Table 2. Cross section dependency test results

Test	Statistics	Probability
Breusch-Pagan LM	53.81467	0.000
Pesaran scaled LM	7.086556	0.000
Pesaran CD	-2.611358	0.000

model in order to see the effects of applied macroeconomic policies on economic output. All variables in the model are taken in logarithmic form.

Model: $LGDP_{it}$= a1LNGROSS + a2LNLABOUR + a3LNTROP+ a4LNENF + LNPAT + u_{it} (1)

EMPIRICAL ANALYSIS

This section includes the cross-section dependency test, the homogeneity test, and the Pooled Mean Group-PMG test introduced by Pesaran et al. (1999). First of all, information about the tests used in econometric analysis are given. Then, the test results are provided and interpreted.

Cross-Section Dependency Test

If there is a cross-sectional dependence between the variables in the econometric analysis, not testing this relationship significantly affects the results of the analysis (Pesaran, 2004). While applying the cross-section dependency test, Breusch and Pagan (1980) LM test is used when the time dimension is larger than the slice dimension, Pesaran (2004) CDLM test is used (Equation 2) when the time dimension is less than the slice dimension, and finally Pesaran (2004) CDLM2 test is used when the time dimension is equal to the slice dimension. In addition, Pesaran et al (2008) developed a preset LM test using finite sample approaches in a heterogeneous panel (Baltagi et al. 2012):

$$CD_{lm} = \sqrt{\frac{1}{n\left(n-1\right)}\sum_{i=1}^{n-1}\sum_{j=i+1}^{n}(T\,\overset{\varsigma^2}{\rho_{ij}} = \pi r^2 - 1)} \qquad \left(2\right)$$

While the null hypothesis of the cross-sectional dependence test denies that "cross-section dependence" exists, the alternative hypothesis favours the existence of "cross-section dependence".

The results of the cross-section dependency test are given in Table (2).

When the probability value is below 0.05 in the cross-sectional dependence test results, the H0 hypothesis is rejected at the 5% significance level, and it is concluded that there is a cross-sectional dependence between the series (Pesaran et al., 2008). Looking at the test results in Table (2), it is determined that there is a cross-sectional dependence between the series across the panel.

Table 3. Homogeneity test results

	Test Statistics	Probability Value
Delta_tilde	1.160	0.246
Delta_tilde_adj	1.357	0.175

Homogeneity Test

Pesaran and Yamagata (2008) homogeneity test is used to test whether the slope coefficients of the variables are homogeneous or not. The null hypothesis of the homogeneity test states that the slope coefficients are homogeneous, while the alternative hypothesis states that the slope coefficients are heterogeneous. If the probability value obtained as a result of the test is greater than 0.10, the null hypothesis is accepted at 10% significance level (Pesaran & Yamagata, 2008). Homogeneity test results are given in Table (3). Before performing the test on whether the slope coefficients of the variables are homogeneous or not, the method developed by Drukker (2003) was used to obtain the first-order serial correlation test recommended by Wooldridge (2010, 2012) for panel data. Since the model includes autocorrelation (F stat. = 3.1e+06; Prob: 0.000) and heteroscedasticity (LR stat. = 29.66; Prob: 0.000), the homogeneity test was performed with the robust version of heteroscedasticity and autocorrelation (HAC) suggested by Blomquist and Westerlund (2016).

Looking at the homogeneity test results in Table (3), the null hypothesis is accepted because the probability values are greater than 0.10. Therefore, it can be concluded that the constant term and slope coefficients are homogeneous.

Panel CADF Unit Root Test

Panel CADF unit root test (known as the second generation unit root test) was used because the cross-sectional dependence relationship is determined between the series used in the study. Panel CADF unit root test developed by Pesaran (2007) is important for a healthier analysis, for it takes into account the cross-sectional dependence. In econometric analysis, the hypothesis that cross-section units are not affected by each other in the presence of shock to the series is unrealistic (Pesaran, 2007).

Pesaran (2007) CADF regression equation is given in formula number 3.

$$y_{it} = \left(1 - \phi_i\right)\mu_i + \phi_i y_{i,t-1} + u_{it}, i = 1,\dots,N; t = 1,\dots,T \quad u_{it} = ◆_i f_t + \varepsilon_{it} \tag{3}$$

While CADF statistics can be calculated for each cross-sectional unit in the CADF unit root test, CIPS statistics can be calculated for the panel as a whole. CADF unit root test can be used when the time dimension is larger than the cross section dimension and vice versa. The hypotheses of the CADF unit root test are given below (Pesaran, 2007: 268).

$$H_0 : \beta_0 = 0 \text{ (The series is not stationary.)} \tag{4}$$

Table 4. Unit root test results

	LNENF	LNGDP	LNGROSS	LNLAB	LNPAT	LNTROP	
SPESIFICATION WITHOUT TREND							
LEVEL	-7.899***	-3.350***	-3.002***	-3.091***	-5.460***	-6.277***	
FIRST DIFFERENCE	-7.154***	-10.478***	-11.187***	-11.187***	-10.759***	-8.693***	
SPESIFICATION WITH TREND							
LEVEL	-7.886***	-0.943	-1.110	-0.975	-3.436***	-5.295***	
FIRST DIFFERENCE	-9.941***	-10.141***	-9.550***	-10.622***	-4.141***	-7.800***	

$$H_1 : \beta_0 < 0, i = 1, 2, \ldots, N_1, \beta_1 = 0, i = N_1 + 1, N_1 + 2, \ldots, N \text{ (The series is stationary.)} \quad (5)$$

The CIPS value calculated for the overall panel is found by averaging the *t* value calculated for each cross-sectional unit (Pesaran, 2007: 276).

$$\mathrm{CIPS}(N,\ T) = t - \mathrm{bar} = N^{-1}\sum_{i=1}^{N} t_i\,(N,\ T) \quad (6)$$

Unit root test results are given in Table (4).

*indicates that the null hypothesis is rejected at * 10%, ** 5% and *** 1% levels.

When the CIPS values are examined as a result of the CADF unit root test, it is determined that the series are stationary at all levels in the specification without trend test. The first differences of the series are taken and they are found to be stationary again. In the Specification with trend test, it is observed that the LN GDP, LN GROSS and LNB series are not stationary at the level; they are stationary in the first degree. This is why it could not be decided whether these variables are stationary at their levels. Hence, these variables are made stationary by taking the first-order differences. Considering the trend-containing specification, it is noted that the null hypothesis "the series are not stationary" could not be rejected for all of the series, but it can be rejected when the first differences are taken into account.

Since it is observed that the series are stationary at different levels, the model is estimated with the PMG (Pooled Mean Group) estimator developed for the Paseran et al. (1999) panel ARDL model.

As shown by the analysis from the Table (5), all other variables, except the inflation variable, are positive and statistically significant in the long run. It is noted that the most influential variable on economic output is openness, while the variable with the least impact is emerging from patent applications. On the other hand, it is clear that the inflation variable is statistically significant at 10% level in the short term, while it is statistically insignificant in the long term. This result can be explained by using Phillips curve analysis. According to the monetarist and New Classical economic view, there is a trade-off

Table 5. PMG test result

DEPENDENT VARIABLE	INDEPENDENT VARIABLES					
LNGDP	**LNGROSS**	**LNLAB**	**LNPAT**	**LNTROP**	**LNINF**	
Long Term Coefficients	.1836397***	.1658237***	.0610544***	.3416471***	.0054297	
Short Term Coefficients	-.0593162*	.1472392***	.1943403***	-.5523613***	.1456838*	
Error Correction Coefficient	-.7017762***					

Note: * indicates significance at the 10%, ** 5%, *** 1% level.

relationship between inflation and unemployment in the short run, while no such a relationship exists in the long run (Bocutoğlu, 2012).

CONCLUSION

Determining the factors affecting the economic output of countries is one of the essential issues in the economic growth literature. When the economics literature is examined, many factors affecting economic growth are taken for granted. The study aims at explaining the effects of capital formation, labor force participation, inflation and openness as macroeconomic policy variables determine economic output in BRICS-T countries. The results of the analysis show that the inflation variable is statistically insignificant in the long run, and when the effects of other variables are considered, all variables are statistically significant in both the short and long run.

According to the results of the analysis, the most influential variable on economic output in BRICS-T countries in the long run is openness. As stated in the study of Asongu, Akpan and Isihak (2018), the reason for this situation can be referred to the fact that countries which are more open to foreign trade are more likely to attract more FDI.

On the other hand, the fact that the inflation variable included in the model as a macroeconomic policy variable is weakly effective in the short run and insignificant in the long run can be explained by using Phillips curve analysis which points out that policies aimed at reducing inflation can be effective in reducing unemployment and increasing output in the short run, but are ineffective in the long run.

REFERENCES

Asongu, S., Akpan, U. S., & Isihak, S. R. (2018). Determinants of foreign direct investment in fast-growing economies: Evidence from the BRICS and MINT countries. *Financial Innovation*, *4*(1), 1–17. doi:10.118640854-018-0114-0

Baltagi, B. H., Feng, Q., & Kao, C. (2012). A Lagrange Multiplier test for cross-sectional dependence in a fixed effects panel data model. *Journal of Econometrics*, *170*(1), 164–177. doi:10.1016/j.jeconom.2012.04.004

Blomquist, J., & Westerlund, J. (2016). Panel bootstrap tests of slope homogeneity. *Empirical Economics, 50*(4), 1359–1381. doi:10.100700181-015-0978-z

Bocutoğlu, E. (2012). *Krizin makro iktisadından makro iktisadın krizine: Eleştirel bir değerlendirme* (No. 2012/106). Discussion Paper.

Burange, L. G., Ranadive, R. R., & Karnik, N. N. (2019). Trade openness and economic growth nexus: A case study of BRICS. *Foreign Trade Review, 54*(1), 1–15. doi:10.1177/0015732518810902

Breusch, T. S., & Pagan, A. R. (1980). The Lagrange Multiplier Test and İts Applications to Model Specification in Econometrics. *The Review of Economic Studies, 47*(1), 239–253. doi:10.2307/2297111

Drukker, D. M. (2003). Testing for serial correlation in linear panel-data models. *The Stata Journal, 3*(2), 168–177. doi:10.1177/1536867X0300300206

Erkişi, K. (2018). Financial Development and Economic Growth in BRICS Countries and Turkey: A Panel Data Analysis. *İstanbul Gelişim Üniversitesi Sosyal Bilimler Dergisi, 5*(2), 1-17.

Fatima, S., Chen, B., Ramzan, M., & Abbas, Q. (2020). The Nexus Between Trade Openness and GDP Growth: Analyzing the Role of Human Capital Accumulation. *SAGE Open, 10*(4), 2158244020967377. doi:10.1177/2158244020967377

Goel, R. K., & Korhonen, I. (2011). *Determinants of economic growth in BRIC countries* (No. 05/2011). Development Research Working Paper Series.

Granger, C. W. (1969). Investigating causal relations by econometric models and cross-spectral methods. *Econometrica, 37*(3), 424–438. doi:10.2307/1912791

Kılıç, J., & Dilber, İ. (2019). Ekonomik Büyüme İle Üretim Faktörleri Arasında Ekonometrik Bir Analiz: Türkiye Örneği (1980-2016) [Econometic Analysis Between Economic Growth And Production Factors: The Case of Turkey (1980-2016)]. *Bilecik Şeyh Edebali Üniversitesi Sosyal Bilimler Dergisi, 4*(1), 149–166. doi:10.33905/bseusbed.475489

Kurt, S., & Kurt, Ü. (2015). Innovation and labour productivity in BRICS countries: Panel causality and co-integration. *Procedia: Social and Behavioral Sciences, 195*, 1295–1302. doi:10.1016/j.sbspro.2015.06.296

Mercan, M., Gocer, I., Bulut, S., & Dam, M. (2013). The effect of openness on economic growth for BRIC-T countries: Panel data analysis. *Eurasian Journal of Business and Economics, 6*(11), 1-14.

Pesaran, M. H. (2004). General Diagnostic Tests for Cross Section Dependence in Panels. *CESifo Working Paper Series*, 1229.

Pesaran, M., Shin, Y., & Smith, R. P. (1999). Pooled Mean Group Estimation of Dynamic Heterogeneous Panels. *Journal of the American Statistical Association, 94*(446), 621–634. doi:10.1080/01621459.1999.10474156

Pesaran, M. H. (2007). A Simple Panel Unit Root Test in the Presence of Cross-Section Dependence. *Journal of Applied Econometrics, 22*(2), 265–312. doi:10.1002/jae.951

Pesaran, M. H., & Yamagata, T. (2008). Testing slope homogeneity in large panels. *Journal of Econometrics, 142*(1), 50–93. doi:10.1016/j.jeconom.2007.05.010

Pesaran, M. H., Ullah, A., & Yamagata, T. (2008). A Bias Adjusted LM Test of Error Cross Section İndependence. *The Econometrics Journal*, *11*(1), 105–127. doi:10.1111/j.1368-423X.2007.00227.x

Shayanewako, V. B. (2018). The relationship between trade openness and economic growth: The case of BRICS countries. *Journal of Global Economics*, *6*(2), 6–10. doi:10.4172/2375-4389.1000289

Streltsov, E. S., Rozhin, A. A., Vosiev, S. S., & Kosnikov, S. N. (2021). The economic potential of the brics countries as a challenge to modern world realities. *Propósitos y Representaciones, 9*(SPE3), 1143.

Raghutla, C. (2020). The effect of trade openness on economic growth: Some empirical evidence from emerging market economies. *Journal of Public Affairs*, *20*(3), e2081.

Wooldridge, J. M. (2010). *Econometric analysis of cross section and panel data*. MIT Press.

Wooldridge, J. M. (2012). *Introductory econometrics: A modern approach*. Cengage Learning.

Yapraklı, S. (2007). *Ticari Ve Finansal Dışa Açıklık ile Ekonomik Büyüme Arasındaki İlişki: Türkiye Üzerine Bir Uygulama. Istanbul University Econometrics and Statistics e-Journal, (5), 67-89.*

KEY TERMS AND DEFINITIONS

HAC: Heteroscedasticity and Autocorrelation.
MINT Countries: Mexico, Indonesia, Nigeria, Turkey.
PMG: Pooled Mean Group.

Chapter 7
The Interaction Among R&D Expenses and Economic Growth Evidence From EU Transition Economies

Omer Faruk Ozturk
Usak University, Turkey

Mahmut Unsal Sasmaz
Usak University, Turkey

ABSTRACT

The research and development (R&D) activities are some of the crucial factors affecting the economic growth through raising the technological development, resource base enlargement, and promotion in the capability of resource utilization. This study analyzed the mutual interplay between R&D investments and economic growth in a sample of the EU transition states by means of causality test. The consequences of causality analysis pointed out a unidirectional causality from R&D expenditures to economic growth in Slovenia and a unidirectional causality from economic growth to R&D expenditures at panel level and in Bulgaria, Croatia, Estonia, and Slovakia.

INTRODUCTION

Economic growth is a crucial determinant underlying level of welfare and one of the main goals for all countries. Technological development and innovation are the significant determinants of economic growth. The key factor behind the technological development and innovation is R&D (R&D) outlays (Erdoğan and Canbay, 2016). The R&D expenditures are important for sustainable long run economic growth, because R&D investments is significant factor underlying innovation development and productivity improvements (Romer, 1994). As a consequence, the countries with higher R&D expenditures have had higher value-added production and economic growth (Gümüş and Çelikay, 2015).

DOI: 10.4018/978-1-7998-9648-7.ch007

Economics science has never disregarded the impact of technological progress on the change of economic dynamics. However, most economists did not accept the factors of technological development, innovation and R&D as inputs to production until the 20th century. But the economic models developed as of 20th century began to include the technological development, innovation, and R&D expenditures in the empirical analyses, because all these factors began to increasingly affect the processes of production, consumption, employment, and economic growth (Doğan and Öcal, 2007).

The continuous technological development is a required to sustain the economic growth (Solow, 1956). Solow growth model is based on a production function with capital and labor and technological development is exogeneous. The new growth theories emphasize the role of technological development in economic growth (Inekwe, 2015). Furthermore, R&D investments make a contribution to intangible capital accumulation and increases in R&D investments foster the technological potential and in turn innovation and economic growth (Celli et al., 2021; Altın and Kaya, 2009).

Technological innovation (product and process innovation) has become an obligation to keep the competitiveness and be successful in the rapidly changing and developing world. For this reason, both firms and countries should attach enough importance to R&D activities to reach a trend of sustainable economic growth. Since R&D activities are an important element of economic growth, it can be said that there is a strong relationship among R&D expenses and economic growth in the world (Altın and Kaya, 2009).

This study investigated the causal interaction among R&D expenses and economic growth in sample of the EU (European Union) transition economies which experienced an economic and institutional transformation. The next part reviewed the literature on the nexus of R&D expenditures and economic growth, and then data and method were described. The following section included the empirical analyses and the study was concluded with Conclusions.

LITERATURE REVIEW

The interaction among R&D expenses and economic growth has been extensively explored in the related empirical literature as seen in Table 1 and the researchers have generally explored the aforementioned relationship in sample of high-income countries and reached a positive effect of R&D expenditures on economic growth.

Goel and Ram (1994) explored the relationship among R&D expenses and economic growth in 52 countries from developing and less developed countries for the period of 1960-1985 by regression analysis and found that R&D expenditures had a positive effect on economic growth, but its statistical significance was low. Furthermore, the impact of R&D expenditures on economic growth was revealed to be stronger in less developing countries.

On the other hand, Freire-Serén (2001) investigated the interaction among R&D expenses and economic growth in 21 OECD members through regression analysis and uncovered that 1% in R&D expenditures led a 0.08% increase in economic growth. Sylwester (2001) also explored the relation among R&D expenses and economic growth in 20 OECD members including G7 economies for the period of 1981-1996 and reached that R&D expenditures had a positive effect on economic growth in the G7 economies, but there was an insignificant relationship between two variables in all sample.

Zachariadis (2004) researched the effect of R&D expenses on growth in 10 OECD members over the 1971-1995 duration via dynamic regression analysis and discovered that increases in R&D expenditures

Table 1. Summary of the literature

Study	Country/Country Group	Impact of R&D on economic growth
Goel and Ram (1994)	52 developing and less developing countries	Positive
Freire-Serén (2001)	21 OECD members	Positive
Sylwester (2001)	20 OECD members	Insignificant in all sample; positive in G7 economies
Zachariadis (2004)	10 OECD members	Positive
Montobbio and Rampa (2005)	9 developing countries	Positive
Seyoum (2005)	in 55 developed and developing countries	Positive
DiPietro and Anoruo (2006)	59 countries	Positive
Braunerhjelm and Thulin (2006)	19 OECD members	Positive
Falk (2007)	OECD members	Positive
Samimi and Alerasoul (2009)	30 developing economies	Insignificant
Genç and Atasoy (2010)	34 countries	Unidirectional causality from R&D expenses to growth
Wang et al. (2013)	23 OECD members and Taiwan	Positive
Silaghi et al. (2014)	CEE countries	Positive
Huňady and Orviska (2014)	26 EU members	Positive
Kacprzyk and Doryn (2014)	EU-28 members	Insignificant
Gümüş and Çelikay (2015)	53 countries	Positive
Inekwe (2015)	66 countries	Positive in upper middle-income countries; insignificant in low-income countries
Freimane and Bāliņa (2016)	EU countries	Positive
Sağlam et al. (2017)	26 developing and developed countries	A significant causality from R&D expenses to growth
Choi and Yi (2018)	105 countries	Positive
Pala (2019)	25 developing countries	Negative
Nair et al. (2020)	OECD	Positive
Olaoye et al. (2021)	Selected African countries	Positive
Ahmad and Zheng (2022)	36 OECD countries	Positive during the boom; negative during the recession

fostered the productivity growth and output. On the other hand, Montobbio and Rampa (2005) explored the relationship between technological progress and export in 9 developing countries over the 1985-1998 duration by means of structural decomposition analysis and found that the countries experiencing the improvements in industries with high increasing technological opportunities had the export gains in high-tech sectors. Seyoum (2005) also explored the determinants of high technology exports in 55 developed and developing countries which had 97% of global high-tecg export via factor and regression analyses and discovered a positive effect of technological infrastructure positively affected the high-tech exports.

DiPietro and Anoruo (2006) explored the effect of creativity and its components (innovation, technology, technology transfer and new businesses) on total export value and export composition in 59 countries and revealed a positive correlation between creativity and its components and export. On the other hand, Braunerhjelm and Thulin (2006) investigated the effect of R&D expenditures and market size on comparative advantages in 19 OECD members over the 1981-1999 duration and reached that 1% increase in R&D expenditures led a 3% increase in high-tech export. Falk (2007) also investigated the relationship between real GPD per capita and R&D expenditures in OECD members for the period of 1970-2004 and found that increases in R&D expenditures of high-tech sectors raised the real GDP per capita.

Samimi and Alerasoul (2009) also researched the interaction among R&D expenses and economic growth in 30 developing economies for the period of 2000-2006 via regression analysis and revealed an insginficiant interaction among R&D expenses and economic growth. Genç and Atasoy (2010) examined the causal interplay among R&D expenses and economic growth in 34 countries over the 1997-2008 duration via causality test and pointed out a unidirectional causality from R&D expenditures to economic growth. On the other hand, Wang et al. (2013) researched the relationship among R&D expenses and economic growth in 23 OECD members and Taiwan over the 1991-2006 duration and reached that high industrial R&D expenditures had a positive effect on real GDP per capita. Silaghi et al. (2014) also explored the effect of public and private sectors' R&D expenditures on economic growth in Central and Eastern European countries over the 1998-2008 duration via dynamic regression analysis and revealed that 1% increase in commercial R&D intensity raisd the conomic growth by 0.050% in the short run and 0.213% in the long run, but public R&D expenditures did not have a significant impact on economic growth.

Huňady and Orviska (2014) researched the relationship among R&D expenses and economic growth in 26 EU members ove the period of 1999-2011 by regression analysis and discovered a positive effect of R&D expenditures on economic growth. On the other hand, Kacprzyk ve Doryn (2014) explored the interaction among R&D expenses and economic growth in EU-28 members over the 1993-2011 duration via dynamic regression analysis and discovered an insignificant interaction between economic growth and R&D expenditures. Gümüş and Çelikay (2015) also researched the relationship among R&D expenses and economic growth in 53 countries over the 1996-2010 duration via cointegration analysis and disclosed a positive effect of R&D expenditures on economic growth in the long term. Furthermore, the growth effect of R&D expenditures was weak in the short term and strong in the long term.

Inekwe (2015) investigated the relationship among R&D expenses and economic growth in 66 countries with different income levels over the 2000-2009 term via dynamic regression analysis and found that R&D expenditures had a positive effect on economic growth in the countries with upper middle income level, but did not have a significant effect on economic growth in the countries with low income level. On the other hand, Freimane and Bāliņa (2016) researched the interaction among R&D expenses and economic growth in the EU countries over the 2000-2013 duration via regression analysis and revealed a positive interaction among R&D expenses and economic growth. On the other hand, Sağlam et al. (2017) examined the causality among R&D expenses and economic growth in 26 countries from developed and develoing economies over the 1996-2014 duration by means of causality tests and pointed out a significant causality from R&D expenditures to economic growth.

DATA AND ECONOMETRIC METHODOLOGY

The study investigated the causal interaction among R&D expenses and economic growth in EU transition states over the 1999-2018 period through Emirmahmutoglu and Kose (2011) causality test. The

Table 2. Dataset description

Variables	Variable Descrip.	Data Source
GRW	GDP per capita growth-annual %	World Bank (2021a)
RD	R&D expenditure -% of GDP	World Bank (2021b)

economic growth was represented by growth rate of GDP per capita based on constant local currency and R&D expenditures was proxied by gross domestic R&D expenditures consisting of capital and current expenditures (outlays on basic research, applied research, and experimental development) in sectors of government, business enterprise, higher education, and private non-profit. All series were annual and provided from database of World Bank as presented in Table 2.

The sample of the study consisted of 11 EU transition states (Bulgaria, Croatia, Czech Republic, Estonia, Hungary, Latvia, Lithuania, Poland, Romania, Slovakia, and Slovenia). The study duration was 1999-2018, because R&D expenditures existed for the 1996-2018 period. The empirical analyses were conducted by means of Stata 14.0 and EViews 10.0

The summary statistics of the dataset were depicted in Table 3. The mean of R&D expenditures was 0.925% of GDP and relatively stable among the countries. On the other hand, the average of economic growth was 3.6644% and exhibited considerable changes among the countries.

Table 3. Summary statistics of the dataset

Variables	Mean	Standard Deviation	Min.	Max.
RD	0.9258	0.4741	0.3526	2.5649
GRW	3.6644	4.1166	-14.4643	12.997

The causality among R&D expenses and economic growth was investigated by means of Emirmahmutoglu and Kose (2011) causality test taking the availability of cross-sectional dependence and heterogeneity into consideration. The Emirmahmutoglu and Kose (2011) causality test is the improved version of Toda-Yamamoto (1995) causality test for heterogeneous panels and takes the availability of cross-sectional dependence and heterogeneity into consideration. Therefore, the series should not be necessary to be stationary (Emirmahmutoglu and Kose, 2011).

Emirmahmutoglu and Kose (2011) causality test allows the lag length to differentiate for each cross-section and decreases the long-term information loss because it models the series with level values (Emirmahmutoglu and Kose, 2011; Toda and Yamamato, 1995). The causality test can be implemented through the following equations:

$\tilde{\Delta}$

$$GRW = \varphi_0^{GRW} + \sum_{k=1}^{k_i+d_{max_i}} A_{21,ik} RD_{it-k} + \sum_{k=1}^{k_i+d_{max_i}} A_{22,ik} GRW_{it-k} + \mu_{0,T}^{GRW} \qquad (2)$$

Table 4. Cross-sectional dependence test outcomes

Test	Test Stat.	Prob.
LM	452.8	0.000
LM adj*	92.12	0.000
LM CD*	20.34	0.000

*two-sided test

In the above equation, k represents the lag length, d_{max} is the maximum integration level for each country. The rejection of $H_0 : \sum_{k=1}^{k_i} A_{12} = 0$ shows that R&D expenditures is Granger cause of economic growth. On the other hand, the rejection of $H_0 : \sum_{k=1}^{k_i} A_{21} = 0$ denotes that R&D expenditures are Granger cause of economic growth. The country level probability values (p_i) is aggregated considering Fisher (1932) and in turn panel level probability value of the causality analysis is obtained. Fisher (1932) test statistic obeys the chi-square distribution with 2N degree of freedom, but critical values for cross-section level causality analysis are derived from bootstrapping.

EMPIRICAL ANALYSIS

Firstly, heterogeneity and cross-sectional dependency of the series was examined in the context of the empirical analysis. Breusch and Pagan (1980) LM test, Pesaran (2004) LM CD test, and Pesaran et al. (2008) LM adj. test were employed to check the existence of cross-sectional dependency. The findings of the aforementioned cross-sectional dependency tests were displayed in Table 4. The test findings indicated that there existed a cross-sectional dependency among the series.

Pesaran and Yamagata (2008) homogeneity tests were employed to test the slope homogeneity of the panel. The findings of the tests displayed in Table 5 revealed that there existed heterogeneity in the panel dataset, The results of both heterogeneity and cross-sectional dependency tests directed us to use a panel causality test considering cross-sectional dependency and heterogeneity.

The stationarity of the series was examined through Pesaran (2007) CIPS (Cross-sectionally augmented IPS (Im- Pesaran-Shin, 2003) unit root test considering the cross-sectional dependence between two series. The test findings were shown in Table 6 and GRW was found to be I (0), and RD was revealed to be I(1).

Table 5. Homogeneity test outcomes

Test	Test Stat.	Prob.
$\tilde{\Delta}_{adj.}$	-0.555	0.579
$\tilde{\Delta}$	-0.511	0.609

Table 6. CIPS panel unit root test

Variables	Level		1. level	
	Const.	Const.+ Trend	Const.	Const. + Trend
GRW	-3.393***	-3.660**-	-5.043***	-5.019***
RD	-1.944	-1.958	-3.674***	-4.045***

*** indicated that it is significant at 1% significance level.

The causal relationship among R&D expenses and economic growth was analyzed by Emirmahmutoglu and Kose (2011) causality test considering the presence of cross-sectional dependency and test findings were shown in Table 7. The causality analysis revealed a one-way significant causality from R&D expenditures to economic growth in Slovenia and a one-way causality from economic growth to R&D expenditures at panel level and in Bulgaria, Croatia, Estonia, and Slovak Republic.

Table 7. Results of causality analysis between RD and GRW

Countries	RD ↛ GRW		GRW↛ RD	
	Test stat.	P val.	Test stat.	P val.
Bulgaria	0.083	0.773	**6.450**	**0.011**
Croatia	2.117	0.347	**6.646**	**0.036**
Czechia	0.434	0.510	0.518	0.472
Estonia	1.003	0.801	**15.794**	**0.001**
Hungary	0.571	0.450	0.005	0.946
Latvia	1.176	0.555	0.723	0.697
Lithuania	0.000	0.987	0.798	0.372
Poland	0.048	0.827	1.867	0.172
Romania	0.096	0.757	0.523	0.470
Slovakia	1.718	0.190	**2.684**	**0.081**
Slovenia	**6.084**	**0.048**	0.769	0.681
Panel	17.566	0.731	**43.714**	**0.004**

A mutual interaction among R&D expenses and economic growth is expected theoretical. However, the researchers have generally investigated the effect of R&D expenditures on economic growth by means of regression analysis and a positive effect of R&D expenditures on economic growth has been discovered to a large extent. Genç and Atasoy (2010) and Sağlam et al. (2017) also discovered a unilateral causality from R&D expenditures to economic growth. However, the researchers have reached these findings for the developed economies. Also, some researchers such as Samimi and Alerasoul (2009) and Kacprzyk and Doryn (2014) discovered a insignificant effect of R&D expenditures on economic growth for developing countries and different income level countries. Our study revealed a unilateral causality from economic growth to R&D expenditures partially in consistent with the related empirical literature. We evaluated that this contradiction can be resulted from very low R&D investment.

CONCLUSION

Reasearch and development investments are crucial determinants of innovation and technological development and in turn economic growth. Therefore, we investigated the interaction between R&D investments and economic growth in sample of the EU transition economies by means of causality analysis. The consequences of the causality analysis pointed out a unidirectional causality from R&D expenditures to economic growth in Slovenia and a unidirectional causality from economic growth to R&D expenditures at panel level and in Bulgaria, Croatia, Estonia, and Slovak Republic.

The researchers have generally conducted the effect of R&D investments on economic growth in developed countries and mainly reached a positive growth effect of R&D investments. However, we revealed a unidirectional causality from economic growth to R&D investments inconsistent with the theoretical findings. The contradiction may be resulted from relatively very low level of R&D investments. In this context, the R&D investments can foster the economic growth after reaching a threshold level over time.

REFERENCES

Ahmad, M., & Zheng, J. (2022). The cyclical and nonlinear impact of R&D and innovation activities on economic growth in OECD economies: A new perspective. *Journal of the Knowledge Economy*, 1–50. doi:10.100713132-021-00887-7

Altın, O., & Kaya, A. A. (2009). Türkiye'de Ar-Ge harcamaları ve ekonomik büyüme arasındaki nedensel ilişkinin analizi. *Ege Academic Review*, *9*(1), 251–259.

Braunerhjelm, P., & Thulin, P. (2006). *Can countries create comparative advantages?* Centre of Excellence for Studies in Science and Innovation (CESIS) Electronic Working Paper Series, Paper No. 61. https://static.sys.kth.se/itm/wp/cesis/cesiswp61.pdf

Breusch, T. S., & Pagan, A. R. (1980). The lagrange multiplier test and its applications to model specification in econometrics. *The Review of Economic Studies*, *47*(1), 239–253. doi:10.2307/2297111

Celli, V., Cerqua, A., & Pellegrini, G. (2021). Does R&D expenditure boost economic growth in lagging regions? *Social Indicators Research*, 1–20. doi:10.100711205-021-02786-5

Choi, C., & Yi, M. H. (2018). The internet, R&D expenditure and economic growth. *Applied Economics Letters*, *25*(4), 264–267. doi:10.1080/13504851.2017.1316819

DiPietro, W. R., & Anoruo, E. (2006). Creativity, innovation, and export performance. *Journal of Policy Modeling*, *28*(2), 133–139. doi:10.1016/j.jpolmod.2005.10.001

Doğan, C., & Öcal, N. (2007). *Yeni iktisat politikaları ve yenilik iktisadına eleştirel yaklaşım. Baskı.* Detay Yayıncılık.

Emirmahmutoglu, F., & Kose, N. (2011). Testing for granger causality in heterogeneous mixed panels. *Economic Modelling*, *28*(3), 870–876. doi:10.1016/j.econmod.2010.10.018

Erdoğan, S., & Canbay, Ş. (2016). İktisadi büyüme ve araştırma & geliştirme (Ar-Ge) harcamaları ilişkisi üzerine teorik bir inceleme. *Muş Alparslan Üniversitesi Sosyal Bilimler Dergisi*, *4*(2), 29–44. doi:10.18506/anemon.16169

Falk, M. (2007). R&D spending in the high-tech sector and economic growth. *Research in Economics*, *61*(3), 140–147. doi:10.1016/j.rie.2007.05.002

Fisher, R. A. (1932). *Statistical methods for research workers* (4th ed.). Oliver and Boyd.

Freimane, R., & Bāliņa, S. (2016). R&D expenditures and economic growth in the EU: A panel data analysis. *Economics and Business*, *29*(1), 5–11. doi:10.1515/eb-2016-0016

Freire-Seren, M. J. (2001). R&D-expenditure in an endogenous growth model. *Journal of Economics*, *74*(1), 39–62. doi:10.1007/BF01231215

Genç, A. G. M. C., & Atasoy, A. G. Y. (2010). Ar & Ge harcamaları ve ekonomik büyüme ilişkisi: Panel veri analizi. *Bilgi Ekonomisi ve Yönetimi Dergisi*, *5*(2), 27–34.

Goel, R. K., & Ram, R. (1994). R&D expenditures and economic growth: A cross-country study. *Economic Development and Cultural Change*, *42*(2), 403–411. doi:10.1086/452087

Gümüs, E., & Çelikay, F. (2015). R&D expenditure and economic growth: New empirical evidence. *The Journal of Applied Economic Research*, *9*(3), 205–217. doi:10.1177/0973801015579753

Huňady, J., & Orviská, M. (2014). The impact of R&D expenditures on innovation performance and economic growth of the country – the empirical evidence. *CBU International Conference Proceedings 2014, 2*, 119–125. 10.12955/cbup.v2.454

Im, K. S., Pesaran, M. H., & Shin, Y. (2003). Testing for unit roots in heterogeneous panels. *Journal of Econometrics*, *115*(1), 53–74. doi:10.1016/S0304-4076(03)00092-7

Inekwe, J. N. (2015). The contribution of R&D expenditure to economic growth in developing economies. *Social Indicators Research*, *124*(3), 727–745. doi:10.100711205-014-0807-3

Kacprzyk, A., & Doryn, W. (2014). Innovation and economic growth in European Union panel data analysis. *Lodz Economics Working Papers, 3*, 1-27.

Montobbio, F., & Rampa, F. (2005). The impact of technology and structural change on export performance in nine developing countries. *World Development*, *33*(4), 527–547. doi:10.1016/j.worlddev.2005.01.001

Nair, M., Pradhan, R. P., & Arvin, M. B. (2020). Endogenous dynamics between R&D, ICT and economic growth: Empirical evidence from the OECD countries. *Technology in Society*, *62*, 101315. doi:10.1016/j.techsoc.2020.101315

Olaoye, I. J., Ayinde, O. E., Ajewole, O. O., & Adebisi, L. O. (2021). The role of R&D (R&D) expenditure and governance on economic growth in selected African countries. *African Journal of Science, Technology, Innovation and Development*, *13*(6), 663–670. doi:10.1080/20421338.2020.1799300

Pala, A. (2019). Innovation and economic growth in developing countries: Empirical implication of swamy's random coefficient model (RCM). *Procedia Computer Science*, *158*, 1122–1130. doi:10.1016/j.procs.2019.09.252

Pesaran, M. H. (2007). A simple panel unit root test in the presence of cross-section dependence. *Journal of Applied Econometrics, 22*(2), 265–312. doi:10.1002/jae.951

Pesaran, M. H. (2004). *General diagnostic tests for cross section dependence in panels* (CESifo Working Paper No. 1229). Academic Press.

Pesaran, M. H., & Yamagata, T. (2008). Testing slope homogeneity in large panels. *Journal of Econometrics, 142*(1), 50–93. doi:10.1016/j.jeconom.2007.05.010

Pesaran, M. H., Ullah, A., & Yamagata, T. (2008). A bias-adjusted LM test of error cross-section independence. *The Econometrics Journal, 11*(1), 105–127. doi:10.1111/j.1368-423X.2007.00227.x

Romer, P. (1994). The origins of endogenous growth. *The Journal of Economic Perspectives, 1*(1), 3–22. doi:10.1257/jep.8.1.3

Sağlam, Y., Egelİ, H. A., & Egeli, P. (2017). Gelişmiş ve gelişmekte olan ülkelerde Ar&Ge harcamaları ve ekonomik büyüme arasındaki ilişki: Panel veri analizi. *Sosyoekonomi, 25*(1), 149–165.

Samimi, A. J., & Alerasoul, S. M. (2009). R&D and economic growth: New Evidence from some developing countries. *Australian Journal of Basic and Applied Sciences, 3*(4), 3464–3469.

Seyoum, B. (2005). Determinants of levels of high technology exports an empirical investigation. *Journal of Competitiveness Studies, 13*(1), 64–79.

Silaghi, M. I. P., Alexa, D., Jude, C., & Litan, C. (2014). Do business and public sector R&D expenditures contribute to economic growth in Central and Eastern European Countries? A dynamic panel estimation. *Economic Modelling, 36*, 108–119. doi:10.1016/j.econmod.2013.08.035

Solow, R. M. (1956). A contribution to the theory of economic growth. *The Quarterly Journal of Economics, 70*(1), 65–94. doi:10.2307/1884513

Sylwester, K. (2001). R&D and economic growth. *Knowledge, Technology & Policy, 13*(4), 71–84. doi:10.1007/BF02693991

Toda, H. Y., & Yamamoto, T. (1995). Statistical inference in vector autoregressions with possibly integrated processes. *Journal of Econometrics, 66*(1-2), 225–250. doi:10.1016/0304-4076(94)01616-8

Wang, D. H. M., Yu, T. H. K., & Liu, H. Q. (2013). Heterogeneous effect of high-tech industrial R&D spending on economic growth. *Journal of Business Research, 66*(10), 1990–1993. doi:10.1016/j.jbusres.2013.02.023

World Bank. (2021a). *GDP per capita growth (annual %)*. https://data.worldbank.org/indicator/NY.GDP.PCAP.KD.ZG

World Bank. (2021b). *R&D expenditure (% of GDP)*. https://data.worldbank.org/indicator/GB.XPD.RSDV.GD.ZS

Zachariadis, M. (2004). R&D-induced Growth in the OECD? *Review of Development Economics, 8*(3), 423–439. doi:10.1111/j.1467-9361.2004.00243.x

ADDITIONAL READING

Ulku, H. (2004). *R&D, innovation, and economic growth: An empirical analysis*. IMF Working Paper No. Issue 185, doi:10.5089/9781451859447.001

Nair, M., Pradhan, R. P., & Arvin, M. B. (2020). Endogenous dynamics between R&D, ICT and economic growth: Empirical evidence from the OECD countries. *Technology in Society*, *62*, 101315. doi:10.1016/j.techsoc.2020.101315

KEY TERMS AND DEFINITIONS

R&D Expenditures (R&D): Gross domestic expenditures on R&D (R&D) consisting of basic research, applied research, and experimental development and include capital and current expenditures in the sectors of business enterprise, government, higher education and private non-profit (World Bank, 2021b).

Real GDP per Capita Growth: Annual percentage growth rate of GDP per capita based on constant local currency (World Bank, 2021a).

Chapter 8
The Relationship Between Technological Development and Economic Growth in Emerging Economies:
Panel Causality Analysis

Funda H. Sezgin
Istanbul-Cerrahpasa University, Turkey

ABSTRACT

Technology creates a difference in production factors, methods, and products, and as a result of these differences increasing production and efficiency, it creates an increase in profit and competitive advantage. Technology is of great importance not only on the basis of companies or sectors, but also on the basis of countries. It also has an important role in determining the development and development levels of countries. For this reason, the use of appropriate technologies at appropriate times is also important in terms of national policies. In the globalizing world economy, technology is decisive for the competition among countries. Technological developments are of great importance as the driving force of growth, especially for emerging economies. The aim of this study is to determine the effect of technological developments on growth in emerging economies with the help of panel causality analysis. As a result of the analysis, one-way causality from technological development to economic growth was determined.

INTRODUCTION

Technology will have the potential and potential to project in production, hero and products, and this growth and the future is expected to be considered. When we examine it in history, you can evaluate that development progresses in parallel with economic growth in the development of investments in technology (Donou-Adonsou, 2019). Technology, especially after the 20th century, automatically consists of capital and production areas that are grown as a kind of capital. Technology is constantly advancing its

DOI: 10.4018/978-1-7998-9648-7.ch008

share in this thinking in terms of impact (Hong, 2017). Countries where technology is not just on the basis of companies or sectors. It is the owner of the payment in the development and development of the countries. The contents of these operating instructions are used. We are in a position to be shown as an example in terms of social life, administration and economies in the country, in the evaluation that they have completed what they have completed in developed and development education even now in countries that have caught technology in the industrial industry in the past (Josheski and Koteski, 2011).

Today, it is emphasized that the phenomenon of growth is related to the level of technology that countries have. Technology; According to the economist, it is a tool that raises the welfare and standard of living of nations, and a measurement technique stuck between resource inputs and production outputs, a set of methods used to produce a good, according to the engineer. In other words, technology is a source of information used to improve the production of existing goods and services, to improve marketing effectiveness, and to produce new goods and services (Bialbao-Osorio and Rodriguez-Pose, 2004). Technology, which has a dynamic structure, is a criterion used in the classification of countries. Industrialization and economic policies determined in developed countries are determined according to technology. The generally accepted view in the world is that there is an important positive relationship between countries' production with advanced technology and their economic growth and development. The aim of this study is to determine the effect of technological developments on growth in emerging economies with the help of panel causality analysis.

TECHNOLOGICAL DEVELOPMENT

The concept of technological development is defined as all kinds of inventions and innovations that enable the production of a new good and the process or method that enables the production of an existing good at a lower cost as a result of the increase in the efficiency of the factors used in the production (Huňady and Orviská, 2014). Technological development is one of the most essential elements for economic growth and international competition. For this reason, companies have to make new product and process innovations based on technology in order to maintain their competitive position. The level of technological development, which is one of the indicators that determine the economic position of nations, is extremely important for countries (Inglesi-Lotz and Gupta, 2015), In this context, the most important indicator that distinguishes developed and developing countries from each other is "Technological Development Levels".

According to Chris Freeman and Luc Soete, the founders of the innovation system, technology is defined as a concept used to express both the knowledge itself and the integrated state of this knowledge within a business system using physical production goods. In addition to the conceptual explanations of the word technology, it is seen that different definitions have been made by many authors and researchers in terms of economics in the academic literature. If a scientific definition is required, technology is generally considered as "a social process that transforms inputs into outputs" (Freeman and Soete, 2003).

In today's world, technology has become an intense environment as a result of rapid change, increasing power shift, competition area and increasing measures of continuity elements in the technological field. As a result of this inevitable transformation, the ratio of research and development expenditures to gross domestic product in the field of technology and innovation, the number of scientists and engineers working in research and development, the number of patents in the field of intellectual and industrial property, the number of scientific publications and finally the communication tools determine the competencies of countries in the field of technology and innovation (Mehran and Reza, 2011). Industries producing high-tech products; plays an important role in productivity, welfare and economic growth. Trade in technological products is very important for a country's competitiveness (Ntuli et al., 2015).

Owning high-tech sectors to contribute to the development of the country's economy is an indication that it has a decisive power in the development of exports with high added value. For countries that implement an export-oriented growth strategy, especially the development of advanced technology constitutes the driving force of economic development and growth (Petrariu, 2013). Countries have to increase their technology/innovation levels in order to increase their development and welfare levels. In this context, R&D investments and R&D studies draw attention as a prerequisite for technological development (Inekwe, 2014).

Technology, which is as old as human history, has become the most important driving force of economy and growth. Technological developments are one of the most important factors affecting economic growth (Samimi and Alerasoul, 2009). At this point, while the countries that produce technology and can use technology in the most efficient way realize economic growth and social and cultural changes faster, countries that cannot catch up with the speed of technological development lag behind this change (Zachariadis, 2003). In this context, small and medium-sized enterprises need to invest in technology in order to increase the innovation aspect of countries. In addition, technological developments have a critical importance on welfare increase and development by triggering the technological change process.

THE RELATIONSHIP OF TECHNOLOGY TRANSFER AND ECONOMIC GROWTH

In the neo-classical view, the relationship between technological development and economic growth was clearly written by Solow for the first time. Solow considers technology as external while making this assessment. According to the economic literature, endogenous growth models, on the other hand, internalized the technological developments that the Solow model accepted as exogenous in 1980 and later, and analyzed the determinant role of technological developments in the economic development process.

The first studies on endogenous growth theories were carried out by Lucas and Romer. Romer identified technological developments as an internal factor in the economy. Lucas, on the other hand, included human capital as an internal factor in Romer's model. Schumpeter considered the role of entrepreneurs in the growth of the capitalist system and the adaptation of technical progress to production by the entrepreneurs, that is, innovations, in his own words, as the most important factor. Here, the innovations mentioned by Schumpeter should not be confused with discoveries and inventions. Innovations refer to the application of any discovery or invention in the commercial field (Hasan and Tucci, 2010).

The emergence of technological innovation is related to creativity. Capitalists invest their own money with the technology they add to production. After a while, they make excessive profits and become a monopoly in the market (Medcof and Lee, 2017). In Marxist theory, the relationship between technology and economic development is explained entirely by class relations.

With the development of technology, capitalists have taken the place of labor under full control in the production process. To maximize their own profits, they increased production and used technology to dominate the worker's time to do the job. In other words, they used technology to increase the productivity of labor (Petruzzelli et al., 2018). Development economics explains technology as an element of dependency. They use it to produce technology from the core countries and to transfer that technology to the developing countries and make them dependent on themselves. The central country producing the technology is in a monopoly position. Since the countries that want to buy the produced technology pay astronomical figures, it makes it easier for the central country to easily control the economies of the surrounding countries (Thuriaux-Alemán et al., 2013). Countries that do not want to put up with these astronomical figures have found the solution to produce their own technology or to shape the technology they have purchased by understanding it very well. Thus, the production of local technologies has become a necessity at this stage.

We can list the technological developments as R&D investments, innovation, developments in information technology, etc. Economic growth, which is one of the most fundamental problems of macroeconomics, is important in terms of affecting the living standard and welfare level of individuals (Verbic et al., 2011). R&D is the key determinant of prosperity and productivity in the long run (Zhou and Luo, 2018). R&D investments create many innovations. This in turn promotes economic growth. In recent years, it has been seen that industrial innovations have played a major role in economic growth and regional development (Wang, 2013).

LITERATURE REVIEW

The main studies in the literature are presented in Table 1.

DATA AND ECONOMETRIC METHODOLOGY

The main purpose of the study is to examine the causality relationship between technological development and economic growth with the help of Dumitrescu-Hurlin Panel Causality Test, through annual data for the 2010-2020 period in emerging economy countries. In the study, technological development was measured using two different indicators, namely R&D expenditures and patent applications. All the series are annual and obtained from World Bank databases.

The study sample includes 17 emerging countries (Brazil, Chile, Colombia, Mexico, Peru, Egypt, Hungary, Poland, Russia, South Africa, Turkey, China, India, Endonesia, Taiwan, Thailand). To analyze the causal relationships between technological development and economic growth panel causality test developed by Dumitrescu and Hurlin (2012) was used. Before carrying out this test, we first tested the existence of cross-sectional dependence between variables employing Breusch-Pagan (1980) (Lagrange Multiplier-LM) and Pesaran (2004) (Cross-section Dependence-CD) and Pesaran, Ullah and Yamagata (2008) (Bias-Adjusted Cross Sectionally Dependence Lagrange Multiplier- CDLM) tests. And then, based on the results of the cross-sectional dependence tests, we performed second generation panel unit root tests of CIPS test. In addition, the homogeneity of delta tilde tests of Pesaran and Yamagata (2008), and the test results were presented in Table 2. Finally, we applied the Dumitrescu-Hurlin (2012) Panel Causality Test.

The Dumitrescu-Hurlin test can predict cross-section dependence and cross-section independence situations. When we examine the traditional panel Granger causality tests, it can be seen that if there is a causal relationship in a sub-group of the variable, due to the lack of cross-sectional information, that is because of the homogeneous null hypothesis. The null hypothesis means that there is no Granger causality relationship in cross-sections, and the alternative hypothesis expresses a Granger causality relationship

Table 1. Literature review

Researcher	Time	Sample	Results
Josheski & Koteski (2011)	1963Q1-1993Q4	G7 Countries	A one-way causality relationship from patent applications to economic growth has been determined.
Gülmez & Yardımcıoğlu (2012)	1990-2010	21 OECD Countries	A bidirectional causality relationship was found between R&D expenditures and economic growth.
Petrariu et al. (2013)	1996-2010	Central and Eastern European countries	A bidirectional causality relationship was found between R&D expenditures and economic growth.
Huňady and Orviska (2014)	2004-2011	26 EU countries	A bidirectional causality relationship was found between R&D expenditures and economic growth.
Tuna et al., (2015)	1990-2013	Turkey	There is no causal relationship between R&D expenditures and economic growth.
Ntuli et al. (2015)	2000-2014	OECD countries	A bidirectional relationship between economic growth and R&D.
Pradhan et al., (2016)	1961-2013	18 Eurozone Countries	Different results were obtained according to the technological development indicator used.
Türedi (2016)	1996-2011	23 OECD Countries	A bidirectional causality relationship was found between R&D expenditures and economic growth. It has been concluded that there is a one-way causality relationship from patent applications to economic growth.
Pradhan et al., (2017)	1970-2016	32 High Income OECD Countries	A bidirectional relationship has been identified between patent applications and economic growth. A unidirectional causality has been determined from economic growth to R&D expenditures.
Hong (2017)	1988-2013	Korea	A bidirectional relationship has been determined between R&D expenditures and economic growth.
Algan et al., (2017)	1996-2015	Turkey	A one-way causality relationship from R&D expenditures to economic growth has been determined. It has been concluded that there is a one-way causality relationship from economic growth to patent applications.
Zaman et al., (2018)	1980-2011	Science and Social Science Top in Areas 20 Countries with Research Output	A bidirectional causality relationship was found between R&D expenditures and economic growth in the USA, China, UK, Japan, India, Switzerland, Taiwan, Sweden and Turkey.
Çütçü & Bozan (2019)	1981-2016	G7 Countries	It has been concluded that there is a one-way causality relationship from economic growth to patent applications.
Shen et al., (2019)	1978-2014	China	A bidirectional relationship has been determined between R&D expenditures and economic growth.

Table 2. Dataset description

Variables	Variables Description	Data Source
GDP	Real GDP (in 2010 constant US dollars)	World Bank
R&D	R&D Expenditures /GDP	World Bank
PA	Patent Applications	World Bank

for at least one cross-section (Dumitrescu and Hurlin, 2012). Dumitrescu and Hurlin (2012) used the following equation for panel causality test considering the linear heterogeneous model:

$$y_{it} = \alpha_i + \sum_{k=1}^{L} \gamma_i^k y_{it-k} + \sum_{k=1}^{L} \beta_i^k x_{it-k} + \varepsilon_{it}, \mathrm{i} = 1,2,\ldots,\mathrm{N} : \mathrm{t} = 1,2,\ldots,\mathrm{T} \tag{1}$$

Where αi denotes individual effects, γ_i^k and β_i^k represents the lag and slope parameters, and L supposed to be the lag orders. We can summarize the model's assumptions as; the individual effects are constant, besides the same lag length in cross-section, the coefficients of slope and lag parameters vary across units and especially a balance panel must be required for the Dumitrescu-Hurlin test. The null and alternative hypotheses equation are as follows:

$$\begin{aligned} &H_0 : \beta_{i1} = \cdots = \beta_{iK} = 0\forall_i = 1,\ldots,N \\ &H_1 = \beta_{i1} = \cdots = \beta_{iK} = 0\forall_i = 1,\ldots,N_1 \\ &\beta_{i1} \neq 0 \text{ or } \beta_{iK} \neq 0\forall_i = N_1 + 1,\ldots,N \end{aligned} \tag{2}$$

When we consider the null hypothesis, it can be seen that there is no Granger causality relationship between variables for all units. In contrast, the alternative hypothesis represents at least one unit that there is evidence of Granger causality between variables. Individual residues are independent for each cross-section unit. Therefore, while the alternative hypothesis supports heterogenous results, the null hypothesis is a heterogenous model providing homogenous results. This test is usually distributed and allows (Dumitrescu and Hurlin, 2012). To determine the outcome of the Dumitrescu-Hurlin panel causality test hypotheses, one can use a test statistic, which is the mean of all test statistics of cross-sectional units.

$$W_{N,T}^{HNC} = \frac{1}{N}\sum_{i=1}^{N} W_{i,T} \left(\text{HNC}: \text{ Homogeneous Non-Causality}\right) \tag{3}$$

Where $W_{i,T}$ represents the test statistics of each cross-sectional unit. In this test, one can obtain two different test statistics based on whether T is greater or less than N. These test statistics are $Z_{N,T}^{HNC}$ and Z_N^{HNC} obtained from $W_{N,T}^{HNC}$. When T>N, we use $Z_{N,T}^{HNC}$ statistics. On the otherhand if T<N we use Z_N^{HNC} statistics. Furthermore, the following equations give these statistics.

$$Z_{N,T}^{HNC} = \sqrt{\frac{N}{2K}}\left(W_{N,T}^{HNC} - K\right)\mathrm{T},\mathrm{N} \to \infty, \mathrm{N}\left(0,1\right) \tag{4}$$

Table 3. Cross-sectional dependence tests and homogeneity test results

Cross-sectional Dependency Test (H_0: There is no cross-sectional dependency)		
Test	**Test Statistics**	**p**
LM (Breusch and Pagan, 1980)	40.210	0.005
LM $_{adj}$ (Pesaran et. al, 2008)	42.543	0.000
LM CD (Pesaran, 2004)	46.392	0.000
Homogeneity test (H_0: Slope coefficients are homogeneous)		
Test	**Test Statistics**	**p**
Delta_tilde	29.463	0.000
Delta_tilde_adj	31.224	0.000

$$Z_N^{HNC} = \frac{\sqrt{N}\left(W_{N,T}^{HNC} - N^{-1}\sum_{i=1}^{N} E\left(W_{i,T}\right)\right)}{\sqrt{N^{-1}\sum_{i=1}^{N} \mathrm{Var}\left(W_{i,T}\right)}} \mathrm{N} \rightarrow \infty, \mathrm{N}\left(0,1\right) \quad (5)$$

EMPIRICAL ANALYSIS

The cross-sectional dependency between the series was analyzed with the LM CD test developed by Pesaran (2004) and the LM adj. test whose deviation was corrected by Pesaran et al. (2008) and the test results are presented in Table 3. Since the probability values of the test results were below 1% and 5%, null hypothesis (there is no cross-sectional dependency) was rejected and it was determined that there was a cross-sectional dependency between the series. In addition, the homogeneity of the co-integration coefficients was tested using the delta tilde and corrected delta tilde tests of Pesaran and Yamagata (2008), and the test results were presented in Table 3. Since the probability values of the test results were below 1% and 5%, null hypothesis (slope coefficients are homogeneous) was rejected and it was determined that the co-integration coefficients were heterogeneous.

In this study, second-generation unit root tests should be used as cross-sectional dependency is determined. The second-generation unit root test of CIPS was used in this study. The results of the CIPS test are given in Table 4.

Table 4. Results of CIPS panel unit root test

Variables	**Level**		**First Difference**	
	Constant	**Constant + Trend**	**Constant**	**Constant + Trend**
GDP	-1.176	-1.289	-7.812*	-8.104*
R&D	-1.548	-1.721	-9.556*	-9.990*
PA	-1.201	-1.280	-8.118*	-8.511*

*indicated that it is significant at 5% significance level.

Table 5. Dumitrescu and Hurlin (2012) causality test results

Null Hypothesis	Test	Statistics	p
DLogGDP does not homogeneously cause DLogR&D	*Whnc*	1.516	0.136
	Zhnc	2.274	0.140
	Ztild	2.311	0.147
DLogR&D does not homogeneously cause DLogGDP	*Whnc*	6.942	0.000
	Zhnc	7.263	0.000
	Ztild	7.822	0.000
DLogGDP does not homogeneously cause DLogPA	*Whnc*	2.351	0.225
	Zhnc	2.886	0.238
	Ztild	3.201	0.353
DLogPA does not homogeneously cause DLogGDP	*Whnc*	9.163	0.000
	Zhnc	9.445	0.000
	Ztild	10.102	0.000

In CIPS tests, the maximum lag length was taken as 1 and the optimal lag length was determined according to the Schwarz information criterion. It is seen that hypothesis zero is rejected at 1% and 5% significance levels. Unit root test results show that the series are not stationary at the level, in other words, the variables are stationary at level I (1).

As can be seen from Table 5; The GDP variable is not the granger cause of the R&D variable. On the other hand, the R&D variable is the granger cause of the GDP variable. Unidirectional causality running from technological development to growth has been determined. The GDP variable is not the granger cause of the PA variable. On the other hand, the PA variable is the granger cause of the GDP variable. Between two variables, unidirectional causality has been obtained from technological development to growth.

CONCLUSION

The aim of the study is to decipher the causal relationship between technological development and economic growth in emerging countries. In the study in which the period 2010-2020 was examined, the panel causality methodology was used. Dumitrescu and Hurlin (2012) Causality Test result, one-way causality was determined from the R&D and PA variables of technological development indicators towards GDP. The growth values of emerging economy countries are not yet at a sufficient level. Therefore, the share allocated from GDP to technological development is less than in developed countries. Probably, R&D expenditures and patent applications supported by the private sector are becoming efficient and successful in creating income. Therefore, one-way causality from R&D and PA variables to GDP was determined. These results were obtained from Josheski & Koteski (2011), Gulmez & Ağıkcıoğlu (2012), Petrariu et al. (2013), Huňady and Orviska (2014), Ntuli et al. (2015), Türedi (2016), Pradhan et al., (2017), Hong (2017), Zaman et al., (2018), Cutcu & Bozan (2019) and Shen et al., (2019) have come out similar with their studies.

Developing countries are obliged to allocate part of their national income to research and development expenditures, which are considered high costs. Although the research and development expenditures of such countries may seem to be a burden on economic growth in the short term, they are an important factor for stable economic growth in the long term. In the developing country group, economic growth up to a certain threshold affects research and development expenditures, and after exceeding this threshold, research and development expenditures affect economic growth.

According to these findings, it is important that countries implement growth policies that prioritize technological development. In this context, government policies such as incentives and tax breaks that support R&D expenditures and patent applications of the private sector in particular may be recommended to be implemented.

For emerging countries, long-term structural plans, efficient technology and innovation policies need to be produced. In particular, universities should be supported in R&D and opportunities should be provided for talented students to realize their ideas. In addition, the number of technoparks in universities should be increased to understand changing paradigms in the world. Lastly, the private sector should be encouraged to increase R&D investments and incentives should be given in this regard.

REFERENCES

Algan, N., Manga, M., & Tekeoğlu, M. (2017). Teknolojik Gelişme Göstergeleri ile Ekonomik Büyüme Arasındaki Nedensellik İlişkisi: Türkiye Örneği. *International Conference on Eurasian Economies*, 332-338. 10.36880/C08.01869

Bialbao-Osorio, B., & Rodriguez-Pose, A. (2004). From R&D to Innovation and Economic Growth in the EU. *Growth and Change*, *35*(4), 434–455. doi:10.1111/j.1468-2257.2004.00256.x

Cütcü, İ., & Bozan, T. (2019). İnovasyon ve Ekonomik Büyüme İlişkisi: G-7 Ülkeleri Üzerine Panel Veri Analizi. *Uluslararası Ekonomi İşletme ve Politika Dergisi*, *3*(2), 289–310.

Donou-Adonsou, F. (2019). Technology, education, and economic growth in sub-saharan Africa. *Telecommunications Policy*, *43*(4), 353–360. doi:10.1016/j.telpol.2018.08.005

Dumitrescu, E., & Hurlin, C. (2012). Testing for Granger non-causality in heterogeneous panels. *Economic Modelling*, *29*(4), 1450–1460. doi:10.1016/j.econmod.2012.02.014

Gulmez, A., & Yardımcıoglu, F. (2012). OECD Ülkelerinde Ar-Ge harcaması ve ekonomik büyüme ilişkisi: Panel eşbütünleşme ve panel nedensellik analizi (1990-2010). *Maliye Dergisi*, *163*, 335–353.

Hasan, I., & Tucci, C. L. (2010). The innovation–Economic growth nexus: Global evidence. *Research Policy*, *39*(10), 1264–1276. doi:10.1016/j.respol.2010.07.005

Hong, J.-P. (2017). Causal Relationship Between ICT R&D Investment and economic growth in Korea. *Technological Forecasting and Social Change*, *116*, 70–75. doi:10.1016/j.techfore.2016.11.005

Huňady, J., & Orviská, M. (2014). The Impact of Research and Development Expenditures on Innovation Performance and Economic Growth of the Country – the Empirical Evidence. *CBU International Conference Proceedings*, *2*, 119-125.

Inekwe, J. N. (2014). The Countribution of R&D Expenditures to Economic Growth in Developing Countries. *Social Indicators Research, 124*(3), 727–745. doi:10.100711205-014-0807-3

Inglesi-Lotz, C. T., & Gupta, R. (2015). Causality Between Research Output and Economic Growth in BRICS. *Quality & Quantity, 49*(1), 167–176. doi:10.100711135-013-9980-8

Josheski, D., & Koteski, C. (2011). The causal relationship between patent growth and growth of GDP with quarterly data in the G7 countries: Cointegration, ARDL and Error Correction Models. *MPRA Paper No., 33153*, 1–21. doi:10.2139srn.1921908

Medcof, J. W., & Lee, T. (2017). The effects of the chief technology officer and firm and industry R&D intensity on organizational performance: CTO and firm and industry R&D on organizational performance. *R & D Management, 47*(5), 767–781. doi:10.1111/radm.12275

Mehran, M., & Reza, M. A. (2011). Comparative Investigation of the Relation of R&D Expenditures to Economic Growth in a Group of the Less Developed Countries and OECD Countries. *Journal of Social and Development Sciences, 2*(4), 188–195. doi:10.22610/jsds.v2i4.668

Ntuli, H., Inglesi-Lotz, R., Chang, T., & Pouris, A. (2015). A Does Research Output Cause Economic Growth or Vice Versa? Evidence from 34 OECD Countries. *Journal of the Association for Information Science and Technology, 66*(8), 1709–1716. doi:10.1002/asi.23285

Pesaran, M. H. (2004). General diagnostic tests for cross section dependence in panels. *CESifo Working Papers, 1233*, 255–260.

Pesaran, M. H. (2007). A Simple panel unit root test in the presence of cross-section dependence. *Journal of Applied Econometrics, 22*(2), 265–312. doi:10.1002/jae.951

Pesaran, M. H., Ullah, A., & Yamagata, T. (2008). A bias-adjusted lm test of error cross-section independence. *The Econometrics Journal, 11*(1), 105–127. doi:10.1111/j.1368-423X.2007.00227.x

Pesaran, M. H., & Yamagata, T. (2008). Testing slope homogeneity in large panels. *Journal of Econometrics, 142*(1), 50–93. doi:10.1016/j.jeconom.2007.05.010

Petrariu, I. R., Bumbac, R., & Ciobanu, R. (2013). Innovation: A path to competitiveness and economic growth. The case of CEE countries. *Theoretical and Applied Economics, 20*(3), 15–26.

Petruzzelli, M. A., Ardito, L., & Savino, T. (2018). Maturity of knowledge inputs and innovation value: The moderating effect of firm age and size. *Journal of Business Research, 86*, 190–201. doi:10.1016/j.jbusres.2018.02.009

Pradhan, R. P., Arvin, M. B., Bahmani, S., & Bennett, S. E. (2017). The ınnovation-growth link in OECD countries: Could other macroeconomic variables matter? *Technology in Society, 51*, 113–123. doi:10.1016/j.techsoc.2017.08.003

Pradhan, R. P., Arvin, M. B., Hall, J. H., & Nair, M. (2016). Innovation, financial development and economic growth in eurozone countries. *Applied Economics Letters, 23*(16), 11411144. doi:10.1080/13504851.2016.1139668

Samimi, A. J., & Alerasoul, S. M. (2009). R&D and Economic Growth: New Evidence from Some Developing Countries. *Australian Journal of Basic and Applied Sciences*, *3*(4), 3464–3469.

Shen, X., Lin, B., & Wu, W. (2019). R&D Efforts, Total Factor Productivity, and the Energy Intensity in China. *Emerging Markets Finance & Trade*, *55*(11), 2566–2588. doi:10.1080/1540496X.2019.1579709

Thuriaux-Alemán, B., Eagar, R., & Johansson, A. (2013). Getting a better return on your innovation investment - Results of the 8th Arthur D. Little global innovation excellence study. Technology and Innovation Management, 1-24.

Tuna, K., Kayacan, E., & Bektaş, H. (2015). The relationship between research & development expenditures and economic growth: The case of Turkey. *Procedia: Social and Behavioral Sciences*, *195*, 501–507. doi:10.1016/j.sbspro.2015.06.255

Türedi, S. (2016). The relationship between R&D expenditures, patent applications and growth: A dynamic panel causality analysis for OECD countries. *Anadolu University Journal of Social Sciences*, *16*(1), 39–48.

Verbič, M., Majcen, B., Ivanova, O., & Čok, M. (2011). R&D and Economic Growth in Slovenia: A Dynamic General Equilibrium Approach with Endogenous Growth. *Panoeconomicus*, *1*(1), 67–89. doi:10.2298/PAN1101067V

Wang, T. L., Yu, T. H.-K., & Liu, H.-Q. (2013). Heterogeneous Effect of High-Tech Industrial R&D Spending on Economic Growth. *Journal of Business Research*, *66*(10), 1990–1993. doi:10.1016/j.jbusres.2013.02.023

Zachariadis, M. (2003). R&D, Innovation, and Technological Progress: A Test of the Schumpeterian Framework without Scale Effects. *The Canadian Journal of Economics. Revue Canadienne d'Economique*, *36*(3), 566–686. doi:10.1111/1540-5982.t01-2-00003

Zaman, K., Khan, H. U. R., Ahmad, M., & Aamir, A. (2018). Research productivity and economic growth: A policy lesson learnt from across the globe. *Indian Economic Review*, *22*(3), 627–641.

Zhou, G., & Luo, Z. (2018). Higher education ınput, technological innovation, and economic growth in China. *Sustainability*, *10*(8), 1–15. doi:10.3390u10082615

Chapter 9
The Effect of Attitudes and Behaviors Towards New Technologies on Performance of Academicians

Lina Karabetyan
Independent Researcher, Turkey

ABSTRACT

Due to the opportunities and conveniences it provides to human life, the use of new technologies is becoming more and more common in daily life, becoming indispensable. With the spread of technology, the increase in the number of people using technology has made it possible to produce new information that creates added value, thanks to the ability to easily access information all over the world to combine and analyze big data. The development of technology and the circulation of knowledge have become important elements of economic and social change. The aim of this study is to determine the effects of attitudes and behaviors towards new technologies on the performance for 450 academicians working in four research universities in Istanbul, for academics who are expected to have high compliance with innovative approaches. As a result of the structural equation model, a positive 38.4% increasing relationship was determined between the attitudes and behaviors towards new technologies and performance.

INTRODUCTION

With the rapid development of science and technology, technological developments manifest in almost every aspect of life in society (Bharadwaj et al., 2013). The ability of people to convey to each other any developments in life enabled societies to take quicker action and become more productive. This situation highlights the connection between education and technology. Today, one of the factors used to measure the development level of a country is its achievements in science and technology (Tondeur et al.,2017a). One of the most important elements in ensuring this development is education.

DOI: 10.4018/978-1-7998-9648-7.ch009

Education, which provides the transfer of knowledge to the society, has also played an important role in terms of transferring the ever-developing technology to societies, the use of developing technology in education and new teaching techniques and methods to be used in the developing process (Voogt et al., 2013). Today, the concepts of education and technology have become concepts that make sense when taken together, rather than when they are handled separately. For this reason, a separate concept coined "educational technology" has emerged, which is a concept that expresses the development and improvement of education and the increase in the quality of education (Scherer et al., 2018). From this point of view, it can be stated today that without educational technology, it will not be possible to increase the quality and efficiency of education.

The contribution of technology use is important for raising qualified students and for efficient education. In universities it is difficult for students to fully grasp theoretical lessons. However, using technological teaching instruments increases the quality of education (Majid, 2014). Academicians, who play an important role in raising qualified and qualified individuals, also have an important role in the effective and productive education process. In this process, effective and efficient use of educational technologies is a rather important issue (King and He, 2006).

Academicians, who are guides and examples to students in higher education, need to use educational technologies effectively and efficiently, and exercise self-efficacy. For students to benefit from educational technologies adequately, to see themselves as competent and to reach the aims aimed in education, academicians must have self-efficacy in terms of technology (Gebre et al., 2014). The teaching staff has an important duty, and it is important for the students, the society and our country that this staff is qualified to meet today's needs. The aim of the study is to determine the effects of attitudes and behaviors towards new technologies on performance for 450 academicians working at four research universities in Istanbul.

CONCEPTUAL FRAMEWORK

Attitude Towards New Technologies

Technology and the innovations it brings are the key to being able to compete with countries which have caught up the information age in today's world. In connection with the advances and development required by modern living, economic growth, technological advancements, changing cultural and social factors prompt major changes in the consumption patterns existing in society (Kirschner, 2015). For example, consumers of new technologies lead connected lives through very dynamic use of technological means such as the World Wide Web, cable TV, networks, phones, satellites, etc. In the 21st century, consumer demands and requirements can be instantly specified and fulfilled, thanks to many information and communication technologies (Dillenbourg, 2016). Hence itis no more possible to imagine a life without all new technologies, specifically information and communication technologies, which facilitate modern life. Effective use of available media has created new purchasing behaviors, which in turn created a new type of consumer today. This new consumer is, in fact, a technology consumer (Eden et al., 2019).

Due to the opportunities and conveniences they provide to human life, the use of new technologies is becoming increasingly widespread, compulsory and indispensable in daily life (Agarwal et al., 2010). While technology creates a bridge to solve real-life problems using scientific methods, new technology means new uncertainty, new complexity, new resource allocation model and new unknown fears. However, these factors may not have the same effect on every person and may vary according to the different characteristics of the users (Van Laar et al., 2019). The group most affected by these changes is younger people who easily adopt technological innovations and developments (Majid, 2014). Doubtlessly, young people in Turkey, form a large and diverse mass with their value judgments, habits, disposition to consumption and new technologies and behaviors just as in the whole world, on the other hand they have become an ever-growing and important consumer group.

Young consumers, who will be the workers and innovators of the future, represent the future of society (Hume, 2009, Claffey, 2006). For this reason, they are defined as the "engine of growth" and "subjects of change" in the world market in the next 20 years (Claffey, 2006). Consumption expenditures, life experience, technological advances, environmental issues, and changes in political frameworks have a significant potential impact on young consumers (Hume, 2009). Especially young people who have better access to products and services equipped with new technological features can be the first adopters and key influencers of emerging technologies (Kirschner and Bruyckere, 2017; Bouwman et al., 2018).

Today, technology is defined as a process that covers the transformation of the data of basic and applied sciences into production within creative processes, their use and the analysis of their social effects (Autio et al., 2018). This approach emphasizes the fact that technology takes place as a process in all kinds of social activities. Technology is a synthesis of creativity and intelligence created by science, art, engineering, economics and social work in order to improve the quality of human life. It is an attempt to do everything better, faster, easier, more economically and more efficiently (Lee and Coughlin, 2015). According to Ertmer et al., (2012), technology is a whole that includes man-made products formed by changing the natural world, is intertwined with many environmental and social elements, inherently involves dilemmas in many issues, has its own characteristics and covers the process from design to production.

According to International Technology Education Association (2008), the characteristics of technology are:

- **Technology is associated with science:** Although there is a relationship between science and technology, the amount of technology which can be classified as "applied science" is very small except for the certainty in high industrial technologies. Technology is specified with different purposes and processes.
- **Technology includes design:** Regarding "design" in the context of technology, 59% of the society has opinions that design consists of "drawings" from a traditional perspective rather than a creative process to solve problems with a contemporary perspective (Bybee, 2000). At the heart of technology is design. The phrase "design is the core of engineering" is a confirmation that all engineering subjects want to embody technology. This design process in technology is a sequential process which starts with the perception of a need, produces ideas, continues with a definition formula with a final solution, and ends with the evaluation of the solution.
- **Technology includes production:** The motivating factor behind all technological activity is the desire to fulfill a need. For this reason, all designs must be produced or realized using prototypes, mass production, or three-dimensional or computer modeling (Jones, 2001).
- **Technology is multidimensional:** Technology does not only include design and manufacturing which involve collaboration between different specialties (e.g., designers, production engineers and material specialists). It may as well include "technologists" who perform many different tasks (such as cooperating with others, acting in budgeting, convincing decision makers, working to deadlines, and communicating with customers).

- **Technology is about values:** Technology is aware of values at every point. Value decisions may require not only the relationship of technology to specific design criteria (e.g., aesthetic, ergonomic and economic judgments, suitability of purpose, and manufacturing convenience), but also its relationship with the rightness or wrongness of a particular solution in ethical terms (Christensen, 2002).

Figure 1. Technology Dimensions and Content
Source: International Technology Education Association (2008)

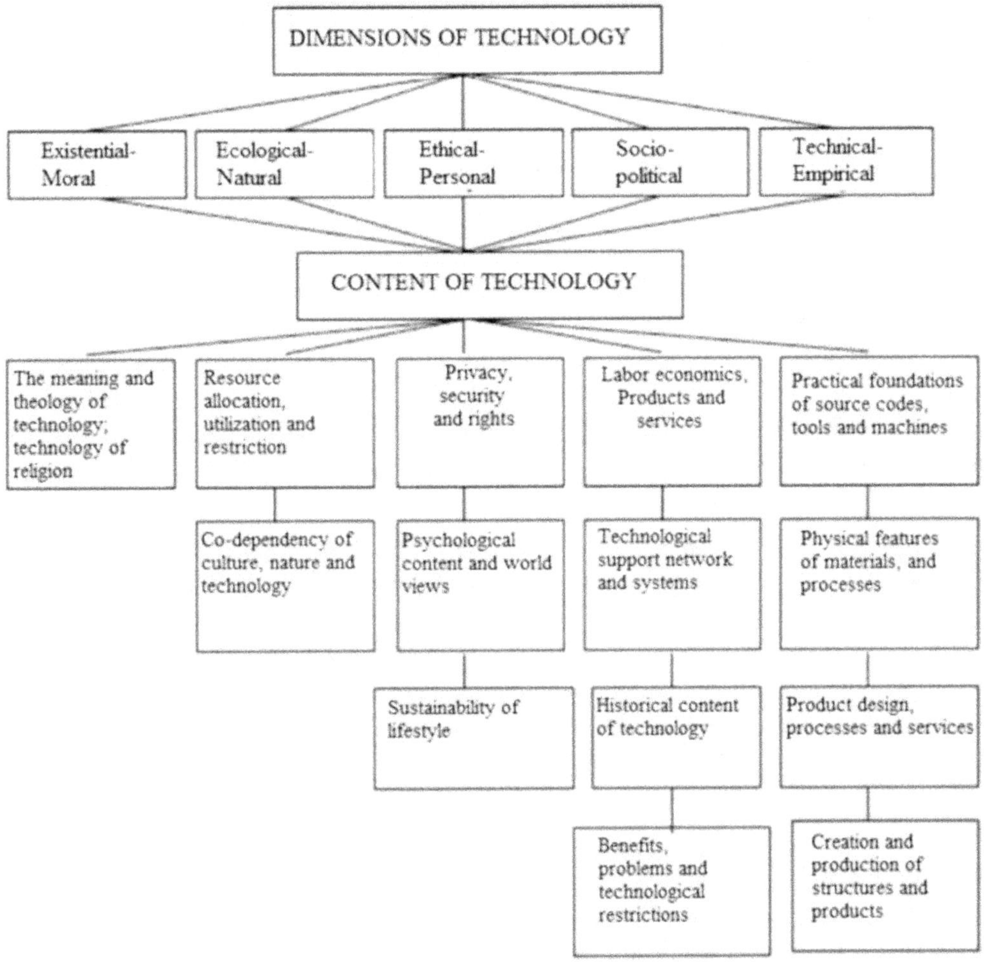

Importance of Attitude Towards New Technologies for Academicians

According to Ball (2008), attitude is “the tendency to react positively or negatively to a certain object, situation, institution, concept or other people”. According to the definition by Rockman (2004), “Attitude is a state of emotional readiness or tendency observed as the acceptance or rejection of a certain person, group, institution or an idea”. According to Dawson and Rakes (2003), besides the importance of using technology in today's education system, teachers' attitudes towards technology are also very important. Dawson and Rakes suggests that teachers who play a leading role in all activities to be carried out in the teaching-learning process need to have a positive attitude towards technology, so they can use technology effectively in learning environments. As stated by Oppenheimer (2003), "Individuals' attitudes towards technology, positive or negative opinions about technology are one of the most important factors in terms of realizing the performance to perform a task."

Teachers and technology constitute two important elements of the learning-teaching process. Because these two elements are important in the education of students. A teacher, who has to carry different roles in today's education system, needs to both benefit from technology and teach the student how to use technology for educational purposes (Livingstone and Sefton-Green, 2016). However, in order for the teaching staff to successfully guide students in the teaching-learning processes in line with the innovations brought by the age, they need to know how to run the technology in the education process (Liu et al., 2016). It is important for the academician to both benefit from technologies in the education process and teach their students to use technologies in accordance with their purpose. By transferring knowledge and experience to the student, the academician can ensure that the process is carried out in a healthy way. According to Sadaf et al., (2012), academicians have to follow the ever-evolving and changing world and get used to changes. At the same time, an academician is in a constant struggle to keep up with the changes in the changing developing world.

The role of academicians is important for young people to keep up with all these changes and to protect their own self, and in order to fulfill these roles well, academicians should not lag behind the times and should constantly renew themselves (Ertmer et al.,2012). In our developing and changing world, new understandings and new models are emerging in education and teachers must keep up with these innovations, and be an effective guide when initiating learners into the world of technology (Knezek and Christensen, (2016). Although academicians seem to be a guide in the education process of students today, we cannot talk about a successful education environment if they cannot fulfill this duty. Teachers should be role models in terms of effectively planning and utilizing educational technologies.

A teacher should be able to plan and use educational technology well and effectively in the classroom, while in this way being a role model for students in using technology. It is considered important that educational technologies are suitable for desired target behaviors and that the teacher is a good role model for his students. Otherwise, educational technologies, which are indisputably beneficial to education, may do more harm than good (Farjon et al., 2019).

Work Performance

Job performance is the results obtained by the employee as a result of fulfilling his/her responsibility within a certain period of time (Ramos-Villagrasa et al., 2019). If the results obtained are positive, it is deemed that the employee fulfills the task assigned to him and exhibits high performance, and if these results are negative, then the employee is considered unsuccessful and displays low performance (Aguinis, 2013). Quantitative and qualitative expression of the point reached by the employee, with reference to the intended goals, is evaluated as work performance (Carlos and Gouveia, 2016). In the most basic sense, work performance is the whole of behaviors displayed at the workplace, in line with purposes and goals defined by the organization (Woehr, 2008). Work performance is the recording and evaluation of the results produced within the scope of a specified job or activity in a specified time period (Viswesvaran and Ones, 2017). The productivity level of the work-related outputs of the employee compared to the other employees with authority and duty shows the work performance (Selenko, 2013). Aguinis (2013), define work performance as "measurable behavior of individuals in relation to organizational goals".

Work performance is the effort spent to achieve a specified goal, task, or job. It mostly describes the output obtained as a result of this effort (Koopmans et al., 2013). Work performance is the difference obtained when the qualitative or quantitative value, which an individual creates in their work activities in line with their personal goals or the goals of their organization, is compared to said goals. If this is a positive difference the work performance is high, if it is a negative difference, the work performance is deemed to be low. The term "organizational performance" refers to the performance of an organization as a whole. However, individual performance is much more important for organizations because organizations can be as good as the sum of the individual performances of their employees (DeNisi and Murphy, 2017). Although the increase in individual performance does not mean an increase in organizational performance, it is an important component and starting point of performance.

STATISTICAL ANALYSIS

The Purpose and the Importance of the Research

The world is going through a very important process of change, with dazzling developments in the areas of science and technology. The frequency of the emergence of technological innovations has increased, and technologies have changed in short periods in production and service industries. This storm of change, especially experienced prominently after the 2000s, has gained even more momentum, which has reached to a point that a newly purchased cutting-edge product is rather very shortly bettered with another product. Rapid developments in science and technology cause revolutionary changes in social, cultural, political and economic fields. It is getting harder and harder to keep up with the pace of these changes and developments in technology.

The increase in purchasing power of young people and their acquaintance with technology at an increasingly early age, as well as their constant interaction with technology, has turned young people into a different target audience than adults for both researchers and producers. With the spreading of communication opportunities and the Internet, young people can be informed very quickly about new developments in the world. In this rapidly progressing process, which we have been experiencing in our transition to the information society, technology is more widely adopted by university students day by day.

The attitudes of students and academicians, which are the most basic components of new technology applications, are of great importance. It is clear that these technologies will be very effective both in increasing academic success and in learning and teaching activities. On the other hand, it is expected that the attitudes and behaviors of employees towards new technologies will create positive outputs that will increase performance. The aim of the study is to determine the effects of attitudes and behaviors towards new technologies on performance for 450 academicians, who are expected to exercise high disposition to new technologies, working at four research universities in Istanbul.

Research Sample

The universe of the study consists of academic staff working in research universities operating in Istanbul. According to the statistics of the number of academicians of the Higher Education Council (HEC) in

Table 1. Research hypotheses

	Hypotheses
H_1 (main hypothesis)	Attitudes and behaviors towards new technologies and performance are statistically significantly correlation.
H_2 (sub hypothesis)	Positive attitudes and behaviors towards new technologies and performance are statistically significantly correlation.
H_3 (sub hypothesis)	Negative attitudes and behaviors towards new technologies and performance are statistically significantly correlation.

2021, the total number of academicians (research assistants, lecturers, doctor lecturers, associate professors, and professors) in state universities in Istanbul is 36,896. "Simple random sampling" was used as the sampling method. Surveys were conducted via e-mail between 15.03.2021 and 15.04.2021 (https://forms.gle/v9VTRwr2E91MYwKnP). Since some participants did not answer most of the questions in the questionnaire during the data entry process, these questionnaires were not included in the analysis process, and a total of 450 questionnaires were used in practice. In the sample size table developed by Yazıcıoğlu and Erdoğan (2004), it was determined that 384 people should be studied for p=0.50 and q=0.50 with a sampling error of 0.05. In this application, analyzes were carried out with 450 samples.

Research Hypotheses

The main hypothesis of the research is that attitudes and behaviors towards new technologies increase performance. The sub-hypothesis is "positive attitudes and behaviors and negative attitudes and behaviors towards technological products and services affect performance". The developed hypotheses are presented in Table 1.

Data Collection Tool

The study is built on a non-experimental quantitative research design and is a relational screening model according to the method of practice. The questionnaire used in the study was prepared using the scales whose validity and reliability were approved in previous studies as a result of a wide-scope literature review. We can explain these scales as follows:

Attitudes and Behaviors Towards New Technologies: Ezer (2008)'s research on "the effects of technological developments on enhancing product features and consumer purchasing behavior" was used in the preparation of the items used to measure attitudes and behaviors towards new technologies. In this study, attitude towards technology is measured with one dimension. There are 11 items in the dimension of attitude towards technology. The Cornbach Alpha value reported in the study by Ezer (2008) is also .88. Five more items were added to this dimension in the Günay (2012) study. Thus, a form consisting of 16 items was used to determine attitudes and behaviors towards advanced technology. As a result of this study, 2 sub-dimensions were obtained as positive attitudes and behaviors (11 items) and negative attitudes and behaviors (5 items) towards technological products and services. Questions prepared in a 5-point Likert style have scores ranging from 1 to 5, with options listed as "(1)-strongly disagree to (5)-strongly agree". A high score on 18 items indicates higher attitudes and behaviors towards new technologies.

Work performance scale: The Employee Performance scale was developed by Kirkman and Rosen (1999) and brought to the literature by Sigler and Pearson (2000). It was adapted into Turkish by Çöl (2008). The scale is unidimensional and consists of 4 articles. It contains no reversing item. The internal consistency coefficient of the scale was obtained in the Çöl (2008) study as 0.82. The prepared scale questions were asked to the participants using the 5-point Likert method, which scales as 1 = Strongly Disagree to 5 = Strongly Agree.

Statistical Methods

The data acquired from the scale utilized in the study were analyzed via IBM SPSS 26.0 and AMOS 25.0 programs. In the first stage, percentage distributions regarding demographic and general information were presented. In the second stage, exploratory factor analysis (EFA) was applied for the scales, and besides, confirmatory factor analysis (CFA) was performed to test construct validity. In the last stage, correlation analysis and structural equation model estimation results were included in order to identify the relationships.

Assumptions and Limitations of the Study

It was assumed that the people participating in the research acted with their true feelings and thoughts while answering the propositions in the scales. It was accepted that each participant answered the survey study voluntarily and answered each statement in the survey correctly and completely. It was also assumed that each participant understood the real meanings of all the words while answering the propositions. There were some difficulties in increasing the sample size in the survey; people were reluctant to participate due to different reasons. The fact that they did not have a positive attitude towards participation in the survey can be considered as an important limitation. In addition, employees who were not aware of the survey and did not check their emails on the specified dates were excluded from the sample. The research is limited to the province of Istanbul.

FINDINGS AND RESULTS

Survey Reliability

For the data obtained from the survey study, Cronbach Alpha, Split, Parallel, Absolute Precise Parallel (strict) tests were carried out as a reliability test. A Cronbach Alpha value above 70% indicates that the survey was successful. Some researchers take this value as 75% (Sezgin, 2016). The fact that other criteria are above 70% indicates that the questionnaire has internal consistency and that the results can be trusted (Sart et al., 2018; Sart 2020). In this study, the results of the reliability analysis of the questionnaire are Cronbach-Alpha = 0.914, Parallel = 0.913, Split = 0.912-0.915, and Strict = 0.914.

Descriptive Statistics

56.8% of the participants were female, and 43.2% were male. 65.4% of the academician were aged 20-30, 23.7% were aged 31-40, 10.0% were aged 41-50, and 0.9% were aged 51 years and over. In terms

Table 2. Exploratory factor analysis results

Attitudes and Behaviors Towards New Technologies Scale	PVE	CA	AVE	CR
Positive Attitudes and Behaviors	35.67%	0.910	0.753	0.909
Negative Attitudes and Behaviors	32.14%	0.909		
KMO= 0.928; Bartlett $\chi 2$= 7963.12 and p= 0.000; Percent of Variance Explained: 67.81%				
Performance Scale	**PVE**	**CA**	**AVE**	**CR**
Performance	73.10%	0.912	0.784	0.911
KMO= 0.930; Bartlett $\chi 2$= 8143.89 and p= 0.000; Percent of Variance Explained: 73.10%				

PVE: Percent of Variance Explained, CA: Cronbach's Alpha Coefficient; AVE: Average Variance Extracted; CR: Construct Reliability

of marital status, 44.3% of the individuals were married, while 55.7% were single. Looking at the participants' employment terms, 3.9% worked less than 1 year, 19.5% between 1-5 years, 24.3% between 6-10 years, 25.6% between 11-20 years, and 26.7% worked for 21 years or more. According to their job positions, 16.9% were research assistant, 27.9% assistant professor, 26.2% associate professor, 22.4% professor and 6.6% lecturer.

Exploratory Factor Analysis

Factor analysis is a multivariate statistics method intended for finding or discovering a small number of unrelated and conceptually significant new variables (i.e. factors, dimensions) by bringing together p number of interrelated variables. After the suitability of the data set was confirmed by the tests, the "Principal Components Analysis" approach was applied via the "Varimax" rotation technique as the factor retention method in order to reveal the factor structure.

As a result of the exploratory factor analysis (EFA): Regarding the factor structure, for the Attitudes and Behaviors Towards New Technologies Scale, 2 factor structure was obtained, which explained 67.81% of the total variance; for the Performance Scale, 1 factor structure was obtained which explained 73.10% of the total variance. Following the EFA, there was no need to eliminate any questions since there was no item below 0.20 in the inference column and no item with anti-image matrix diagonal values below 0.50.

Confirmatory Factor Analysis

Confirmatory factor analysis (CFA) is utilized to express multivariate statistical analyses containing latent structures denoted by a large number of observable or measurable variables. CFA is a factor analysis technique utilized to question whether the factors revealed as a result of Exploratory Factor Analysis (EFA) are appropriate for the structure of the factors revealed as a result of the hypotheses. While EFA is utilized to examine which variable groups are highly correlated with which factors, CFA is employed to determine whether the variable groups contributing to the k number of identified factors are sufficiently represented by the said factors.

In Table 3, X^2 /sd= 2.11, a "good fit" decision was made since it met the condition 3. NFI=0.934 resulted in the range of 0.94-0.90, thus an "acceptable fit"; other results were obtained as TLI (NNFI)= 0.979 was 0.95, a "good fit"; IFI= 0.986 was 0.95, a "good fit"; CFI= 0.960 was 0.97, an "acceptable

Table 3. CFA model fit indices

Measurement (Fit Statistic)	Good Fit	Acceptable Fit	Research Model Value	Fit Status
General Model Fit				
X^2 /sd	≤3	≤4-5	2.11	Good fit
Comparative Fit Statistics				
NFI	≥0.95	0.94-0.90	0.934	Acceptable fit
TLI (NNFI)	≥0.95	0.94-0.90	0.979	Good fit
IFI	≥0.95	0.94-0.90	0.986	Good fit
CFI	≥0.97	≥0.95	0.960	Acceptable fit
RMSEA	≤0.05	0.06-0.08	0.023	Good fit
Absolute Fit Indices				
GFI	≥0.90	0.89-0.85	0.930	Good fit
AGFI	≥0.90	0.89-0.85	0.949	Good fit
Residual-Based Fit Index				
RMR	≤0.05	0.06-0.08	0.031	Good fit

fit"; RMSEA= 0.023 was 0.05, a "good fit"; GFI= 0.930 was 0.90, a "good fit"; AGFI= 0.949 was 0.90, a "good fit"; and RMR= 0.031 was 0.05, thus it was a "good fit".

Correlation Analysis

The results of the correlation analysis for the dimensions of the scales under examination are given in Table 4.

Table 4. Mean, standard deviation values, and correlation matrix

	Mean	Sd.	1	2	3	4
1- PAB	3.979	0.712	1			
2- NAB	2.257	1.109	-0.326*	1		
3- NTAB	4.013	0.744	0.394*	-0.383*	1	
4- PER	3.892	0.512	0.361*	-0.347*	0.411*	1

PAB: positive attitudes and behaviors NAB: negative attitudes and behaviors
NTAB: Attitudes and Behaviors Towards New Technologies
PER: performance
*p <0.01

Correlation analysis was executed to exhibit the relationships among the variables. At the end of the analysis, significant ($p<0.01$) and relationships were observed among all the variables. Among the structures, the strongest relationship emerged between PER and NTAB ($r= 0.411$, $p<0.01$), and the weakest relationship emerged between NAB and PAB ($r= -0.326$, $p<0.01$).

Table 5. SEM model estimation results

Structural Relation	Direction	Estimated Coefficient	Std. Error	t-statistic	p	Result
PAB → PER	+	0.317	0.084	3.773	0.000*	Significant relationship
NAB → PER	-	-0.402	0.095	4.231	0.000*	Significant relationship
NTAB → PER	+	0.384	0.081	4.740	0.000*	Significant relationship

*p<0.01

Structural Equation Modeling

Structural equation modeling (SEM) is a statistical technique used to test models in which causal relationships and correlation relationships between observed variables and latent variables coexist; it is a multivariate method that is formed by combining analyses such as variance and covariance analyses, factor analysis, and multiple regression in order to predict interdependency relationships. Considering the goodness of fit criteria for SEM, it was found that X^2 /sd= 2.25, a "good fit" decision was made because it met the condition ≤3. NFI=0.945 resulted in 0.94-0.90, thus an "acceptable fit"; other results were obtained as TLI (NNFI)= 0.983 was ≥ 0.95, a "good fit"; IFI = 0.989 was ≥ 0.95, a "good fit"; CFI= 0.988 was ≥ 0.97, an "acceptable fit"; RMSEA= 0.015 was ≤0.05, a "good fit"; GFI= 0.945 was ≥ 0.90, a "good fit"; AGFI= 0.956 was ≥ 0.90, a "good fit"; and RMR= 0.024 was ≤0.05, thus it was a "good fit". SEM estimates fit criteria yielded the result "acceptable" for only one criterion; others revealed that a "good fit" was attained and the model was appropriate for interpretation.

According to the SEM results, significant relationships were obtained among the variables. PAB has a statistically significant positive effect on PER (β=0.317; p<0.01). NAB has a statistically significant negative effect on PER (β= -0.402; p<0.01). NTAB has a statistically significant positive effect on PER (β= 0.384; p<0.01). According to the coefficient sizes, the NAB variable is most effective on the PER variable.

CONCLUSION

This study aims to determine academicians' interest in and knowledge regarding new technologies, their disposition towards using products with contemporary technological features and the effects of this interest, knowledge, and disposition on their performance. Science and technology have spread into our daily lives and have become a part of our daily life from banks to homes, from clothing to food. As long as technology and science play this role, society needs to gain sufficient foresight in this area. In particular, academicians, as trainers, should have knowledge and skills regarding technological products and services, as well as products and services with new technologies.

As a result of the correlation analysis carried out in the study, a positive and significant relationship of 41.1% was determined between attitudes and behaviors towards new technologies and performance.

As a result of SEM analysis, a positive and significant relationship was determined between attitudes and behaviors towards new technologies and performance ($\beta=0.384$; $p<0.01$).

According to the sub-hypotheses, a positive and significant relationship was determined between positive attitudes and behaviors towards new technologies and performance ($\beta=0.317$; $p<0.01$). A significant negative correlation was determined between negative attitudes and behaviors towards new technologies and performance ($\beta=-0.402$; $p<0.01$). Negative attitudes and behaviors towards new technologies have a negative effect on performance.

For this reason, young people, who are potentially and practically most affected by social and technological changes and developments, should gain a perspectives which enable them to analyze the benefits and drawbacks of technological developments. In this respect, academicians should act as role models. As with every innovation, new technologies that make our lives easier bring with them negativities such as uncertainty, complexity and waste of resources. Therefore, students and academicians, who act as a change factor affecting society and culture, should act in awareness of the positive and negative sides of new technology. Thus, thanks to these abilities, they will have the opportunity to positively affect their environment and shape their future. In order for young people to act consciously about technology and consumption, they should be informed through information and communication technologies regarding changing and developing technologies, areas where technology is widely used in society, and the positive and negative effects of new technologies on society and the environment.

The research has a certain sample limit due to cost and time constraints. For this reason, in order to generalize the findings to the whole society, it would be more beneficial to reach the whole society by extending the coverages of new research on this subject to more regions and settlements throughout the country, and to include more universities in these researches. In addition, further studies should separately examine students and academicians in order to demonstrate differences between generations, and determine changes in the results over time by periodically repeating research of this kind. In this context, we believe that a sample which involves all occupational groups will be useful.

REFERENCES

Adler, S., Campion, M., Colquitt, A., Grubb, A., Murphy, K., Ollander-Krane, R., & Pulakos, E. D. (2016). Getting rid of performance ratings: Genius or folly? A debate. *Industrial and Organizational Psychology: Perspectives on Science and Practice*, *9*(2), 219–252. doi:10.1017/iop.2015.106

Agarwal, R., Gao, G., DesRoches, C., & Jha, A. K. (2010). Research commentary-The digital transformation of healthcare: Current status and the road ahead. *Information Systems Research*, *21*(4), 796–809. doi:10.1287/isre.1100.0327

Aguinis, H. (2013). *Performance management*. Pearson Prentice Hall.

Autio, E., Nambisan, S., Thomas, L. D., & Wright, M. (2018). Digital affordances, spatial affordances, and the genesis of entrepreneurial ecosystems. *Strategic Entrepreneurship Journal*, *12*(1), 72–95. doi:10.1002ej.1266

Ball, D. L., Thames, M. H., & Phelps, G. (2008). Content knowledge for teaching: What makes it special? *Journal of Teacher Education*, *59*(1), 389–407. doi:10.1177/0022487108324554

Bharadwaj, A., El Sawy, O., Pavlou, P., & Venkatraman, N. (2013). Digital business strategy: Toward a next generation of insights. *Management Information Systems Quarterly*, *37*(2), 471–482. doi:10.25300/MISQ/2013/37:2.3

Bouwman, H., Nikou, S., Molina-Castillo, F. J., & de Reuver, M. (2018). The impact of digitalisation on business models. *Digital Policy. Regulation & Governance*, *20*(2), 105–124. doi:10.1108/DPRG-07-2017-0039

Bybee, R. W. (2000). Achieving technological literacy: A national imperative. *Technology Teacher*, *60*(1), 23–28.

Carlos, V. S., & Gouveia, R. (2016). Development and validation of a self-reported measure of job performance. *Social Indicators Research*, *126*(1), 279–307. doi:10.100711205-015-0883-z

Christensen, R. (2002). Effects of technology integration education on the attitudes of teachers and students. *Journal of Research on Technology in Education*, *34*(4), 411–433. doi:10.1080/15391523.2002.10782359

Çöl, G. (2008). Algılanan Güçlendirmenin İş Gören Performansı Üzerine Etkileri. *Dogus University Journal*, *9*(1), 35–46.

Dawson, C., & Rakes, G. C. (2003). The influence of principals' technology training on the integration of technology into schools. *Journal of Research on Technology in Education*, *36*(1), 29–49. doi:10.1080/15391523.2003.10782401

DeNisi, A. S., & Murphy, K. R. (2017). Performance appraisal and performance management: 100 years of progress? *The Journal of Applied Psychology*, *102*(3), 421–433. doi:10.1037/apl0000085 PMID:28125265

Dillenbourg, P. (2016). The evolution of research on digital education. *International Journal of Artificial Intelligence in Education*, *26*(2), 544–560. doi:10.100740593-016-0106-z

Eden, R., Jones, A. B., Casey, V., & Draheim, M. (2019). Digital transformation requires workforce transformation. *MIS Quarterly Executive*, *18*(1), 1–17. doi:10.17705/2msqe.00005

Ertmer, P. A., Ottenbreit-Leftwich, A. T., Sadik, O., Sendurur, E., & Sendurur, P. (2012). Teacher beliefs and technology integration practices: A critical relationship. *Computers & Education*, *59*(2), 423–435. doi:10.1016/j.compedu.2012.02.001

Ezer, G. (2008). *Teknolojik Gelişme ile Artan Ürün Özellikleri ve Tüketici Satın Alma Davranışına Etkileri* (Unpublished Master's thesis). Istanbul Technical University, Institute of Science and Technology.

Farjon, D., Smits, A., & Voogt, J. M. (2019). Technology integration of pre-service teachers explained by attitudes and beliefs, competency, access, and experience. *Computers & Education*, *130*, 81–93. doi:10.1016/j.compedu.2018.11.010

Gebre, E., Saroyan, A., & Bracewell, R. (2014). Students' engagement in technology rich classrooms and its relationship to professors' conceptions of effective teaching. *British Journal of Educational Technology*, *45*(1), 83–96. doi:10.1111/bjet.12001

Günay, G. (2012). Effect of New Technologies On The Purchasing Trends of Young People. *Akademik Bakis Dergisi*, *29*(1), 1–20.

International Technology Education Association. (2008). *Advancing excellence in technological literacy:Student assessment, Professional development, and program standards*. Author.

Jones, A. (2001). Theme issue: Developing research in technology education. *Research in Science Education*, *31*(1), 3–14. doi:10.1023/A:1012658211512

King, W. R., & He, J. (2006). A meta-analysis of the technology acceptance model. *Information & Management*, *43*(6), 740–755. doi:10.1016/j.im.2006.05.003

Kirkman, B. L., & Rosen, B. (1999). Beyond Self-Management: Antecedents and Consequences of Team Empowerment. *Academy of Management Journal*, *42*, 58–74.

Kirschner, P. A. (2015). Do we need teachers as designers of technology enhanced learning? *Instructional Science*, *43*(2), 309–322. doi:10.100711251-015-9346-9

Kirschner, P. A., & de Bruyckere, P. (2017). The myths of the digital native and the multitasker. *Teaching and Teacher Education*, *67*, 135–142. doi:10.1016/j.tate.2017.06.001

Knezek, G., & Christensen, R. (2016). Extending the will, skill, tool model of technology integration: Adding pedagogy as a new model construct. *Journal of Computing in Higher Education*, *28*(3), 307–325. doi:10.100712528-016-9120-2

Koopmans, L., Bernaards, C. M., Hildebrandt, V. H., De Vet, H. C. W., & Van der Beek, A. J. (2013). Measuring individual work performance: Identifying and selecting indicators. *Work (Reading, Mass.)*, *48*(2), 229–238. doi:10.3233/WOR-131659 PMID:23803443

Lee, C., & Coughlin, J. F. (2015). Perspectıve: older adults' adoption of technology: An integrated approach to identifying determinants and barriers. *Journal of Product Innovation Management*, *32*(5), 747–759. doi:10.1111/jpim.12176

Liu, C. C., Wang, P. C., & Tai, S. J. D. (2016). An analysis of student engagement patterns in language learning facilitated by web 2.0 technologies. *ReCALL*, *28*(2), 104–122. doi:10.1017/S095834401600001X

Livingstone, S., & Sefton-Green, J. (2016). *The Class: Living and Learning in the Digital Age*. New York University Press. doi:10.18574/nyu/9781479884575.001.0001

Majid, N. A. A. (2014). Integration of web 2.0 tools in learning a programming course. *The Turkish Online Journal of Educational Technology*, *13*(4), 88–94.

Oppenheimer, T. (2003). *The Flickering Mind: The False Promise of Technology in the Classroom and How Learning Can Be Saved*. Random House.

Ramos-Villagrasa, P. J., Barrada, J. R., Fernández-del-Río, E., & Koopmans, L. (2019). Assessing Job Performance Using Brief Self-report Scales: The Case of the Individual Work Performance Questionnaire. *Journal of Work and Organizational Psychology*, *35*(3), 195–205. doi:10.5093/jwop2019a21

Rockman, I. F. (2004). *Integrating Information Literacy into the Higher Education Curriculum: Practical Models for Transformation*. Jossey-Bass.

Sadaf, A., Newby, T. J., & Ertmer, P. A. (2012). Exploring factors that predict preservice teachers' intentions to use web 2.0 technologies using decomposed theory of planned behavior. *Journal of Research on Technology in Education*, *45*(2), 171–195. doi:10.1080/15391523.2012.10782602

Sart, G. (2020). Bireysel Girişimcilik Eğilimi Ölçeğinin Geliştirilmesi: Geçerlik ve Güvenirlik Çalışması. *International Journal of Applied Economic and Finance Studies*, *1*(5), 58–72.

Sart, G., Sezgin, F. H., & Demir, N. (2018). Mobbingin Mesleki Tükenmişlik Algısı Üzerine Etkileri: Kadın Akademisyenler Örneği. *Beykoz Akademi Dergisi*, *6*(1), 118–135. doi:10.14514/BYK.m.21478082.2018.6/1.117-135

Scherer, R., Tondeur, J., Siddiq, F., & Baran, E. (2018). The importance of attitudes toward technology for pre-service teachers' technological, pedagogical, and content knowledge: Comparing structural equation modeling approaches. *Computers in Human Behavior*, *80*, 67–80. doi:10.1016/j.chb.2017.11.003

Selenko, E., Mäkikangas, A., Mauno, S., & Kinnunen, U. (2013). How does job insecurity relate to self-reported job performance? Analysing curvilinear associations in a longitudinal sample. *Journal of Occupational and Organizational Psychology*, *86*(4), 522–542. doi:10.1111/joop.12020

Sezgin, F. H. (2016). Bayesci Faktör Analizi ve Maslach Tükenmişlik Envanteri Uygulaması. *International Conference on Scientific Cooperation for the Future in the Social Sciences (USAK),* 1283-1296.

Sigler, T. H., & Pearson, C. M. (2000). Creating an empowering culture: Examining the relationship between organizational culture and perceptions of empowerment. *Journal of Quality Management*, *5*(1), 27–52. doi:10.1016/S1084-8568(00)00011-0

Tondeur, J., Pareja-Roblin, N., van Braak, J., Voogt, J., & Prestridge, S. (2017a). Preparing beginning teachers for technology integration in education: Ready for take-off? *Technology, Pedagogy and Education*, *26*(2), 157–177. doi:10.1080/1475939X.2016.1193556

Van Laar, E., Van Deursen, A. J. A. M., Van Dijk, J. A. G. M., & Haan, J. (2017). The relation between 21st-century skills and digital skills: A systematic literature review. *Computers in Human Behavior*, *72*, 577–588. doi:10.1016/j.chb.2017.03.010

Viswesvaran, C., & Ones, D. S. (2017). Job performance: Assessment issues in personnel selection. In A. Evers, N. Anderson, & O. Voskuijl (Eds.), *The Blackwell handbook of personnel selection* (pp. 354–375). Wiley. doi:10.1002/9781405164221.ch16

Voogt, J. M., Fisser, P., Pareja Roblin, N., Tondeur, J., & Van Braak, J. (2013). Technological pedagogical content knowledge - a review of the literature. *Journal of Computer Assisted Learning*, *29*(2), 109–121. doi:10.1111/j.1365-2729.2012.00487.x

Woehr, D. J. (2008). On the relationship between job performance and ratings of job performance: What do we really know? *Industrial and Organizational Psychology: Perspectives on Science and Practice*, *1*(2), 161–166. doi:10.1111/j.1754-9434.2008.00031.x

ADDITIONAL READING

Åkesson, M., Sørensen, C., & Eriksson, C. I. (2018). Ambidexterity under digitalisation: A tale of two decades of new media at a Swedish newspaper. *Scandinavian Journal of Management*, *34*(3), 276–288. doi:10.1016/j.scaman.2018.06.004

DiMaria-Ghalili, R. A., Ostrow, L., & Rodney, K. (2005). Webcasting: A new instructional technology in distance graduate nursing education. *The Journal of Nursing Education*, *44*(1), 11–18. doi:10.3928/01484834-20050101-03 PMID:15673169

Ma, W. M., Andersson, R., & Streith, K. O. (2005). Examining user acceptance of computer technology: An empirical study of student teachers. *Journal of Computer Assisted Learning*, *21*(6), 387–395. doi:10.1111/j.1365-2729.2005.00145.x

Schepers, J., & Wetzels, M. (2007). A meta-analysis of the technology acceptance model: Investigating subjective norm and moderation effects. *Information & Management*, *44*(1), 90–103. doi:10.1016/j.im.2006.10.007

Tondeur, J., Van Braak, J., Ertmer, P. A., & Ottenbreit-Leftwich, A. (2017b). Understanding the relationship between teachers' pedagogical beliefs and technology use in education: A systematic review of qualitative evidence. *Educational Technology Research and Development*, *65*(3), 555–575. doi:10.100711423-016-9481-2

Willermark, S. (2018). Technological pedagogical and content knowledge: A review of empirical studies published from 2011 to 2016. *Journal of Educational Computing Research*, *56*(3), 315–343. doi:10.1177/0735633117713114

Chapter 10
Identification of Factors Affecting the Exports of High-Tech Products:
A Panel Data Analysis

Hacer Handan Demir
Istanbul Gelisim University, Turkey

ABSTRACT

Innovation activities, which have been on a rapid increase, impact countries' degrees of development. Countries that are able to produce and export advanced technology are one step ahead of other countries in terms of international competition. For this reason, exports of high-tech products and related determining factors have become an issue that needs to be addressed. The aim of this study is to examine the determinants of high technology product exports between 2010-2020 for the BRICS-T developing country group using panel regression analysis. As a result of the analysis, GDP and R&D were specified as the most influential variables on exports of high-tech products. A GDP variable of 29.1%, R&D variable 28.9%, FDI variable 16.5%, EMP variable 13.5%, and finally, an ICT variable of 12.8% positively affect high technology product exports in terms of statistics. For developing countries, it is important to improve policies that increase income as well as achieve higher levels of R&D.

INTRODUCTION

The surging international trade and the increase in the diversity of commercial activities accelerated capital movement between countries, and hence speed of technological developments has considerably increased (Awokuse and Christopoulos, 2009). The development of technology affects many industries such as economy, education, security and health. Technology contributes to reducing waste of time and costs for individuals, companies and even countries. Therefore, today, use of technology has become inevitable in all the lives of individuals; technological development has become a vital target for countries

DOI: 10.4018/978-1-7998-9648-7.ch010

as well. Countries are aware that the more high-tech products they produce and export, the better they will develop in terms of economy (Castellani and Fassio, 2017).

We can define products which are based on high technology as “products light in physics, but heavy in price”. Due to this nature, products based on high technology provide extremely high added value to their economy, and therefore, high technology production is one of the factors which act as an indicator for the difference in terms of development between countries today (Fagerberg, 2000). Therefore, countries that have completely established their infrastructure investments in terms of technology production can be one step ahead of other countries in terms of development. For this reason, export products and the industries that are at the forefront of exports differ between countries. In this context, the production and export of high-tech products increases the export revenues of the countries that have adopted the export-based growth strategy and constitutes an extremely important source of financing for the growth and development of the countries (Ekananda and Parlinggoman, 2017). Therefore, the desire to be a producer of advanced technology has become a main goal of both developed and developing countries. If it has advanced technology, a country will be able to produce products with high added value, gain competitive power in international markets, as well as effectively export its products (Archibugia and Cocoa, 2005).

One of the main goals of developing countries which to increase their growth rates is to provide financial resources to their economy by producing and exporting products with high added value and advanced technology (Sandu and Ciocanel, 2014). In addition, production of high-tech products may increase, as well as reduce the development differences between countries. For this reason, it is crucially important that more resources be directed to producing high technology products, and better concentrating on relevant R&D activities, which has become vitally important for developing countries (Usman, 2017).

In literature, high technology production and export, as well as production of high technology goods, have been attributed to a variety of factors by different researchers for different reasons. These factors may differ according to the economic conditions of a country. Factors which affect a country’s high technology exports may yield different results in different countries. From this point of view, the purpose of this study is to examine the determinants of high technology product exports between 2010-2020 for the developing country group BRICS-T using panel regression analysis.

CONCEPTUAL FRAMEWORK

The Importance of High Technology Production

The ability of a country to produce and export this technology are among the factors which indicate the development level of that country. Many countries are comparatively insufficient in this regard, which leads to a development problem (Teodora and Marinela, 2011). Countries that can produce their own technology increase their production amounts, implementing their growth in line with their plans. Countries that cannot achieve this need positive developments that high technology will bring about in their economies to reach the level of developed countries by increasing their production (Vogel and Wagner, 2010).

Ownership of high technology elements provides many important advantages to countries. Among these advantages, contributions of high technology to economic growth is the most prominent advantage (Satrovic, 2018). Infrastructure investments aimed at developing technology, especially in developed countries, gradually emerged as one of the most important factors of economic growth and became the basis of technological developments. Technological developments and innovations, on the other hand, contribute to the increase in the production potential of companies, and this situation enables productivity increases and thus increases in production volume (Gorodnichenko et al., 2010). In other words, positive developments in technology enable the production factors to be used more effectively by providing efficiency in the production process, which contributes to the acceleration of economic growth, as well as development, and improves life quality and standards of individuals (Mani, 2004).

In this context, we can say that a technology-intensive production process will provide a significant amount of economic input, rapid economic development and growth process for the country where production is realized. In addition, the ability of a country to produce high-tech products plays an important role in eliminating income and economic growth differences between countries (Gani, 2009). In addition, the high added value of high-tech products and introduction of these products to the world market through export, contribute to the increase of the export income of the country and the realization of economic growth (Sertić et al., 2015). At this point, we can say that the export of high technology products not only for developed countries but also for developing countries contributes significantly to the economic growth of countries.

Recently, the export of high technology products has become one of the determining factors of economic growth due to the high added value of these products. For this reason, care should be taken to ensure that production for the manufacturing industry is carried out in a technology-intensive manner in order to increase the export revenues of the countries. High technology production also earns countries and companies competitive power in international markets (Mehrara et al., 2017). In our rapidly developing, changing and globalizing world, competition between countries has become much more prominent, especially in the fields of science, industry and technology (Bustos, 2011). For this reason, countries have to constantly renew their technological infrastructure and use their know-how and communication technologies much more effectively and efficiently in order to gain competitive advantage in international markets (Hu, 2017).

In addition, countries should implement mechanisms to facilitate foreign investors, in the form of tax reductions, alleviating bureaucratic obstacles and providing infrastructure opportunities in order to encourage foreign companies with the opportunities to produce high-tech products to invest in their own countries in case of insufficiency of capital (Kinoshita, 2000). These regulations will make foreign investors feel economically secure and important, thus attracting foreign investors to a country. Hence the increase in foreign investments involving technology will make significant contributions to the development of the technology infrastructure of the country. The ability of a country to produce and export its own technology enables that country to develop economically and socially, and therefore to get ahead of other countries (Zhang and Cui, 2018). Today, the development level of a country is not only evaluated according to the type and amount of products produced in its industries, but also according to whether these products are produced with high technology or not. For this reason, countries that can produce information and technology have a more important place within the context of the world economy compared to other countries (Yang, 2017). The ability to produce own technology also provides countries with the opportunity to increase their own production amounts and substantiate their economic growth as they plan. Countries that fail to achieve this need high technology and the positive economical developments that the use of high technology will bring about to help complete their development processes and reach the economic and social level of developed countries. When the factors affecting the country's high-tech product exports are examined, it can be seen that very different results emerge in different countries (Mehrara et al., 2017).

Determinants of High-Tech Product Exports

Examining the relations between innovation activities and international trade realized within the scope of high technology and economic performance requires focusing on high technology trade. Maintaining their level of development, having a say in the field of high technology in terms of the sector and producing with high export value are among the important determinants of the economic growth of both developed and developing countries (Fu et al., 2012). The concept of high technology refers to the goods and services obtained through innovation. In this respect, high technology supply gains importance with the technological superiority of companies or industries (Sandu and Ciocanel, 2014). According to OECD, the "high-tech" status of a product is determined by the intensity of R&D investments in the manufacturing of that product. Thus, in addition to R&D expenditures, the efficiency of research within this scope is of great importance. In other words, the more R&D efforts can turn into new ideas and new products, the more efficient they will be. The most important characteristic of high-tech products is their high-income elasticity (Aali Bujari and Venegas Martínez, 2016).

When the studies in the literature focusing on the determinants of high-tech product exports are examined, it was noticed that variables such as economic growth, R&D expenditures, number of patent applications, fixed capital investment, number of qualified employments, openness rate and foreign direct investments are taken into account.

Economic growth; the positive and significant relationship between high technology exports and economic growth was proven by many studies in the economics literature. The high added value of high-tech products increases the export income of a country and ensures the realization of economic growth. In this respect, it is observed that technological development and the production of high technology products have an increasing importance within the scope of the economic growth and international trade of a country (Falk, 2009).

R&D expenditures; R&D and innovation intensity form the basis of high technology exports. The share of R&D expenditures in national income is necessary to increase competitiveness in global markets and to ensure continuity of innovation capacity (Saleem and Sial, 2015). The analyzes made in this context determined that R&D expenditures have a positive effect on the export of high technology products. Hence while the reason for companies to make their R&D expenditures is to increase their future profits, the purpose on a country basis is to become stronger in the international competitive environment (Khachoo and Sharma, 2017).

Number of patent applications; an important indicator in terms of technological development, a patent grants all related rights on new products and production techniques to its owner. It is striking that the number of patent applications obtained as a result of R&D expenditures is quite high in high-tech product exporting countries. An increase in the number of patent applications indicates that new technologies are being produced, technology is developing, and the number of new products is increasing in parallel. In this regard, China is a leading country (Fan and Zhao, 2019).

Fixed capital investment; it is known that China, which has a high level of fixed capital investment, is also a country which exports high-tech products. Therefore, fixed capital investments are considered as a determining factor in the export of high-tech products (Zahonogo, 2016).

Number of qualified employments; the number of qualified employment (human capital) is one of the determining variables in the export of high technology products. The more the share of human capital (qualified workforce with post-graduate and doctorate degrees) in a population of a country is, the more high-tech products that country can produce, hence be able to increase its exports (Pece et al., 2005).

Openness ratio; is another variable addressed in empirical studies within the scope of high-tech product exports is the openness ratio. Openness increases the export performance of high-tech products. It is reported that high technology exporting countries have high openness rates. Therefore, openness to international trade has a positive and significant effect on high technology exports (Tebaldi, 2011).

Foreign direct investments; inflows were used, as indicators, in many studies conducted within the scope of determinants of high-tech product exports. Analyses determined that foreign direct investments have a positive and significant effect on the export of high technology products. In this study, those that do not cause multicollinearity among the influential variables, which are frequently used in the literature, were determined and included in the model (Ekananda and Parlinggoman, 2017).

LITERATURE REVIEW

ECONOMETRIC ANALYSIS

The Purpose and the Importance of the Study

One of the most important economic development goals of globalizing economies is to increase their export performance by way of high quality and competitive production. Due to the gradual increase in international trade volume and increasing openness rates, economic growth is significantly affected by the export performance of countries. In this context, as stated in the export-oriented growth theories, being competitive in exports started gaining importance. Opening to foreign markets with low price competition based on cheap labor can lead to negative developments in the terms of foreign trade, resulting in a decrease in the earnings from foreign trade. For this reason, it has become an important purpose to produce and export products with high added value. The concept of high technology refers to the goods and services obtained through innovation. In this respect, high technology supply gains importance with the technological superiority of companies or industries. High technology has recently started to be regarded as a source of wealth, as opposed to dominant resource-based industries, contributing to economic growth. Therefore, it is of great importance for developing countries. The aim of this study is to examine the determinants of export of high technology products for the BRICS-T group of countries, whose economic structures are similar, with the help of panel regression analysis.

Econometric Method

In the first stage of the study, homogeneity test and cross-section dependency test were applied. In the other stage, first generation and second-generation stationarity tests were applied. First generation unit root tests, which included Im et al (2003), Maddala and Wu (1999) and Choi (2001) tests, and the second-

Table 1. Empirical studies examining the factors determining the export of high-tech products

Autor	Country and Period	Method	Results
Anaruo and Di Pietro (2006)	59 countries	Panel Regression Analysis	A country's creativity, innovation, technological situation, technology transfer from other countries affects exports positively.
Erdil et al (2009)	131 countries underdeveloped and developing (1995 - 2006)	Generalized Method of Moments (GMM)	Exports of information communication exports has a positive effect on growth.
Falk (2009)	22 OECD Countries (1980 - 2004)	GMM Analysis Method	The share of high technology exports is significantly correlated with GDP per working age population.
Uysal (2010)	146 countries including Turkey (1980 - 2008)	Panel Cointegration and Dynamic Panel Data Analysis	There is a relation between exports of information and communication technologies and economic growth, and between high and medium-high income countries. No relationship was found in the low and middle-low income groups.
Lee and Hong (2010)	71 Countries (1970 - 2004)	Literature	The growth of high-tech exporting countries is faster than others.
Kılavuz et al. (2012)	22 Developing countries (1998 - 2006)	Panel Data Analysis	High-tech product exports and investment increases positively affected economic growth.
Türedi (2013)	Turkey and 53 countries (1995 - 2008)	Panel Data Analysis	Increase in information technology exports positively affects economic growth.
Göçer (2013)	11 Asian Countries (1996 - 2012)	Panel Data Analysis	A positive relationship was found between R&D and exports of high technology, information communication technologies, total exports and economic growth.
Ismail (2013)	10 Asian countries (Excluding 2004 to 2009, and the years 2007 and 2008)	Gravity Model	Innovations are key factors in high-tech exports.
Gökmen and Turen (2013)	15 EU member countries (1995 - 2010)	Panel Causality Test and Granger Causality Test	There is a positive relationship between high technology export and economic growth.
Saray and Hark (2015)	OECD Countries (2004 - 2013)	Generalized Method of Moments (GMM)	It was determined that the most important determinant of high-tech competitive power is the level of productivity.
Alagöz et al. (2016)	E7 Countries	Literature review	There is a positive relationship between R&D and exports of high technology products.
Çetin (2016)	Newly industrialized 7 countries (1996 - 2013)	Granger Causality and Fixed Random Effects Estimation methods	R&D positively affects the export of high-tech products positively
Yıldız (2017)	BRICS countries and Turkey (2005 - 2014)	Panel Data Analysis	The increase in high-tech exports has an enhancing effect on economic growth.
Kızılkaya et al. (2017)	12 developing countries (2000 - 2012)	Panel Data Analysis	Foreign direct capital and openness affect the export of high technology products positively.
Moraes and Luna (2018)	Latin America and the Caribbean (2005-2015)	Panel Data Analysis	In the study, it was determined that foreign direct investment inflows in Latin America and the Caribbean were not an important indicator in terms of explaining the growth of high technology exports.
Buzdağlı et al. (2019)	18 Growing Economy (1996-2016)	Panel Data Analysis	In the study, the determinants of export of high-tech goods were determined as openness and the capacity to produce patents.

generation panel unit root test, the CADF unit root test, were used. In the next stage, Breush-Pagan test, Chow test and Hausman test were applied to determine which panel regression method should be used. As a result of the tests, analyzes were carried out for the fixed effects model. Green's covariance test and Wooldridge autocorrelation test were used to test the assumptions.

Sample and Data

In the study, the relations between the factors affecting the export of high-tech products for the BRICS-T country group (Brazil, Russia, India, China, South Africa and Turkey), where countries have similar economic structures, will be discussed. Analyzes were carried out for the annual data for the period

Table 2. Definitions of variables

Variable	Impression	Definition
R&D expenditures/GDP (%)	R&D	Independent Variable
Foreign direct investments	FDI	Independent Variable
Qualified Employment Rate-Higher Education Graduate (%)	EMP	Independent Variable
Gross domestic product	GDP	Independent Variable
ICT access index	ICT	Independent Variable
Exports of high-tech products (percent-% of production exports)	HTPE	Dependent Variable

between 2010 and 2020, for which country data for each variable can be found in full. Eviews version 10.0 and Stata version 16.0 package programs were used for analysis. Data used in the study www. It was obtained from the worldbank.org data site and is given in Table 2.

Model:

$$HTPE=\beta 0+\beta 1 R\&D_{it}+\beta 2 FDI_{it}+\beta 3 EMP_{it}+\beta_4 GDP_{it}+\beta 5 ICT_{it}+\varepsilon_{it}$$

Research Hypotheses

The hypotheses of the study are presented in Table 3.

Cross-Section Dependency and Homogeneity Tests

For cross-sectional dependence, Pesaran (2004) LM CD test and the deviation-corrected LM adj test in Pesaran et al (2008) study were applied. Since $p<0.05$ for both tests, H0 was rejected and H1 hypothesis indicating the cross-sectional dependence was accepted. On the other hand, homogeneity test was applied with the help of Pesaran and Yamagata (2008) delta tilde and corrected delta tilde tests. As the result of the test was $p<0.05$, Ho was rejected and H1 hypothesis indicating heterogeneity was accepted.

First and Second Generation Unit Root Test Results

First generation unit root tests are divided into two as homogeneous and heterogeneous models. Since the coefficients are heterogeneous, Im, Pesaran and Shin (2003), Maddala and Wu (1999), Choi (2001) first generation unit root tests" based on the heterogeneous model assumption will be used.

Table 3. Research hypotheses

H	Hypotheses
H_1	R&D expenditures/GDP (%) and high-tech product exports are statistically significantly related.
H_2	Foreign direct investments and exports of high-tech products are statistically significantly related.
H_3	The rate of skilled employment and exports of high-tech products are statistically significantly related.
H_4	Gross domestic product and exports of high-tech products are statistically significantly related.
H_5	ICT access index and high-tech product exports are statistically significantly related.

Table 4. Cross section dependency and homogeneity test results

Cross-section dependency test (H_0: There is no cross section dependency)		
Test	**Test statistic**	**p-value**
LM (Breusch and Pagan (1980)	43.564	0.002
LM_{adj} (Pesaran et al. (2008)	40.213	0.001
LM CD (Pesaran (2004)	39.559	0.000
Homogeneity test (H_0: Slope coefficients are homogeneous)		
Test	**Test statistic**	**p-value**
Delta_tilde	20.342	0.000
Delta_tilde_adj	22.894	0.000

All variables have a unit root at their level values. It is determined that they are stationary for the first order difference, I (1). Second generation unit root tests will be applied due to cross section dependency. The CADF test developed by Pesaran (2007) was used.

For the second generation unit root test CADF, the lag length is taken as 1 according to the Schwarz information criterion. As a result of the test, it was observed that the series were not stationary at the level but were stationary for the first order difference.

Panel Regression Estimation Results

Three different methods, namely pooled, fixed and random effects models are used for panel regression analysis. There is a requirement for some pre-tests to choose between them (Baltagi, 2005:78). Chow and Breush-Pagan (BP) tests were used for method selection. "While the H00 hyp$_0$thesis is pooled regression (pooled) and the H1 hyp$_0$thesis is the fixed effects model (SEM) for the Chow test, the H0 hyp$_0$thesis is pooled regression and the H1 is $_r$andom effects model (TEM) for the BP test."

The result of the tests indicate that the H0 h$_y$pothesis was rejected. Because of this situation, the Hausman test was applied to choose between TEM and SEM models.

"**H0:** There is incidental effect (TEM)"

"**H1**$_:$ There is no incidental effect (SEM)"

According to the Hausman test, H_1 was accepted and the SEM model was suitable. In the estimation phase of the regression analysis, different solution algorithms were utilized and solutions were realized with the "*Cross section SUR algorithm*" with the smallest total square of error.

As can be seen in the regression outputs, the independent variables have 78.3% explanatory power for the HTPE variable. Present independent variables affect the HTPE variable positively. Significant panel regression estimation results are briefly listed according to their coefficient sizes as follows:

- Among the independent variables, it is the GDP variable that has a high impact on HTPE. The GDP variable increases the HTPE variable by 29.1%.
- The second effective variable is R&D. The R&D variable increases the HTPE variable by 28.9%.
- The third effective variable is FDI. The FDI variable increases the HTPE variable by 16.5%.
- The fourth effective variable is EMP. The EMP variable increases the HTPE variable by 13.5%.
- The fifth effective variable is ICT. The ICT variable increases the HTPE variable by 12.8%.

Table 5. First generation panel unit root test results

Variables		Im et al. (2003)	Maddala and Wu (1999)	Choi (2001)
R&D	Level	-1.193(0.126)	9.563 (0.135)	-0.988(0.142)
	∇	-6.883(0.001)*	30.461(0.000)*	-8.506(0.000)*
FDI	Level	-0.910(0.119)	8.946(0.147)	-1.257(0.150)
	∇	-7.215(0.002)*	34.550(0.002)*	-9.505(0.000)*
EMP	Level	-1.216(0.137)	8.452 (0.145)	-0.912(0.155)
	∇	-9.397(0.001)*	43.157(0.000)*	-8.493(0.000)*
GDP	Level	-0.911(0.106)	10.308(0.139)	-0.835(0.167)
	∇	-8.604(0.000)*	41.583(0.000)*	-8.202(0.000)*
ICT	Level	-0.887(0.118)	10.339(0.125)	-1.290(0.136)
	∇	-8.345(0.001)*	38.266(0.000)*	-7.052(0.000)*
HTPE	Level	-1.099 (0.120)	13.901(0.144)	-1.253(0.151)
	∇	-9.322 (0.000)*	44.589(0.000)*	-9118(0.000)*

Note: The ∇ notation indicates first-order difference, and the * notation, the stationarity state. The deterministic specification of tests includes constant and trend. Probability values are indicated in parentheses. Tests were conducted for significance at the 0.05 level. The null hypothesis of the tests is that there is a unit root. The optimal lag length was determined using the Schwarz information criterion.

Wooldridge (2002) autocorrelation test was used to test the assumptions of the model, whereby it was determined that there was no autocorrelation. The Greene heteroscedasticity test indicated that the model results in which the assumptions were provided as a result of the presence of homoskedacity were interpretable.

Table 6. Second generation panel CADF unit root test results

Variables	Level		1st order difference	
	Constant	Constant+ Trend	Constant	Constant+ Trend
R&D	-1.127	-1.248	-8.520*	-8.343*
FDI	-1.515	-1.721	-9.641*	-9.865*
EMP	-1.209	-1.315	-8.597*	-8.933*
GDP	-1.322	-1.476	-9.224*	-9.460*
ICT	-0.945	-1.097	-6.595*	-7.547*
HTPE	-1.066	-1.194	-8.489*	-9.302*

*Stationary variable for 0.05

Table 7. Panel regression estimation method selection test results

Test	Probability (p)	Decision
Chow (F test)	0.000	H_0 red
BP (X^2 test)	0.003	H_0 red

Table 8. Hausman test results

Test Summary	Chi-square Statistics	d.f.	Probability (p)
Cross-section random	637.289	2	0.000
Period random	517.493	2	0.000
Cross-section and period random	488.560	2	0.001

CONCLUSION

Today, economies are able to grow thanks to technology and innovation. In other words, the effective use of technology enables countries to take a step towards development and growth and gain strength in global competition by increasing productivity in both domestic and foreign markets. Therefore, high technology products and their export increase the level of economic development of countries.

In this study, the determining factors in the export of high technology products within the scope of selected BRICS-T countries were investigated. In the study, panel regression analysis was applied on the basis of annual data for the period between 2010-2020. According to the analysis results obtained in the study, the independent variables considered a 78.3% explanatory power for exports of high technology products, which is the dependent variable. The variables highest associated with exports of high-tech products were determined as GDP and R&D. A GDP variable of 29.1%, R&D variable 28.9%, FDI variable 16.5%, EMP variable 13.5% and finally an ICT variable of 12.8% positively affect high technology product exports in terms of statistics.

It has now become a necessity for developing countries that implement an export-oriented growth strategy to use high technology for economic development and growth. It is of great importance to be able to use technology effectively in order to increase efficiency and keep up with global competition. Therefore, increasing the share of products that require high technology in total production and increasing

Table 9. Panel regression estimation results

Dependent Variable: DLnHTPE				
Method: Panel EGLS (bidirectional fixed effects)				
Sample: 2011 - 2020				
Number of Horizontal Sections: 6				
Rates	**Coefficient**	**Std. Error**	**t-statistic**	**Possibility**
DLNR&D	0.289	0.052	5.557	0.000*
DLnFDI	0.165	0.026	6.346	0.000*
DLnEMP	0.135	0.024	5.625	0.001*
DLnGDP	0.291	0.042	6.928	0.002*
DLnICT	0.128	0.037	3.459	0.000*
Constant	1.547	0.183	8.453	0.000*
R^2 = 0.783 F_{ist} = 25.49 F(p) = 0.000 DW = 2.09 Wooldridge (p)=0.163 Greene Heteroskedasticity Test (p)=0.219				

*A significant variable at the 0.05 level, "D" denotes a 1st order difference.

their economic growth are among the objectives of the countries intending to increase their economic growth. In countries that are unable to produce their own technologies and have a low share of R&D expenditures in their national income, implementation of incentive policies in terms of foreign direct investment, production, management skills and technology transfer is of vital importance for developing countries to achieve their goals. in this regard

In this respect, developing countries should increase the importance they attach to R&D activities and focus more on scientific and technical studies. As a result, in these countries, significant progress can be achieved in the export of high-tech products by developing policies on science and technology issues and by providing more financial support to researchers. First of all, there is a need to train qualified workforce that can lead the transformation in the industry since the people working in this context are qualified (high education level) profiles. In addition to providing financial support to these researchers, it is also important to make legal arrangements for innovation that encourages technological engagement. Apart from this, tax reductions, reduction of bureaucracy, use of low-interest loans and similar arrangements should be realized in order to encourage foreign investors to invest in high technology transfer to developing countries. In developing countries, it is of great importance to increase the number of techno-cities, to provide financial support to the researchers these cities, and to make legal arrangements to ensure the development of the existing technological structure in order to develop the technological infrastructure and ensure technological development.

In these countries, it is essential for the state administration to ensure investments in strategic sectors that will produce high-tech products, on the one hand, and to create a workforce capable of producing qualified and high-value-added products, on the other. Thus, qualified, high quality and high value-added products can be obtained.

REFERENCES

Aali Bujari, A., & Venegas Martínez, F. (2016). Technological Innovation and Economic Growth in Latin America. *Mexican Journal of Economics and Finance*, *11*(2), 77–89.

Anoruo, E., & DiPietro, W. R. (2006). Creativity, innovation, and export performance. *Journal of Policy Modeling*, *28*(2), 133–139. doi:10.1016/j.jpolmod.2005.10.001

Archibugia, D., & Cocoa, A. (2005). Measuring technological capabilities at the country level: A survey and a menu for choice. *Research Policy*, *34*(2), 175–194. doi:10.1016/j.respol.2004.12.002

Awokuse, T., & Christopoulos, D. (2009). Nonlinear dynamics and the exports-output growth nexus. *Economic Modelling*, *26*(1), 184-190. .econmod.2008.06.009 doi:10.1016/j

Baltagi, B. H. (2005). *Econometric Analysis of Panel Data* (3rd ed.). John Wiley & Sons Ltd.

Breusch, T. S., & Pagan, A. R. (1980). The Lagrange Multiplier Test and Its Applications to Model Specification in Econometrics. *The Review of Economic Studies*, *47*(1), 239–253. doi:10.2307/2297111

Bustos, P. (2011). Trade liberalization, exports, and technology upgrading: Evidence on the impact of MERCOSUR on Argentinian firms. *The American Economic Review*, *101*(1), 304–340. doi:10.1257/aer.101.1.304

Castellani, D., & Fassio, C. (2017). *Export innovation: The role of new imported inputs and multinationality. Innovation Studies, No. 2017/16*. Lund University.

Cetin, R. (2016). Yeni sanayileşen ülkelerde ar-ge harcamaları ve yüksek teknoloji ürünü ihracatı arasındaki ilişkinin panel veri analizi yöntemi ile incelenmesi. *İktisat Fakültesi Mecmuası, 66*(2), 30-43.

Choi, I. (2001). Unit root tests for panel data. *Journal of International Money and Finance, 20*(2), 249–272. doi:10.1016/S0261-5606(00)00048-6

Ekananda, M., & Parlinggoman, D. J. (2017). The role of high-tech exports and of foreign direct investments (FDI) on economic growth. *European Research Studies Journal, 20*(4A, 4A), 194–212. doi:10.35808/ersj/828

Erdil, E., Turkcan, B., & Yetkiner, İ. H. (2009). *Does information and communication technology sustain economic growth? The underdeveloped and developing countries case*. Science and Technology Policies Research Center, TEKPOL Working Paper Series 09/03.

Fagerberg, J. (2000). Technological progress, structural change and productivity growth: A comparative study. *Structural Change and Economic Dynamics, 11*(4), 393–411. doi:10.1016/S0954-349X(00)00025-4

Falk, M. (2009). High-tech exports and economic growth in industrialized countries. *Applied Economics Letters, 16*(10), 1025–1028. doi:10.1080/13504850701222228

Fan, C., & Zhao, Y. (2019). Analysis on the Evolution of Innovation Efficiency of High-tech Industry and Its Influencing Factors -Taking Zhongguancun Science and Technology Park as an Example, *Modern. Management Science, 1*(1), 6–8.

Fu, D., Wu, Y., & Tang, Y. (2012). Does Innovation Matter for Chinese High-Tech Exports? A FirmLevel Analysis. *Frontiers of Economics in China, 7*(2), 218–245.

Gani, A. (2009). Technological achievement, high technology exports and growth. *Journal of Comparative International Management, 12*(2), 31–47.

Gocer, İ. (2013). Ar-Ge harcamalarının yüksek teknolojili ürün ihracatı, dış ticaret dengesi ve ekonomik büyüme üzerindeki etkileri. *Maliye Dergisi, 165*(2), 215–240.

Gokmen, Y., & Turen, U. (2013). The Determinants of high technology exports volume: A panel data analysis of EU-15 countries. *International Journal of Management, Economics and Social Sciences, 2*(3), 217–232.

Gorodnichenko, Yu., Svejnar, J., & Terrel, K. (2010). Globalization and innovation in emerging markets. *American Economic Journal. Macroeconomics, 2*(2), 194–226. doi:10.1257/mac.2.2.194

Hu, H. (2017). Analysis of Factors Affecting the Growth of Cross-Strait High-Tech Products Trade-Based on Modified CMS Model. *International Economic and Trade Exploration, 4*(1), 13–23.

Im, K. S., Pesaran, M. H., & Shin, Y. (2003). Testing for unit roots in heterogeneous panels. *Journal of Econometrics, 115*(1), 53–74. doi:10.1016/S0304-4076(03)00092-7

Ismail, N. W. (2013). Innovation and High-Tech Trade in Asian Countries. *International Conference on Recent Developments in Asian Trade Policy and Integration, 1*(1), 1-19.

Khachoo, Q., & Sharma, R. (2017). FDI and Incumbent R&D Behavior: Evidence From Indian Manufacturing Sector. *Journal of Economic Studies (Glasgow, Scotland)*, *44*(3), 380–399. doi:10.1108/JES-10-2015-0188

Kinoshita, Y. (2000). *R&D and Technology Spillovers via FDI: Innovation and Absorptive Capacity.* William Davidson Institute Working Paper No.349.

Kizilkaya, O., Sofuoglu, E., & Ay, A. (2017). Yüksek teknolojili ürün ihracatı üzerinde doğrudan yabancı sermaye yatırımları ve dışa açıklığın etkisi: Gelişmekte olan ülkelerde panel veri analizi. *Doğuş Üniversitesi Dergisi*, *18*(1), 63–78. doi:10.31671/dogus.2018.22

Lee, J.-W., & Hong, K. (2010). *Economic Growth in Asia: Determinants and Prospects.* Asian Development Bank Economics Working Paper Series No. 220.

Maddala, G. S., & Wu, S. (1999). A comparative study of unit root tests with panel data and a new simple test. *Oxford Bulletin of Economics and Statistics, Special Issue*, *61*(S1), 631–652. doi:10.1111/1468-0084.0610s1631

Mani, S. (2004). Exports of high technology products from developing countries: Are the figures real or are they statistical artefacts? *Innovation, Learning, and Technological Dynamism of Developing Countries*, *1*(1), 12–47.

Mehrara, M., Seijani, S., & Karsalari, A. R. (2017). Determinants of high-tech export in developing countries based on bayesian model averaging. *Zbornik Radova Ekonomskog Fakulteta u Rijeci*, *35*(1), 199–215.

Moraes, J., & Luna, I. (2018). *Dynamic and determinants of high technology exports in Latin America and the Caribbean: a network and a panel data analysis.* III Encontro Nacional de Economia Industrial e Inovação. doi:10.5151/enei2018-26

Pece, M. A., Ecaterina, O. S. O., & Salisteanu, F. (2015). Innovation and Economic Growth: An Empirical Analysis for CEE Countries. *Procedia Economics and Finance*, *26*, 461–467. doi:10.1016/S2212-5671(15)00874-6

Pesaran, M. H. (2004). *General diagnostic tests for cross section dependence in panels.* CESifo Working Papers 1229. Retrieved from https://www.cesifo.org/en/publikationen/2004/working-paper/general-diagnostic-tests-cross-section-dependence-panels doi:10.17863/CAM.5113

Pesaran, M. H. (2007). A simple panel unit root test in the presence of cross-section dependence. *Journal of Applied Econometrics*, *22*(2), 265–312. doi:10.1002/jae.951

Pesaran, M. H., Ullah, A., & Yamagata, T. (2008). A bias-adjusted LM test of error cross-section independence. *The Econometrics Journal*, *11*(1), 105–127. doi:10.1111/j.1368-423X.2007.00227.x

Pesaran, M. H., & Yamagata, T. (2008). Testing slope homogeneity in large panels. *Journal of Econometrics*, *142*(1), 50–93. doi:10.1016/j.jeconom.2007.05.010

Saleem, A., & Sial, M. H. (2015). Exports-Growth Nexus in Pakistan Cointegration and Causality Analysis. *Pakistan Economic and Social Review*, *53*(1), 17–46.

Sandu, S., & Ciocanel, N. (2014). Impact of R&D and innovation on high-tech export. *Procedia Economics and Finance, 15*(1), 80–90. doi:10.1016/S2212-5671(14)00450-X

Satrovic, E. (2018). Economic output and high-technology export: Panel causality analysis. *International Journal of Economic Studies, 4*(3), 55–63.

Sertić, M. B., Vučković, V., & Perić, B. Š. (2015). Determinants of manufacturing industry exports in European Union Member States: A panel data analysis. *Economic Research-Ekonomska Istraživanja, 28*(1), 384–397. doi:10.1080/1331677X.2015.1043781

Tebaldi, E. (2011). The Determinants of High tech Exports. A Panel Data Analysis. *Atlantic Economic Journal, 39*(4), 349–353. doi:10.100711293-011-9288-9

Teodora, M. I., & Marinela, S. R. (2011). An Investigation of Longrun Relationship Between Economic Growth, Investment and Export in Romania. *Annals of Faculty of Economics, 1*(1), 316–321.

Turedi, S. (2013). Bilgi ve iletişim teknolojilerinin ekonomik büyümeye etkisi: Gelişmiş ve gelişmekte olan ülkeler için panel veri analizi. *Gümüşhane Üniversitesi Sosyal Bilimler Elektronik Dergisi, 4*(7), 298–322.

Usman, M. (2017). Impact of high-tech exports on economic growth: Empirical evidence from pakistan. *Journal on Innovation and Sustainability, 8*(1), 91–105. doi:10.24212/2179-3565.2017v8i1p91-105

Uysal, H. A. (2010). *ICT Development and Economic Growth: An Analysis of Cointegrating and Causal Relationships with Panel Data Approach* (Unpublished Master Thesis). School of Architecture and the Built Environment,Royal Institute of Technology, Stockholm, Sweden.

Vogel, A., & Wagner, J. (2010). Higher productivity in importing German manufacturing firms: Self-selection, learning from importing, or both? *Review of World Economics, 145*(4), 641–665. doi:10.100710290-009-0031-4

Waithe, K., Lorde, T., & Francis, B. (2011). Export-led growth: A case study of Mexico. *International Journal of Business. Human Technology, 1*(1), 33–44.

Wooldridge, J. M. (2010). *Econometric Analysis of Cross Section and Panel Data* (2nd ed.). The MIT Press.

Yang, F. (2017). The Positive Influence of High-tech Product Export on Economic Growth in Liaoning Province. *Journal of Simulation, 5*(4), 7–9.

Yildiz, U. (2017). BRICS Ülkeleri ve Türkiye'de Yüksek Teknoloji İhracatı ve Ekonomik Büyüme İlişkisinin Panel Veri Analizi. *Dumlupınar Üniversitesi Sosyal Bilimler Dergisi, 53*, 26–34.

Yokota, K., & Tomohara, A. (2010). Modeling FDI-Induced Technology Spillovers. *The International Trade Journal, 24*(1), 5–34. doi:10.1080/08853900903442897

Zahonogo, P. (2016). Trade and economic growth in developing countries: Evidence from SubSaharan Africa. *Journal of Africa Trade, 3*(1-2), 41–56. doi:10.1016/j.joat.2017.02.001

Zhang, D., & Cui, X. (2018). Research on the Open Development and Industrial Security of China's High-tech Industry. *International Trade, 12*(1), 19–22.

ADDITIONAL READING

Afzal, M., & Hussain, I. (2010). Export-Led Growth Hypothesis: Evidence from Pakistan. *Journal of Quantitative Economics*, *8*(1), 130–147.

Sultanuzzaman, M. R., Fan, H., Mohamued, E. A., Hossain, M. I., & Islam, M. A. (2019). Effects of Exportand Technology on Economic Growth: Selected Emerging Asian Economies, Economic Research-. *Ekonomska Istrazivanja*, *32*(1), 2515–2531. doi:10.1080/1331677X.2019.1650656

Telatar, O. M., Değer, M. K., & Doğanay, M. A. (2016). Teknoloji Yoğunluklu Ürün İhracatının Ekonomik Büyümeye Etkisi: Türkiye Örneği (1996:Q1-2015:Q3). *Atatürk Üniversitesi İktisadi ve İdari Bilimler Dergisi*, *30*(4), 921–934.

Usman, M. (2017). Impact of High-Tech Exports on Economic Growth: Empirical Evidence from Pakistan, Journal on Innovation and Sustainability. *RISUS*, *8*(1), 91–105. doi:10.24212/2179-3565.2017v8i1p91-105

Vohra, R. (2001). Export and Economic Growth: Further Time Series Evidence From Less-Developed Countries. *International Advances in Economic Research*, *7*(3), 345–350. doi:10.1007/BF02295403

KEY TERMS AND DEFINITIONS

Panel Data Analysis: Panel data it is the gathering of cross-sectional observations of units such as individuals, countries, firms, households in a certain period of time and analyzing them for the purpose of analysis with any statistical method.

Technological Development: Any invention and product innovation that enables a new good to be produced, and a process innovation or method that enables an existing good to be produced at a lower cost as a result of the increase in the efficiency of the factors used in its production.

Chapter 11
The Relationship of Technological Change With Economic Growth From the Perspective of Institutional Economics

Yahya Can Dura
https://orcid.org/0000-0002-5662-7748
Istanbul Gelisim University, Turkey

Cengizhan Güler
Istanbul Gelisim University, Turkey

ABSTRACT

The relationship between economic growth, technological change, and institutions has been the subject of various theoretical evaluations. In this chapter, the relationship in question will be examined in the context of the systematics of thought of two great thinkers, J. A. Schumpeter and T. Veblen. In this study, evaluations are made by theoretically putting Schumpeter, who examines the effects of economic growth and institutional structure as the dominant factor of the change brought about by technological development, at one end of the spectrum and Veblen, who states that the structure of institutions and society is more dominant in technological change, on the other side.

INTRODUCTION

The problem of the source of the capital accumulation of the society and the steady increase of this accumulation has always been an important focus in the economic literature. At this point, the mission of technology as a resource, in terms of economic growth, has indisputably been among the main topics of

DOI: 10.4018/978-1-7998-9648-7.ch011

almost all periods. So much so that even schools at different ends of economics have created an intense theoretical debate on the functions of technology in economics.

Here, the role of technological progress in growth, especially as an accelerator of capital accumulation, is emphasized in the capitalist economic order. New products and new markets have been seen as the result of technology and progress in this field. In the second half of the 20th century, theoretical studies on growth started to include the technology parameter in their modeling, first externally and then internally. There has been a process that has evolved from the Solow-Swan Growth Model, in which technology is externally accepted, to growth models (Romer and Lucas), where knowledge, that is, technological progress, is internally accepted. At this point, technology is accepted as the most important power in growth theories.

In order to comprehend the importance of technology and innovation necessary for technological change today, consulting the views of two pioneering scientists, Veblen and Schumpeter, who analyzed these phenomena for the first time with their economic and social aspects, will add an intellectual depth to the subject. The main point of this study is to discuss the ways in which both thinkers approach technology and institutions by making a synthesis.

In fact, all these discussions are lived on the individual and his behavior patterns. In that case, it would be useful to start the technology issue with a gradual introduction, from the perspective of Veblen and Schumpeter, through the individual.

The debate on whether individuals are rational beings who act with the profit motive in the economics literature, which has not been reached a consensus, is still up-to-date. The discussion in question also changed the economic theory and included a human figure that adapts its behavior to the changes experienced instead of the human figure exhibiting rational behavior in the theoretical models here. In this sense, Veblen and Schumpeter's approaches to economic theory can be positioned at both ends of the spectrum. In Schumpeter, this approach takes place as an evolutionary process with the creative response that accompanies the creative destruction process in the market brought about by technological change. In this context, economic units act with a profit motive in the market, in a way that constantly moves the market and every area touched by the economy in a world where the basic paradigm is mostly established on the axis of economic relations. The function of the institutional structure in this process is to reveal the creative destruction-response processes. According to Schumpeter, the economic reflection of this behavior pattern also creates the growth dynamics in a given economy.

On the other hand, in Veblen, which can be positioned at the other end of the spectrum, economic units are far from being rational in their behavior but have distortions such as conspicuous consumption. This understanding of irrationality, unlike Schumpeter, combines with the assumption that individuals do not act together with the profit motive. In this context, while the effect of the institutional structure on technological change and economic growth in Schumpeter presents a more passive structure, in Veblen, technological change and economic growth are integrated with the institutional structure. The main reason for this is that the institutional structure in a country reflects the thinking habits and lifestyles of the society. Another important point is that while the basic dynamic of technological change in Schumpeter is the dominance of the market, Veblen considers the technological change process as a social development process in a way. In this context, institutional development and technological change accompanying the process of social change provide economic growth.

In the light of the explanations, rationality, which can generally be presented as a linear behavior pattern brought by the profit motive in Schumpeter, is considered as possible in an economy with a market economy, while Veblen bases his thoughts on the fact that technological change will occur in parallel with the development of a society. The role of institutions, on the other hand, is opened to discussion in different contexts, depending on their effectiveness and passivity.

VEBLEN'S SYSTEM OF THOUGHT AND THE ROLE OF INSTITUTIONS

Veblen is an important economist and sociologist who researches the institutional framework of the capital system and its effects on the development process and societies, and is considered to be the pioneer of institutional economics, with a viewpoint based on the critique of the new theoretical capitalism (Skousen, 2014; 275-283).

We can explain Veblen's interest in the phenomena of "institution, institutional structure, technology and economic development" with its economic and sociological aspects, and his focus on the concepts of wealth-poverty in this context, with the environmental factors in which he grew up. Veblen was born into a Norwegian immigrant family and had a difficult childhood and youth. He is in a state of constant anger at the injustice and opposition between the poor and wealthy segments of society in his country. He attributes the success of the rich not to their abilities, but to the advantage of "being rich already". The question always remains in mind: the rich, why are they rich, and what talents can explain such accumulation and wealth (Galbraith, 2004).

Veblen has meticulously built his critique of industrial capitalism on the capitalist class itself and its basic instincts. He defines this class as those in the grip of a predatory and ruthless instinct for profit, risk-taking, leisure, and competition (Veblen, 1899).

This angry attitude, which he initiated over the capitalist class, is actually an open criticism of established economics through the refutation of the invisible hand and natural order presuppositions by using the power of philosophy by Veblen. Veblen, who criticizes the emphasis on the utilitarian aspect of the individual and the hedonistic approach in classical economists, states that isolating the individual will also isolate the science of economics, render it stagnant and dysfunctional. However, in economics, the individual cannot be separated from the social structure and is based on the social context, and the determinant of the society is also at the forefront in his preferences and decisions (Şenalp, 2007; 54).

Veblen embodies institutions in the form of generally accepted ways of thinking and behavior, instead of defining them as restrictions on individual actions in the classical sense. Thus, Veblen defines the phenomenon of institution as the power that shapes the preferences, decisions and values of the individual who embodies his desires, tendencies and desires (Rutherford, 2001). This quality, which Veblen attributes to the concept of institution, almost legitimizes his stance against the hedonist dimension in which established economics positions the individual. According to him, personal interests can never be the determinant of an individual's behavior (Kazgan, 2000).

Veblen opposes highlighting the hedonistic and self-interested side of the individual and shaping the theoretical framework in economics from this point of view. However, on the other hand, he claimed that institutions are a product of the habits of individuals, and that institutional change is a result of the thinking habits and behaviors of the individual who is a part of the society. Therefore, in Veblen, the institutional structure cannot be separated from the individual, his habits and behavioral patterns. Therefore, economics should take individual behaviors into the field of study and formulate it in the context of individual behaviors. Institutional change is a product of individual behavior (Veblen, 1909).

Veblen dealt with the economics with an evolutionist approach, and in this respect, he constantly criticized Classical Economics for its static feature. Therefore, he was skeptical of concepts such as "natural/normal" and opposed the understanding of economics, which is contrary to human nature and genetics, and which is not based on the individual (Veblen, 1919).

VEBLEN'S THEORY OF SOCIAL CHANGE, TECHNOLOGY AND ECONOMIC GROWTH

Veblen, from a Darwinian point of view, dealt with the processes of change and transformation in economic and social behavior and defended the view that this is a natural result. The Darwinian process that applies to species is adapted to social and institutional structures in Veblen. Veblen claims that in economics, there is no final point, the most correct and/or optimal results, and therefore forward-oriented processes do not always lead to modern results. Seeing technology, individual habits, their experiences and engineers as indispensable for industrial production, Veblen believes that technological progress is important for the development processes of both institutions and society, especially through engineers. The mastery and curiosity instincts of engineers and workers constitute the main source of technology, which has a role in the development of civilization and societies (Kaymaz and Eren, 2018: 202-205).

Veblen's Darwinian evolutionary approach shapes his theory of social change, in which the phenomenon of technological progress comes to the fore. The creative actions of the individual are themselves the drivers of institutional and social change. However, these actions essentially turn into a social action and become a stock value at the end of a cumulative process (Veblen, 1946: 103). This stock emerging at this point and the technical actions taken by the society by using this stock itself will lead to an economic progress, development and growth. Technological progress, or in other words, the technological development that occurs as a result of the technical actions of the society, creates social life styles, its rules, rules and culture, which are considered as institutions. In short, the formation processes of institutions in Veblen cannot be separated from technological progress and change, they are shaped under its influence.

From this point of view, the answer to the following question should be sought: How and in what way will the technological development process work? Veblen seeks an answer to this question again through the institutional structure. Institutional structures, embodied by technological development, are composed of organizational forms for material life determined by the productive forces formed with technological progress. In other words, technology has the feature of determining the structure of material life and determining the habits of thought of the society. Institutions are a reflection of society's habits of thought, and these habits change only with technology. However, there are also forms in which institutions, that is, habits of thought, transform into established rules and resist change, which are called "stupid institutions" in Veblen. On the other hand, there are dynamic technical institutions. Change is the work of these institutions (Gürkan, 2007: 237-242).

Technology also has a significant impact on economic parameters, with the effect of triggering institutional structures and change processes. It should also be emphasized that the technological progress in Veblen is accelerated by the technical actions of the individual and these actions are essentially the result of his natural tendencies-instincts. These instincts, on the other hand, consist of two opposing sides, the peaceful and the predatory. In fact, the above-mentioned categorization of institutions is a product of these instincts. Stupid institutions, the predatory instincts of the individual; dynamic technical institutions are the results of peaceful instincts. While the former is against change, the latter is the source of change. Veblen defines a lower category "mastery instinct" in the formation of dynamic technical institutions fed by peaceful instincts that are the source of technological progress. According to Veblen, this is instinct, which reflects the production and development tendencies of the individual and is the main source of the technological development process (Rutherford, 1998: 463-476).

Institutions that undertake the task of transferring the economic actions of the society formed by individuals to future generations also constitute the infrastructure of technological progress. Technological progress, on the other hand, expresses the future material conditions, welfare and economic growth of that society in general (Young and Ekiz, 2021: 127).

While Veblen defines institutions as habits of thought, he attributes the change in these habits to technological progress. Therefore, technological change and transformation is required for institutional change and transformation. According to Veblen, established economics lacks the ability to describe and analyze the phenomena of social and economic transformation. However, Veblen attributes this transformation to technological progress that supports economic growth and, on the other hand, to rules or traditional institutions that hinder this progress. Technology and institutions, which are the determinants of the material conditions of the society, affect the actions of economic agents, and this effect directly affects the growth of the society and its economy. According to Veblen, while technology affects growth positively; especially traditional institutions create a restraining effect (Derya, 2021: 102).

THE CONCEPT OF CREATIVE DESTRUCTION AS THE ENGINE OF ECONOMIC GROWTH IN SCHUMPETER

In the neo-classical economic theory, the profit-making behavior of the firms, which is the ultimate goal, is explained together with the changes in price in a competitive market economy. Despite the dominant theoretical approach of the time, the book Capitalism, Socialism and Democracy, written by Schumpeter in 1942, examines the dynamics within economic systems and bases that the basic dynamic of the competitive element in a capitalist economy comes not from changes in prices, but from a relatively uncertain continuous innovation process. While the continuous innovation process, which can be considered as an external factor developing within a given economy, refers to the process in which old methods are replaced by new ones, in other words, technological change, this approach is conceptualized as creative destruction.

In the portrait drawn by the concept of creative destruction, the basic locomotive of a capitalist economy is the elimination process, which is provided with the reward and punishment system that it contains in the process of continuous change. In the context of the continuous evolution of the structure of economic activities, a capitalist economy is also in constant change and evolution by its nature. While the pioneers of this change process gain by increasing their activities in the market, those who cannot integrate become the losers of the change. The main thrust of this dynamism is the entrepreneurial factor. Entrepreneurship factor undertakes a risky task by carrying a new good or service to the market by operating with the data of the present time and the ever-changing uncertain structure of the future. The success of the risk taken means the success of the role undertaken by the entrepreneurs by transferring the outputs of the said change to the market with the profit motive. As a result of a successful transfer process, change can be achieved in the given economy.

According to Schumpeter, the risks that must be taken in order for the creative destruction activity to occur are not only the nature of the constantly changing economic activity. Because it is based on a creation process, the activity in question may cause reductions in total output on a firm basis in the short run. In this sense, creative destruction, in which intellectual activity plays a major role, may require the renunciation of resources allocated to current production for future advantage. As another result of this situation, companies may be placed in a short-term monopoly position among market actors due to the advantages they have gained with technological change in the process of creative destruction.

While the economic activity, whose structure has changed as a result of the development of production technologies, creates new business lines in the market, some business lines are deleted from the market, causing a structural change in the labor market. The gap between business lines that have been deleted from the market and the integration process for new business lines can also present a temporary unemployment problem. In this context, according to Schumpeter, the outcome of the process in question is that the phenomenon of economic development that will develop as a result of creative destruction can be moderated with the opportunities to be given to those who are socially unemployed.

According to Schumpeter, which is relatively negative at first glance, the issue of monopoles as a phenomenon that develops in the natural flow of the process is also closely related to creative destruction. When examined in this context, it is seen that a given market economy is quite far from the situation of perfect competition. With Schumpeter's observations and evaluations, it has been concluded that short-term monopolies are formed in the evolutionary and dynamic process caused by creative destruction, unlike the perfect competition market. The mechanism that causes this situation can be listed as follows.

- The introduction of a product unfamiliar to consumers.
- Launch of a new production method that has not been tested before.
- The emergence of a new product market that did not exist before or as a new variation of an existing market.
- Capturing of new supply source.
- The creation of a monopoly situation or the end of a monopoly situation with a new organizational structure (Schumpeter, 1911: 139).

According to the flow chart above, the process in question creates a temporary monopoly in the sense that new production methods do not become widespread. In this sense, regardless of the interventions of the institutional structure, monopolization may lose its power with the spread of new production methods in the market, and on the other hand, new production techniques can end a certain monopoly by offering an alternative to existing monopoles.

It is concluded that while the potential for short-term negative situations is high with the creative destruction conceptualized after the constant change dynamics of capitalism, which accompanies a dynamic and evolutionary process in general terms, the total output increases, in other words, economic growth is achieved with the technological methods developed in the long term.

ECONOMIC GROWTH, CREATIVE DESTRUCTION AND INSTITUTIONS IN SCHUMPETER

The economic growth provided by the economic activity in which companies are integrated into the creative destruction process, whether consciously or unconsciously, covers a significant part of the process in question by Schumpeter. In addition, when the creative destruction process is only associated with economic value in a limited context, the whole of reality cannot be grasped. In order to grasp the reality in today's world, it should be mentioned that the basic paradigm of relations in the global relations network in which modernity prevails is economic. In this context, the phenomenon of creative destruction, which is the main engine of economic growth, has a close relationship with intellectual accumulation.

The economic growth provided by the economic activity in which companies are integrated into the creative destruction process, whether consciously or unconsciously, covers a significant part of the process in question by Schumpeter. In addition, when the creative destruction process is only associated with economic value in a limited context, the whole of reality cannot be grasped. In order to grasp the reality in today's world, it should be mentioned that the basic paradigm of relations in the global relations network in which modernity prevails is economic. In this context, the phenomenon of creative destruction, which is the main engine of economic growth, has a close relationship with intellectual accumulation.

Since a capitalist economy is pregnant with relatively uncertain changes in an evolutionary way, the political structure and the behavior of the institutional structures that will subsequently come into being against the uncertainty brought about by a dynamic society are also effective in the process of economic growth. It is highly probable that the institutional structures created under the influence of authoritarian political powers naturally try to impose a static and relatively conservative society structure, not the changes brought about by a dynamic society. In this context, the direction of the relationship between the creative destruction activity, which is the main dynamo of economic growth, and the institutional structure can directly affect economic growth. Countries where the link between political powers and institutional structures is relatively low may act less ideologically in order not to hinder the dynamism of the change process brought about by creative destruction. The phenomenon of whether the regulatory and potentially restrictive role played by institutions in economic activity is established in the ideological context, and in this sense, the process of creative destruction and economic growth are in constant interaction with each other.

It is seen in the sense of a more general reality that; the existence of the relationship that a country's democratic institutions lead to the creative destruction process is much more evident. The authors, Acemoglu and Robinson (2012) & (2020), who grounded the relationship in question with a historical background in their work, also explained the existence of the relationship in the context of creative destruction in a society and their subsequent economic growth and prosperity. In this sense, the authors went beyond the restrictive argument stating that only good institutional structures lead to economic growth and revealed the relationship of the above-mentioned creative destruction process with various institutional structures in the historical process.

The Roles, Structural Factors and Creative Destruction and Response of Institutions in the Creative Destruction Process

The ways in which institutions affect technological changes in the shadow of creative destruction in economic terms can be examined under two headings. The first of these is the structural factors of institutions that can be the subject of historical evaluations throughout the ages, while the second is the concept of knowledge-based economic organization specific to the twentieth and twenty-first centuries.

Structural factors, which can be considered as the first factor, are closely related to the irreversibility of investments. Investments made due to their irreversible nature are based on the profits planned to be obtained in the future periods. In this sense, well-established contracts and intellectual property rights encourage innovative investments (Egidi, 1995). The important point here is the strong institutional structure required for legally guaranteed rights. A strong institutional structure needs to provide order in social functioning. On the contrary, as theorized by Acemoglu & Robinson (2020), the authoritarian nature of strong institutional structures can hinder the intellectual accumulation required by the creative destruction process.

On the other hand, the main reason behind the desire of authoritarian institutional structures to influence or control the creative destruction process is the dynamic creative response concept that will develop after this process. The concept of creative response, which can be explained as the continuity of the creative destruction process on the basis of firms or individuals, causes a continuous process of social and economic change in a given society (Schumpeter, 1947). In this context, the dynamic social structure that will be brought about by the changes that occur due to the innovation process in question may contradict the controlling policies of authoritarian governments. Apart from controlling policies, internalized creative destruction also changes the direction of the wealth distribution belonging to the privileged class in the society in the context of its negative impact on the social status quo. In this context, together with the redistribution of the wealth of the established status quo as a result of the economic growth achieved in the process of innovative technological change, the tensions peculiar to creative destruction and the ever-changing balance situations causes the necessity of constant change in institutional structures.

Uncertainty, Information and Institutions

The asymmetrical distribution of information in the society reveals the value of the information factor in an economy organized on the basis of knowledge. As a result of the effort to reach and obtain information, the value of information in an economy is formed. Individuals, firms, governments, etc. In the capitalist economy, where the uncertainty factor resulting from the eccentricity of the movements of the segments engaged in economic activity is seen as a risk factor, access to information provides benefits in reducing the uncertainty in question. In this context, it is important to be able to access and use the limited information factor in order to make an economic decision rationally (Hayek, 1945).

The heterogeneity of information distribution at various levels of society plays an important role in the complexity of economic systems. The disadvantageous situation of the information that individuals cannot reach can be tolerated, together with the information that can be accessed by the public, provided by the complex and uncertain behavior network that is formed as a result of the production of information in relation to the economically known and unknown phenomena.

In an environment of uncertainty in the context of the limits of access to information, the creative destruction process can be affected by decisions and signals in the direction of the course of economic policy, by providing the necessary information in the coordination process of institutions, by arranging predictable procedures (Loasby, 2002: 48). As mentioned in the previous section, because creative destruction is an activity within time but outside the practices of time, the potential risk is greater than in a traditional investment activity. In this context, in economies where the institutional structure is relatively weak, factors such as financial underdevelopment, lack of contract habitat and political narrow-mindedness can damage the fragility of the dynamic situation brought about by the new technological transformation that will replace the old one (Caballero & Hammour, 2000). The main reason behind the fact that the regulatory practices that cannot be provided by the weak institutional structures in question lead to the formation of a more stagnant and insufficient market structure to trigger technological change, is that the creative destruction activity develops outside the practices that do not exist in a given economy or sector. In this context, the institutional assurances and opportunities provided in both production and market presentation of an output that does not exist in the market will contribute to a healthy creative destruction and response process.

On the other hand, when it is considered as an active market factor as well as being a regulator, institutions can redistribute information by regulating the information distribution in the society with the opportunities they have. The process of regulating the distribution of information is important because the dominant information distribution, which is seen as the basic factors of the dynamic structures of economic systems with complexity and uncertainty, is heterogeneous at various levels of society. With this situation, the redistribution of available information stocks of individuals occurs. In this context, in the investment process planned for creative destruction, which is the cycle of technological change and innovation, as a result of meeting an unmet need or demand for information, institutions make the natural uncertainty dynamics of the market economy relatively predictable with their regulatory effect on the distribution of information.

CONCLUSION

The phenomenon of economic growth has a very fundamental characteristic, both in theory and in terms of increasing the welfare of societies. In this context, the intellectual pursuit of how societies can increase economic growth has been continuously studied by classical economic theory in the literature of economics.

Schumpeter and Veblen made important theoretical contributions to economic growth from different perspectives on the classical economic approach. Technological change occupies an important place in both authors and plays a fundamental role in the economic growth process. According to Schumpeter, while the creative destruction that determines the technological development process has a structure that develops within the system but affects the market as if it were an external factor, Veblen evaluates the technological development together with the development of the society and states that technological development and economic growth emerge as its output. In this context, while Schumpeter states that the expanding knowledge in the society is realized as a result of the profit motive of the firms trying to gain superiority in the market conditions, Veblen prioritizes the technological development with the social development. Both authors critically approached the established economic theory of the time with different evaluations, and as a result of these criticisms, they reached a common conclusion about the importance of technological development on economic growth. When the dynamics of this inference are evaluated, the approaches of Schumpeter and Veblen differ from each other.

Technology, which is also defined as the process of social accumulation in Veblen, is an important variable that determines social evolution. Veblen, who dealt with technological change together with social transformation, saw it as an internal phenomenon and linked the emergence of capitalism with technological development. In the perspective of Veblen, who sees technology as a dynamic factor, while the individual is the factor that determines institutional change, technological progress is seen as a cause of institutional change. In any case, there is a strong relationship between technology and the individual. Therefore, the individual, the human element, is the source of technology and growth. There are strong relationships between technology and the instincts of the individual, his habits and thought patterns, and institutions. But the direction of these relations is not very clear. In fact, causality is always bidirectional. The individual causes technological change, but on the other hand, technological progress leads to institutional change by changing the thinking habits and patterns of the individual and society.

According to Schumpeter, the entrepreneurial factor has a great importance in innovation and technological development, which are the main drivers of economic growth. In Veblen, on the other hand, entrepreneurship is considered together with the evolution of the capital accumulation process, and unlike Schumpeter, it is not seen as a cause of technological change but as a part of the profit increase process at the firm level. However, the common point in both is the direct and/or indirect effect of the entrepreneur on the technology phenomenon.

In terms of the above evaluations and the overall study, it is seen that although the context of the importance attributed to technological change by two important economists is valid for economic growth, technical development also brings disadvantages. In this sense, neither Veblen's technological development, which is articulated with the development of society, nor Schumpeter's creative destruction, which has a transformative effect on society, does not occur clearly. Contrary to this situation, the institutional structures can use it's growing technical knowledge as a function that facilitates management and increases control. In other words, beyond the cases where the source of the technical progress brought about by technological change comes out of a transformed social structure or is channeled to the society as a transformative activity, technological change can continue its existence in the institutional structure in order to preserve the current status quo.

REFERENCES

Acemoglu, D., & Robinson, J. A. (2012). *Why nations fail: The origins of power, prosperity, and poverty*. Currency.

Acemoglu, D., & Robinson, J. A. (2020). *The narrow corridor: States, societies, and the fate of liberty*. Penguin Books.

Batabyal, A. A., & Yoo, S. J. (2018). Schumpeterian creative class competition, innovation policy, and regional economic growth. *International Review of Economics & Finance*, *55*, 86–97. doi:10.1016/j.iref.2018.01.016

Caballero, R. J., & Hammour, M. (2000). *Creative destruction and development: Institutions, crises, and restructuring*. Academic Press.

Derya, H. (2021). Kurumsal İktisadın Katkıları Üzerine Değerlendirme. In *Kurumsal İktisat: Kurallar ve Kurumların İktisadi Gelişme Açısından Önemi içinde* (pp. 99–121). Astana Yayınları.

Egidi, M. (1995). *The "Creative Destruction" in Economic and Political Institutions*. Academic Press.

Florida, R. (2002). *The rise of the creative class* (Vol. 9). Basic Books.

Galbraith, J. K. (2004). *Ekonomik Gelişmeler Tarihi: Kuşku Çağı, Altın Kitaplar, 3*. Basım.

Genç, H. (2021). Kurumsal İktisat: Metodolojik ve Terminolojik Temeller. In *Kurumsal İktisat: Kurallar ve Kurumların İktisadi Gelişme Açısından Önemi içinde* (pp. 123–138). Astana Yayınları.

Gürkan, C. (2007). Veblen, Schumpeter ve Teknoloji. In *Kurumsal İktisat içinde* (pp. 237–281). İmge Kitabevi.

Hayek, F. A. (1945). The use of knowledge in society. *The American Economic Review*, *35*(4), 519–530.

Kaymaz, V., & Eren, E. (2018). Modern Zamanlar ve Veblen. *Yildiz Social Science Review, 4*(2), 201-212. Retrieved from https://dergipark.org.tr/tr/pub/yssr/issue/41948/442677

Kazgan, G. (2000). *İktisadi Düşünce veya Politik İktisadın Evrimi* (Vol. 9). Basım, Remzi Kitapevi.

Loasby, B. (2002). *Knowledge, institutions and evolution in economics*. Routledge. doi:10.4324/9780203459096

Pérez, C. (2009). *Technological revolutions and techno-economic paradigms*. TOC (No. 20). TUT Working Paper.

Rutherford, M. (1998). Veblen's Evolutionary Programme: A Promise Unfulfilled. *Cambridge Journal of Economics*, *22*(4), 463–477. doi:10.1093/oxfordjournals.cje.a013729

Rutherford, M. (2001). Association Institutional Economics: Then and Now. *The Journal of Economic Perspectives, 15*(3), 173-194.

Schumpeter, J. A. (1947). The creative response in economic history. *The Journal of Economic History*, *7*(2), 149–159. doi:10.1017/S0022050700054279

Şenalp, M. G. (2007). Dünden Bugüne Kurumsal İktisat. In *Kurumsal İktisat içinde* (pp. 45–92). İmge Kitabevi.

Shumpeter, J. (1911). *The Theory of Economic Development: An Inquiry into Profits*. Capital, Credit, Interest, and the Business Cycle.

Shumpeter, J. (1942). *Capitalism, socialism and democracy.*

Skousen, M. (2009). *İktisadi Düşünce Tarihi: Modern İktisadın İnşası. Adres Yayınları, 6.*

Veblen, T. (1899). *The Theory of the Leisure Class: An Economic Study of Institutions*. The Macmillan Company.

Veblen, T. (1909). The Limitations of Marginal Utility. *Journal of Political Economy*, *17*(9), 620-636.

Veblen, T. (1919). *The Place of Science in Modern Civilization and Other Essays*. Huebsch.

Veblen, T. (1946). *The Instinct of Workmanship: And the State of the Industrial Arts*. The Viking Press.

Chapter 12
Evaluation of the Development Level of Provinces in Turkey and Incentives for Research and Development

Ahmet Tekin
Eskisehir Osmangazi University, Turkey

Esra Doğan
Eskisehir Osmangazi University, Turkey

ABSTRACT

The aim of this study is to reveal the relationship between the support provided for research and development (R&D) within the scope of the investment incentive system and innovation registration on the basis of spatial differences, taking into account regional development differences. In this direction, an empirical evaluation is made to reveal whether the level of incentives provided for R&D and the level of innovation in Turkey on the basis of 81 provinces differ in the context of socio-economic development level. As a result of the analysis, it is seen that 81 provinces are divided into five clusters.

INTRODUCTION

Research and Development (R&D) in Turkey is supported within financial incentive practices, a fundamental fiscal policy tool. In this direction, implementations were carried out based on different laws and regulations. Technology Development Zones Law dated 26/6/2001 and numbered 4691 and Law on Supporting Research, Development and Design Activities dated 28/2/2008 and numbered 5746 are regulations with specific purposes for R&D (Doğan, 2020: 95). Following these regulations, rendering specific support for R&D became the main objective with the Decree No. 15199 on State Aids in Investments, which came into force in 2009, and the Decree on State Aids in Investments, No. 3305, which came into force in 2012, and repealed the former decision.

DOI: 10.4018/978-1-7998-9648-7.ch012

The aim of this study is outlined in an article of the Decree on State Aids in Investments (No. 2012/3305), which follows as "This Decision's purpose is, in line with the targets envisioned in the development plans and annual programs, to determine the procedures and principles regarding conduction the preservation to investments with high added value, boosting production and employment, promoting regional and strategic investments with high research and development content that will increase international competitiveness, enhancing international direct investments, reducing regional development differences, clustering and supporting investments for environmental conservation and research and development activities." In this direction, the study aims to reveal the relationship between the support provided to R&D and innovation registration based on spatial differences within the scope of the Investment Incentive System, taking into account regional development differences. The regions within the scope of the decree are divided into six tiers according to the socio-economic development level of the 81 provinces in Turkey. This classification is involved in the Socio-Economic Development Ranking (SEGE) Studies emerging as one of the monitoring and evaluation tools of regional development policies. The last of these studies has been the SEGE-2017 report. Fifty-two variables in total were applied in the report within the scope of 8 main categories: demography, employment, education, health, competitive and innovative capacity, financial accessibility, and quality of life. In this classification, the first tier consists of the provinces with the best socio-economic development level, and the sixth consists of the worst. When the supporting elements of Decision No. 2012/3305, which is based on this classification, are examined, the classification's importance becomes clear (Doğan, 2021:414).

In this context, firstly, the relevant literature's summary is presented comparatively, later empirical findings are presented, and the study is concluded with a policy proposal developed by these findings.

LITERATURE

In the literature, R&D Incentives have a place in the empirical literature, especially in the context of their relationship with R&D expenditures at the firm level and evaluations made in the context of legislation. This situation can be said to arise from the expectation that R&D incentives will decrease the R&D costs of the companies and consequently increase the R&D expenditures. Although it is stated that these studies measuring the effectiveness of R&D incentives are limited on the basis of country samples (Takalo et al., 2013), there is a wider literature for other countries (Acconcia and Cantabene, 2018; Ernst and Spengel, 2011; Freitas et al., 2017; Guellec and Pottelsberghe, 2000; Hall and Van Reenen, 2000; Huang, 2009; Takalo et al., 2013; Thomson, 2009; Wang and Tsai, 1998; Yang et al., 2012), especially when compared to the case of Turkey (Ersungur et al., 2018; Göçer, 2014; Kutbay and Öz, 2017; Şimşek et al., 2004).

On the other hand, the relationship between R&D incentives and their main purpose is discussed within macro and micro scales. Accordingly, besides studies in which the relationship between the level of innovation, which is the main purpose of R&D incentives, and the level of R&D incentives in accordance with the legal legislation are handled with country-based macro data (Colombo, 2019), there are also cross-country comparative studies (Jaumotte and Pain, 2005; Pradhan et al., 2017; Sarıdoğan, 2021; Tüylüoğlu and Saraç, 2012; Westmore, 2013). In micro-level studies, the relationship between the level of firms benefiting from R&D incentives and their innovation levels is presented using micro data sets containing firm data on a country basis (Bérubé and Mohnen, 2009; Cappelen et al. 2012; Czarnitzki et al. 2011; Chen and Zhang, 2019; Hanel, 2003; Radas et al., 2015). On the other hand, studies carried out in Turkey address the relationship between R&D and innovation directly and address the factors determining innovation indirectly (Çakın and Özdemir, 2018; Çetin and Gedik, 2017; Demirdöğen, 2019; Doğan, 2020; Kılıç and Keklik, 2012; Mercan et al. 2011; Şahbaz and Tanyeri, 2018). Based on the relevant literature, this study examines the relationship between R&D incentives and innovation in Turkey only at the provincial level. The distribution of R&D incentives and the level of innovation by provinces are evaluated by considering the socio-economic development levels of the provinces. Accordingly, this study is planned to make two main contributions to the literature. First of all, the relationship between R&D incentives and innovation is examined directly and specifically on the scale of Turkey, contributing to the macro-scale studies in the literature with the Turkish sample. Secondly, it is aimed to contribute to the literature from a methodological perspective by examining the scale of Turkey at the provincial level, revealing the importance of province-based differentiations and thus spatial differences.

EMPIRICAL EVALUATION

In this section, an empirical evaluation is executed to reveal whether the level of incentives provided for R&D in Turkey and the level of innovation differ in terms of the level of socio-economic development. Consecutively, information regarding the scope of the research, the method applied, and the evaluation of the findings is presented in the study.

Scope of the Research

Scope of the Research is the total investment amount within the scope of incentives for R&D investments within the scope of the Investment Incentive System of 81 provinces in Turkey, which is constantly changing in the 2007-2019 period, the number of applications for innovation (patent, utility model, trademark, design) presented to the Turkish Patent and Trademark Office, the approval rate of these applications, and data regarding the socio-economic development level of the categorically variable provinces (SEGE 2017)[1]. In this context, the Turkish Patent and Trademark Office statistics, the Investment Incentive Data Set of the Ministry of Industry and Technology, and the Socio-Economic Development Ranking of Provinces and Regions (SEGE 2017) report were utilized to compose a proper assessment for the purpose of the research.

Research Method

Clustering method analysis is applied to examine the distribution of incentives provided to R&D, the level of innovation applied and realized, and the level of socio-economic development with 81 provinces in Turkey.

Cluster analysis is applied to divide units, variables or units and variables into homogeneous groups by using measurements calculated based on distance, closeness, similarity, or differences (Ozdamar 2018, 228). Within the scope of clustering analysis, there are two primary clustering methods: progressive and non-progressive. In progressive clustering, both units and variables form clusters with different levels of similarity to each other. In non-progressive methods, only units are clustered. (Ozdamar 2018, 321). Although progressive and non-progressive clustering methods vary, in this study, firstly, a two-stage (progressive) clustering method was used to determine the number of clusters, and then the K-Means Method, which is the most extensively used non-progressive clustering method, was preferred.

This method is preferred because the study aims to cluster the units and in this direction, and the most commonly used method is the K-Means Method. In this method, the intention is to divide the continuous p-variable data sets obtained from a large number of units into k clusters to minimize the sum of squares within the cluster.

p= $(p_1, p_2, \ldots, p_n)$ and q=$(q_1, q_2, \ldots, q_n)$

$$\sqrt{\sum_{i=1}^{n}(p_i - q_i)^2} = \sqrt{(p_1 - q_1)^2 + (p_2 - q_2)^2 + \ldots + (p_n - q_n)^2}$$

However, it is sufficient to predetermine the cluster numbers of the data without calculating distance or similarity matrix (Özdamar 2018, 323). On the other hand, in order to apply this method, it is necessary to determine the number of clusters first. Both theoretical assumptions and technical methods can be used to determine the number of clusters (Kodinariya and Makvana, 2013, 90). In the study, Akaike information criterion and cluster quality values are examined to determine the number of clusters.

In this context, the Akaike information criterion and cluster quality values are examined to determine the number of clusters in 81 provinces where the level of incentives provided to R&D, the level of innovation applied and achieved, and the level of socioeconomic development are used as variables within the scope of the study. Following the determination of the number of clusters, ANOVA analysis of variance results is evaluated to reveal the determinant effect of the variables on cluster formation and the findings related to cluster characteristics based on variables such as cluster averages and distance between clusters, applying the K Means Method. Subsequently, within the scope of all the findings, the distribution of the provinces in the context of clusters is examined.

Findings of the Research

The tree graph, which results from the hierarchical clustering analysis carried out to ascertain the number of clusters, determining the distance between the provinces and the connections between the clusters they form, is given below.

The findings obtained from the two-stage clustering analysis to ascertain the number of clusters is given below.

It was decided that 81 provinces should be divided into 5 clusters, considering the findings obtained as a result of the two-stage clustering analysis, which evaluates whether the number of graphics and clusters obtained using the Akaike Information Criteria is acceptable or not. Hence, the results obtained applying the K Mean Technique are given below.

When the cluster centers are examined, while the fourth cluster has the highest value for the socio-economic development level category (the socio-economic development level is bad), it is observed that the second and fifth clusters have the lowest values (socio-economic development level is good). While investments within the scope of R&D incentives are significantly higher in the first cluster, they are at the lowest level in the fourth cluster. The number of innovative applications and the rate of approved applications is highest in the fifth cluster and lowest in the fourth cluster. Relationships between clusters are evaluated through the table below, which summarizes the distance between cluster centers.

Figure 1. Dendrogram

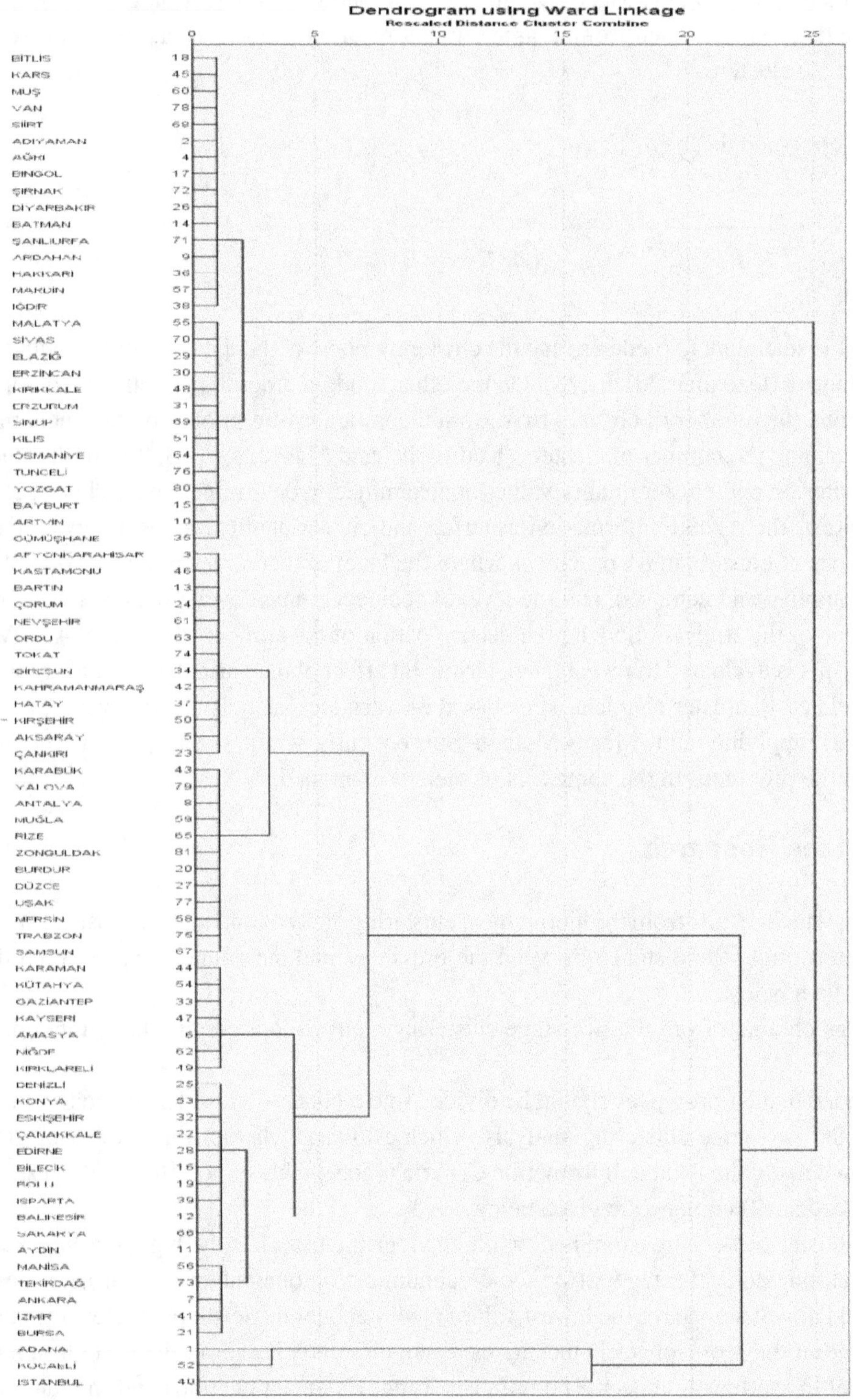

Figure 2. Akaike information criterion

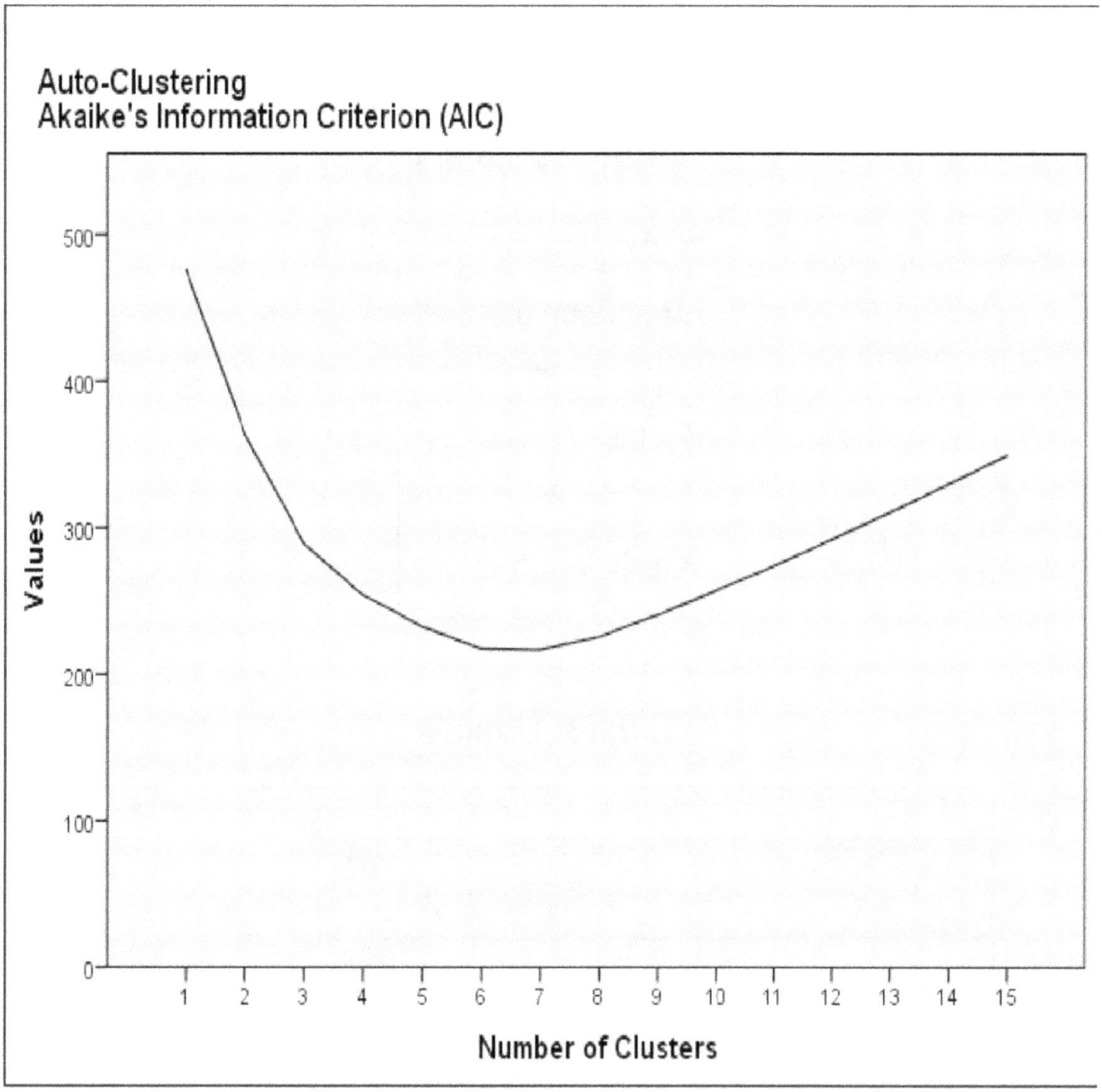

As the distance value increases, the similarity value between the clusters decreases. Accordingly, the two closest clusters are the second and third clusters, and the two farthest clusters are the first and fifth clusters.

The findings obtained with Table 1 and Table 2 become more understandable through the figure below.

It is seen that all clusters differ significantly from other clusters. Accordingly, it can be stated that homogeneous structures are formed in the context of the combination of variable values with each other. However, the first cluster differs significantly from other clusters in terms of incentive rate and the fifth cluster in terms of incentive rate and the number of innovative applications. On the other hand, although the averages of the second, third and fourth clusters seem close, they differ significantly in terms of all variables.

Figure 3. Cluster quality

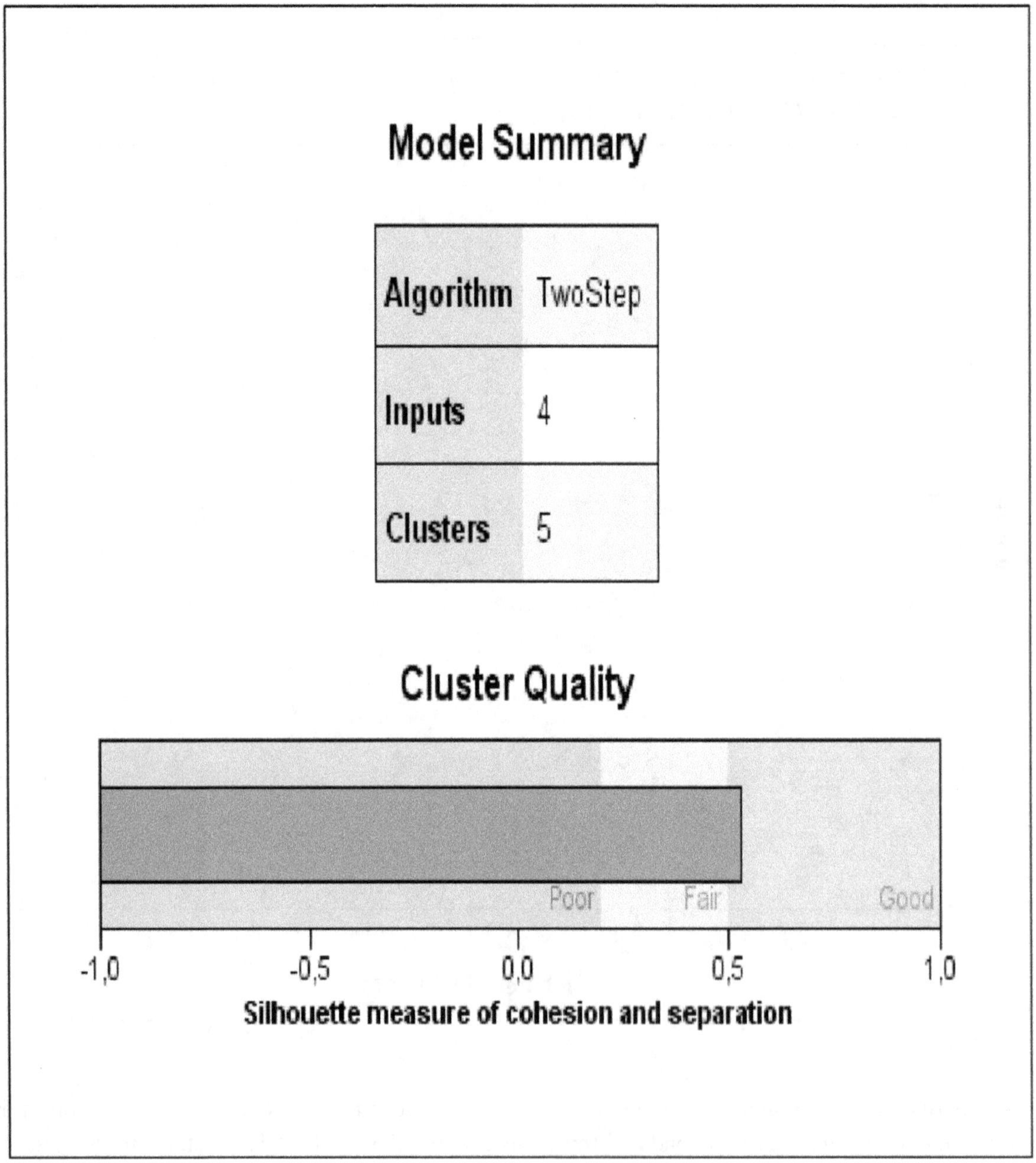

When the analysis of the variance table is examined, it is seen that all of the variables contributed to the clustering at a significant probability level ($p<0.05$).

As a result of the analyzes made within the scope of the clustering method, the clusters where 81 provinces are located are presented and evaluated through the table below.

The principal characteristics of each cluster and consequently the provinces in each cluster based on the associated variables will be addressed through the last cluster centers (Table 1), the distance between

Table 1. Final cluster centers

	Cluster				
	1	2	3	4	5
Zscore (SEDL)	-,41971	-1,61258	-,61315	,88599	-1,61258
Zscore (INCENTIVE)	7,25722	1,36490	-,16394	-,27052	1,99336
Zscore (APPLICATION)	,02681	,58468	-,10401	-,20825	8,60326
Zscore (REGISTRATION RATIO)	,22643	,89520	,60644	-,75940	,95699

the cluster centers (Table 2), and the Last Cluster Centers Variable Values (Figure 4) and the evaluations made in these contexts.

- While the amount of incentives in the first cluster (Adana) is significantly higher than in other clusters, the number of innovative applications and registration rates is considerably lower.
- In the second cluster (Ankara, Bursa, İzmir, Kocaeli, Tekirdağ), both the number of incentives and the number of innovative applications and registration rates are high.
- Although the number of incentives and the number of innovative applications is low in the third cluster (37 provinces), the registration rate is high.
- In the fourth cluster (37 provinces), both the number of incentives and the number of innovative applications and registration rates are low (the opposite of the second cluster).
- In the fifth cluster (Istanbul), the number of innovative applications is significantly higher than the other clusters, while the number of incentives and registration rates is also high.

When the clusters are handled comparatively; The second (Ankara, Bursa, İzmir, Kocaeli, Tekirdağ) and fifth (Istanbul) clusters consist of provinces with relatively high incentives and registration rates. Nevertheless, the core difference between these clusters is the difference in the number of incentive applications, despite similar incentive and registration rates. Accordingly, it can be stated that incentives are more effective in the second cluster.

Contrary to these clusters, in the first (Adana) cluster, it is recognized that the positive effect of the incentives is not satisfactory. The third and fourth clusters, where most of the provinces (74 provinces) are included, have the opposite feature in terms of the incentive-innovation relationships. Although the incentive rate and the number of innovative applications are close, the registration rate is high in the third cluster (close to the second and fifth clusters); significantly lower in the fourth cluster. The main

Table 2. Distances between final cluster centers

Cluster	1	2	3	4	5
1		6,075	7,435	7,707	10,160
2	6,075		1,973	3,505	8,043
3	7,435	1,973		2,034	9,033
4	7,707	3,505	2,034		9,589
5	10,160	8,043	9,033	9,589	

Figure 4. Final cluster centers

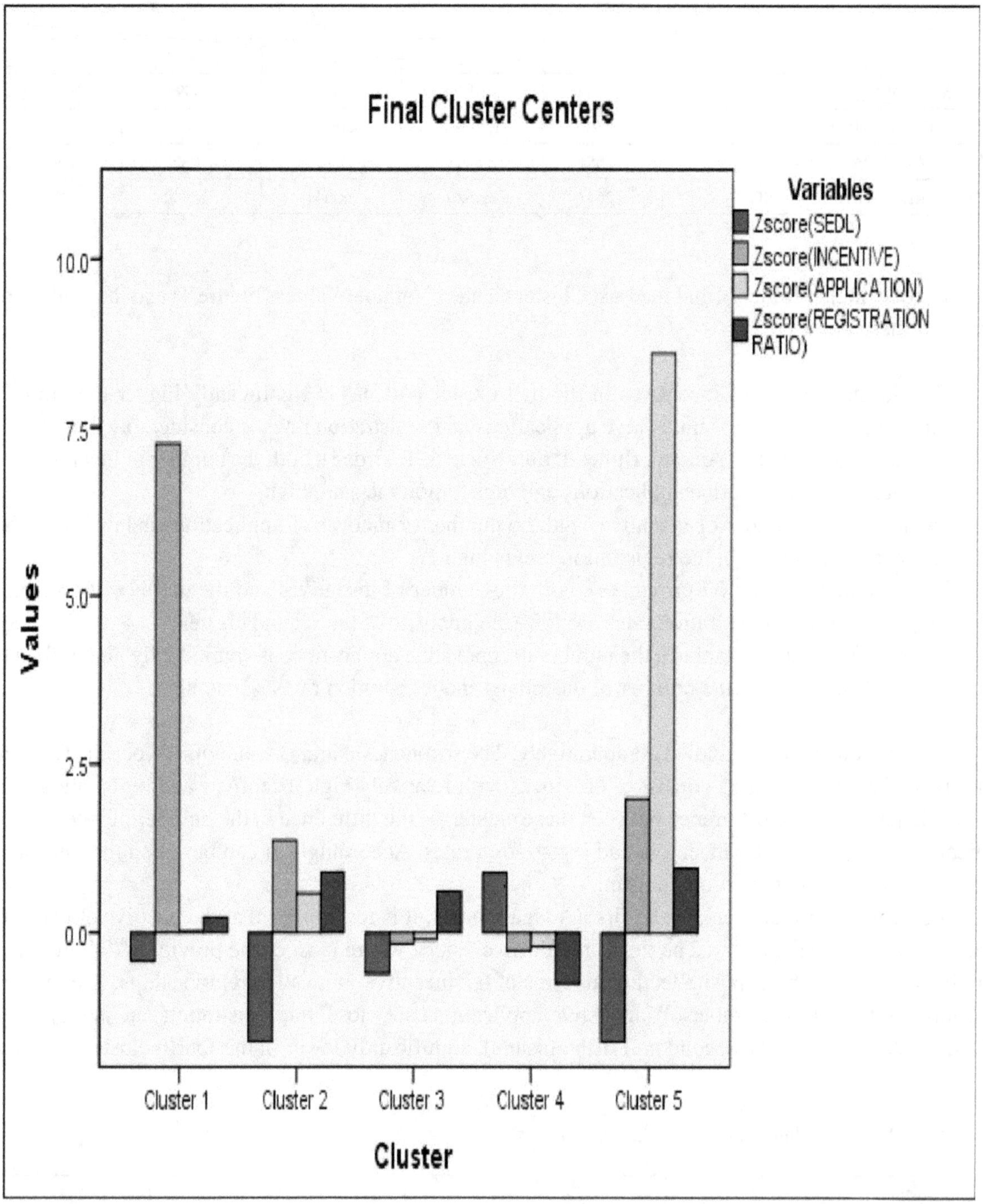

contrast between these clusters is their socio-economic development levels. The third cluster provinces have a good socio-economic development level similar to other clusters; the fourth cluster provinces, on the other hand, have the worst socio-economic development level.

Table 3. ANOVA

	Cluster		Error		F	Sig.
	Mean Square	df	Mean Square	df		
Zscore(SEDL)	14,683	4	,280	76	52,472	,000
Zscore (INCENTIVE)	17,414	4	,136	76	127,968	,000
Zscore(APPLICATION)	19,433	4	,030	76	650,874	,000
Zscore (REGISTRATION RATIO)	9,980	4	,527	76	18,923	,000
The F tests should be used only for descriptive purposes because the clusters have been chosen to maximize the differences among cases in different clusters. The observed significance levels are not corrected for this and thus cannot be interpreted as tests of the hypothesis that the cluster means are equal.						

Based on these findings, when all clusters are examined as a whole, it is concluded that although the incentive rate has a differentiating effect among the provinces, the innovation registration rate is clearly higher in provinces with a good socio-economic development level.

CONCLUSION

With the Law on Technology Development Zones dated 26/6/2001 and numbered 4691, and the Law on Supporting Research, Development and Design Activities dated 28/2/2008 and numbered 5746, as well as the Decision on State Aids in Investments, numbered 2012/3305, supporting R&D investments within the incentive system has gained a specific purpose. However, the fact that regional development differences are among the main objectives, especially within the scope of Decision numbered 2012/3305, revealed the necessity of implementing the Decision in line with both objectives. Accordingly, socio-economic development levels became the main criteria during the implementation phase of the Decision.

Within the scope of this study, an empirical analysis was conducted at the level of 81 provinces in Turkey in order to evaluate the effectiveness of the implementation phase of the relevant decision. Provinces were categorized by cluster analysis method, taking into account their socio-economic development levels, on the basis of the relationship between the total amount of investment made within the scope of supports for R&D investments within the Investment Incentive System, representing the level

Table 4. Clusters of provinces

Clusters	Provinces
Cluster 1	Adana
Cluster 2	Ankara, Bursa, İzmir, Kocaeli, Tekirdağ
Cluster 3	Afyonkarahisar, Amasya, Antalya, Aydın, Balıkesir, Bartın, Bilecik, Bolu, Burdur, Çanakkale, Çorum, Denizli, Düzce, Edirne, Eskişehir, Gaziantep, Hatay, Isparta, Karabük, Karaman, Kastamonu, Kayseri, Kırklareli, Kırşehir, Konya, Kütahya, Manisa, Mersin, Muğla, Niğde, Rize, Sakarya, Samsun, Trabzon, Uşak, Yalova, Zonguldak
Cluster 4	Adıyaman, Ağrı, Aksaray, Ardahan Artvin, Batman, Bayburt, Bingöl, Bitlis, Çankırı, Diyarbakır, Elazığ, Erzincan, Erzurum, Giresun, Gümüşhane, Hakkari, Iğdır, Kahramanmaraş, Kars, Kırıkkale, Kilis, Malatya, Mardin, Muş, Nevşehir, Ordu, Osmaniye, Siirt, Sinop, Sivas, Şanlıurfa, Şırnak, Tokat, Tunceli, Van, Yozgat
Cluster 5	İstanbul

of R&D, the number of innovation applications (patent, utility model, trademark, design) made to the Turkish Patent and Trademark Office, representing the level of innovation, and the rate of approval of these applications. In the five-cluster categorization, Adana was separated from other clusters due to the significant increase in the number of incentives, while Istanbul was separated from the other clusters due to its relatively high rate of innovation practices. The majority of the provinces (74 provinces) were gathered in two clusters that differ by their socio-economic development level. This situation reveals that the provinces show significant similarities in terms of the number of incentives for R&D and innovation application levels. Nevertheless, the categorical distinction between these provinces is due to the differences in socio-economic development levels and innovation registration rates. In the context of these provinces, it is seen that the innovation registration rate cannot be directly related to the incentive level. Indeed, the existence of a separate cluster covering the provinces of Ankara, Bursa, Izmir, Kocaeli, and Tekirdag also supports this situation. Although this cluster, which differs significantly from all others, has a very close innovation rate with the third cluster consisting of 37 provinces, unlike that cluster, the level of incentive is quite high. From this point of view, it can be concluded that there is no generally accepted relationship between innovation and the level of incentives within the scope of R&D in Turkey.

In this context, the present study on the relationship between the incentive level and innovation at the provincial level in Turkey reveals that the regional development gap is the primary determinant. Accordingly, it can be said that the objective of R&D in Decision No. 2012/3305 mainly depends on the realization of the policies narrowing the regional development gap. In this direction, two main policy recommendations are presented as a result of the present findings. First of all, during the implementation phase of Decision No. 2012/3305, the coordination of R&D incentives should not be carried out independent of the regional development difference, and the socio-economic development levels of the provinces should not be disregarded. Secondly, it is thought that impact assessment analyzes in incentive policies should be made by taking into account spatial comparisons, and incentives should be directed accordingly.

REFERENCES

Acconcia, A., & Cantabene, C. (2018). Liquidity and Firms' Response to Fiscal Stimulus. *Economic Journal. Revue Economique et Sociale*, *128*(613), 1759–1785. doi:10.1111/ecoj.12499

Bérubé, C., & Mohnen, P. (2009). Are Firms that Receive R&D Subsidies More Innovative? *Can. J. Econ. Can. Econ. Assoc.*, *42*(1), 206–225. doi:10.1111/j.1540-5982.2008.01505.x

Çakın, E., & Özdemir, A. (2018). Kobi'lerde İnovasyon Performansını Etkileyen Faktörlerin Bulanık Dematel Tabanlı Analitik Ağ Süreci (BDANP) Yöntemiyle Analizi ve Bir Uygulama. *Dokuz Eylül Üniversitesi Sosyal Bilimler Enstitüsü Dergisi*, *20*(4), 559–586. doi:10.16953/deusosbil.293170

Cappelen, A., Raknerud, A., & Rybalka, M. (2012). The effects of R&D Tax Credits Onpatenting and Innovations. *Research Policy*, *41*(2), 334–345. doi:10.1016/j.respol.2011.10.001

Çetin, K., & Gedik, H. (2017). İşletmelerde İnovasyona Etki Eden Faktörler: Karaman İli Örneği. *Uluslararası Yönetim İktisat ve İşletme Dergisi*, *13*(13), 160–172.

Chen, Z., & Zhang, J. (2019). Types of Patents and Driving Forces Behind the Patent Growth in China. *Economic Modelling*, *80*, 294–302. doi:10.1016/j.econmod.2018.11.015

Colombo, D. G. (2019). Brazilian Innovation Tax Policy and International Investment: Evidence From United States Multinationals and International Patent Applications. *Análise Econômica, Porto Alegre, 37*(74), 61-90.

Czarnitzki, D., Hanel, P., & Rosa, J. M. (2011). Evaluating the Impact of R&D Tax Credits on Innovation: A Microeconometric Study on Canadian Firms. *Research Policy*, *40*(2), 217–229. doi:10.1016/j.respol.2010.09.017

Demirdöğen, S. (2019). İşletmelerin İnovasyon Yapmalarına Engel olan Faktörlerin Belirlenmesine Yönelik Bir Araştırma: Erzincan Organize Sanayi Bölgesi Örneği. *Erciyes Üniversitesi İktisadi ve İdari Bilimler Fakültesi Dergisi*, (54), 417–446. doi:10.18070/erciyesiibd.521871

Doğan, E. (2020). Türkiye'de İnovasyonu Belirleyen Faktörler: 5746 ve 4691 Sayılı Kanunlar Kapsamında Bir Değerlendirme. In Ş. Karabulut (Ed.), *Kamu Politikalarında Mali ve İktisadi Yapıdaki Dönüşüm: Yerelden Globale Teori, Beklentiler ve Uygulama* (pp. 95–117). Gazi Kitapevi.

Doğan, E. (2021). The Purpose-Spesific Structure of Decree on State Aids for Investments: A Comparision of Regions Classified as Socioeconomic Development Level via Copras Method. *BILTURK. The Journal of Economics and Related Studies*, *3*(3), 410–426. doi:10.47103/bilturk.937305

Ernst, C., & Spengel, C. (2011). *Taxation, R&D Tax Incentives and Patent Application in Europe.* ZEW Discussion Paper No. 11, 0-24. doi:10.2139/ssrn.1805762

Ersungur, Ş. M., & Takım, A. (2018). Türkiye'de Teşvik Sisteminin Yapısı, Sorunları ve Etkinliği Üzerine Bir Politika Önerisi: Tek Bir Uygulamacı Kuruluş Sorunları Çözer Mi? *Atatürk Üniversitesi İktisadi ve İdari Bilimler Dergisi*, *32*(3), 725–744.

Freitas, I. B., Castellacci, F., Fontana, R., Malerba, F., & Vezzulli, A. (2017). Sectors and the Additionality Effects of R&D Tax Credits: A Cross-Country Microeconometric Analysis. *Research Policy*, *46*(1), 57–72. doi:10.1016/j.respol.2016.10.002

Göçer, İ., Kutbay, H., Gerede, C., & Aslan, R. (2014). Vergi Teşviklerinin Ar-Ge ve İnovasyona Etkisi: Panel Eş Bütünleşme ve Nedensellik Analizi. *Maliye Dergisi*, (167), 163–183.

Guellec, D., & Pottelsberghe, B. (2000). *The Impact of Public R&D Expenditure on Business R&D.* STI Working Papers, No. 4.

Hall, B. H., & Reenen, J. W. (2000). How Effective are Fiscal Incentives for R&D? A New Review of the Evidence. *Research Policy*, *29*(4-5), 449–469. doi:10.1016/S0048-7333(99)00085-2

Hanel, P. (2003). *Impact of Government Support Programs on Innovation by Canadian Manufacturing Firms*. Centre interuniversitaire de recherche sur lascience et la technologie (CIRST), ca-hier de recherche.

Huang, C.-H. (2009). *Three Essays on The Innovation Behaviour of Taiwan'S Manufacturing Firms.* Graduate Institute of Industrial Economics, National Central University.

Jaumotte, F., & Pain, N. (2005). An Owerview of Public Policies to Support Innovation. *OECD Economics Department Working Papers,* (456). doi:10.1787/18151973

Kodinariya, T. M., & Makwana, P. R. (2013). Review on Determining Number of Cluster in K-Means Clustering. *International Journal (Toronto, Ont.)*, *1*(6), 90–95.

Kutbay, H., & Öz, E. (2017). Ar-Ge Harcamalarının Ekonomik Büyüme Üzerine Etkisi: Türkiye ve Seçilmiş Ülkelerde Vergi Teşvikleri Boyutuyla Ekonometrik Analizi. *Maliye Dergisi*, *173*, 331–361.

Mercan, B., Göktaş, D., & Gömleksiz, M. (2011). AR-GE Faaliyetleri ve Girişimcilerin İnovasyon Üzerindeki Etkileri: Patent Verileri Üzerinde Bir Uygulama. *PARADOKS Ekonomi Sosyoloji ve Politika Dergisi*, *7*(2), 27–44.

Ministry of Industry and Technology. (2019). *İllerin ve Bölgelerin Sosyo-Ekonomik Gelişmişlik Sıralaması Araştırması Sege-2017*. https://www.sanayi.gov.tr/merkez-birimi/b94224510b7b/sege/2017-il/date:30.04.2021

Ministry of Industry and Technology. (2021). *Yatırımlarda Devlet Yardımları Hakkında Karar*. https://www.sanayi.gov.tr/mevzuat/diger/mc0403018201/date:30.04.2021

Ministry of Industry and Technology. (2021). *Yatırım Teşvik Uygulamaları*. https://www.sanayi.gov.tr/destek-ve-tesvikler/yatirim-tesvik-sistemleri/md0103011615/

Ministry of Industry and Technology. (2021). *Yatırım Teşvik Verisi (01.01.2001-31.03.2021)*. https://sanayi.gov.tr/istatistikler/yatirim-istatistikleri/mi1304021615/

Özdamar, K. (2018). *Paket Programlar ile İstatistiksel Veri Analizi Cilt 2*. Nisan Kitabevi.

Pradhan, R. P., Arvin, M. B., Bahmani, S., & Bennett, S. E. (2017). The Innovation-Growth Link in OECD Countries: Could Other Macroeconomic Variables Matter? *Technology in Society*, *51*, 113–123. doi:10.1016/j.techsoc.2017.08.003

Radas, S., Anić, I. D., Tafro, A., & Wagner, V. (2015). The Effects of Public Support Schemes on Small And Medium Enterprises. *Technovation*, *38*, 15–30. doi:10.1016/j.technovation.2014.08.002

Şahbaz, A., & Tanyeri, M. (2018). Küçük ve Orta Büyüklükteki İşletmelerde İnovasyona Yönelik Tutumlar ve İnovasyon Engelleri: Çanakkale İlinde Kobi'ler Üzerine Bir Araştırma. *ÇOMÜ Uluslararası Sosyal Bilimler Dergisi*, *3*(2), 233-263. doi:10.31454/usb.476867

Sarıdoğan, H. Ö. (2021). Vergi Teşviklerinin İnovasyon Üzerindeki Etkisinin Panel Sur Yöntemi ile Analizi. *Abant Sosyal Bilimler Dergisi*, *21*(2), 221–241. doi:10.11616/basbed.vi.857270

Seçilmiş, N., & Konu, A. (2019). OECD Ülkelerinde Ar-Ge Teşvikleri ve İnovasyon İlişkisi Üzerine Ampirik Bir İnceleme. *Kahramanmaraş Sütçü İmam Üniversitesi Sosyal Bilimler Dergisi*, *16*(2), 686–702. doi:10.33437/ksusbd.533175

Şimşek, M., & Yazıcı, R. (2004). İhracat Teşviklerinin Etkinliğini Ölçmeye Yönelik Bir Analiz: Bilecik Ve Eskişehir Örneği. *Osmangazi Üniversitesi Sosyal Bilimler Dergisi*, *5*(2), 121–140.

Takalo, T., Tanayama, T., & Toivanen, O. (2013). Estimating the Benefits of Targeted R&D Subsidies. *The Review of Economics and Statistics*, *95*(1), 255–272. doi:10.1162/REST_a_00280

Thompson, R. (2009). *Tax policy and the Globalisation of R&D.* The Australian National University Working Papers in Trade and Development, Working Paper No. 2009/03.

Tüylüoğlu, Ş., & Saraç, Ş. (2012). Gelişmiş ve Gelişmekte olan Ülkelerde İnovasyonun Belirleyicileri: Ampirik Bir Analiz. *Eskişehir Osmangazi Üniversitesi İİBF Dergisi*, *7*(1), 39–74.

Wang, J.-C., & Tsai, K.-H. (1998). The Impact of Research and Development Promotion Schemes in the Taiwanese Electronic Component Industry. *R&D Management*, *28*(2), 119–124. doi:10.1111/1467-9310.00088

Yang, C. H., Huang, C. H., & Hou, T. C. T. (2012). Tax Incentives and R&D Activity: Firm-Level Evidence from Taiwan. *Research Policy*, *41*(9), 1578–1588. doi:10.1016/j.respol.2012.04.006

ENDNOTE

1 In the SEGE (2017) report, the provinces are divided into six categories; and the first category consists of the provinces with the best socioeconomic development level, the sixth category consists of the provinces with the worst socioeconomic development level.

Chapter 13
Use of Augmented Reality Technology in Marketing

Ümmü Saliha Eken Inan
https://orcid.org/0000-0001-6442-3000
Selcuk University, Turkey

ABSTRACT

Augmented reality technology is accepted in different fields today. Marketing is one of the areas where this new generation technology is widely used. This technology, which enables customers to gain experience between the virtual world and the real world, regardless of time and place, in order to ensure sustainable purchasing behavior, should be considered as a gateway to the changing world of marketing. In addition to its use in the fields of augmented reality, health, defense, education, engineering, architecture, media, it has also been effective in the acceptance of institutions/organizations, brands, and social media by wider customers/users. Provided that this technology is implemented in all marketing strategies, it contributes to gaining competitive advantage in the market. In this chapter, augmented reality technology will be discussed first. In the rest of the chapter, the application of this technology to marketing strategies will be explained with examples.

INTRODUCTION

The marketing field, which is constantly developing and evolving with innovations, has provided integration with digital instruments while using traditional instruments. At the present time, consumers have come to follow the rapidly changing technology at the same speed, and they have even created a driving force for businesses to adapt to innovations. Of course, different positive/negative events in the world have different reflections on individuals, businesses and societies. Thanks to technology, individuals can be instantly informed about different developments and can change their lifestyles, consumption perceptions and habits accordingly. In particular, some wishes and needs have completely differentiated due to generational difference. At the present time, individuals continue their lives both in the real world and in the virtual world. Individuals/customers who adopt the virtual world and adapt to this technology discovered a dimension closer to reality than virtuality when they met with augmented reality technol-

DOI: 10.4018/978-1-7998-9648-7.ch013

ogy. Augmented reality is a technology that has the potential to facilitate communication and interaction between the physical and digital worlds (Alimamy et al., 2017) that creates value for both customers and businesses.

Augmented reality can be seen as a tool that supports applications in different fields. It requires a clear understanding of technology and technology (Craig, 2013) as a tool that mediates information communication between humans and computers, humans and humans, and computers and humans. The increasing dependence of people on technology has mediated businesses to turn more towards these tools and move customer interactions to these environments in order to gain competitive advantage.

In this context, Augmented Reality (AR); It is a promising technological tool (Rejeb et al., 2021) as well as an environment for expanding consumer experiences that enhances interaction by stimulating consumers' senses, generating positive reactions on consumers through trust, entertainment and enjoyment. Especially in the entertainment industry, users who use virtual reality and are accustomed to virtual environments can grasp the difference between augmented reality and virtual reality. AR uses some of the hardware used in virtual reality and it is as if virtual reality tries to rival the real world, but augmented reality respectfully integrates the real world (Feiner, 2002).

With augmented reality, you can add to the physical world and create a unique consumer experience. Therefore, the use of augmented reality interface in the field of marketing, beyond its use in different sectors, is important for businesses. In line with this importance, applications related to the use of augmented reality technology in the field of marketing will be mentioned in this section. A summary of previous work will be presented and AR will be explained in the study. In addition, applications in the field of marketing will be exemplified.

LITERATURE REVIEW

Javornik (2016), in her study investigating two augmented reality applications and consumer reactions against media features, firstly investigated the role of AR technology and consumer interaction, and then evaluated the measurement elements of perceived magnification in increasing AR applications as a prominent media feature. Interaction on brand websites; evaluated in the context of consumers' cognitive, affective and behavioral responses explained by their online streaming experiences, and stated that the perceived augmentation represents a suitable concept for understanding consumer responses to AR features, while the increase mediates consumers' emotional responses and behavioral intentions.

Yaoyuneyong et al. (2016), in their study on augmented reality marketing, examined consumer preferences and attitudes towards hypermedia print ads. In their study, they determined eight different parameters to compare consumer attitudes and preferences with three different advertising formats. These; attitude towards advertising, informativeness, entertainment, discomfort, advertising value, time-labor, innovation and advertising effectiveness. The ad formats compared are traditional print ad, quick response code (QR) hypermedia print ad (QRH), and augmented reality print ad (ARH). In the study, they concluded that ARH print advertising is effective on consumer attitudes and preferences and creates a perception of more information, innovation and effectiveness.

Seeing augmented reality as a new marketing strategy, Gallordo et al. (2018) state that an application can be created in line with the customers' changing the features they want according to their tastes and needs in their study where they propose the development of an augmented reality application that allows customers to preview the product they want to buy in real time. In the proposal, the application included in a catalog consisting of living room, dining room and bedroom furniture; They offer customers the opportunity to change size, color, texture properties interactively. They state that this will result in the customer taking the leading role and ensuring their full participation.

Ng and Ramasamy (2018) aimed to measure the driving forces of AR and the future trend of AR marketing in their study in Malaysia. They preferred Social, Technological, Environmental, Economic and Political Values (STEEPV), which is a foresight methodology tool, as a method of determining what the driving forces are in AR. Using the impact-uncertainty analysis, they tried to identify the two most important driving forces. As a result, they determined that the *'need for interrelationship between virtual and real'* and *'technological knowledge production'* are the two most important driving forces.

In their study on how different AR applications can improve service brand personality, Plotkina et al. (2021), using the experimental plan, investigated how attitudes towards AR applications and the location and orientation of the AR application contribute to customers' perceptions of brand personality. As a result of the research, it has been determined that applications that are not location-specific and that can be performed virtual trials are evaluated more positively for the customer and the brand is perceived as more exciting, sincere, competent and sophisticated. They also concluded that AR *'apps also improve perceptions of brand personality on innovative and adventure-oriented shoppers'*.

Scholz and Smith (2015) focused on the active and passive components of Augmented Reality in their work. They examined the basic design decisions that managers need to make in planning AR campaigns. In this way, they made suggestions to help marketers realize various consumer interactions. Interactions; they grouped them as user-brand participation, user-user participation and user-bystander participation and presented the actions they defined with the abbreviation ENTANGLE.

Sung (2021), in her study in the USA, wanted to test the effectiveness of AR advertising on two experimental groups in the context of a holiday mobile application. The study investigated consumer interest in AR mobile app ads by measuring shared social experience and purchase intentions. The first experimental group consists of students, and the second experimental group consists of general consumers. As a result, she stated that in AR mobile application ads, immersive new brand experiences turn into positive purchase intentions for both groups and that these experiences are shared in relation to viral marketing behavior as a social experience, resulting in brand approval.

Wang et al. (2015) conducted a study on the purchase of hats by customers from an online shopping site in their study in Taiwan. In the study, an experimental platform with augmented reality function was used, which allows customers to try on hats virtually. The same experiment was compared to another shopping experience that gave participants a choice without using augmented reality technology. However, as a result, it was revealed that the participants preferred to use the augmented reality embedded system.

Bulearca and Tamarjan (2010), in their study on the benefits of Augmented Reality Experiential Marketing (AREM) for brands and companies, stated that it is not only a short-term *'bright target'* sign, but also an experiential marketing form that will provide long-term customer satisfaction. They also concluded that this experience will create customer loyalty/loyalty and increase the purchase intention, and that customers will carry out positive word of mouth (VOM) marketing action.

Scholz and Duffy (2018) investigated the adventure of incorporating the Sephora brand *into the private areas and self-perceptions of consumers* with an application, with the slogan 'We are at home'. Normally AR applications; While it is widely accepted in the public sphere, they tested whether the rate of acceptance in private areas will be less due to privacy/privacy, or whether it will be more accepted in the friendly, familiar, casual and comfortable atmosphere of their homes. Two different themes were used here. While the 'outside-in' effect was taken into account in theme 1, the 'inside-out' effect was taken into account in theme 2. As a result, both ‘outside-in’ and ‘inside-out’ effects have determined that consumers provide a hedonic space that allows them to experience the application fluently and to revive social relations by integrating their own facial features with branded content.

In their study, Hinsch et al. (2020) focused on how AR applications inspire users. Explaining the harmony and the effect of the stimulus, they concluded that the more surprising and wonderful the stimulus is, the greater the harmony, and the more inspiring the experience. Thus, they state that augmented reality applications are inspiring experiences for users.

In their study on how *‘Magic Mirror’* will affect the customer experience as a new augmented reality application, Jovernik et al. (2016) examined the attitudes and feedback of smart device users towards using the *‘magic mirror’* application. The image of a person’s face on the screen of the built-in device used in the study can be used by aligning add-ons such as make-up and accessories, that is, by superimposing them. Unlike other applications, Magic Mirror opens the door to an extraordinary user experience by allowing the camera to face forward, allowing the images to be superimposed on the real rather than the virtual. Users can really feel like they are wearing make-up, the effect looks quite realistic, but they have come to the conclusion that users hesitate for a while as to whether the technique is original or not.

Liao (2014) also shared the applications they created for companies that use augmented reality as a virtual living room solution for retail purposes, at ARE2012, which was realized by the coming together of various sectors. He stated that in past experiments with users placing AR glasses on their faces, a stagnant toy market reached a 17% increase in sales in the same year after the application, as a result of the applications made in the Lego retail store, and that the rate of customers benefiting from technology opportunities is quite high. In the study, it is reported that 210 million copies of the IKEA digital catalog application were distributed and six hundred thousand people used this application to look at furniture.

AUGMENTED REALITY AND AR TECHNOLOGY WITH ITS CONCEPTUAL DIMENSIONS

Augmented reality work was also started by Ivan Sutherland in 1968 as the first virtual reality system and continued with the invention of the first conceptual tablet computer (called Dynabook) by Alan Kay in 1972. Motorola, the first mobile phone, was invented by Dr Martin Cooper in 1973, and the laptop computer was invented in 1982. In 1992, Tom Caudell and David Mizell coined the term ‘augmented reality’ to refer to the superposition of computer-presented material over the real world. In 1993, Loomis and colleagues developed a prototype of an outdoor navigation system for the visually impaired, transforming a notebook into a differential GPS system. receiver and a head-mounted electronic compass (Arth et al., 2015). Years after the AR system was first used, thanks to its primitive prototype in the form of a head-mounted caged head, in the 1980s, it began to be used by the US air force in the analysis of complex systems in areas such as repair and maintenance services of advanced AR systems. In the study carried out by Boeing Corporation with scientists in order to make it easier for workers to assemble wiring harnesses during breakdown and maintenance periods and to prevent errors, the AR system was used effectively thanks to a head-mounted helmet and information transfer to glasses (Feiner, 2002).

Augmented Reality is an experience developed with computer-generated content connected to specific locations/events in the real world (Yuen et al., 2011), allowing virtual images to be superimposed on top of physical objects in real time (Zhou et al., 2008), 3D objects to be created in real time. It is a technology in which 3D is integrated into the real environment (Azuma, 1997). However, unlike virtual reality, augmented reality; allows users to benefit from the interaction of virtual images with real objects in the physical environment. In this way, it can be used in different application areas such as entertainment, medicine, education, art and production. AR is not only capable of producing useful and enjoyable experiences, but can also inspire consumers with the experiences it provides (Hinsch et al., 2020).

The augmented reality system complements the real world with objects created by computers that seem to coexist on the same plane as the real world. AR system has a number of features (Azuma et al., 2001), these are;

- Combines real and virtual objects in a real environment;
- Works interactively and in real time;
- İs expressed as aligning real and virtual objects with each other.

Thanks to AR, which enables the blending of high-quality and rich content with the real world, marketers provide personalized experiences to consumers and support sensory marketing strategies, but not only supports the visual senses, but also activates subliminal triggers, enabling the formation of vivid memories (Rejeb et al., 2021).

Augmented Reality Technology; It is a study area that provides the interaction between the real world and data such as GPS, graphics, audio and video created in the virtual environment (Zachary et al., 1997). In augmented reality, a technology is used that allows the addition of desired digital information to the physical world. It is mentioned about a technology that makes possible a world in which digital information add-ons that increase the physical world are things that cannot normally be seen, heard, felt or touched (Craig, 2013).

Thanks to this technology, it is possible to decide how to position the shelves in an empty store, how to group the products, which in-store arrangement will provide a more enjoyable shopping experience for the customer, and more arrangements can be made. The store can be painted in different colors, browsed through the store, canceled all edits and rearranged. Trials can be carried out until the most pleasant shopping atmosphere is achieved. Besides, thanks to AR technology, a mechanic can see instructions on how to repair defective equipment, a surgeon can obtain X-ray images of a patient during surgery, firefighters can avoid invisible dangers in a burning building, soldiers can see enemy positions with the help of drones, or a computer gamer. he can fight aliens on his way to work (Feiner, 2002).

In augmented reality technology, high-performance computers and mobile devices with android or IOS operating systems are needed, which will enable the production of data in three dimensions and computer aided, as well as the synchronized production of images with intense details and projected onto the user screen (Bilici and Özdemir, 2020). Thanks to the screens (HMDS), smart glasses, laptop computers, and barcode readers attached to the users' heads, a small image or a stored information, visual can be accessed. HDMS devices; they are in two categories as optical transparent and video transition (Feiner, 2002). These technologies are called 'head-ups' and are used by fighter jet/race car pilots. In addition, similar features are used in new generation vehicles.

In augmented reality technology, there is a need for software interfaces that will bring together the augmented environment and the real environment. The software infrastructure is image recognition-based such as data matrix, logo, labels, and wireless network connections are global positioning tracking-based systems compatible with 4.5G technology. Today, thanks to smart phones/tablets with data matrix and/or barcode reader applications, it is possible to access information stored on restaurants, printed publications and visual servers.

Augmented reality applications have become widely available on portable and mobile devices, such that in audio-visual media; news, entertainment, sports, and other aspects of our lives, especially in areas such as electronic commerce, travel, and marketing (Yuen et al., 2011). In addition, wearable technologies in AR applications such as smart lenses, smart watches and rabbit eyes, which are called Rabbit Eye, are seen as the most exciting developments in this technology. Platforms that provide AR services to brands, such as Blippar, offer an interactive digital experience that enables seeing every material or object in the real environment, three-dimensional animations, campaigns, coupons and sweepstakes via IOS/Android phones and tablets without scanning or taking a picture of it (Küçüksaraç & Sayımer, 2016).

THE USE OF AUGMENTED REALITY TECHNOLOGY IN MARKETING

Augmented reality is used in many fields such as education, medicine, tourism, architecture, city planning, sports, mapping, etc. Since the marketing field is a constantly changing and developing field that requires constant interaction with people, augmented reality has become an indispensable tool of this field with its different combinations. In fact, the concept of AR in the literature has begun to be considered as a marketing method on its own, and this is called Augmented Reality Marketing (ARM). AR marketing can enhance and expand on traditional marketing approaches ranging from advertising to content marketing to storytelling. In this sense, AR marketing can be applied to technologies provided by businesses, such as virtual mirrors in stores, or to mobile devices such as tablets or smart glasses provided by users (Rauschnabel et al., 2019).

Augmented Reality Marketing (ARM) is a customer-facing interface for the application of digital marketing technologies in physical environments, a unique set of digital possibilities that it offers beyond existing marketing approaches in traditional media, starting from the theory of *'embedded cognition'* (Chylinski et al., 2020). Rauschnabel et al. (2019) define augmented reality marketing as a strategic concept that integrates digital information or objects into the subject's physical world, often together with other media, to reveal, express or demonstrate consumer benefits to achieve corporate goals.

Businesses that want to maintain their market shares in an intensely competitive environment must adapt to the continuous change in the external environment (Gümrah et al., 2021). In the field of marketing, AR technology comes to life in different applications. To list them briefly (Bilici, 2015);

- Gamification with augmented reality
- Face, body recognition, virtual mirror applications in the retail industry
- Augmented reality applications in the automotive industry
- Augmented reality applications in furniture and decoration industry
- Augmented reality applications in the field of advertising
- Augmented reality applications in tourism marketing, appears as.

Gamification (Gamification with Augmented Reality Technology)

In gamification carried out on mobile platforms; Labeling retail products has the potential to entertain customers, encourage and accelerate repurchase, retain customers, and contribute to in-store interaction (Hofacker et al., 2016). In the gamification process, users point their mobile devices or iPads towards the digital content brochures, application compatible packaging or product, leading to the game. It is

Figure 1. Sturbucks cup magic for Valentine's Day
Source: Smashapp, 2011 *Date of access:12.01.2022*

an application used by businesses that want to attract the attention of customers who are bored with routine applications, and to differentiate their products, brands and promotions with different applications, to provide customer experience and to increase their visibility on social platforms. In this regard, Mc Donalds' Monopoly, Café Crown's gamification with Selçuk Erdem through Blippar, Starbucks' "Sturbucks Cup Magic", "Sturbucks Cup Magic for Valentine's Day" applications are the most popular gamifications. Of course, here, brands realize both the level of entertainment and rewarding in order to increase interaction. When users participate in these applications, they also have experiences and gains such as coupons, rewards and entertainment.

Face, Body Recognition, Virtual Mirror Applications in the Retail İndustry

When it is mentioned, the first thing that comes to mind is the "*Magic Mirror*" applications. Magic mirror; It is the form of taking the image of a person's face or body, which appears on the screen, in motion, from different angles, through the camera typically used for a video conference, and superimposing add-ons such as make-up, clothing, accessories, glasses on these images (Jovernik et al., 2016), aligning them. is defined. This is magic or illusion; It begins with the perception of a person's facial features in a two-dimensional, motion-sensitive lens. AR face recognition application was first realized by the AR virtual make-up technology provider ModiFace with the SEPHORA brand in 2014 (Tidy, n.d.).

The products subject to shopping can be applied with the help of a 3D augmented reality mirror that can be simulated on the user in real time and in three dimensions. There are examples of the application in different brands. Brands such as GAP, Shiseido, Flormar, Ray-Ban, Burberry, Lacoste, Sephora offer this application to their customers.

Augmented Reality Applications in the Automotive İndustry

İt is an application that allows accessing three-dimensional images of vehicles, adding desired modules, changing from the color of the vehicle to its accessories, configuring, and synchronizing devices with iOS/Android features on digital catalogs. In addition, among the technical features of the vehicles, AR compatible options with Head-up-Display feature and reflected on the glass can be offered. In most vehicles, there are assistant applications that increase the driving quality with the assistant application,

Figure 2. Sephora 3D augmented reality application
Source: Tidy, n.d., Accessed: 11.01.2022

360-degree vision with in-car cameras, and enhancement applications that detect driver features. Many brands such as Mercedes, Tesla, Audi, Ferrari, BMW, Volvo, Range Rover are leading this practice in the sector. With AR target guidance; images such as pre-turn, driving maneuver, and house numbers can be included.

Augmented Reality Applications in Furniture and Decoration İndustry

People give importance to the decoration of their homes in the same way they give importance to clothes, accessories, cosmetics and their appearance. The presence of objects that will reflect themselves in every place they live is the beauty that appeals to the souls of people rather than the beauty added to the interiors. Harmony is also important for spaces. An inappropriate furniture or accessory may cause deterioration of the ambiance. However, it may not always be easy for consumers to change furniture, likewise, it may not be possible to meet this demand of customers who come with a request to change furniture that has been purchased for furniture dealers and that has not adapted to their homes. Therefore,

Figure 3. Mercedes AR catalog

Figure 4. Mercedes bike AR catalog
Sources:https://www.campaigntr.com/mercedes-benzden-arac-aksesuarlari-icin-artirilmis-gerceklik-uygulamasi/Access Date: 11.01.2022.

in the furniture and decoration industry, AR technology, which enables customers to see virtual interior design ideas in real time, can increase mutual satisfaction and reduce costs.

The first initiative in this regard was started by IKEA, and then many brands from furniture to accessories offered this application to their customers.

Augmented Reality Applications in Advertising

Advertising, which is the sub-component of the promotion strategy from the marketing mix elements, has many functional features such as giving information about the product, attracting the attention of potential customers, showing the difference from competing products and services, creating a brand image and spreading brand slogans. Augmented Reality ads convey context-sensitive information but do so in a way that provides users with an enjoyable and interactive experience (Sung & Cho, 2012).

Figure 5. IKEA AR application
Source: Artırılmış Gerçeklik, 2017 Access date: 12.01.2022

Figure 6. Coca Cola advertisement

While the messages that are created convey information, they also provide interaction on the product, the benefits that the product will provide from purchasing, its difference from the equivalent products, the formation of the intention of the customers to prefer that product, that is, the acquisition of a positive purchasing attitude. In addition, they include some social messages and issues that will raise awareness, in accordance with the understanding of social marketing. When Picture 6 is examined, the social message can be understood.

Picture 6 shows an augmented reality advertisement designed in collaboration with Coca-Cola and WWF. This ad was presented in the Arctic Home Campaign in collaboration with Coca-Cola and WWF. The campaign launched to protect polar bears and their habitats has real-time awareness raising experience with augmented reality technology (Ergün, 2018) at the Science Museum in London.

Figure 7. Domestos advertisement
Source: *WWF International, 2013.*
Access date: 12.01.2022

Figure 8. Edirne Selimiye Mosque
Source: SOLVOTEK, 2017, Access date: 12.01.2022

Augmented Reality Applications in Tourism Marketing

The tourism sector is a complex structure that includes different sub-fields in itself. The main purpose of tourism enterprises is to provide the highest income (Garda, 2014). Tourism marketing differs from traditional product and service marketing. Because providing an authentic, fun, educational and informative experience in tourism involves a delicate balance, augmented reality needs to provide an unobtrusive experience that delivers the right amount of information (Cranmer et al., 2020). The range of products and services in tourism is also wide. Many types of tourism can be counted, such as cultural tourism, art tourism, winter tourism, sports tourism, health tourism, congress tourism. Tourists need driving forces that will influence their decision making with such a wide range of products. Before traveling for tourism purposes, the historical texture, natural beauties, gastronomic richness, promotion of activities, accommodation and transportation opportunities as well as the experience offered by three-dimensional augmented reality applications will also be effective in their purchasing decision.

CONCLUSION

The plane between virtuality and reality has been populated more closely by computer-generated objects since the day Pokémon Go entered human life. As technology advances, the alignment between augmented reality and the real world begins to fade and become astonishing.

Maintaining our presence in the real world and having fun, learning, playing games or socializing in virtual worlds; shows that virtual reality technology is limited to games and simulations used in different fields. Today, we experience the augmented reality of objects created by computers connected to specific locations in the real world. These experiences are systems that require a three-dimensional infrastructure and are compatible with them. Applications appear in different fields. It can be used in health, science, art, sports, education, marketing, etc. Since marketing is an area that requires constant interaction with customers, different augmented reality applications are encountered in the sector.

Brands; They use AR effectively to provide the best customer experience and increase their brand value. While some brands use AR glasses, wearable technology, and wearable headgear, some brands can create more customer value by including their customers in the design experience. These increases are important not only for differentiation, but also because they will contribute to both the reduction of costs and the growth of the target market. While AR technology continues to exist in the entertainment sector, it also makes a name for itself with different applications in the decoration, fashion, cosmetics, automotive and tourism sectors.

Businesses with hardware and software infrastructures adapt quickly to this technology and implement various applications. One of the most important marketing strategies for an industry is the promotion strategy. AR applications reduce advertising costs and provide greater visibility with real-time experiences. These applications are also effective in the emergence of innovative ideas, as they allow customers to design their own products.

The purchasing decision is a painful dimension for some customers, but with AR applications, real-time face and body recognition and magic mirror applications can shorten the decision process of customers. The same is true for home decoration products. Since the harmony of the products and their stance in the space can be monitored in real time, and also the opportunity to try different color options at the same time, customer satisfaction increases.

One of our most basic needs is the need to eat and drink. Thanks to AR applications that allow us to see the digital menu, choose the ingredients, and capture the real portion size, we gain the experience of accessing the right information at the right time. In addition, the existence of AR technology applied for properties subject to real estate marketing shows that this technology is effectively utilized in all areas of marketing.

REFERENCES

Arth, C., Gruber, L., Grasset, R., Langlotz, T., Mulloni, A., Schmalstieg, D., & Wagner, D. (2015). *The history of mobile augmented reality. In Developments in mobile AR over the last almost 50 years, Inst.* For Computer Graphics and Vision Graz University of Technology.

Azuma, R. T. (1997). A survey of augmented reality. *Presence*, *6*(4), 355–385. doi:10.1162/pres.1997.6.4.355

Azuma, R., Baillot, Y., Behringer, R., Feiner, S., Julier, S., & MacIntyre, B. (2001). Recent advances in augmented reality. *IEEE Computer Graphics and Applications*, *21*(6), 34–47. doi:10.1109/38.963459

Alimamy, S., Deans, K. R., & Gnoth, J. (2017). ' Augmented reality: Uses and future considerations in marketing. In R. Benlamri & M. Sparer (Eds.), *Leadership, Innovation and Entrepreneurship as Driving Forces of Global Economy. Springer Proceedings in Business and Economics* (pp. 705–712). Springer. doi:10.1007/978-3-319-43434-6_62

Bilici, F. (2015). *Pazarlamada artırılmış gerçeklik ve karekod teknolojileri:Tüketicilerin artırılmış gerçeklik teknoloji algılamaları üzerine bir alan araştırması*. Yüksek Lisans Tezi, Uludağ Üniversitesi Sosyal Bilimler Enstitüsü.

Bilici, F., & Özdemir, E. (2020). Tüketicilerin artırılmış gerçeklik teknolojilerini kullanma niyeti üzerinde teknolojik hazır bulunuşluğun rolü. *International Social Mentality and Researcher Thinkers Journal, 6*(37), 2046–2060. doi:10.31576mryj.669

Bulearca, M., & Tamarjan, D. (2010). Augmented reality: A sustainable marketing tool? *Global Business and Management Research, 2/3*, 237–252.

Chylinski, M., Heller, J., Hilken, T., Keeling, I. D., Mahr, D., & de Ruyter, K. (2020). Augmented reality marketing: A technology-enabled approach to situated customer experience. *Australasian Marketing Journal, 28*(4), 374–384. doi:10.1016/j.ausmj.2020.04.004

Craig, A. B. (2013). Understanding Augmented Reality. Morgan Kaufmann.

Cranmer, E. E., Dieck, M.C.T., & Fountoulaki, P. (2020). Exploring the value of augmented reality for tourism. *Tourism Management Perspective, 35.*

Ergün, F. (2018). *Artırılmış gerçeklik reklam sektörünü nasıl etkiler?* https://fikretergunblog.wordpress.com/2018/03/13/artirilmis-gerceklik-reklam-sektorunu-nasil-etkiler/

Feiner, S. K. (2002). Augmented Reality: A New Way of Seeing. *Scientific American, 286*(4), 48–55. https://www.jstor.org/stable/26059641)

Gallardo, C., Rodriguez, S. P., Chango, I. E., Quevedo, W. X., Santana, J., Acosta, A. G., Tapia, J. C., & Andaluz, V. H. (2018). Augmented reality as a new marketing strategy. *International Conference on Augmented Reality, Virtual Reality and Computer Graphics*, 351-362. 10.1007/978-3-319-95270-3_29

Garda, B. (2014). *Macera turizmi pazarlaması, özel ilgi turizminin yeni yüzü*. Çizhi Kitabevi.

Gümrah, A., İnan, Ü.S.E., & Garda, B. (2021). Hizmet pazarlaması ve muhasebe verileri: Turizm işletmelerinde bir uygulama. In Sosyal, Beşeri ve İdari Bilimler Alanında Uluslararası Araştırmalar VIII. Eğitim Yayınevi.

Hinsch, C., Felix, R., & Rauschnabel, P. A. (2020). Nostalgia beats the wow-effect: Inspiration, awe and meaningful associations in augmented reality marketing. *Journal of Retailing and Consumer Services, 53*, 101987. doi:10.1016/j.jretconser.2019.101987

Hofacker, C. F., de Ruyter, K., Lurie, N. H., Manchanda, P., & Donaldson, J. (2016). Gamification and mobile marketing effectiveness. *Journal of Interactive Marketing, 34*, 25–36. doi:10.1016/j.intmar.2016.03.001

Javornik, A. (2016). 'It's an illusion, but it looks real!' Consumer affective, cognitive and behavioural responses to augmented reality applications. *Journal of Marketing Management, 32*(9-10), 987-1011.

Javornik, A., Rogers, Y., Moutinho, A. M., & Freeman, R. (2016). Revealing the Shopper Experience of Using a "Magic Mirror" Augmented Reality Make-Up Application. *DIS '16: Proceedings of the 2016 ACM Conference on Designing*. 10.1145/2901790.2901881

Küçüksaraç, B., & Sayımer, İ. (2016). Deneyimsel pazarlama aracı olarak artırılmış gerçeklik: Türkiye'deki marka deneyimlerinin etkileri üzerine bir araştırma. İstanbul Üniversitesi İletişim Fakültesi Dergisi, 2, 73-95.

Liao, T. (2014). Augmented or admented reality? The influence of marketing on augmented reality technologies. *Information Communication and Society*, *18*(3), 310–326. doi:10.1080/1369118X.2014.989252

Ng, C. C. & Ramasamy, C. (2018). Augmented Reality Marketing in Malaysia- Future Scenarios. *Social Sciences, 7*(11).

Plotkina, D., Dinsmore, J., & Racat, M. (2021). Improving service brand personality with augmented reality marketing. *Journal of Services Marketing*. https://www.emerald.com/insight/content/doi/10.1108/JSM-12-2020-0519/full/html#abstract

Rauschnabel, P. A., Felix, R., & Hinsch, C. (2019). Augmented reality marketing: How mobile AR-apps can improve brands through inspiration. *Journal of Retailing and Consumer Services*, *49*, 43–53. doi:10.1016/j.jretconser.2019.03.004

Rejeb, A., Rejeb, K., & Treibimaier, H. (2021). How augmented reality impacts retail marketing: A state-of-the-art review from a consumer perspective. *Journal of Strategic Marketing*, 1–31. doi:10.1080/0965254X.2021.1972439

Scholz, J., & Smith, A. N. (2015). Augmented reality: Designing immersive experiences that maximize consumer engagement. *Business Horizons*, *59*(2), 149–161. doi:10.1016/j.bushor.2015.10.003

Scholz, J., & Duffy, K. (2018). We are at home: How augmented reality reshapes mobile marketing and consumer-brand relationships. *Journal of Retailing and Consumer Services*, *44*, 11–23. doi:10.1016/j.jretconser.2018.05.004

Sung, E. C. (2021). The effects of augmented reality mobile app advertising: Viral marketing via shared social experience. *Journal of Business Research*, *122*, 75–87. doi:10.1016/j.jbusres.2020.08.034

Sung, J., & Cho, K. (2012). User experiences with augmented reality advertising applications: Focusing on perceived values and telepresence based on the experiential learning theory. *Human Centric Technology and Service in Smart Space*, *182*, 9–15. doi:10.1007/978-94-007-5086-9_2

Yaoyuneyong, G., Foster, J., Johnson, E., & Johnson, D. (2016). Augmented reality marketing: Consumer preferences and attitudes toward hypermedia print ads. *Journal of Interactive Advertising*, *16*(1), 16–30. doi:10.1080/15252019.2015.1125316

Yuen, S. C. Y., Yaoyuneyong, G., & Johnson, E. (2011). Augmented reality: An overview and five directions for AR in education. *Journal of Educational Technology Development and Exchange, 4*(1).

Wang, C.-H., Chiang, Y.-C., & Wang, M.-J. (2015). Evaluation of an augmented reality embedded on-line shopping system. *Procedia Manufacturing*, *3*, 5624–5630. doi:10.1016/j.promfg.2015.07.766

Zachary, W., Ryder, J., Hicinbothom, J., & Bracken, K. (1997). The use of executable cognitive models in simulation- based intelligent embedded training. *Proceeding of the Human Factors and Ergonomics Society Annual Meeting*, 41(2), 1118-1122. 10.1177/107118139704100287

Zhou, F., Duh, H. B.-L., & Billinghurst, M. (2008). Trends in augmented reality tracking, interaction and display: A review of ten years of ISMAR. *7th IEEE/ACM International Symposium on Mixed and Augmented Reality (ISMAR).*

Gerçeklik, A. (2017). IKEA Place Uygulamasıyla Eşyaları Evinizin İçinde Görün. *Dijital Ajanslar*. Retrieved from https://www.dijitalajanslar.com/ikeanin-artirilmis-gerceklik-uygulamasiyla-esyalari-evinizin-icinde-gorun/

Smashapp. (2011). *Starbucks Cup Magic*. YouTube. https://www.youtube.com/watch?v=n7dEshkTri4

Tidy, J. (n.d.). Sephora+ModiFace Launch The World's First 3D Augmented Reality Mirror in Milan. *PRWeb*. Retrieved from http://www.prweb.com/pdfdownload/11881669.pdf

Türkiye, C. (2012). *Mercedes Benz'den araç aksesuarları için artırılmış gerçeklik uygulaması*. Retrieved from https://www.campaigntr.com/mercedes-benzden-arac-aksesuarlari-icin-artirilmis-gerceklik-uygulamasi/

WWF International. (2013). *WWF - Coca-Cola Arctic Home Campaign - Augmented Reality | WWF*. Youtube. Retrieved from https://www.youtube.com/watch?v=h2Jg8ryVk1k&list=RDCMUC5MDIy3yhWDrx0MyDo4QmYg https://www.webtekno.com/sektorel/domestos-sanal-gerceklik-reklami-h7409.html

SOLVOTEK. (2017). *Selimiye Camii, Edirne 3D lazer tarama (nokta bulutu animasyonu)*. YouTube. Retrieved from https://www.youtube.com/watch?v=b9OltaxADgU

ADDITIONAL READING

Barhorst, J. B., McLean, G., Shah, E., & Mack, R. (2021). Blending the real World and the virtual World: Exploring the role of flow in augmented reality experiences. *Journal of Business Research*, *122*, 423–436. doi:10.1016/j.jbusres.2020.08.041

Wedel, M., Bigne, E., & Zhang, J. (2020). Virtual and augmented reality: Advancing research in consumer marketing. *International Journal of Research in Marketing*, *37*(3), 443–465. doi:10.1016/j.ijresmar.2020.04.004

Chapter 14
Sustainable Tourism and the COVID-19 Crisis

Betül Garda
https://orcid.org/0000-0002-2406-6448
Social Science Vocational School, Selcuk University, Turkey

ABSTRACT

Sustainable tourism is an approach in which the environment is protected from deterioration and change and cultural integrity, ecological process, biological diversity, and life support systems are maintained. Resources are managed so that the needs of hosts and tourists are met and that future generations can meet the same needs. Sustainable tourism is expected to minimize the negative effects of tourism development on society and the environment and to have an impact on the local economy, the preservation of natural and cultural heritage, and the quality of life of hosts and visitors through tourism. The concept of "sustainable tourism" focuses on the principles that should be adopted while carrying out activities for the development of different types of tourism.

INTRODUCTION

Tourism, which has a dynamic structure, is a strong industry that adapts rapidly to the changes that occur as a result of globalization and technological developments and provides great contributions to the economy of countries such as employment opportunities, productivity increase and foreign exchange inflow. The tourism sector, along with petrochemistry and automotive, is among the three sectors that generate the highest income in the world economy (Bezirgan & Bezirgan, 2021: 1). Therefore, the tourism industry is an important competitive tool that should be considered in terms of sustainable development.

The understanding of the global village consisting of a single and large world market, which gained momentum with the liberalization in world markets, has increased the interdependence of countries. Therefore, political instability, terrorist incidents, epidemics or climate crises that occur in any region as a result of intense industrialization cause a crisis in the whole world economy. The crisis, which we can describe as a loss of order resulting from any reason, can uncontrollably change all the balances in the regions under its influence. Therefore, it has devastating effects on the tourism industry, which is open to

DOI: 10.4018/978-1-7998-9648-7.ch014

environmental changes, has a complex and fragile economic structure. The tourism industry has to implement emergency plans in order not to disturb the balance in every crisis period with a massive impact.

In addition to the epidemics caused by the SARS, MERS, EBOLA viruses that emerged in previous years, the negative effects caused by the COVID-19 epidemic, which started to show its effect in late December 2019, affected the whole world. In this period of economic crisis and uncertainty, both health and marketing-oriented measures to be applied in terms of tourism businesses are very important for the continuity of the sector and to overcome the crisis with the least damage. Although the crisis has devastating effects, it can be overcome by turning threats into opportunities as a result of a professional management approach and the implementation of effective strategies (Çeti & Ünlüönen, 2019:110).

In times of crisis, marketing strategies should be redefined according to consumer expectations and emergency measures. When tourism businesses make the necessary arrangements in their marketing components with the awareness of the emergency, they can overcome the crisis period harmlessly and even increase their profitability levels. Achieving this success depends on the careful examination of consumer behavior during the crisis (Köylüoğlu et al., 2020), the realistic determination of external environmental conditions, and the effective implementation of emergency plans.

The biggest threat faced by tourism enterprises during economic crisis periods is that the income obtained from the activities of the enterprise is lower than the total costs, which are compulsory expenses for creating touristic products (Erol, 2008: 153). When it comes to reducing costs, the first limitation that comes to mind is to reduce the marketing and advertising budgets that damage the corporate image. the other hand, in order to combat the crisis, it is a more rational alternative to develop alternative tourism types with fixed customer potential such as sports tourism, accessible tourism, green tourism, thermal tourism, cultural tourism and congress tourism and protect their tourism potential.

The crisis, which started in late December 2019 due to the COVID-19 epidemic and affected the whole world, has put the tourism industry in a great impasse due to local and international travel restrictions, curfews, the cessation of the activities of food and beverage (Aydın & Doğan, 2020).

In 2019, the contribution of tourism to the world economy was 10.9% of GDP and about 30% of exports. The tourism industry has had a significant impact on the development of related industries due to its feature of providing services in connection with other sectors. 1.5 billion people participated in tourism events in 2019, hence the direct, indirect and multiplier effects of the travel and tourism industry accounted for 10.3% of global GDP (US$ 8.9 trillion). According to UNWTO, as of October 2020, 100% of destinations worldwide have travel restrictions related to Covid-19. According to the World Tourism Organization, the number of international international arrivals decreased by 70% in the first eight months of 2020. The most significant decrease in arrivals from abroad was observed in the Asia-Pacific region in January-April 2020 as 51%. This was followed by Europe with 44%, Middle East 40%, America 36% and Africa 35%. It has been noted that the losses in tourism revenues in this context are 730 billion dollars, which is more than eight times the losses suffered by the tourism sector in 2009 due to the global economic and financial crisis (UNWTO, 2020).

This crisis, which still continues to negatively affect international tourism despite vaccination efforts, has made it necessary for the tourism industry to develop measures to ensure sustainability. Based on the logic that every crisis contains certain opportunities, the COVID-19 pandemic may also be an opportunity for the tourism industry to become more sustainable (Muller, 2021). The Sustainability Leaders Project (Florian, 2020) argues that for sustainability, the COVID-19 crisis is a positive development in the tourism industry that will result in a rethinking of the management of oversaturated destinations, better communication and stronger implementation of online communication. Tourism business managers who are quick to implement organizational change can take advantage of this crisis and turn crisis learning into strategies and actions to build more resilient and sustainable businesses. Moreover, at the country level, the crisis can be regarded as an opportunity to design specific policies that support and promote sustainability in tourism.

The tourism industry has always been affected by natural, political and economic crises. For this reason, tactics and strategies have been developed over the years to ensure sustainability and alleviate the consequences of the crisis. However, the crisis caused by the Covid-19 pandemic is different and unique in many ways. Due to this crisis, primarily, a decrease is observed in the activities of travel, hotel management and related tourism businesses all over the world. Secondly, the ongoing crisis is causing radical changes in many tourism segments. In addition, due to the complexity of predicting pandemic development, it is difficult to analyze the future status and development of the tourism industry (Ritchie & Jiang, 2019).

Today, while the Covid-19 epidemic continues, first problems that governments should urgently address is to determine the severity of the economic recession caused by Covid-19. Secondly; The rapid creation of growth and recovery scenarios is to be addressed. Finally, is determine whether the developing crisis will have a long-term structural effect and to create precautionary packages (World Commission on Environment and Development, 1987). The pandemic created by COVID-19 has been changed the tourism industry and the environments in which it operates. Measures taken within the framework of the protection of social health and differentiating business models will carry the service quality to different dimensions in the tourism sector and make sustainability permanent after the crisis (Higgins-Desbiolles, 2020).

The restriction of travel at the global level in the COVID-19 epidemic has positively affected the natural environment by reducing greenhouse gas emissions that cause destruction in nature. In this context, the pandemic has created an opportunity to redesign sustainable tourism models. However, a more responsible and sustainable approach to tourism will be possible by redefining social rights and benefits, not because of a pandemic that shook the world (Abbas et al., 2021). In the light of the experiences gained from the crisis, tourism stakeholders should approach sensitive issues such as environmental destruction due to excessive tourism, economic exploitation, overpopulation and climate change with more sensitive sustainable development models. The challenge facing the tourism industry is an opportunity to navigate the crisis towards sustainable tourism transformation (Gössling et al., 2020). However, when the restriction is lifted, it is possible that the sensitivity of tourism stakeholders to social and environmental issues will disappear in order to regain their economic power. Because small and medium-sized tourism enterprises, which are sensitive to actions based on sustainability and social benefit, will not be able to support the change of their business models with a sustainable approach without the incentives of the governments (Elliott, 2020). As a result, this recent COVID-19 global crisis shows that the tourism industry is obliged to develop a long-term sustainable vision that considers social and environmental factors. Otherwise, problems such as climate change and health crises may bring recurrent risks and bring the global economy to a point of no return.

CONCEPT OF SUSTAINABLE TOURISM

Sustainability is a complex concept with many dimensions. The concept of sustainability, which is used in many ecological, social, political, health and economic fields, has become a concept that should be given more importance since the 1970s. Mass tourism, which increased its speed with the effect of globalization and technological development, and heavy industries that developed after the industrial revolution, in addition to the benefits they provide, have begun to threaten the lives of future generations by causing destruction on the environment. The deterioration resulting from rapid population growth and excessive consumption of natural resources has made it necessary to protect the environment and has created a reaction against excessive and unconscious consumption. In this context, sustainability is defined as "meeting today's needs without harming the living standards of future generations". Sustainability, which literally means "to sustain, to nurture", is the protection of resources in order to continue to meet our unlimited needs and desires with scarce resources in the world. In this context, people and the environment form the focal point of sustainability (WCED, 1987: 43).

Sustainable Development is the raising of living standards, as well as the activation of the use of environmental resources and the continuity of this improvement. Sustainable development is programming the life of today in a way that will allow the needs of future generations to be met by establishing a balance between human and nature. The necessity of environmental protection for sustainable development was first emphasized at the Stockholm Conference in 1972, which Turkey also attended. Later, in the report prepared by the International Union for Conservation of Natural Resources (IUCN) in 1980, by the United Nations Commission in 1983, and by the World Commission on Environmental Development in 1987, attention was drawn to the concept of sustainability, and it was aimed to maintain the harmony between human and environment by preparing strategic plans for sustainable development on a global scale. These studies contribute to the development of international cooperation and coordination (UNWTO, n.d.).

In 1992, the United Nations held the Environment and Development Conference called the Rio Summit with 172 countries and 17 thousand participants. In the conference, national governments agreed on environmental issues within the framework of "restructuring the world economic system according to the principles of sustainable development in which ecological values are protected". In addition, plans were made to implement the solutions produced with the financial support of organizations such as the United Nations and the World Bank (Butler, 1999).

At the United Nations World Sustainable Development Summit in 2002; Issues such as biodiversity, the impact of globalization on countries, inequalities in income distribution were discussed, and joint decisions were made on issues such as protection of natural resources, development of democracy and balanced income distribution on a global scale. Sustainable development studies is focus on the relationship between human and environment and strategies are developed within the framework of the following objectives (Agca, n.d.):

- Creating a new vision for global development
- To improve the conditions of use of ecosystems that are likely to be degraded and depleted.
- Increasing the welfare level of developing countries
- Ensuring coordination between the public and private sectors
- To take the necessary measures to ensure that future generations have quality living standards.

Sustainability in tourism, which is one of the largest industries in the world, today and in the future potential tourists's; It is the tourism plan and principles that include the measures to be taken so that they can continue to meet their needs and wishes such as curiosity, information, learning, entertainment, rest and getting away from the monotony of daily life (Bahar & Kozak, 2005).

According to World Tourism Organization (UNWTO, 1998) sustainable tourism; It defines it as "resource management planning by considering the continuation of biological diversity and vital systems while the tourism industry responds to current and potential demands today and in the future". The environmental damage caused by excessive resource use has made the sustainability of tourism a matter of discussion. After the 1990s, alternative solutions have been started to be determined for a tourism development that does not harm the ecological system.

The purposes that form the basis of Sustainable Tourism can be listed as follows (Sustainable Tourism for Development Guidebook, 2013):

- Sustainable use of resources: As a result of the sustainable use of resources, the understanding of providing long-term benefits will be adopted and the environment will be protected in the long term.
- Conservation and maintenance of biological, cultural and social diversity: Ecological diversity will ensure that regions receive a share from tourism in the long term. The point to be considered here is that tourism activities can adapt to different cultural identities. Otherwise, the economic benefit that the region expects from tourism may need to be spent on resolving the damages that may arise due to cultural conflict. As a result, tourism may lose its source over time and sustainability may disappear.
- Preventing excessive consumption of biological, cultural and social resources and reducing waste, thus preventing long-term environmental damage: Reducing the rate of excessive consumption and industrial waste will reduce the costs that will occur due to environmental destruction in the long term. In addition, it increases the quality of tourism services. Planning, considering the touristic carrying capacities of the regions, will provide economic benefits in the long run.
- Protection of social and cultural identity: Social and cultural identity is the source of tourism and the reason for touristic activities in the region. It is an indispensable element for the realization of sustainable development. The corruption that will emerge in societies that have lost their cultural identity will cause irreparable damage in every respect and future generations will face the danger of extinction.
- Including tourism in the development plans of the countries: Environmental impact assessments will be made and solutions for possible problems will be put forward with the inclusion of tourism in the development plans of the countries. Thus, the long-term sustainability of tourism will be ensured. Observing the change in the social environment and making the plans in accordance with the conditions will increase the quality of tourism in the long run and minimize the damages it causes.
- Supporting local economies by including them in planning: Tourism provides benefits such as foreign currency input to local economic development, incentives for new investments, new employment opportunities and high-income levels. In addition, by preventing the dangers such as planned tourism activities, environmental wear caused by excessive capacity use, and depletion of resources, the values that contribute economically to local economies are secured.
- Training and informing personnel in order to ensure that the local people receive a share from tourism: The realization of promotional and training activities for the local people in cooperation with the public and private sectors will create social synergy. As a result of education and promotional activities, local people will look at tourism from a more positive perspective, their self-confidence will increase as an educated employee, and their income level and living standards

will increase with the creation of new job opportunities. Sustainable tourism will make a positive contribution to providing individual freedom by informing the local community.

- Ensuring coordination between the tourism industry and the public within the framework of a responsible tourism approach: The share to be taken from the tourism industry can be increased with an effective coordination between the society, public and private institutions. It will be easier evaluate the opportunities that can provide economic benefits and prevent possible threats by conducting joint studies.
- Planning of responsive tourism: Social marketing understanding will be beneficial in establishing a balance between the ecological elements of the region. As a result of the harmonious activities that emerged, visitor satisfaction will increase and positive contributions will be made to the reputation of the region. The point to be considered here is to prevent the increase in the number of visitors as a result of positive opinions from causing excessive capacity use.

CURRENT STATE OF TOURISM INDUSTRY ON COVID-19 PANDEMİC

The tourism industry, which is extremely susceptible to epidemics, has been severely affected by SARS (2003), MERS (2012), EBOLA (2014) and today the COVID-19 crises (Guerava & Richards, 2019). Outbreaks have an immediate impact on the tourism industry and are also long-term. The epidemic reduces tourism demand as soon as it occurs and continues after the severity of the disease decreases. The impact of the epidemic has devastating effects both for tourists who are concerned about their safety and because of the restrictions imposed by countries with tourist attractions. Thus, epidemics negatively affect economic development, reduce people's income and lead to a decrease in their ability to spend on tourism. The impact of epidemics varies depending on the psychological characteristics of the tourism market, behavioral patterns, economic conditions and geographical location. This shows that tourism destinations should have a clearer and different orientation for each segment of the market that is suitable for them in different epidemic times.

Restrictions on tourism services implemented by countries to combat epidemics threaten the existence of tourism businesses. This situation obliges the tourism enterprises to implement the precautionary packages aimed at reducing the layoff and marketing costs. Therefore, it causes a decrease in employment in the tourism industry in the long run, and affects the sustainability of the tourism industry by bringing along disruptions in the supply and distribution system as a chain reaction.

The impact of an epidemic on the tourism industry; varies depending on the severity, size and duration of the epidemic. It may take years for the tourism industry to return to normal conditions after a global pandemic. For example, it took two years for countries affected by the SARS 2003 outbreak to normalize their tourism activities (Guerava & Richards, 2019). The COVID-19 outbreak has a global impact and new versions are constantly emerging. The COVID-19 pandemic not only reduces the mobility of potential tourists, but also causes local people to view tourists as potential spreaders of disease and do not want them in their resorts.

The experience of previous epidemic crises shows how important countries and businesses are to the recovery of the tourism industry. Faced with the threats of epidemics to the tourism industry, countries are responding quite similarly to steps from containing the spread of the disease to gradually revitalizing the tourism industry to restoring trust among visitors (Guerava & Richards, 2019). In other words, in order to build trust in tourists, it is very important to create an image of a country that can control the epidemic during and after the epidemic. Due to the complex structure of the tourism industry, efforts to create this image should be carried out at the national level with the cooperation of the public and private sectors. While long-term solutions to the COVID-19 pandemic are not clear, in the short term, focusing on reducing costs is the most common response. Short-term solutions such as stopping costly services, implementing reasonable personnel policies, reducing operating costs in general, restructuring businesses' debts, quarterly business plans, reorganizing the market, restructuring the supply system, and using credit are currently implemented by the majority of businesses.

COPING WITH COVID-19 PANDEMİC

The experience of previous epidemic crises shows how important countries and businesses are to the recovery of the tourism industry. Faced with the threats of epidemics to the tourism industry, countries are responding quite similarly to steps from containing the spread of the disease to gradually revitalizing the tourism industry to restoring trust among visitors (Guerava & Richards, 2019). In other words, in order to build trust in tourists, it is very important to create an image of a country that can control the epidemic during and after the epidemic. Due to the complex structure of the tourism industry, efforts to create this image should be carried out at the national level with the cooperation of the public and private sectors. While long-term solutions to the COVID-19 pandemic are not clear, in the short term, focusing on reducing costs is the most common response. Short-term solutions such as stopping costly services, implementing reasonable personnel policies, reducing operating costs in general, restructuring businesses' debts, quarterly business plans, reorganizing the market, restructuring the supply system, and using credit are currently implemented by the majority of businesses.

TRENDS OF SUSTAINABLE TOURISM MARKETING DURING THE COVID-19 ERA

Digital Marketing Strategies

The COVID-19 pandemic has accelerated the digitization of processes in the tourism industry (Antonio & Rita, 2021). Digital marketing, which is one of the most successful marketing methods of today, is used effectively in the tourism industry. During the COVID-19 pandemic, the most important issue is that the tourism industry uses its marketing budgets effectively and conveys its messages clearly through appropriate channels. In times of crisis, it is necessary to conduct research by making the best use of the previous data available. Because the tourism market is complex and unpredictable in such periods. Search engines, e-mail and social media are extremely effective in the decision-making process of users who have the intention to travel but have not yet made the choice of destination. The focus of the created campaign should be to build trust in the potential consumer. All types of tourism businesses need to analyze market trends before starting their marketing campaigns. Thus, time loss can be prevented and necessary measures can be taken to ensure the safety of the environment during the pandemic period. The points to be considered in digital marketing campaigns in times of crisis are as follows (Hotelogix, 2021):

- The marketing content used by the business in their operations should be updated before the season starts. Materials such as photos, videos, references, reviews about the services of the enterprise in the digital environment should be reviewed and made available to the current market. Blog sessions should be created on the website where users can share their experiences. It would also be appropriate to analyze the traffic on the website for potential market analysis. In line with the analyzes made, adding new services and products to be created in cooperation with local businesses will be effective in attracting users and making reservations.
- Shooting videos containing service promotions for use on social media is an important tool in digital marketing. Videos are one of the most popular types of content. In the COVID-19 era, video marketing is used extensively as a tool to build consumer trust. Posting videos of blog posts or trust-building certificates on social media and using screenshots as images is an ideal way to engage your audience. Synergy can be created by getting support from employees and customers to create these videos.
- During the COVID-19 period, a webinar should be planned or a frequently asked questions (FAQ) video should be created. Scheduling and conducting web sessions; It is an effective marketing tactic in answering frequently asked questions about opportunities, advantages, new products and services within the tourism business. Creating an FAQ video highlighting the latest changes in hygiene and sanitation and posting it on the website and social media platforms such as TikTok and YouTube will attract the attention of the target audience.
- An effective digital marketing practice requires the development of an online review strategy. Responding to the comments and feedback on the website on a daily basis is an indication of the importance that the business attaches to customer satisfaction. Staff should be provided with ongoing training in handling customer feedback, resolving customer service issues, and measuring monthly review reports. Especially for negative comments, sample response texts will make the staff's job easier at the beginning. Online image management is as important as customer service delivery.
- To attract customers, your website and your business "Google My Business" application should be updated. Adding the measures, guidelines, and campaigns about COVID-19 to Google My Business will help build trust in potential consumers.
- It is a powerful tactic to connect with people and build trust by contacting your old customers again during the pandemic, to get their suggestions about your hygiene and sanitation practices that you share on social media and on your website, and to chat.
- Existing data should be analyzed periodically to measure the effectiveness of your digital marketing applications. By examining online analytics and potential client data, the distinguishing features, wishes and needs of the target audience can be determined, and a roadmap can be created for campaigns and price offers.

Regain Passenger Trust

The first step to understand and prioritize passengers' concerns during the COVID-19 era; is to empathize with them. Basic customer expectations for travel in this period is hygiene standards, flexibility in ticket cancellations, a consistent and easily accessible information system, and reliability. Traveling is not just entry and arrival, it is also an experience. In order to make this experience positive, the passenger should be informed in detail about the measures taken to prevent illness at every stage of the journey. If an interactive communication is established with the passengers and the needs and priorities of the customers are determined and grouped with the travel information systems to be created, it can be ensured that each passenger has a unique experience. In this context, it is imperative to use digital tools to quickly react to changing conditions and provide personalized interactions to customers.

Second step; is to create consistent solutions related to the entire journey. Today's COVID-19 measures are under the control of private and government agencies involved in the transportation industry. All stakeholders need to work holistically, collaboratively across the value chain to meet customer expectations and address their fears and concerns and develop a safe travel solution during and after COVID-19 (Schmiedbaur & Lauwerier, 2020). Informing customers about all possibilities regarding travel and destination security, their rights relating to trip cancellation an important step to build trust. It can be clearly seen that the current COVID-19 crisis has enabled the improvement of service quality in the tourism industry if customers' needs for flexibility, consistency, predictability and hygiene are fully met.

Special Interest Tourism (SIT)

The closure of borders, lockdowns and travel restrictions due to COVID_19 devastated the tourism economy worldwide (Butler, 2020). Thus, mass tourism has been severely restricted as it leaves people vulnerable to health hazards (Hall et al., 2020). For this reason, there have been great changes in consumer demands and preferences. In this period, the changing expectations of the consumer should be analyzed correctly and preparations should be made accordingly. This change resulting from the pandemic crisis has drawn the attention of tourism stakeholders all over the world to the review of practices related to tourism destinations and alternative tourism types that can be effective in reviving tourism. Niche products relating to nature tourism (İnan, 2019) and cultural tourism within the scope of special interest tourism; It will create a sense of confidence in consumers as it allows traveling in small groups with a lower risk of infection and easy control.

Revitalizing Domestic Tourism

As a result of the global financial crisis caused by COVID-19, domestic tourism will increase its importance in the tourism industry. Various studies on developing countries show that domestic tourists are more likely to purchase locally produced goods and services. Local tourists prefer small-scale businesses. In addition, their participation in social development initiatives is higher (Kozak & Kim, 2019). Domestic travel, which includes visiting friends and relatives and other social activities, distributes tourists to areas not frequented by international tourists and promotes more balanced regional development.

Reducing Uncertainty

In the specific case of the COVID-19 pandemic, the way to increase perceived control over risks and reduce uncertainty is to limit travel by tourist groups that are difficult to control, such as international visitors. During this period, mass travel was banned in many countries as it was a major risk factor. With the resumption of international travel tourists have been seek assurance that the potential risk of infection is under control and that their tourism experience is not dangerous. Therefore, the main purpose of marketing initiatives related to touristic products is to change the risk perceptions of tourists and to restore trust (Scott et al., 2008). The way to reduce this uncertainty is to increase control, trust and knowledge. The management of risk perception can be ensured by continuous information provided by tourism enterprises and the public.

SafeTravels Stamp

One of the recovery protocols created in the COVID-19 era with the WTTC members, governments, healthcare professionals and other industries is the SafeTravels stamp. The protocol is aimed to establish common standards to ensure the safety of the workforce and passengers as the tourism industry transitions to a new normal. The SafeTravels Stamp was created to identify destinations and businesses around the world that have adopted the SafeTravels health and hygiene global standard protocols. Thus, uncertainty will be eliminated and trust will be re-established (World Travel and Tourism Council, n.d.).

CONCLUSION

COVID-19 crisis is the biggest pandemic in the last hundred years that has affected the whole world, has had a significant impact on the world economy and has a devastating impact on the tourism industry. This damage has been further increased by travel restrictions and social distancing rules, anxiety in crowded environments and fear of infection, reducing tourism demand. The tourism industry has reached a global impasse and has turned to special interest tourism events for small groups and sustainable business models for the domestic market.

All countries have adopted the best health measures, labor market measures, financial measures and fiscal measures to combat the effects of the crisis. As vaccination campaigns begin to be successful, the tourism industry must focus on gaining public trust, strengthening its brands and adapting operations, which are still characterized by many restrictions. Continuous improvement of the new business models that create is important for the continuation of sustainable tourism after the end of the pandemic.

Increasing the quality of touristic products globally and avoiding excessive tourism will contribute to the protection of tourism revenues of developed countries and to increase the share of developing countries from tourism. Thus, the imbalance of income distribution between countries will be eliminated and global sustainable development will be focused on under equal conditions. The support of all tourism stakeholders in the restructuring of tourism and the creation of sustainable and flexible business models in a constantly changing competitive environment is a necessary prerequisite for the world to achieve a social and economic balance environment.

REFERENCES

Abbas, J., Mubeen, R., Iorember, P. T., Raza, S., & Mamirkulova, G. (2021). Exploring The Impact of COVID-19 on Tourism: Transformational Potential and Implications For a Sustainable Recovery Of The Travel And Leisure Industry. *Current Research in Behavioral Sciences*, *2*, 100033. doi:10.1016/j.crbeha.2021.100033

Agca, B. (n.d.). *World Sustainable Development Summit (Johannesburg, 26 August - 4 September 2002).* Ministry of Foreign Affairs of the Republic of Turkey. Retrieved from https://www.mfa.gov.tr/dunya-surdurulebilir-kalkinma-zirvesi_johannesburg_-26-agustos---4-eylul-2002_.tr.mfa

Aydın, B., & Doğan, M. (2020). Yeni Koronavirüs (Covıd-19) Pandemisinin Turistik Tüketici Davranışları ve Türkiye Turizmi Üzerindeki Etkilerinin Değerlendirilmesi. *Pazarlama Teorisi ve Uygulamaları Dergisi*, *6*(1), 93–115.

Bahar, O., & Kozak, M. (2005). *Küreselleşme Sürecinde Uluslararası Turizm ve Rekabet Edebilirlik.* Detay Yayıncılık.

Bezirgan, E., & Bezirgan, M. (2021). The Effects of COVID-19 Pandemics to Turkey's Tourism: A Research on the Interbank Card Center Data. In The Evaluations and Researches in Social Sciences and Humanities. Livre de Lyon.

Butler, R. (1999). Sustainable tourism: A state-of-the-art review. *Tourism Geographies*, *1*(1), 1, 7–25. doi:10.1080/14616689908721291

Butler, R. (2020). Tourism – resilient but vulnerable as "the times they are a changing" in the "new normality". *Worldwide Hospitality and Tourism Themes*, *12*(6), 663–670. doi:10.1108/WHATT-07-2020-0063

Çeti, B., & Ünlüönen, K. (2019). Salgın Hastalıklar Sebebiyle Oluşan Krizlerin Turizm Sektörü Üzerindeki Etkisinin Değerlendirilmesi. *AHBVÜ Turizm Fakültesi Dergisi*, *22*(2), 109–128.

Elliott, C. (2020). What Will Travel Be Like After The Coronavirus? *Forbes*. Retrieved from: https://www.forbes.com/sites/christopherelliott/2020/03/18/what-will-travel-be-like-after-the-coronavirus/?sh=49d89dde3329

Erol, M. (2010). Ekonomik Kriz ve Kobiler. *Journal of Entrepreneurship and Development*, *5*(1), 165–181.

Florian. (2020). *Corona Pandemic: What it Means for the Sustainable Tourism Community.* Sustainability Leaders Project. Retrieved from https://sustainability-leaders.com/what-corona-pandemic-means-for-sustainable-toursim/

Gössling, S., Scott, D., & Hall, C. M. (2020). Pandemics, tourism and global change: A rapid assessment of COVID-19. *Journal of Sustainable Tourism*, *29*(1), 1–20. doi:10.1080/09669582.2020.1758708

Guerava, G., & Richards, D. (2019). *Crisis Readiness.* Global Rescue and World Travel and Tourism Council. Retrieved from https://www.globalrescue.com/grmkt_resources/pdfs/Crisis-Readiness-Final.pdf

Hall, C. M., Scott, D., & Gössling, S. (2020). Pandemics, transformations and tourism: Be careful what you wish for. *Tourism Geographies*, *22*(3), 577–598. doi:10.1080/14616688.2020.1759131

Higgins-Desbiolles. (2020). The end of global travel as we know it: an opportunity for sustainable tourism. *The Conversation*. Retrieved from: https://theconversation.com/the-end-of-global-travel-as-we-know-it-an-opportunity-for-sustainable-tourism-133783

Hotelogix. (2021). Post COVID-19 Hospitality: 8 Proven Digital Marketing Strategies For Smart Hoteliers. *Hospitalitynet*. Retrieved from https://www.hospitalitynet.org/news/4106616.html

İnan, Ü. S. E. (2019). *İşletmelerde Uygulanan Pazarlama Stratejilerinin Rekabet Gücüne Etkisi*. Eğitim Yayınevi.

Köylüoğlu, S., & Gümrah, A., & İnan, Ü.S.E. (2020). Analysis of the Effect of Expectation Theory on Consumer Behavior with the Mental Accounting Dimension. *Journal of Euromarketing*, *29*(1-2), 56–71.

Kozak, M., & Kim, S. (2019). Revisiting choice sets for overseas pleasure vacations: Comparison of short-haul and long-haul destinations. *Journal of Destination Marketing & Management*, *14*, 100388. doi:10.1016/j.jdmm.2019.100388

Muller, T. (2021). *Why the Corona Virus Crisis Is a Unique and Once in a Lifetime Opportunity for Destinations and the Tourism Industry*. https://voyagesafriq.com/2020/03/23/why-the-corona-virus-crisis-is-a-unique-and-once-in-a-lifetime-opportunity-for-destinations-and-the-tourism-industry/

Ritchie, B. W., & Jiang, Y. (2019). A review of research on tourism risk, crisis and disaster management: Launching the Annals of Tourism Research curated collection on tourism risk, crisis and disaster management. *Annals of Tourism Research, Elsevier*, *79*(C), 102812. doi:10.1016/j.annals.2019.102812

Schmiedbaur, M., & Lauwerier, S. (2020). Rebuilding trust in air-traveling in times of a global pandemic. *Star*. Retrieved from: https://star.global/posts/air-travel-experience

Scott, N., Laws, E., & Prideaux, B. (2008). Tourism crises and marketing recovery strategies. *Journal of Travel & Tourism Marketing*, *23*(2–4), 1–13. doi:10.1300/J073v23n02_01

Sustainable Tourism for Development Guidebook. (2013). *UNWTO*. Retrieved from https://www.e-unwto.org/doi/pdf/10.18111/9789284415496

UNWTO. (2020). *International tourism growth continues to outpace the global economy*. World Tourism Organization. Retrieved from https://www.unwto.org/international-tourism-growth-continues-to-outpace-the-economy

UNWTO. (n.d.). *International tourism and COVID-19*. World Tourism Organization. Retrieved from: https://www.unwto.org/international-tourism-and-covid-19

World Commission on Environment and Development. (1987). *Our Common Future (BrundlandReport)*. https://www.are.admin.ch/are/en/home/media/publications/sustainabledevelopment/brundtland-report.html

World Travel and Tourism Council. (n.d.). *'Safe Travels': Global Protocols & Stamp for the New Normal*. Retrieved from https://wttc.org/COVID-19/SafeTravels-Global-Protocols-Stamp

Chapter 15
The COVID-19 Pandemic and Agricultural Futures in the USA:
Evidence From a Dynamic Fourier Quantile Causality Test

Ugur Korkut Pata
Osmaniye Korkut Ata University, Turkey

Onder Ozgur
Ankara Yildirim Beyazit University, Turkey

Veli Yilanci
Faculty of Political Sciences, Canakkale Onsekiz Mart University, Turkey

Muhammed Sehid Gorus
https://orcid.org/0000-0002-7614-4567
Ankara Yildirim Beyazit University, Turkey

ABSTRACT

This study aims to examine the impact of the COVID-19 pandemic on various agricultural commodity futures (cocoa, coffee, corn, cotton, soybean meal, soybeans, sugar, and wheat) in the United States for the period from January 24, 2020, to July 6, 2021, considering oil prices as a control variable. Specifically, the study employs a novel Fourier quantile causality test and its time-varying form. The results show that the causal relationships between COVID-19 cases and agricultural commodity futures are highly time-varying. The empirical findings also demonstrate that COVID-19 has the strongest causal effect on coffee futures, followed by sugar, soybeans, and corn. In contrast, the impact of COVID-19 on cocoa and cotton futures is relatively limited. The causal effect of COVID-19 on agricultural futures is more pronounced at lower quantiles and in the spring and summer months. In general, COVID-19 has significant predictive power for the six agricultural commodity futures over 100 days in the analysis period, with the exception of cocoa and cotton.

DOI: 10.4018/978-1-7998-9648-7.ch015

INTRODUCTION

The global economy was hit by the COVID-19 pandemic in late 2019. Most governments have adopted stringent economic and social policies to prevent the spread of COVID-19, including restrictions on mass gatherings, internal and/or international travel restrictions, school closures, etc. (Cheng et al. 2020). Although these measures helped to slow the virus from spreading, they had a significant economic impact. According to Aggarwal et al. (2021), the stringent lockdown measures led to difficulties in conducting day-to-day business. As a result, most industries, including agriculture, were severely impacted by the virus' effects.

COVID-19 has harmed the agricultural market by disrupting agricultural commodity demand and supply (Elleby et al. 2020). COVID-19 has a greater impact on demand for agricultural products than on supply due to its limited accessibility (Siche et al. 2020). On the one hand, due to the closure of schools, workplaces, hotels, and restaurants, demand for agricultural commodities has decreased. The demand for agricultural goods has decreased as the unemployment rate has risen and per capita income has decreased (Varshney et al. 2020). Rising food costs and income losses due to COVID -19 threaten food access and food security in developed and developing countries, with long-term implications (FAO, 2020). In addition, trade restrictions on agricultural goods (Casey and Cimino-Isaacs, 2020) and labor and logistical restrictions (Varshney et al. 2020) have worsened agricultural supply chains. On the other hand, the agricultural sector is supported by the increasing demand for food from consumers who need to eat at home and fill their pantries. Governments around the world have taken action to protect the viability of the food supply chain by attaching importance to the need for food in difficult pandemic conditions (Gray, 2020).

The combined effects of demand and supply disturbances increase food prices in the short-run, and the theoretical implications of COVID-19 on food inflation are widely recognized (Akter, 2020). Similarly, COVID-19 is highly likely to affect agricultural futures prices. In this context, this study aims to examine the impacts of the COVID-19 outbreak on the eight main agricultural futures prices (cocoa, coffee, corn, cotton, soybean meal, soybeans, sugar, and wheat) for the United States from January 24, 2020, to July 6, 2021. This study utilizes the COVID-19 cases (million people) in the United States as an indicator of pandemic severity. In addition, this study adds crude oil prices as a control variable in the model. Crude oil prices have a key role in agricultural price modeling. According to Wang et al. (2020), oil products are used for the production, transportation, and trade of agricultural commodities. Therefore, an increase in crude oil prices affects agricultural commodity prices through the change in demand and/or supply.

During the period under study, agricultural commodity futures prices have been very volatile. Prices for corn, coffee, and cocoa, in particular, fluctuated dramatically (see Figure A.1.). Besides, COVID-19 cases increased multifold. Although the number of cases did not reach triple digits by the end of February 2020, it exceeded 33 million by the end of June 2021. Besides, crude oil prices were negatively affected by the pandemic in the early stages of the outbreak. On June 22, 2020, crude oil prices were $56.76 per barrel, compared to the minus $36.98 per barrel on April 20, 2020. After this date, crude oil prices started to increase gradually. These trends in agricultural commodity prices, crude oil prices, and the number of COVID-19 cases led us to study the causal linkage between these variables in a time-varying environment for the United States.

This paper proposes and employs the *time-varying Fourier quantile causality test* to determine the causal relationship between the COVID-19 cases and agricultural futures prices. This method aims to combine three main approaches in causality analysis: the Fourier approximation, the time-varying analysis, and the quantile analysis. This novel methodology has several advantages over existing time-series methods. First, it considers possible instabilities, such as the change of direction or the existence of causality in different time periods. Second, it allows the existence of causality to be examined over the entire conditional distribution of the dependent variable. Third, the method considers the gradual structural shifts in the data. In comparison to the existing empirical literature, all these advantages may make the empirical results derived from this study more reliable.

The rest of the paper consists of four main sections. Section 2 reviews the empirical literature on oil prices-agricultural prices-coronavirus pandemic, while Section 3 introduces the dataset and methodology. Section 4 exhibits the empirical results, while Section 5 presents the conclusion and policy implications.

LITERATURE REVIEW

Many studies in the literature have addressed the nexus between oil prices and agricultural prices. Some of these studies show that oil price shocks have no influence on the change of agricultural commodity prices. In contrast, some parts of the literature have found that oil price shocks are not neutral to agricultural commodity prices. As a result, the literature on the relationship between oil prices and agricultural commodity prices is inconclusive. The outbreak of the COVID-19 pandemic, on the other hand, had an impact on both oil and agricultural prices, raising researchers' awareness of the current connection. Since this study analyzes the link between confirmed COVID-19 cases and agricultural prices considering oil prices, this paper splits the literature into two parts.

The first part of this section provides and review of studies that have examined the link between oil prices and agricultural prices in the pre-pandemic period.

Campiche et al. (2007) looked at the relationship between crude oil prices and agricultural commodities from 2003 to 2007. The authors found that crude oil and agricultural commodity prices had no long-run cointegration relationship from 2003 to 2005. However, their findings revealed that corn and soybean prices were cointegrated during the 2006-2007 sub-period. Nazlioglu (2011) showed that linear causality analysis did not reveal any significant relationship between world oil prices and agricultural commodity prices. In contrast, his study revealed a nonlinear causal linkage between oil and agricultural prices, demonstrating the non-neutrality of oil prices on agricultural prices. Nazlioglu and Soytas (2011) found no significant short-run and long-run impact of oil price shocks on agricultural commodity prices in Turkey between January 1994 and March 2010. Similarly, Reboredo (2012) demonstrated the neutrality of oil prices on agricultural prices and showed no significant contagion effect between crude oil and agricultural product markets. Conversely, Nazlioglu and Soytas (2012) provided evidence of the non-neutrality of world oil prices on prices of various agricultural products. Rezitis (2015) also found evidence favoring the significant role of crude oil prices on international agricultural commodity prices.

Fowowe (2016) examined the linkage between oil prices and agricultural commodity prices from January 2003 to January 2014 in South Africa. This study found no cointegration and causality relationship between oil and agricultural prices and verified that agricultural commodity prices are neutral to global oil prices. Another study proposed by Fasanya et al. (2019) analyzed the relationship between oil prices and agricultural commodity prices in Nigeria using linear and nonlinear models from January 1997 to December 2016. The results of the linear model suggested that oil prices contribute positively to agricultural commodity prices. The authors also found that asymmetric impacts and structural breaks significantly affect the linkage between oil and agricultural commodity prices. Gokmenoglu et al. (2020) also examined the dynamic nexus between oil and agricultural commodity prices and found that oil prices significantly drive agricultural commodity prices in Nigeria. Su et al. (2019) also proposed a dynamic causality analysis on the nexus of oil and agricultural commodity prices. The authors analyzed the period between January 1990 and February 2017. In their time-varying causality setting, they found a bidirectional causal relationship between oil and agricultural commodity prices.

Koirala et al. (2015) worked with the Copulas method and used data from March 2011 to September 2012 to analyze the correlation between energy future prices and agricultural commodity prices in the United States. Their findings indicated that energy futures prices are highly correlated with agricultural commodity prices, and the rise in energy prices leads to an increase in agricultural commodity prices. In another study for the USA, McFarlane (2016) found a significant cointegration relationship between crude oil and agricultural prices over the period 1995 to 2012. For China, Ma et al. (2015) analyzed the impact of oil price shocks on agricultural product prices. Their study used data from June 2002 to August 2013, and impulse-response analysis demonstrated that agricultural commodity prices are agricultural product prices of oil price shocks in the short-run. Similarly, their causality analysis showed that changes in oil prices are not significant for agricultural prices in the long-run.

The second part of this section introduces the review of studies concentrating on agricultural commodity prices and oil prices nexus by considering the impact of COVID-19 in the pandemic period.

Elleby et al. (2020) performed a recursive-dynamic partial equilibrium model to analyze the impact of energy price volatility on the global agricultural commodity markets. The results of their scenario model suggest that energy price volatility has a greater impact on biodiesel prices. However, the simulation results demonstrated that grain prices are less affected by energy price volatility. Beckman and Countryman (2021) also used a computable general equilibrium model to estimate the macroeconomic impact of COVID-19 due to agricultural production and trade. Their results indicated that the combined impact of the agricultural shock is higher than the share of the agricultural production in the USA economy during the COVID-19 period.

Mouloudj et al. (2020) focused on the impact of COVID-19 on food security in developed and developing countries. The authors found that the COVID-19 pandemic hurts food security in most of the developed and developing countries. However, poorer and war-affected countries experienced massive food shortages during the pandemic period. Rawal and Verma (2020) confirmed that lockdowns during the period of COVID-19 resulted in disruptions in agricultural product markets, and farmers suffered massive losses. In contrast, Varshney et al. (2020) argued that agricultural markets in India were more resilient to the COVID-19 shock due to policy support.

Ezeaku and Asongu (2020) found that international commodity prices responded differently by commodity group following the COVID-19 pandemic outbreak. The authors demonstrated that agricultural commodity prices fall significantly between December 2019 and April 2020. However, grain and cereal prices remain quieter than the raw material and oil prices during this period. Wang et al. (2020) analyzed the correlation between crude oil and agricultural futures during the COVID-19 period. They confirmed that the correlation of these two futures became more robust in the pandemic period.

Kotyza et al. (2021) examined the relationship between sugar prices and the volatility in the stock market index volatility in the USA. Their study mainly concentrated on whether the COVID-19 pandemic significantly affects the relationship between sugar prices and stock market uncertainty. The authors used data from 2000 to 2020 and concluded that the COVID-19 did not significantly affect the nexus between sugar prices and stock market uncertainty. Cariappa et al. (2021) analyzed the impact of the

COVID-19 pandemic on the prices of key food commodities from November 2019 to August 2020 in India. They found that lockdowns, transportation restrictions, and supply chain disruptions led to an increase in wholesale and retail food prices during this period. Shruthi and Ramani (2021) used the variance causality test to analyze the linkage between oil and commodity markets. Their findings indicated that oil market volatility is transmitted to agricultural commodity prices in the post-pandemic period.

Borgards et al. (2021) used daily data from November 2019 to June 2020 and concentrated on the overreaction behavior of various commodity futures prices. The authors utilized a dynamic and non-parametric model and verified the overreaction hypothesis in commodity prices during the COVID-19 period. Their findings indicated that agricultural commodities are less overreactive than precious metals and energy commodities. Ezeaku et al. (2021) examined the impact of oil market shocks on agricultural commodity prices and used the structural VAR model during the recent pandemic. They worked with daily data covers the period from December 2, 2019, to October 1, 2020. Their findings demonstrated that agricultural commodity prices respond differently to oil market shocks. They also found that the cumulative response of agricultural commodities becomes much weaker over time. Finally, Sun et al. (2021) used the bootstrap panel causality test to examine the causality linkage between oil and agricultural commodity prices pre-and post-pandemic. Their findings demonstrated a significant bidirectional causal relationship between oil and agricultural commodity prices and confirmed the non-neutrality of oil price shocks on agricultural commodity prices.

As can be seen from the above review, there is recent literature on the impact of the COVID-19 pandemic and the related lockdowns and restrictions on agricultural commodity prices. Different from the literature, this study offers some obvious methodological advantages and thus contributes to the debates on agricultural futures markets. Since the changes in COVID-19 and agricultural prices are a very dynamic process, the time-varying Fourier quantile causality test used in the study allows us to more precisely determine the predictive power of COVID -19 for agricultural commodity futures.

DATA AND ECONOMETRIC METHODOLOGY

Data

The data used in this study covers the period from January 24, 2020, to July 6, 2021, with daily frequency. The data were compiled from three different sources. The number of COVID-19 cases in the United States (million people) was obtained from Our World in Data (2021), agricultural commodity futures for cocoa, coffee C, corn, cotton no. 2, soybean meal, soybeans, sugar no. 11, and wheat were derived from Investing (2021), and crude oil prices (USD per barrel) were collected from the U.S. Energy Information Administration (2021). This paper converts the data to a logarithmic scale and report some descriptive statistics for the data in Table 1.

For agricultural commodity futures, it can be seen that the highest mean and median is that of cocoa, followed by soybeans, wheat, and corn. In addition, the statistics in Table 1 show that cocoa, coffee, corn, soybean meal, soybeans, and wheat are positively skewed, while cotton, sugar, COVID-19 cases, and oil prices are negatively skewed. COVID-19 cases, oil prices, cocoa, and coffee futures exhibit excess kurtosis. Jarque-Bera test statistics and probability values strongly reject the null hypothesis of normality. In other words, all series are not normally distributed. This finding motivates the use of a quantile causality test instead of the standard mean-based linear Granger causality test (Balcilar et al.

Table 1. Descriptive statistics

Variables	Mean	Median	Std. Dev.	Skewness	Kurtosis	JB	p-value	Observations
lnCocoa	7.819	7.804	0.073	0.671	2.941	27.388	0.000	364
lnCoffee	4.777	4.775	0.135	0.426	2.521	14.488	0.001	364
lnCorn	6.063	5.980	0.268	0.547	1.948	34.921	0.002	364
lnCotton	4.253	4.232	0.160	-0.066	1.908	18.321	0.003	364
lnSoybean-meal	5.850	5.871	0.164	0.041	1.366	40.552	0.004	364
lnSoybeans	6.999	6.957	0.223	0.242	1.442	40.341	0.005	364
lnSugar	2.633	2.676	0.170	-0.384	2.044	22.809	0.006	364
lnWheat	6.371	6.369	0.112	0.144	1.959	17.681	0.007	364
lnCOVID-19	14.637	15.881	4.025	-2.205	6.837	518.345	0.008	364
lnCrudeOil	3.786	3.781	0.363	-1.202	4.960	146.025	0.009	364

Note: JB denotes the Jarque and Bera (1980)'s test statistics.

2017; Bahloul et al. 2018), as the application of the quantile causality test can provide robust estimates for non-normally distributed skewness (Troster et al. 2018; Yahya et al. 2020).

Methodology

Granger's (1969) causality test can be used to determine whether past and present values of one variable (e.g., X) have predictive power for the future values of another variable (e.g., Y). There have been significant improvements in the concept of causality, particularly in the last two decades. For example, several causality tests have been added to the literature to account for structural changes in the causality relationship. While Enders and Jones (2016) propose to test the causality nexus in a vector autoregressive model that is augmented with a Fourier function to consider multiple structural changes, Nazlioglu et al. (2016) suggest using the Fourier function in the lag-augmented VAR model to address pretest bias following Toda and Yamamoto (1995). Balcilar et al. (2010) and Yilanci and Bozoklu (2014) propose to examine the causality relationship in a time-varying framework to consider possible instabilities, such as changing the direction or existence of causality in different time periods. Besides, Jeong et al. (2012), Troster (2018), and Song and Taamouti (2020) suggest testing the causality relationship in quantiles. Testing causality in quantiles enables us to explore the existence of causality over the entire conditional distribution of the dependent variable. Moreover, this approach is robust to outliers and is also more convenient than linear alternatives when the residuals are not Gaussian distributed (see Uribe and Guillen, 2020). This study aims to combine these three approaches and suggest a new causality test that allows testing causality in different quantiles by allowing multiple structural changes via a Fourier function in a time-varying framework.

To apply the newly suggested test, this study first estimate the following model:

$$Y_t = \beta_0 + \beta_1 \sin\left(\frac{2\pi kt}{T}\right) + \beta_2 \cos\left(\frac{2\pi kt}{T}\right) + \sum_{i=1}^{p+1} \alpha_{1i} Y_{t-i} + \sum_{i=1}^{p+1} \alpha_{2i} X_{t-i} + e_t \quad (1)$$

where t, T, k, and p respectively denote a trend term, the sample size, the optimal frequency of the Fourier function, and the optimal lag length, respectively. The paper determines the values of k and p endogenously. To find the optimal value of frequency, this study estimates Eq. (1) for each value of $k \in \{1, 2, ..., 5\}$ and choose the *k* that minimizes the sum of squared residuals. After determining *k*, this paper chooses the *p* using Akaike information criterion. While Nazlioglu et al. (2016) follow Toda and Yamamoto (1995) and augments Eq. (1) with maximal integration levels of the variables, this investigation follow the suggestion of Dolado and Lutkepohl (1996) and augment Eq. (1) with one lag.

After determining the optimal values of frequency (k^*) and lag length (p^*), following Cheng et al. (2021), this paper estimates Eq. (1), by employing the quantile regression approach:

$$Q_{Y_t}(\tau|Z) = \beta_0(\tau) + \beta_1(\tau)\sin\left(\frac{2\pi k^* t}{T}\right) + \beta_2(\tau)\cos\left(\frac{2\pi k^* t}{T}\right) + \sum_{i=1}^{p^*+1}\alpha_{1i}(\tau)Y_{t-i} + \sum_{i=1}^{p^*+1}\alpha_{2i}(\tau)X_{t-i} + e_t$$

where τ shows the chosen quantile and Z denotes covariates matrix. The paper uses the modified simplex algorithm of Barrodale and Roberts (1973) to estimate the coefficients. To test the null hypothesis of X_t does not cause Y_t in the τ th quantile ($H_0 : \alpha_{2,1}(\tau) = \alpha_{2,2}(\tau) = ... = \alpha_{2,p^*}(\tau) = 0, \quad \forall \tau \in (0,1)$), this paper computes the following test statistic as in Eq. (2):

$$W = \frac{\left[T\left(\hat{\alpha}_2(\tau)'\left(\hat{\Omega}(\tau)\right)^{-1}\hat{\alpha}_2(\tau)\right)\right]}{\tau(1-\tau)} \tag{2}$$

where $\hat{\Omega}(\tau)$ indicates the $\hat{\alpha}_2(\tau)$'s consistent variance-covariance estimator matrix. To uncover the instabilities in the causality relationship, this study follows Yilanci and Kilci (2021) and use the Fourier quantile (FQ) causality test in rolling windows, as the rolling estimation approach is superior to other dynamic approaches (see Stock and Watson (1996)). To use the FQ test in a dynamic framework, this paper first determine the subsample size employing the following formula (see Phillips et al. 2015):

$$s = \left[T\left(0.01 + 1.8 / \sqrt{T}\right)\right]$$

In the next step, this investigation applies the dynamic FQ (DFQ) test considering changing subsamples as;

1, 2, 3, …, s.
2, 3, 4, …, s+1
3, 4, 5, …, s+2

Thus, both the first and last observations are changing in every step. While the first observation is excluded from the subsample, a new observation is added to the subsample. This approach continues until the last observation is added to the sample. To obtain the necessary critical values, this study runs bootstrap simulations and compute the following ratio to detect the instabilities in the causality relationship:

$$DFQ = \frac{\text{The FQ test statistic in the given subsample}}{\text{Bootstrap critical value}} \tag{3}$$

If the DFQ in Eq. (3) is greater than one, it implies the null of no-causality in the given subsample must be rejected; otherwise, one cannot reject the null. Since the inspection of the graphical illustration of the DFQ ratios for the consecutive subsamples provides useful information to the researcher for detecting the instabilities, this paper illustrates the DFQ rations over the analysis period.

EMPIRICAL RESULTS

This study first use the FQ causality test and present the results in Table 2. The results show that there is causality from COVID-19 to corn and coffee prices at 0.2 and 0.6 quantiles, respectively. There is no causal relationship between the other six agricultural commodities and COVID-19.

However, these results may not reflect reality. The relationship between COVID-19 and commodity prices may take a time-varying form. Therefore, this paper also examine the causal relationships between COVID-19 and agricultural prices in time-varying form and present the results for each agricultural commodity in Figure 1-8.

Figure 1 shows the impact of COVID-19 on coffee prices. At lower quantiles, COVID-19 has the largest impact on coffee prices in the winter months. There is unidirectional causality from COVID-19 to coffee prices on December 21, 23, 24, and 28, 2020; January 7, 8, 11, 12, 13, 21, 26, 27, 28, and 29, 2021; and February 1, 3, 5, 10, 11, 12, 16, 17, 18, 19, and 22, 2021. Besides, there are fewer causal relationships at upper quantiles. Similar to the lower quantiles, the effects of COVID-19 on coffee prices during the winter months are strongest for the upper quantiles. There is a unidirectional causality running from COVID-19 to coffee prices on December 7, 8, 9, 21, 22, 23, and 24, 2020; January 6, 8, 11, 12, 13, 19, and 20, 2021; and February 3, 5, 10, 16, 17, and 19, 2021.

Figure 2 represents the impact of COVID-19 on coffee prices. At the lower quantiles, COVID-19 has the most impact on coffee prices in the summer of 2020. There is a unidirectional causality from COVID-19 to coffee prices on June 3, 4, 8, 10, 11, 12, 15, 16, 18, 24, 25, and 26, 2020; July 8, 9, 10, 13, 14, 15, 16, 17, 20, 23, 27, and 31, 2020; and August 20, 21, 24, 25, 26, 27, and 31, 2020. More causal relationships can be found for upper quantiles than for lower quantiles. In addition, the impact of COVID-19 on coffee prices is larger than that of cocoa in both quantile groups. At high quantiles, COVID-19 has a greater impact on coffee prices in the spring of 2020 than in other periods. A unidirectional causality is going from COVID-19 to coffee prices on March 18, 19, 20, 23, 24, 27, 30, and 31, 2020; April 6, 7, 8, 9, 13, 14, 15, 16, 17, 20, 21, 22, 24, and 30, 2020; and May 5, 6, 7, 12, 13, 14, 15, and 21, 2020. When the lower and upper quantiles are evaluated together, it is seen that COVID-19 has a significant impact on coffee prices in the spring and summer of 2020.

Figure 3 presents the impact of COVID-19 on corn prices. At low quantiles, COVID-19 has the most impact on corn prices in spring 2020. A unidirectional causality from COVID-19 to coffee prices is confirmed on March 18, 20, and 31, 2020; on April 1, 6, 7, 8, 9, 13, 14, 15, 16, 20, 21, 23, 24, 27, 28, 29, and 30, 2020, and on May 1, 4, 5, 6, 7, 8, 11, 12, 13, 14, 20, 21, 22, 26, 27, and 29, 2020. Similarly, at high quantiles, the most intense relationship between COVID-19 and corn prices is in the spring of 2020. There is unidirectional causality from COVID-19 to coffee prices on March 18, 24, 25, 26, 27, and

Table 2. Results of Fourier quantile causality test

Model: Agricultural Commodity Futures = *f* (COVID-19 cases, crude oil prices)				
Quantile	**Wald stat.**	**10% CV**	**5% CV**	**1% CV**
H_0: COVID19 does not Granger cause Cocoa prices				
0.2	0.769	16.675	20.308	27.721
0.4	5.836	15.036	18.004	22.640
0.6	0.984	14.768	17.001	21.344
0.8	1.501	15.045	17.572	24.088
H_0: COVID19 does not Granger cause Coffee prices				
0.2	5.679	11.562	16.242	35.376
0.4	0.995	15.684	20.977	33.050
0.6	23.634***	22.764	28.274	39.997
0.8	14.237	25.327	30.387	45.194
H_0: COVID19 does not Granger cause Corn prices				
0.2	5.654***	5.624	7.052	9.469
0.4	1.718	3.666	4.485	6.600
0.6	0.135	2.367	3.169	5.354
0.8	0.340	1.841	2.573	4.104
H_0: COVID19 does not Granger cause Cotton prices				
0.2	6.325	17.989	21.272	27.883
0.4	6.435	17.900	21.326	28.292
0.6	5.812	19.354	23.107	29.064
0.8	22.439	25.377	29.332	40.688
H_0: COVID19 does not Granger cause Soybean-meal prices				
0.2	9.450	17.439	20.700	26.473
0.4	4.302	15.592	17.794	21.980
0.6	6.613	14.768	16.911	22.728
0.8	8.203	14.330	17.423	24.961
H_0: COVID19 does not Granger cause Soybeans prices				
0.2	0.049	11.129	13.042	18.345
0.4	0.139	11.020	12.831	17.236
0.6	0.834	12.905	15.259	20.144
0.8	0.404	17.938	21.385	29.123
H_0: COVID19 does not Granger cause Sugar prices				
0.2	1.446	20.733	23.993	32.381
0.4	7.453	22.722	25.297	30.895
0.6	8.239	22.018	25.099	32.272
0.8	2.276	22.373	26.667	34.425
H_0: COVID19 does not Granger cause Wheat prices				
0.2	1.284	7.810	9.683	14.031
0.4	1.902	8.670	10.287	15.601
0.6	5.122	10.148	12.149	16.699
0.8	6.472	13.481	17.038	25.383
Note: *** shows significance at 10% level. CV: critical value.				

Figure 1. Results of time-varying Fourier causality test for COVID-19-Cocoa nexus

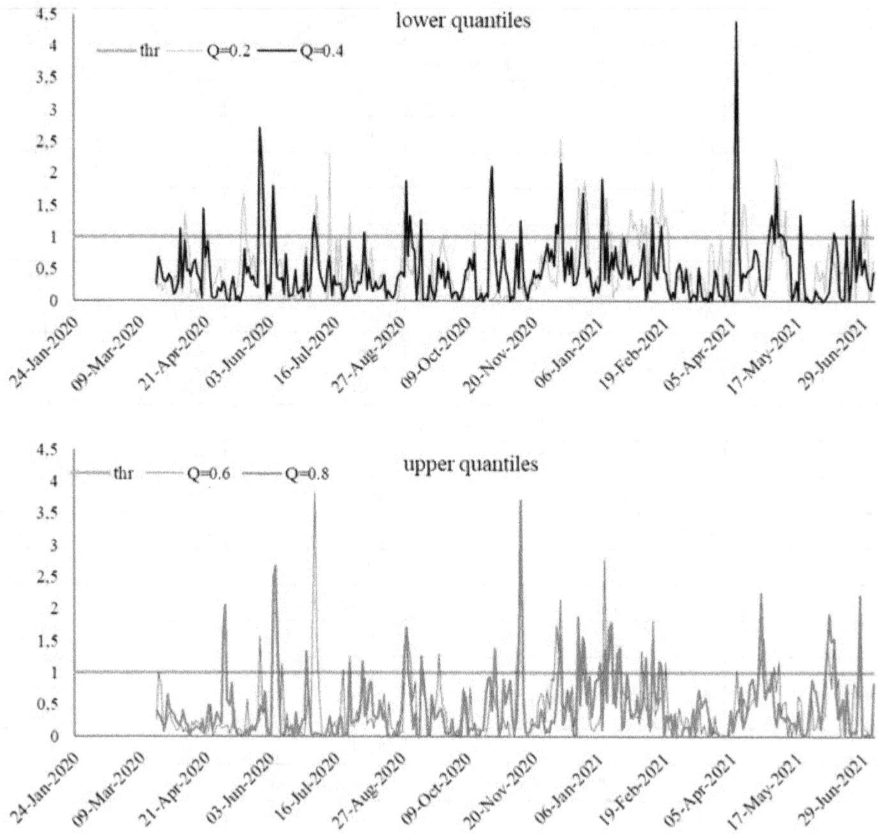

31, 2020; on April 1, 2, 3, 9, and 23, 2020 and on May 6, 7, 8, 9, 10, 11, 12, 13, 14, 15, 18, 20, 21, 22, 26, 27, 28, and 29, 2020. According to these findings, COVID-19 affects corn prices more than cocoa prices and less than coffee prices.

The impact of COVID-19 on cotton prices is presented in Figure 4. At the low quantiles, COVID-19 has the largest impact on cotton prices in the spring months of 2020. There is unidirectional causality running from COVID-19 to cotton prices on March 25, 2020; on April 3, 7, 8, 9, 13, 16, 17, 18, 20, 21, 22, 23, 24, 27, and 28, 2020, and on May 6, 19, 20, 21, 22, 26, 27, and 29, 2020. At high quantiles, COVID-19 is more effective on cotton prices than at low quantiles. Meanwhile, at higher quantiles, COVID-19 has the greatest impact on cotton prices in summer 2020. There is unidirectional causality running from COVID-19 to cotton prices on June 1, 3, 9, 10, 11, 17, 18, 19, and 30, 2020; on July 1, 2, 7, 8, 9, 10, 21, 29, and 30, 2020, and on August 5, 11, 12, 13, 24, 26, and 28, 2020. Although the effect of COVID-19 on cotton prices is stronger than the impact on cocoa prices, it is quite small compared to corn and coffee.

The causal effects of COVID-19 on soybeans are shown in Figure 5. At both low and high quantiles, COVID-19 has the largest causal effect on soybeans in the summer of 2020. A unidirectional causality is going from COVID-19 cases to soybeans futures on Jun, 1, 9, 10, 11, 16, 17, 25, 26, and 30, 2020; on July 6, 9, 17, 20, 21, 22, 23, 24, 27, 28, 29, 30, and 31, 2020; and on August 3, 4, 5, 6, 7, 10, 11, 12,

Figure 2. Results of time-varying Fourier causality test for COVID-19-Coffee nexus

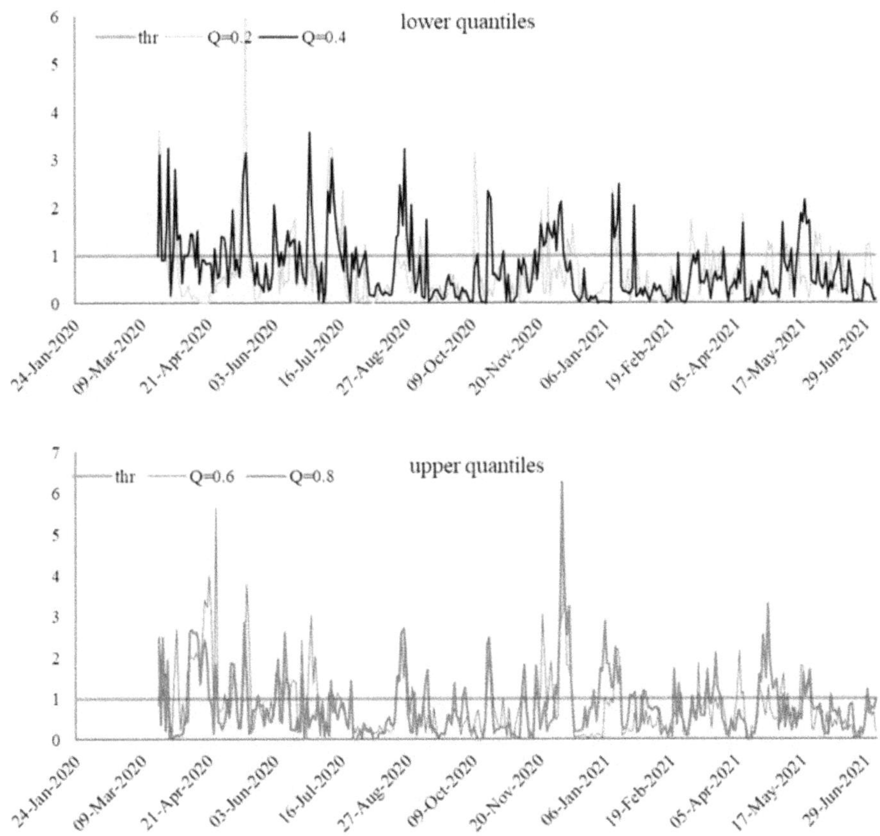

13, 17, 24, 25, 26, 27, 28, and 31, 2020. Soybeans futures prediction power of COVID-19 is less than coffee but higher than cocoa, corn, and cotton.

The causal effects of COVID-19 cases on soybean meal are presented in Figure 6. The causal effect of COVID-19 is greater in low quantiles than in high quantiles. For the low quantiles (0.2 - 0.4), causality is found to be strongest in summer 2020. The null of no-causality from COVID-19 cases to soybean meal futures is rejected on June 2, and 9, 2020; on July 13, 16, 20, 21, 22, 23, 24, 27, 28, 29, 30, and 31, 2020, and on August 3, 4, 5, 6, 7, 11, 12, 19, 21, 25, 27, 28, and 31, 2020. Similarly, the most intense causal relationship for high quantiles (0.6-0.8) is in summer 2020. There is unidirectional causality from COVID-19 to soybean meal futures on July 2, 6, 16, 17, 20, 21, and 23, 2020; on August 3, 4, 5, 6, 7, 10, 12, 13, 14, 18, 21, 24, 25, 26, 27, 28, and 31, 2020. Moreover, the results show that the predictive power of COVID-19 is higher for soybean- meal futures than for cocoa and cotton.

Figure 7 illustrates the causal effects of COVID-19 on sugar. At higher quantiles, COVID-19 has greater predictive power for sugar futures. For both high and low quantiles, COVID-19 has the largest impact in the spring of 2021. At low quantiles, there is unidirectional causality from COVID-19 cases to sugar futures prices on March, 2, 4, 9, 26, 29 and 31, 2021; on April 1, 5, 6, 7, 8, 16, 21, 22, 23, 26, 27, 28, 29, and 30, 2021; and on May, 3, 4, 5, 6, 7, 10, 11, 12, 13, 14, 17, 18, 19, 20, 21, 24, 25, 26, 27, and 28, 2021. At high quantiles, the null hypothesis of no-causality is rejected on March, 2, 4, 9, 10,

Figure 3. Results of time-varying Fourier causality test for COVID-19-Corn nexus

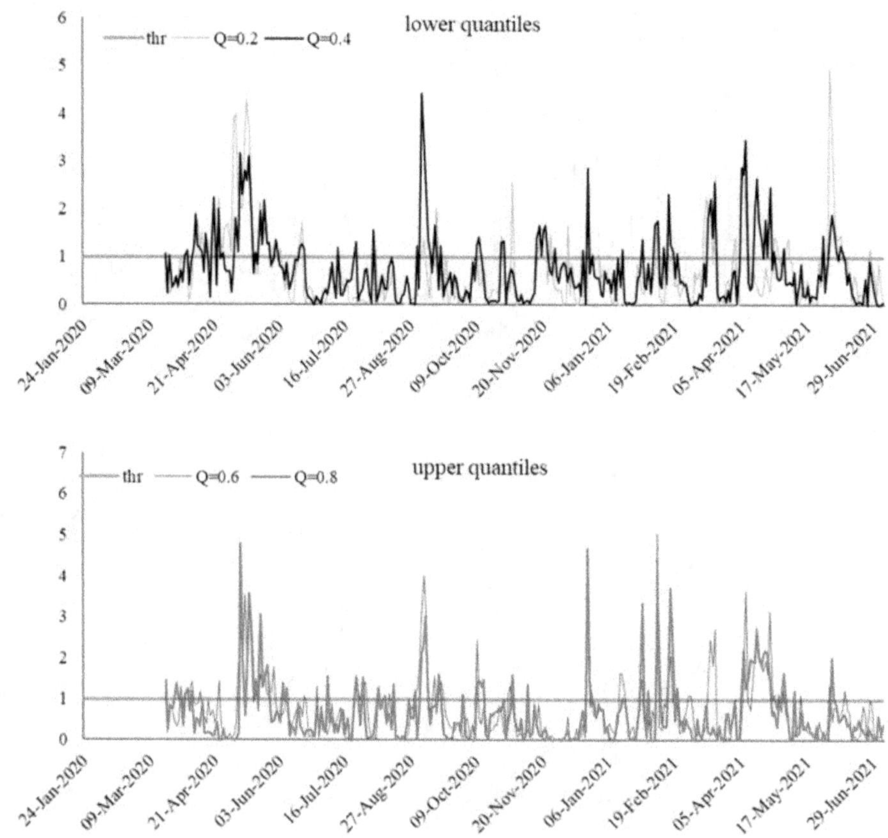

and 18, 2021; on April 1, 13, 16, 20, 21, 22, 23, 26, 27, 28, 29, and 30, 2021; and on May, 3, 4, 5, 6, 7, 10, 11, 12, 13, 14, 17, 18, 19, 20, 21, 25, 26, 27, and 28, 2021. In addition to coffee and soybeans, the findings show that COVID-19 cases also have a significant causal effect on sugar futures.

Finally, Figure 8 presents the causal effect of COVID-19 on wheat futures. COVID-19 has the largest causal effect on wheat in summer 2020. At lower quantiles, COVID-19 causes wheat futures on June 11 and 24, 2020; on July 6, 7, 8, 9, 10, 13, 14, 15, 16, 17, 21, 28, 29, and 30, 2020; and on August 6, 7, 12, 14, 18, 19, 20, 21, 24, 25, 26, 27, and 31, 2020. At higher quantiles, unidirectional causality runs from COVID-19 to wheat futures on June 4, 11, 26, 29, and 30, 2020; on July 7, 8, 9, 10, 13, 14, 15, 16, 17, 21, and 28, 2020; and on August 7, 12, 13, 18, 19, 20, 21, 24, 25, 26, and 27, 2020. The results show that the causal effect of COVID-19 on wheat is more than just cotton and cocoa.

In summary, the COVID-19 pandemic has a significant causal impact on agricultural futures. In this analysis with 364 daily observations, COVID-19 had a causal effect on all agricultural futures prices except cocoa and cotton futures over 100 days in the analysis period (see Table A.1). COVID-19 cases are the cause of changes in futures prices for coffee, sugar, and soybeans in particular. The performance of these three agricultural commodity futures during COVID-19 is somewhat different (see Fig. A.1.). While sugar prices bottomed out in the second quarter of 2020 and then showed an upward trend, coffee prices fluctuated until the fourth quarter of 2020 and then had an increasing trend. Soybean futures

Figure 4. Results of time-varying Fourier causality test for COVID-19-Cotton nexus

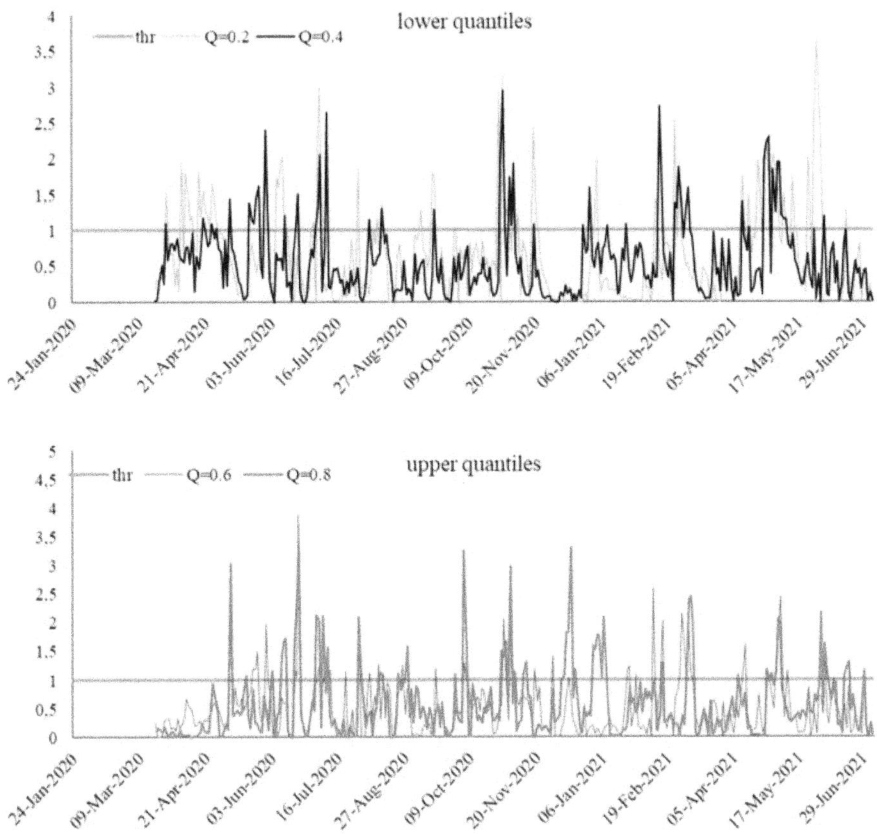

prices, on the other hand, followed a stable course until the third quarter of 2020 and then showed an increasing trend. These trend changes have a time-varying causal effect on COVID-19 cases.

CONCLUSION AND POLICY SUGGESTION

The COVID-19 pandemic has had a devastating impact on economy all across the world. Lockdowns and restrictions have disrupted supply networks, resulting in commodity price volatility. COVID-19-induced lockdowns and limitations have had a negative impact on agricultural goods. As a result, verified COVID-19 cases are likely to affect agricultural commodity prices.

Although COVID-19 has an impact on a variety of commodities, this article examines the impact of the COVID-19 pandemic on eight agricultural commodities' future prices (cocoa, coffee, corn, cotton, soybean meal, soybeans, sugar, and wheat) in the United States on a daily basis. Oil prices are also used as a control variable in the study.

The study provides insights at the association between COVID-19 cases and agricultural commodity futures prices using the Fourier quantile causality test. The analysis concentrates on four different quantiles (0.2, 0.4, 0.6, 0.8). The main finding of the first empirical step is that there is no causal relation-

Figure 5. Results of time-varying Fourier causality test for COVID-19-Soybeans nexus

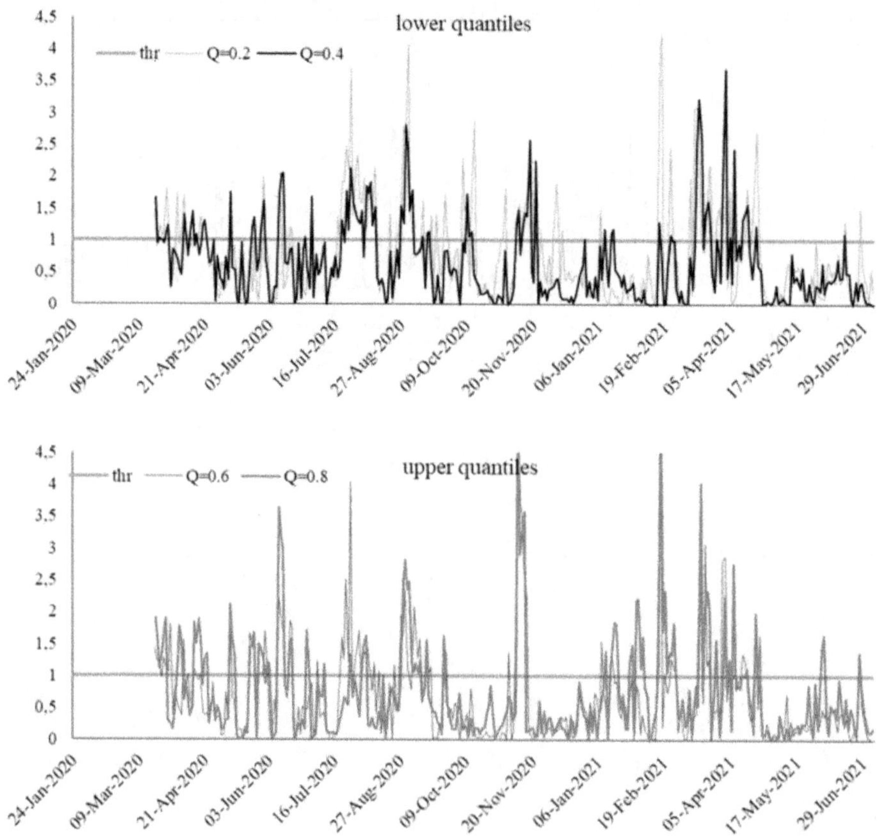

ship between COVID-19 cases and agricultural futures for six out of eight commodities. Therefore, one might conclude that the first empirical specification provides evidence of the neutrality of COVID-19 on agricultural commodity futures in the United States.

However, it is reasonable to assume that the relationship between COVID-19 and agricultural prices is dynamic and that the linkage between these variables may change over time. Therefore, in the second step of our empirical configuration, this paper utilizes the Fourier quantile causality test in a time-varying form. The inclusion of time-varying components demonstrated that strong causation exists between COVID-19 and agricultural commodity futures for six out of eight agricultural commodities during one-third of the study period. As a result, the second specification in a time-varying form has demonstrated that COVID-19 cases on agricultural commodity futures are not neutral.

Our empirical findings have some policy implications for investors and policymakers. For investors, these empirical outcomes could lead them to better anticipate the reaction of agricultural futures to future disturbances. The existence of the heterogeneous response of agricultural commodity future prices might urge investors about portfolio diversification. In addition, the response of futures of various agricultural commodities varies over the COVID-19 period. Therefore, these results might indicate the importance of portfolio allocation for investors and portfolio managers.

Figure 6. Results of time-varying Fourier causality test for COVID-19-Soybean meal nexus

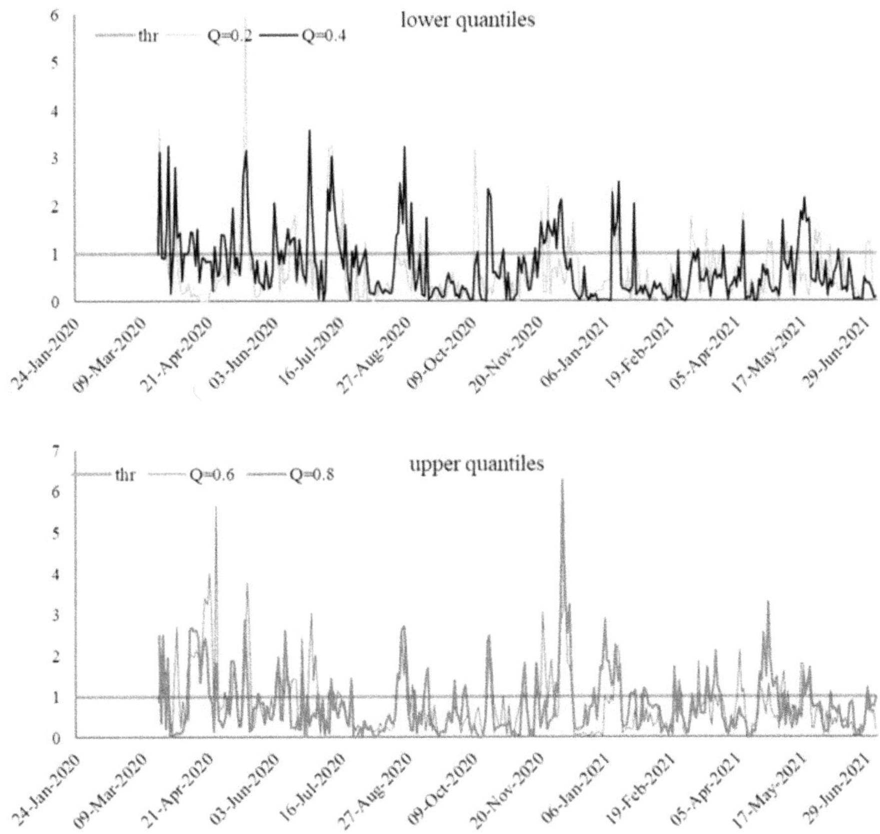

The devastating effects of the COVID-19 pandemic have heightened public awareness of government policy. As the pandemic has increased uncertainties and created instabilities in the market, governments are expected to restore confidence in the economies. Also, the sharp response of agricultural commodity futures to the COVID-19 cases urges policymakers to provide secure supply chains for agricultural commodities in the face of such exogenous shocks. Governments can also help affected industries to improve their value chains by providing financial assistance.

Since environmental threats are also potential candidates to increase uncertainty in the agricultural sector and damage supply chains, policymakers should also keep climate change concerns in mind to overcome problems, as is the case with the COVID-19 pandemic. The link between COVID-19 and agricultural commodity prices also warns central banks about agricultural price transmission to the headline inflation rate. Therefore, monetary authorities need to monitor unfavorable shocks to mitigate the impact of such shocks in maintaining price stability and financial stability.

Finally, international organizations must also take precautions to prevent disruptions in supply chains and ensure the security of global trade in times of pandemic.

Further research could address the analysis of the transmission mechanism through which the COVID-19 induced disruptions affect agricultural commodity prices.

Figure 7. Results of time-varying Fourier causality test for COVID-19-Sugar nexus

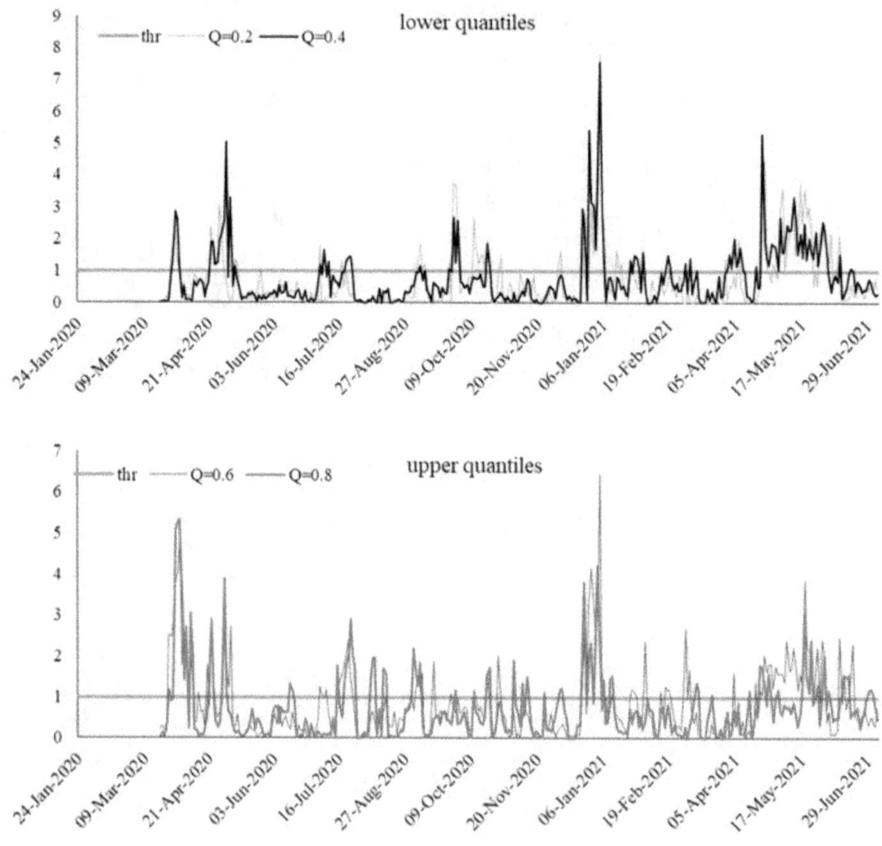

ACKNOWLEDGMENT

The authors extend sincere gratitude to:

• The Editor and the International Editorial Advisory Board (IEAB) of this book who initially desk reviewed, arranged a rigorous double/triple blind review process and conducted a thorough, minute and critical final review before accepting the chapter for publication.

• All anonymous reviewers who provided very constructive feedbacks for thorough revision, improvement, extension and fine tuning of the chapter.

• All colleagues, assistants and well-wishers who assisted the authors to complete this task.

Figure 8. Results of time-varying Fourier causality test for COVID-19-Wheat nexus

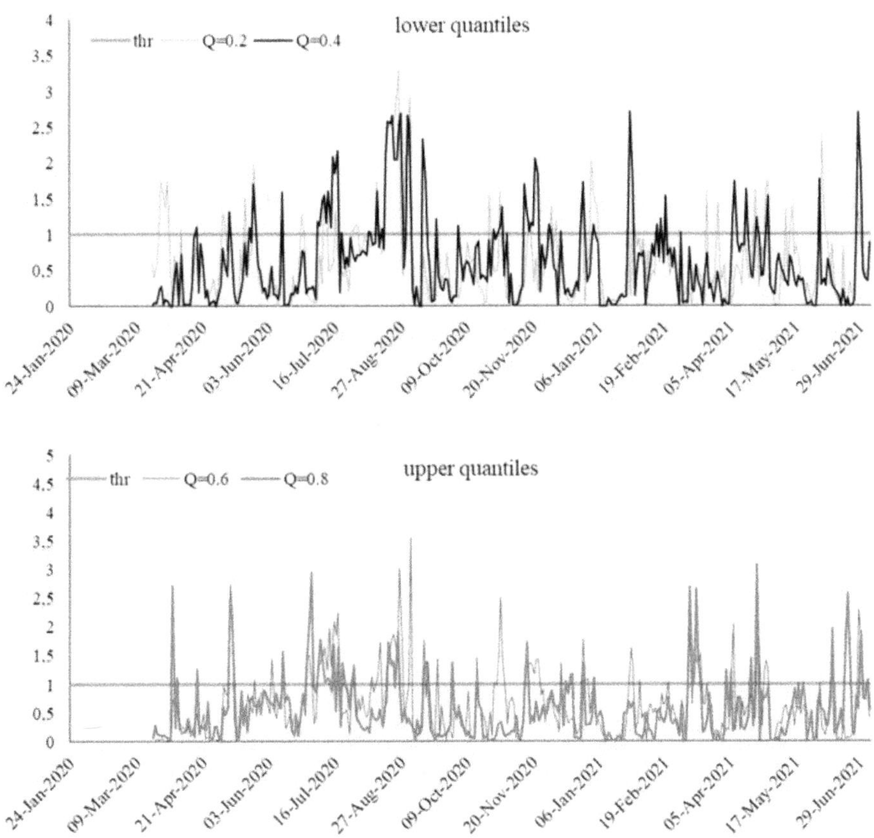

REFERENCES

Aggarwal, S., Nawn, S., & Dugar, A. (2021). What caused global stock market meltdown during the COVID pandemic–Lockdown stringency or investor panic? *Finance Research Letters*, *38*, 101827. Advance online publication. doi:10.1016/j.frl.2020.101827

Akter, S. (2020). The impact of COVID-19 related 'stay-at-home'restrictions on food prices in Europe: Findings from a preliminary analysis. *Food Security*, *12*(4), 719–725. doi:10.100712571-020-01082-3 PMID:32837638

Bahloul, W., Balcilar, M., Cunado, J., & Gupta, R. (2018). The role of economic and financial uncertainties in predicting commodity futures returns and volatility: Evidence from a nonparametric causality-in-quantiles test. *Journal of Multinational Financial Management*, *45*, 52–71. doi:10.1016/j.mulfin.2018.04.002

Balcilar, M., Bekiros, S., & Gupta, R. (2017). The role of news-based uncertainty indices in predicting oil markets: A hybrid nonparametric quantile causality method. *Empirical Economics*, *53*(3), 879–889. doi:10.100700181-016-1150-0

Balcilar, M., Ozdemir, Z. A., & Arslanturk, Y. (2010). Economic growth and energy consumption causal nexus viewed through a bootstrap rolling window. *Energy Economics*, *32*(6), 1398–1410. doi:10.1016/j.eneco.2010.05.015

Barrodale, I., & Roberts, F. D. (1973). An improved algorithm for discrete l1 linear approximation. *SIAM Journal on Numerical Analysis*, *10*(5), 839–848. doi:10.1137/0710069

Beckman, J., & Countryman, A. M. (2021). The Importance of Agriculture in the Economy: Impacts from COVID-19. *American Journal of Agricultural Economics*, *103*(5), 1595–1611. Advance online publication. doi:10.1111/ajae.12212 PMID:33821008

Borgards, O., Czudaj, R. L., & Van Hoang, T. H. (2021). Price overreactions in the commodity futures market: An intraday analysis of the Covid-19 pandemic impact. *Resources Policy*, *71*, 101966. Advance online publication. doi:10.1016/j.resourpol.2020.101966

Campiche, J. L., Bryant, H. L., Richardson, J. W., & Outlaw, J. L. (2007). Examining the evolving correspondence between petroleum prices and agricultural commodity prices. In *Agricultural and Applied Economics Association Conferences* (No. 381-2016-22070). 10.22004/ag.econ.9881

Cariappa, A. A., Acharya, K. K., Adhav, C. A., Sendhil, R., & Ramasundaram, P. (2021). Impact of COVID-19 on the Indian agricultural system: A 10-point strategy for post-pandemic recovery. *Outlook on Agriculture*, *50*(1), 26–33. doi:10.1177/0030727021989060

Casey, C. A., & Cimino-Isaacs, C. D. (2020). *Export restrictions in response to the COVID-19 pandemic*. Congressional Research Service, No. IF11551 (Version 5).

Cheng, C., Barceló, J., Hartnett, A. S., Kubinec, R., & Messerschmidt, L. (2020). COVID-19 government response event dataset (CoronaNet v.1.0). *Nature Human Behaviour*, *4*(7), 756–768. doi:10.103841562-020-0909-7 PMID:32576982

Cheng, K., Hsueh, H. P., Ranjbar, O., Wang, M. C., & Chang, T. (2021). Urbanization, coal consumption and CO_2 emissions nexus in China using bootstrap Fourier Granger causality test in quantiles. *Letters in Spatial and Resource Sciences*, *14*(1), 31–49. doi:10.100712076-020-00263-0

Dolado, J. J., & Lütkepohl, H. (1996). Making Wald tests work for cointegrated VAR systems. *Econometric Theory*, *15*(4), 369–386. doi:10.1080/07474939608800362

Elleby, C., Domínguez, I. P., Adenauer, M., & Genovese, G. (2020). Impacts of the COVID-19 pandemic on the global agricultural markets. *Environmental and Resource Economics*, *76*(4), 1067–1079. doi:10.100710640-020-00473-6 PMID:32836856

Enders, W., & Jones, P. (2016). Grain prices, oil prices, and multiple smooth breaks in a VAR. *Studies in Nonlinear Dynamics and Econometrics*, *20*(4), 399–419. doi:10.1515nde-2014-0101

EzeakuH.AsonguS. (2020). Covid-19 and Cacophony of coughing: Did International commodity Prices catch influenza? *European Xtramile Centre of African Studies* (WP/20/040). doi:10.2139/ssrn.3636399

Ezeaku, H. C., Asongu, S. A., & Nnanna, J. (2021). Volatility of international commodity prices in times of COVID-19: Effects of oil supply and global demand shocks. *The Extractive Industries and Society*, *8*(1), 257–270. doi:10.1016/j.exis.2020.12.013

FAO. (2020). *Novel Coronavirus (COVID-19)*. https://www.fao.org/2019-ncov/q-and-a/impact-on-food-and-agriculture/en/

Fasanya, I. O., Odudu, T. F., & Adekoya, O. (2019). Oil and agricultural commodity prices in Nigeria: New evidence from asymmetry and structural breaks. *International Journal of Energy Sector Management, 13*(2), 377–401. doi:10.1108/IJESM-07-2018-0004

Fowowe, B. (2016). Do oil prices drive agricultural commodity prices? Evidence from South Africa. *Energy, 104*, 149–157. doi:10.1016/j.energy.2016.03.101

Gokmenoglu, K. K., Güngör, H., & Bekun, F. V. (2020). Revisiting the linkage between oil and agricultural commodity prices: Panel evidence from an Agrarian state. *International Journal of Finance & Economics*. Advance online publication. doi:10.1002/ijfe.2083

Granger, C. W. (1969). Investigating causal relations by econometric models and cross-spectral methods. *Econometrica, 37*(3), 424–438. doi:10.2307/1912791

Gray, R. S. (2020). Agriculture, transportation, and the COVID-19 crisis. *Canadian Journal of Agricultural Economics/Revue Canadienne D'agroeconomie, 68*(2), 239-243. doi:10.1111/cjag.12235

Investing. (2021). https://www.investing.com/search/?q=futures&tab=quotes

Jarque, C. M., & Bera, A. K. (1980). Efficient tests for normality, homoscedasticity and serial independence of regression residuals. *Economics Letters, 6*(3), 255–259. doi:10.1016/0165-1765(80)90024-5

Jeong, K., Härdle, W. K., & Song, S. (2012). A consistent nonparametric test for causality in quantile. *Econometric Theory, 28*(4), 861–887. doi:10.1017/S0266466611000685

Koirala, K. H., Mishra, A. K., D'Antoni, J. M., & Mehlhorn, J. E. (2015). Energy prices and agricultural commodity prices: Testing correlation using copulas method. *Energy, 81*, 430–436. doi:10.1016/j.energy.2014.12.055

Kotyza, P., Czech, K., Wielechowski, M., Smutka, L., & Procházka, P. (2021). Sugar prices vs. financial market uncertainty in the time of crisis: Does COVID-19 induce structural changes in the relationship? *Agriculture, 11*(2), 93. Advance online publication. doi:10.3390/agriculture11020093

Ma, Z., Xu, R., & Dong, X. (2015). World oil prices and agricultural commodity prices: The evidence from China. *Agricultural Economics, 61*(12), 564–576. doi:10.17221/6/2015-AGRICECON

McFarlane, I. (2016). Agricultural commodity prices and oil prices: Mutual causation. *Outlook on Agriculture, 45*(2), 87–93. doi:10.1177/0030727016649809

Mouloudj, K., Bouarar, A. C., & Fechit, H. (2020). The impact of COVID-19 pandemic on food security. *Les Cahiers du CREAD, 36*(3), 159–184.

Nazlioglu, S. (2011). World oil and agricultural commodity prices: Evidence from nonlinear causality. *Energy Policy, 39*(5), 2935–2943. doi:10.1016/j.enpol.2011.03.001

Nazlioglu, S., Gormus, N. A., & Soytas, U. (2016). Oil prices and real estate investment trusts (REITs): Gradual-shift causality and volatility transmission analysis. *Energy Economics, 60*, 168–175. doi:10.1016/j.eneco.2016.09.009

Nazlioglu, S., & Soytas, U. (2011). World oil prices and agricultural commodity prices: Evidence from an emerging market. *Energy Economics*, *33*(3), 488–496. doi:10.1016/j.eneco.2010.11.012

Nazlioglu, S., & Soytas, U. (2012). Oil price, agricultural commodity prices, and the dollar: A panel cointegration and causality analysis. *Energy Economics*, *34*(4), 1098–1104. doi:10.1016/j.eneco.2011.09.008

Our World in Data. (2021). *Country-by-country data on confirmed cases*. https://ourworldindata.org/covid-cases

Phillips, P. C., Shi, S., & Yu, J. (2015). Testing for multiple bubbles: Historical episodes of exuberance and collapse in the S&P 500. *International Economic Review*, *56*(4), 1043–1078. doi:10.1111/iere.12132

Rawal, V., & Verma, A. (2020). Agricultural Supply Chains during the COVID-19 Lockdown. *SSER Monograph*, *20*(1), 1–26.

Reboredo, J. C. (2012). Do food and oil prices co-move? *Energy Policy*, *49*, 456–467. doi:10.1016/j.enpol.2012.06.035

Rezitis, A. N. (2015). The relationship between agricultural commodity prices, crude oil prices and US dollar exchange rates: A panel VAR approach and causality analysis. *International Review of Applied Economics*, *29*(3), 403–434. doi:10.1080/02692171.2014.1001325

Shruthi, M. S., & Ramani, D. (2021). Statistical analysis of impact of COVID 19 on India commodity markets. *Materials Today: Proceedings*, *37*, 2306–2311. doi:10.1016/j.matpr.2020.07.729 PMID:32837924

Siche, R. (2020). What is the impact of COVID-19 disease on agriculture? *Scientia Agropecuaria*, *11*(1), 3–6. doi:10.17268ci.agropecu.2020.01.00

Song, X., & Taamouti, A. (2020). Measuring Granger Causality in Quantiles. *Journal of Business & Economic Statistics*, *39*(4), 1–42. doi:10.1080/07350015.2020.1739531

Stock, J. H., & Watson, M. W. (1996). Evidence on structural instability in macroeconomic time series relations. *Journal of Business & Economic Statistics*, *14*(1), 11–30.

Su, C. W., Wang, X. Q., Tao, R., & Oana-Ramona, L. (2019). Do oil prices drive agricultural commodity prices? Further evidence in a global bio-energy context. *Energy*, *172*, 691–701. doi:10.1016/j.energy.2019.02.028

Sun, Y., Mirza, N., Qadeer, A., & Hsueh, H. P. (2021). Connectedness between oil and agricultural commodity prices during tranquil and volatile period. Is crude oil a victim indeed? *Resources Policy*, *72*, 102131. Advance online publication. doi:10.1016/j.resourpol.2021.102131

Toda, H. Y., & Yamamoto, T. (1995). Statistical inference in vector autoregressions with possibly integrated processes. *Journal of Econometrics*, *66*(1-2), 225–250. doi:10.1016/0304-4076(94)01616-8

Troster, V. (2018). Testing for Granger-causality in quantiles. *Econometric Reviews*, *37*(8), 850–866. doi:10.1080/07474938.2016.1172400

Troster, V., Shahbaz, M., & Uddin, G. S. (2018). Renewable energy, oil prices, and economic activity: A Granger-causality in quantiles analysis. *Energy Economics*, *70*, 440–452. doi:10.1016/j.eneco.2018.01.029

Uribe, J. M., & Guillen, M. (2020). *Quantile regression for cross-sectional and time series data: Applications in energy markets using R.* Springer Nature. doi:10.1007/978-3-030-44504-1

U.S. Energy Information Administration. (2021). *Petroleum & Other Liquids.* https://www.eia.gov/petroleum/data.php

Varshney, D., Roy, D., & Meenakshi, J. V. (2020). Impact of COVID-19 on agricultural markets: Assessing the roles of commodity characteristics, disease caseload and market reforms. *Indian Economic Review, 55*(1), 83–103. doi:10.100741775-020-00095-1 PMID:32863419

Wang, J., Shao, W., & Kim, J. (2020). Analysis of the impact of COVID-19 on the correlations between crude oil and agricultural futures. *Chaos, Solitons, and Fractals, 136*, 109896. Advance online publication. doi:10.1016/j.chaos.2020.109896 PMID:32421108

Yahya, M., Ghosh, S., Kanjilal, K., Dutta, A., & Uddin, G. S. (2020). Evaluation of cross-quantile dependence and causality between non-ferrous metals and clean energy indexes. *Energy, 202*, 117777. Advance online publication. doi:10.1016/j.energy.2020.117777

Yilanci, V., & Bozoklu, Ş. (2014). Price and trade volume relationship in Turkish stock market: A time-varying asymmetric causality analysis. *Ege Academic Review, 14*(2), 211–220.

Yilanci, V., & Kilci, E. N. (2021). The role of economic policy uncertainty and geopolitical risk in predicting prices of precious metals: Evidence from a time-varying bootstrap causality test. *Resources Policy, 72*, 102039. Advance online publication. doi:10.1016/j.resourpol.2021.102039

KEY TERMS AND DEFINITIONS

Agricultural Commodities: They are crops produced on farms or plantations such as corn, cotton, sugar, and wheat.

COVID-19 Pandemic: It is an ongoing global pandemic of coronavirus disease caused by severe acute respiratory syndrome coronavirus 2 (SARS-CoV-2).

Fourier Approximation: It is a method that considers the gradual structural (instead of sharp breaks) shifts in the series.

Futures: It is a standardized legal agreement to buy or sell something at a predetermined price at a certain time in the future. The buyer must purchase, or the seller must sell the underlying asset at the set price.

Granger Causality: It is a statistical hypothesis test that is developed for determining whether one series is useful in forecasting another or not.

Public Restrictions: It covers restrictions on mass gatherings, internal and international travel restrictions, and school closures to slow down the epidemic.

Quantile: A quantile is where a sample is divided into equal-sized, adjacent, subgroups.

APPENDIX

Table 3. Causality dates

Cocoa		Coffee			
Lower (71)	Upper (55)	Lower (113)		Upper (138)	
1. 02-Apr-2020	1. 19-Mar-2020	1. 18-Mar-2020	58. 12-Oct-2020	1. 18-Mar-2020	70. 10-Nov-2020
2. 06-Apr-2020	2. 01-May-2020	2. 19-Mar-2020	59. 13-Oct-2020	2. 19-Mar-2020	71. 11-Nov-2020
3. 07-Apr-2020	3. 04-May-2020	3. 20.Mar-2020	60. 20-Oct-2020	3. 20-Mar-2020	72. 18-Nov-2020
4. 20-Apr-2020	4. 27-May-2020	4. 23-Mar-2020	61. 21-Oct-2020	4. 23-Mar-2020	73. 19-Nov-2020
5. 14-May-2020	5. 04-Jun-2020	5. 24-Mar-2020	62. 29-Oct-2020	5. 24-Mar-2020	74. 20-Nov-2020
6. 15-May-2020	6. 05-Jun-2020	6. 25-Mar-2020	63. 18-Nov-2020	6. 27-Mar-2020	75. 23-Nov-2020
7. 27-May-2020	7. 08-Jun-2020	7. 27-Mar-2020	64. 20-Nov-2020	7. 30-Mar-2020	76. 24-Nov-2020
8. 28-May-2020	8. 10-Jun-2020	8. 30-Mar-2020	65. 23-Nov-2020	8. 31-Mar-2020	77. 27-Nov-2020
9. 29-May-2020	9. 25-Jun-2020	9. 31-Mar-2020	66. 24-Nov-2020	9. 06-Apr-2020	78. 30-Nov-2020
10. 04-Jun-2020	10. 30-Jun-2020	10. 01-Apr-2020	67. 25-Nov-2020	10. 07-Apr-2020	79. 01-Dec-2020
11. 05-Jun-2020	11. 01-Jul-2020	11. 03-Apr-2020	68. 27-Nov-2020	11. 08-Apr-2020	80. 02-Dec-2020
12. 01-Jul-2020	12. 02-Jul-2020	12. 07-Apr-2020	69. 30-Nov-2020	12. 09-Apr-2020	81. 03-Dec-2020
13. 02-Jul-2020	13. 21-Jul-2020	13. 08-Apr-2020	70. 01-Dec-2020	13. 13-Apr-2020	82. 04-Dec-2020
14. 06-Jul-2020	14. 24-Jul-2020	14. 09-Apr-2020	71. 02-Dec-2020	14. 14-Apr-2020	83. 07-Dec-2020
15. 13-Jul-2020	15. 03-Aug-2020	15. 14-Apr-2020	72. 03-Dec-2020	15. 15-Apr-2020	84. 08-Dec-2020
16. 16-Jul-2020	16. 28-Aug-2020	16. 24-Apr-2020	73. 04-Dec-2020	16. 16-Apr-2020	85. 09-Dec-2020
17. 20-Jul-2020	17. 31-Aug-2020	17. 29-Apr-2020	74. 07-Dec-2020	17. 17-Apr-2020	86. 10-Dec-2020
18. 24-Jul-2020	18. 01-Sep-2020	18. 30-Apr-2020	75. 08-Dec-2020	18. 20-Apr-2020	87. 11-Dec-2020
19. 04-Aug-2020	19. 02-Sep-2020	19. 01-May-2020	76. 10-Dec-2020	19. 21-Apr-2020	88. 28-Dec-2020
20. 28-Aug-2020	20. 10-Sep-2020	20. 06-May-2020	77. 14-Dec-2020	20. 22-Apr-2020	89. 31-Dec-2020
21. 31-Aug-2020	21. 22-Sep-2020	21. 12-May-2020	78. 11-Jan-2021	21. 24-Apr-2020	90. 04-Jan-2021
22. 10-Sep-2020	22. 27-Oct-2020	22. 13-May-2020	79. 12-Jan-2021	22. 30-Apr-2020	91. 05-Jan-2021
23. 24-Sep-2020	23. 27-Oct-2020	23. 14-May-2020	80. 13-Jan-2021	23. 05-May-2020	92. 06-Jan-2021
24. 14-Oct-2020	24. 07-Dec-2020	24. 15-May-2020	81. 14-Jan-2021	24. 06-May-2020	93. 07-Jan-2021
25. 23-Oct-2020	25. 08-Dec-2020	25. 18-May-2020	82. 26-Jan-2021	25. 07-May-2020	94. 08-Jan-2021
26. 26-Oct-2020	26. 09-Dec-2020	26. 03-Jun-2020	83. 24-Feb-2021	26. 12-May-2020	95. 11-Jan-2021
27. 12-Nov-2020	27. 21-Dec-2020	27. 04-Jun-2020	84. 04-Mar-2021	27. 13-May-2020	96. 12-Jan-2021
28. 07-Dec-2020	28. 22-Dec-2020	28. 08-Jun-2020	85. 05-Mar-2021	28. 14-May-2020	97. 13-Jan-2021
29. 08-Dec-2020	29. 23-Dec-2020	29. 10-Jun-2020	86. 08-Mar-2021	29. 15-May-2020	98. 14-Jan-2021
30. 09-Dec-2020	30. 24-Dec-2020	30. 11-Jun-2020	87. 09-Mar-2021	30. 21-May-2020	99. 22-Jan-2021
31. 10-Dec-2020	31. 06-Jan-2021	31. 12-Jun-2020	88. 15-Mar-2021	31. 03-Jun-2020	100. 25-Jan-2021
32. 21-Dec-2020	32. 08-Jan-2021	32. 15-Jun-2020	89. 18-Mar-2021	32. 04-Jun-2020	101. 26-Jan-2021
33. 23-Dec-2020	33. 11-Jan-2021	33. 16-Jun-2020	90. 24-Mar-2021	33. 05-Jun-2020	102. 29-Jan-2021
34. 24-Dec-2020	34. 12-Jan-2021	34. 18-Jun-2020	91. 25-Mar-2021	34. 09-Jun-2020	103. 01-Feb-2021
35. 28-Dec-2020	35. 13-Jan-2021	35. 24-Jun-2020	92. 08-Apr-2021	35. 10-Jun-2020	104. 02-Feb-2021
36. 07-Jan-2021	36. 19-Jan-2021	36. 25-Jun-2020	93. 23-Apr-2021	36. 11-Jun-2020	105. 22-Feb-2021
37. 08-Jan-2021	37. 20-Jan-2021	37. 26-Jun-2020	94. 26-Apr-2021	37. 12-Jun-2020	106. 24-Feb-2021
38. 11-Jan-2021	38. 03-Feb-2021	38. 08-Jul-2020	95. 27-Apr-2021	38. 15-Jun-2020	107. 25-Feb-2021
39. 12-Jan-2021	39. 05-Feb-2021	39. 09-Jul-2020	96. 04-May-2021	39. 16-Jun-2020	108. 04-Mar-2021
40. 13-Jan-2021	40. 10-Feb-2021	40. 10-Jul-2020	97. 05-May-2021	40. 19-Jun-2020	109. 09-Mar-2021
41. 21-Jan-2021	41. 16-Feb-2021	41. 13-Jul-2020	98. 06-May-2021	41. 23-Jun-2020	110. 12-Mar-2021
42. 26-Jan-2021	42. 17-Feb-2021	42. 14-Jul-2020	99. 10-May-2021	42. 24-Jun-2020	111. 15-Mar-2021
43. 27-Jan-2021	43. 19-Feb-2021	43. 15-Jul-2020	100. 13-May-2021	43. 25-Jun-2020	112. 18-Mar-2021
44. 28-Jan-2021	44. 07-Apr-2021	44. 16-Jul-2020	101. 14-May-2021	44. 26-Jun-2020	113. 19-Mar-2021
45. 29-Jan-2021	45. 21-Apr-2021	45. 17-Jul-2020	102. 17-May-2021	45. 29-Jun-2020	114. 22-Mar-2021
46. 01-Feb-2021	46. 22-Apr-2021	46. 20-Jul-2020	103. 18-May-2021	46. 30-Jun-2020	115. 23-Mar-2021
47. 03-Feb-2021	47. 23-Apr-2021	47. 23-Jul-2020	104. 19-May-2021	47. 08-Jul-2020	116. 24-Mar-2021
48. 05-Feb-2021	48. 29-Apr-2021	48. 27-Jul-2020	105. 20-May-2021	48. 09-Jul-2020	117. 06-Apr-2021
49. 10-Feb-2021	49. 30-Apr-2021	49. 31-Jul-2020	106. 25-May-2021	49. 10-Jul-2020	118. 07-Apr-2021
50. 11-Feb-2021	50. 04-May-2021	50. 20-Aug-2020	107. 26-May-2021	50. 14-Jul-2020	119. 08-Apr-2021
51. 12-Feb-2021	51. 04-Jun-2021	51. 21-Aug-2020	108. 27-May-2021	51. 15-Jul-2020	120. 19-Apr-2021
52. 16-Feb-2021	52. 07-Jun-2021	52. 24-Aug-2020	109. 04-Jun-2021	52. 22-Jul-2020	121. 20-Apr-2021
53. 17-Feb-2021	53. 08-Jun-2021	53. 25-Aug-2020	110. 10-Jun-2021	53. 20-Aug-2020	122. 21-Apr-2021
54. 18-Feb-2021	54. 09-Jun-2021	54. 26-Aug-2020	111. 14-Jun-2021	54. 21-Aug-2020	123. 22-Apr-2021
55. 19-Feb-2021	55. 25-Jun-2021	55. 27-Aug-2020	112. 29-Jun-2021	55. 24-Aug-2020	124. 23-Apr-2021
56. 22-Feb-2021		56. 31-Aug-2020	113. 30-Jun-2021	56. 25-Aug-2020	125. 26-Apr-2021
57. 06-Apr-2021		57. 10-Sep-2020		57. 26-Aug-2020	126. 27-Apr-2021
58. 07-Apr-2021				58. 27-Aug-2020	127. 28-Apr-2021
59. 12-Apr-2021				59. 31-Aug-2020	128. 29-Apr-2021
60. 13-Apr-2021				60. 01-Sep-2020	129. 03-May-2021
61. 28-Apr-2021				61. 09-Sep-2020	130. 04-May-2021
62. 30-Apr-2021				62. 10-Sep-2020	131. 06-May-2021
63. 03-May-2021				63. 28-Sep-2020	132. 14-May-2021
64. 04-May-2021				64. 02-Oct-2020	133. 17-May-2021
65. 07-May-2021				65. 05-Oct-2020	134. 18-May-2021
66. 18-May-2021				66. 19-Oct-2020	135. 19-May-2021
67. 09-Jun-2021				67. 20-Oct-2020	136. 20-May-2021
68. 17-Jun-2021				68. 21-Oct-2020	137. 04-Jun-2021
69. 22-Jun-2021				69. 28-Oct-2020	138. 29-Jun-2021
70. 28-Jun-2021					
71. 30-Jun-2021					

Table 4. Causality dates (continued)

Corn				Cotton			
Lower (118)		Upper (107)		Lower (98)		Upper (86)	
1. 18-Mar-2020		1. 18-Mar-2020		1. 25-Mar-2020		1. 06-May-2020	
2. 20-Mar-2020		2. 24-Mar-2020		2. 03-Apr-2020		2. 15-May-2020	
3. 31-Mar-2020		3. 25-Mar-2020		3. 07-Apr-2020		3. 20-May-2020	
4. 01-Apr-2020		4. 26-Mar-2020		4. 08-Apr-2020		4. 21-May-2020	
5. 06-Apr-2020		5. 27-Mar-2020		5. 09-Apr-2020		5. 22-May-2020	
6. 07-Apr-2020		6. 31-Mar-2020		6. 13-Apr-2020		6. 29-May-2020	
7. 08-Apr-2020		7. 01-Apr-2020		7. 16-Apr-2020		7. 01-Jun-2020	
8. 09-Apr-2020		8. 02-Apr-2020		8. 17-Apr-2020		8. 03-Jun-2020	
9. 13-Apr-2020		9. 03-Apr-2020		9. 20-Apr-2020		9. 09-Jun-2020	
10. 14-Apr-2020		10. 09-Apr-2020		10. 21-Apr-2020		10. 10-Jun-2020	
11. 15-Apr-2020		11. 23-Apr-2020		11. 22-Apr-2020		11. 11-Jun-2020	
12. 16-Apr-2020		12. 06-May-2020		12. 23-Apr-2020		12. 17-Jun-2020	
13. 20-Apr-2020	72. 17-Dec-2020	13. 07-May-2020		13. 24-Apr-2020		13. 18-Jun-2020	
14. 21-Apr-2020	73. 21-Dec-2020	14. 08-May-2020		14. 27-Apr-2020		14. 19-Jun-2020	
15. 23-Apr-2020	74. 23-Dec-2020	15. 11-May-2020		15. 28-Apr-2020		15. 30-Jun-2020	
16. 24-Apr-2020	75. 24-Dec-2020	16. 12-May-2020		16. 06-May-2020		16. 01-Jul-2020	
17. 27-Apr-2020	76. 29-Dec-2020	17. 13-May-2020		17. 19-May-2020		17. 02-Jul-2020	
18. 28-Apr-2020	77. 14-Jan-2021	18. 14-May-2020	72. 08-Feb-2021	18. 20-May-2020		18. 07-Jul-2020	
19. 29-Apr-2020	78. 28-Jan-2021	19. 15-May-2020	73. 09-Feb-2021	19. 21-May-2020		19. 08-Jul-2020	
20. 30-Apr-2020	79. 05-Feb-2021	20. 18-May-2020	74. 16-Feb-2021	20. 22-May-2020		20. 09-Jul-2020	
21. 01-May-2020	80. 08-Feb-2021	21. 20-May-2020	75. 17-Feb-2021	21. 26-May-2020		21. 10-Jul-2020	
22. 04-May-2020	81. 11-Feb-2021	22. 21-May-2020	76. 18-Feb-2021	22. 27-May-2020		22. 21-Jul-2020	
23. 05-May-2020	82. 16-Feb-2021	23. 22-May-2020	77. 19-Feb-2021	23. 29-May-2020	72. 01-Mar-2021	23. 29-Jul-2020	
24. 06-May-2020	83. 17-Feb-2021	24. 26-May-2020	78. 22-Feb-2021	24. 01-Jun-2020	73. 03-Mar-2021	24. 30-Jul-2020	
25. 07-May-2020	84. 18-Feb-2021	25. 27-May-2020	79. 01-Mar-2021	25. 05-Jun-2020	74. 04-Mar-2021	25. 05-Aug-2020	
26. 08-May-2020	85. 22-Feb-2021	26. 28-May-2020	80. 02-Mar-2021	26. 08-Jun-2020	75. 09-Apr-2021	26. 11-Aug-2020	
27. 11-May-2020	86. 10-Mar-2021	27. 29-May-2020	81. 12-Mar-2021	27. 09-Jun-2020	76. 14-Apr-2021	27. 12-Aug-2020	
28. 12-May-2020	87. 11-Mar-2021	28. 04-Jun-2020	82. 15-Mar-2021	28. 10-Jun-2020	77. 20-Apr-2021	28. 13-Aug-2020	
29. 13-May-2020	88. 12-Mar-2021	29. 08-Jun-2020	83. 16-Mar-2021	29. 11-Jun-2020	78. 21-Apr-2021	29. 24-Aug-2020	72. 27-Apr-2021
30. 14-May-2020	89. 15-Mar-2021	30. 18-Jun-2020	84. 17-Mar-2021	30. 12-Jun-2020	79. 23-Apr-2021	30. 26-Aug-2020	73. 28-Apr-2021
31. 20-May-2020	90. 16-Mar-2021	31. 26-Jun-2020	85. 05-Apr-2021	31. 18-Jun-2020	80. 26-Apr-2021	31. 28-Aug-2020	74. 30-Apr-2021
32. 21-May-2020	91. 17-Mar-2021	32. 06-Jul-2020	86. 06-Apr-2021	32. 19-Jun-2020	81. 27-Apr-2021	32. 17-Sep-2020	75. 03-May-2021
33. 22-May-2020	92. 30-Mar-2021	33. 22-Jul-2020	87. 07-Apr-2021	33. 30-Jun-2020	82. 28-Apr-2021	33. 30-Sep-2020	76. 04-May-2021
34. 26-May-2020	93. 05-Apr-2021	34. 23-Jul-2020	88. 08-Apr-2021	34. 02-Jul-2020	83. 29-Apr-2021	34. 06-Oct-2020	77. 05-May-2021
35. 27-May-2020	94. 06-Apr-2021	35. 24-Jul-2020	89. 09-Apr-2021	35. 06-Jul-2020	84. 30-Apr-2021	35. 07-Oct-2020	78. 07-May-2021
36. 29-May-2020	95. 07-Apr-2021	36. 28-Jul-2020	90. 12-Apr-2021	36. 09-Jul-2020	85. 03-May-2021	36. 29-Oct-2020	79. 01-Jun-2021
37. 01-Jun-2020	96. 08-Apr-2021	37. 29-Jul-2020	91. 13-Apr-2021	37. 29-Jul-2020	86. 04-May-2021	37. 30-Oct-2020	80. 03-Jun-2021
38. 02-Jun-2020	97. 13-Apr-2021	38. 06-Aug-2020	92. 14-Apr-2021	38. 05-Aug-2020	87. 05-May-2021	38. 02-Nov-2020	81. 04-Jun-2021
39. 03-Jun-2020	98. 14-Apr-2021	39. 11-Aug-2020	93. 15-Apr-2021	39. 07-Aug-2020	88. 06-May-2021	39. 04-Nov-2020	82. 09-Jun-2021
40. 16-Jun-2020	99. 15-Apr-2021	40. 13-Aug-2020	94. 16-Apr-2021	40. 11-Aug-2020	89. 07-May-2021	40. 06-Nov-2020	83. 16-Jun-2021
41. 17-Jun-2020	100. 16-Apr-2021	41. 17-Aug-2020	95. 19-Apr-2021	41. 13-Aug-2020	90. 12-May-2021	41. 12-Nov-2020	84. 17-Jun-2021
42. 18-Jun-2020	101. 20-Apr-2021	42. 31-Aug-2020	96. 20-Apr-2021	42. 08-Sep-2020	91. 21-May-2021	42. 13-Nov-2020	85. 18-Jun-2021
43. 13-Jul-2020	102. 21-Apr-2021	43. 01-Sep-2020	97. 21-Apr-2021	43. 09-Sep-2020	92. 24-May-2021	43. 19-Nov-2020	86. 29-Jun-2021
44. 22-Jul-2020	103. 22-Apr-2021	44. 02-Sep-2020	98. 22-Apr-2021	44. 16-Sep-2020	93. 26-May-2021	44. 02-Dec-2020	
45. 23-Jul-2020	104. 26-Apr-2021	45. 03-Sep-2020	99. 26-Apr-2021	45. 17-Sep-2020	94. 27-May-2021	45. 09-Dec-2020	
46. 04-Aug-2020	105. 27-Apr-2021	46. 04-Sep-2020	100. 28-Apr-2021	46. 30-Sep-2020	95. 28-May-2021	46. 10-Dec-2020	
47. 05-Aug-2020	106. 28-Apr-2021	47. 08-Sep-2020	101. 30-Apr-2021	47. 28-Oct-2020	96. 01-Jun-2021	47. 11-Dec-2020	
48. 01-Sep-2020	107. 30-Apr-2021	48. 09-Sep-2020	102. 07-May-2021	48. 29-Oct-2020	97. 03-Jun-2021	48. 14-Dec-2020	
49. 02-Sep-2020	108. 03-May-2021	49. 11-Sep-2020	103. 12-May-2021	49. 30-Oct-2020	98. 17-Jun-2021	49. 16-Dec-2020	
50. 03-Sep-2020	109. 04-May-2021	50. 14-Sep-2020	104. 01-Jun-2021	50. 02-Nov-2020		50. 29-Dec-2020	
51. 04-Sep-2020	110. 26-May-2021	51. 16-Sep-2020	105. 02-Jun-2021	51. 03-Nov-2020		51. 30-Dec-2020	
52. 08-Sep-2020	111. 01-Jun-2021	52. 17-Sep-2020	106. 03-Jun-2021	52. 04-Nov-2020		52. 31-Dec-2020	
53. 09-Sep-2020	112. 02-Jun-2021	53. 18-Sep-2020	107. 10-Jun-2021	53. 05-Nov-2020		53. 04-Jan-2021	
54. 11-Sep-2020	113. 03-Jun-2021	54. 01-Oct-2020		54. 06-Nov-2020		54. 05-Jan-2021	
55. 14-Sep-2020	114. 04-Jun-2021	55. 09-Oct-2020		55. 10-Nov-2020		55. 06-Jan-2021	
56. 15-Sep-2020	115. 07-Jun-2021	56. 12-Oct-2020		56. 18-Nov-2020		56. 07-Jan-2021	
57. 17-Sep-2020	116. 08-Jun-2021	57. 13-Oct-2020		57. 19-Nov-2020		57. 22-Jan-2021	
58. 21-Sep-2020	117. 09-Jun-2021	58. 14-Oct-2020		58. 20-Nov-2020		58. 25-Jan-2021	
59. 09-Oct-2020	118. 25-Jun-2021	59. 29-Oct-2020		59. 23-Nov-2020		59. 28-Jan-2021	
60. 12-Oct-2020		60. 30-Oct-2020		60. 22-Dec-2020		60. 09-Feb-2021	
61. 26-Oct-2020		61. 02-Nov-2020		61. 28-Dec-2020		61. 16-Feb-2021	
62. 27-Oct-2020		62. 11-Nov-2020		62. 31-Dec-2020		62. 26-Feb-2021	
63. 02-Nov-2020		63. 21-Dec-2020		63. 08-Jan-2021		63. 01-Mar-2021	
64. 17-Nov-2020		64. 22-Dec-2020		64. 22-Jan-2021		64. 02-Mar-2021	
65. 18-Nov-2020		65. 23-Dec-2020		65. 10-Feb-2021		65. 04-Mar-2021	
66. 19-Nov-2020		66. 13-Jan-2021		66. 11-Feb-2021		66. 05-Mar-2021	
67. 20-Nov-2020		67. 14-Jan-2021		67. 12-Feb-2021		67. 08-Mar-2021	
68. 23-Nov-2020		68. 15-Jan-2021		68. 16-Feb-2021		68. 07-Apr-2021	
69. 25-Nov-2020		69. 27-Jan-2021		69. 24-Feb-2021		69. 09-Apr-2021	
70. 30-Nov-2020		70. 28-Jan-2021		70. 25-Feb-2021		70. 12-Apr-2021	
71. 08-Dec-2020		71. 02-Feb-2021		71. 26-Feb-2021		71. 26-Apr-2021	

Table 5. Causality dates (continued)

Soybeans				Soybean-meal			
Lower (122)		Upper (116)		Lower (105)		Upper (84)	
1. 18-Mar-2020		1. 18-Mar-2020		1. 19-Mar-2020		1. 19-Mar-2020	
2. 19-Mar-2020		2. 19-Mar-2020		2. 20-Mar-2020		2. 25-Mar-2020	
3. 20-Mar-2020		3. 20-Mar-2020		3. 25-Mar-2020		3. 30-Mar-2020	
4. 23-Mar-2020		4. 23-Mar-2020		4. 26-Mar-2020		4. 01-Apr-2020	
5. 24-Mar-2020		5. 24-Mar-2020		5. 30-Mar-2020		5. 02-Apr-2020	
6. 25-Mar-2020		6. 25-Mar-2020		6. 06-Apr-2020		6. 23-Apr-2020	
7. 26-Mar-2020		7. 26-Mar-2020		7. 07-Apr-2020		7. 30-Apr-2020	
8. 01-Apr-2020		8. 27-Mar-2020		8. 08-Apr-2020		8. 07-May-2020	
9. 03-Apr-2020		9. 01-Apr-2020		9. 17-Apr-2020		9. 19-May-2020	
10. 06-Apr-2020		10. 02-Apr-2020		10. 21-Apr-2020		10. 02-Jul-2020	
11. 08-Apr-2020	72. 12-Oct-2020	11. 03-Apr-2020		11. 23-Apr-2020		11. 06-Jul-2020	
12. 09-Apr-2020	73. 13-Oct-2020	12. 06-Apr-2020		12. 24-Apr-2020		12. 16-Jul-2020	
13. 13-Apr-2020	74. 14-Oct-2020	13. 08-Apr-2020		13. 05-May-2020		13. 17-Jul-2020	
14. 14-Apr-2020	75. 03-Nov-2020	14. 14-Apr-2020	72. 05-Nov-2020	14. 06-May-2020		14. 20-Jul-2020	
15. 15-Apr-2020	76. 10-Nov-2020	15. 15-Apr-2020	73. 10-Nov-2020	15. 07-May-2020		15. 21-Jul-2020	
16. 16-Apr-2020	77. 11-Nov-2020	16. 16-Apr-2020	74. 11-Nov-2020	16. 19-May-2020		16. 23-Jul-2020	
17. 17-Apr-2020	78. 12-Nov-2020	17. 17-Apr-2020	75. 12-Nov-2020	17. 22-May-2020		17. 03-Aug-2020	
18. 20-Apr-2020	79. 13-Nov-2020	18. 21-Apr-2020	76. 13-Nov-2020	18. 02-Jun-2020		18. 04-Aug-2020	
19. 21-Apr-2020	80. 16-Nov-2020	19. 22-Apr-2020	77. 16-Nov-2020	19. 09-Jun-2020		19. 05-Aug-2020	
20. 22-Apr-2020	81. 17-Nov-2020	20. 07-May-2020	78. 17-Nov-2020	20. 13-Jul-2020	72. 27-Jan-2021	20. 06-Aug-2020	
21. 07-May-2020	82. 18-Nov-2020	21. 08-May-2020	79. 07-Jan-2021	21. 16-Jul-2020	73. 03-Feb-2021	21. 07-Aug-2020	
22. 21-May-2020	83. 23-Nov-2020	22. 11-May-2020	80. 11-Jan-2021	22. 20-Jul-2020	74. 04-Feb-2021	22. 10-Aug-2020	
23. 22-May-2020	84. 25-Nov-2020	23. 20-May-2020	81. 13-Jan-2021	23. 21-Jul-2020	75. 17-Feb-2021	23. 12-Aug-2020	
24. 28-May-2020	85. 04-Dec-2020	24. 21-May-2020	82. 14-Jan-2021	24. 22-Jul-2020	76. 24-Feb-2021	24. 13-Aug-2020	
25. 29-May-2020	86. 07-Dec-2020	25. 22-May-2020	83. 15-Jan-2021	25. 23-Jul-2020	77. 01-Mar-2021	25. 14-Aug-2020	
26. 01-Jun-2020	87. 08-Dec-2020	26. 27-May-2020	84. 19-Jan-2021	26. 24-Jul-2020	78. 02-Mar-2021	26. 18-Aug-2020	
27. 09-Jun-2020	88. 10-Dec-2020	27. 28-May-2020	85. 27-Jan-2021	27. 27-Jul-2020	79. 04-Mar-2021	27. 21-Aug-2020	
28. 10-Jun-2020	89. 24-Dec-2020	28. 29-May-2020	86. 28-Jan-2021	28. 28-Jul-2020	80. 08-Mar-2021	28. 24-Aug-2020	
29. 11-Jun-2020	90. 06-Jan-2021	29. 01-Jun-2020	87. 01-Feb-2021	29. 29-Jul-2020	81. 09-Mar-2021	29. 25-Aug-2020	
30. 16-Jun-2020	91. 08-Jan-2021	30. 02-Jun-2020	88. 02-Feb-2021	30. 30-Jul-2020	82. 10-Mar-2021	30. 26-Aug-2020	72. 18-Mar-2021
31. 17-Jun-2020	92. 13-Jan-2021	31. 03-Jun-2020	89. 04-Feb-2021	31. 31-Jul-2020	83. 11-Mar-2021	31. 27-Aug-2020	73. 19-Mar-2021
32. 25-Jun-2020	93. 14-Jan-2021	32. 09-Jun-2020	90. 16-Feb-2021	32. 03-Aug-2020	84. 12-Mar-2021	32. 28-Aug-2020	74. 22-Mar-2021
33. 30-Jun-2020	94. 16-Feb-2021	33. 10-Jun-2020	91. 17-Feb-2021	33. 04-Aug-2020	85. 15-Mar-2021	33. 31-Aug-2020	75. 23-Mar-2021
34. 17-Jul-2020	95. 17-Feb-2021	34. 11-Jun-2020	92. 19-Feb-2021	34. 05-Aug-2020	86. 16-Mar-2021	34. 01-Sep-2020	76. 29-Mar-2021
35. 20-Jul-2020	96. 23-Feb-2021	35. 16-Jun-2020	93. 22-Feb-2021	35. 06-Aug-2020	87. 17-Mar-2021	35. 02-Sep-2020	77. 30-Mar-2021
36. 21-Jul-2020	97. 24-Feb-2021	36. 17-Jun-2020	94. 23-Feb-2021	36. 07-Aug-2020	88. 18-Mar-2021	36. 03-Sep-2020	78. 06-Apr-2021
37. 22-Jul-2020	98. 25-Feb-2021	37. 26-Jun-2020	95. 24-Feb-2021	37. 11-Aug-2020	89. 19-Mar-2021	37. 04-Sep-2020	79. 08-Apr-2021
38. 23-Jul-2020	99. 08-Mar-2021	38. 06-Jul-2020	96. 25-Feb-2021	38. 12-Aug-2020	90. 29-Mar-2021	38. 08-Sep-2020	80. 20-Apr-2021
39. 24-Jul-2020	100. 10-Mar-2021	39. 09-Jul-2020	97. 26-Feb-2021	39. 19-Aug-2020	91. 30-Mar-2021	39. 09-Sep-2020	81. 28-May-2021
40. 27-Jul-2020	101. 11-Mar-2021	40. 21-Jul-2020	98. 12-Mar-2021	40. 21-Aug-2020	92. 01-Apr-2021	40. 10-Sep-2020	82. 02-Jun-2021
41. 28-Jul-2020	102. 12-Mar-2021	41. 22-Jul-2020	99. 15-Mar-2021	41. 25-Aug-2020	93. 05-Apr-2021	41. 11-Sep-2020	83. 29-Jun-2021
42. 29-Jul-2020	103. 15-Mar-2021	42. 23-Jul-2020	100. 17-Mar-2021	42. 27-Aug-2020	94. 06-Apr-2021	42. 14-Sep-2020	84. 06-Jul-2021
43. 30-Jul-2020	104. 17-Mar-2021	43. 24-Jul-2020	101. 18-Mar-2021	43. 28-Aug-2020	95. 08-Apr-2021	43. 15-Sep-2020	
44. 31-Jul-2020	105. 18-Mar-2021	44. 27-Jul-2020	102. 19-Mar-2021	44. 31-Aug-2020	96. 12-May-2021	44. 23-Sep-2020	
45. 03-Aug-2020	106. 19-Mar-2021	45. 29-Jul-2020	103. 24-Mar-2021	45. 01-Sep-2020	97. 17-May-2021	45. 02-Oct-2020	
46. 04-Aug-2020	107. 24-Mar-2021	46. 30-Jul-2020	104. 29-Mar-2021	46. 02-Sep-2020	98. 19-May-2021	46. 05-Oct-2020	
47. 05-Aug-2020	108. 25-Mar-2021	47. 31-Jul-2020	105. 30-Mar-2021	47. 04-Sep-2020	99. 20-May-2021	47. 15-Oct-2020	
48. 06-Aug-2020	109. 26-Mar-2021	48. 03-Aug-2020	106. 01-Apr-2021	48. 09-Sep-2020	100. 07-Jun-2021	48. 23-Oct-2020	
49. 07-Aug-2020	110. 29-Mar-2021	49. 04-Aug-2020	107. 06-Apr-2021	49. 10-Sep-2020	101. 09-Jun-2021	49. 26-Oct-2020	
50. 10-Aug-2020	111. 30-Mar-2021	50. 05-Aug-2020	108. 12-Apr-2021	50. 11-Sep-2020	102. 10-Jun-2021	50. 03-Dec-2020	
51. 11-Aug-2020	112. 06-Apr-2021	51. 06-Aug-2020	109. 13-Apr-2021	51. 21-Sep-2020	103. 11-Jun-2021	51. 07-Dec-2020	
52. 12-Aug-2020	113. 12-Apr-2021	52. 07-Aug-2020	110. 14-Apr-2021	52. 22-Oct-2020	104. 22-Jun-2021	52. 09-Dec-2020	
53. 20-Aug-2020	114. 13-Apr-2021	53. 11-Aug-2020	111. 20-Apr-2021	53. 23-Oct-2020	105. 23-Jun-2021	53. 11-Dec-2020	
54. 25-Aug-2020	115. 14-Apr-2021	54. 13-Aug-2020	112. 21-Apr-2021	54. 26-Oct-2020		54. 14-Dec-2020	
55. 26-Aug-2020	116. 16-Apr-2021	55. 17-Aug-2020	113. 22-Apr-2021	55. 18-Nov-2020		55. 16-Dec-2020	
56. 27-Aug-2020	117. 19-Apr-2021	56. 24-Aug-2020	114. 02-Jun-2021	56. 19-Nov-2020		56. 21-Dec-2020	
57. 28-Aug-2020	118. 20-Apr-2021	57. 27-Aug-2020	115. 03-Jun-2021	57. 20-Nov-2020		57. 31-Dec-2020	
58. 31-Aug-2020	119. 21-Apr-2021	58. 28-Aug-2020	116. 25-Jun-2021	58. 23-Nov-2020		58. 06-Jan-2021	
59. 01-Sep-2020	120. 27-May-2021	59. 31-Aug-2020		59. 24-Nov-2020		59. 20-Jan-2021	
60. 02-Sep-2020	121. 16-Jun-2021	60. 01-Sep-2020		60. 25-Nov-2020		60. 28-Jan-2021	
61. 03-Sep-2020	122. 25-Jun-2021	61. 02-Sep-2020		61. 01-Dec-2020		61. 04-Feb-2021	
62. 11-Sep-2020		62. 03-Sep-2020		62. 14-Dec-2020		62. 08-Feb-2021	
63. 15-Sep-2020		63. 04-Sep-2020		63. 18-Dec-2020		63. 24-Feb-2021	
64. 16-Sep-2020		64. 08-Sep-2020		64. 21-Dec-2020		64. 02-Mar-2021	
65. 17-Sep-2020		65. 09-Sep-2020		65. 28-Dec-2020		65. 03-Mar-2021	
66. 21-Sep-2020		66. 10-Sep-2020		66. 29-Dec-2020		66. 04-Mar-2021	
67. 25-Sep-2020		67. 15-Sep-2020		67. 31-Dec-2020		67. 11-Mar-2021	
68. 28-Sep-2020		68. 16-Sep-2020		68. 04-Jan-2021		68. 12-Mar-2021	
69. 07-Oct-2020		69. 17-Sep-2020		69. 06-Jan-2021		69. 15-Mar-2021	
70. 08-Oct-2020		70. 25-Sep-2020		70. 20-Jan-2021		70. 16-Mar-2021	
71. 09-Oct-2020		71. 28-Sep-2020		71. 26-Jan-2021		71. 17-Mar-2021	

Table 6. Causality dates (continued)

Sugar				Wheat			
Lower (108)		Upper (130)		Lower (100)		Upper (89)	
1. 25-Mar-2020		1. 24-Mar-2020		1. 23-Mar-2020		1. 31-Mar-2020	
2. 26-Mar-2020		2. 25-Mar-2020		2. 24-Mar-2020		2. 02-Apr-2020	
3. 27-Mar-2020		3. 26-Mar-2020		3. 25-Mar-2020		3. 16-Apr-2020	
4. 30-Mar-2020		4. 27-Mar-2020		4. 26-Mar-2020		4. 07-May-2020	
5. 31-Mar-2020		5. 30-Mar-2020		5. 27-Mar-2020		5. 08-May-2020	
6. 22-Apr-2020		6. 31-Mar-2020		6. 06-Apr-2020		6. 22-May-2020	
7. 23-Apr-2020		7. 01-Apr-2020	72. 06-Jan-2021	7. 16-Apr-2020		7. 04-Jun-2020	
8. 24-Apr-2020		8. 02-Apr-2020	73. 07-Jan-2021	8. 04-May-2020		8. 11-Jun-2020	
9. 27-Apr-2020		9. 03-Apr-2020	74. 11-Jan-2021	9. 05-May-2020		9. 26-Jun-2020	
10. 28-Apr-2020		10. 06-Apr-2020	75. 12-Jan-2021	10. 07-May-2020		10. 29-Jun-2020	
11. 29-Apr-2020		11. 07-Apr-2020	76. 26-Jan-2021	11. 18-May-2020		11. 30-Jun-2020	
12. 30-Apr-2020		12. 08-Apr-2020	77. 27-Jan-2021	12. 20-May-2020		12. 06-Jul-2020	
13. 01-May-2020		13. 14-Apr-2020	78. 28-Jan-2021	13. 22-May-2020		13. 07-Jul-2020	
14. 05-May-2020		14. 20-Apr-2020	79. 03-Feb-2021	14. 26-May-2020		14. 08-Jul-2020	
15. 07-May-2020		15. 21-Apr-2020	80. 12-Feb-2021	15. 11-Jun-2020		15. 09-Jul-2020	
16. 08-May-2020		16. 22-Apr-2020	81. 17-Feb-2021	16. 24-Jun-2020		16. 10-Jul-2020	
17. 26-May-2020		17. 23-Apr-2020	82. 18-Feb-2021	17. 06-Jul-2020		17. 13-Jul-2020	
18. 02-Jul-2020	72. 07-Apr-2021	18. 29-Apr-2020	83. 19-Feb-2021	18. 07-Jul-2020		18. 14-Jul-2020	
19. 07-Jul-2020	73. 08-Apr-2021	19. 30-Apr-2020	84. 02-Mar-2021	19. 08-Jul-2020		19. 15-Jul-2020	
20. 09-Jul-2020	74. 16-Apr-2021	20. 01-May-2020	85. 04-Mar-2021	20. 09-Jul-2020		20. 16-Jul-2020	
21. 17-Jul-2020	75. 21-Apr-2021	21. 04-May-2020	86. 09-Mar-2021	21. 10-Jul-2020		21. 17-Jul-2020	
22. 21-Jul-2020	76. 22-Apr-2021	22. 05-May-2020	87. 10-Mar-2021	22. 13-Jul-2020	72. 04-Jan-2021	22. 21-Jul-2020	
23. 22-Jul-2020	77. 23-Apr-2021	23. 12-Jun-2020	88. 18-Mar-2021	23. 14-Jul-2020	73. 05-Jan-2021	23. 28-Jul-2020	
24. 23-Jul-2020	78. 26-Apr-2021	24. 15-Jun-2020	89. 01-Apr-2021	24. 15-Jul-2020	74. 26-Jan-2021	24. 07-Aug-2020	
25. 04-Sep-2020	79. 27-Apr-2021	25. 02-Jul-2020	90. 13-Apr-2021	25. 16-Jul-2020	75. 27-Jan-2021	25. 12-Aug-2020	
26. 08-Sep-2020	80. 28-Apr-2021	26. 06-Jul-2020	91. 16-Apr-2021	26. 17-Jul-2020	76. 28-Jan-2021	26. 13-Aug-2020	
27. 10-Sep-2020	81. 29-Apr-2021	27. 08-Jul-2020	92. 20-Apr-2021	27. 21-Jul-2020	77. 29-Jan-2021	27. 18-Aug-2020	72. 31-Mar-2021
28. 25-Sep-2020	82. 30-Apr-2021	28. 15-Jul-2020	93. 21-Apr-2021	28. 28-Jul-2020	78. 12-Feb-2021	28. 19-Aug-2020	73. 05-Apr-2021
29. 29-Sep-2020	83. 03-May-2021	29. 16-Jul-2020	94. 22-Apr-2021	29. 29-Jul-2020	79. 17-Feb-2021	29. 20-Aug-2020	74. 06-Apr-2021
30. 30-Sep-2020	84. 04-May-2021	30. 17-Jul-2020	95. 23-Apr-2021	30. 30-Jul-2020	80. 19-Feb-2021	30. 21-Aug-2020	75. 16-Apr-2021
31. 01-Oct-2020	85. 05-May-2021	31. 20-Jul-2020	96. 26-Apr-2021	31. 06-Aug-2020	81. 02-Mar-2021	31. 24-Aug-2020	76. 21-Apr-2021
32. 12-Oct-2020	86. 06-May-2021	32. 21-Jul-2020	97. 27-Apr-2021	32. 07-Aug-2020	82. 18-Mar-2021	32. 25-Aug-2020	77. 22-Apr-2021
33. 13-Oct-2020	87. 07-May-2021	33. 22-Jul-2020	98. 28-Apr-2021	33. 12-Aug-2020	83. 25-Mar-2021	33. 26-Aug-2020	78. 26-Apr-2021
34. 14-Oct-2020	88. 10-May-2021	34. 23-Jul-2020	99. 29-Apr-2021	34. 14-Aug-2020	84. 06-Apr-2021	34. 27-Aug-2020	79. 27-Apr-2021
35. 15-Oct-2020	89. 11-May-2021	35. 24-Jul-2020	100. 30-Apr-2021	35. 18-Aug-2020	85. 07-Apr-2021	35. 02-Sep-2020	80. 28-Apr-2021
36. 16-Oct-2020	90. 12-May-2021	36. 27-Jul-2020	101. 03-May-2021	36. 19-Aug-2020	86. 13-Apr-2021	36. 11-Sep-2020	81. 20-May-2021
37. 19-Oct-2020	91. 13-May-2021	37. 05-Aug-2020	102. 04-May-2021	37. 20-Aug-2020	87. 14-Apr-2021	37. 14-Sep-2020	82. 02-Jun-2021
38. 20-Oct-2020	92. 14-May-2021	38. 06-Aug-2020	103. 05-May-2021	38. 21-Aug-2020	88. 20-Apr-2021	38. 15-Sep-2020	83. 10-Jun-2021
39. 21-Oct-2020	93. 17-May-2021	39. 07-Aug-2020	104. 06-May-2021	39. 24-Aug-2020	89. 21-Apr-2021	39. 21-Sep-2020	84. 18-Jun-2021
40. 28-Oct-2020	94. 18-May-2021	40. 13-Aug-2020	105. 07-May-2021	40. 25-Aug-2020	90. 27-Apr-2021	40. 30-Sep-2020	85. 21-Jun-2021
41. 04-Dec-2020	95. 19-May-2021	41. 14-Aug-2020	106. 10-May-2021	41. 26-Aug-2020	91. 28-Apr-2021	41. 15-Oct-2020	86. 22-Jun-2021
42. 07-Dec-2020	96. 20-May-2021	42. 01-Sep-2020	107. 11-May-2021	42. 27-Aug-2020	92. 10-May-2021	42. 27-Oct-2020	87. 28-Jun-2021
43. 21-Dec-2020	97. 21-May-2021	43. 02-Sep-2020	108. 12-May-2021	43. 31-Aug-2020	93. 13-May-2021	43. 29-Oct-2020	88. 29-Jun-2021
44. 22-Dec-2020	98. 24-May-2021	44. 03-Sep-2020	109. 13-May-2021	44. 01-Sep-2020	94. 02-Jun-2021	44. 30-Oct-2020	89. 02-Jul-2021
45. 24-Dec-2020	99. 25-May-2021	45. 04-Sep-2020	110. 14-May-2021	45. 02-Sep-2020	95. 03-Jun-2021	45. 02-Nov-2020	
46. 28-Dec-2020	100. 26-May-2021	46. 08-Sep-2020	111. 17-May-2021	46. 11-Sep-2020	96. 04-Jun-2021	46. 16-Nov-2020	
47. 29-Dec-2020	101. 27-May-2021	47. 09-Sep-2020	112. 18-May-2021	47. 14-Sep-2020	97. 07-Jun-2021	47. 17-Nov-2020	
48. 30-Dec-2020	102. 28-May-2021	48. 16-Sep-2020	113. 19-May-2021	48. 21-Sep-2020	98. 25-Jun-2021	48. 18-Nov-2020	
49. 31-Dec-2020	103. 01-Jun-2021	49. 28-Sep-2020	114. 20-May-2021	49. 05-Oct-2020	99. 28-Jun-2021	49. 19-Nov-2020	
50. 04-Jan-2021	104. 02-Jun-2021	50. 30-Sep-2020	115. 21-May-2021	50. 23-Oct-2020	100. 29-Jun-2021	50. 20-Nov-2020	
51. 05-Jan-2021	105. 03-Jun-2021	51. 12-Oct-2020	116. 25-May-2021	51. 27-Oct-2020		51. 23-Nov-2020	
52. 06-Jan-2021	106. 04-Jun-2021	52. 13-Oct-2020	117. 26-May-2021	52. 28-Oct-2020		52. 24-Nov-2020	
53. 14-Jan-2021	107. 10-Jun-2021	53. 20-Oct-2020	118. 28-May-2021	53. 29-Oct-2020		53. 09-Dec-2020	
54. 19-Jan-2021	108. 17-Jun-2021	54. 21-Oct-2020	119. 01-Jun-2021	54. 30-Oct-2020		54. 11-Dec-2020	
55. 25-Jan-2021		55. 27-Oct-2020	120. 03-Jun-2021	55. 02-Nov-2020		55. 15-Dec-2020	
56. 27-Jan-2021		56. 05-Nov-2020	121. 10-Jun-2021	56. 04-Nov-2020		56. 16-Dec-2020	
57. 28-Jan-2021		57. 11-Nov-2020	122. 11-Jun-2021	57. 16-Nov-2020		57. 22-Dec-2020	
58. 29-Jan-2021		58. 13-Nov-2020	123. 14-Jun-2021	58. 17-Nov-2020		58. 23-Dec-2020	
59. 02-Feb-2021		59. 25-Nov-2020	124. 15-Jun-2021	59. 18-Nov-2020		59. 24-Dec-2020	
60. 18-Feb-2021		60. 07-Dec-2020	125. 16-Jun-2021	60. 19-Nov-2020		60. 28-Dec-2020	
61. 19-Feb-2021		61. 08-Dec-2020	126. 17-Jun-2021	61. 20-Nov-2020		61. 31-Dec-2020	
62. 02-Mar-2021		62. 21-Dec-2020	127. 18-Jun-2021	62. 23-Nov-2020		62. 27-Jan-2021	
63. 04-Mar-2021		63. 22-Dec-2020	128. 29-Jun-2021	63. 24-Nov-2020		63. 28-Jan-2021	
64. 09-Mar-2021		64. 23-Dec-2020	129. 30-Jun-2021	64. 02-Dec-2020		64. 02-Feb-2021	
65. 26-Mar-2021		65. 24-Dec-2020	130. 01-Jul-2021	65. 03-Dec-2020		65. 22-Feb-2021	
66. 29-Mar-2021		66. 28-Dec-2020		66. 07-Dec-2020		66. 08-Mar-2021	
67. 30-Mar-2021		67. 29-Dec-2020		67. 09-Dec-2020		67. 10-Mar-2021	
68. 31-Mar-2021		68. 30-Dec-2020		68. 22-Dec-2020		68. 11-Mar-2021	
69. 01-Apr-2021		69. 31-Dec-2020		69. 23-Dec-2020		69. 12-Mar-2021	
70. 05-Apr-2021		70. 04-Jan-2021		70. 30-Dec-2020		70. 15-Mar-2021	
71. 06-Apr-2021		71. 05-Jan-2021		71. 31-Dec-2020		71. 18-Mar-2021	

Figure 9. Time plots of agricultural commodity futures

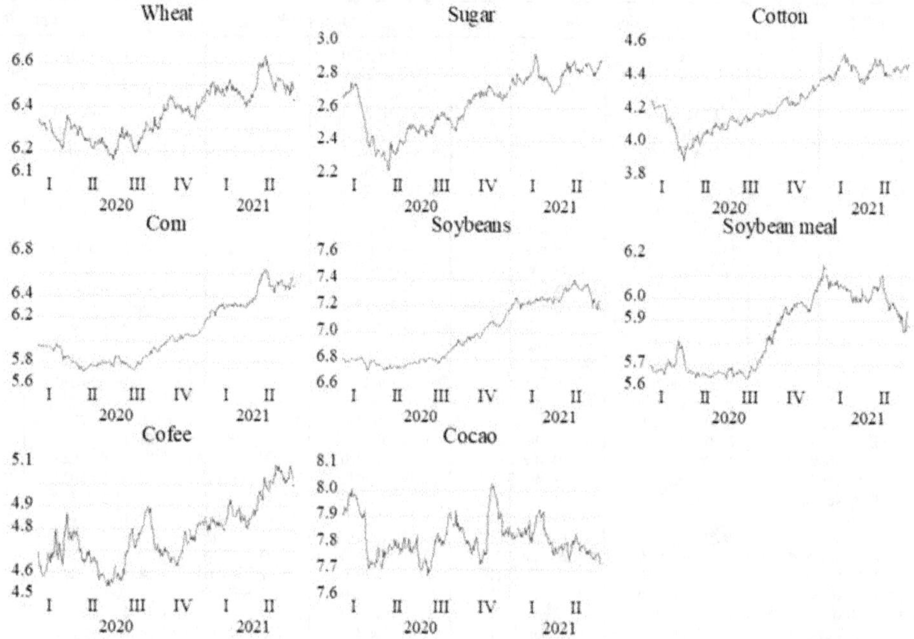

Chapter 16
Secure Smart Grid Management Maturity Within Big Data

Zühre Aydın Yenioğlu
https://orcid.org/0000-0002-5992-4983
Energy Market Regulatory Authority, Turkey

Vildan Ateş
Ankara Yıldırım Beyazıt University, Turkey

ABSTRACT

Smart energy systems of smart energy grid and meters are effective on operational processes and regulations in terms of security, continuity, and remote effective management. For a better development of smart grid, in which the data volume and complexity increases rapidly, smart energy management security plans should be implemented for efficiency and reliability of the network. Big data in energy systems plays an important role both in assessing the capacity needed and in making smarter investments to manage energy demand and supply. In this chapter, a novel secure smart energy management maturity model is presented in the context of capacity planning, demand forecasting, predictive maintenance, software optimization, network optimization, detecting and preventing threats, disaster recovery, and business intelligence and data visualization on which security criterias should be considered, planned, and managed for smart grids including big data. Relevant international big data and smart grid standards have been proposed for security, continuity, and performance in smart networks.

INTRODUCTION

Energy is the basic ingredient of many vital services that increase the quality of our lives and enable economic and social development, such as transportation, electricity, heating, food preservation and cooking, lighting, communication, commercial and industrial processes. There are certain needs for the secure supply of energy, which is essential for sustainable development. These requirements are depends on enough, affordable, safe, on time, clean and uninterrupted energy supply.

DOI: 10.4018/978-1-7998-9648-7.ch016

The energy security issue has been one of the most important issue of the world's nations since the 1800's. While energy security defines accession and protection of energy resources in the past, today this definition has changed with the rapid decline of energy reserves, climate change and cyber war. The new energy security paradigm will be based on resource diversity through the consumption of renewable energy sources and local resources and will be based on smart energy security. Within the energy security concept; "security of energy supply" means long term availability of energy resources. The most important primary energy resources like oil, gas and coal are often located away from the consumption areas and another component of energy security concept; "reliability of energy supply" depends on management of networks, technical issues and regulation regarding access to them. It could be mentioned 'reliability of energy supply' as 'security of delivery of energy supply'. Reliability of energy supply concerns the degree to which consumers could rely on a regular and reliable delivery of energy supply. Security also depends on external parameters, that may lead to supply interruptions. The availability of energy resources and energy management security depends on security and maintenance of energy supply. In regards of energy resources, a distinction should be made between; oil and coal and network bounded gas and electricity. Coal is imported for the purpose of electricity generation. Although reserves of coal are distributed around the world, there are only limited number of countries are exporting oil. So that, a special international emergency programme has applied to the oil security (Barton et al. 2004).

When discussing the security of electricity supply, two issues should be considered to guarantee long term supply. They are; investments on generation and network and dependency on one primary energy source. The legal instruments ensuring reliability include consumer protection and the regulation of the infrastructure supplying consumers. The Asia Pacific Center for Energy Studies recommends that the analysis of energy security is classified under four main headings: Availability, accessibility, affordability and social acceptability (APERC, 2007).

The International Energy Agency (IEA) determines energy security as the useability of affordable energy resources. However, from the perspective of policy makers and academics, energy security emerges as a multidimensional and very meaningful phenomenon and might have different meanings for different countries. Each country makes the definition of energy security for itself and different issues come to the fore in the short and long term. For example long-term energy security for a particular country might be ensured by creating the right energy infrastructure with the necessary environmental sensitivity and guaranteeing energy imports with long-term contracts, while another country may plan in a way that will meet its energy needs entirely with its own local resources. In summary; study could state that; the concept of energy security has many meanings such as; political factors, economic indicators, technical threats, environmental factors. According to these issues; considering the energy security concepts as dimensions of energy security, essential metrics of related dimensions and impacts of these metrics on energy security are inevitable issues.

Dealing with security threats in energy systems, smart meters and big data issues could be considered in the concept of energy security. Smart grid serves for better reliable, efficient, and secure power grid. Smart grid is characterized by; consumers, real time pricing, generation, energy sources incorporation into the grid, energy efficiency and security. With the development of technology and the understanding of its benefits, countries have turned into smart grid investments. Many governments have set targets and implemented programs related to smart grid. The main target of smart grid projects implemented in the World and it has been to use energy efficiently by reducing the loss and leakage rate. In addition, other main targets are; generating energy from renewable sources such as wind and sun, reducing carbon emissions, improving power lines, establishing advanced measurement infrastructure, integrating electric vehicles and smart buildings and establishing smart management systems. Although smart grid projects require high budget costs, they could pay for themselves in a few years with the savings and benefits gained. Within the scope of the Telegestore project, which started in 2000 and was completed in 2005, Italy was the country that took the first step regarding smart grids. With this project, 27 million meters were replaced with remotely readable smart meters. In the meeting held by the EU, it was emphasized that the electricity infrastructure needed a major transformation in line with the climate change and energy policy targets for 2020. Optimizing, strengthening and upgrading existing networks, increasing grid security, developing the internal energy market, raising awareness of energy savings, improving energy efficiency and integrating renewable energy production into the system are of great importance. To achieve these goals, it is not enough to just build new lines and transformers. With the integration of information and communication technologies into smart energy management systems, it is necessary to transform the entire electrical system into a smart structure for sustainability and security.

The chapter emphasizes the importance and role of big data and big data security through secure smart energy management in smart grids. Technical threats as security threats in energy security and role of big data have a big role for solutions on energy security. In this perspective, this chapter presents a research of big data included grid with the emphasis of big data security in smart grids, presents the importance of big data in energy securıty within big data security threats, big data operational tools and big data analytics. In addition end of the chapter a secure smart energy management maturity model metamorphosis is proposed and within the metamorphosis the smart grid security objectives and requirements are explained.

The chapter is organized as following sub sections: an literature review of big data security in smart grid is given in "Background". Description of imrtance of big data in smart grid is provided in " The Importance of Data in Energy Security". "Big Data in Smart Grid" overviews big data opportunities and technologies. In "A Smart Grid Security Objectives and Requirements" section, paper discusses the data management issues for smart grid security depends on energy security. In the "Secure Smart Energy Management Maturity Model Metamorphosis" section, there is a new recommendation of smart energy management maturity model metamorphosis through, capacity planning, demand forecasting, predictive maintenance, software optimization, network optimization, detecting and preventing threats, disaster recovery and business intelligence and data visualization for monitoring. Finally, "Solutions and Recommendations" sub section states recommendations on the phases, techniques and technical requirements for applying and deploying secure energy management factors for smart grids.

BACKGROUND

This sub section reveals a review of literature in the context of; smart grid capacity planning, demand forecasting, predictive maintenance, software optimization, network optimization, detecting and preventing threats, disaster recovery and business intelligence and data visualization for monitoring.

Big data is firstly defined with its three V's as Volume (amount), Velocity (speed) and Variety (heterogenity) of data (Laney, 2001). According to Asia Pacific Energy Research Centre (2007) the energy supply, energy security relates with availability of resources, ability of energy supply to meet current energy demand, energy resource and energy supplier diversification, fuel reserves within the availability of energy transportation infrastructure and geopolitical concerns surrounding resource acquisition. It also determines sustainable and integrated energy sector development planning by integrated energy and energy resource planning, energy statistics, energy database developement, technical power supply options, power sector economics, socio economic analysis and methodology, energy environment relationships, various energy development scenarios, regulatory incentives, energy pricing and supply demand management.

Fan, Weber, Barroso and Bramlett (2007) presented the large power usage characteristics and mentioned that even in optimized applications there is a distinction between achieved and opportunities for energy savings are significant. According to them, power usage rates and activity rate could guide the way of energy management and energy policies. Farhangis (2010), presented a review of smart grid communication technniques such as ZigBee, WLAN, WiMAX, Power Line Communication (PLC) and is demostrated comparison of communication infrastructure standards.

Du (2011) studied on probabilistic analysis at searching more reliable peak loads than deterministic analysis, and it provides estimation of prospects of overloads, these are crucial parameters in grid asset capacity planning. This research provides deeper insights on technical uncertainties in smart grid, hence capacity planning process is very important. Cherp and Jewell (2011) focused on three factors on energy security; such as, sovereignty, robustness, resilience. Ekanayake, Liyanage, Wu, Yokoyama and Jenkins (2012) researched authentication, encryption and decryption and cyber security standards through smart grid information security. Shawkat Ali and Azad (2013) demonstrated that smart grid provides the facilities for the energy consumers for sensible and efficient power usage. Hence, in the implementation phase, energy demand management is very important. Energy demand scheduling is an efficient step to apply demand management. It is an automated way to change the demand from peak to off peak therefore the demand curve is flattened. To tune and optimize the demand scheduling, the accurate demand forecasting comes into play to facilitate electricity demand management.

Nafi, Ahmed, Gregory and Datta (2016) identified the difficulties between the power and communication systems. The situation of smart grid related machine to machine communication system design is determined and recommendations are provided for traffic features. Zhou, Fu and Yang (2016) presented a wide study of big data driven smart energy management, discussed the sources and characteristics of energy big data and found out the difficulties of big data driven smart energy management. They also focused on databases and database administration, data integration, data processing, data analysis, database tuning and optimization and data security. Khan, Rehman, Arif, Aftab and Jadoon (2016) studied on a hybrid communication model that suggested for reliable communication between smart meter and its control system. Escobedo, Jacome and Arroyo-Figueroa (2016) presented a proposed framework for the application of business intelligence and data analytics to help the decision making processes of smart grid system to provide reliable and timely information for better decisions within data mining and data analytics. Refaat, Abu-Rub and Mohamed (2016) highlighted the big data problems and difficulties that related with smart energy management systems and manage decisions in smart grid networks. Bhattacharya and Sinha (2017) developed an artificially intelligent system that could analyze the grid information at any time and monitor the health of the system within the models and proposed machine learning techniques as recurrent neural networks.

Otuoze, Mustafa and Lariks (2018) discussed smart grid security threats and for focusing on the security and resiliency issues threats. For providing adoptation to various conditions of system network, implementation, analysis, simulations of suitable models and optimization of related tools are needed. These could be taken care of in planning and operational level for a reliable, optimized and secured smart grid system. According to this study; for smart grid systems' data amangement security; critical generation, transmission, distribution networks, consumer's load profile data and performance indicators as the characteristics of management equipment must be collected, processed, analysed and simulated to assess the systems' reliability and maintenance with existing systems' installations and upgrades. Sharma, Mahela and Agarwal (2018) mentioned that, when an error is occured on the distribution process of smart grid, the preventive relay should respond swiftly to isolate the faulted line for the stability of the rest of the system. Reliable estimation of fault processes are desirable for examination, optimization and maintenance of the related fault and next faulties. Chhaya, Sharma, Kumar and Bhagwatikar (2018) described that complicated infrastructure of smart grid communication architecture needs tuning of different factors of communication protocols for network performance improvement. The primitive layered method being used for existing communication networks cannot serve the neccesities of complicated smart grid network. El Mrabet, Kaabouch, El Ghazi and El Ghazi (2018) reviewed the security requirements of smart grid systems through cyber security and investigated a number of significant cyber threats in smart grid to diagnose the potential vulnerabilities along with their impact. They proposed a novel cyber security methodology as a solution to show intrusion, counter attacks and deploy suitable countermeasures. Radoglou-Grammatikis, and Sarigiannidis (2019) studied on Supervisory Control and Data Acquisition (SCADA) systems and developed metering architecture. Improvement of Intrusion Detection System (IDS) and Intrusion Prevention System (IPS), could provide a robust and secured line of defense in communication network, by enlarging the operation of the encryption and authorization processes. That is, when a cyberattack achieves to solve the encryption and authorization cautions, the IDS or IPS could timely inform the responsible administrator or might carry out logical preventive countermeasures. According to them; an efficient countermeasure against different cyberattacks is the Intrusion Detection And Prevention System (IDPS). Bikmetov, Raja, Kazi, Sane, and Shevchenko (2019) researched needed energy capacity planning in smart microgrids and divided energy loads into two groups: "dynamic" and "slowly-changing". Dynamic energy loads are scheduled according to their current time energy demand depended on machine to machine interactions accessible via Internet of Things (IoT) sensors implementation. Thomas, Reji, Mathew and Aswin (2020) proposed an application to determine the accurate location of the error by co-ordinate operation of an adaptive sensor and relays. In their study, a communication controller platform is implemented to detect and communicate the unexpected cases and reported it to system administrator at remote station.

THE IMPORTANCE OF BIG DATA IN ENERGY SECURITY

Data in energy security has a critical role in energy market operations such as delivering energy and managing consumption and generation. Availability of accurate information, reliable data and security of data are critical factors of successful energy security. Reliable energy data is fundamental for improving effective and essential energy economics and policies. Accurate decision making and long term planning through investments are necessities in energy security. Collection and monitoring of related sectors' data provide accurate energy statistics and reports. Associated energy indicators or parameters should be in assessments for deciding energy efficiency within true measures in development. Hence, consistent and timely data in energy provide an accurate and unique platform for desired energy policies, clean energy applications and energy security.

Monitoring energy operations and evaluation of energy efficiency get together the energy security and big data issues. Concerns on cyber attacks, security issues on databases and data availability increase the dependency on network and database security such as; collected safety big data sets. Big data advantages

Figure 1. 5 V's of big data
(Laney, 2001)

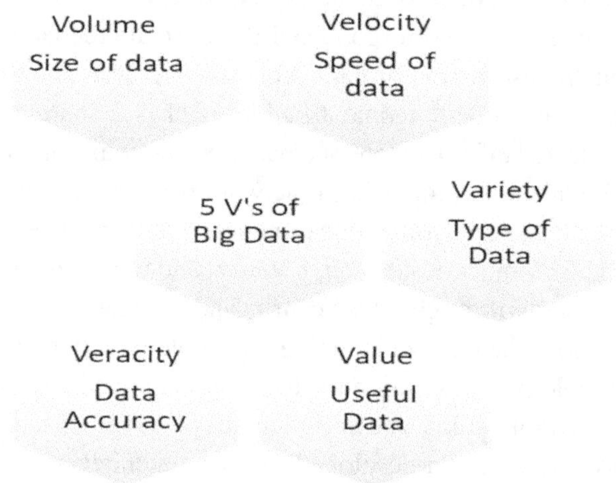

in the energy sector could be summarized as; providing supply demand balance, improving monitoring, analysing risks and opportunities, reporting for accurate energy policies. The collection, and usage of these data sets are what the system realizes as big data. Big data was determined by five Vs as in Figure 1: Volume, Velocity, Variety, Value and Veracity (Laney, 2001).

Big data analysis is the improvement of advanced data analytic methodologies on large volume of data. Advanced data analytics techniques are generally emphasized as; data mining, machine learning, language processing, data visualization, statistical analysis and so on.

A review of the data operation within big data analytics is shown in Figure 2. It indicates three levels: internal data, big data analytics and output as processed data that is needed information. Big data analytics have core processes as data collection, data preprocessing, data storage and data analysis (Hu, Wen, Chua & Li 2014).

Big data driven energy management systems, improves energy operations reliability and energy efficiency, provides accurately forecast demand, optimize energy consumption and generation, increase customer satisfaction.

BIG DATA IN SMART GRIDS

Since current smart grid systems could be demonstrated in the big data's five Vs, these systems might be determined through big data driven systems. A smart grid system has an improved interactive two way communications technology that provides different sub-systems, such as Advanced Metering Infrastructure (AMI) and Wide-Area Monitoring Systems (WAMS). It is obvious that a smart grid might produce a huge amount of data. Actual data from the smart grid systems could be produced in terabytes because of the huge scale of the power network grid. Therefore the velocity of current data is rising notably. In addition, the smart grid has different data sources that range from intelligent electronic devices to specialized commercial databases, weather data of various types, lightning detection data, seismic

Figure 2. Big data analytics and data processing
(Hu, Wen, Chua & Li 2014)

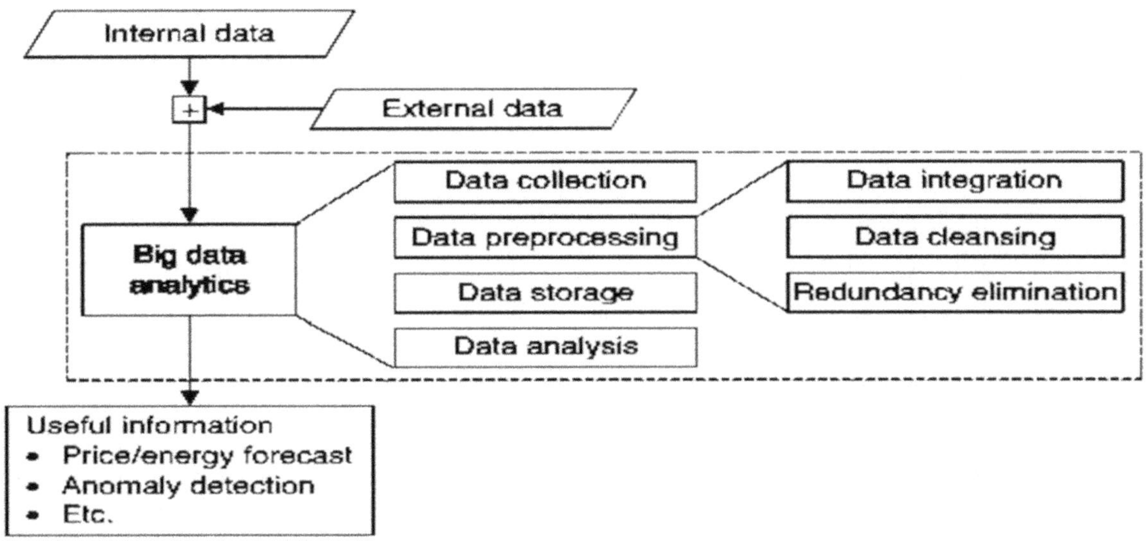

data, fire detection data, electricity market data, vegetation and soil data and so on (Kezunovic,2017). In summary; smart grid data is collected from meters, sensors, devices, mobile data terminals, intelligent electronic devices, distributed energy resources, customer devices and historical data. The operation and management of massive data in the smart grid requires the data analytics solutions used in big data technologies. Data in the smart grid requires to be related, reliable, transparent, organized, aggregated, processed and analyzed to gain expected grid intelligence (Mahmoud Daneshman, 2017). Big data security, secure energy management, cyber energy security and energy demand and supply are concerns which addresses big data solutions, due to the large number of devices in the communications technology. The smart grid technology aims to achieve efficient grid operations and to decrease greenhouse gas emissions. Cybersecurity should not threaten the performance and efficiency of the smart grid, since rising in energy consumption and energy demand provided by big data. There should be secure enery management systems within big data solutions and cyber attack measures.

Big data in the field of energy could be categorized in two groups; suplementary data and electric utility data (Refaat, Abu-Rub & Mohamed, 2016). Supplementary data implies to all data sources which are applicable for systems including big data applications as geographical information system (GIS), global positioning system (GPS) (Refaat, Abu-Rub & Mohamed, 2016). A smart grid could present utilities conserve energy, decrease costs, increase reliability, clearness and transparency.

Electricity utility data enables all of smart grid data and indicates SCADA data, Phasor Measurement Units (PMU) data, smart meter data, Intelligent Electronic Devices (IEDs) data, Digital Protective Relay (DPR) data, Digital Fault Recorder (DFR) data, Sequence of Event Recorder (SER) data, AMI data, management and maintenance data for current infrustructure and Automated Metering Reading (AMR) data (Nafi, Ahmed, Gregory & Datta, 2016). Figure 3 presents data sources that are used for big data energy systems.

Smart grid, internet of things and cloud computing are essential three technologies of big data implementations in the energy sector. Smart grid is an electricity network technology that intelligently

Figure 3. Energy data sources within big data
(Nafi, Ahmed, Gregory & Datta, 2016)

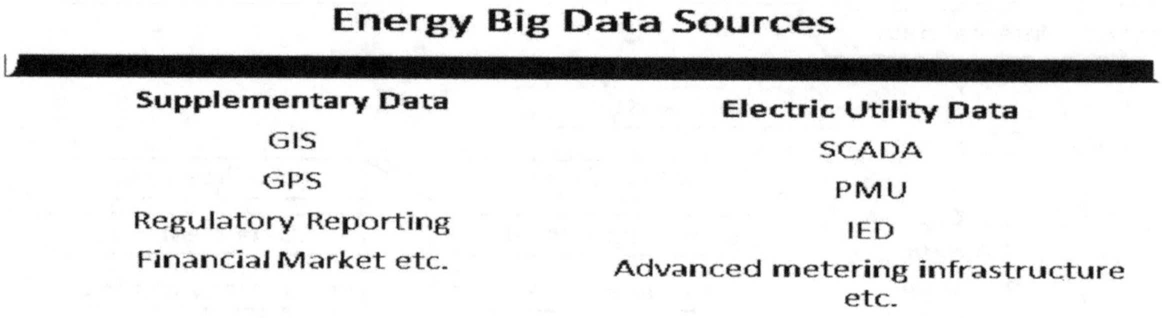

joins the operations of generators and subscribers of it for delivering efficient, sustainable and secure electricity supplies. Smart Grid is a generation power network that has a massive data flow from massive data sources, distributed and automated components and enables to perform timely balancing of supply and demand by computing characteristics (Nafi, Ahmed, Gregory & Datta, 2016).

The smart grid system design and infrastructure might meet cyber or data security threats and attacks, terrorism and unexpected natural disasters and so on (Otuoze, Mustafa & Lariks, 2018). When a smart grid has trouble with these threats and attacks then it might have possible outcomes such as; power system blackouts, IT operations faulties, careless data visualization or monitoring of the current system's situation, damaged consumer devices, energy market conflicts and untransparency. The threats, attacks and problems could be summarized as; data theft, physical damage, malware attacks in the cyber systems, system malfunctioning; distributed control devices vulnerability, lack of physical protection against sudden environmental disasters; inadequate control mechanisms for cyber threats. (Otuoze, Mustafa & Lariks, 2018). Threats relates with different forms of attacks which could be occur by systems either naturally or artificially.

SMART GRID BIG DATA SECURITY OBJECTIVES AND REQUIREMENTS

There are different data protection technologies used in the scope of security attacks in the smart grids. Because, energy security within the concept of big data, leads to needed safe system for safe energy trading. Smart grid big data security objectives are data confidetaiality, data integrity and data availability whereas requirements are privacy, authentication, authorization, accountability and surviveability (Pandey & Misra, 2016).

To be successful in smart energy processes within big data, a big data driven smart energy operation could be shown as in Figure 4. Through smart energy management organization might gain data driven methods that provide market operational efficiency, investment controls, system realiability, secure energy management, desired energy efficiency, consumer engagement and service improvement.

Smart grid security threats could be summarized as technical and nontechnical sources in energy management security such as; technical sources threats, infrastructural threats, cyber attacks, technical operational threats, systems' data management threats, nontechnical sources of smart grid threats,

Figure 4. Big data driven smart energy management life cycle
(Zhou, Fu & Yang, 2016).

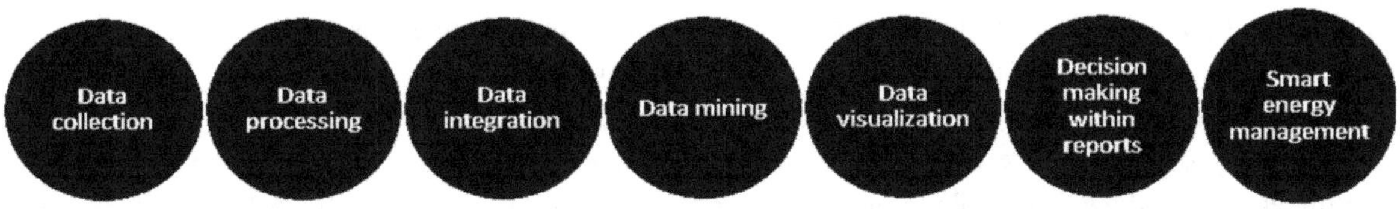

environmental threats, regulatory policy problems. Securing smart grid includes; authorization, authentication, encryption, detect policy violations, logging events and auditing data principles. Cybersecurity solutions are part of required maintaining of a prevented smart grid system. There are several roles that analytical models could contribute to the security of smart grid in the context of gathering intelligence, determining industrial control system weaknesses and vulnerabilities, determining real-time faulties, predicting and preventing possible attacks and security gaps, measuring threat rates and characteristics.

Big data solutions enable repeatable detection and preventing algorithms with both structured and unstructured data sources, indicate storage technologies and identify both internal and external threats.

In addition, the key concepts of establishing big data security solutions in energy management systems could be summarized as;

- Analyzing and identifying information security concerns and assess the role of big data analytics,
- Determining the roles of storage and processing,
- Creating proactive smart energy systems that prevent and detect all attacks,
- Enabling data and information sharing with including other utilities and cybersecurity assets,
- Proving the value of big data analytics with test operations.

A secured smart grid should be reliable, actual, confidential; should have integrity and efficiency, authentication mechanism, robustness, reliability, resiliency and indicates maturing energy utilities and assets. In the context of data security; huge speed and massive volume of data from smart grid services forms the basis for the big data analytics for disaster recovery management. Recovering big data collections, after unexpected events is an important data protection strategy for continuous, secure and sustainable smart grid technologies.

SECURE SMART ENERGY MANAGEMENT MATURITY MODEL METAMORPHOSIS

In this section of the chapter, as a result of these smart energy monitoring through secure smart energy management maturity model metamorphosis are presented and proposed. Maturity model metamorphosis consist of capacity planning, demand forecasting, predictive maintenance, software optimization, network optimization, detecting and preventing threats, disaster recovery, business intelligence and data visualization.

Capacity Planning in Smart Grid

Significant operations have been made to develop data centers of energy systems for efficiency and capacity project. These operations predominantly are efforts around evaluation of energy consumption within data centers and efforts to decrease the energy used by data centers.

Electricity demand and supply for Distribution Network Operators (DNOs) in grid asset is more complicated since the capacity planning, significantly at low voltage. Accurately peak loads, forecasting of overloads, which are very important components in grid asset capacity planning operation. Energy demand and supply in DNOs should provide adequate network capacity to supply peak demand (Du, 2011).

The electrical power system has been 'vertically' operated including of transmission system that transfers electricity from large scale generating plants over long distances and distribution system that distributes electricity to consumers. The distribution system being very extensive supplying large amounts of loads (Ekanayake, Liyanage, Wu, Yokoyama & Jenkins, 2012).

Peak grid power consumption is generally a matter for databases as it might influence the power infrastructure of grid power providers. Agreements are often heavily impacted by peak usage (Fan, Weber. Barroso & Bramlett, 2007) and might impose penalties for exceeding an agreed upon peak.

Various criterias and benchmarks have been implemented for evaluating different grid performance indicators. Grid performance could be measured within power outages, network losses, population served, consumer tariffs and unification of generation capacity. Unification of renewable generation capacity solution indicates load control and peak avoidance in smart grid.

The aim and distinct characteristics of capacity planning in smart grid systems are the actual time measurement of the Total Load Profile (TLP) for a residential area of energy users with an sufficient accuracy. The TLP measurements are depend on the initial data and actual time factors, such as; single load profile (LP), consumer requirements and priorities, supply and demand rates, planned energy capacity, current energy tariffs.

One of the significant caharacteristic of the actual time measurement of TLP is dividing all energy loads into two groups: dynamic loads and slowly changing loads. The key features for division method is the duration of load's Operation Cycle (OC) with respect to the established time window. Depend on these features, the loads with relatively short OCs are considered as dynamic loads and scheduled actual demand basis. While the loads with relatively long or continuously periodic OCs are considered as slowly changing loads and established for the whole duration of scheduling time window (Bikmetov, Raja, Kazi, Sane & Shevchenko, 2019).

Demand Forecasting in Smart Grid

Changes and uncertainty in climate and the variety of natural events causes much energy production to meet the consumer consumption. The smart grid system enables two way communications between the electricity suppliers and consumers. Within the application of smart grid system, supply and demand management going to play an important role for system accuracy and transperancy. Demand and capacity planning is an efficient way for demand control at the customer side. It is an automated and intelligent way to shift a part of the demand from peak to off peak hence, the demand curve is flattened. To tune the demand scheduling, the accurate energy consumption model of the consumers is significiant. Optimization of energy consumption pattern of the consumers is where the demand forecasting comes into play (Shawkat Ali & Azad, 2013).

Energy consumer supply and demand control is a methodology to motivate the electricity consumers to use less energy on the peak time so as to decrease the investment on electricity generation and provide a reliable and accurate supply. The representative measures for demand forecasting and management are presented by Government of South Australia, Department for Energy and Mining, (2021) within below items:

- In the context of pricing changes, the price of the electricity should be made cheaper during the off the peak. The customers should be received incentive for decreasing electricity consumption rates during peak times.
- Within the direct load control; load shedding operation managed where the utility decrease the energy usage of customers by controlling their home appliances usage by direct load control. The customers should be offered incentives for relieve the local peak by cutting energy usage.
- Customers should be offered incentives for a better electricity consumption. Smart meters offer in home monitoring and display, therefore consumers could follow their electricity usage rates and have better and greater management on electricity consumption during peak times.
- Distributed generation solutions should be supported in where electricity is produced, such as solar panels or wind turbines to minimise the local peak demand.
- Electricity customers should be encouraged to set up a power storage system along with their own solar panels that could supply the additional electricity demand during the peak time to avoid blackout in the grid.

Predictive Maintenance in Smart Grid

The most important objective of smart grid system is to meet continuous electricity service to the customers. In addition, energy issues and unexpected disturbances within the grid frequently due to power blackouts and that has influences on the system dependability and customer satisfaction. In smart energy grids, four significant issues might occur in a distribution network. These issues are a line to line fault (LLF), a three phase to ground fault (LLLGF), a single line to ground fault (SLGF), and a double line to ground fault (DLGF) (Bhattacharya & Sinha, 2017; Sharma, Mahela & Agarwal, 2018). The single line to ground fault is the most common fault detected in smart grid distribution system networks (Thomas, Reji, Mathew & Aswin 2020).

Implemented methodologies for fault prediction in the power distribution grids, utilizing modern methods and technologies developments are crucial for predictive maintenance in smart grid systems. Prediction of faults and critical events might pave the way for better performance and planning. Implementing predictive maintenance in a smart grid distribution network system should include following opportunities: Maximizing productivity, optimizing the grid operation, tuning smarter network operation and maintenance, minimizing unexpected error, fault and outage, making smarter and proactive maintenance strategies, planning proactive and efficient maintenance and performance management, predicting faults, critical events, applying outage management systems, speeding up the fault location, restoration and reconfiguration operations, reducing total maintenance costs, scheduling proactive maintenance methodology, evaluating predictive maintenance options for optimal response, activating self healing smart grid system and tracking network maintenance system automatically.

Software Optimization in Smart Grid

Today, many industries use software systems as a basic component. Time loss, error rate and test time might increase during manual tests performed to ensure software quality. Test automation studies are carried out to minimize such situations. The efficient and fast execution of the tests make an important contribution to the software development processes. Test automation is seen as an important software element to meet this need. Automation, on the other hand, provides a remarkable benefit along with time and cost savings. Software security is the set of technical practices that must be followed in order to protect software, systems and applications against the risk of hacking and malicious attacks. Software security includes evaluating, detecting and minimizing vulnerabilities, protecting the system without attack if possible. Ensuring continuity in energy management system, preserving vitality, continuing to operate smoothly, preventing data theft are concerns of software security and secure software development. In order to avoid problems, software security must be ensured. The security of a system software should be ensured by the precautions and techniques to be taken against threats during and after the development of your software. The main purpose is to detect and intervene before security vulnerabilities occur. Otherwise, energy system is vulnerable to attacks. In this case, it will cause disruption of energy supply, loss of data, loss of cost and security vulnerabilities.

Enhanced meter infrastructures are systems that collect, measure and analyze energy usage information. In addition, it provides the communication of the system with electricity, gas, heat and water meters, so that the need is requested or planned. In these systems, hardware, software, communication, consumer energy display and controllers, are used by consumer connected systems, as counter information management software.

Smart grid implements high speed and automatic regulators, innovative software for managing and monitoring the records, and linking utility and users in two directions. The flexiblity of smart grid communication networks is becoming a curicial problem in software planning and grid network components. Monitoring, sharing and altering the messages communicated over the grid infrastructure are in the middle for hackers.

The objective of the energy management systems' software optimization is to enhance energy efficiency, planning next day for supply demand balance. Within grid extensions, there should be development and optimization of smart grid software for customer's benefit and healthy secure energy management system. Secure smart grid software maintanence processes are; optimization of software algorithms for grid capacity planning, tools for evaluating transfer capacities, models for tunned utilization of hydro power and thermal power plants and optimization and update software.

Application level software optimization for smart grids is a significant issue, and that provides secure smart grid framework hence improving smart grid success. Software optimization in smart grid could develop capacity and scalability of the application and also decrease its energy consumption and increase performance and security. In order to discover security vulnerabilities and take necessary measures in the concept of software optimization in smart grids, code reviewing analyzes, update operations and secure code development should be made and a roadmap should be drawn as a result of the analysis. Software security improvement should be done by taking necessary actions with the roadmap.

Network Optimization in Smart Grid

A distributed data infrastructure is used for the Internet Protocol (IP) based communication network of smart grids. Infrastructure is provided with an adaptive software. This infrastructure is based on a distributor subscriber model that provides low latency and realizability for the smart grid. If all the economic, physical and digital technology requirements are met, the smart grid will work efficiently.

Electrical grid implies a network that carries electricity from power plants to customer assets. Smart Grid is a digestion of electrical and communication groundwork. Smart Grid is qualified by two way interaction flow of electricity and processed data. It is a complicated network with hierarchical infrastructure. Materialization of a smart grid infrastructure architecture necessitates various types of communication standards and protocols. Communication network standards and protocols are modified and established on the basis of layered approach. Each layer is planned to generate an obvious functionality in unification with other layers. Layered approach could be engineered with cross layer approach for performance improvement.

The power grid development of the world is enhaced a significant and harsh transformation through intelligent grid technology. A classical power grid has the gaps such as; reliability, remote monitoring and management, automation, sensing, disaster recovery, security, and efficiency (Gungor, Lu & Hancke, 2010). Smart grid technology provides reliable electricity distribution through actual time monitoring and management of generation, transmission, and distribution operations. Sensing, communication, and automation are the core componenets of a smart grid infrastructure (Cecati, Citro, Piccolo & Siano, 2011). Internet development has presented the way for smart grid design, implementation and deployment. Smart grid standards indicates hierarchical and heterogeneous layer standards. Smart grid has three important hierarchical layers such as; Home Area Network (HAN) for consumer premises, Neighbourhood Area Network (NAN) and Wide Area network (WAN). HAN comprises Wireless Sensor Network (WSN), home appliances, smart meters, renewable energy resources and so on for its operation (Saputro, Akkaya & Uludag, 2012).

IEEE 802.11, IEEE 802.15.1, IEEE 802.15.4, and IEEE 802.16 network standards could be used for HAN. NAN is a unification of HAN and suitable for distribution automation. WAN shelters HAN and NAN for monitoring and management of communication network (Xu, 2009). WAN is a massive network covering management of generation, transmission, distribution, and utilization of entire grid.

Therefore, smart grid is characterized by unification of different communication standards and complicated infrastructure.

Communication protocols should be designed by using layered implementation in that each layer represents a specific function in agreement with the rest of the layers. Cross layer optimization could be achieved for performance development of indicators within various network layers or exchange of data between diferent network layers. Diverse set of network parameter optimization of related layer could be resulted in overall network performance tunning.

Cross layer optimization presents synergy between different layers for the development of network optimization and performance. It is a unification and optimization of different layers that finds out dependence between layers. Figure 5 shows the conceptual diagram of cross layer design (Chhaya, Sharma, Kumar & Bhagwatikar, 2018).

In this context a smart grid network optimization should be optimized according to different layer dependencies and unification and related parameter performances.

Figure 5. Conceptual diagram of cross layer optimization
(Chhaya, Sharma, Kumar & Bhagwatikar, 2018)

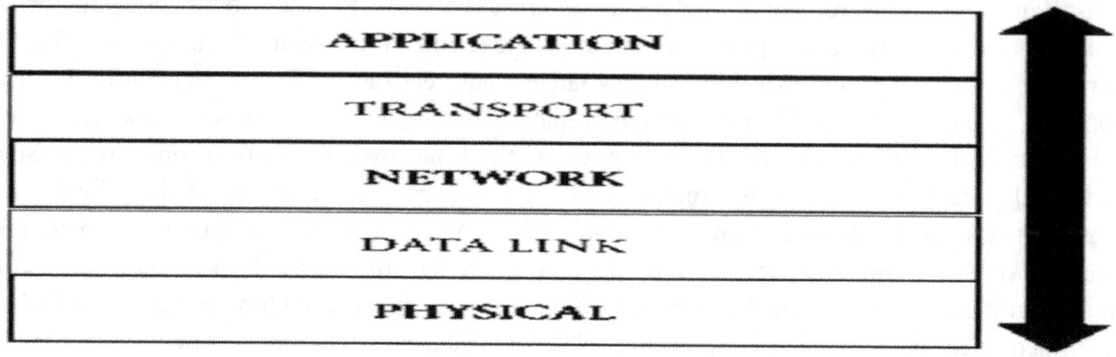

Detecting and Preventing Threats in Smart Grid

Smart Grid has crucial security difficulties, since it unions heterogeneous communication networks such as industrial devices, Internet of Things (IoT) devices, wireless components and Wireless Sensor Networks (WSNs) characterized by different security threats (Khan, Rehman, Arif, Aftab& Jadoon, 2016, El Mrabet, Kaabouch, El Ghazi & El Ghazi, 2018). In addition, the integration of smart meters with other devices, that communicate with each other includes more security concerns. On the other hand, the development of SCADA systems, increase the potential threats, if these systems don't indicate modernized and modified security solutions. The smart grid security intrusions target on the availability, integrity and confidentiality of assets. Moreover, various types of Denial of Service (DoS) attacks target to damage the network services and cause important disservice such as power outage. It is harmful for the avalability of the smart grid. By DoS attacks accessing information actually might be disabled.

In the context of big data, false data injection attacks could delete or alter the data of smart meters in order to succeed damage the massive databases. Furthermore, among the various types of cyberattacks, man in the middle, advanced persistent threat zero-day attacks that might violate the privacy of the systems and threaten the smart grid infrastructure. An IDS and IPS might operate defense in communication networks, by improving the operation of the encryption and authorization methodologies. IDS or IPS could actually inform the security administrator or perform necessary preventive countermeasures. By the integretion of IDS and IPS, Intrusion Detection and Prevention System (IDPS) developed for security within privacy. Detecting and preventing threats in smart grid is possible by the requirements of IDPS systems for the smart grid.

Contribution and advices of this section is summarized for smart grid security as in below:

- Do a comprehensive and comparative analysis of IDPS devoted to protecting smart grid.
- Determine actual IDPS weaknesses and identfying the security requirements of IDPS especially to detect and prevent the communication infrastructure failures or cyber-attacks.
- Choose approprite IDPS according to smart grid type and attributes.
- Update, tune and optimize the system software infrastructure.
- Use secure software development technologies.

- Apply relevant international standards (ISO/IEC 27001, ISO/IEC 27002, ISO/IEC 27031 for ISO/IEC 24762).

Disaster Recovery in Smart Grid

Recovering big data collections, after unexpected events, includes more than database backups. While literature focuses on security technologies of data, there is a very little attention on the Big Data Disaster Recovery (BDDR) issue. This section determines building effective BDDR strategy for databases with Big Data Clusters (BDC). Database Disaster Recovery (DR) is the process of restoring data backups after disasters that destroy or damage IT infrastructure. Organizations should have a DR life cycle management plans through IT operations. Because, DR projects prevent destroying organizational data that drive business, and these projects do restore database operations in time for getting back to business operations. An effective BDDR plan should include off-site and on-site database backups, a document of BDDR project processes for big data recovery, data transformation tools to be punctual and fast, data capture services for business continuity, big data analytics tools for ideal backup and disaster recovery projects and ensuring quality and usability of backups and recovered files.

Backing up business data to a remote location as off-site backups is a data loss prevention process and it is the most essential DR step for data protection and database security. This DR step provides unharmed business data in the event that destroys IT infrastructure as a physical disaster. However, off-site business data backups are not adequate on their own to ensure data loss prevention within reliable DR. Through data security in a DR system, restoring production data operations quickly in a broader big data disaster recovery strategy is essential. Quick restoring of backup file is possible with on-site backups from on-site servers. Verifying the quality of off-site and on-site data backups and recovered files is important for data security and efficient DR. Data backup and recovery answer data security requirements if they are free of data damage and errors. This means data quality within data security that is provided by DR strategies.

Big data involved databases deal with long time restoring plans that move data from backup locations to production servers. In DR systems, big data databases may need data backup transformations such as converting stored backup data format to a different format in production. Hence, IT infrastructure should have good data transformation tools during disaster recovery. Flowing of data is possible, but capturing data is difficult during a disaster. During a disaster, to ensure maintaining continuous capture of data, even interrupted analytics operations, having operable backup storage locations, preparing backup locations that have enough capacity to handle big data, verifying backups are important cases for undamaged secure data.

During an unexpected IT infrastructure failure or event, there should be processes and next steps for capturing, restoring and flowing data in a DR plan in place. For quick and efficient disaster recovery a business database backup and recovery plan should be included in a playbook, which involves flowcharts and steps of recovering from a disaster. Playbook makes related disaster recovery tools meet with related business needs.

Since big data is determined by its volume, variety, velocity, variability, the accuracy, the amount of data produced and stored, the variety and type of data, the rate at which data is produced and processed, the inaccuracy of the dataset, and the quality of the data are key concepts of it. The captured data on smart grids shows the relationship between big data concepts and smart grid systems.

In emergency management, the speed and volume of data from smart grid services pose a major challenge for big data analytics. Big data services are another challenge in addition to ever-evolving technologies, privacy, security and regulatory concerns, and due to these challenges, detailed research and international collaborations are required in this emerging scope. Other challenges in big data analytics for disaster management are overestimation, data noise, inaccurate data, and imprecise data.

Big data from smart grids will become increasingly suitable for disaster management due to the advanced sensors and their ongoing growth. Therefore, the big data analytics of smart grid in disaster recovery management as a novel technology has a number of pitfalls that needs detailed analyze by experts from related fields. For efficient use of big data in disaster management, local attendance and guidance by emergency management professionals should be ensured.

Preparedness, technical and planned response, recovery and prevention life cycle items are appropriate and planned operational strategies for a sudden disaster and for a disaster management playbook. Smart grids are approprite for maintaining electricity provision during or after a natural disaster if organization planned these cases:

Before disaster events; testing with simulations, preapering requirement analysis, making risk analysis and risk reduction for sudden disasters are prevention methodologies. Readiness according to risk analysis results is a part of playbook within detection, monitorin, forecasting and post disaster experiences.

After disaster events; damage evaluation and post disaster response could be a good guide for relieve the system. In addition planned reconstruction of infrastructure and services provides could allow quick and less damaged system recovery. All of these disaster management life cycle cautions and playbook items are presented in the study of Alexander (2002) as in below Figure 6. These cautions should include data loss prevention phase in it and should be implemented in smart grid with big data disaster recovery management phases and playbooks.

Business Intelligence and Data Visualization in Smart Grid

Smart grid system uses inteligent techniques and various information technologies in the context of modernization of electrical networks. The development of smart grid data interest with its multidisciplinary nature motivates the need for solutions coming from various fields of knowledge. Because of complicated and heterogeneity of the smart grid and its massive volume of information, data analytics within business intelligence appear to be important techniques applied to the various issues that arise in the smart grid development. Applications of data analytics within business intelligence in big data included smart grid databases enable processes of security for distribution system and to have available and actual information to make better decisions, to reduce the number of accidents and incidents in grid infrastructure. This section of the chapter is devoted to overview the most relevant challenges addressed by the smart grid technologies and how data analytics within business intelligence systems could contribute to their achievement as an element of secure smart energy management maturity model metamorphosis.

Distributed data, data stream, and timeseries data are much related to smart grid system since its nature of distributiveness and its relations with various data streams and time series data from different data sources such as; smart meters, sensors, and power system machinery. Big data analytics within business intelligence treat big data analytics. In the context of smart grid there are implementations of discovering subpatterns in a dataset with frequent pattern mining technique; finding causes of data interactions with association rule mining that could be derived from the frequent patterns technique; classifying instances in a dataset into predefined class labels with supervised learning classification technique; organizing

Figure 6. Disaster recovery life cycle
(Alexander, 2002)

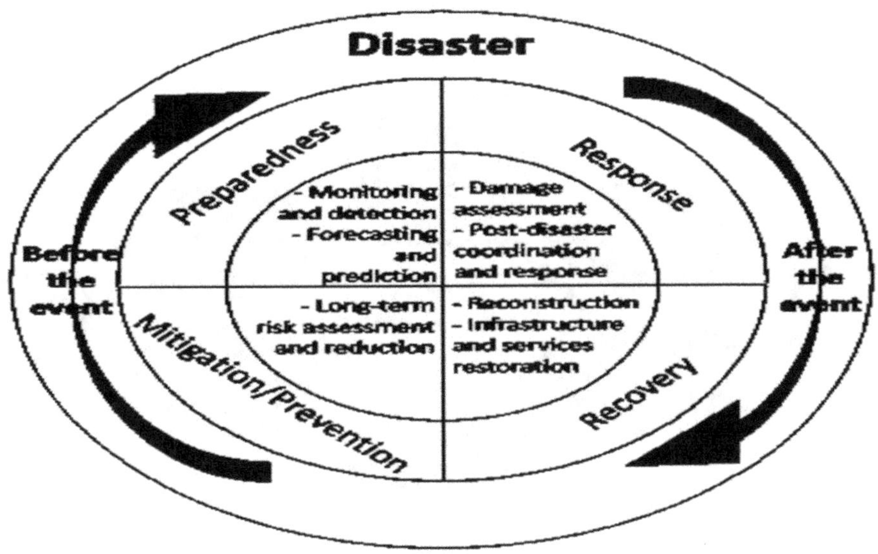

similar instances in a dataset into groups which are unpredefined with unsupervised learning clustering technique; predicting the value of the target attribute that is dependent variable based on the values of independent variables with supervised learning regression technique; identifying abnormal instances, which indicate errors and require further research with supervised, unsupervised, or semi-supervised learning outlier detection technique.

These concepts of big data analytics within business intelligence were studied by Escobedo-Briones, Jacome-Grajales and Arroyo-Figueroa (2016) and figured out as below in Figure 7.

Implementation of big data analytics within business intelligence technologies in smart grids provide the benefits of actual and reliable data security, time reducing in making decisions, displaying and monitoring situation of the security implementations, doing deeply analysis as a conclusion of consolidated past, actual and experienced information, decreasing faulties and outages with dashboards and reports, reducing investments occured by accidents and in number of days lost because of accidents.

Data visualization of big data analytics within business intelligence could be obtained from the frontend applications through of dashboards, decision making systems and reports. The dashboards, decision making systems and reports should provide a tool or a development for managers and system administrators to navigate through needed, reliable and actual information.

SOLUTIONS AND RECOMMENDATIONS

The primary aim of smart grid systems is providing the reliable, continuos and secure ditrubition of electricity. Actual electricity system designs and abilities have to be successful in supplying security and continuity by preventing the grid against sudden attacks, system outages and disasters. Cybersecurity, network and software security requirements of power systems should be implemented.

Figure 7. Data analytics within business intelligence technologies and their applications in smart grid (Escobedo-Briones, Jacome-Grajales & Arroyo-Figueroa, 2016)

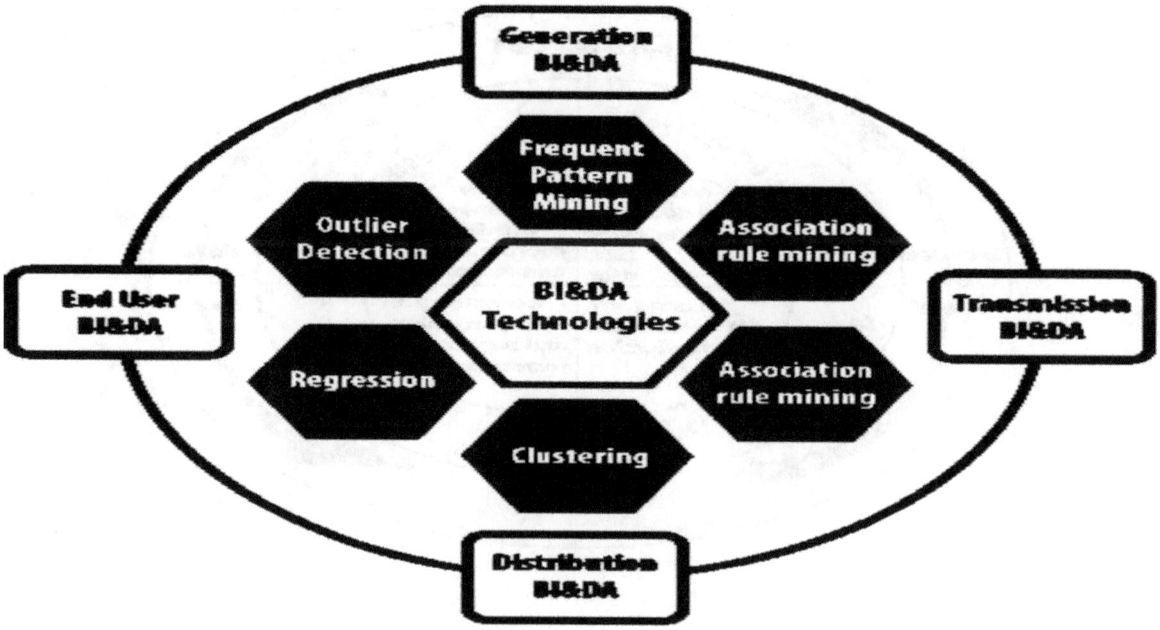

Mature security standards and best practices could facilitate smart grid operations. IEC; is an international standards community that organize and publishes international standards on technologies related to electricity and electronics. The International Electrotechnical Commission (IEC) standard for "Information security for power system control operations" is an essential requirement for secure smart grid system. IEEE Standard P2030 includes knowledge base terminology, features, assessment criterias and implementation of engineering principles to smart grid operations of the electric system with end-use applications (IEEE Std 2030, 2011).

The IEC has presented over a hundred standards relevant to the smart grid systems. Continuous improvement of the smart grid and the massive scale of the cyber system and big data, require standards and regulations within the smart grid communications infrastructure and security. A selected standards for the big data included smart grid security are presented as recommendations in Table 1.

On the other hand there are different ways for securing big data such as; encrypting data both at rest and in motion, separating encrypted data, using the Kerberos network authentication protocol, using secure automation.

In the context of recommendations for regulators and policy makers there should be encouraging the development of Electricity Continuity Planning (ECP) and Electricity Continuity System (ECS) that provide sudden disasters have been considered, and plans have been developed for the restoration of energy supply. In addition, during the development of disaster recovery plans, regulators should realize the interaction of outages between the energy supply system and utilities. Policy makers should consider the achievements from distributed generation, load management and microgrid technologies, removing regulatory barriers. Utilities, industry and researchers should develope ECP to reestablish operations after widespread electricity outages. Such plans includes the implementation of local generation, the priority of

Table 1. IEEE and IEC security standards for big data involved smart grid

IEEE and IEC Security standards for Big Data involved Smart Grid	
IEEE 2030	Different types of methodologies and best practices for Smart Grid.
IEEE 1402	Methodologies to reduce human intrusions on electric power supply.
IEC 60870	Supervisory and data acquisition telecontrol systems in electrical engineering and power system automation implementation.
IEC 61334	Continuous and reliable power network line communications by electricity meters and SCADA.
IEC 61850	Unified solution of the communication aspect of substation automation.
IEC 61968	Information exchanges between electrical distribution systems standard.
IEC 61970	Energy system management application program interface (EMS-API), Common information model (CIM) base, CIM static transmission network model profiles.
IEC 62056	International standard versions of the electricity metering data exchange specification.
IEC 62351	Security requirements for network and system management.
IEC 62357	Energy systems management and related information exchanges standards.
ISO/IEC 17799	A general guidlines and principles for implementing, maintaining and developing information security management in an organization.

loads, and other key service dependencies and they are likely to rely on standards that concluded in Table 1. These standards have the resilience of a particular facility against security and natural disasters issue.

Smart grids are based on more quality real-time data collection. This type of system could include the analysis of big data by computers for very fast decisions and rapid analysis by humans. It prevents events and repairs itself. All these are possible with an advanced counter structure and key components. These counters are; demand management, greater integration of renewable resources, efficient use of resources both on the production and consumption side, energy saving and price advantage, system balance benefits. Within these concerns smart grids structure has three key components; incident prevention, self-healing network and advanced counter infrastructure.

In addition, for achieving energy big data maturity for energy security and sustainability there should be implemention of the energy operations metamorphosis of Figure 8 which is a proposed secure smart energy management maturity model metamorphosis of the chapter. These metamorphosis emphasize the importance and the role of technical threats as security threats in energy security and show the role of big data as a solution for energy security. Figure 8 metamorphosis items should be implemented through the related security and management standards of Table 1.

FUTURE RESEARCH DIRECTIONS

Future research in smart grid security area within big data should be on big data sets and related supervised learning models to supply needed decisions. Efficient and secure big data analytics considering scale of the bid data included grid, efficient and cost-effective services could be a future research issue. With big data included analytics and supervised and unsupervised machine learning algorithms, energy future predictions could be made to improve power demand response, performance and operational efficiency of the grid. In smart grid services efficiency and security is important issues to be considered

Figure 8. A proposed secure smart energy management maturity model metamorphosis

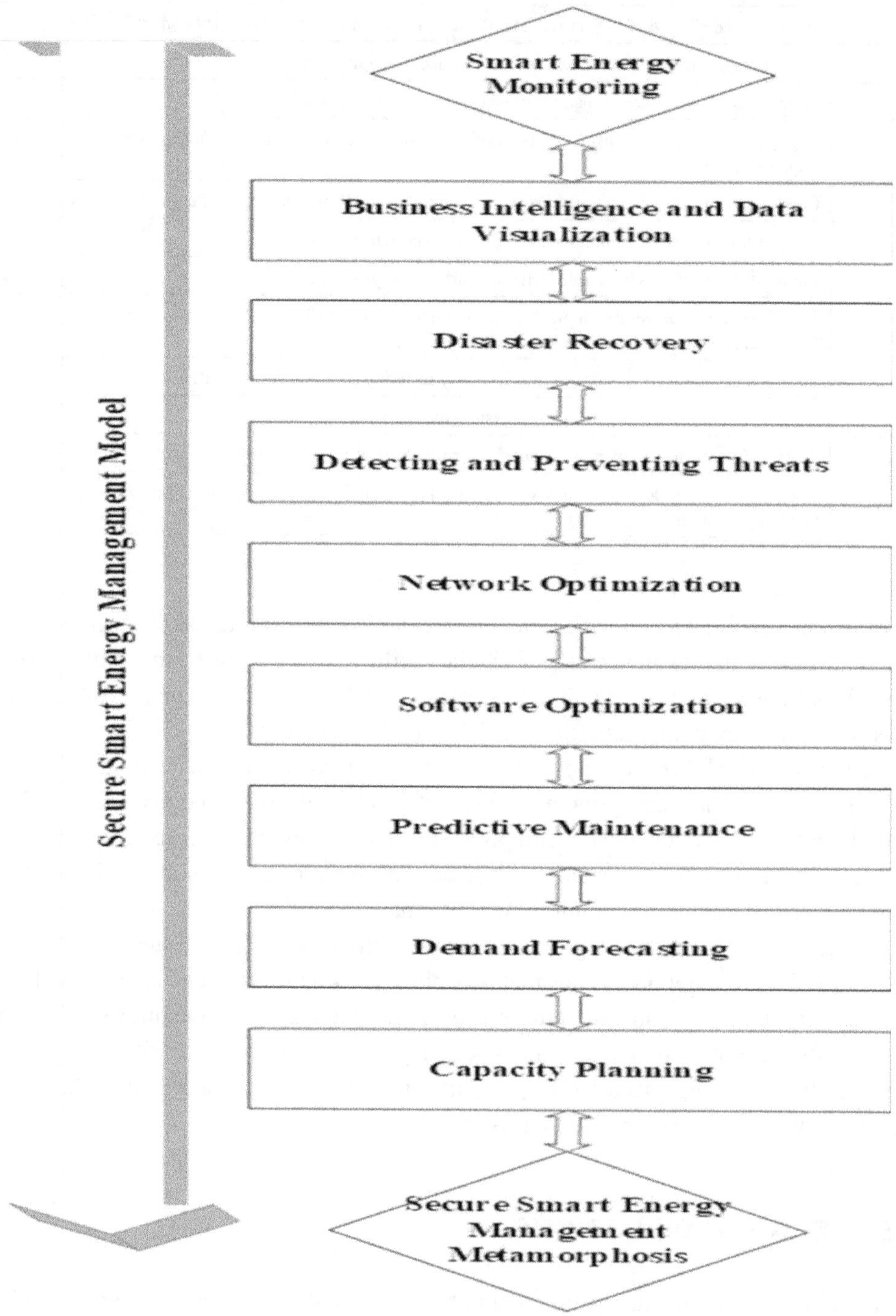

when enhancing methodologies for big data included system solutions. Hence, the privacy of consumers might be protected. Moreover; big data standards and capability maturity models (CMMs) and related

IEEE, ISO and IEC security, plan and management standards integration model for big data involved smart grid could be developed for future researches.

CONCLUSION

This chapter points out energy security threats, maturity metamorphosis and related standards in energy systems through smart meters and big data issues. There is a discussion of security difficulties, solutions and recommendations for the big data included smart grid system. The difficulties from the reported requirements of techniqual issues and also from the actual processes in the smart grid. Providing security by the security and management standards of IEEE, ISO and IEC, might be used as a playbook and guideline for proactive security planning. Smart grid communications network security requirements depends on optimized private or public network applications. In additon, actual optimization and tuning techniques, related standards, plans and reviewed regulations are required to secure the smart grid communications infrastructure.

ACKNOWLEDGMENT

This research received no specific grant from any funding agency in the public, commercial, or not-for-profit sectors.

REFERENCES

Aleh, C., & Jewell, J. (2011). The three perspectives on energy security: Intellectual history, disciplinary roots and the potential for integration. *Current Opinion in Environmental Sustainability*, *3*(4), 202–212. doi:10.1016/j.cosust.2011.07.001

Alexander, D. E. (2002). *Principles of emergency planning and management*. Oxford University Press on Demand.

APERC. (2007). Quest for energy security in the 21st Century: resources and constraints. Asia Pacific Energy Research Centre.

Barker, S., Mishra, A., Irwin, D., Cecchet, E., Shenoy, P., & Albrecht, J. (2012). Smart*: An open data set and tools for enabling research in sustainable homes. *SustKDD, 111*(112), 108.

Barton, J. P., & Infield, D. G. (2004). Energy storage and its use with intermittent renewable energy. *IEEE Transactions on Energy Conversion*, *19*(2), 441–448. doi:10.1109/TEC.2003.822305

Bhattacharya, B., & Sinha, A. (2017). Intelligent Fault Analysis in Electrical Power Grids. *Proceedings of the IEEE 29th International Conference on Tools with Artificial Intelligence (ICTAI)*. 10.1109/ICTAI.2017.00151

Bikmetov, R., Raja, M., Kazi, K., Sane, T., & Shevchenko, N. (2016, October). Dynamic energy capacity planning for distributed resources in Smart Microgrids. In *2016 HONET-ICT* (pp. 159-163). IEEE.

Cecati, C., Citro, C., Piccolo, A., & Siano, P. (2011). Smart operation of wind turbines and diesel generators according to economic criteria. *IEEE Transactions on Industrial Electronics*, *58*(10), 4514–4525. doi:10.1109/TIE.2011.2106100

Chhaya, L. K., Sharma, P., Kumar, A., & Bhagwatikar, G. (2018). Cross layer optimization and simulation of smart grid home area network. Modelling and Simulation in Engineering.

Danahy, J. (2009). *The coming smart grid data surge*. Retrieved from: http:// www.smartgridnews.com/story/coming-smart-grid-data-surge/2009-10-05

Du, W. (2011). Probabilistic analysis for capacity planning in smart grid at residential low voltage level by Monte-Carlo method. *Procedia Engineering*, *23*, 804–812. doi:10.1016/j.proeng.2011.11.2585

Ekanayake, J., Liyanage, K., Wu, J., Yokoyama, A., & Jenkins, N. (2012). *The smart grid: Technology and applications*. John Wiley & Sons, Ltd. doi:10.1002/9781119968696

El Mrabet, Z., Kaabouch, N., El Ghazi, H., & El Ghazi, H. (2018). Cyber-security in smart grid: Survey and challenges. *Computers & Electrical Engineering*, *67*, 469–482. doi:10.1016/j.compeleceng.2018.01.015

Escobedo, G., Jacome, N., & Arroyo-Figueroa, G. (2016). *Business intelligence and data analytics to support the operation of smart grid. Conference: Special Session on Recent Advancement in IoT, Big Data and Security*. doi:10.5220/0005936604890496

Escobedo-Briones, G., Jacome-Grajales, N., & Arroyo-Figueroa, G. (2016). Business Intelligence and Data Analytics (BI&DA) to Support the Operation of Smart Grid - Business Intelligence and Data Analytics (BI&DA) for Smart Grid. *Proceedings of the International Conference on Internet of Things and Big Data (1): RAIBS*, 489-496.

Fan, X., Weber, W. D., & Barroso, L. A. (2007). Power provisioning for a warehouse-sized computer. *ACM SIGARCH Computer Architecture News*, *35*(2), 13–23. doi:10.1145/1273440.1250665

Farhangis, H. (2010). Smart grid communication technologies. *IEEE Power & Energy Magazine*, *8*, 18–28.

Government of South Australia, Department for Energy and Mining. (2021). *Managing peak demand*. Retrieved from: https://www.sa.gov.au/topics/energy-and-environment/energy-supply/managing-peak-demand

Gungor, V. C., Lu, B., & Hancke, G. P. (2010). Opportunities and challenges of wireless sensor networks in smart grid. *IEEE Transactions on Industrial Electronics*, *57*(10), 3557–3564. doi:10.1109/TIE.2009.2039455

Hu, H., Wen, Y., Chua, T. S., & Li, X. (2014). Toward scalable systems for big data analytics: A technology tutorial. *Access, IEEE*, *2*, 652–687. doi:10.1109/ACCESS.2014.2332453

IEEE Std 2030 (2011), Guide for Smart Grid Interoperability of Energy Technology and Information Technology Operation with the Electric Power System (EPS), and End-Use Applications and Loads, IEEE Standards Association.

Kezunovic, M. (2017). *Big data applications in smart grids: benefits and challenges*. IEEE Smartgrid.

Khan, F., Rehman, A. U., Arif, M., Aftab, M., & Jadoon, B. K. (2016). A survey of communication technologies for smart grid connectivity. *Electron. Elect. Eng. (ICE Cube)*, 256–261.

Laney, D. (2001). 3D data management: Controlling data volume, velocity and variety. *META Group Research Note, 6*(70), 1.

Mahmoud Daneshman, K. J. L. (2017). *Big challenges for big data in the smart grid era*. Retrieved from https://www.ecnmag.com/blog/2017/ 04/big-challenges-big-data-smart-grid-era

Nafi, N., Ahmed, S. K., Gregory, M. A., & Datta, M. (2016). A survey of smart grid architectures, applications, benefits and standardization. *Journal of Network and Computer Applications*, *76*, 23–36. doi:10.1016/j.jnca.2016.10.003

Otuoze, A. O., Mustafa, M. W., & Lariks, R. M. (2018). Smart grids security challenges: Classification by sources of threats. *Journal of Electrical Systems and Information Technology*, *5*(3), 468–483. doi:10.1016/j.jesit.2018.01.001

Pandey, R. K., & Misra, M. (2016, December). Cyber security threats—smart grid infrastructure. In *2016 National Power Systems Conference (NPSC)* (pp. 1-6). IEEE.

Radoglou-Grammatikis, P. I., & Sarigiannidis, P. G. (2019). Securing the smart grid: A comprehensive compilation of intrusion detection and prevention systems. *IEEE Access: Practical Innovations, Open Solutions*, *7*, 46595–46620. doi:10.1109/ACCESS.2019.2909807

Refaat, S. S., Abu-Rub, H., & Mohamed, A. (2016, December). Big data, better energy management and control decisions for distribution systems in smart grid. In *2016 IEEE International Conference on Big Data (Big Data)* (pp. 3115-3120). IEEE.

Saputro, N., Akkaya, K., & Uludag, S. (2012). A survey of routing protocols for smart grid communications. *Computer Networks*, *56*(11), 2741–2771. doi:10.1016/j.comnet.2012.03.027

Sharma, R., Mahela, O. P., & Agarwal, S. (2018) Detection of power system faults in distribution system using stockwell transform. *Proceedings of the IEEE International Students' Conference on Electrical, Electronics and Computer Science (SCEECS).*

Shawkat Ali, A. B. M., & Azad, S. (2013). Demand forecasting in smart grid. *Green Energy and Technology*, *132*, 135–150.

Thomas, P., Reji, A. G., Mathew, A., & Aswin, D. (2020). Stand alone distribution feeder inter area fault location identification system for Indian utility. In *Proceedings of the 2020 IEEE 5th International Conference on Computing Communication and Automation (ICCCA)* (vol. 30–31, pp. 258–262). 10.1109/ICCCA49541.2020.9250916

Xu, X. (2009). *Introduction to Smart Grid*. China Electric Power Press.

Zhou, K., Fu, C., & Yang, S. (2016). Big data driven smart energy management: From big data to big insights. *Renewable & Sustainable Energy Reviews*, *56*, 215–225. doi:10.1016/j.rser.2015.11.050

ADDITIONAL READING

Butt, O. M., Zulqarnain, M., & Butt, T. M. (2021). Recent advancement in smart grid technology: Future prospects in the electrical power network. *Ain Shams Engineering Journal, 12*(1), 687–695. doi:10.1016/j.asej.2020.05.004

Chehri, A., Fofana, I., & Yang, X. (2021). Security risk modeling in smart grid critical infrastructures in the era of big data and artificial intelligence. *Sustainability, 13*(6), 3196. doi:10.3390u13063196

Khurana, H., Hadley, M., Lu, N., & Frincke, D. A. (2010). Smart-grid security issues. *IEEE Security and Privacy, 8*(1), 81–85. doi:10.1109/MSP.2010.49

Skopik, F., & Smith, P. (2015). *Smart Grid Security: Innovative Solutions for a Modernized Grid* (1st ed.). Elsevier.

Tomar, A., & Kandari, R. (2021). *Advances in Smart Grid Power System Network, Control and Security*. Elsevier.

Wang, F., Lei, Z., Yin, X., Li, Z., Cao, Z., & Wang, Y. (2018). *Information security in the smart grid: Survey and challenges in Geo-Spatial Knowledge and Intelligence* (H. Yuan, J. Geng, C. Liu, F. Bian, & T. Surapunt, Eds.). Springer.

Wei, F., Wan, Z., & He, H. (2019). Cyber-attack recovery strategy for smart grid based on deep reinforcement learning. *IEEE Transactions on Smart Grid, 11*(3), 2476–2486. doi:10.1109/TSG.2019.2956161

Zhang, H., Liu, B., & Wu, H. (2021). Smart grid cyber-physical attack and defense: A review. *IEEE Access: Practical Innovations, Open Solutions, 9*, 29641–29659. doi:10.1109/ACCESS.2021.3058628

KEY TERMS AND DEFINITIONS

Demand Forecasting: Predicting the demand with data analytics tools for energy requirements.

Disaster Recovery: Regaining and relieving the IT infrastructure of an organization after an unexpected natural disaster event.

Energy Management System (EMS): A remote computer-aided development tool that used by power system operators to monitor, manage, and serve optimal energy.

Energy Security: Providing affordable, available, reliable and continuos energy supply from sustainable energy resources by ensuring global energy adequacy.

Network Optimization: Implementing tools, techniques and best practices to enhance network performance and security.

Smart Grid: An intelligent electrical grid that involves a variety of advanced smart metering infrastructure.

Smart Grid Security: Software, network and grid infrastructure security issues within standards, controls, plans and caution management criterias.

Software Optimization: Modifying a software system for more efficiency, performance and security.

Chapter 17
The Transformation Framework:
The Role of Artificial Intelligence for Military Strategies (RAI4MS)

Antoine Trad
https://orcid.org/0000-0002-4199-6970
IBISTM, France

ABSTRACT

It is known that geopolitical knowledge, conflicts, wars, and military investments are the backbone for flourishing global economies' evolution, stagnation, or failure. Military and defence organizations are those who drive major intelligence-based technology transformation and innovation trends. Countries, military environments, and organizations (or simply entities) are increasingly using complex and intelligent technologies, like artificial intelligence (AI). One of the most complex military tasks and geopolitical risks is using AI to balance and coordinate in real-time the following military technology artefacts: autonomous and fixed objects, financial and resources capabilities, combative and morale statuses, mass management, information technology and data, developing military scenarios, evolution of demography, and others. Therefore, the stability and evolution of an entity depends on the role of artificial intelligence for military strategies (RAI4MS).

INTRODUCTION

It not a secret that conflicts, wars and military investments are the backbone for major global economies' evolution, stagnation or failure. Military organizations are the ones who drive major AI based technological transformation and innovation trends. The most known case is the internet, where USA's Defense Advanced Research Projects Agency (DARPA), developed technologies for interlinking packet networks to support communication protocols that was called the Internetting project; and today this concept is known as the Internet… AI based military technology transformation and innovation projects are based on major financing capabilities, ideology and also on the factor of demography. *Entities*, are increasingly using complex technologies to gain geopolitical and hence economical advantage. Trans-

DOI: 10.4018/978-1-7998-9648-7.ch017

formed *Entities*, have to face new challenges and geopolitical Risks (gRisk), when implementing their AI decision systems, complex infrastructure, organizational concept and Information and Communication System (ICS). One of the most important gRisks is related to finding the right balance between, AI based Military Technology (AIbMT), military strategy, financial capabilities, geopolitical knowledge, combative status and the evolution of demography. Therefore, the stability of an Entity depends a holistic strategy, like the one proposed in this article, the RAI4MS to support the *Entity's* transformation projects. The RAI4MS includes a methodology and a concept to manage the *Entity's* geological stability and tries to detect the main gRisk, which is that an *Entity* may lose the sense of reality, by thinking that only AIbMT and financial investments will solve all types of military conflicts. RAI4MS and automated tactics are the basis of managing modern warfare, in which technology strategy includes the design, planning, coordination, preparing and directing military activities to meet the *Entity's* main geopolitical, economic and military objectives. Tactical scenarios implement strategy by short-term and long-term decisions on the *Entity's* troops activities and the usage of technology and weapons in confrontations. The known military specialist *Carl von Clausewitz* defines tactics as: *Tactics is the art of using troops in battle; strategy is the art of using battles to win the war.* Winning a war open new markets and business opportunities… Strategy, technology and tactics, however, have been used differently in different periods of history. The main change in the usage of these terms in evolution of technology, is the notion of scope and the nature of warfare, as well as the context of the *Entities* in conflict and the development of technologies. Strategy means, *the art of the general* (from the Greek term *strategos*), which originally meant just planning of a military campaign. Therefore, until the 17th and 18th centuries strategy included various military issues, like, building fortifications, maneuver and supply. In the 19th and 20th centuries, nations have witnessed the rise of mass ideologies, vast conscript armies, global alliances and ultra-rapid technological change, which made RAI4MS become practically similar to *grand strategy*, that is based on planning and the optimal usage of the *Entity's* main pools of resources that includes: human, military, technological, economic and political resources. The actual change in the scope and meaning of RAI4MS and automated tactics is due to the vast changes and evolution of technologies. Tactics is a very complex activity that is used to be distinguished from strategy because the two are interdependent; and in the 20th century, tactics has been redefined as *operational strategy*. RAI4MS includes limited tactics' possibilities; which depends on the size, training and the morale of armed forces, type and volume of weapons available, terrain, weather, demography, technological capacities, quality and location of enemy armed forces… Tactics are very dependent on strategic considerations (Cheyney, 2021); where today, technological capacities are probably the most important ones. *Entity's* technology or ICS capacities, enables the processing and coordination of its various organizations, which have a large set of applications and resources. These applications are used in order to serve people, leaders and executive management, who are supported by a Decision Making System (DMS). The DMS and technology evolutions have enabled to the transformation of monolithic legacy systems. Such a transformed systems needs an optimal RAI4MS that includes the following factors and areas: 1) The design of the needed AIbMT; 2) Manage and control financial capabilities; 3) Build geopolitical knowledge; 4) Enhance combative moral and status; and 5) The evolution of demography. These factors and areas are interrelated and their disbalance may create major setbacks and even major defeats, like in the cases the Western armies, losing ground in the Middle East Area (MEA) and other parts of the world. The loss of the sense of reality, by relying only on AIbMT and financial conflicts will offer easy victories to the *Entities* enemies. Humans and their sustainable demography, stay the *Entities* and its military's armed forces, major asset and the used technology is just an auxiliary factor. *Entity's* defense capability process operates in parallel with many other management, security, policy, regulatory and governance frameworks. RAI4MS' central element is Enterprise Architecture (EA) that was introduced in Defense strategies, to support their ICS. Many *Entities* embraced EA to support their defense and government strategies. The RAI4MS comprises a set of templates and diagrammatic forms. USA' Department of Defense (DoD) Architecture Framework (DoDAF), that uses an EA based approach (DoDAF 2010); however, the RAI4MS differs greatly from DoDAF because of its holistic approach (Hue, 2014). This article's Research and Development Project (RDP) will offer a resultant set of recommendation to support the RAI4MS.

THE RESEAECH AND DEVELOPMENT PROJECT

This article's Research Question (RQ) is: "Can an RAI4MS, support an *Entity* transformation project by innovating its AIbMT capacities?" The main RAI4MS gaps are related to the facts on *Entities'* capacities to support financially, the defined sets of RAI4MS requirements and also the *Entity's* stability requirements… *This chapter and the author's works research complex topics in cross-functional domains, therefore it is assumed that the respectable reader has sufficient knowledge in the noted keyword. It is not a simplistic quantitative analysis and it is based on an adapted mixed method.*

The Research's Literature Review

The author's RDP and framework are very mature in the domains of Transformation Projects (simply a *Project)* risk management and strategy design. The Research's Literature Review (RLR) result is that a small number of relevant scholar resources exist on the RQ and its related subjects, with the only exception of The Open Group Architecture Framework (TOGAF) that relates to various strategies, concepts, technology areas and interfaces to standard frameworks; but there is a relevant and important gap, between existing concepts and the RAI4MS. The knowledge and methodology gaps exist, mainly because of the lack of a holistic approach, where there is practically no insight on a holistic approach to design an RAI4MS for *Projects*. In this article the following resources are used: 1) Various articles related to *Entity* security risk management; 2) The author's general works and framework, the *Transformation Research Architecture Development framework (TRADf)*; 3) An initial set of factors; 4) A large set of RAI4MS related literature, standards and frameworks; and 5) Uses an empirical engineering method, which far more than just literature scanning and concrete engineering projects.

Empirical Engineering Methods

The RDP uses an empirical engineering method, which is optimal various types of engineering projects like RAI4MS based *Projects* (Easterbrook, Singer, Storey, & Damian, 2008). The main goal is to deliver a holistic approach for an interactive mixed method based on factors and Heuristics Decision Tree (HDT).

Critical Success Area

Critical Success Area (CSA) is a set of Critical Success Factors (CSF) where a CSF is a set of KPIs. A KPI corresponds to a single *Project* or RAI4MS requirement. For a RAI4MS requirement, an analyst identifies an initial set of CSFs. CSFs are the most important relation between an RAI4MS construct, organizational predisposition and the DMS (Trad, & Kalpić, 2020b). Therefore, CSFs reflect control areas that must meet strategic goals and defined constraints. Measurements are used to evaluate gRisks in each CSA, where CSFs can be internal or external. For a given military problem type, the RAI4MS analyst, must identify the initial set of CSFs to be used for the DMS and its HDT. Hence the CSFs are the most important mapping/relation between the RAI4MS, AIbMT status, organizational predisposition and DMS; that can a subject for attacks or global crime schemes (Peterson, 2011). The proposed RAI4MS delivers a set of recommendations and solutions for the global transformation process.

Selecting Entity RAI4MS CSFs

Selecting the *Entity's* RAI4MS CSFs is based on the following facts and resources: 1) ICS; 2) Actors and boundaries; 3) Used and connected components; 4) Technical and military functional requirements; 5) Established national defense strategies, objectives and goals; 5) Applied defense and security policies; 6) Sustainability, robustness, proactivity and competition; 7) Geopolitical, national/societal and geoeconomical statuses; and their correlation; 8) Behavioral sciences, propaganda and parapsychology mirage, which can alienate the main objectives; and 9) The *Entity's* Organized Global Predators' Pattern (EOGPP) for destabilizations and attacks, where the targeted domains, can be national destabilizations & civil-wars, national security, finance, logistics, geopolitics or other; it can be even used for a combination of these fields. Determination and the evaluation of major gRisks, is affected by many CSFs and their relation/correlation is therefore essential. *Entities* must defend their organizations, AI & ICS, assets, and resources; so that an external actor or aggressor using an EOGPP scheme has to be detected and deterred to access to the *Entity's* internals. The *Entity* must be capable to defend its internal territory, organizations, systems and national objectives, and must build an RAI4MS to identify and block any external incursion or supplicated EOGPP attempts to damage the *Entity*. Therefore, the main objective is to block and to have information, security and technology services that identifies probable aggressors (or other types of attack patterns) attempts. Besides classical attacks the RAI4MS must be aware of other types of organized asymmetric attacks like: 1) Cyberwarfare; 2) Cyberterrorism; 3) Cyberhooliganism; 4) Cyberfinance attacks; 5) Terrorism groups acting like armies; 6) Destabilization propaganda; 7) Information and spying service; and others. Just analyzing data and historical events is a partial, limited and offers static solutions, there is a need for a dynamic proactive qualitative heuristics' method like the author's HDT algorithm. There is also a need to control the activities and behavior of terrorist groups, which can be an important part of the *Entity's* internals; and to proactively detect any probable violations, like in the case of France. Possible internal or external attacks can be modelled by using: RAI4MS, spying and information services, skilled special forces, responsibilities & awareness and defined ethics.

The Architecture Development Method and Defence Strategy

As already mentioned, major *Entities* are using technologies and methodologies as the kernel of their AI based Defense Strategy (AIbDS), like the case of EA in the form of DoDAF (DoDAF 2010) The RAI4MS focuses on the design of AIbDS for an *Entity*. In the actual age of distributed fast changes, geopolitical instability, intelligence, complexity, knowledge, economy, AI and technology (Gardner, 1999), RAI4MS becomes the most important objective, in order to offer a concept that includes the HDT that supports a wide class of AIbDS problem types, and that is a major benefit (Markides, 2011). The RAI4MS synchronizes with the Architecture Development Method (ADM) to deliver juts-in-time solutions. The RAI4MS defines AIbDS capabilities to protect the *Entity* from attacks by: 1) Localizing gaps in the infrastructures and ICS; 2) Review of detection and real-time AIbDS solutions; 3) Block cumulative attacks; 4) Defining an RAI4MS and AIbDS to locate potential weaknesses; 5) Build a robust RAI4MS; 6) Integrate AIbDS in in all *Project* requirements; 6) Block EOGPP attacks; and 8) Apply qualification procedures in the ADM (Clark, 2002). TOGAF's ADM is the most used EA delivery process and this article presents which AIbDS artifacts are relevant to ADM's phases, this makes AIbDS an integrated part of the EA. This enables, security framework like SABSA to interface TOGAF, to provide common EA models to improve information exchange between *Project* experts. *TRADf* englobes TOGAF, other standard methodologies and artifacts, which facilitates the *Project*.

RAI4MS' Fundaments

Today the world is witnessing unprecedented technological change and new adversaries with different alliances, have emerged, alongside traditional threats; these facts might change the world-wide order; mainly due to substantial and rapidly modernizing militaries and their RAI4MS. The unfortunate evolution of terrorist groups and non-state militias who have access to sophisticated technologies and weapons. Military Technology Research and Development (MTRD) has become a major CSF in the global RAI4MS competition. New MTRD and RAI4MS domains are emerging from the intersection of various scientific domains. New technologies are developing and are adopted faster than before. Weaker adversaries like terrorist groups have become capable of developing an RAI4MS to gain military and geopolitical advantage. *Entity's* RAI4MS needs to confront these new facts and prepare the right tactics and above all, courage. RAI4MS needs to set long term objectives, building future capabilities, taking risks, improving scientific and technological literacy, collaborating effectively and managing huge volumes of data. The RAI4MS needs to mitigate gRisks by applying MTRD that supports military capabilities and continuing to maintain critical economic capabilities that are crucial for *Entity's* national security (MOD, 2020).

RAI4MS Principles of Warfare

Entity's military leaders and specialists throughout history have formulated the most important strategic and tactical concepts of warfare, like for example: 1) Napoleon I, developed 115 principles; and 2) The Confederate general Nathan Bedford Forrest had only one: *Get there first with the most men*. The common principles are: objective, offensive, surprise, security, unity of command, economy of force, mass and maneuver. Military forces, must have a well-defined objectives that must be followed despite possible difficulties. Only offensive operations, in which exploiting the initiative will use objectives. Offensives increase the possibility of surprise and security (protection against surprise activities). RAI4MS control of command and cooperation, is crucial to follow the objectives, the capacity to use *Entity's* forces effectively and to optimization critical phases. Maneuver consists of manners on how troops can be deployed and moved to support offensive, mass and surprise activities; a known case, that illustrates these principles was used in World War II (WWII), when the Allied forces launched an offensive on Europe, by using a combined command and they have effectively massed their forces in England, and have deceived Germans regarding the point of invasion and have set a maneuver called *Operation Overlord* in action respecting the principle of mass (Cheyney, 2021).

RAI4MS Manoeuvres

Classification of actual military types of maneuvers and their variations are a part of the RAI4MS. New technology and weapons have not drastically changed classical types of offensive maneuvering, like: penetration, envelopment, defensive-offensive maneuvers and turning movements. The penetration, is one of the oldest maneuver types and is a main attack that attempts to penetrate enemy lines, while secondary attacks on other enemy lines prevent the freeing of enemy's reserves. Defensive-offensive maneuvers include attack from a defensive position after the attacking enemy has been slowed down. Turning maneuvers are indirect approaches that attempt to swing wide around an enemy's flank to threaten its supply and communication lines (Cheyney, 2021).

The Historical and Theoretical Development of RAI4MS

The historical roots of strategy and tactics date back to the origins of human warfare and the development of large-scale empires. Dense tactical infantry formation of overlapping shields called the phalanx, for example, existed in an early form in ancient Sumer (3000 BCE). The development of strategy and tactics is related to the growth, spread and clash of civilizations. Technological evolution is the base for modern state power, ideology and nationalism. The Mediterranean area is the origin of modern military strategy and tactics; like in the cases of Philip II (382 BCE) and Alexander the Great (356 BCE) and Hannibal (247 BCE) of Carthage, who established the first strides of military strategy. Philip combined infantry, cavalry and primitive artillery into a trained, organized and maneuverable army supported by engineers and a rudimentary signaling system. The Middle Ages saw the decline of military strategy, with the exception of the Mongol conqueror Genghis Khan. Medieval tactics was based on defensive fortifications and armored cavalry.

The Emergence of Modern Warfare

The emergence of modern warfare is related to the following historical facts (Cheyney, 2021):

- King of Sweden, Gustav II Adolf, is considered as the *father of modern tactics* because he transformed military maneuvering tactics. He headed a disciplined national army and the transformation resulted in small, mobile units armed with maneuverable firepower.
- Frederick II of Prussia, transformed his armed forces by mastering initiative and mass, using small units; he faced mighty coalitions using a strategy of flexible interior lines that can re assemble in a superior armed force to strike the enemy.
- Napoleon I is considered to be the inventor of modern warfare; the French Revolution created mass organized army with flexible divisions. Napoleon designed and planned his military campaigns and optimally maneuvered his armies to the selected battle field. His tactics and strategy were based on initial provocations and massive bombardments, which were followed by massive armed forces attacks on the enemy's flanks.
- The 19th century brought major theory and RAI4MS transformations. Napoleon's inventions in the fields of strategy and tactics were adopted by theorists of war, like the Prussian general Carl von Clausewitz and the French general Antoine Jomini. Clausewitz's emphasized the close relationship between warfare and *Entity's* policy and the importance of the factor of mass, economy

of force and the elimination of adversary armed forces. Whereas Jomini, emphasized conquering adversary territory using planned, fast and precise geometric maneuvers. Jomini's RAI4MS and AIbDS theories influenced French armies in North America, Clausewitz's approach was influential on the Prussian military strategists of the 19th century, like Helmuth von Moltke, who was the master mind of the victory in the Franco-Prussian War of 1870; and on Alfred von Schlieffen, known for his *Schlieffen plan*, which was used in the war against Russia and the weakening of France, during World War I (WWI).

- The 19th century was an age of major technological transformations that heavily changed the scope of tactics and strategy; and hence the RAI4MS. This was noticed in the first total war, USA's Civil War, in which railroads and steamships increased their volume, reach and speed of mobilization and of conscription; and that needed major technological artifacts and infrastructure. RAI4MS became warfare's major support and the evolution of firepower needed new tactical transformations, like: heavy artillery that had to be installed behind frontlines, massed brigades became ineffective, horse-based cavalry became limited to reconnaissance and infantry began to use trenches, hand grenades and land mines. Telegraph communications linked various distant armed units and made global scale RAI4MS and automated tactics possible. In USA's Civil War, the North used global and systemic strategy by: blockading divisions of the Confederacy, destruction of the Confederate armies and supplies... The North was backed by much superior financial, industrial, technological and human power, which were the key CSFs in its victory against the South. The automation of guns, which were transformed in *machine guns* at the end of the 19th century made a decisive effect in WWI.
- WWI and WWII, which have seen the birth of trench tactics to Nuclear Strategy, where WWI saw the emergence of immense, rapid, national mobilizations and classical offensive maneuvers, but after various attempts to destroy their enemies and after the *Battle of the Marne*, static trench warfare ruled over all WWI battlefields. Total war needed, the total national involvement in war efforts, which crippled them. In this phase, two key technological developments modelled RAI4MS' visions of the 1920s and 1930s; the use of air force, that was advocated by the theorists like, Giulio Douhet, Billy Mitchell, Henry Arnold and Hugh Trenchard. Their vision was based on the fact that air force alone, can make a decisive victory, by: 1) Striking the enemy forces; and 2) Strategic bombardment, with massive attacks on cities, industries, lines of communication and supply chains. This RAI4MS was used by the Allied forces during WWII. Another major evolution was the development of motorized armored vehicles, like tanks which became the cavalry of modern warfare and was advocated by: B. H. Liddell Hart, Charles de Gaulle and J. F. C. Fuller. Germanic Nazis were the first to use the tactical offensive combination of air force and tank power in warfare, which was labelled: *blitzkriegs*.

AI based Defence Strategies

An AIbDS must reorganize the government, orient the *Entity* and rally allies to defend and prepare the phase of AIbDS for conflict. To build AIbDS against AI-enabled threats and to simplify digital dependence by transforming vulnerabilities into potential *Entity's* security weaknesses. Adversaries are using AI based systems to enhance Cyberattacks and are storing data on the *Entity*. This type of foreign interference demanded transformation steps to ensure resilience and the *Entity* needs to confront disinformation. The AIbDS needs to secure data sources and prioritize investments, gRisk management and legislation procedures. The *Entity* should leverage AI-enabled Cyberdefence to protect against AI based Cyberattacks; and biosecurity has to be a top priority in national security policy. Transform national intelligence. *Entity's* AIbDS should integrate AI capabilities in all its organizational processes. AIbDS will benefit from AI more than any other technology and the *Entity* needs to enhance its *Managers* and teams skills, leverage open-source and public information. To improve insights, *Entities* need to develop innovative AIbMT concepts to human-machine collaboration by using AI to support the DMS. This new phase of warfare will transform the world, where an option is to design the *Project* or to be defeated. The use of AIbMT in all *Entity's* defence elements will grow and the frequency of transformation and innovation will continue to increase. Adversaries are determined to use AI capabilities and China is determined to gain world AI leadership. Advances in AIbMT gives important strategic advantages. The main principles to be established are: increase investments, improve national security applications, redesign the *Entity's* organizational structure, forge partnerships, build coalitions and build talents (NSCAI, 2020).

RAI4MS' INTEGRATION

AI's Usage

AI is playing a crucial role in military applications and infrastructure; in which it enhances software applications, overall productivity, reduce end-user workload and operate faster than human factors or semi-automated environments. AIbMT research is continuously improving the *Entity's* defence capabilities, explainabilities, proactivity and resilience. The *Entity's* military has to enforce AIbMT and other related technologies. If AIbMT is not given the priority adversaries will take the advantage and might attack and maybe defeat the *Entity*. However, we must resist the allure of this resurgent technology. Integrating and using AIbMT based systems in complex domains and making them deliver geopolitical critical decisions enables the situation for disastrous conflicts and eventual defeats; therefore actually, the human factor stays responsible for key critical decisions. Given in account the high probability that an *Entity* will be exposed to AIbMT based attacks and if there is a current lack of resilience in the *Entity's* AI based defense and technology, an eminent attack is to be expected; and therefore, best domains to invest in military AI are those that used for defence. AIbMT and AIbDS tools and environments are constantly controlled by human experts, who have secure information (inputs and outputs), which can support the *Entity's* military and satisfying concerns about defence vulnerabilities. AIbMT environments might include systems like, medical-imaging diagnostic tools, maintenance-failure prediction applications, and fraud-detection programs; all these environments and tools can provide support to the military and can limit gRisks that can be: adversarial attacks, biased data, context misunderstanding, internal instability and more. AIbMT and AIbDS are not commercial environments sponsored by technology marketing groups world but are the ones that are needed for the near and long term (Maxwell, 2020).

Designing the RAI4MS

Entity's internals, like boundaries, organizations, applications, ICS, assets & resources and processes; are designed, developed and implemented with an important level of security. Depending on the ecosystem and geopolitical context of the *Entity*, major domains (or CSAs) can be divided into subdomains (or CSFs). An important *Entity* domain is global communication management and national territory that can be divided into the following AIbDS sub-domains: 1) Fixed national area and communication network; 2) External passages and communication interfaces; 3) Autonomous devices like drones and tanks; 4) Mobile or ad hoc networks; and 5) Sophisticated spying services. Creating the classification domains (or CSAs) is to reduce complexity in defining EA main RAI4MS and AIbDS objectives, like, security breaches, gRisks, threats and other.

Cyberwarfare, Cybersecurity Constraints and Characteristics

The main Cyberwarfare, Cybersecurity constraints and characteristics are:

- Information security, includes the protection of *Entity's* information against unauthorized disclosure, modification or deletion, whether these operations are accidental or intentional.
- According to S. 1900, *Cyberterrorism Preparedness Act of 2002*, Cybersecurity is *Information: assurance, security, technology disaster recovery and privacy.*

The Applied Holistic Mathematical Model for RAI4MS

The Applied Holistic Mathematical Model for AIbMT (AHMM4AIbMT) nomenclature is showed in Figure 1, in a simplified form to be understandable on the cost of a holistic formulation vision (Trad, & Kalpić, 2020a). The RAI4MS uses the AHMM4AIbMT that is formalized as shown in Figure 1, and AHMM4AIbMT's main artefacts are:

- Basic AIbDS actions = support sovereignty, integrity and secrecy in the face of Cyberwarfare, attacks, incursions and failures with the goal of protecting *Entity's* assets and territory.
- RAI4MS = A set of basic AIbDS actions to counter Cyberwarfare, attacks and major failures.
- National territory and Cyberspace = Includes the territory, AI & ICS and its networks.
- National Security and Cybersecurity = security of national territory, Cyberspace + the defined goals of protecting assets.
- Organizational Security and Cybersecurity = includes national territory + Cyberspace + Cybertechnology + Cybersecurity.
- *Entity* (or national) Security and Cybersecurity = $\sum$ Organizational Security and Cybersecurity.

The Role of Defence Strategy

USA's DoD constant technology priorities jeopardizes its capacity to win a long-term technology competition, it needs a systematic and holistic approach, an RAI4MS in order to prioritize technology change and investments. Today's ICS' evolution is the leading trend and the highest DoD's priority is RAI4MS for digital technologies developed by the private sector. The DoD must invest in major AIbMTs, such as hypersonics or directed energy weapons, which have real operational values. Technology is the artifact needed to achieve military superiority, but alone it cannot give a decisive advantage and is an enabler for gaining superiority. Combined with the right organization, training and concepts for war activities, technological advantages can make combats asymmetric, but the human factor is the decisive CSF. By using advanced AIbMT like, GPS and precision-guided weapons, the USA defeated Iraq's army dur-

Figure 1. The AHMM4AIbMT nomenclature

Basic Mathematical Model's (BMM) Nomenclature

Iteration	= An integer variable **"*i*"** that denotes a *Project/ADM iteration*	
microRequirement	= KPI	(B1)
CSF	= Σ KPI	(B2)
Requirement	= CSF = $\bigcup$ microRequirement	(B3)
CSA	= Σ CSF	(B4)
microKnowledgeArtefact	= $\bigcup$ knowledgeItem(s)	(B4)
neuron	= action->data + microKnowledgeArtefact	(B5)
microArtefact / neural network	= $\bigcup$ neurons	(B6)
microArtefactScenario	= $\bigcup$ microartefact	(B9)
AI/Decision Making	= $\bigcup$ microArtefactScenario	(B10)
microEntity	= $\bigcup$ microArtefact	(B7)
Entity or Enterprise	= $\bigcup$ microEntity	(B8)
EnityIntelligence	= $\bigcup$ AI/Decision Making	(B11)
BMM(*Iteration*) as an instance	= EnityIntelligence(*Iteration*)	(B12)

ing the Persian Gulf War. But afterwards the USA was fatigued and chased out, which confirms that technology must be accompanied by the human, demography and ideology CSFs. Today *Entities* invest in long-range ballistic and cruise missiles, integrated in air defenses, counter-space weapons to blind military spy satellites and Cyberweapons to disable logistics. The USA must transform its RAI4MS and AIbDS to face military aggressions. RAI4MS and AIbDS should include new technologies, like AI to make AIbMT more autonomous; for that RAI4MS must adopt today's technology landscape. Military technology is driven by the private sector because the military does not have the resources to support avantgarde technologies; the USA has a 700 billion USD defense budget. The RAI4MS must support long-term AIbMT competition. Actual DoD's RAI4MS priorities might jeopardize national stability; and it needs a coherent long-term approach. The RAI4MS is not person-driven approach, but a framework for identifying military priorities. The current person-driven approach MUST be replaced by a strategic process for setting military priorities. The dominant technology is the ICS, which is leading to exponential growth in digital capabilities (networks, data, and computing power). The RAI4MS must incorporate this trend to outcompete adversaries (Scharre, & Riikonen, 2020).

Figure 2. The AHMM4AIbMT nomenclature

AHMM's Application and Instantiation for National Security and AIbDS

Domain	= AIbMT	(14)
AHMM(*Domain*)	= $\bigcup$ ADMs + BMMs(*Domain*)	(15)

Figure 3. The MTRD trends

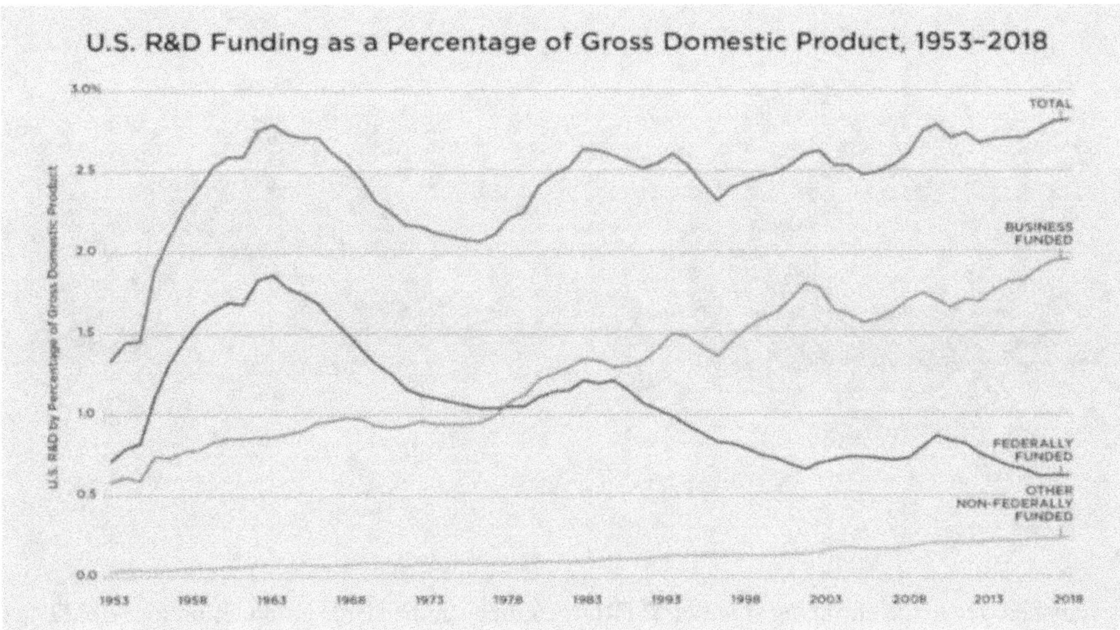

N-Tiered Approach

The RAI4MS focuses on digital and information technologies, which are mature in the commercial sector, can be used for military objectives. RAI4MS' capabilities is seeing important changes in the fields of: Cyber, electronic warfare, sensors, data, networks, cloud computing, AI, autonomy/robotics, genomics, biotech and synthetic biology.

Major Military Technologies

The RAI4MS recommends to invest in major AIbMTs, such as directed energy weapons or hypersonic missiles, when there is clear military operational value. Non-digital technologies such as materials, optics, energy and power are improving, but not as fast as ICS, and they are less likely to offer transformative changes in warfare.

The RAI4MS recommends also to invest in paradigm-shifting *wild card* technologies that have a low-likelihood of reaching operationally relevant maturity, like quantum technologies (quantum computing, communications and sensing), brain-computer interfaces, AI and nanotechnology; supporting these areas can be important changes in these areas. The RAI4MS supports N-tiered investment strategy for critical technologies. As shown in Figure 3, the current global MTRD trends in ICS and the rationale for this RAI4MS. USA' MTRD ecosystem has shifted dramatically over the past several decades and the DoD is not the dominant player in MTRD's landscape. In the 1960s, the USA funded two-thirds of the MTRD and the DoD alone funded about half of national MTRD. As shown in Figures 3 and 4, today, the DoD contributes with one-tenth of USA's MTRD and its overall share has declined to less than one quarter, where the private sector has filled the rest. DoD's drive on global technology development

Figure 4. The MTRD trends

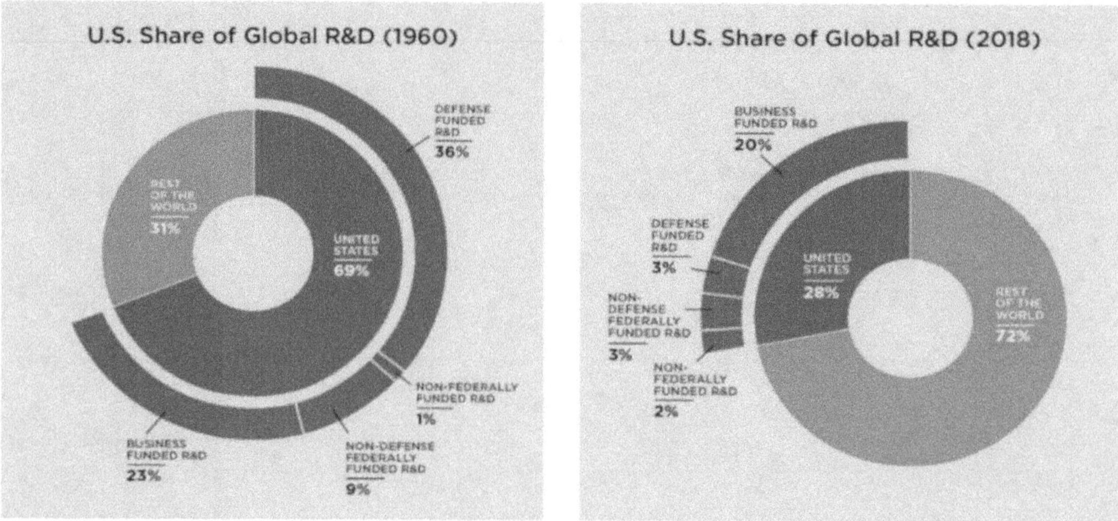

has vanished due to the shrinking share of MTRD spending. In the fierce competition for AIbMT lead, the most important CSF is the *Entity's* capacity to combine national public spending, demography and ideology; that explains USA's decline and China's fulgurant dominance.

ICS' Revolution and Dominance

The most important CSF and trend in the global ICS' ecosystem is the information dominance and revolution. ICS has an exponential growth in various areas, like: data, networks, AI and processing power... There are about 22 billion connected devices today, with an annual growth of 10 percent. Internet of Things (IoT) devices include, smart meters, medical devices and industrial applications, are growing fast. These IoT devices generate data that is managed across the network that trafficked 250+ exabytes per month in 2020. Internet Protocol (IP) traffic is growing fast, at a rate of 26 percent per year and is expected to increase to nearly 400 exabytes per month by 2022. As shown in Figure 5, ICS processing power for AI *Projects* has increased 300,000-fold from 2012 to 2018, which is doubling every few months. This growth in ICS contrasts with its growth in physical attributes (speed, range, scalability, payload, endurance). The most important changes in military competition will come partially from evolution of AIbMT capabilities; and the RAI4MS has to include the abilities to sense the environment, process and transmit information and make just-in-time decisions. Military technology include mainly: Helicopters, planes, tanks, submarines and missiles and the role of AI will make a difference.

Avantgarde AIbMT

The RAI4MS promote a systematic approach for determining which AIbMT will support military dominance. Investments are financially driven by business managers and that endangers military lead. The RAI4MS and AIbDS have to prioritize CSAs to enable a systematic and holistic approach and should adopt an N-tiered strategy. ICS and other CSFs will dramatically transform military competition, because of:

Figure 5. AI projects' trends

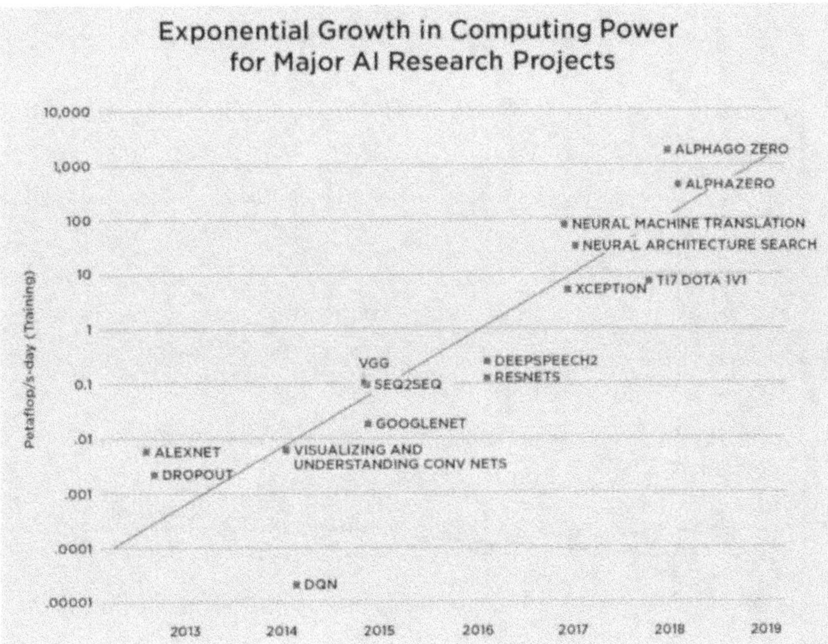

Cyber, electronic warfare and other. Public investments in AIbMT is a crucial CSF. Some ICS areas lack commercial interest and the *Entity* needs to invest in them, like high-energy lasers, hypersonic missiles…

Major AIbMT

There are major AIbMTs that do not have financial benefits and such cases the RAI4MS proposes, to invest and develop them, because non tangible CSF can be the most crucial ones. RAI4MS intangible values include: high-energy lasers, hypersonic missiles, stealth, armor and above all the human CSF. The progress of specific AIbMTs is slow compared to ICS' evolution, like materials, optics, energy and power, which present important technological growth rates. The RAI4MS must consider AIbMTs which will not bring financial benefits, but rather intangible transformative benefits to military activities; the intangible effects will be felt on the longer-term.

RAI4MS' Technology Strategy

As already mentioned, investments alone in right is not recommended, an *Entity* must enforce its AIbMT's capabilities along with other intangible CSFs. AIbMT is a crucial CSF for economic competitiveness and financial benefits, which is supported by political and military capacities; but also, by mammothlike companies like Google and others.

As shown in Figure 6, China will overtake the USA in national MTRD activities, knowing that China is already a leader in various domains, like: AI, genomics and quantum technologies. The RAI4MS must support a national technology concept that manages the *Entity's* government, private sector and allies, in order to be ready for competition. Between the years 1998 and 2018, China's national MTRD

Figure 6. Spending by major players

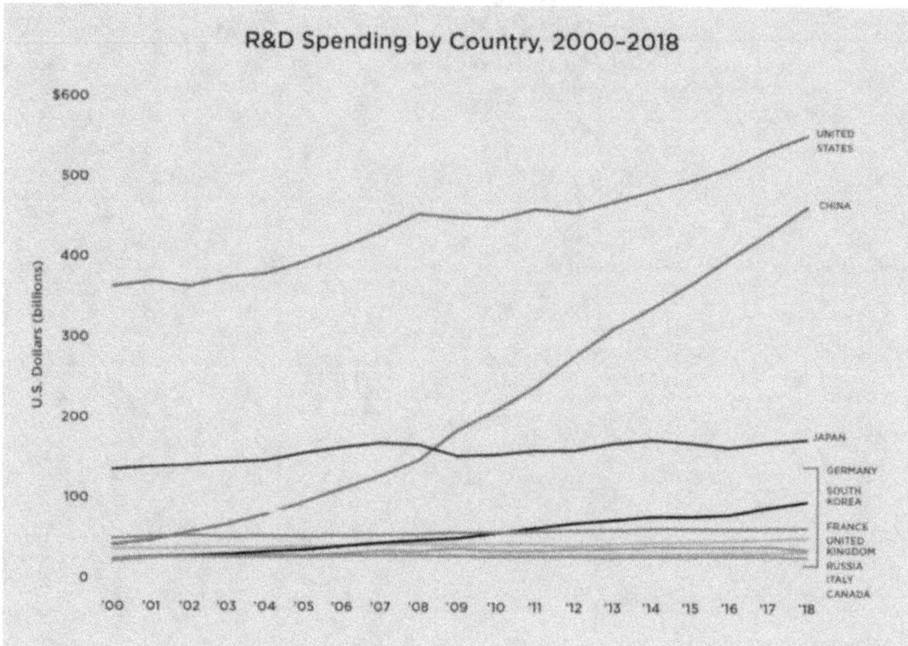

spending had an average of 15 percent annually and it is closing the gap with the USA. USA's MTRD spending was 13 times that of China's in 1998 and China surpassed the USA in 2020. *Allen Institute for Artificial Intelligence*, confirms that China overtook the USA in the most-cited 50 percent of AI research papers in 2019 and will surpass the USA in the most-cited 1 percent of AI research papers by 2025. The RAI4MS must encourage the public sector and its important priorities are: increasing MTRD spending; improving human capital through science; technology, engineering and mathematics education; and accepting high-qualified immigration. There is also a need to: improve data, processing resources; integrating existing standards; enforce policy and regulatory ecosystem. Partnerships and alliances are needed for a global technology ecosystem that becomes mature and in the same time stays competitive, open and secure. A global technology ecosystem dominated by China would be a major change and an important challenge for the West.

Cyberwarfare

Since WWII, the primary RAI4MS and tactical advances is the emergence of amphibious warfare. The principal significance of that phase that was supported by massive coalitions dedicated to build a major offensive against Germanic Nazis. The development of nuclear warfare, which continued after WWII, introduced a new RAI4MS based on nuclear strategy and tactics; that introduced immense destructive possibilities, meant also that warfare had limited RAI4MS goals. The use of conventional tactics with technologically very advanced arms, would predominate in *limited* wars that followed WWII. That resulted in the need to keep wars limited and that has produced an RAI4MS pattern based on: small, mobile special forces, armed with light but sophisticated weapons and trained in guerrilla tactics, that can be rapidly used and rapidly withdrawn from hostile regions (Cheyney, 2021).

Cyberattacks and Protection

The possible types of Cyberattacks are: 1) Denial-of-Service (DoS) and Distributed Denial-of-Service (DDoS) attacks; 2) Man-in-the-Middle (MitM) attacks are simple types of digital attacks; 3) Phishing and spear-phishing, are attacks in which Cybercriminals target the ICS by email attachments; 4) Drive-by attack or Drive by download attacks; 5) Password attack, password cracking or dictionary attacks are attacks by Cyberhackers; 6) Structured Language Query (SQL) injection attack; 7) Cross-Site-Scripting (XSS) attacks are injections, in which malicious scripts are injected in trusted websites; and 8) Eavesdropping attack, also known as a sniffing or snooping attacks. The most common motivations for Cyberattacks are: geopolitical changes, financial greediness, lack of ethics, immoral education and other. Financial greediness can drive to major criminal acts, like, the gigantic financial irregularities, which are related to fraud and money laundering that damage many *Entities*, and this case it is related to major global financial institutions, like the Union des Banques Suisse (UBS) (Stupples, Sazonov, & Woolley, 2019), in which 32 trillion US dollars are *hidden*. Under the cover of bank secrecy… An *Entity's* RAI4MS may counter these types of threats: 1) Cybercrime, which includes a single Cyberattacker or groups, attacking *Entities* for financial gains or to cause damage; 2) Cyberattack, often involves politically motivated information gathering for various ideological purposes; and 3) Cyberterrorism, it is used to undermine the ICS and to cause panic; it originates from various anonymous groups. The RAI4MS proposed actions and predispositions used to support the *Entity's* global stability, security and to reduce gRisks of possible Cyberattacks and to offer possible protections. A Cybersecurity attack is possible when the attacker gains the right to attack. These rights must be hardened in order to avoid the following scenarios: 1) Systemic password management; 2) Using screen lock and face recognition when mowing away; 3) Block the used of email attached files from anonymous email address; 4) Not using anti-virus software, 5) Sharing personal info (and client or server nodes); 6) Not reporting security loops to company; 7) Not using proper paper Documents; 8) Non-secured digital Data (while at rest and in motion); 9) Unsecured way of Information handling; and 10) Providing of information over phone (Trad, 2021a).

Cyberterrorism

Cyberterrorism is a premeditated, political (or ideological) motivated attack against ICSs, software applications/programs and data storages that result in major damages, sabotage activities and even in violence.

Financial Cybercrime Schemes

The integration of Finance for Technologies (FinTech) and ICS is crucial for an *Entity* and its financial controls critical system(s). Today such FinTech standards and fields are robust, resilient and can be applied as automated synchronized (block) chains; to enable the traditional financial environments to become a part of a networked financial world. FinTech platforms can be applied to support an RAI4MS and gRisks mitigation, in order to avoid locked-in situations. EOGPP locked-in scenarios, when building the financial structure of the future transformed *Entity*, must be blocked. The *Project* team and RAI4MS must be cautious of eventual financial locked-in situation(s), which is a major stability and RAI4MS problem. Even though some countries like Switzerland offer attractive financial and tax package(s), this country applies a coordinated legal and financial locked-in trap; it is sealed and represents an unwritten concept that can at any moment sweep out the financial resources from an *Entity* and even powerful countries like the USA, UK and France; and can ruin many like Lebanon, who saw its richness dilapidated by Swiss banks. This locked-in Swiss EOGPP model, combines: 1) Specific culture and mentality; 2) The power of Swiss law; 3) Too Big to Fail state banks; 4) Banking secrecy that protects financial crimes; 5) Ultraliberal economy; 6) rejection of local and global standards; and laws; 7) Isolationism and racism; and 8) A finance supportive political environment for collective plundering. Swiss banks and other Swiss financial institutions are under no supervision what so ever; and are free to hit and run. That indirectly makes this *Entity* the financial and malware industry's super protector that sets up fortifications against any possible legal intrusion; even when these institutions are executing massive irregular, criminal and illegal activities. The author refers to this phenomenon as an instance of the Black Swan phenomena or simply the directed Swiss Black Swan, which *Entity's* (and countries) should try to avoid and penalize. It is probably wiser to pay more taxes and social services then to face such phenomena and traps (International Monetary Fund, 2009; Taleb, 2012). The major problem with combating such a EOGPP based system that is has a hermetically closed environment, characterized by the following: 1) Police and information services, block any attempt to pursue financial criminal acts; 2) The legal system, ignores any attempt to investigate financial criminal acts; 3) Legal support too expensive, to discourage any action of law enforcing; 4) Psychological harassment, to discredit investigators; 5) Intolerance and discrimination, to block any foreign request; 6) A powerful global network, to embed and hide various dubious operations; 7) Financial guerrilla-like and hit and run tactics, to confiscate wealth; and 8) Occurrence of financial locked-in situations and corrupt politicians. Financial havens target to become leaders in FinTech, which is not very assuring; because FinTech should combat state criminality and enforce global security and international law. It is recommended to avoid any form of financial and technological collaboration with EOGPP oriented *Entities*.

Secure Development and Operations

The Development and Operations (DevOps) processes must continuously update the *Entity's* infrastructure patches, software applications, operating system… The *Entity* should benefit from the latest methodologies that support applications' changes and which can be opportunities for Cyberattacks, that makes security a critical CFS. To enforce RAI4MS against Cyberattacks, Secure DevOps (SecDevOps) can be integrated with the ADM. SecDevOps integrates security in the *Project*, by using sets of best practices designed to support *Entities'* implementation processes. Applications' implementation is coordinated by SecDevOps process managed by agile methodologies. The RAI4MS uses agile methodologies to identify patterns for managing requirements (Mees, 2017; Trad, 2021a).

The Legal Constraints

The RAI4MS supports the *Entity's* legal integration and constraints and in order to achieve this legal support, CSFs are selected and asserted, to monitor the used artefacts. These CSFs manage the differences in Cybertechnologies' local and international laws. An *Entity* must have the capacity to proactively recognize erroneous Cybertransactions and Cyberattacks, in a systemic manner (Daellenbach & McNickle, 2005).

BIOWARFARE

Biowarfare can be defined as an intentional application of biological artefacts, like, bacteria, viruses, fungi and toxins, as military weapons in warfare activities. The organized apllication of microorganisms, like toxins, is an ancient military discipline that is today reinvented.

Biotech as a Major Military Technology

The Chinese People's Liberation Army (PLA) is conducting MTRD on gene editing, human performance enhancement, viruses and other, which is a new type of warfare and advances in biotechnology and genetic engineering have various applications in medicine and in alarming implications in AIbMTs. China's RAI4MS has highlighted biology as a major priority and the PLA is a forefront of expanding and exploiting this AIbMT knowledge. PLA's key interests are reflected in strategic writings and MTRD that presents advances in biology are contributing to changing the form and nature of warfare, that is formulated as follows:

- In the 2010's, War for Biological Dominance publication, Guo Jiwei, a professor with the Third Military Medical University, emphasizes the impact of biology on future warfare.
- In 2015, then-president of the Academy of Military Medical Sciences, He Fuchu argued that biotechnology will become the new *strategic commanding heights* of national defense, from biomaterials to *brain control* weapons. Maj. Gen. He, has since become the vice president of the Academy of Military Sciences, which leads China's military science enterprise…
- Biology is among seven *new domains of warfare* discussed in a 2017 book by Zhang Shibo, a retired general and former president of the National Defense University, who concludes: *Modern biotechnology development is gradually showing strong signs characteristic of an offensive capability*, including the possibility that *specific ethnic genetic attacks* could be employed.
- The 2017's edition of Science of Military Strategy, a textbook published by the PLA's National Defense University, which is authoritative, debuted a section about biology as a domain of military struggle, similarly mentioning the potential for new kinds of biological warfare to include *specific ethnic genetic attacks*.
- Following these lines of RAI4MS approaches, the PLA is pursuing military applications for biology and looking into promising intersections with other disciplines, including brain science, supercomputing and AI. Since 2016, the Central Military Commission has funded projects on military brain science, advanced biomimetic systems, biological and biomimetic materials, human performance enhancement, and *new concept* biotechnology.

The Role of AI

The intersection of AIbMT, biotechnology, finance and AI can be a strategic Synergy. The complexity and the huge human genome characteristics, need immense big data infrastructure, that in turn needs AI and machine learning to analyze these characteristics. In 2016, the strategic value of genetic information, influenced the Chinese government to create the *National Genebank*, which is the largest genetic information database; its goal is to *develop and utilize China's valuable genetic resources, safeguard national security in bioinformatics, and enhance China's capability to seize the strategic commanding heights* in domains related to biotechnology and probably biowarfare (Kania, & Vorndick, 2019).

The Evolution

Today Cyberattacks, biowarfare and misinformation, traditional military forces are complemented by less visible assets and national capabilities. Globalization and global connectivity have made *Entities* very vulnerable to attacks. A set of new AIbMT that includes Cybertechnologies, electronics and drone warfare are available to terrorist organizations. *Entities* like, Russia, US and China, are developing offensive weapons in space. This is a major concern for international communications, critical intelligence, surveillance and navigation; also, to *Entity's* infrastructures, mobile phones to stock markets. Estimating the evolution of warfare possibilities, has raised crucial questions on the type of equipment needed to support the *Entity's* army, and the profile of soldiers and their needed skills. There is a need to try to create peace in the Cyber world, rather than in the traditional world; which is a military challenge. The majority of military capabilities are now in Cyberspace and the *Entity* needs to protect that space. The major CSF is the that distance is becoming increasingly irrelevant as a security barrier. Therefore, the *Integrated Review and associated Defence Review* argues that the UK should shift its focus from traditional military equipment, like aircraft carriers and tanks, and to invest in AIbMT, quantum computing, robotics, space and Cyberspace. Traditional warfare is changing and is becoming more technical and precise and in the same time less formal, seeing a shift from traditional battle grounds to a type of hybrid warfare, centered on disinformation, mainly done in grey zones just below the threshold of open conflict areas. An AIbDS needs a flexible army and less instances of physical conflicts. The positive evolution is that there will be fewer physical casualties, but the consequences of AIbMT based engagements, tend to leave lasting psychological impact; like in the case where serving soldiers can be deployed to control groups or individuals prior to an attack. This type of personal involvement leads to the increase in mental stress for the *Entity's* armed forces. Although modern warfare is getting further back from traditional front lines, by using drones, but it is getting closer by inflicting moral injuries... Public attitudes and opinions are changing and there is a desire for a consensual decision prior to military actions and awareness of impacts of warfare. Public's ambivalence to warfare is affected by the wars in the middle east and that this has had an impact on recruitment. Actually, the lack of confidence in the morality of warfare and the increased skills requirement, pushes people not join the armed forces (FIMT, 2021).

RAI4MS' ADVANCED TOPICS

Nuclear modernization has become one of the least priorities and the actual priorities are: Hypersonics; Directed energy; Command, control, and communications; Space offense and defence, Cybersecurity; AI and machine learning; Missile defence; Quantum science and computing; Microelectronics; Autonomy (which replaced nuclear weapons). But RAI4MS' modernization priorities are: AI and machine learning; Biotechnology; Autonomy; Cyber; Directed energy; Fully networked command; Microelectronics; Quantum; Hypersonics; 5G; and Space technologies. AI and autonomy are probably the number one priority for any RAI4MS (Kania, & Vorndick, 2019).

Capacity Building – Skill and Competence Development

The ADM supports the RAI4MS to create best practices and *Entity*-specific security capabilities, which supports EA and security experts to avoid missing critical gRisks, and this article offers recommendations on the needed skills to carry out AIbDS activities. The AIbDS is treated as a separate domain within the EA, which fully integrates it. AIbDS is the enforcement of the *Entity's* security policies which includes the following skills and characteristics (The Open Group, 2011b): 1) Security methodology; 2) Management of viewpoints; 3) To design non-normative flows through the ICS; 4) To design single-purpose components; and 5) To develop EA, AIbDS and ICS models.

Guidance on Security for the Architecture Domains

RAI4MS' Security (RAI4MSS) requirements are pervasive in all EA domains and to all ADM phases. The RAI4MSS focuses mainly on the infrastructure that is not visible to other functions; it also focuses on the protection of the ICS and *Entity's* assets. AIbDS manages single-purpose components and measures the quality of the ICS and the common artifacts are: 1) AI rules for handling of data/information assets; 2) Defined RAI4MSS policies, 3) Codified data/information assets' ownership and custody; 4) gRisk analysis documentation; and 5) Data classification policy documentation. The RAI4MSS has its own unique building blocks, collaborations and interfaces; these blocks must interface with the *Entity's* ICS in an optimal manner, in order to support RAI4MSS' policies and to avoid interfering with ICS operations. RAI4MSS is effective to design and implement controls in the *Target Architecture* in the initial development cycle to support reengineering development and deployment. The RAI4MSS manages the normal flow of application's fallout, abnormal flows, failure modes and the possibilities in which the ICS and applications can be interrupted or attacked. All *Entities* have security concerns and they should dedicate an RAI4MSS to support the *Project*. In all ADM phases, recommendations are given on RAI4MSS' management (The Open Group, 2011b).

Security Monitoring and Logs

The RAI4MSS is not dedicated to any specific AIbMT environment and it offers to support: 1) Performance and availability; 2) Reliability and recovery; 3) Attack's tracing; and 4) Cybersecurity fundaments. The ICS is controlled and monitored in real-time, using the *Entity's* Unified Logging Subsystem (EULS) and is integrated in order to support the RAI4MSS. EULS' exist and are powerful monitoring subsystems that support the presentation, sorting and tuning of stored logs. EULSs can be designed to analyses, collect and store security related data from various ICS sources to support the central logging system. An ICS continuously needs to manage massive central logging system that persists: event logs, sorts security logs for security purposes and system performances.

RAI4MS' Steps for Enhancements

RAI4MS' Steps for Enhancements the *Entity* must (Morgan, Boudreaux, Lohn, Ashby, Curriden, Klima, & Grossman, 2020): 1) Organize, prepare train and equip national armies in order to prevail in the world's context in which AIbMT systems are prominent in all domains of possible confrontations: 2) Understand how to treat and integrate the ethical concerns required by *Managers,* leaders, AI technologists the private sector and the *Entity's* public; 3) Organize public campaigns to inform main stakeholders of the *Entity's* military commitment to mitigating ethical gRisks related AI, in order to avoid public resistance and any resulting national limitations; 4) Prepare and follow discussions of *Entity's* national security experts involved in UN's Convention on Certain Conventional Weapons and to track the evolving positions held by stakeholders in the international community; 5) To seek ambitious AIbDS cooperation and policy alignment with all allies and partners, with respect regarding the development and usage of AIbMT; and 6) Explore confidence-building and gRisk mitigation/reduction procedures with major powers like the USA, China, Russia and other *Entities* attempting to develop AIbMT and AIbDS.

PROOF OF CONCEPT

The Implementation Environment

RAI4MS' PoC was implemented using *TRADf* which was developed exclusively by the author and uses microartefacts on the basis of the fine-grained granularity approach of the "1:1" mapping design and concept; and was developed using the following resources and tools: 1) Microsoft Visual Studio .NET/C#, system scripting and C/C++; and 2) Java Enterprise Edition development environments (Trad, 2021a).

The Literature Review's Outcome

The RLR and phase 1's outcomes support the PoC, by using of the author's archive of an important set of references and links that are analysed using a specific interface; where each link can then be reviewed, archived, weighted parsed into an Excel file. After selecting the sets of CSA/CSFs, tags are linked to various microartefacts scenarios. A CSF is implemented as an item, in an Excel file; where all its details are defined; these actions conclude phase 1. In this PoC (or it phase 2), the HDT is used to deliver solutions to concrete RAI4MS problems. The HDT process is an iterative *rule of thumb* and a guide to implement RAI4MS problem solving using a goal function and constraints. The RAI4MS uses the AHMM4AIbMT instance to manage microartefacts mechanics', which in turn uses the internal initial sets of CSFs' that are used in phases 1 and 2.

The RAI4MS-S' CSFs Phase 1

All other CSAs' CSFs values are defined by the RAI4MS expert. Based on the RLR and the related evaluation processes (phase 1) the most important CSFs are used and processed by the internal HDT and the results are presented in Table 1 (Trad & Kalpić, 2020a). As shown in Table 1, this fact keeps all CSAs that helps to make this work's conclusion. If the automated evaluation of RLR outcomes is successful, then this ends phase 1 and afterwards phase 2 starts to complete the PoC. As shown in Table 1, the results justify (an average of 8.50) the usage of the RAI4MS and how it can be used with the PoC's final phase (or phase 2); where the described process is applied to the CSAs. A RAI4MS problem is selected and an HDT process is launched to find a set of solutions.

Table 1. The ACS's CSFs that have an average of 9.0

Critical Success Factors	KPIs	Weightings
The Research and Development Project	ROBUST	From 1 to 10. **10 Selected**
RAI4MS Fundaments	ROBUST	From 1 to 10. **10 Selected**
RAI4MS Integration	POSSIBLE	From 1 to 10. **09 Selected**
RAI4MS Advanced Topics	POSSIBLE	From 1 to 10. **08 Selected**
AI based Cyberwarfare	COMPLEX	From 1 to 10. **07 Selected**
AI based Biowarfare	COMPLEX	From 1 to 10. **07 Selected**

Linking the Applied Case Study – Integration and Unification

Phase 2 starts with the selection of the Case Studies (CS) from the following list of possible cases:

- ***Cyber, Internet related technologies … CS_IoT.***
- Economy, Growth or the CS_EcoSys.
- ***Conflict, political, religious, ethnical and other or the CS_EthnoPol.***
- ***Geopolitics, basics, analysis and transformation or the CS_GeoPol.***
- ***Finance, governance, law and technology category or the CS_FinTech.***
- (In)dependence, external resources, man power, agriculture… CS_InpFact

The Architecture Method's Phases' Integration, Setup and Selecting Factors

The phase 2 implementation setup looks as follows:

- Sub-phase A or the *Architecture Vision* phase's goals, establishes a data architecture.
- Sub-phase B or the *Business Architecture* phase shows how the RAI4MS target architecture.
- Sub-phase C or the *Gap Analysis* phase uses the *Application Communication Diagram.*
- Sub-phase D or the *Target Technology Architecture and Gap Analysis* phase shows the end RAI4MS's concept implementation; where here is limited.
- Sub-phases E and F, or the *Implementation and Migration Planning*; where the transition architecture, proposing possible intermediate situation and evaluates RAI4MS's integration status.

Experiment's Processing on a Concrete Tree Node

In phase 2, the HDT is used, to find a combination of HDT's action, used to solve an RAI4MS problem related to this chapter's RQ. A specifically selected CSF is linked to a RAI4MS problem type and a related set of actions; where the processing starts in the root node. Each RAI4MS problem, like this case the PRB_RAI4MS_ EOGPP RAI4MS problem, has the following set of actions: 1) ACT_RAI4MS_Define_ProblemType; 2) ACT_RAI4MS_Verify_ProblemType; 3) ACT_RAI4MS_Match_ProblemType 4) ACT_RAI4MS_Validate_ProblemType… For this RAI4MS related PoC, the author has selected the CSF_RAI4MS_ESTIMATION as the active CSF, taken from the previously defined Tables or the RAI4MS's CSAs. In this PoC the goal is to find solutions related to this selected CSF's related RAI4MS problems. Such RAI4MS problems can be only researched with the HDT based mixed-model that is very similar to the (re)scheduling of *Project's* activities. Solving the given RAI4MS problem is done by a set of actions and delivers solutions.

Selected Node Solution in Phase 2

The frameworks scripts make up the processing logic of the RAI4MS problems and is supported by a set of actions. Where these actions are processed in the DMS background to support microartefacts that are called by the HDT's engine actions, which deliver the solution and the flow of steps. This RDP, the AHMM4AIbMT and its related CSAs/CSFs were selected as demonstrated previously, and interact.

Experiment's Processing on a Concrete Tree Node

The HDT is applied to a specific CSF that is mapped to a specific RAI4MS problem and a set of linked actions, to deliver results in the form of solutions. The selected RAI4MS problem is related to *the detection of EOGPP activities*. The hyper HDT approach is used, to find a combination of HDT's action, used to solve an RAI4MS problem related to this chapter's RQ. A specifically selected CSF is linked to a RAI4MS problem type and a related set of RAI4MS actions; where the processing starts in HDT's root node. Each RAI4MS problem, like in this case, the selected RAI4MS problem, has the following set of actions: RAI4MS_Init, RAI4MS _Eval and others …

Selected Node Solution in Phase 2

The scripts make up the processing logic of the defined RAI4MS problems and are supported by a set of actions. Where these actions are processed in the background by the use of microartefacts that are called by HDT's actions, which deliver the solutions.

CONCLUSION

Because of a just passing score, 8.50, Table 1 shows that RAI4MS's implementation is a risky transformation process and that an inhouse only methodology and framework, like *TRADf*, can be built. In this article, the author proposes the following set of managerial recommendations:

- The RAI4MS supports the AIbMT and AIbDS in order to ensure an efficient global defense concept.
- Public AIbMT and AIbDS should replace private sectors' investments.
- ADM's integration in the RAI4MS enables the automation of all its activities.
- Conflicts, wars and military investments are the backbone of major economies.
- Military organizations are the ones who drive major AI based technological transformation trends.
- RAI4MS has to find the right balance between military: technology, strategy, investments, geopolitical knowledge, combative status and the evolution of demography
- RAI4MS and automated tactics are the basis of managing modern warfare.

- Humans and their sustainable demography are *Entities*' main CSFs; even concerning the need of intelligence.
- *Entities* are using AI based technologies and methodologies as the kernel of their AIbDS.
- Modern biotechnology is showing dangerous offensive capabilities...
- Applications' development and operations are coordinated by using the SecDevOps.
- FinTech would make financial operations more embedded and abstract.
- Avoid any form of collaboration with doubtful financial EOGPP oriented organizations.
- Cyberattacks and Cyberwarfare are advancing quickly especially the domains of Biotech and Cybertechnologies.
- *TRADf* englobes TOGAF and indirectly SABSA and other standard methodologies and artifacts, which facilitates the transformation process.

REFERENCES

Cheyney, S. (2021). *Strategy and Tactics, Military*. Scholastic Inc.

Clark, D. (2002). *Enterprise Security: The Manager's Defense Guide*. Addison-Wesley Professional.

Daellenbach, H., McNickle, D., & Dye, Sh. (2012). *Management Science - Decision-making through systems thinking* (2nd ed.). Plagrave Macmillian.

DODAF. (2010). *Deputy Chief Information Officer, The DoDAF Architecture Framework Version 2.02*. U.S. Department of Defense. https://dodcio.defense.gov/dodaf20.aspx

Easterbrook, S., Singer, J., Storey, M., & Damian, D. (2008). *Guide to Advanced Empirical Software Engineering-Selecting Empirical Methods for Software Engineering Research*. Springer.

FIMT. (2021). *Changing Characteristics of Conflict*. FIMT. https://www.liftingoursights.org.uk/trends/changing-characteristics-of-conflict/

Gardner, H. (1999). *Intelligence Reframed: Multiple Intelligences for the 21st Century*. Basic Books.

Hue, M. (2014). A Review of Enterprise Architecture Use in Defence. Defence Systems Integration Technical Advisory. Joint and Operations Analysis Division. Defence Science and Technology Organisation. Australian Government. Department of Defence.

International Monetary Fund. (2009). Switzerland: Financial Sector Assessment Program - Detailed Assessment of Observance of Financial Sector Standards and Codes. International Monetary Fund, 5, 170.

Kania, E., & Vorndick, W. (2019). *Weaponizing Biotech: How China's Military Is Preparing for a 'New Domain of Warfare*. Government Media Executive Group LLC.

Markides, C. (2011, March). Crossing the Chasm: How to Convert Relevant Research Into Managerially Useful Research. *The Journal of Applied Behavioral Science*, *47*(1), 121–134. doi:10.1177/0021886310388162

Maxwell, P. (2020). Artificial intelligence is the future of warfare (just not in the way you think). Modern War Institute.

Mees, W. (2017). *Security by Design in an Enterprise Architecture Framework*. NATO.

MOD. (2020). *MOD Science and Technology Strategy 2020*. Government UK.

Morgan, F., Boudreaux, B., Lohn, A., Ashby, M., Curriden, Ch., Klima, K., & Grossman, D. (2020). *Military Applications of Artificial Intelligence-Ethical Concerns in an Uncertain World*. RAND Corporation.

NSCAI. (2020). *Final Report National Security Commission on Artificial Intelligence*. NSC.

Peterson, S. (2011). *Why it Worked: Critical Success Factors of a Financial Reform Project in Africa*. Faculty Research Working Paper Series. Harvard Kennedy School.

Scharre, P., & Riikonen, A. (2020). Defense Technology Strategy. Center for a New American Security.

Stupples, B., Sazonov, A., & Woolley, S. (2019). UBS Whistle-Blower Hunts Trillions Hidden in Treasure Isles. Bloomberg-Economics. *Bloomberg*. Reviewed in November 2019 https://www.bloomberg.com/news/articles/2019-07-26/ubs-whistle-blower-hunts-trillions-hidden-in-treasure-islands

Taleb, N. (2012). *Antifragile: Things that gain from disorder*. Library of Congress Cataloguing-in-Publication Data. Nassim Nicholas Taleb.

The Open Group. (2011a). *The TOGAF Framework*. The Open Group.

The Open Group. (2011b). *Security Architecture and the ADM*. The Open Group. https://pubs.opengroup.org/architecture/togaf91-doc/arch/chap21.html

Trad, A. (2021a). The Security Management Concept (SMC). *STF Conference*. Turkey.

Trad, A., & Kalpić, D. (2020a). *Using Applied Mathematical Models for Business Transformation*. IGI Global. doi:10.4018/978-1-7998-1009-4

Chapter 18
Business Architecture and Transformation Projects:
Enterprise Holistic Security Risk Management (ESRM)

Antoine Trad
https://orcid.org/0000-0002-4199-6970
IBISTM, France

ABSTRACT

Enterprise security risk management (ESRM) is a planned strategy that identifies and assesses possible security problems that may jeopardize the enterprise's growth, assets, sustainability, or defined objectives. The ESRM supports the process of identifying the set of security risks to be monitored actively and to deliver scenarios of efficient actions. It also offers recommendations to senior managers and stakeholders in the form of routine and executive actions and reports. In this chapter, the author implemented his research on a specific mixed method that is supported by a heuristics component, the applied holistic mathematical model for enterprise security risk management (AHMM4ESRM). The AHMM4ESRM can be also used for financial, operations, and governance services to detect various types of irregularities.

INTRODUCTION

Business environments, governments and organizations (or simply *Entities*) are increasingly using Cybertechnologies to become Cyberentities. The transformed Cyberentity, has to face new challenges, dangers and security Risks (sRisk), when implementing its infrastructure and Information and Communication System (ICS). One of the most important sRisks is the stability of an *Entity* in an unsafe and unstable ecosystem that is mainly based on the ICS. Therefore, the security of an *Entity* should have a holistic concept like the ESRM for an *Entity* transformation project (or simply *Project*). The ESRM includes a methodology and a concept to manage security for *Entities*, which includes classical and Cybersecurity. Cybersecurity is employed in the *Entity*'s architecture and operations processes. *Entity's* transformation

DOI: 10.4018/978-1-7998-9648-7.ch018

has many tangible advantages and unfortunately has also many risks and pitfalls. *Entity's* main sRisks are: data, assets and resources platform security, but there is a whole set of other types of ICS and domain sRisks. *Entities* are more or less sensitive on classical attacks and Cyberattacks, depending on the size of the *Entity*, volume of transactions, data management and the applied agility. In order to identify classified *Entity's* security breaches like data leaking, the proposed ESRM proposes a systematic and holistic approach to ICS' resources protection that includes Cybersecurity mechanisms. Cybersecurity is essential for ensuring the *Entity's* sensitive information, assets and resources protection from a probable use of personal information that can be leaked and can be used by hackers. *Entities* are facing excessive requests to optimize their assets and minimize sRisks, to guarantee sustainability, optimize costs, support frequent transformation initiatives and to integrate legal, security and governance frameworks. The ESRM is supported by a Decision Making System for ESRM (DMS4ESRM) for planning, inventory and risk mitigation activities. The DMS4ESRM, uses Artificial Neural Networks (ANN) based heuristics reasoning engine that is optimal for solving complex problems. The DMS4ESRM is domain agnostic and uses a holistic approach and is based on a reasoning concept that is a qualitative method that manages, weighting mechanisms, rates Critical Success Factor (CSF) sets, actions and solutions (Capecchi, Buscema, Contucci, D'Amore, 2010). Hence the CSFs are the most important mapping/relation between the ESRM, financial status, organizational predisposition and DMS4ESRM; that can a subject for Cyberattacks or global crime schemes (Peterson, 2011). The ESRP uses scenarios that are sets of services and rules to manage sRisks which can have a fatal impact on capital markets. The AHMM4ESRM considers sRisks (or *exposures*) measurable and transmits the profits and losses to the *bottom-line* process (Trad, & Kalpić, 2020a). *Entities* face a set of barriers and difficult situations, which need the management of sRisks using a specialized framework to support their activities. sRisks may include CSFs related to: reputation, routine operational procedures, legal and human resources management, financial, the risk of failure of internal controls systems related to the Sarbanes-Oxley Act (SOX) and global governance. The ESRM focuses on assessing sRisks and using the DMS4ESRM to estimate possible dangers and to offer solutions. Solutions, include just-in-case alternatives for routine activities and practices to manage potential security problems. A *Project* integrates various objects, like ESRM managers and/or the creation of a department for risk management supported by a quality control team (Kenton, 2020). Possible ESRM risks are: 1) Hazard risks, which include risks that present a high level of threat to life, health or property; 2) Financial risks, refer to risks that are directly related to money; 3) Strategic risks are risks that affect or are created by strategic decisions; 4) Operational and security risks are risks that influence the *Entity;* 5) ESRM main fields and background.

BACKGROUND AND FOCUS

Entity's ICS enables the processing large groups of applications and their related data storages with optimal performance and sometimes in hyper-time, in order to serve clients and executive management, who are supported by a DMS4ESRM. The DMS4ESRM and Cybertechnologies' evolutions have enabled to the transformation of legacy mainframe systems where most of the *Entity*'s transactions and data storages are found. Such a distributed n-tiered architecture needs an optimal ESRM that includes a security integration pattern, which is be crucial for: 1) Achieving and maintaining sustainability; 2) Competitiveness; 3) Providing the flow of transactions related to money; 4) Achieving profitability; and 5) Ensuring *Entity's* robustness (Vulić, Prodanović, & Tot, 2019). This chapter's background combines: ESRM, ESRP,

Enterprise Architecture (EA), AHMM4ESRM, technology management and *Project* fields. Building ESRPs for ESRM is a major strategic objective, where the ESRP is agnostic to a specific domain. The ESRM uses industry standards, like the ICS modelling methodologies and Architecture Development Method (ADM) (The Open Group, 2011a). The *Project* manager or ESRM manager (the term *Manager* will be used) can apply the ESRP to facilitate the integration of the ESRM in the transformed *Entity*. The ESRP uses Artificial Intelligence (AI) capacities and governance components, the ESRP is a part of the Risk management module (Rm). The Rm is a part of this Research & Development Project's (RDP) framework, called the Transformation, Research and Architecture Development framework (*TRADf*). The *Project* uses a Natural Language Programming (NLP) for prototyping the ESRP by using a set of atomic Building Blocks (aBB) in the form of services (or microartefacts). The RDP uses a Research Literature Review's (RLR), a qualitative methodology and a Proof of Concept (PoC).

THE REASEARCH METHOD AND CONCEPT

For this chapter the Research Question (RQ) is: "Can an ESRM and ESRP, support a business transformation project and minimize the related security risks of failure?"

The Research's Literature Review

RLR's results show that a small number of relevant scholar resources exist on the RQ and its related subjects, with the exception of the Open Group Architecture Framework (TOGAF). The author considers that his RDP works, are pioneering and the most relevant finding is that there is an important gap, between *Projects* goals and the ESRM. The knowledge gap exists, mainly because of the existing RLR on failure rates and on ESRM, where there is practically no insight on a holistic approach to design an ESRP for the ESRM. In the RLR the following resources are used: 1) Various chapters related to *Entity* asset and security risk management; 2) The author's general works and framework; 3) *TRADf*, which is used to support ESRM's integration; 4) An initial set of CSFs; and 5) Uses empirical engineering methods. This chapter is based on the RDP's maturity in the domains of risk management and asset management; and the most important related works are: 1) The Business Transformation Framework and Enterprise Architecture Framework for Managers in Business Innovation: The Alignment of Enterprise Asset Management and Enterprise Architecture Methodologies (Trad, 2021a); 2) The Business Transformation Framework and Enterprise Architecture Framework: Organizational Asset Management in the Lebanese Context (Trad, 2021b); 3) Business Transformation and Enterprise Architecture: The Holistic Project Asset Management Concept (Trad, & Kalpić, 2021a); and 4) The Security Management Concept (SMC) (Trad, 2021c).

Empirical Engineering Methods

The RDP uses an empirical engineering method, which is optimal various types of engineering projects like AI based transformations (Easterbrook, Singer, Storey, & Damian, 2008). The RDP main goal is to deliver a holistic approach for an interactive mixed method. Method's validity checks if the RDP is credible as a contribution to scientific knowledge. An experiment or a PoC is a concept that contains design artefacts, Critical Success Areas (CSA) and a software prototype to verify the RQ. The PoC uses an Applied Case Study (ACS) from the insurance domain (The Open Group, 2011a).

Critical Success Areas

A CSA is a set of CSFs where a CSF is a set of KPIs. A KPI corresponds to a single ESRM requirement. For a ESRM requirement, an analyst identifies an initial set of CSFs. CSFs are the most important relation between an ESRM construct, organizational predisposition and the DMS4ESRM. Therefore, CSFs reflect performance areas that must meet strategic goals and defined security constraints. Measurements are used to evaluate performance in each CSA, where CSFs can be internal and/or external. An RDP identifies ESRM's important CSFs through: 1) the RLR; 2) the PoC; and 3) a survey, which collects evidence. The results can confirm success or failure. The significant differences of the *Project's* CSAs, is sorted by weighting and rating mechanisms. A *Project* team searches for a consensus on the most important CSFs (Zhao, Hwang, & Low, 2013). Selecting the *Entity's* security CSFs is based on the following facts and resources (Trad, 2021c): 1) ICS; 2) Actors and boundaries; 3) Used and connected components; 4) Technical and functional security requirements; 5) Well defined business and organizational strategies, objectives and goals; 5) Applied security policies; 6) Sustainability and competition; 7) Geopolitical and geoeconomical statuses; and their correlation; 8) Behavioral sciences and parapsychology mirage, which can alienate the main objectives; and 9) The *Entity* Organized Global Predators' Pattern (EODPP) for Cyberattacks, where the targeted domains, can be security, finance, logistics, geopolitics or other; it can be even used for a combination of these fields. Determination and the evaluation of major sRisk is affected by many CSFs and their relation/correlation is therefore essential. *Entities* must defend their ICS, assets, resources, Business Process Models (BPM), data storages; so that an external actor using an EODPP has to detected and deterred to access to its internals. Such an unauthorized access can be fatal and very difficult to prove. The *Entity* must be capable to defend its internal sub-systems and objectives, like data consistency, accuracy and reliability and must build an ESRM to identify and block any EODPP attempts to damage the *Entity*. Therefore, the main objective is to block and to have security controls that identifies EODPP (or other types of attack patterns) attempts, like unauthorized and even criminal activities. Besides classical Cybersecurity, the EODPP must be aware of other types of organized asymmetric attacks like: 1) Cyberwarfare; 2) Cyberterrorism; 3) Cyberhooliganism; 4) Cyberfinance attacks; and others. Just analyzing data is a partial, limited and is a static solution, there is a need for a dynamic proactive qualitative heuristics' method like the author's Heuristics Decision Tree (HDT) algorithm. There is also a need to control the activities and behavior of persons (and groups), which are an important part of the *Entity's* internals and to proactively detect any probable violations. Possible violations can be modelled to deliver controlled access to *Entity's* internals through: political backup, spying services, assigned roles, responsibilities & credentials, and defined standards.

The Author's Applied Framework

The ESRM asses and governs the enterprise's assets using the ESRP; and a global management concept of assets is optimal for the ESRM that can be applied in many fields. The ESRP is managed by ADM's phases, where each ESRP microartefact circulates through its phases. The ESRP microartefacts contain their sets of CSFs. In this chapter, sections from previous works are reused to improve the understand-

Figure 1. The COSO framework
(IIA, 2004, Curtis, & Carey, 2012).

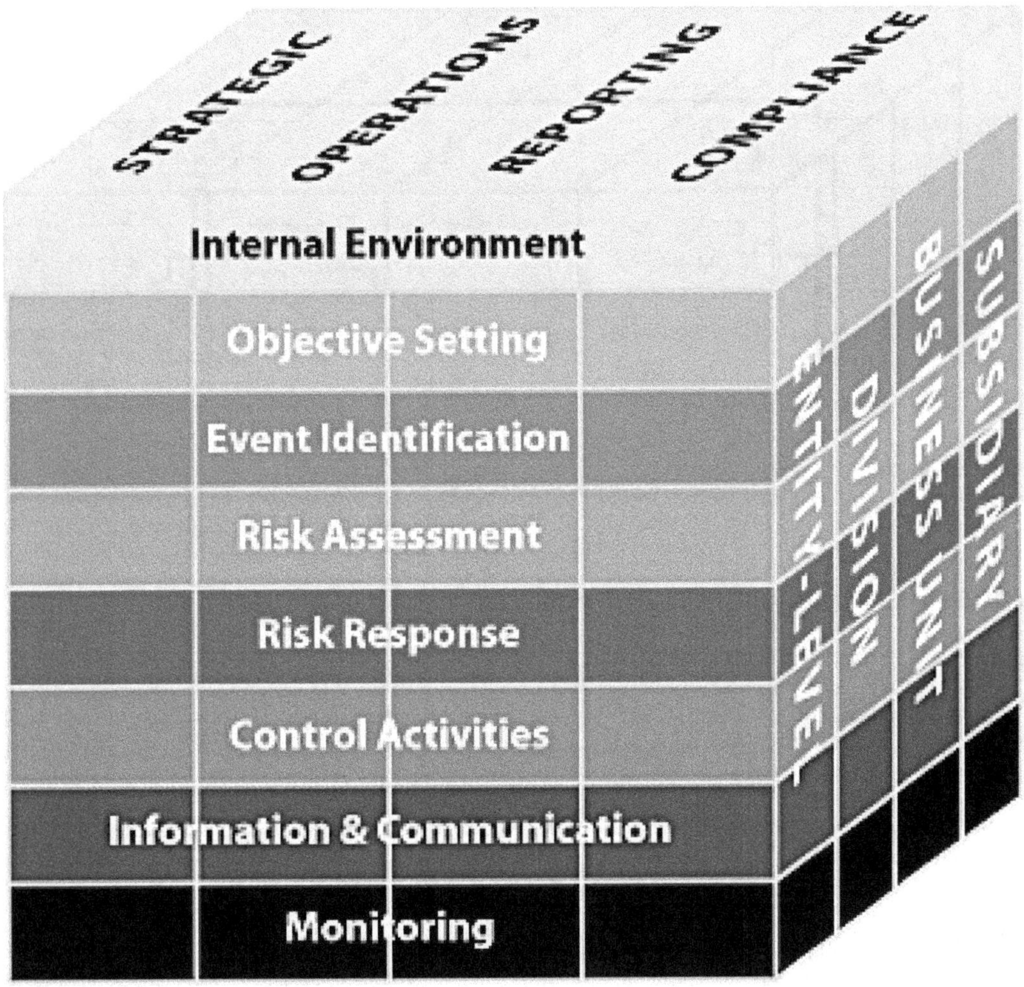

ing of this complex subject. *TRADf* interfaces various market risk frameworks like the Committee of Sponsoring Organizations of the Treadway Commission (COSO), which is shown in Figure 1.

The ESRM is *a process, effected by an entity's board of directors, management and other personnel, applied in strategy setting and across the enterprise, designed to identify potential events that may affect the entity, and manage risks to be within its risk appetite, to provide reasonable assurance regarding the achievement of entity objectives...* This COSO framework defines basic important components, proposes a common language and offers a roadmap for enterprise risk management and the ESRM. Enterprise objectives can have the following CSAs: 1) Strategic; 2) Operations; 3) Reporting; and 4) Compliance. And the following key CSF: 1) Organizational design of business; 2) Establishing an ESRM organization; 3) Performing risk assessment; 4) Determining overall risk possibilities; 5) Identifying risk responses; 6) Communication of risk results; and 7) Monitoring (IIA, 2004, *Curtis, & Carey, 2012).*

Figure 2. Types of economic risks
(Kiseleva, Karmanov, Korotkov, Kuznetsov, & Gasparian, 2018).

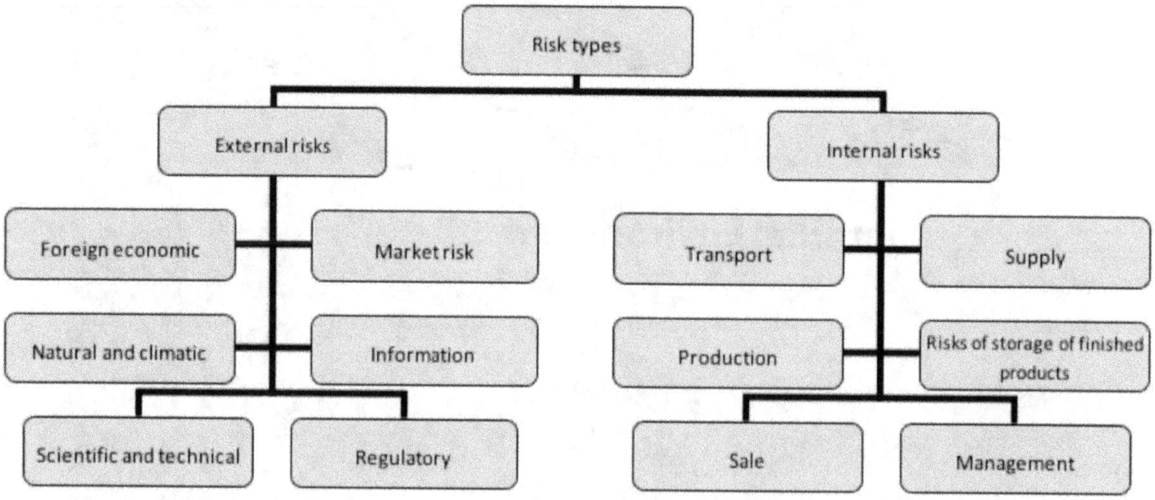

Enterprise Risk Management and Security

ESRM's integration is complex and needs massive use of tools and technology to radically improve performance and ensure tangible benefits by using ESRP integration and scripting. Accountant oriented ESRM scripting promotes off-shoring and ruthless growth, can have a negative effect on *Projects*, because they may promote confused and contradictory conclusions. ESRMs are of strategic importance and if a *Project* is successful, the transformed *Entity* will excel. Transformed *Entities* with an efficient ESRM, automates sRisks' management, by using the ESRP which is in turn supported by the ADM. The *Entity* chooses a strategy to achieve its goals and tries to finds ways to avoid sRisks. Evaluation of sRisks and the definition of the probability of hazardous events and the choice of solutions is specific to *Entity* and its eco-system. sRisks are, in most cases, difficult to discover and classify, due to their diversity and complexity. There are various types of sRisks that are related with each application domain. sRisks' neutralization is a technical, financial and mathematical process for the implementation of decisions for the transformation measures. The ESRM structures sRisks by using CSAs, weights them and uses delimiters to select the related CSFs. The ESRM analysis the CSAs by applying scenarios for mitigation. ESRM system's key principles are: 1) Principle of integration using a systemic and holistic approach; 2) Principle of continuity using a set of procedures; and 3) Principle of validity, provides an analysis of the ratio of costs to reduce possible sRisks. Figure 2, shows an example sRisk classification that is used in economic practice (Kiseleva, Karmanov, Korotkov, Kuznetsov, & Gasparian, 2018).

The ESRM Knowledge Management System

The Knowledge Management System for the ESRM's (KMS4EAM) main goal, is to manage sRisk information items; this is achieved by using a distributed access to knowledge. KMS4EAM's characteristics are:

- The KMS4EAM is based on a pool on coordinated knowledge services. ESRP microartefacts are responsible for the manipulation and processing knowledge items.
- Weightings' concept enables the ESRP support the security subsystem that delivers answers in the form of sRisk values.
- ESRP actions map to various KMS4EAM processes, which are responsible for the implementation of mechanisms needed to deliver knowledge items.
- The KMS4EAM manages security knowledge item that uses scripts, which are responsible for the manipulation of intelligence and control of various KMS4EAM processes.
- sRisk knowledge items map to CSFs and microartefact(s) and are classified in specific CSAs; to be used by the DMS4ESRM.

The DMS4ESRM

The DMS4ESRM is conceptually based on a mixed method, combining Action Research (AR) with ANN to support the HDT and directed quantitative analysis. The author believes that qualitative, quantitative and other methods can be united in a single holistic reasoning method. This process inspects and learns from configurable intelligent microartefacts that are the skeleton of the DMS4ESRM. A DMS4ESRM must be managed by existing audit or governance frameworks, where the *Manager's* configures various types of sRisks. These sRisks are estimated by DMS4ESRM's actions to deliver possible solutions. DMS4ESRM actions' map to the governance processes, which are responsible for the implementation of governance needed to adjust the business objectives. DMS4ESRM's implementation of governance mechanisms identifies critical ESRM risks. Risk types are managed as CSFs, where these types might need many iterations to be tuned. ESRM is a crucial topic within an *Entity*, resulting in important investments on implementing sRisk solutions, where complex technologies may cause *Project* failures and defining the right set CSF may reduce the sRisk of *Project* failures. The RLR showed that the *Project* starts with CSFs' definition (Gibson, 2012).

The AHMM4ESRM

The AHMM4ESRM is domain agnostic and contains a configurable reasoning module. The AHMM4ESRM supports a microartefact based ADM. The ESRP uses the following CSAs: 1) ESRM's concept; 2) ICS' integration; 3) Legal and governance frameworks; and 4) Financial aspects. ESRM's financial assets' component integration uses a CSA which represents the following sub-systems: 1) Information Technology Asset Management (ITAM); 2) Hardware Asset Management (HAM); and 3) Software Asset Management (SAM). For asset related risk activities, tools may have different structures and interfaces, like Oracle's SAM one. Therefore, the problem lies in integrating such heterogenous tools in the *Entity's* ICS, which might create an unmanageable system. Building the right EA paradigm using an ESRP, facilitates such an integration. Knowing that the ADM has a governance phase which is optimal for the ESRM's integration. In turn, CSAs contain the selected CSFs that relate to unique standardized tags like the Asset IDentifier (AID) that managed by the ESRM. An ACS is used to present ESRM's integration feasibility.

Table 1. The RDP's CSFs that have an average of (rounded) 9.40

Critical Success Factors	KPIs	Weightings
CSF_ESRM_RDP_Modelling	Complex	From 1 to 10. **09 Selected**
CSF_ESRM_RDP_CFS	PossibleClassification	From 1 to 10. **10 Selected**
CSF_ESRM_RDP_RLR	Exists	From 1 to 10. **09 Selected**
CSF_ESRM_RDP_ADM	IntegrationPossible	From 1 to 10. **09 Selected**
CSF_ESRM_RDP_ICS	AdvancedStage	From 1 to 10. **09 Selected**
CSF_ESRM_RDP_Governance	Advanced	From 1 to 10. **09 Selected**
CSF_ESRM_RDP_Transformation_TRADf	IntegrationPossible	From 1 to 10. **10 Selected**
CSF_ESRM_RDP_Leading_Governance	Possible	From 1 to 10. **10 Selected**

valuation

RDP' CSFs Evaluation

Based on the RLR, the most important RDP's CSFs are used and evaluated as shown in Table 1.

THE ACS

ICS Infrastructure

The RDP uses mainly an ACS, developed by the Open Group as a reference study for its frameworks, and it offers the capability to implement *Project* components, like the ESRM. The ACS is based on the insurance company named ArchiSurance (Jonkers, Band & Quartel, 2012a). The author recommends that the readers refer to the original ACS to understand the construct, which is used in the PoC. ESRP instances are used by the ACS, which presents the possibilities on how to integrate the ArchiSurance's ESRM. ArchiSurance ESRM's main goals are to: 1) Offer an ICS to support feasible solutions; 2) offer ESRP based solutions: 3) Select a jump start objective; 4) Build ESRM pool of microartefacts; and 5) Prepare RDP's next phase; if phase one was successful, the PoC selects an ESRM problem from the ACS for phase two.

Integrating CSFs

A CSF and its KPI enumerations are measurable and mapped to a weighting that are estimated in the RDP's first iteration and then tuned in the next ADM iterations, to support the ESRM (Felfel, Ayadi, & Masmoudi, 2017). The complexity lies in how to define the main ESRP goals, in order to integrate the ESRM and how to interrelate the different business, ICS and other *Project's* components; where the ADM is the *Project's* skeleton.

The Architecture Development Method and Security

This ADM supports *Projects'* integration and presents the influence of an ESRP to support ESRM's development. In this RDP, distributed AI, complexity, knowledge management, economic and financial models, complex business models and avant-garde technologies, are supported by an ANN based HDT. This HDT is a module used in RDP's Phase 2 (Markides, 2015). *TRADf's* modules synchronize their activities with the ADM, where the ESRM and its internal components are interfaced with all activated ADM phases. The ESRM focuses on the design of security controls' integration in the ICS. In the actual age of distributed intelligence, complexity, knowledge, economy and technology (Gardner, 1999), security becomes the most important objective. The ESRM offers a concept that includes the HDT that supports a wide class of security problem types, and that is its major benefit (Markides, 2011). The ESRM synchronizes with the ADM. The ESRM defines security capabilities to protect the *Entity* from attack by: 1) Localizing gaps in the infrastructures of partners; 2) Review of detection, and real-time security solutions; 3) Block cumulative attacks; 4) Defining a security strategy to locate potential weaknesses; 5) Build a robust defense; 6) Integrate security in transactions; 6) EODPP attacks; and 8) Apply qualification procedures in the ADM (Clark, 2002).

CSFs' Evaluation in Phase 1

Based on the CSF review and *TRADf's* evaluation processes, the evaluation is done with the relation and influence of sRisks on the ESRM. Based on the CSF review process, the important ACS' CSFs are used and evaluated and the results are presented in Table 2. In this chapter, the deductions are done by using the analysis of each CSA of a total of 7, where a *TRADf's* NLP script is used, in which all its CSFs are stored and appear in Table's 1 column. The *TRADf's* background scripts, calculate the weightings and ratings (known as the KPIs). KPI values originate from enumerated sets; and they are tuned and stored in column 2. This RDP proposes a standardized and automated manner to evaluate RLRs that is an evolution in regard to the very subjective method. If the automated RLR's evaluation is successful, only then the experiment (or Phase 2) can be started. *TRADf* and its RDP, can automate complex RDPs in phase 1, and estimate the values for each selected KPI, as described in the in the associated works; on how to use CSA, CSF, KPI processing in RDPs. As shown in Table 2, the results justify (average of 9.30) the usage of the ACS in the final PoC (or phase 2). This process is applied to the next six CSAs and their tables. This section's results show clearly the uniqueness *TRADf* in integrating a standard ACS using a mapping structure; the closest comparable framework is TOGAF which does really tackle mapping that is the most complex topic.

ACS' CSFs Evaluation

Based on the RLR, the most important ACS' CSFs are used and evaluated as shown in Table 2.

THE ICS

Global or holistic *Entity* agility is achieved by combining various methodologies to promote business and technological agility.

Table 2. The ACS's CSFs that have an average of (rounded) 9.30

Critical Success Factors	KPIs	Weightings
CSF_ESRM_ACS_Modelling	Complex	From 1 to 10. **09 Selected**
CSF_ESRM_ACS_ACS	PossibleClassification	From 1 to 10. **10 Selected**
CSF_ESRM_ACS_RLR	Exists	From 1 to 10. **09 Selected**
CSF_ESRM_ACS_ADM	IntegrationPossible	From 1 to 10. **09 Selected**
CSF_ESRM_ACS_ICS	AdvancedStage	From 1 to 10. **09 Selected**
CSF_ESRM_ACS_Specific_Topics	Advanced	From 1 to 10. **08 Selected**
CSF_ESRM_ACS_Transformation_TRADf	IntegrationPossible	From 1 to 10. **10 Selected**
CSF_ESRM_ACS_InsuranceCase	Possible	From 1 to 10. **10 Selected**

valuation

Internet of Things, Telecommunication and Infrastructure Control-the Glue

For ESRM's distributed modules, standards like the Institute of Electrical and Electronic Engineers' (IEEE) architectural framework for the Internet of Things (IoT), can be used. The standard offers a reference model defining relationships between *Entity's* risk management modules (BSI, 2015). IoT and mobile infrastructure has been innovated to interconnect ESRM's endpoints, to create a virtual and global environment. In these virtually interconnected ESRMs, standard business applications, endpoints and mobile apps collaborate in real-time, using standard technologies and methodologies.

Reference EA Models and Their Phases

The intent of ESRP's reference EA models is to support *Projects* with an implementation and vendor agnostic paradigm with enhanced interoperable and dynamic blueprint. Technological and business implementation agnostic concepts promote: 1) Avoiding locked-in concepts; 2) Integrate various sRisk management platforms; 3) Certification and compliancy policies; 4) Modularity structures; and 5) A market structure agnostic concept. The ADM manages the *Project's* development iterations and its interaction with the ESRM, which care also for sRisks' valuations.

ESRM's Standards

To manage agile *Project's* modules, including ESRM, an adequate mapping concept must integrate existing standards, which have the following levels: 1) Strategic; 2) Financial; 3) Process; and 4) Technical. These standards and tooling environments, support the ESRM using an iterative bottom-up approach. Without the use of the ESRP, an ESRM system can: 1) Become siloed and have poor performance; 2) Lack scalability; 3) Fail, become un-usable and un-maintainable; 4) Fail in producing a successful ESRM functionalities. The ESRM interfaces various market risk frameworks like the COSO, which is shown in

Figure 1. *Entities* today, use various market business and technology standards, which include security Standards (sStandard), like, TOGAF/Sherwood Applied Business Security Architecture (SABSA), ISO 27000, NIST, which contain major security requirements and constraints for maintaining sRisk at an acceptable level. The integration of sStandards can lead to the neglect security requirements arising from the specifical characteristics of an *Entity* or its BPM aspects. An *Entity* needs an *Entity* transformation framework that include sStandards module to manage sRisks. sRisks needs to be integrated using a methodological holistic approach for security in the context of a distributed ICS that communicates to other external systems.

ADM's Integration

An AI based reorganization of an ESRM, makes it ready to integrate the local and global economies. ESRM based systems are exponentially increasing in number and importance, so the need to interface their data and functions, becomes a major priority. The hyper-evolution of, new ESRM scenarios and applications makes sRisk centric to *Entities*. AI supports scalable ESRM; insuring the interoperability between natively incompatible automation technologies, ICS, various sRisk apps (Miori & Russo, 2014). ADM's integration in the ESRM and *Project,* enables the automation of all their activities. The ADM encloses cyclic iterations; where all its phases log information to a unified logging system. ESRM systems are not dedicated to any specific business environment and offer information on: 1) sRisk activities; 2) Reliability; and 3) *Entity's* assets security.

ESRP's Microartefacts

The ESRP is a structural concept that supports ESRM's implementations: 1) It offers a set of predefined ESRP objects; 2) It describes its responsibilities and the content of sRisk microartefacts; 3) It defines the software artefacts for these ESRM modules; 4) It defines a ESRM engineering model; and 5) It includes the description of the relationships between the different ESRP objects. ESRP components support the ESRM by interfaces to handle various types of ESRM endpoints. The usage of endpoints provides some of the mechanisms needed to make ESRP tuneable with CSFs. Where an ESRP microartefact is an instance of a building block that can interact with other *Project*s microartefacts in a synchronized manner. A microartefact uses the ADM to assist in grouping of the needed services.

Security Building Blocks

The ESRM handles various types of sRisk management mitigation interfaces, like by using Financial Technology (FinTech) to deliver interactive financial evaluation services. The usage of AI based financial endpoints provides some of the technologies intended to make ESRM open to many resources' internal and external information endpoints (Ravanetti, 2016). The main danger effecting *Entity'* assets is organized Fintech fraud and financial crimes.

FinTech Fraud, Electronic Payments and Finance

FinTech transformations can make finance abstract and impossible to trace; institutions in some predator organizations that have the culture of financial secrecy and arbitral confiscation. Such predators, would be tempted to use FinTech to obfuscate the origins of money. ESRM systems use FinTech, to transform them, where automating economy and digitalization of financial services are fundamental by transforming the legacy sRisk management system. The evolution of FinTech, is un-linear in different environments. ESRM systems need to transform the interaction with financial institutions to automate crucial ESRM services. The technology transformation of Deutsche Bank, Raiffeisenbank, Hana-Bank and Bank Group are good examples of such *Projects* (Makarchenko, Nerkararian & Shmeleva, 2016).

Legal Aspects

The European commission defines a legislation to govern businesses, sRisks and their assets' and security risk management. Progress has been done in these fields. European commission's member states have implemented and enforced sRisks and assets' risk management in national practices. ESRM transactions that generate value, have to be security, legally asserted, traced and their periodic summaries are reported to ESRM's *Managers*. *Entities* and their ESRMs are orthogonal to security requirements, where the *Entity's* ICS' roles define security of the ESRM. ESRM's legal interests, resources and accesses, should be managed by *Managers* who are assisted by an EA and a security framework. Then, the *Entity* can integrate ESRM's access management to transaction's execution system. The regulation for the transaction's security and law needs qualified time-stamps for robust certifications like those used in the European Union (European Union, 2014). The RLR showed that international law on ESRM's security is inefficient and archaic. Avant-garde's *Entities* are hesitant to implement ESRM related international law that is based on the emergence of non-government norm-making initiatives. These *Entities* insist on their traditional central legal system that marginalizes the inter-state governance of the global sphere (Mačák, 2016).

The Accounting Sub-System

The ESRM should be supported by a multimodal accounting sub-system that minimizes the dependencies between various business partners with minimized risks. An important ESRM CSF that can be integrated, is the ratio of cost before and after *Project's* completion. *Project's* financial outcomes have to be controlled in real-time and reports must be delivered to the executive *Manager(s)*. The ESRP supports automated accounting which uses mapping between ESRM activities and the accounting subsystem, as shown in Figure 3 (Xiaohong, 2011).

The accounting sub-system, to support financial, ESRM and accountancy activities. The ESRM uses an accounting sub-system for the following types of assets related operations: 1) Support day-to-day operations; 2) Transaction processing; 3) Support for DMS4ESRM operations; 4) Trend analyses; 5) Quantitative and qualitative data operations; 6) estimate sRisks damage; and 7) Help in fulfilling stewardships role.

ESRM Processes

ESRM's processes are a set of co-ordinated activities, as shown in Figure 4. There are various descriptions of these processes and this set represents the 7Rs and 4Ts of risks to be managed are: 1) Recognition or the identification of risks; 2) Ranking or the evaluation of risks; 3) Responding to significant risks; 4)

Figure 3. The accounting subsystem structure
(Xiaohong, 2011).

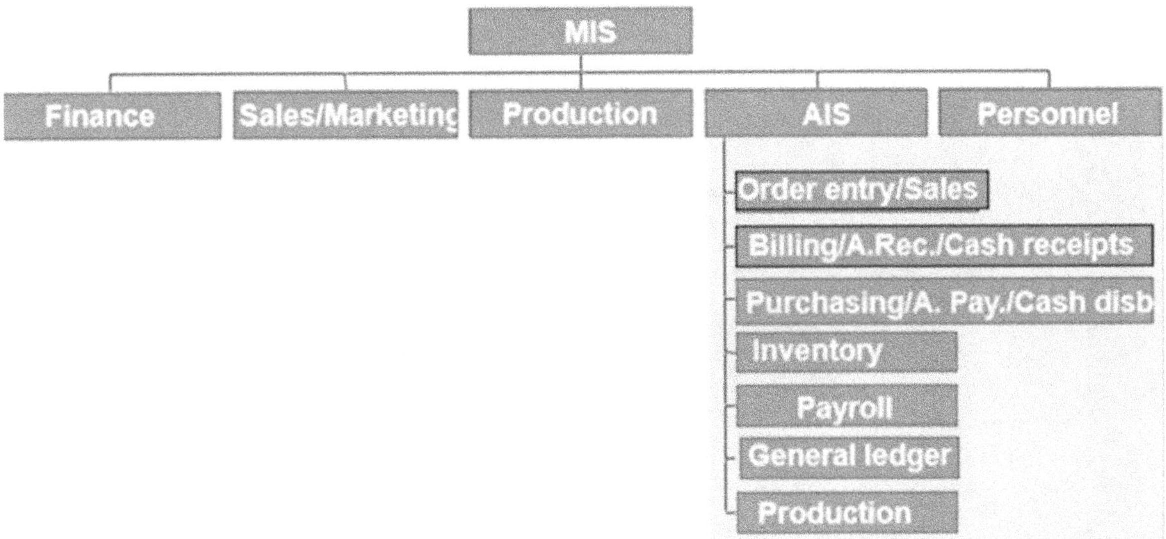

Tolerate; 5) Treat; 6) Transfer; 8) Terminate; 9) Resourcing controls; 10) Reaction planning; 11) Reporting and monitoring of risk performances; and 12) Reviewing risk management frameworks (Airmic, 2010).

ICS' CSFs Evaluation

Based on the RLR, the most important ICS' CSFs are used and evaluated as shown in Table 3.

EA BASED ENTERPRISE RISM MANAGEMENT APPROACH

Risk Management Aspects

Using ESRM to discover sRisk aspects mitigation measures, that are strongly related to EA and the defined transformation strategy. ESRM is supported by an evaluation of the impact of sRisks by the use of DMS4ESRM. A *Project* incorporates ESRM approach that supports risk and security policies that include step by step approach into the *Entity's* operational control measures. This EA driven approach, starts in the *Project's* multiple points in the cycle, depending on the used top-down or a more bottom-up approach. An EA phase includes the following actions: 1) To assess sRisks that covers discovered risk types, like, Cyberattacks, technology, business related risks; 2) To define control measures, using a combination of sRisks and control measures, which can be modeled with artefacts of the ArchiMate language's motivation extension that includes: assessment, goal and requirement; 3) To implement control procedures to control sRisks. EA is a step where the *Project* shifts from design to model the implementation; 4) To execute and monitor the implemented control procedures, monitoring accumulates statistics of the effectiveness of the implemented control procedures; 5) To analyze the vulnerabilities, monitoring delivers the insights on the effectiveness of implemented controls, like, pen-testing. This

Figure 4. Risk architecture, strategy and protocols
(Airmic, 2010).

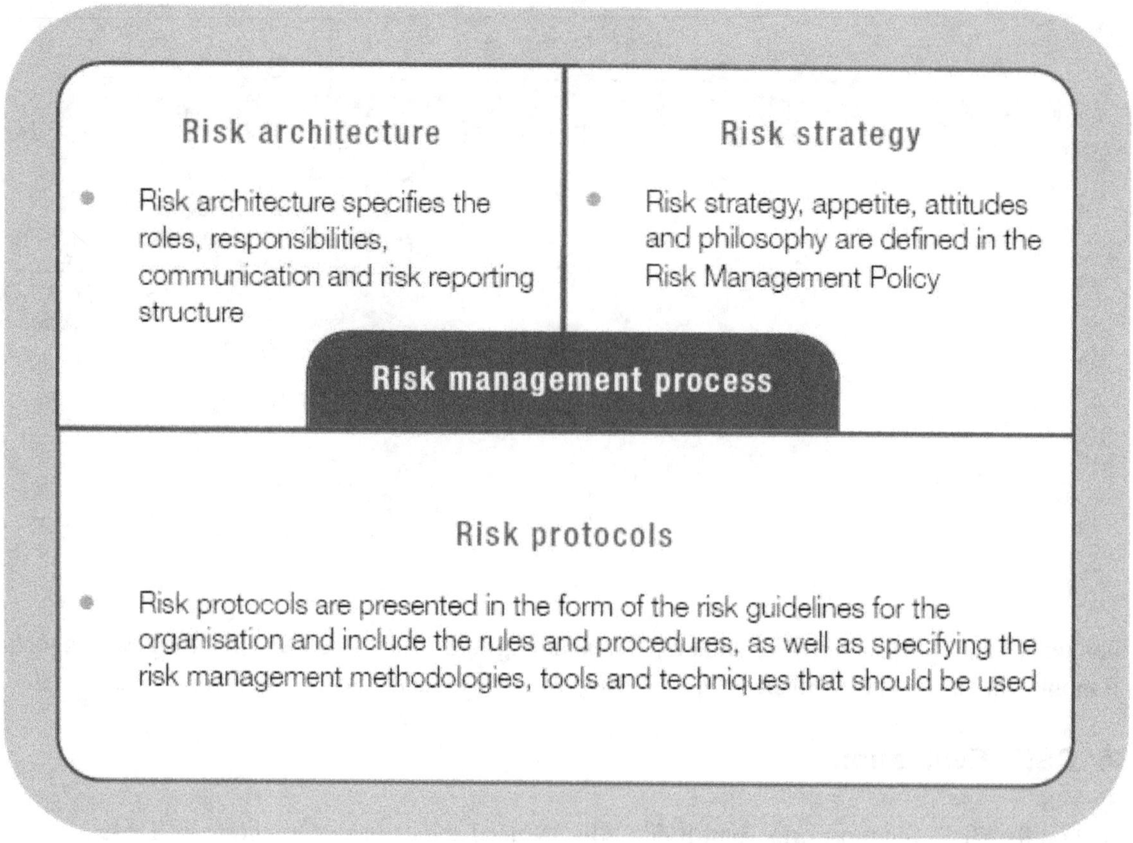

activity determines which vulnerabilities (or CSFs) are dangerous and the link is implemented between the vulnerabilities and identified sRisks, by using EA models; and 6) To identify external and internal threats (Kroese, 2014).

Top Down vs. Bottom Up

A top-down approach starts with the identification of threats and discovering the sRisks, in the form of CSFs, which are the stubs for ESRM's design and implementation of control procedures. A bottom-up approach, typically starts with monitoring and execution procedures, which investigates the actual *Project's* environment. *Entities* use EA capabilities coupled with a top-down approach offering the following benefits: 1) Systematic analysis of threats; 2) Integrates design of control measures; 3) EA's support to analyze risks; 4) Translates risk and security decisions into concrete change actions. These benefits integrate security in the *Entities'* components and makes DMS4ESRM discover operational sRisk impacts and costs.

Table 3. The ICS' CSFs that have an average of (rounded) 9.0

Critical Success Factors	KPIs	Weightings
CSF_ESRM_ICS_GUID_Integration	Standard	From 1 to 10. **09 Selected**
CSF_ESRM_ICS_TRADf_Standards	AdvancedState	From 1 to 10. **10 Selected**
CSF_ESRM_ICS_Services	Supported	From 1 to 10. **09 Selected**
CSF_ESRM_ICS_Accounting	Exists	From 1 to 10. **08 Selected**
CSF_ESRM_ICS_IoT	Stable	From 1 to 10. **09 Selected**
CSF_ESRM_ICS_Finance	ExistingSupport	From 1 to 10. **09 Selected**
CSF_ESRM_ICS_Security	Complex	From 1 to 10. **08 Selected**
CSF_ESRM_ICS_Automation	Supported	From 1 to 10. **09 Selected**
CSF_ESRM_ICS_EARP	Supported	From 1 to 10. **09 Selected**
CSF_ESRM_ICS_Control_Procedures	Supported	From 1 to 10. **10 Selected**

valuation

ESRM, EA and Governance

The ESRM proposes a holistic alignment between ESRP, Governance and EA activities, in order to provide a systematic support to map and trace identified sRisks to EA artifacts, supporting the *Project's* strategy of an *Entity*. The relationships between ESRM and EA needs modelling in order to manage sRisks' characteristics. ESRM defines a set of principles and foundations to design and implement of ESRM processes. The ESRM is not focused on any specific domain and it is not possible to make recommendations on the use of ESRM processes or the optimal control procedures for the identified risks. As shown in Figure 5, there are standards for ESRM processes that are based on the principle that a process operates at different levels. ESRM processes are characterized by a set of policies and procedures applied to assess (identifying, analyzing and evaluating), treat, monitor and review discovered risks. The main processes are: 1) To define the strategic objectives and criteria (internal and external) to determine the level of acceptability; and 2) As *Entity* are exposed to a set of threats and vulnerabilities a definition of a normal behavior, must be defined. The identification process discovers risks; the analysis process examines the nature and severity of the identified sRisks; and the evaluation process compares the severity of sRisks with the implemented risk criteria; in order to decide if the sRisks are acceptable, tolerable or to apply appropriate controls to handle them (Barateiro, Antunes, & Borbinha, 2012).

EA Based Risk Management

EA models provide descriptions of complex *Project* solutions and are an optimal approach to handle the dynamic and increasingly complex implementations. IEEE (Std. 1471-2000, which has also become ISO/IEC 42010:2007), defines EA as: ...*the fundamental organization of a system, embodied in its com-*

Figure 5. Risk management process
(Barateiro, Antunes, & Borbinha, 2012).

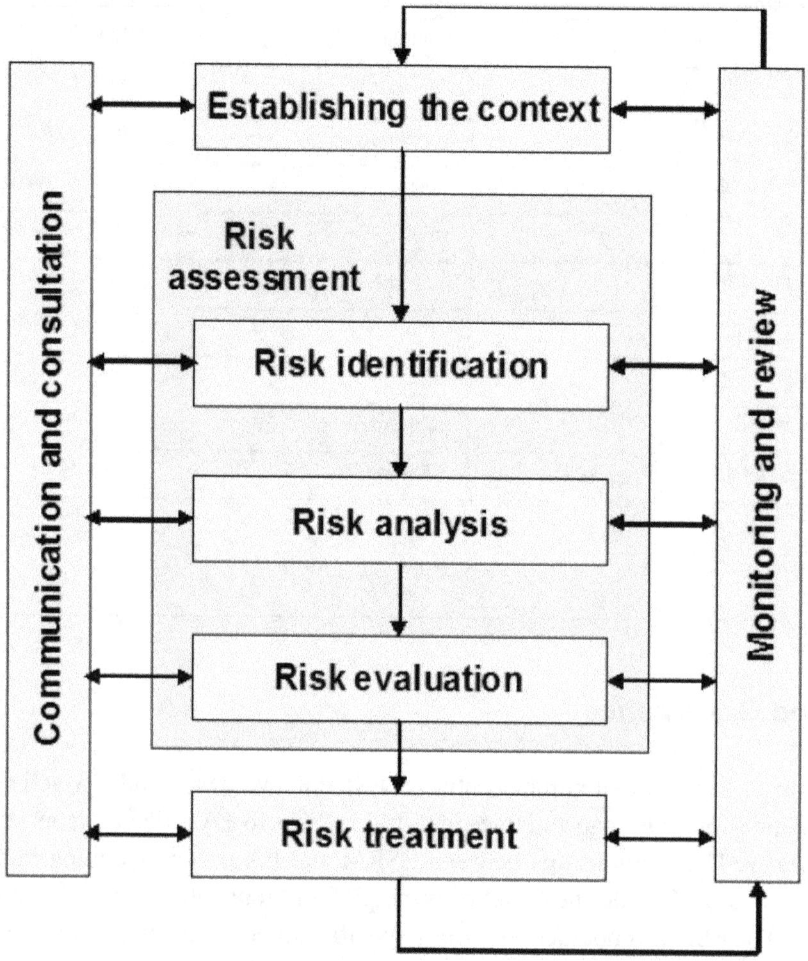

ponents, their relationships to each other and the environment, and the principles governing its design and evolution... EA considers that: 1) An Entity system has a precise mission and has an environment which influences it; 2) It has stakeholders who are concerned with the system's and its mission; 3) Its concern are those interests that pertain to the system's development, its operation, or any other aspects that are critical or otherwise important to one or more stakeholders; 4) A system is a set of EA models which includes a rationale for its architecture; and 5) Its description is related with the stakeholders of the system and deals with several viewpoints (functional and nonfunctional aspects of stakeholders' concerns). As shown in Figure 6, TOGAF supports the *Project's* development using seven modules. The core of TOGAF is the ADM, which consists of a cyclical process divided in nine phases. After a preliminary phase in which the context, relevant guidelines, standards and main goals are identified, the main process starts with the elaboration of an architecture vision and the principles that directs ESRM system's implementation. The vision phase provides the jumpstart for ESRM's developing the busi-

Figure 6. The ADM Process
(Barateiro, Antunes, & Borbinha, 2012).

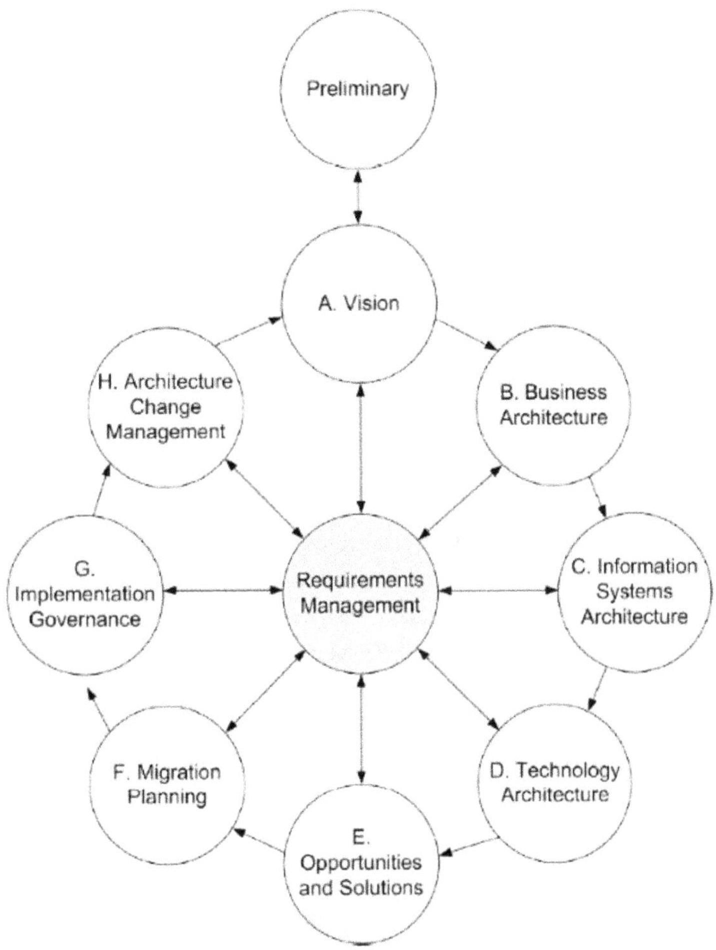

ness architecture, information systems architecture, and technology architecture (Barateiro, Antunes, & Borbinha, 2012).

EA's CSFs Evaluation

Based on the RLR, the most important EA's CSFs are used and evaluated as shown in Table 4.

AHMM4ESRM'S SUPPORT

The AHMM4ESRM is ESRM's basic structure and is based on various mathematical disciplines, development methods and engineering standards (Trad, & Kalpić, 2020a).

Table 4. The EA's CSFs that have an average of (rounded) 9.70

Critical Success Factors	AHMM enhances: KPIs	Weightings
CSF_ESRM_EA_CSF_Initialization&Setup	Feasible	From 1 to 10. **10 Selected**
CSF_ESRM_EA_IntegrationProcesses	Supported	From 1 to 10. **10 Selected**
CSF_ESRM_EA_Phases	Supported	From 1 to 10. **10 Selected**
CSF_ESRM_EA_Requirements	MappingAutomated	From 1 to 10. **09 Selected**
CSF_ESRM_EA_EARP	Supported	From 1 to 10. **09 Selected**

valuation

Risk Response Strategies for Enterprise Asset Risk Management

Projects' Managers, select the optimal ESRM strategies and that are the following types: 1) Risk avoidance; 2) Risk reduction, where mitigation of the severity of losses; 3) Alternative actions to offer possible actions to reduce risks; 4) Share the actions of transferring risks to third parties; and 5) Risk acceptance, is the willingness to accept their consequences. ESRM critical capabilities include (Pratap, & Predovich, (2020): 1) Risk analysis; 2) Risk remediation; 3) Compliance content mapping; 4) Workflow design; 5) User experience; 5) Board and senior executive reporting; 6) Basic and advanced integrations; 7) Digital asset discovery; and 8) Near-real-time assessment. Figure 7 shows the major trends concerning ESRM

ESRM'S Basic Elements

The ESRM identifies and assesses various strategic and main risks to guaranty *Entity's* security and includes the following elements: 1) Strategy settings; 2) sRisk's identification; 3) sRisks assessment; 4) sRisks response; and 5) Communication and monitoring.

The Artefacts' Model for Security

The Applied Holistic Mathematical Model for ESRM and Cybersecurity (AHMM4ESRM) nomenclature is showed in a simplified form to be easily understandable on the cost of a holistic formulation vision (Trad, & Kalpić, 2020b). The ESRM uses the AHMM4ESRM that is formalized as shown in Figure 8; and the main artefacts and characteristics are:

- Basic protection actions = support availability, integrity and secrecy of the ICS and its networks in the face of Cyberattacks, accidents and failures with the goal of protecting operations and *Entity's* assets and resources.
- Security = A set of basic protection actions to counter Cyberattacks and major failures.
- Cyberspace = Includes the ICS and its networks.
- Cybersecurity = security of Cyberspace + the defined goals of protecting operations and assets.

Figure 7. The magic quadrant for risk management
(Pratap & Predovich, 2020).

- Organizational Cybersecurity = includes Cyberspace + Cybertechnology + Cybersecurity.
- *Entity* (or national) Cybersecurity = $\sum$ Organizational Cybersecurity.

The Enterprise Model

As shown in Figure 8, the symbol $\sum$ indicates summation of all the relevant named set ESRM related members, while the indices and the set cardinality have been omitted. The summation should be understood in a broader sense, more like set union. The AHMM4ESRM uses Service Oriented Architecture (SOA) to support the ESRP based ESRM and is in this RDP, represented in a simplified form. The ESRM's interfaces are based on the ADM and uses SOA to enable agility, business benefits and infrastructure scalability. These facts can be formalized in a AHMM4ESRM that needs the formulas shown in Figure

Figure 8. The AHMM4ESRM nomenclature

Basic Mathematical Model's (BMM) Nomenclature

Iteration	= An integer variable "*i*" that denotes a *Project/ADM iteration*	
microRequirement	= KPI	(B1)
CSF	= Σ KPI	(B2)
Requirement	= CSF = $\bigcup$ microRequirement	(B3)
CSA	= Σ CSF	(B4)
microKnowledgeArtefact	= $\bigcup$ knowledgeItem(s)	(B4)
neuron	= action->data + microKnowledgeArtefact	(B5)
microArtefact / neural network	= $\bigcup$ neurons	(B6)
microArtefactScenario	= $\bigcup$ microartefact	(B9)
AI/Decision Making	= $\bigcup$ microArtefactScenario	(B10)
microEntity	= $\bigcup$ microArtefact	(B7)
Entity or Enterprise	= $\bigcup$ microEntity	(B8)
EnityIntelligence	= $\bigcup$ AI/Decision Making	(B11)
BMM(*Iteration*) as an instance	= EnityIntelligence(*Iteration*)	(B12)

9. The EA based AHMM4ESRM (EAHMM4ESRM) is the combination of an EA and AHMM4ESRM that can be modelled using the following formula:

EAHMM4ESRM = EA + AHMM4ESRM (16).

The ESRM Transformation Model

The ESRM transformation model is the combination of an EAHMM4ESRM and IterationGap that can be modelled using the following formula:

Project = EAHMM4ESRM + IterationGap (17).

The *Project's* model is based on a concurrent and synchronized infrastructure using threads.

Figure 9. The AHMM4ESRM main formulas

AHMM's Application and Instantiation for Security

Domain	= SMC	(14)
AHMM(*Domain*)	= $\bigcup$ ADMs + BMMs(*Domain*)	(15)

Table 5. The AHMM4ESRM's CSFs that have an average of (rounded) 9.30

Critical Success Factors	KPIs	Weightings
CSF_ESRM_AHMM4ESRM_TRADf_Integration	Feasible	From 1 to 10. **09 Selected**
CSF_ESRM_AHMM4ESRM_InitialPhase_CSFs	Stable	From 1 to 10. **10 Selected**
CSF_ESRM_AHMM4ESRM_PoCPhase	Complex	From 1 to 10. **09 Selected**
CSF_ESRM_AHMM4ESRM_Qualitative&Quantitative	Complex	From 1 to 10. **09 Selected**
CSF_ESRM_AHMM4ESRM_Final_Instance	VerifiedModel	From 1 to 10. **09 Selected**
CSF_ESRM_AHMM4ESRM_EA_Integration	Synchronized	From 1 to 10. **10 Selected**
CSF_ESRM_AHMM4ESRM_EARP_Interfacing	Stable	From 1 to 10. **09 Selected**

valuation

The Role of AHMM4ESRM Choreography

A *Project* is related to: transformations, sRisk management, process modelling and EA. All these mentioned fields need choreography capability that in turn is based on the HDT that uses microartefacts. The AHMM4ESRM is composed of a large number of interconnected neurons, to solve a specific ESRM (or other *Project*) problems. ESRM units are connected to each other, like nodes of the HDT and there is a real number associated with each connection, which are called weightings (Stergiou, & Siganos, 2015).

AHMM4ESRM's CSFs Evaluation

Based on the RLR, the most important AHMM4ESRM's CSFs are evaluated as shown in Table 5.

ESRM BASED TRANSFORMATION

Melvin Conway cited: "*...organizations which design systems ... are constrained to produce designs which are copies of the communication structures of these organizations*", where the ESRM produces a set of AI microartefacts that are based on CSFs. CSFs map to the *Entity's* structure and its ICS (James, Grinter, & Grinter, 1999). The ESRM processing, is supported by a non-predictive DMS4ESRM that depends on the selected CSFs, like the types of assets, types of sRisks, financial situation, types of process models, internal political influences, etc. A *Project* should be adapted to handle complex ESRM requirements that can generate complex designs and eventual problems that can be the source of unpredictability and sRisks... ESRM problems can be measured and weighted; while its internal financial sRisks are not simply measurable. This explains the difficulty of estimating sRisks of a consequential set of requirements.

Figure 10. The ANN based HDT
(Capecchi, Buscema, Contucci, & D'Amore, 2010)

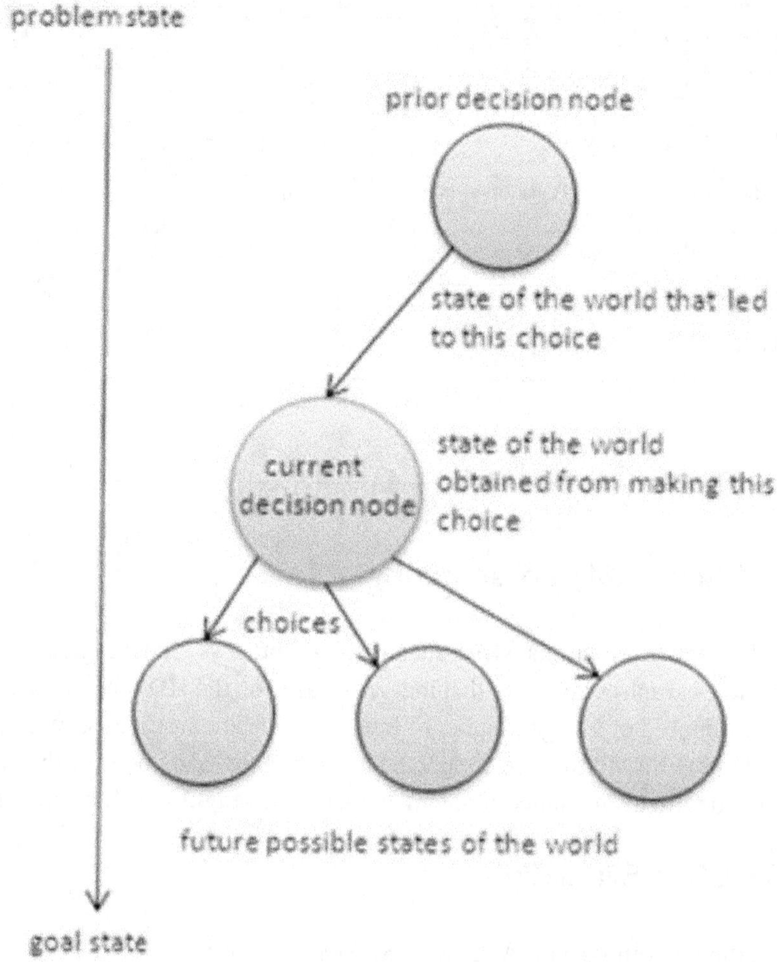

A Holistic Model

DMS4ESRM is used to generate sets of weightings for possible actions (AI microartefacts). Weightings' concept enables ESRP's to support an ESRM that delivers solutions in the form of security management recommendations. The DMS4ESRM is responsible for the HDT based approach for ESRM problem solving, as shown in Figure 10. The ESRM adopts a holistic systemic approach which can give an *Entity* important competitive business advantages and it is not a secret that AI based microartefacts management are the basis of a successful *Project.* ESRP's building blocks are based on microartefacts (and services) that uses the ADM.

Resources and CSFs

The one-to-one modelling concept is used to assemble the needed ESRM units, sRisk types and assets' fragility. This modelling concept is *Project's* used to manage ESRP instances in the implementation phase. The *Project* identifies the initial set of CSFs which reflects the performance areas that map to the major strategic goals. ESRM's integration is a major paradigm shift and is very complex to implement. An ESRM can give an *Entity* the important competitive advantages. The ESRM manages sRisks related to the following types of assets: 1) Tangible assets are mainly physical and measurable; and 2) Intangible assets are nonphysical assets and are mainly intellectual (knowledge) assets.

The Role of Assets Management

A *Project* focuses on all implementation aspects, like, transformation activities, assets' related sRisk management and EA. The key element of this paradigm is the novel structure of the ESRM that is based on EA, AHMM4ESRM and DMS4ESRM. The DMS4ESRM is composed of a number of interconnected modules needed to solve a specific ESRM problem, as shown in Figure 11. ESRM units are connected to each other like nodes in the HDT and there is a real number associated with each connection, which are called weightings used in ESRM (Soft Expert, 2018).

Integrated Decision Making

ESRM's integration process is supported by the DMS4ESRM to support an agile approach to the *Entity's* assets related sRisk mitigation. ESRP's structure is based on the following concepts: 1) The sRisk object is a conceptual representation; 2) AHMM4ESRM is an abstraction of the ESRM's structure and capacities; 3) The ESRM is responsible for processing of sRisk activities; and 4) The use of existing *Project's* modules.

Proactive Financial Crimes Detection, Anti-Locked-In and Assets' Protection

A Major Risk-FinTech Fraud

The ESRM that can handle various types of FinTech risks and sRisks. Institutions in some countries with the culture of financial secrecy, would be tempted to use FinTech to obfuscate the origins of money and other assets, like in the concrete cases: 1) Paula Ramada estimated the amount of lost money due to the benchmark of interest rates debacle is estimated at $300 trillion in financial instruments, ranging from mortgages to student loans (Ramada, 2013). FinTech would make such operations more embedded and abstract; 2) FinTech is the technology that aims to change the traditional financial environment in the delivery of interactive financial services; 3) Blockchain is a FinTech framework that supports crypto-currency like the Bitcoin; Bitcoin supports exchange of currencies in a digital encryption form; and 4) organized financial irregularities' tactics can be used to destroy its opponents' assets.

Figure 11. Asset management system
(Soft Expert, 2018).

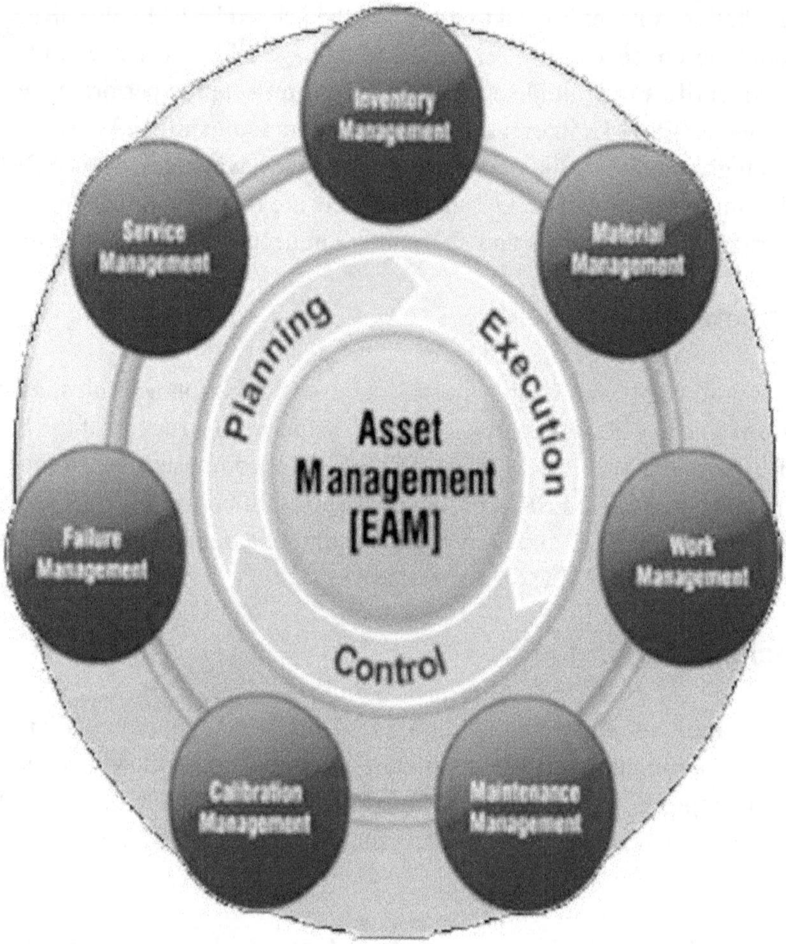

Predator's Lock In

The predator's locked-in model combines: 1) The power of financial institutions; 2) Too Big to Fail banks; 3) Banking secrecy; 4) Ultraliberal economy; 5) Rejection of local and global standards; and 6) A specific political environment.

Building an Adequate Strategy

When building the financial structure of the *Project* team and EA specialists must pay attention to risky financial locked-in situation(s). Even though some predator organizations offer an attractive financial conditions and tax packages, these organizations apply a legal and financial locked-in trap. It is an unwritten concept that can at any moment sweep out the enterprise of its financial resources. The peak of such behavior is the Fraud scandal of the bank UBS that was hit with a historic fine and the incredible delict was openly supported and protected by the Swiss Federal Court that makes the Swiss banks' financial

Figure 12. ESRM in an Entity's risk management concept
(Barateiro, Antunes, & Borbinha, 2012).

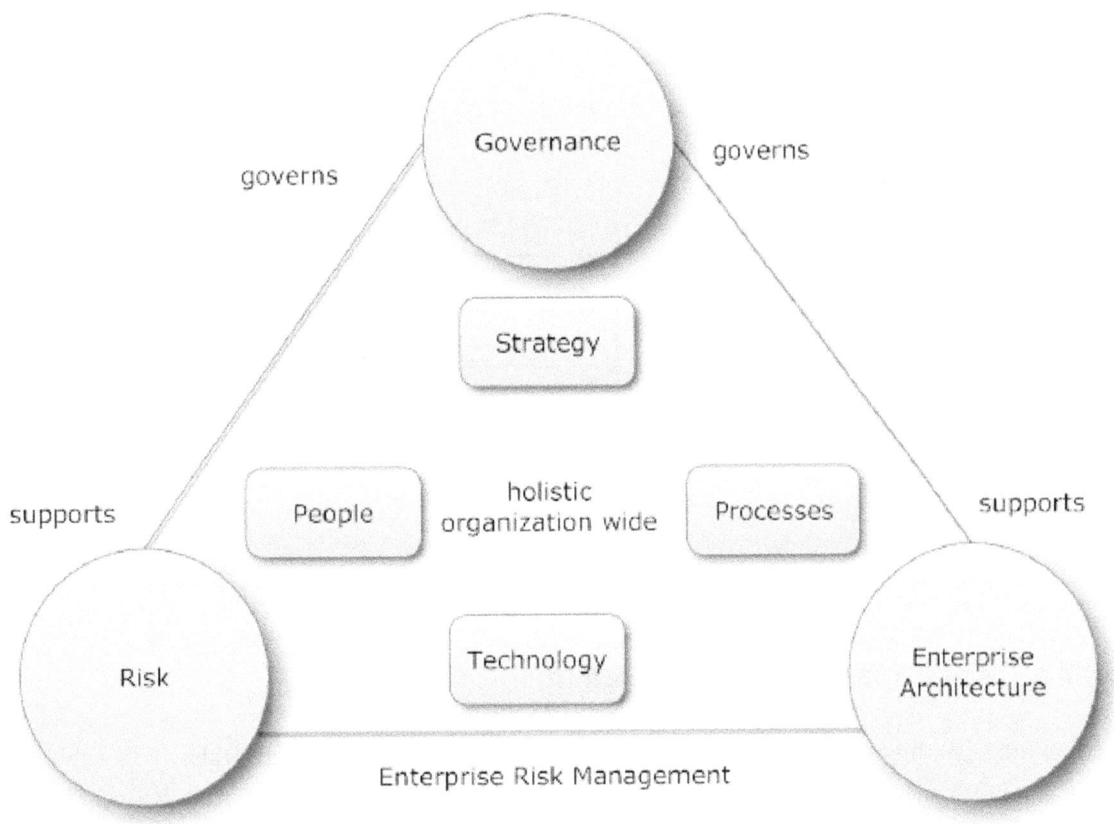

irregularities a state model, protect by the law. Here a dilemma and a question can be asked, how such a country can be a synonym of honesty and anti-corruption… (Alderman, 2019; Tagliabuejune, 1986).

ESRM'S Concept

This chapter proposes an alignment between the ESRM, ICS, Governance and EA activities. The main goal is to provide a systematic support to map and trace discovered sRisks to *Entity* assets and artifacts that are modeled using EA. Supporting an overall ESRM strategy of an *Entity,* and Figure 11, shows the main concept. Governance processes ensure the control when moving from strategic planning to operative implementation activities and this demands guidance and transparency that is supported by EA's ADM. EA is used to discover deficiencies, show complex and risky interactions between strategies, global processes, SOA services and infrastructure, providing a base for complex analysis (either by Governance or ESRM activities). The concept proposes an integrated view of Governance, ESRM and EA to support an *Entity* to be efficient and reliable. This enables the DMS4ESRM to control risks optimally. *Entities* are modelled using EA which uses artifacts (like, data models, business models, strategies, platform plans, organizational structure…) (Barateiro, Antunes, & Borbinha, 2012).

Table 6. The ESRM's Transformation CSFs that have an average of (rounded) 9.0

Critical Success Factors	AHMM enhances: KPIs	Weightings
CSF_ESRM_Transformation_Integration	Possible	From 1 to 10. **10 Selected**
CSF_ESRM_Transformation_EA_Structure	Feasible	From 1 to 10. **09 Selected**
CSF_ESRM_Transformation_(in)_Tangible_Values	ManagementEnabled	From 1 to 10. **09 Selected**
CSF_ESRM_Transformation_Decision_Capacities	Feasible	From 1 to 10. **09 Selected**
CSF_ESRM_Transformation_HolisticApproach	Supported	From 1 to 10. **09 Selected**
CSF_ESRM_Transformation_TRADf_Support	ComplexButFeasible	From 1 to 10. **08 Selected**
CSF_ESRM_Transformation_EARP	Possible	From 1 to 10. **09 Selected**
CSF_ESRM_Transformation_Skills	Exisiting	From 1 to 10. **10 Selected**
CSF_ESRM_Transformation_ExistingStatus	Transformable	From 1 to 10. **08 Selected**
CSF_ESRM_Transformation_Control_Procedures	Supported	From 1 to 10. **09 Selected**
CSF_ESRM_Transformation_Tracking_Auditing	Feasible	From 1 to 10. **09 Selected**

valuation

ESRM's Transformation CSFs Evaluation

Based on the RLR, the important ESRM's Transformation CSFs are evaluated as shown in Table 6.

ESRM'S USAGE AND INTEGRATION

Security Requirements

The optimal ESRP should fit in the *Entity's* EA model that in turn is based on best practices. The resultant global ESRP is a mixture of technical solutions, business & organizational engineering and global security concepts. TOGAF includes sub-frameworks in the form of interfaces, like the SABSA to handle global security requirements (Unwin, 2013).

Global Security Domains

Governance defines the interaction between various components and their Cyber or ICS security that understands the security of: 1) Data; 2) Technology resources; 3) Networks; 4) Web and Internet infrastructure; and 5) Applications, development and operations.

Designing the ESRM

Entity's internals, like boundaries and ICS, resources and BPM instances are designed, various application domains can be designed, developed and implemented. Depending on the context, eco-system and complexity of the *Entity*, major domains (or CSAs) can be divided into subdomains (or CSFs). An important *Entity* domain is the *Entity's* global network management that can be divided into the following sub-domains: 1) Fixed network; 2) External interfaces; and 3) Mobile or ad hoc networks. Creating the classification domains (or CSAs) is to reduce complexity in defining EA main security objectives, like, security requirements, sRisks, threats and controls. Other design security objectives can be: 1) Costs and finance; 2) Performance and speed; 3) Ease of use; 4) Open EA using services; 5) Backward compatibility; 6) Use of CSFs and KPIs as metrics to measure security; 7) Cyberspace is global and international; 8) EODPP attacks; and 9) The Private sector owns almost all Cyberspace most infrastructure. Classifying CSAs can be complex because many domains overlap. Security requirements engineering is done by applying the following phases (Vulić, Prodanović, & Tot, 2019): 1) Phase I - Preparation for defining security requirements; 2) Phase II - Security vulnerability analysis; 3) Phase III - Threats' modelling; 4) Phase IV - Determination of security requirements; 5) Phase V - sRisks assessment; 6) Phase VI - Categorization and prioritization; and 7) Phase VII - Preparation of documentation.

The Levels of Damage

Security damages can be very important and USA's Federal Bureau of Investigation (FBI) officials estimated the attacks caused 1.7 billion USDs in damage. And *Entities* are increasingly dependent on Cybertechnologies like: 1) Direct internet; 2) Communication (Email, IM, VoIP); 3) Commerce (business, banking, e-commerce and other); 4) Control and management systems (*Entity* public utilities and other); 5) Information and entertainment services; 6) Sensitive data stored on the cloud; 7) Indirectly by using Cybertransactions and BPM; 8) The right policy; and 9) Biz, Edu, Gov domains have replaced manual processes with BPM based ones. The scale of damage is probably much more important, because EODPP misdeeds are never condemned and huge amounts of money and assets are hidden (Stupples, Sazonov, & Woolley, 2019).

Cybersecurity Constraints and Characteristics

The main Cybersecurity Constraints and Characteristics are:

- Security, includes the protection of the *Entity's* information against unauthorized actions.
- According to H.R. 4246, *Cyber Security Information Act*, Cybersecurity is: *The vulnerability of any computing system, software program, or critical infrastructure to, or their ability to resist, intentional interference, compromise, or incapacitation through the misuse of, or by unauthorized means ...*
- According to S. 1901, *Cybersecurity Research and Education Act of 2002*, Cybersecurity is: *Information assurance, including scientific, technical, management, or any other relevant disciplines required to ensure computer and network security, including, but not limited to, a discipline related to the following functions*: 1) Secure *Entity's* ICS and its wide network administration and operations; 2) Support *Entity's* security engineering by using the ESRM; 3) Support *Entity's* ICS Information assurance and products' acquisition; 4) Apply cryptography; 5) Integrate threats and vulnerability assessment, including sRisks management; 6) ESRM should use a holistic Cyberspace security approach; 7) Secure Development and Operations (DevOps) of ICS

emergency support teams; 8) Cybersecurity training, education and management; 9) ICS and EA forensics; 10) Defensive ICS DevOps; and 11) The use of ESRM to block ESRM attempts.

- According to S. 1900, *Cyberterrorism Preparedness Act of 2002*, Cybersecurity is: *Information assurance, including information security, information technology disaster recovery and information privacy*.

Types of Attacks

The possible types of Cyberattacks are:

- Denial-of-Service (DoS) and Distributed Denial-of-Service (DDoS) attacks, are attacks where Cyberhackers block an ICS from serving legitimate requests.
- Man-in-the-Middle (MitM) attacks are simple types of digital attacks where a Cybercriminal intercepts communication between two routers in order to leak data.
- Phishing and spear-phishing, are attacks in which Cybercriminals target the ICS by email attachments.
- Drive-by attack or Drive by download attacks, refer to malicious application that can be installed on the ICS.
- Password attack are attacks by Cyberhackers that are able to determine usernames and passwords.
- Structured Language Query (SQL) injection attack used to control the ICS.
- Cross-Site-Scripting (XSS) attacks are injections, in which malicious scripts are injected in trusted websites.
- Eavesdropping attack, also known as a sniffing or snooping attacks, is based on stealing information as it is transmitted over ICS.

Motivation for Attacks

The most common motivations for Cyberattacks are: financial greediness, lack of ethics, immoral education and other. Financial greediness can drive to major criminal acts, like, the gigantic financial irregularities, which are related to fraud and money laundering that damage many countries, and this case it is related to major global financial institutions, like the Union des Banques Suisse (UBS) (Stupples, Sazonov, & Woolley, 2019), in which 32 trillion US dollars are *hidden*. Under the cover of bank secrecy…

ESRM's Layers

The ESRM manages and analyzes the following security layers:

- Network, platform and infrastructure security.
- Application, software and services security.
- Information and data security.
- Operational security.
- Cloud Security.
- Hacking WIFI possibilities and building the right security policies.
- Financial security barriers, against EODPP schemes.

- EA security.

Protection Against Attacks

An *Entity* may counter these types of threats: 1) Cybercrime, which includes a single Cyberattacker or groups, attacking *Entities* for financial gains or to cause damage; 2) Cyberattack, often involves politically motivated information gathering for various ideological purposes; and 3) Cyberterrorism, it is used to undermine the ICS and to cause panic; it originates from various anonymous groups. The ESRM proposed actions and predispositions used to support the *Entity's* global security and to reduce sRisks of possible Cyberattacks and to offer possible protections, like in the following forms:

- Spread information and knowledge to all *Entity's* organizations, units and personnel related to sRisks of *Social Engineering Attacks* (SEA) and common social engineering scams.
- An *Entity* has to build modules: to support the ESRM, to limit information leaks, to control 3rd party sRisks and 4th party sRisks.
- Use EA models and the ESRM to avoid important spending like uses local security tools.

A Cybersecurity attack is possible when the attacker gains the right to attack. These rights must be hardened in order to avoid the following scenarios: 1) Systemic password management; 2) Using screen lock and face recognition when mowing away; 3) Block the used of email attached files from anonymous email address; 4) Not using anti-virus software, 5) Sharing personal info (and client or server nodes); 6) Not reporting security loops to company; 7) Not using proper paper Documents; 8) Non-secured digital Data (while at rest and in motion); 9) Unsecured way of Information handling; and 10) Providing of information over phone.

Types of Hackers and Attackers

Cyberattacks are increasing due to global connectivity and usage of complex distributed services, like Web services. The lack of ESRM can be a serious threat and an open door for Cyberhackers' activities. A Cyberhacker is a person who gains access to the ICS, usually by getting access to administrative part of the ICS to access controls. The Cyberhacker can be: White Hat, Grey Hat and Black Hat; and their descriptions are:

- White Hat: these experienced hackers have the license for hacking.
- Grey Hat: they are commissioned by *Entities* to attack them, in order to verify their security.
- Black Hat: these are criminal Cyberhackers and perform unethical misdeeds by hacking *Entities*.

The ESRM contains controls to block Cyberhackers but it cannot totally block all their activities. Optimized and holistic ESRM controls, ensure that complex passwords and firewalls management can improve security. Firewalls and antivirus systems are not enough to secure an *Entity,* because there a need for ESRP.

ESRM'S MAIN ARTEFACTS

Managing Passwords

The ESRM ensures *Entity's* passwords' management that have a complex pattern and which cannot be hacked easily. An ICS actor should have different user names, security dongles and passwords for different systems. That can be enforced by voice, biometric or visual recognition mechanisms.

Firewalls

A firewall is an important EA, ESRM and Cybersecurity element, which is used to protect an *Entity's* distributed network(s) from Cyberattacks in the form of malware and other types of dangers. There are many types of firewalls and they have different security capabilities; therefore, the ESRM defines a firewall metamodel.

Secure Development and Operations

To block Cyberattacks, Secure DevOps (SecDevOps) can be integrated with the ADM. SecDevOps integrates security in the development and operations processes, by using sets of best practices designed to support *Entities'* implementation processes. Applications development and operations are coordinated by a secure DevOps process managed by agile methodologies. SecDevOps manages developers, operations and security team members. The ESRM uses agile SecDevOps procedures to identify patterns for managing transformation and development of requirements (Mees, 2017).

Antivirus, Viruses and Worms

Antivirus software applications are used to detect and remove threats known as viruses. The main recommendation is to keep *Entity's* applications and modules updated for the *Entity's* optimal defense strategy and concept. A Virus is a piece of software that is installed on the *Entity's* ICS without an official approval and operates without official control. The ESRM proposes various security controls to protect the ICS against Cyberattacks, like viruses, worms or trojan horses. Cyberattackers and Cybercriminals use ICS' vulnerabilities to install pirate code like worms, in the *Entity's* database(s), by using badly intentioned SQL instructions. Such misdeeds give Cybercriminals, access to profitable login credentials information.

Emails

Electronic mails (Email) can be dangerous, because they may contain attachments, when opened can launch applications or scripts that can modify the ICS. The main recommendation, is not to open email attachments from unknown, spam or anonymous expeditors. Email attachments could be infected with malware or any kind of spyware software. It also recommended not to use embedded hyperlinks in emails that are issued by anonymous senders or unknown web links. These are the common patterns in which malware is dispatched on ICS' endpoints.

Wireless Fidelity

ICS' mobile endpoints should block: 1) The connections to open Wireless Fidelity (WIFI) connections in public serviced sections; and 2) It should also block unauthorized smart devices like cellphones from connecting to the ICS. Connections to unprotected network endpoints makes ICS nodes vulnerable and Cyberattackers may use *Man-in-the-Middle* tactics and this the most popular types of WIFI Cyberattacks; where on open WIFI network endpoints, Cyberattackers can *sniff* network packets. In ESRM and Cybersecurity, a Man-In-The-Middle, Monster-In-The-Middle, Machine-In-The-Middle, MitM or Person-In-The-Middle (PITM), in which Cyberattackers secretly listen and can alter the communications between endpoints.

Malware

The term Malware derives from *MALicious software*, which is an application that infects and damages the ICS without authorized permissions; the ESRM should use the following mechanisms to block: 1) Viruses by integrating Antivirus modules that also block Malicious intrusions; 2) *Activate Network Threat Protection* strategies; 3) Firewall installations; and 4) Trojan horses' detection. Trojan horses are email Malwares which make multiple installations on the ICS in order to leak information and make substantial damages. These types of viruses are the most damaging ones.

Capacity Building – Skill and Competence Development

The ADM supports the ESRM to create best practices and *Entity*-specific security capabilities. The ESRM supports EA and security experts to avoid missing critical security pitfalls, and this chapter offers recommendations on the needed skills to carry out ESRP activities. The ESRP is treated as a separate architecture domain within the EA, which fully integrates it. ESRP is the enforcement of the *Entity's* security policies which includes the following ESRP skills and characteristics (The Open Group, 2011b): 1) Security methodology; 2) Management of discrete views and viewpoints; 3) To design non-normative flows through the ICS; 4) To design single-purpose components; and 5) To develop EA, ESRP and ICS models.

Guidance on Security for the Architecture Domains

Security requirements are pervasive in all EA domains and to all ADM phases. Security focuses mainly on the infrastructure that is not visible to the *Entity's* business function. ESRM focuses on the protection of the ICS and *Entity's* assets. ESRP manages single-purpose components and measures the quality of the ICS. Common ESRP artifacts can include: 1) Business rules for handling of data/information assets; 2) Defined security policies, 3) Codified data/information assets' ownership and custody; 4) sRisk analysis documentation; and 5) Data classification policy documentation. The *Entity security* view of the EA has its own unique building blocks, collaborations and interfaces. These security-unique blocks must interface with the *Entity's* ICS in an optimal manner, in order to support its security policies and to avoid interfering with ICS operations. ESRP is effective to design and implement security-specific controls in the *Target Architecture* in the initial development cycle to support reengineering development and deployment. The ESRM manages the normal flow of application's fallout, abnormal flows, failure modes and the possibilities in which the ICS and applications can be interrupted or attacked. All *Entities* have security concerns and they should dedicate a security architect to support the *Entity's* transformation process. In all ADM phases, recommendations are given on security-specific management. ESRP decisions are traceable to business and policy decisions and their sRisk management. The areas of concern for the ESRP are (The Open Group, 2011b):

- Authentication: The substantiation of the identity to the *Entity*.
- Authorization: The definition and enforcement of permitted capabilities for a person whose identity has been established.
- Audit: The ability to provide forensic data confirming that the ICS has been used in accordance with ESRP policies.
- Assurance: The ability to test the EA and its security attributes, which are required to support security policies.
- Availability: The *Entity's* ability to function without services' interruption despite malicious events.
- Asset Protection: The protection of information and assets from loss and resources from unauthorized and unintended use.
- Administration: The ability to add and change security policies and to add or change the persons related to the ICS.
- sRisk Management: The *Entity's* attitude and tolerance for sRisks.

Security Monitoring and Logs

The ESRM is not dedicated to any specific environment and it offers to support: 1) Performance and availability; 2) Reliability and recovery; 3) Attack's tracing; and 4) Cybersecurity fundaments. The ICS is controlled and monitored in real-time, using the *Entity's* Unified Logging Subsystem (EULS) and is integrated in order to support the ESRM. EULS' exist and are powerful monitoring subsystems that support the presentation, sorting and tuning of stored logs. EULSs can be designed to analyses, collect and store security related data from various ICS sources to support the central logging system. An ICS continuously needs to manage massive central logging system that persists: event logs, sorts security logs for security purposes and system performances.

The Legal Constraints

The ESRM supports the *Entity's* legal integration and constraints and in order to achieve this legal support, CSFs are selected and asserted, to monitor the used artefacts. These CSFs manage the differences in Cyberbusiness' local and international laws. An *Entity* or Cyberbusiness environment must have the capacity to proactively recognize erroneous Cybertransactions and Cyberattacks, in a systemic manner (Daellenbach & McNickle, 2005).

Cybertransactions' Security Violations

The European commission defines a legislation to govern *Entity's* Cyberbusiness activities; and progress has been done in this direction. European commission's member states have implemented and enforced

Cyberlaws related to national practices. Cybertransactions outcomes have to be continually legally asserted, verified, traced and their periodic summaries are reported to the *Entity's* executive management (Fu & Mittnight, 2015). Cyberbusinesses are orthogonal to global Cybersecurity requirements, where the *Entity's* role defines the responsibility of its resources. Management of the *Entity's* legal interests, resources and accesses, should be managed by EA, ESRP and security experts. Thus, the Cyberbusiness structure is an important consideration in the legal assertion and access management of Cybertransaction's security. The regulation for the Cybertransaction's security and law needs qualified time-stamps for robust electronic certification like those used in the European Union (European Union, 2014).

Cybertransaction Law

Cybertransaction is influenced by the Uniform Law Commissioners who promulgated the Uniform Electronic Transactions Act in 1999. It is the first adaptable effort to prepare a Cyberlaw for *Entity's* Cyberbusiness and electronic government activities. Many *Entities* have adopted Cyberbusiness and electronic government regulations. The Uniform Electronic Transactions Act represents the first effort in providing some standardized rules to govern Cybertransactions and Cyberlaws (The Uniform Law Commissioners, 2015). Facts show that international law on global security is inefficient and are in an agonizing state. Advanced states are hesitant to integrate international law that is based on the emergence of non-government norm-making initiatives. States insist on their traditional central legal system that marginalizes the inter-state governance of Cyberspace (Mačák, 2016).

Cyberbusiness Legislation Monitoring

The integration of the ESRM is done with the use of TOGAF's standardized legal environment. This legal environment supports data protection laws, contract law, procurement law, fraud law and many other legislation domains to counter EODPP misdeeds, which are the most fatal types of crimes and Cybercrimes.

Financial Cybercrime Schemes

The integration of Finance for Technologies (FinTech) and ICS is crucial for an *Entity* and its financial controls critical system(s). Today such FinTech standards and fields are robust, resilient and can be applied as automated synchronized (block) chains; to enable the traditional financial environments to become a part of a networked financial world. FinTech platforms can be applied to support an ESRM and sRisks mitigation, in order to avoid locked-in situations. EODPP related locked-in, when building the financial structure of the future transformed *Entity*, the *Project* team and ESRM must be cautious of eventual financial locked-in situation(s), which is a major security problem. Even though some countries like Switzerland offer attractive financial and tax package(s), this country applies a coordinated legal and financial locked-in trap; it is sealed and represents an unwritten concept that can at any moment sweep out the financial resources from an *Entity* and even powerful countries like the USA, UK and France. This locked-in Swiss EODPP model, combines: 1) Specific culture and mentality; 2) The power of Swiss law; 3) Too Big to Fail state banks; 4) Banking secrecy that protects financial crimes; 5) Ultra-liberal economy; 6) rejection of local and global standards; and laws; 7) Isolationism and racism; and 8) A finance supportive political environment for collective plundering. Swiss banks and other Swiss financial institutions are under no supervision what so ever; and are free to hit and run. That indirectly makes this *Entity* the financial and malware industry's super protector that sets up fortifications against any possible legal intrusion; even when these institutions are executing massive irregular, criminal and illegal activities. The author refers to this phenomenon as an instance of the Black Swan phenomena or simply the directed Swiss Black Swan, which *Entity's* (and countries) should try to avoid and penalize. It is probably wiser to pay more taxes and social services then to face such phenomena and traps (International Monetary Fund, 2009; Taleb, 2012). The major problem with combating such a system is that some countries have hermetically closed system characterized by the following attitudes: 1) Police and information services, blocking any attempt to pursue financial criminal acts; 2) The legal system, ignoring any attempt to investigate financial criminal acts; 3) Legal support too expensive, to discourage any action of law enforcing; 4) Psychological harassment, to discredit investigators; 5) Intolerance and discrimination, to block any foreign request; 6) A powerful global network, to embed and hide various dubious operations; 7) Financial guerrilla-like and hit and run tactics, to confiscate wealth; and 8) Occurrence of financial locked-in situations. Some financial haven states target to become leaders in FinTech, which is not very assuring; because FinTech should combat state criminality and enforce global security international law. It is recommended to avoid any form of financial and technological collaboration with EODPP oriented *Entities*.

ESRM's Usage and Integration CSFs Evaluation

Based on the RLR, the important ESRM's Integration CSFs are evaluated as shown in Table 7.

THE MODEL'S IMPLEMENTATION

ESRM Design and Implementation

An important prerequisite for the ESRM's PoC is the use of existing standards; in this case TOGAF and UML are used. These standards include microartefacts to be used to integrate ESRM modules in the existing *Project* processes, like design, development and operations....

To identify the sets of CSFs and test RQ's hypothesis of whether CSFs affect ESRM's integration, the PoC uses a mixed qualitative and quantitative method. The analytical process is illustrated in Figure 13. As shown in the figure 1, the PoC firstly uses phase 1 based on heuristic decision tables using CSFs for ESRM. Phase 1 is used to rank the relative importance of CSFs for ESRM based on their evaluation (Quang Phu, & Thi Yen Thao, 2017).

The Proof of Concept – Phase 1

The PoC is based on the CSFs' binding to a specific research resources, where the ESRM was prototyped using *TRADf*. The reasoning model represents the relationships between this RDP's requirements, microartefacts and selected CSFs. PoC's interfaces were achieved using Microsoft Visual Studio .NET environment and *TRADf*. The ESRM uses calls to ESRP microartefacts, to execute various actions related to sRisks. CSFs were selected and evaluated (using the DMS4ESRM) in this chapter's tables; and the results are illustrated in Table 8. Table 8, shows that the ESRM is not an independent component and

Table 7. The ESRM's Integration CSFs that have an average of 8.3

Critical Success Factors	KPIs	Weightings
CSF_ESRM_Integration_Requirements	Standard	From 1 to 10. **09 Selected**
CSF_ESRM_Integration_Design	AdvancedState	From 1 to 10. **10 Selected**
CSF_ESRM_Integration_Damages	Exists	From 1 to 10. **08 Selected**
CSF_ESRM_Integration_Cybersecurity	Exists	From 1 to 10. **08 Selected**
CSF_ESRM_Integration_Layers	Complex	From 1 to 10. **08 Selected**
CSF_ESRM_Integration_TypesOfAttacks	Complex	From 1 to 10. **08 Selected**
CSF_ESRM_Integration_Artefacts	Partial	From 1 to 10. **08 Selected**
CSF_ESRM_Integration_Skills	Complex	From 1 to 10. **08 Selected**
CSF_ESRM_Integration_EA_Models	Supported	From 1 to 10. **09 Selected**
CSF_ESRM_Integration_Control_Procedures	VeryComplex	From 1 to 10. **07 Selected**

valuation

in fact it is strongly bonded to *Project's* and *Entity's* overall risk concept. The model's main constraint is that CSAs having an average result below 7.5 will be ignored. This fact leaves the ESRM's CSAs (marked in green) to make this work's conclusions; and drops the CSAs marked in red, which means that the *Project* and ESRM transformation is feasible, but will face major difficulties.

The Proof of Concept – Phase 2

EA's Setup and Related CSFs

The Phase's 2 implementation major settings look as follows:

- Sub-phase A or the Architecture Vision phase's goals, establishes a data architecture.
- Sub-phase B or the Business Architecture phase shows how the ESRP target architecture realizes the key requirements.
- Sub-phase C shows and uses the Application Communication Diagram.
- Sub-phase D or the Target Technology Architecture shows the end ESRP infrastructure.
- Sub-phases E and F, Implementation and Migration Planning; the transition architecture, proposing possible intermediate situation and evaluates the ESRP status.

The AI based microartefacts have mappings to specific ESRM resources and where the ESRM defines relationships between the security requirements and microartefacts.

Figure 13. RDP's flow
(Quang Phu, & Thi Yen Thao, 2017).

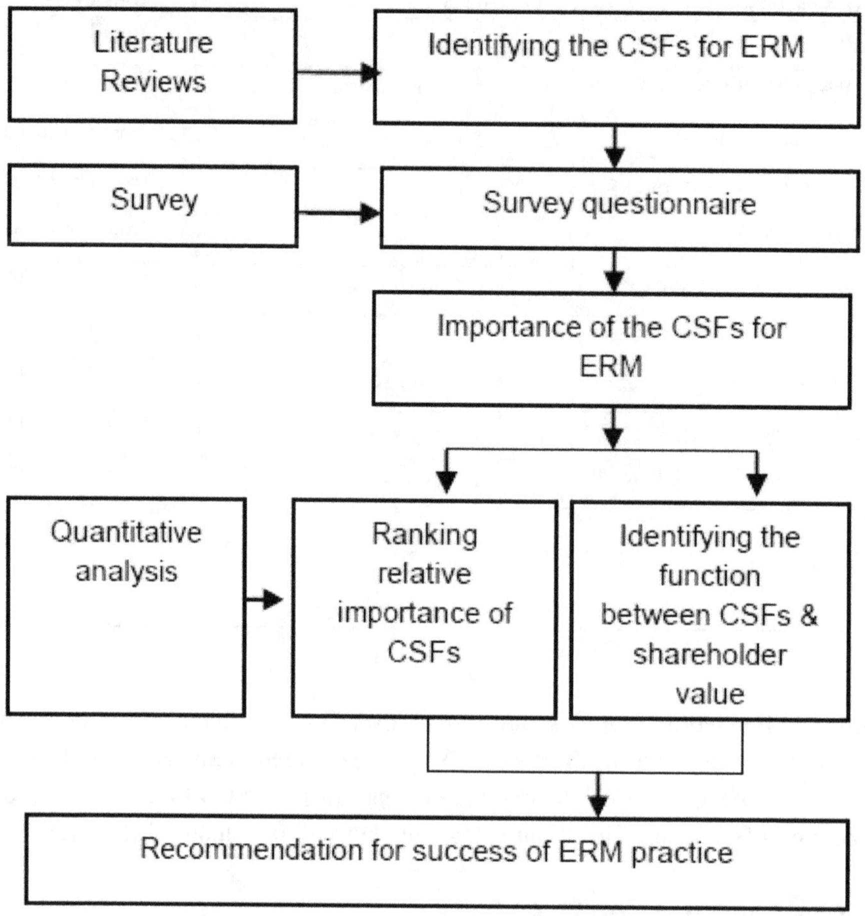

Processing Control on a Concrete Node

The DMS4ESRM tries to solve an ESRM request, where its CSF is linked to a security problem type and a related set of actions that starts to be processed at a specific HDT node. For this goal, the CSF_ESRM_Control_Procedure was selected from the ESRM CSA and delivered solutions related to the problem. Solving the given security problem involves the determination of actions and related solutions for multiple activities for the ESRM team. These mixed models are based on quantitative analysis, beam search and grounded hyper-heuristics; that is in fact a dual-objective of the DMS4ESRM solves the problem using the following steps:

- Relating the ACS' resources to CSF_ESRM_Control_Procedure that is done in Phase 1.
- Link the selected node to the mixed modules and deliver the root node of the HDT.
- The DMS4ESRM engine is configured, weighted and tuned using configuration information.

Table 8. The ESRM PoC's phase 1 outcome is 9.15

CSA Category of CSFs/KPIs	Influences transformation management	Average Resu
The Research Method and Concept	Possible	From 1 to 10 9.40
The Applied Case Study Integration	Possible	From 1 to 10 9.30
The Usage of the Architecture Development Method	FullyIntegrated	From 1 to 10 9.70
The Information and Communication Technology System	Transformable	From 1 to 10 9.00
The Mathematical Model's Integration	Possible	From 1 to 10 9.30
The ESRM Transformation Process	Feasible	From 1 to 10 9.00
The ESRM Usage and Integration	Complex	From 1 to 10 8.30
Evaluate First Phase		

- The HDT starts with the initial CSF_ESRM_Control_Procedure and then finds the set of solutions in the form of possible improvements.
- Once the *TRADf's* interface is activated to implement the needed microartefact scripts to process the defined six CSAs.

Node Solution

These scripts support AHMM4ESRM's instance that are processed in the background to deliver sRisk value. The AHMM4ESRM uses data services that are called by the DMS4ESRM actions, which deliver solutions.

SOLUTION AND RECOMMENDATIONS

In this chapter, the author proposes the following set of ESRM's architecture, technical and managerial recommendations:

- A *Project* must build a holistic EA concept in order to ensure an efficient ESRP based ESRM.
- Efforts are applied to integrate the ICS to support sRisk operations and the problem is the alignment of various modules.

- ESRMs replace traditional sRisk management systems in order to improve accountability.
- ESRM should fit in the *Entity's* EA framework.
- The ADM's integration in an ESRM enables the automation of all its activities.
- *Entity's* assets and stability are orthogonal to security and legal requirements. Concepts must be built to evaluate sRisks.
- It is recommended to avoid collaboration with doubtful financial and assets management organizations.

FUTURE RESEARCH DIRECTIONS

The *TRADf* future research will focus on the evolution of the system's intelligence.

CONCLUSION

This RDP phase is part of a series of publications related to *Projects*, ESRM and EAs; and is based on mixed AR model; where CSFs and areas are offered to help *Managers* to decrease the chances of ESRM's integration failure. In this chapter, the focus is on evaluating sRisks. ESRM and EA alignment is security driven. The concept describes a structured relationship between: security, assets, risks, finance, EA, technical constraints and security solutions to support the long-term needs of the *Project*. The ESRP based ESRM's integration in the end system and the most important recommendation that was generated by previous RDP phases was that the *Manager* must be an architect of adaptive business systems. In this chapter, the PoC is based on the CSFs' binding to a specific RDP resources, the DMS4ESRM, RQ, and selected CSFs; and the result is that ESRM is feasible and the main complexity lies in ESRM's integration and transformation. Because of the score, 9.15, Table 8 shows that ESRM's implementation is possible but is a risky transformation process and that an inhouse only methodology and framework can be built. In this chapter, the author proposes the following set of managerial recommendations:

- The ESRM supports an ESRP in order to ensure an efficient global security concept.
- Cybertechnologies should replace traditional exchanges in order to improve productivity and to enforce in real-time security.
- Cybersecurity should fit in the *Entity's* global EA framework.
- ADM's integration in the ESRM enables the automation of all its activities.
- Security constraints are controlled and monitored by the EULS.
- FinTech would make financial operations more embedded and abstract.
- *Entities* are orthogonal to global security requirements.
- To avoid any form of financial collaboration with doubtful financial EODPP oriented organizations.

ACKNOWLEDGMENT

In a work as large as this research project, technical, typographical, grammatical, or other kinds of errors are bound to be present.

REFERENCES

Airmic. (2010). *A structured approach to Enterprise Risk Management (ERM) and the requirements of ISO 31000.* Alarm-The Institute of Risk Management.

Alderman, L. (2019). French Court Fines UBS $4.2 Billion for Helping Clients Evade Taxes. *The New York Times*. https://www.nytimes.com/2019/02/20/business/ubs-france-tax-evasion.html

Barateiro, J., Antunes, G., & Borbinha, J. (2012). Manage Risks through the Enterprise Architecture. *45th Hawaii International Conference on System Sciences.*

BSI. (2015). *Architectural framework for the Internet of Things, for Smart Cities.* BSI.

Capecchi, V., Buscema, M., Contucci, P., & D'Amore, D. (2010). *Applications of Mathematics in Models, Artificial Neural Networks and Arts: Mathematics and Society*. Springer Science & Business Media. doi:10.1007/978-90-481-8581-8

Clark, D. (2002). *Enterprise Security: The Manager's Defense Guide*. Addison-Wesley Professional.

Curtis, P., & Carey, M. (2012). *Committee of Sponsoring Organizations of the Treadway Commission-Risk Assessment in Practice*. Deloitte & Touche LLP.

Daellenbach, H., McNickle, D., & Dye, Sh. (2012). *Management Science - Decision-making through systems thinking* (2nd ed.). Plagrave Macmillian.

Easterbrook, S., Singer, J., Storey, M., & Damian, D. (2008). *Guide to Advanced Empirical Software Engineering-Selecting Empirical Methods for Software Engineering Research.* Springer.

European Union (2014). Regulation (EU) No 910/2014 of the European Par lament and of the Council - on electronic identification and trust services for electronic transactions in the internal market and repealing Directive 1999/93/EC The European Par lament and of the Council – Regulation. European Union.

Felfel, H., Ayadi, O., & Masmoudi, F. (2017). Pareto Optimal Solution Selection for a Multi-Site Supply Chain Planning Problem Using the VIKOR and TOPSIS Methods. *International Journal of Service Science, Management, Engineering, and Technology*. . doi:10.4018/IJSSMET.2017070102

Fu, Zh., & Mittnight, E. (2015). *Critical Success Factors for Continually Monitoring, Evaluating and Assessing Management of Enterprise IT*. ISACA.

Gardner, H. (1999). *Intelligence Reframed: Multiple Intelligences for the 21st Century*. Basic Books.

Gibson, M. (2012). *Critical success factors for the implementation of an operational risk management system for south African financial services organisations (Master of Commerce)*. Business Management. University of South Africa.

IIA. (2004). *Enterprise Risk Management — Integrated Framework*. The Institute of Auditors.

International Monetary Fund. (2009). Switzerland: Financial Sector Assessment Program - Detailed Assessment of Observance of Financial Sector Standards and Codes. International Monetary Fund, 5, 170.

James, D., Grinter, H., & Grinter, R. (1999). Splitting the Organization and Integrating the Code: Conway's Law Revisited. Bell Laboratories, Lucent Technologies. *Proceedings, International Conference on Software Engineering*, 85-95.

Jonkers, H., Band, I., & Quartel, D. (2012a). *ArchiSurance Case Study*. The Open Group.

Kenton, W. (2020). Enterprise Risk Management (ERM). *Investopedia*. https://www.investopedia.com/terms/e/enterprise-risk-management.asp

Kiseleva, I., Karmanov, M., Korotkov, A., Kuznetsov, V., & Gasparian, M. (2018). Risk management in business: Concept, types, evaluation criteria. Revista ESPACIOS. *ISSN*, *0798*, 1015.

Kroese, R. (2014). *Enterprise Risk Management Approach*. Bizzdesign. https://bizzdesign.com/blog/enterprise-risk-management-approach/

Mačák, K. (2016). Is the International Law of Cyber Security in Crisis? Law School-University of Exeter. Exeter, United Kingdom. In *Cyber Power. 8th International Conference on Cyber Conflict*. NATO CCD COE Publications.

Makarchenko, M., Nerkararian, S., & Shmeleva, S. (2016). How Traditional Banks Should Work in Smart City. *Communications in Computer and Information Science*. 10.1007/978-3-319-49700-6_13

Markides, C. (2011, March). Crossing the Chasm: How to Convert Relevant Research Into Managerially Useful Research. *The Journal of Applied Behavioral Science*, *47*(1), 121–134. doi:10.1177/0021886310388162

Markides, C. (2015). Research on Business Models: Challenges and Opportunities. *Advances in Strategic Management*, *33*, 133–147. doi:10.1108/S0742-332220150000033004

Mees, W. (2017). *Security by Design in an Enterprise Architecture Framework*. NATO.

Miori, V., & Russo, D. (2014). Domotic Evolution towards the IoT. *28th International Conference on Advanced Information Networking and Applications Workshops*. 10.1109/WAINA.2014.128

Peterson, S. (2011). *Why it Worked: Critical Success Factors of a Financial Reform Project in Africa*. Faculty Research Working Paper Series. Harvard Kennedy School.

Pratap, K., & Predovich, B. (2020). *Magic Quadrant for IT Risk Management*. Gartner Inc.

Quang Phu, T., & Thi Yen Thao, H. (2017). Enterprise Risk Management Implementation: The Critical Success Factors For Vietnamese Construction Companies. *Journal of Multidisciplinary Engineering Science Studies*.

Ramada, P. (2013). How much did allegedly rigged interest rate (Libor) cost? Academic Press.

Ravanetti, A. (2016). *Switzerland Bank on Fintech with Lighter Regulations*. Crowd Valley. https://news.crowdvalley.com/news/switzerland-bank-on-fintech-with-lighter-regulations

Soft Expert. (2018). *Enterprise Asset Management.* https://www.softexpert.com/solucao/enterprise-asset-management-eam/

Stergiou, C., & Siganos, D. (2015). *Neural Networks.* https://www.doc.ic.ac.uk/~nd/surprise_96/journal/vol4/cs11/report.html

STS. (2018). *Enterprise asset management.* STS. http://www.stsolutions-global.com/enterprise-asset-management.html

Stupples, B., Sazonov, A., & Woolley, S. (2019). UBS Whistle-Blower Hunts Trillions Hidden in Treasure Isles. Bloomberg-Economics. *Bloomberg*. Reviewed in November 2019 https://www.bloomberg.com/news/chapters/2019-07-26/ubs-whistle-blower-hunts-trillions-hidden-in-treasure-islands

Taleb, N. (2012). Antifragile: Things that gain from disorder. Academic Press.

The Open Group. (2011b). *The TOGAF Framework*. The Open Group.

The Uniform Law Commissioners. (2015). *Electronic Transactions Act Summary*. The Uniform Law Commissioners.

Tiwari, D. (2017). *Architecture Development Method.* The Open Group. https://pubs.opengroup.org/architecture/togaf9-doc/arch/chap05.html

Trad, A. (2021a). *The Business Transformation Framework and Enterprise Architecture Framework for Managers in Business Innovation: The Alignment of Enterprise Asset Management and Enterprise Architecture Methodologies*. IGI Global. doi:10.4018/978-1-5225-8229-8.ch001

Trad, A. (2021b). *The Business Transformation Framework and Enterprise Architecture Framework: Organisational Asset Management in the Lebanese Context.* IGI Global. doi:10.4018/978-1-7998-4459-4.ch030

Trad, A. (2021c). The Security Management Concept (SMC). *STF Conference*. Turkey.

Trad, A., & Kalpić, D. (2020a). *Using Applied Mathematical Models for Business Transformation.* IGI Global. doi:10.4018/978-1-7998-1009-4

Trad, A., & Kalpić, D. (2020b). *An Applied Mathematical Model for Business Transformation and Enterprise Architecture-The Holistic Global Security Management System (HGSMS)*. IGI Global.

Trad, A., & Kalpić, D. (2021a). *Business Transformation and Enterprise Architecture: The Holistic Project Asset Management Concept (HPAMC)*. IGI Global.

Unwin, D. (2013). *Security Architecture-Enterprise Architecture*. Business Aspect.

Vulić, I., Prodanović, R., & Tot, I. (2019). An Example of a Methodology for Developing the Security of a Distributed Business System. In *Advances in Economics, Business and Management Research,* volume 108. *5th IPMA SENET Project Management Conference (SENET 2019)*. Atlantis Press. 10.2991enet-19.2019.34

Xiaohong, C. (2011). *Research on E-Commerce Transaction Cost-Benefit Characteristics and Evaluation Approaches.* Management and Service Science (MASS), *2011 International Conference*, Wuhan. China.

Zhao, X., Hwang, B., & Low, S. (2013). *Exploring Critical Success Factors for Enterprise Risk Management in Chinese Construction Firms*. Academic Press.

Compilation of References

Aali Bujari, A., & Venegas Martínez, F. (2016). Technological Innovation and Economic Growth in Latin America. *Mexican Journal of Economics and Finance*, *11*(2), 77–89.

Abbas, J., Mubeen, R., Iorember, P. T., Raza, S., & Mamirkulova, G. (2021). Exploring The Impact of COVID-19 on Tourism: Transformational Potential and Implications For a Sustainable Recovery Of The Travel And Leisure Industry. *Current Research in Behavioral Sciences*, *2*, 100033. doi:10.1016/j.crbeha.2021.100033

Abdurrahman, Gebru, & Bezabih. (2015, May). Sensor Based Automatic Irrigation Management System. *International Journal of Computer and Information Technology, 4*(3). https://www.ijcit.com/archives/volume4/issue3.

Abel, G. J., Brottrager, M., Crespo Cuaresma, J., & Muttarak, R. (2019). Climate, conflict, and Forced Migration. *Journal of Global Environmental Change*, *54*, 239–249. doi:10.1016/j.gloenvcha.2018.12.003

Acconcia, A., & Cantabene, C. (2018). Liquidity and Firms' Response to Fiscal Stimulus. *Economic Journal. Revue Economique et Sociale*, *128*(613), 1759–1785. doi:10.1111/ecoj.12499

Acemoglu, D., & Robinson, J. A. (2012). *Why nations fail: The origins of power, prosperity, and poverty*. Currency.

Acemoglu, D., & Robinson, J. A. (2020). *The narrow corridor: States, societies, and the fate of liberty*. Penguin Books.

Adler, S., Campion, M., Colquitt, A., Grubb, A., Murphy, K., Ollander-Krane, R., & Pulakos, E. D. (2016). Getting rid of performance ratings: Genius or folly? A debate. *Industrial and Organizational Psychology: Perspectives on Science and Practice*, *9*(2), 219–252. doi:10.1017/iop.2015.106

Agarwal, R., Gao, G., DesRoches, C., & Jha, A. K. (2010). Research commentary-The digital transformation of healthcare: Current status and the road ahead. *Information Systems Research*, *21*(4), 796–809. doi:10.1287/isre.1100.0327

Agca, B. (n.d.). *World Sustainable Development Summit (Johannesburg, 26 August - 4 September 2002)*. Ministry of Foreign Affairs of the Republic of Turkey. Retrieved from https://www.mfa.gov.tr/dunya-surdurulebilir-kalkinma-zirvesi_johannesburg_-26-agustos---4-eylul-2002_.tr.mfa

Aggarwal, S., Nawn, S., & Dugar, A. (2021). What caused global stock market meltdown during the COVID pandemic–Lockdown stringency or investor panic? *Finance Research Letters*, *38*, 101827. Advance online publication. doi:10.1016/j.frl.2020.101827

Agrawal, S., & Das, M. L. (2011, December). *Internet of Things — A Paradigm Shift Of Future Internet Applications.* https://ieeexplore.ieee.org/document/6153246

Aguinis, H. (2013). *Performance management*. Pearson Prentice Hall.

Ahmad, M., & Zheng, J. (2022). The cyclical and nonlinear impact of R&D and innovation activities on economic growth in OECD economies: A new perspective. *Journal of the Knowledge Economy*, 1–50. doi:10.100713132-021-00887-7

Ahmed, M. (2019). *How climate change exacerbates the refugee crisis and what can be done about it.* World Economic Forum. Retrieved from https://www.weforum.org/agenda/2019/06/how-climate-change-exacerbates-the-refugee-crisis-and-what-can-be-done-about-it/

Airmic. (2010). *A structured approach to Enterprise Risk Management (ERM) and the requirements of ISO 31000.* Alarm-The Institute of Risk Management.

Akter, S. (2020). The impact of COVID-19 related 'stay-at-home'restrictions on food prices in Europe: Findings from a preliminary analysis. *Food Security, 12*(4), 719–725. doi:10.100712571-020-01082-3 PMID:32837638

Alderman, L. (2019). French Court Fines UBS $4.2 Billion for Helping Clients Evade Taxes. *The New York Times.* https://www.nytimes.com/2019/02/20/business/ubs-france-tax-evasion.html

Aleh, C., & Jewell, J. (2011). The three perspectives on energy security: Intellectual history, disciplinary roots and the potential for integration. *Current Opinion in Environmental Sustainability, 3*(4), 202–212. doi:10.1016/j.cosust.2011.07.001

Alexander, D. E. (2002). *Principles of emergency planning and management.* Oxford University Press on Demand.

Algan, N., Manga, M., & Tekeoğlu, M. (2017). Teknolojik Gelişme Göstergeleri ile Ekonomik Büyüme Arasındaki Nedensellik İlişkisi: Türkiye Örneği. *International Conference on Eurasian Economies*, 332-338. 10.36880/C08.01869

Alimamy, S., Deans, K. R., & Gnoth, J. (2017). ' Augmented reality: Uses and future considerations in marketing. In R. Benlamri & M. Sparer (Eds.), *Leadership, Innovation and Entrepreneurship as Driving Forces of Global Economy. Springer Proceedings in Business and Economics* (pp. 705–712). Springer. doi:10.1007/978-3-319-43434-6_62

Al-Mulali, U., Sheau-Ting, L., & Ozturk, I. (2015). The global move toward internet shopping and it's influence on pollution: An empirical analysis. *Environmental Science and Pollution Research International, 22*(13), 9717–9727. doi:10.100711356-015-4142-2 PMID:25631741

Altın, O., & Kaya, A. A. (2009). Türkiye'de Ar-Ge harcamaları ve ekonomik büyüme arasındaki nedensel ilişkinin analizi. *Ege Academic Review, 9*(1), 251–259.

Altinoz, B., Vasbieva, D., & Kalugina, O. (2020). The effect of information and communication technologies and total factor productivity on co2 emissions in top 10 emerging market economies. *Environmental Science and Pollution Research International.* Advance online publication. doi:10.100711356-020-11630-1 PMID:33201509

Amri, F., Zaied, Y. B., & Lahouel, B. B. (2019). ICT, total factor productivity, and carbon dioxide emissions in Tunisia. *Technological Forecasting and Social Change, 146*, 212–217. doi:10.1016/j.techfore.2019.05.028

APERC. (2007). Quest for energy security in the 21st Century: resources and constraints. Asia Pacific Energy Research Centre.

Arçelik. (2020). Retrieved from https://www.arcelikglobal.com/media/6365/arcelik_2020surdurulebilirlikraporu_yoneticiozeti.pdf

Archibugia, D., & Cocoa, A. (2005). Measuring technological capabilities at the country level: A survey and a menu for choice. *Research Policy, 34*(2), 175–194. doi:10.1016/j.respol.2004.12.002

Arnell, N. W. (1998). Climate change and water resources in Britain. *Climatic Change, 39*(1), 83–110. doi:10.1023/A:1005339412565

Arth, C., Gruber, L., Grasset, R., Langlotz, T., Mulloni, A., Schmalstieg, D., & Wagner, D. (2015). *The history of mobile augmented reality. In Developments in mobile AR over the last almost 50 years, Inst.* For Computer Graphics and Vision Graz University of Technology.

Aselsan. (n.d.). Retrieved from https://www.aselsan.com.tr/tr/cozumlerimiz/enerji-sistemleri

Asongu, S. A. (2018). ICT, openness and CO2 emissions in Africa. *Environmental Science and Pollution Research International*, *25*(10), 9351–9359. doi:10.100711356-018-1239-4 PMID:29349735

Asongu, S., Akpan, U. S., & Isihak, S. R. (2018). Determinants of foreign direct investment in fast-growing economies: Evidence from the BRICS and MINT countries. *Financial Innovation*, *4*(1), 1–17. doi:10.118640854-018-0114-0

Autio, E., Nambisan, S., Thomas, L. D., & Wright, M. (2018). Digital affordances, spatial affordances, and the genesis of entrepreneurial ecosystems. *Strategic Entrepreneurship Journal*, *12*(1), 72–95. doi:10.1002ej.1266

Awokuse, T., & Christopoulos, D. (2009). Nonlinear dynamics and the exports-output growth nexus. *Economic Modelling*, *26*(1), 184-190. .econmod.2008.06.009 doi:10.1016/j

Ayaz, Ammad-Uddin, Sharif, Mansour, & Aggoune. (2019). Internet-of-Things (IoT)-Based Smart Agriculture: Toward Making the Fields Talk. In *New Technologies For Smart Farming 4.0: Research Challenges And Opportunities*. https://ieeexplore.ieee.org/document/8784034

Aydın, B., & Doğan, M. (2020). Yeni Koronavirüs (Covıd-19) Pandemisinin Turistik Tüketici Davranışları ve Türkiye Turizmi Üzerindeki Etkilerinin Değerlendirilmesi. *Pazarlama Teorisi ve Uygulamaları Dergisi*, *6*(1), 93–115.

Azuma, R. T. (1997). A survey of augmented reality. *Presence*, *6*(4), 355–385. doi:10.1162/pres.1997.6.4.355

Azuma, R., Baillot, Y., Behringer, R., Feiner, S., Julier, S., & Maclntyre, B. (2001). Recent advances in augmented reality. *IEEE Computer Graphics and Applications*, *21*(6), 34–47. doi:10.1109/38.963459

Bahar, O., & Kozak, M. (2005). *Küreselleşme Sürecinde Uluslararası Turizm ve Rekabet Edebilirlik*. Detay Yayıncılık.

Bahloul, W., Balcilar, M., Cunado, J., & Gupta, R. (2018). The role of economic and financial uncertainties in predicting commodity futures returns and volatility: Evidence from a nonparametric causality-in-quantiles test. *Journal of Multinational Financial Management*, *45*, 52–71. doi:10.1016/j.mulfin.2018.04.002

Balcilar, M., Bekiros, S., & Gupta, R. (2017). The role of news-based uncertainty indices in predicting oil markets: A hybrid nonparametric quantile causality method. *Empirical Economics*, *53*(3), 879–889. doi:10.100700181-016-1150-0

Balcilar, M., Ozdemir, Z. A., & Arslanturk, Y. (2010). Economic growth and energy consumption causal nexus viewed through a bootstrap rolling window. *Energy Economics*, *32*(6), 1398–1410. doi:10.1016/j.eneco.2010.05.015

Ball, D. L., Thames, M. H., & Phelps, G. (2008). Content knowledge for teaching: What makes it special? *Journal of Teacher Education*, *59*(1), 389–407. doi:10.1177/0022487108324554

Baltagi, B. H. (2005). *Econometric Analysis of Panel Data* (3rd ed.). John Wiley & Sons Ltd.

Baltagi, B. H., Feng, Q., & Kao, C. (2012). A Lagrange Multiplier test for cross-sectional dependence in a fixed effects panel data model. *Journal of Econometrics*, *170*(1), 164–177. doi:10.1016/j.jeconom.2012.04.004

Barateiro, J., Antunes, G., & Borbinha, J. (2012). Manage Risks through the Enterprise Architecture. *45th Hawaii International Conference on System Sciences*.

Barker, S., Mishra, A., Irwin, D., Cecchet, E., Shenoy, P., & Albrecht, J. (2012). Smart*: An open data set and tools for enabling research in sustainable homes. *SustKDD*, *111*(112), 108.

Barrodale, I., & Roberts, F. D. (1973). An improved algorithm for discrete l1 linear approximation. *SIAM Journal on Numerical Analysis*, *10*(5), 839–848. doi:10.1137/0710069

Barton, J. P., & Infield, D. G. (2004). Energy storage and its use with intermittent renewable energy. *IEEE Transactions on Energy Conversion, 19*(2), 441–448. doi:10.1109/TEC.2003.822305

Batabyal, A. A., & Yoo, S. J. (2018). Schumpeterian creative class competition, innovation policy, and regional economic growth. *International Review of Economics & Finance, 55*, 86–97. doi:10.1016/j.iref.2018.01.016

Beckman, J., & Countryman, A. M. (2021). The Importance of Agriculture in the Economy: Impacts from COVID-19. *American Journal of Agricultural Economics, 103*(5), 1595–1611. Advance online publication. doi:10.1111/ajae.12212 PMID:33821008

Berger, T., Amann, C., Formayer, H., Korjenic, A., Pospichal, B., Neururer, C., & Smutny, R. (2014). Impacts of urban location and climate change upon energy demand of office buildings in Vienna, Austria. *Building and Environment, 81*, 258–269. doi:10.1016/j.buildenv.2014.07.007

Berkhout, F., & Hertin, J. (2001). *Impacts of ınformation and communication technologies on environmental sustainability: Speculations and evidence.* Report to the OECD. https://www.oecd.org/sti/inno/1897156.pdf

Bérubé, C., & Mohnen, P. (2009). Are Firms that Receive R&D Subsidies More Innovative? *Can. J. Econ. Can. Econ. Assoc., 42*(1), 206–225. doi:10.1111/j.1540-5982.2008.01505.x

Bezirgan, E., & Bezirgan, M. (2021). The Effects of COVID-19 Pandemics to Turkey's Tourism: A Research on the Interbank Card Center Data. In The Evaluations and Researches in Social Sciences and Humanities. Livre de Lyon.

Bharadwaj, A., El Sawy, O., Pavlou, P., & Venkatraman, N. (2013). Digital business strategy: Toward a next generation of insights. *Management Information Systems Quarterly, 37*(2), 471–482. doi:10.25300/MISQ/2013/37:2.3

Bhattacharya, B., & Sinha, A. (2017). Intelligent Fault Analysis in Electrical Power Grids. *Proceedings of the IEEE 29th International Conference on Tools with Artificial Intelligence (ICTAI).* 10.1109/ICTAI.2017.00151

Bialbao-Osorio, B., & Rodriguez-Pose, A. (2004). From R&D to Innovation and Economic Growth in the EU. *Growth and Change, 35*(4), 434–455. doi:10.1111/j.1468-2257.2004.00256.x

Bikmetov, R., Raja, M., Kazi, K., Sane, T., & Shevchenko, N. (2016, October). Dynamic energy capacity planning for distributed resources in Smart Microgrids. In *2016 HONET-ICT* (pp. 159-163). IEEE.

Bilici, F. (2015). *Pazarlamada artırılmış gerçeklik ve karekod teknolojileri:Tüketicilerin artırılmış gerçeklik teknoloji algılamaları üzerine bir alan araştırması.* Yüksek Lisans Tezi, Uludağ Üniversitesi Sosyal Bilimler Enstitüsü.

Bilici, F., & Özdemir, E. (2020). Tüketicilerin artırılmış gerçeklik teknolojilerini kullanma niyeti üzerinde teknolojik hazır bulunuşluğun rolü. *International Social Mentality and Researcher Thinkers Journal, 6*(37), 2046–2060. doi:10.31576mryj.669

Blomquist, J., & Westerlund, J. (2016). Panel bootstrap tests of slope homogeneity. *Empirical Economics, 50*(4), 1359–1381. doi:10.100700181-015-0978-z

Boadi, S. A., & Owusu, K. (2019). Impact of climate change and variability on hydropower in Ghana. *African Geographical Review, 38*(1), 19–31. doi:10.1080/19376812.2017.1284598

Bocutoğlu, E. (2012). *Krizin makro iktisadından makro iktisadın krizine: Eleştirel bir değerlendirme* (No. 2012/106). Discussion Paper.

Borgards, O., Czudaj, R. L., & Van Hoang, T. H. (2021). Price overreactions in the commodity futures market: An intraday analysis of the Covid-19 pandemic impact. *Resources Policy, 71*, 101966. Advance online publication. doi:10.1016/j.resourpol.2020.101966

Bouwman, H., Nikou, S., Molina-Castillo, F. J., & de Reuver, M. (2018). The impact of digitalisation on business models. *Digital Policy. Regulation & Governance*, *20*(2), 105–124. doi:10.1108/DPRG-07-2017-0039

Braunerhjelm, P., & Thulin, P. (2006). *Can countries create comparative advantages?* Centre of Excellence for Studies in Science and Innovation (CESIS) Electronic Working Paper Series, Paper No. 61. https://static.sys.kth.se/itm/wp/cesis/cesiswp61.pdf

Breusch, T. S., & Pagan, A. R. (1980). The lagrange multiplier test and its applications to model specification in econometrics. *The Review of Economic Studies*, *47*(1), 239–253. doi:10.2307/2297111

Brundtland, G. (1987). *Ortak Geleceğimiz Dünya Çevre ve Kalkınma Komisyonu*. Raporu, Türkiye Çevre Sorunları Vakfı.

BSI. (2015). *Architectural framework for the Internet of Things, for Smart Cities*. BSI.

Bulearca, M., & Tamarjan, D. (2010). Augmented reality: A sustainable marketing tool? *Global Business and Management Research*, *2/3*, 237–252.

Burange, L. G., Ranadive, R. R., & Karnik, N. N. (2019). Trade openness and economic growth nexus: A case study of BRICS. *Foreign Trade Review*, *54*(1), 1–15. doi:10.1177/0015732518810902

Busby, J. W. (2007). *Climate Change and National Security: An Agenda for Action*. Report to the Council on Foreign Relations, C.S.R. No. 32. Retrieved from https://cdn.cfr.org/sites/default/files/report_pdf/ClimateChange_CSR32%20%281%29.pdf

Bustos, C., Willshire, J., Carrera, D. A., Becker, T., & Chase, J. C. (2021). *Shelter from the Storm: Policy Options to Address Climate-Induced Migration from the Northern Triangle*. Harvard Immigration and Refugee Clinical Program, H.L.S. Immigration Project, the University Network for Human Rights, Yale Immigrant Justice Project, and Yale Environmental Law Association. Retrieved from https://static1.squarespace.com/static/5b3538249d5abb21360e858f/t/6092e7854c5e4362887c0197/1620240265281/Shelter_Final_5May21.pdf

Bustos, P. (2011). Trade liberalization, exports, and technology upgrading: Evidence on the impact of MERCOSUR on Argentinian firms. *The American Economic Review*, *101*(1), 304–340. doi:10.1257/aer.101.1.304

Butler, R. (1999). Sustainable tourism: A state-of-the-art review. *Tourism Geographies*, *1*(1), 1, 7–25. doi:10.1080/14616689908721291

Butler, R. (2020). Tourism – resilient but vulnerable as "the times they are a changing" in the "new normality". *Worldwide Hospitality and Tourism Themes*, *12*(6), 663–670. doi:10.1108/WHATT-07-2020-0063

Bybee, R. W. (2000). Achieving technological literacy: A national imperative. *Technology Teacher*, *60*(1), 23–28.

Caballero, R. J., & Hammour, M. (2000). *Creative destruction and development: Institutions, crises, and restructuring*. Academic Press.

Çakın, E., & Özdemir, A. (2018). Kobi'lerde İnovasyon Performansını Etkileyen Faktörlerin Bulanık Dematel Tabanlı Analitik Ağ Süreci (BDANP) Yöntemiyle Analizi ve Bir Uygulama. *Dokuz Eylül Üniversitesi Sosyal Bilimler Enstitüsü Dergisi*, *20*(4), 559–586. doi:10.16953/deusosbil.293170

Campiche, J. L., Bryant, H. L., Richardson, J. W., & Outlaw, J. L. (2007). Examining the evolving correspondence between petroleum prices and agricultural commodity prices. In *Agricultural and Applied Economics Association Conferences* (No. 381-2016-22070). 10.22004/ag.econ.9881

Capecchi, V., Buscema, M., Contucci, P., & D'Amore, D. (2010). *Applications of Mathematics in Models, Artificial Neural Networks and Arts: Mathematics and Society*. Springer Science & Business Media. doi:10.1007/978-90-481-8581-8

Cappelen, A., Raknerud, A., & Rybalka, M. (2012). The effects of R&D Tax Credits Onpatenting and Innovations. *Research Policy, 41*(2), 334–345. doi:10.1016/j.respol.2011.10.001

Cariappa, A. A., Acharya, K. K., Adhav, C. A., Sendhil, R., & Ramasundaram, P. (2021). Impact of COVID-19 on the Indian agricultural system: A 10-point strategy for post-pandemic recovery. *Outlook on Agriculture, 50*(1), 26–33. doi:10.1177/0030727021989060

Carlos, V. S., & Gouveia, R. (2016). Development and validation of a self-reported measure of job performance. *Social Indicators Research, 126*(1), 279–307. doi:10.100711205-015-0883-z

Casey, C. A., & Cimino-Isaacs, C. D. (2020). *Export restrictions in response to the COVID-19 pandemic.* Congressional Research Service, No. IF11551 (Version 5).

Castellani, D., & Fassio, C. (2017). *Export innovation: The role of new imported inputs and multinationality. Innovation Studies, No. 2017/16.* Lund University.

Cecati, C., Citro, C., Piccolo, A., & Siano, P. (2011). Smart operation of wind turbines and diesel generators according to economic criteria. *IEEE Transactions on Industrial Electronics, 58*(10), 4514–4525. doi:10.1109/TIE.2011.2106100

Celli, V., Cerqua, A., & Pellegrini, G. (2021). Does R&D expenditure boost economic growth in lagging regions? *Social Indicators Research*, 1–20. doi:10.100711205-021-02786-5

CEMA. (2019, September). *Digital Farming: What Does It Really Mean?* https://www.cema-agri.org/publication/digital-farming-what-does-it-really-mean

Çeti, B., & Ünlüönen, K. (2019). Salgın Hastalıklar Sebebiyle Oluşan Krizlerin Turizm Sektörü Üzerindeki Etkisinin Değerlendirilmesi. *AHBVÜ Turizm Fakültesi Dergisi, 22*(2), 109–128.

Cetin, R. (2016). Yeni sanayileşen ülkelerde ar-ge harcamaları ve yüksek teknoloji ürünü ihracatı arasındaki ilişkinin panel veri analizi yöntemi ile incelenmesi. *İktisat Fakültesi Mecmuası, 66*(2), 30-43.

Çetin, K., & Gedik, H. (2017). İşletmelerde İnovasyona Etki Eden Faktörler: Karaman İli Örneği. *Uluslararası Yönetim İktisat ve İşletme Dergisi, 13*(13), 160–172.

Chang, C. L., & Liao, C. S. (2012). Parameter sensitivity analysis of artificial neural network for predicting water turbidity. *International Journal of Geological and Environmental Engineering, 6*(10), 657–660.

Cheng, C., Barceló, J., Hartnett, A. S., Kubinec, R., & Messerschmidt, L. (2020). COVID-19 government response event dataset (CoronaNet v.1.0). *Nature Human Behaviour, 4*(7), 756–768. doi:10.103841562-020-0909-7 PMID:32576982

Cheng, K., Hsueh, H. P., Ranjbar, O., Wang, M. C., & Chang, T. (2021). Urbanization, coal consumption and CO_2 emissions nexus in China using bootstrap Fourier Granger causality test in quantiles. *Letters in Spatial and Resource Sciences, 14*(1), 31–49. doi:10.100712076-020-00263-0

Chen, Z., & Zhang, J. (2019). Types of Patents and Driving Forces Behind the Patent Growth in China. *Economic Modelling, 80*, 294–302. doi:10.1016/j.econmod.2018.11.015

Cheyney, S. (2021). *Strategy and Tactics, Military.* Scholastic Inc.

Chhaya, L. K., Sharma, P., Kumar, A., & Bhagwatikar, G. (2018). Cross layer optimization and simulation of smart grid home area network. Modelling and Simulation in Engineering.

Chikankar, Mehetre, & Das. (2015, April). *An Automatic Irrigation System Using ZigBee In Wireless Sensor Network.* https://ieeexplore.ieee.org/document/7086997

Chikankar, P. B., Mehetre, D., & Das, S. (2015). An automatic irrigation system using ZigBee in wireless sensor network. *International Conference on Pervasive Computing (ICPC)*, 1-5. 10.1109/PERVASIVE.2015.7086997

Choi, C., & Yi, M. H. (2018). The internet, R&D expenditure and economic growth. *Applied Economics Letters*, *25*(4), 264–267. doi:10.1080/13504851.2017.1316819

Choi, I. (2001). Unit root tests for panel data. *Journal of International Money and Finance*, *20*(2), 249–272. doi:10.1016/S0261-5606(00)00048-6

Christensen, R. (2002). Effects of technology integration education on the attitudes of teachers and students. *Journal of Research on Technology in Education*, *34*(4), 411–433. doi:10.1080/15391523.2002.10782359

Chuang, C. C., & Sue, D. C. (2005). Performance effects of combined cycle power plant with variable condenser pressure and loading. *Energy*, *30*(10), 1793–1801. doi:10.1016/j.energy.2004.10.003

Chylinski, M., Heller, J., Hilken, T., Keeling, I. D., Mahr, D., & de Ruyter, K. (2020). Augmented reality marketing: A technology-enabled approach to situated customer experience. *Australasian Marketing Journal*, *28*(4), 374–384. doi:10.1016/j.ausmj.2020.04.004

Clark, D. (2002). *Enterprise Security: The Manager's Defense Guide*. Addison-Wesley Professional.

Climate Refugee. (n.d.). *Cambridge English Dictionary*. Retrieved January 30, 2022, from https://dictionary.cambridge.org/us/dictionary/english/climate-refugee

Çöl, G. (2008). Algılanan Güçlendirmenin İş Gören Performansı Üzerine Etkileri. *Dogus University Journal*, *9*(1), 35–46.

Colombo, D. G. (2019). Brazilian Innovation Tax Policy and International Investment: Evidence From United States Multinationals and International Patent Applications. *Análise Econômica, Porto Alegre*, *37*(74), 61-90.

Coulibaly, P., Anctil, F., & Bobée, B. (2000). Daily reservoir inflow forecasting using artificial neural networks with stopped training approach. *Journal of Hydrology (Amsterdam)*, *230*(3-4), 244–257. doi:10.1016/S0022-1694(00)00214-6

Craig, A. B. (2013). Understanding Augmented Reality. Morgan Kaufmann.

Cranmer, E. E., Dieck, M.C.T., & Fountoulaki, P. (2020). Exploring the value of augmented reality for tourism. *Tourism Management Perspective, 35*.

Crook, J. A., Jones, L. A., Forster, P. M., & Crook, R. (2011). Climate change impacts on future photovoltaic and concentrated solar power energy output. *Energy & Environmental Science*, *4*(9), 3101–3109. doi:10.1039/c1ee01495a

Curtis, P., & Carey, M. (2012). *Committee of Sponsoring Organizations of the Treadway Commission-Risk Assessment in Practice*. Deloitte & Touche LLP.

Cütcü, İ., & Bozan, T. (2019). İnovasyon ve Ekonomik Büyüme İlişkisi: G-7 Ülkeleri Üzerine Panel Veri Analizi. *Uluslararası Ekonomi İşletme ve Politika Dergisi*, *3*(2), 289–310.

Czarnitzki, D., Hanel, P., & Rosa, J. M. (2011). Evaluating the Impact of R&D Tax Credits on Innovation: A Microeconometric Study on Canadian Firms. *Research Policy*, *40*(2), 217–229. doi:10.1016/j.respol.2010.09.017

Daellenbach, H., McNickle, D., & Dye, Sh. (2012). *Management Science - Decision-making through systems thinking* (2nd ed.). Plagrave Macmillian.

Danahy, J. (2009). *The coming smart grid data surge*. Retrieved from: http:// www.smartgridnews.com/story/coming-smart-grid-data-surge/2009-10-05

Dawson, C., & Rakes, G. C. (2003). The influence of principals' technology training on the integration of technology into schools. *Journal of Research on Technology in Education, 36*(1), 29–49. doi:10.1080/15391523.2003.10782401

Değirmenci, B., & Aytekin, M. (2021). Çalışanların Çevreci Davranışları Merinos A.Ş. Uygulaması. Gazi Kitabevi.

Dehghan Shabani, Z., & Shahnazi, R. (2019). Energy consumption, carbon dioxide emissions, information and communications technology, and gross domestic product in Iranian economic sectors: A panel causality analysis. *Energy, 169*, 1064–1078. doi:10.1016/j.energy.2018.11.062

Demirdöğen, S. (2019). İşletmelerin İnovasyon Yapmalarına Engel olan Faktörlerin Belirlenmesine Yönelik Bir Araştırma: Erzincan Organize Sanayi Bölgesi Örneği. *Erciyes Üniversitesi İktisadi ve İdari Bilimler Fakültesi Dergisi*, (54), 417–446. doi:10.18070/erciyesiibd.521871

DeNisi, A. S., & Murphy, K. R. (2017). Performance appraisal and performance management: 100 years of progress? *The Journal of Applied Psychology, 102*(3), 421–433. doi:10.1037/apl0000085 PMID:28125265

Derya, H. (2021). Kurumsal İktisadın Katkıları Üzerine Değerlendirme. In *Kurumsal İktisat: Kurallar ve Kurumların İktisadi Gelişme Açısından Önemi içinde* (pp. 99–121). Astana Yayınları.

Dillenbourg, P. (2016). The evolution of research on digital education. *International Journal of Artificial Intelligence in Education, 26*(2), 544–560. doi:10.100740593-016-0106-z

DiPietro, W. R., & Anoruo, E. (2006). Creativity, innovation, and export performance. *Journal of Policy Modeling, 28*(2), 133–139. doi:10.1016/j.jpolmod.2005.10.001

DODAF. (2010). *Deputy Chief Information Officer, The DoDAF Architecture Framework Version 2.02*. U.S. Department of Defense. https://dodcio.defense.gov/dodaf20.aspx

Doğan, C., & Öcal, N. (2007). *Yeni iktisat politikaları ve yenilik iktisadına eleştirel yaklaşım. Baskı.* Detay Yayıncılık.

Doğan, E. (2020). Türkiye'de İnovasyonu Belirleyen Faktörler: 5746 ve 4691 Sayılı Kanunlar Kapsamında Bir Değerlendirme. In Ş. Karabulut (Ed.), *Kamu Politikalarında Mali ve İktisadi Yapıdaki Dönüşüm: Yerelden Globale Teori, Beklentiler ve Uygulama* (pp. 95–117). Gazi Kitapevi.

Doğan, E. (2021). The Purpose-Spesific Structure of Decree on State Aids for Investments: A Comparision of Regions Classified as Socioeconomic Development Level via Copras Method. *BILTURK. The Journal of Economics and Related Studies, 3*(3), 410–426. doi:10.47103/bilturk.937305

Dolado, J. J., & Lütkepohl, H. (1996). Making Wald tests work for cointegrated VAR systems. *Econometric Theory, 15*(4), 369–386. doi:10.1080/07474939608800362

Donou-Adonsou, F. (2019). Technology, education, and economic growth in sub-saharan Africa. *Telecommunications Policy, 43*(4), 353–360. doi:10.1016/j.telpol.2018.08.005

Drukker, D. M. (2003). Testing for serial correlation in linear panel-data models. *The Stata Journal, 3*(2), 168–177. doi:10.1177/1536867X0300300206

Dumitrescu, E., & Hurlin, C. (2012). Testing for Granger non-causality in heterogeneous panels. *Economic Modelling, 29*(4), 1450–1460. doi:10.1016/j.econmod.2012.02.014

Durmayaz, A., & Sogut, O. S. (2006). Influence of cooling water temperature on the efficiency of a pressurized-water reactor nuclear-power plant. *International Journal of Energy Research, 30*(10), 799–810. doi:10.1002/er.1186

Du, W. (2011). Probabilistic analysis for capacity planning in smart grid at residential low voltage level by Monte-Carlo method. *Procedia Engineering, 23*, 804–812. doi:10.1016/j.proeng.2011.11.2585

Easterbrook, S., Singer, J., Storey, M., & Damian, D. (2008). *Guide to Advanced Empirical Software Engineering-Selecting Empirical Methods for Software Engineering Research.* Springer.

Ebner, D., & Baumgartner, R. (2006). The Relationship Between Sustainable Development and Corporate Social Responsibility. *Corporate Responsibility Research Conference, 4*(5-9), 1-17.

Eden, R., Jones, A. B., Casey, V., & Draheim, M. (2019). Digital transformation requires workforce transformation. *MIS Quarterly Executive, 18*(1), 1–17. doi:10.17705/2msqe.00005

Egidi, M. (1995). *The "Creative Destruction" in Economic and Political Institutions.* Academic Press.

Ekananda, M., & Parlinggoman, D. J. (2017). The role of high-tech exports and of foreign direct investments (FDI) on economic growth. *European Research Studies Journal, 20*(4A, 4A), 194–212. doi:10.35808/ersj/828

Ekanayake, J., Liyanage, K., Wu, J., Yokoyama, A., & Jenkins, N. (2012). *The smart grid: Technology and applications.* John Wiley & Sons, Ltd. doi:10.1002/9781119968696

El Mrabet, Z., Kaabouch, N., El Ghazi, H., & El Ghazi, H. (2018). Cyber-security in smart grid: Survey and challenges. *Computers & Electrical Engineering, 67*, 469–482. doi:10.1016/j.compeleceng.2018.01.015

Elleby, C., Domínguez, I. P., Adenauer, M., & Genovese, G. (2020). Impacts of the COVID-19 pandemic on the global agricultural markets. *Environmental and Resource Economics, 76*(4), 1067–1079. doi:10.100710640-020-00473-6 PMID:32836856

Elliott, C. (2020). What Will Travel Be Like After The Coronavirus? *Forbes.* Retrieved from: https://www.forbes.com/sites/christopherelliott/2020/03/18/what-will-travel-be-like-after-the-coronavirus/?sh=49d89dde3329

Emirmahmutoglu, F., & Kose, N. (2011). Testing for granger causality in heterogeneous mixed panels. *Economic Modelling, 28*(3), 870–876. doi:10.1016/j.econmod.2010.10.018

Enders, W., & Jones, P. (2016). Grain prices, oil prices, and multiple smooth breaks in a VAR. *Studies in Nonlinear Dynamics and Econometrics, 20*(4), 399–419. doi:10.1515nde-2014-0101

Erdemir Çevresel Sürdürülebilirlik Raporu. (n.d.). *Kurumsal.* Retrieved from https://www.erdemir.com.tr/kurumsal/

Erdil, E., Turkcan, B., & Yetkiner, İ. H. (2009). *Does information and communication technology sustain economic growth? The underdeveloped and developing countries case.* Science and Technology Policies Research Center, TEKPOL Working Paper Series 09/03.

Erdoğan, S., & Canbay, Ş. (2016). İktisadi büyüme ve araştırma & geliştirme (Ar-Ge) harcamaları ilişkisi üzerine teorik bir inceleme. *Muş Alparslan Üniversitesi Sosyal Bilimler Dergisi, 4*(2), 29–44. doi:10.18506/anemon.16169

Ergün, F. (2018). *Artırılmış gerçeklik reklam sektörünü nasıl etkiler?* https://fikretergunblog.wordpress.com/2018/03/13/artirilmis-gerceklik-reklam-sektorunu-nasil-etkiler/

Erkişi, K. (2018). Financial Development and Economic Growth in BRICS Countries and Turkey: A Panel Data Analysis. *İstanbul Gelişim Üniversitesi Sosyal Bilimler Dergisi, 5*(2), 1-17.

Ernst, C., & Spengel, C. (2011). *Taxation, R&D Tax Incentives and Patent Application in Europe.* ZEW Discussion Paper No. 11, 0-24. doi:10.2139/ssrn.1805762

Erol, M. (2010). Ekonomik Kriz ve Kobiler. *Journal of Entrepreneurship and Development, 5*(1), 165–181.

Ersungur, Ş. M., & Takım, A. (2018). Türkiye'de Teşvik Sisteminin Yapısı, Sorunları ve Etkinliği Üzerine Bir Politika Önerisi: Tek Bir Uygulamacı Kuruluş Sorunları Çözer Mi? *Atatürk Üniversitesi İktisadi ve İdari Bilimler Dergisi, 32*(3), 725–744.

Ertmer, P. A., Ottenbreit-Leftwich, A. T., Sadik, O., Sendurur, E., & Sendurur, P. (2012). Teacher beliefs and technology integration practices: A critical relationship. *Computers & Education, 59*(2), 423–435. doi:10.1016/j.compedu.2012.02.001

Escobedo-Briones, G., Jacome-Grajales, N., & Arroyo-Figueroa, G. (2016). Business Intelligence and Data Analytics (BI&DA) to Support the Operation of Smart Grid - Business Intelligence and Data Analytics (BI&DA) for Smart Grid. *Proceedings of the International Conference on Internet of Things and Big Data (1): RAIBS*, 489-496.

Escobedo, G., Jacome, N., & Arroyo-Figueroa, G. (2016). *Business intelligence and data analytics to support the operation of smart grid. Conference: Special Session on Recent Advancement in IoT, Big Data and Security.* doi:10.5220/0005936604890496

European Commission. (2012). *Generational Renewal in EU Agriculture: Statistical Background.* https://www.europeansources.info/record/rural-development-in-the-eu-statistical-and-economic-information/

European Council. (2008). *Climate change and international security.* Joint Paper from the High Representative and the European Commission to the European Council, S113/08. Retrieved from https://www.consilium.europa.eu/uedocs/cms_data/docs/pressdata/en/reports/99387.pdf

European Union (2014). Regulation (EU) No 910/2014 of the European Par lament and of the Council - on electronic identification and trust services for electronic transactions in the internal market and repealing Directive 1999/93/EC The European Par lament and of the Council – Regulation. European Union.

EuropeYou Asociación. (2020). *What is Information and Communication Technology?* https://europeyou.eu/es/what-is-informationand-communication-technology

Ezeaku, H. C., Asongu, S. A., & Nnanna, J. (2021). Volatility of international commodity prices in times of COVID-19: Effects of oil supply and global demand shocks. *The Extractive Industries and Society, 8*(1), 257–270. doi:10.1016/j.exis.2020.12.013

EzeakuH.AsonguS. (2020). Covid-19 and Cacophony of coughing: Did International commodity Prices catch influenza? *European Xtramile Centre of African Studies* (WP/20/040). doi:10.2139/ssrn.3636399

Ezer, G. (2008). *Teknolojik Gelişme ile Artan Ürün Özellikleri ve Tüketici Satın Alma Davranışına Etkileri* (Unpublished Master's thesis). Istanbul Technical University, Institute of Science and Technology.

Fagerberg, J. (2000). Technological progress, structural change and productivity growth: A comparative study. *Structural Change and Economic Dynamics, 11*(4), 393–411. doi:10.1016/S0954-349X(00)00025-4

Falk, M. (2007). R&D spending in the high-tech sector and economic growth. *Research in Economics, 61*(3), 140–147. doi:10.1016/j.rie.2007.05.002

Falk, M. (2009). High-tech exports and economic growth in industrialized countries. *Applied Economics Letters, 16*(10), 1025–1028. doi:10.1080/13504850701222228

Fan, C., & Zhao, Y. (2019). Analysis on the Evolution of Innovation Efficiency of High-tech Industry and Its Influencing Factors -Taking Zhongguancun Science and Technology Park as an Example, *Modern. Management Science, 1*(1), 6–8.

Fant, C., Schlosser, C. A., & Strzepek, K. (2016). The impact of climate change on wind and solar resources in southern Africa. *Applied Energy, 161*, 556–564. doi:10.1016/j.apenergy.2015.03.042

Fan, X., Weber, W. D., & Barroso, L. A. (2007). Power provisioning for a warehouse-sized computer. *ACM SIGARCH Computer Architecture News*, *35*(2), 13–23. doi:10.1145/1273440.1250665

FAO. (2020). *Novel Coronavirus (COVID-19)*. https://www.fao.org/2019-ncov/q-and-a/impact-on-food-and-agriculture/en/

Farhangis, H. (2010). Smart grid communication technologies. *IEEE Power & Energy Magazine*, *8*, 18–28.

Farjon, D., Smits, A., & Voogt, J. M. (2019). Technology integration of pre-service teachers explained by attitudes and beliefs, competency, access, and experience. *Computers & Education*, *130*, 81–93. doi:10.1016/j.compedu.2018.11.010

Farooq, M. S., Riaz, S., Abid, A., Umer, T., & Zikria, Y. B. (2020, February 12). Electronics | Free Full-Text | Role Of IoT Technology In Agriculture: A Systematic Literature Review. *MDPI*. https://www.mdpi.com/2079-9292/9/2/319

Fasanya, I. O., Odudu, T. F., & Adekoya, O. (2019). Oil and agricultural commodity prices in Nigeria: New evidence from asymmetry and structural breaks. *International Journal of Energy Sector Management*, *13*(2), 377–401. doi:10.1108/IJESM-07-2018-0004

Fatima, S., Chen, B., Ramzan, M., & Abbas, Q. (2020). The Nexus Between Trade Openness and GDP Growth: Analyzing the Role of Human Capital Accumulation. *SAGE Open*, *10*(4), 2158244020967377. doi:10.1177/2158244020967377

Feiner, S. K. (2002). Augmented Reality: A New Way of Seeing. *Scientific American*, *286*(4), 48–55. https://www.jstor.org/stable/26059641)

Felfel, H., Ayadi, O., & Masmoudi, F. (2017). Pareto Optimal Solution Selection for a Multi-Site Supply Chain Planning Problem Using the VIKOR and TOPSIS Methods. *International Journal of Service Science, Management, Engineering, and Technology*. . doi:10.4018/IJSSMET.2017070102

FIMT. (2021). *Changing Characteristics of Conflict*. FIMT. https://www.liftingoursights.org.uk/trends/changing-characteristics-of-conflict/

Finnveden, G., Hauschild, M., Ekvall, T., Guinee, J., Heijungs, R., Hellweg, S., Koehler, A., Pennington, D., & Suh, S. (2009). Recent Developments In Life Cycle Assessment. *Journal of Environmental Management*, *91*(1), 1–21. doi:10.1016/j.jenvman.2009.06.018 PMID:19716647

Fisher, R. A. (1932). *Statistical methods for research workers* (4th ed.). Oliver and Boyd.

Florian. (2020). *Corona Pandemic: What it Means for the Sustainable Tourism Community*. Sustainability Leaders Project. Retrieved from https://sustainability-leaders.com/what-corona-pandemic-means-for-sustainable-toursim/

Florida, R. (2002). *The rise of the creative class* (Vol. 9). Basic Books.

Food Insecurity. (n.d.). *Merriam-Webster Dictionary*. Retrieved January 31, 2022, from https://www.merriam-webster.com/dictionary/food%20insecurity

Forced Migration. (n.d.). *Definitions.net*. Retrieved January 31, 2022, from https://www.definitions.net/definition/forced+migration

Fordotosan. (2020). Retrieved from https://www.fordotosan.com.tr/documents/Documents/Surd_Raporlari/2020_surduruleklilik_raporuv1.pdf

Fowowe, B. (2016). Do oil prices drive agricultural commodity prices? Evidence from South Africa. *Energy*, *104*, 149–157. doi:10.1016/j.energy.2016.03.101

Freimane, R., & Bāliņa, S. (2016). R&D expenditures and economic growth in the EU: A panel data analysis. *Economics and Business*, *29*(1), 5–11. doi:10.1515/eb-2016-0016

Freire-Seren, M. J. (2001). R&D-expenditure in an endogenous growth model. *Journal of Economics*, *74*(1), 39–62. doi:10.1007/BF01231215

Freitas, I. B., Castellacci, F., Fontana, R., Malerba, F., & Vezzulli, A. (2017). Sectors and the Additionality Effects of R&D Tax Credits: A Cross-Country Microeconometric Analysis. *Research Policy*, *46*(1), 57–72. doi:10.1016/j.respol.2016.10.002

Fu, D., Wu, Y., & Tang, Y. (2012). Does Innovation Matter for Chinese High-Tech Exports? A FirmLevel Analysis. *Frontiers of Economics in China*, *7*(2), 218–245.

Fu, Zh., & Mittnight, E. (2015). *Critical Success Factors for Continually Monitoring, Evaluating and Assessing Management of Enterprise IT*. ISACA.

Gaetani, M., Huld, T., Vignati, E., Monforti-Ferrario, F., Dosio, A., & Raes, F. (2014). The near future availability of photovoltaic energy in Europe and Africa in climate-aerosol modeling experiments. *Renewable & Sustainable Energy Reviews*, *38*, 706–716. doi:10.1016/j.rser.2014.07.041

Galbraith, J. K. (2004). *Ekonomik Gelişmeler Tarihi: Kuşku Çağı, Altın Kitaplar, 3*. Basım.

Gallardo, C., Rodriguez, S. P., Chango, I. E., Quevedo, W. X., Santana, J., Acosta, A. G., Tapia, J. C., & Andaluz, V. H. (2018). Augmented reality as a new marketing strategy. *International Conference on Augmented Reality, Virtual Reality and Computer Graphics*, 351-362. 10.1007/978-3-319-95270-3_29

Gani, A. (2009). Technological achievement, high technology exports and growth. *Journal of Comparative International Management*, *12*(2), 31–47.

Garanti Bank. (2020). Retrieved from https://surdurulebilirlik.garantibbva.com.tr/surdurulebilirlik-yaklasimimiz/

Garda, B. (2014). *Macera turizmi pazarlaması, özel ilgi turizminin yeni yüzü*. Çizhi Kitabevi.

Gardner, H. (1999). *Intelligence Reframed: Multiple Intelligences for the 21st Century*. Basic Books.

Gatimbu, K., & Ogada, M., Budambula, N., & Kariuk, S. (2018). *Environmental Sustainability And Financial Performance Of The Small-Scale Tea Processors in Kenya. Business Strategy & the Environment, 27*(8), 1765-1771.

Gebre, E., Saroyan, A., & Bracewell, R. (2014). Students' engagement in technology rich classrooms and its relationship to professors' conceptions of effective teaching. *British Journal of Educational Technology*, *45*(1), 83–96. doi:10.1111/bjet.12001

Gedik, Y. (2020). Kurumsal Sosyal Sorumluluk: Tanımları, Tarihi, Teorileri, Boyutları ve Avantajları Üzerine Kuramsal Bir Çerçeve. *Haliç Üniversitesi Sosyal Bilimleri Dergisi, 3*(2), 265-304. Retrieved from https://dergipark.org.tr/en/pub/husbd/issue/58132/776380

Gedik, Y. (2020). Sosyal, Ekonomik Ve Çevresel Boyutlarla Sürdürülebilirlik Ve Sürdürülebilir Kalkınma. *Uluslararası Ekonomi Siyaset İnsan ve Toplum Bilimleri Dergisi*, *3*(3), 196–215.

Genç, A. G. M. C., & Atasoy, A. G. Y. (2010). Ar & Ge harcamaları ve ekonomik büyüme ilişkisi: Panel veri analizi. *Bilgi Ekonomisi ve Yönetimi Dergisi*, *5*(2), 27–34.

Genç, H. (2021). Kurumsal İktisat: Metodolojik ve Terminolojik Temeller. In *Kurumsal İktisat: Kurallar ve Kurumların İktisadi Gelişme Açısından Önemi içinde* (pp. 123–138). Astana Yayınları.

Geopolitics. (n.d.). *Merriam-Webster Dictionary*. Retrieved January 31, 2022, from https://www.merriam-webster.com/dictionary/geopolitics

Gerçeklik, A. (2017). IKEA Place Uygulamasıyla Eşyaları Evinizin İçinde Görün. *Dijital Ajanslar*. Retrieved from https://www.dijitalajanslar.com/ikeanin-artirilmis-gerceklik-uygulamasiyla-esyalari-evinizin-icinde-gorun/

GeSI. (2008). SMART 2020: Enabling The Low Carbon Economy In *The İnformation Age*. The Climate Group on behalf of the Global eSustainability Initiative (GeSI). https://gesi.org/research/download/7

Giaritelli, A. (2021, July). *Migrants arrive to the U.S. border from all over the world: We are seeing a permanent change*. Retrieved from https://news.yahoo.com/migrants-arrive-us-border-over-100100416.html?fr=sycsrp_catchall

Gibson, M. (2012). *Critical success factors for the implementation of an operational risk management system for south African financial services organisations (Master of Commerce)*. Business Management. University of South Africa.

Gocer, İ. (2013). Ar-Ge harcamalarının yüksek teknolojili ürün ihracatı, dış ticaret dengesi ve ekonomik büyüme üzerindeki etkileri. *Maliye Dergisi*, *165*(2), 215–240.

Göçer, İ., Kutbay, H., Gerede, C., & Aslan, R. (2014). Vergi Teşviklerinin Ar-Ge ve İnovasyona Etkisi: Panel Eş Bütünleşme ve Nedensellik Analizi. *Maliye Dergisi*, (167), 163–183.

Goel, R. K., & Korhonen, I. (2011). *Determinants of economic growth in BRIC countries* (No. 05/2011). Development Research Working Paper Series.

Goel, R. K., & Ram, R. (1994). R&D expenditures and economic growth: A cross-country study. *Economic Development and Cultural Change*, *42*(2), 403–411. doi:10.1086/452087

Gokmenoglu, K. K., Güngör, H., & Bekun, F. V. (2020). Revisiting the linkage between oil and agricultural commodity prices: Panel evidence from an Agrarian state. *International Journal of Finance & Economics*. Advance online publication. doi:10.1002/ijfe.2083

Gokmen, Y., & Turen, U. (2013). The Determinants of high technology exports volume: A panel data analysis of EU-15 countries. *International Journal of Management, Economics and Social Sciences*, *2*(3), 217–232.

Gorodnichenko, Yu., Svejnar, J., & Terrel, K. (2010). Globalization and innovation in emerging markets. *American Economic Journal. Macroeconomics*, *2*(2), 194–226. doi:10.1257/mac.2.2.194

Gössling, S., Scott, D., & Hall, C. M. (2020). Pandemics, tourism and global change: A rapid assessment of COVID-19. *Journal of Sustainable Tourism*, *29*(1), 1–20. doi:10.1080/09669582.2020.1758708

Government of South Australia, Department for Energy and Mining. (2021). *Managing peak demand*. Retrieved from: https://www.sa.gov.au/topics/energy-and-environment/energy-supply/managing-peak-demand

Granger, C. W. (1969). Investigating causal relations by econometric models and cross-spectral methods. *Econometrica*, *37*(3), 424–438. doi:10.2307/1912791

Gray, R. S. (2020). Agriculture, transportation, and the COVID-19 crisis. *Canadian Journal of Agricultural Economics/Revue Canadienne D'agroeconomie, 68*(2), 239-243. doi:10.1111/cjag.12235

Grecequet, M., Dewaard, J., Hellmann, J. J., & Abel, G. J. (2017). Climate Vulnerability and Human Migration in Global Perspective. *Journal of Sustainability, 9*(5). Retrieved from https://www.mdpi.com/2071-105/9/5/720/htm

Gries, T., Grundmann, R., Palnau, I., & Redlin, M. (2017). Innovations, growth and participation in advanced economies-a review of major concepts and findings. *International Economics and Economic Policy*, *14*(2), 293–351. doi:10.100710368-016-0371-1

Guellec, D., & Pottelsberghe, B. (2000). *The Impact of Public R&D Expenditure on Business R&D*. STI Working Papers, No. 4.

Guerava, G., & Richards, D. (2019). *Crisis Readiness*. Global Rescue and World Travel and Tourism Council. Retrieved from https://www.globalrescue.com/grmkt_resources/pdfs/Crisis-Readiness-Final.pdf

Gulmez, A., & Yardımcıoglu, F. (2012). OECD Ülkelerinde Ar-Ge harcaması ve ekonomik büyüme ilişkisi: Panel eşbütünleşme ve panel nedensellik analizi (1990-2010). *Maliye Dergisi*, *163*, 335–353.

Gümrah, A., İnan, Ü.S.E., & Garda, B. (2021). Hizmet pazarlaması ve muhasebe verileri: Turizm işletmelerinde bir uygulama. In Sosyal, Beşeri ve İdari Bilimler Alanında Uluslararası Araştırmalar VIII. Eğitim Yayınevi.

Gümüs, E., & Çelikay, F. (2015). R&D expenditure and economic growth: New empirical evidence. *The Journal of Applied Economic Research*, *9*(3), 205–217. doi:10.1177/0973801015579753

Günay, G. (2012). Effect of New Technologies On The Purchasing Trends of Young People. *Akademik Bakis Dergisi*, *29*(1), 1–20.

Gungor, V. C., Lu, B., & Hancke, G. P. (2010). Opportunities and challenges of wireless sensor networks in smart grid. *IEEE Transactions on Industrial Electronics*, *57*(10), 3557–3564. doi:10.1109/TIE.2009.2039455

Gürkan, C. (2007). Veblen, Schumpeter ve Teknoloji. In *Kurumsal İktisat içinde* (pp. 237–281). İmge Kitabevi.

Hall, B. H., & Reenen, J. W. (2000). How Effective are Fiscal Incentives for R&D? A New Review of the Evidence. *Research Policy*, *29*(4-5), 449–469. doi:10.1016/S0048-7333(99)00085-2

Hall, C. M., Scott, D., & Gössling, S. (2020). Pandemics, transformations and tourism: Be careful what you wish for. *Tourism Geographies*, *22*(3), 577–598. doi:10.1080/14616688.2020.1759131

Hanel, P. (2003). *Impact of Government Support Programs on Innovation by Canadian Manufacturing Firms*. Centre interuniversitaire de recherche sur lascience et la technologie (CIRST), ca-hier de recherche.

Hasan, I., & Tucci, C. L. (2010). The innovation–Economic growth nexus: Global evidence. *Research Policy*, *39*(10), 1264–1276. doi:10.1016/j.respol.2010.07.005

Haseeb, A., Xia, E., Saud, S., Ahmad, A., & Khurshid, H. (2019). Does information and communication technologies improve environmental quality in the era of globalization? an empirical analysis. *Environmental Science and Pollution Research International*, *26*(9), 8594–8608. doi:10.100711356-019-04296-x PMID:30710332

Hayek, F. A. (1945). The use of knowledge in society. *The American Economic Review*, *35*(4), 519–530.

Higgins-Desbiolles. (2020). The end of global travel as we know it: an opportunity for sustainable tourism. *The Conversation*. Retrieved from: https://theconversation.com/the-end-of-global-travel-as-we-know-it-an-opportunity-for-sustainable-tourism-133783

Higon, D. A., Gholami, R., & Shirazi, F. (2017). ICT and environmental sustainability: A global perspective. *Telematics and Informatics*, *34*(4), 85–95. doi:10.1016/j.tele.2017.01.001

Himesh, S. (2018, September). *Digital Revolution And Big Data: a New Revolution In Agriculture*. Research Gate. https://www.researchgate.net/publication/327572166

Hinsch, C., Felix, R., & Rauschnabel, P. A. (2020). Nostalgia beats the wow-effect: Inspiration, awe and meaningful associations in augmented reality marketing. *Journal of Retailing and Consumer Services*, *53*, 101987. doi:10.1016/j.jretconser.2019.101987

Hofacker, C. F., de Ruyter, K., Lurie, N. H., Manchanda, P., & Donaldson, J. (2016). Gamification and mobile marketing effectiveness. *Journal of Interactive Marketing*, *34*, 25–36. doi:10.1016/j.intmar.2016.03.001

Holding, T. (2020). *Surdurulebilirlik Raporu*. Retrieved from https://www.tekfen.com.tr/Uploads/pdfs/318202191845964surdurulebilirlik-raporu-2020-web.pdf

HoldingD. (n.d.). Retrieved from https://www.doganholding.com.tr/surdurulebilirlik/cevre-ile-ilgili-projeler/

Hong, J.-P. (2017). Causal Relationship Between ICT R&D Investment and economic growth in Korea. *Technological Forecasting and Social Change*, *116*, 70–75. doi:10.1016/j.techfore.2016.11.005

Hossain, M. S., Rahaman, S., Kor, A.-L., Andersson, K., & Pattison, C. (2017). A Belief Rule Based Expert System for Datacenter PUE Prediction under Uncertainty. *IEEE Transactions on Sustainable Computing*, *2*(2), 140–153. doi:10.1109/TSUSC.2017.2697768

Hotelogix. (2021). Post COVID-19 Hospitality: 8 Proven Digital Marketing Strategies For Smart Hoteliers. *Hospitalitynet*. Retrieved from https://www.hospitalitynet.org/news/4106616.html

Hridoy, M. S., Islam, R. U., Hossain, M. S., & Andersson, K. (2017, December). *A Web Based Belief Rule Based Expert System for Assessing Flood Risk*. ACM. https://dl.acm.org/doi/10.1145/3151759.3151807

Huang, C.-H. (2009). *Three Essays on The Innovation Behaviour of Taiwan'S Manufacturing Firms*. Graduate Institute of Industrial Economics, National Central University.

Hue, M. (2014). A Review of Enterprise Architecture Use in Defence. Defence Systems Integration Technical Advisory. Joint and Operations Analysis Division. Defence Science and Technology Organisation. Australian Government. Department of Defence.

Hu, H. (2017). Analysis of Factors Affecting the Growth of Cross-Strait High-Tech Products Trade-Based on Modified CMS Model. *International Economic and Trade Exploration*, *4*(1), 13–23.

Hu, H., Wen, Y., Chua, T. S., & Li, X. (2014). Toward scalable systems for big data analytics: A technology tutorial. *Access, IEEE*, *2*, 652–687. doi:10.1109/ACCESS.2014.2332453

Humanitarian Crisis. (2013, May). *Complex Humanitarian Emergency Program, Education and Training*. Retrieved January 31, 2022, from https://globalhealthsciences.ucsf.edu/education-training/complex-humanitarian-emergency-program

Huňady, J., & Orviská, M. (2014). The impact of R&D expenditures on innovation performance and economic growth of the country – the empirical evidence. *CBU International Conference Proceedings 2014*, *2*, 119–125. 10.12955/cbup.v2.454

Huňady, J., & Orviská, M. (2014). The Impact of Research and Development Expenditures on Innovation Performance and Economic Growth of the Country – the Empirical Evidence. *CBU International Conference Proceedings*, *2*, 119-125.

Ibrahim, S., Ibrahim, M., & Attia, S. (2014). The impact of climate changes on the thermal performance of a proposed pressurized water reactor: nuclear-power plant. *International Journal of Nuclear Energy*.

IEEE Std 2030 (2011), Guide for Smart Grid Interoperability of Energy Technology and Information Technology Operation with the Electric Power System (EPS), and End-Use Applications and Loads, IEEE Standards Association.

IIA. (2004). *Enterprise Risk Management — Integrated Framework*. The Institute of Auditors.

Im, K. S., Pesaran, M. H., & Shin, Y. (2003). Testing for unit roots in heterogeneous panels. *Journal of Econometrics*, *115*(1), 53–74. doi:10.1016/S0304-4076(03)00092-7

İnan, Ü. S. E. (2019). *İşletmelerde Uygulanan Pazarlama Stratejilerinin Rekabet Gücüne Etkisi*. Eğitim Yayınevi.

Inekwe, J. N. (2015). The contribution of R&D expenditure to economic growth in developing economies. *Social Indicators Research*, *124*(3), 727–745. doi:10.100711205-014-0807-3

Inglesi-Lotz, C. T., & Gupta, R. (2015). Causality Between Research Output and Economic Growth in BRICS. *Quality & Quantity*, *49*(1), 167–176. doi:10.100711135-013-9980-8

International Monetary Fund. (2009). Switzerland: Financial Sector Assessment Program - Detailed Assessment of Observance of Financial Sector Standards and Codes. International Monetary Fund, 5, 170.

International Technology Education Association. (2008). *Advancing excellence in technological literacy:Student assessment, Professional development, and program standards*. Author.

Investing. (2021). https://www.investing.com/search/?q=futures&tab=quotes

İşbank. (2020). Retrieved from https://www.isbank.com.tr/contentmanagement/IsbankSurdurulebilirlik/pdf/2020EntegreRaporu.pdf

Ismail, N. W. (2013). Innovation and High-Tech Trade in Asian Countries. *International Conference on Recent Developments in Asian Trade Policy and Integration*, *1*(1), 1-19.

James, D., Grinter, H., & Grinter, R. (1999). Splitting the Organization and Integrating the Code: Conway's Law Revisited. Bell Laboratories, Lucent Technologies. *Proceedings, International Conference on Software Engineering*, 85-95.

Jarque, C. M., & Bera, A. K. (1980). Efficient tests for normality, homoscedasticity and serial independence of regression residuals. *Economics Letters*, *6*(3), 255–259. doi:10.1016/0165-1765(80)90024-5

Jaumotte, F., & Pain, N. (2005). An Owerview of Public Policies to Support Innovation. *OECD Economics Department Working Papers,* (456). doi:10.1787/18151973

Javornik, A. (2016). 'It's an illusion, but it looks real!' Consumer affective, cognitive and behavioural responses to augmented reality applications. *Journal of Marketing Management, 32*(9-10), 987-1011.

Javornik, A., Rogers, Y., Moutinho, A. M., & Freeman, R. (2016). Revealing the Shopper Experience of Using a "Magic Mirror" Augmented Reality Make-Up Application. *DIS '16: Proceedings of the 2016 ACM Conference on Designing*. 10.1145/2901790.2901881

Jeong, K., Härdle, W. K., & Song, S. (2012). A consistent nonparametric test for causality in quantile. *Econometric Theory*, *28*(4), 861–887. doi:10.1017/S0266466611000685

John, Palaparthy, Sarik, Baghini, & Kasbekar. (2015, March). *Design And Implementation of a Soil Moisture Wireless Sensor Network*. https://ieeexplore.ieee.org/abstract/document/7084901/.

Jones, A. (2001). Theme issue: Developing research in technology education. *Research in Science Education*, *31*(1), 3–14. doi:10.1023/A:1012658211512

Jonkers, H., Band, I., & Quartel, D. (2012a). *ArchiSurance Case Study*. The Open Group.

Jorgenson, D. W. (2001). Information technology and the US economy. *The American Economic Review*, *91*(1), 1–32. doi:10.1257/aer.91.1.1

Josheski, D., & Koteski, C. (2011). The causal relationship between patent growth and growth of GDP with quarterly data in the G7 countries: Cointegration, ARDL and Error Correction Models. *MPRA Paper No.*, *33153*, 1–21. doi:10.2139srn.1921908

Kacprzyk, A., & Doryn, W. (2014). Innovation and economic growth in European Union panel data analysis. *Lodz Economics Working Papers, 3*, 1-27.

Kania, E., & Vorndick, W. (2019). *Weaponizing Biotech: How China's Military Is Preparing for a 'New Domain of Warfare*. Government Media Executive Group LLC.

Kaplan, M. A. (2020). *The Social Political and Environmental Forces Contributing to the Immigration Crisis at the Texas-Mexico Border.* In M. Kearney, A. Knopp, A. N. Zavaleta, & T. D. Knight (Eds.), *Fresh Studies in Rio Grande Valley History* (Vol. 17, pp. 233–254). The U.T.B. Regional History Series, The University of Texas Rio Grande Valley. Retrieved from https://drtonyzavaleta.com/the-social-political-and-environmental-forces-contributing-to-the-immigration-crisis-at-the-texas-mexico-border-fresh/

Kardemir 2020 Sustainability Report. (2020). Retrieved from https://www.kardemir.com/dosyalar/ Sayfalar/1338/05082021/2021080508550667_Sayfalar_1338_05082021.pdf?v=eb7ea1d2_a131_7764_d20d_1028a70f35c0

Kaygusuz, K. (2003). Energy policy and climate change in Turkey. *Energy Conversion and Management, 44*(10), 1671–1688. doi:10.1016/S0196-8904(02)00170-X

Kaymaz, V., & Eren, E. (2018). Modern Zamanlar ve Veblen. *Yildiz Social Science Review, 4*(2), 201-212. Retrieved from https://dergipark.org.tr/tr/pub/yssr/issue/41948/442677

Kazgan, G. (2000). *İktisadi Düşünce veya Politik İktisadın Evrimi* (Vol. 9). Basım, Remzi Kitapevi.

Kenton, W. (2020). Enterprise Risk Management (ERM). *Investopedia*. https://www.investopedia.com/terms/e/enterprise-risk-management.asp

Kezunovic, M. (2017). *Big data applications in smart grids: benefits and challenges*. IEEE Smartgrid.

Khachoo, Q., & Sharma, R. (2017). FDI and Incumbent R&D Behavior: Evidence From Indian Manufacturing Sector. *Journal of Economic Studies (Glasgow, Scotland), 44*(3), 380–399. doi:10.1108/JES-10-2015-0188

Khadam, U., Iqbal, M. M., Alruily, M., Al Ghamdi, M. A., Ramzan, M., & Almotiri, S. H. (2020). Text Data Security And Privacy In the Internet Of Things: Threats, Challenges, And Future Directions. *Wireless Communications and Mobile Computing, 2020*, 1–15. doi:10.1155/2020/7105625

Khajehpour, H., Norouzi, N., & Fani, M. (2021). An exergetic model for the ambient air temperature impacts on the combined power plants and its management using the genetic algorithm. *International Journal of Air-Conditioning and Refrigeration, 29*(1), 2150008. doi:10.1142/S2010132521500085

Khan, F., Rehman, A. U., Arif, M., Aftab, M., & Jadoon, B. K. (2016). A survey of communication technologies for smart grid connectivity. *Electron. Elect. Eng. (ICE Cube)*, 256–261.

Kılıç, J., & Dilber, İ. (2019). Ekonomik Büyüme İle Üretim Faktörleri Arasında Ekonometrik Bir Analiz: Türkiye Örneği (1980-2016) [Econometic Analysis Between Economic Growth And Production Factors: The Case of Turkey (1980-2016)]. *Bilecik Şeyh Edebali Üniversitesi Sosyal Bilimler Dergisi, 4*(1), 149–166. doi:10.33905/bseusbed.475489

Kim, K. (2019). Elasticity of substitution of renewable energy for nuclear power: Evidence from the Korean electricity industry. *Nuclear Engineering and Technology, 51*(6), 1689–1695. doi:10.1016/j.net.2019.04.005

King, W. R., & He, J. (2006). A meta-analysis of the technology acceptance model. *Information & Management, 43*(6), 740–755. doi:10.1016/j.im.2006.05.003

Kinoshita, Y. (2000). *R&D and Technology Spillovers via FDI: Innovation and Absorptive Capacity*. William Davidson Institute Working Paper No.349.

Kirkman, B. L., & Rosen, B. (1999). Beyond Self-Management: Antecedents and Consequences of Team Empowerment. *Academy of Management Journal, 42*, 58–74.

Kirschner, P. A. (2015). Do we need teachers as designers of technology enhanced learning? *Instructional Science, 43*(2), 309–322. doi:10.100711251-015-9346-9

Kirschner, P. A., & de Bruyckere, P. (2017). The myths of the digital native and the multitasker. *Teaching and Teacher Education, 67*, 135–142. doi:10.1016/j.tate.2017.06.001

Kiseleva, I., Karmanov, M., Korotkov, A., Kuznetsov, V., & Gasparian, M. (2018). Risk management in business: Concept, types, evaluation criteria. Revista ESPACIOS. *ISSN, 0798*, 1015.

Kizilkaya, O., Sofuoglu, E., & Ay, A. (2017). Yüksek teknolojili ürün ihracatı üzerinde doğrudan yabancı sermaye yatırımları ve dışa açıklığın etkisi: Gelişmekte olan ülkelerde panel veri analizi. *Doğuş Üniversitesi Dergisi, 18*(1), 63–78. doi:10.31671/dogus.2018.22

Klimova, A., Rondeau, E., Andersson, K., Porras, J., Rybin, A., & Zaslavsky, A. (2016). An international Master's program in green ICT as a contribution to sustainable development. *Journal of Cleaner Production, 135*, 223–239. doi:10.1016/j.jclepro.2016.06.032

Knezek, G., & Christensen, R. (2016). Extending the will, skill, tool model of technology integration: Adding pedagogy as a new model construct. *Journal of Computing in Higher Education, 28*(3), 307–325. doi:10.100712528-016-9120-2

Koch, H., Vögele, S., Hattermann, F., & Huang, S. (2014). Hydro-climatic conditions and thermoelectric electricity generation–Part II: Model application to 17 nuclear power plants in Germany. *Energy, 69*, 700–707. doi:10.1016/j.energy.2014.03.071

Kodinariya, T. M., & Makwana, P. R. (2013). Review on Determining Number of Cluster in K-Means Clustering. *International Journal (Toronto, Ont.), 1*(6), 90–95.

Koirala, K. H., Mishra, A. K., D'Antoni, J. M., & Mehlhorn, J. E. (2015). Energy prices and agricultural commodity prices: Testing correlation using copulas method. *Energy, 81*, 430–436. doi:10.1016/j.energy.2014.12.055

Koopmans, L., Bernaards, C. M., Hildebrandt, V. H., De Vet, H. C. W., & Van der Beek, A. J. (2013). Measuring individual work performance: Identifying and selecting indicators. *Work (Reading, Mass.), 48*(2), 229–238. doi:10.3233/WOR-131659 PMID:23803443

Kotyza, P., Czech, K., Wielechowski, M., Smutka, L., & Procházka, P. (2021). Sugar prices vs. financial market uncertainty in the time of crisis: Does COVID-19 induce structural changes in the relationship? *Agriculture, 11*(2), 93. Advance online publication. doi:10.3390/agriculture11020093

Köylüoğlu, S., & Gümrah, A., & İnan, Ü.S.E. (2020). Analysis of the Effect of Expectation Theory on Consumer Behavior with the Mental Accounting Dimension. *Journal of Euromarketing, 29*(1-2), 56–71.

Kozak, M., & Kim, S. (2019). Revisiting choice sets for overseas pleasure vacations: Comparison of short-haul and long-haul destinations. *Journal of Destination Marketing & Management, 14*, 100388. doi:10.1016/j.jdmm.2019.100388

Kroese, R. (2014). *Enterprise Risk Management Approach*. Bizzdesign. https://bizzdesign.com/blog/enterprise-risk-management-approach/

Küçüksaraç, B., & Sayımer, İ. (2016). Deneyimsel pazarlama aracı olarak artırılmış gerçeklik: Türkiye'deki marka deneyimlerinin etkileri üzerine bir araştırma. İstanbul Üniversitesi İletişim Fakültesi Dergisi, 2, 73-95.

Kurt, S., & Kurt, Ü. (2015). Innovation and labour productivity in BRICS countries: Panel causality and co-integration. *Procedia: Social and Behavioral Sciences, 195*, 1295–1302. doi:10.1016/j.sbspro.2015.06.296

Kutbay, H., & Öz, E. (2017). Ar-Ge Harcamalarının Ekonomik Büyüme Üzerine Etkisi: Türkiye ve Seçilmiş Ülkelerde Vergi Teşvikleri Boyutuyla Ekonometrik Analizi. *Maliye Dergisi, 173*, 331–361.

Laczko, F., & Aghazarm, C. (2009). *Migration, Environment, and Climate Change: Assessing the evidence*. International Organization for Migration. Retrieved from https://publications.iom.int/system/files/pdf/migration_and_environment.pdf

Laney, D. (2001). 3D data management: Controlling data volume, velocity and variety. *META Group Research Note, 6*(70), 1.

Lee, J.-W., & Hong, K. (2010). *Economic Growth in Asia: Determinants and Prospects.* Asian Development Bank Economics Working Paper Series No. 220.

Lee, C., & Coughlin, J. F. (2015). Perspective: older adults' adoption of technology: An integrated approach to identifying determinants and barriers. *Journal of Product Innovation Management, 32*(5), 747–759. doi:10.1111/jpim.12176

Lee, J. W., & Brahmasrene, T. (2014). ICT, CO2 emissions and economic growth: Evidence from a panel of ASEAN. *Global Economic Review, 43*(2), 93–109. doi:10.1080/1226508X.2014.917803

Liao, T. (2014). Augmented or admented reality? The influence of marketing on augmented reality technologies. *Information Communication and Society, 18*(3), 310–326. doi:10.1080/1369118X.2014.989252

Linnerud, K., Mideksa, T. K., & Eskeland, G. S. (2011). The impact of climate change on nuclear power supply. *Energy Journal, 32*(1). Advance online publication. doi:10.5547/ISSN0195-6574-EJ-Vol32-No1-6

Li, S., Deng, H., & Zhang, K. (2019). The İmpact Of Economy On Carbon Emissions: An Empirical Study Based On The Synergistic Effect Of Gender Factors. *International Journal of Environmental Research and Public Health, 16*(19), 2–16. doi:10.3390/ijerph16193723 PMID:31581715

Liu, C. C., Wang, P. C., & Tai, S. J. D. (2016). An analysis of student engagement patterns in language learning facilitated by web 2.0 technologies. *ReCALL, 28*(2), 104–122. doi:10.1017/S095834401600001X

Livingstone, S., & Sefton-Green, J. (2016). *The Class: Living and Learning in the Digital Age.* New York University Press. doi:10.18574/nyu/9781479884575.001.0001

Loasby, B. (2002). *Knowledge, institutions and evolution in economics.* Routledge. doi:10.4324/9780203459096

Lu, W. C. (2018). The impacts of information and communication technology, energy consumption, financial development, and economic growth on carbon dioxide emissions in 12 Asian countries. *Mitigation and Adaptation Strategies for Global Change, 23*(1), 1351–1365. doi:10.100711027-018-9787-y

Mačák, K. (2016). Is the International Law of Cyber Security in Crisis? Law School-University of Exeter. Exeter, United Kingdom. In *Cyber Power. 8th International Conference on Cyber Conflict.* NATO CCD COE Publications.

Maddala, G. S., & Wu, S. (1999). A comparative study of unit root tests with panel data and a new simple test. *Oxford Bulletin of Economics and Statistics, Special Issue, 61*(S1), 631–652. doi:10.1111/1468-0084.0610s1631

Mahmood, N., Wang, Z., & Zhang, B. (2020). The role of nuclear energy in the correction of environmental pollution: Evidence from Pakistan. *Nuclear Engineering and Technology, 52*(6), 1327–1333. doi:10.1016/j.net.2019.11.027

Mahmoud Daneshman, K. J. L. (2017). *Big challenges for big data in the smart grid era.* Retrieved from https://www.ecnmag.com/blog/2017/ 04/big-challenges-big-data-smart-grid-era

Majid, N. A. A. (2014). Integration of web 2.0 tools in learning a programming course. *The Turkish Online Journal of Educational Technology, 13*(4), 88–94.

Makarchenko, M., Nerkararian, S., & Shmeleva, S. (2016). How Traditional Banks Should Work in Smart City. *Communications in Computer and Information Science*. 10.1007/978-3-319-49700-6_13

Malavade & Akulwar. (2016). *Role of IoT in Agriculture*. https://www.iosrjournals.org/iosr-jce/papers/Conf.16051/Volume-1/

Mani, S. (2004). Exports of high technology products from developing countries: Are the figures real or are they statistical artefacts? *Innovation, Learning, and Technological Dynamism of Developing Countries*, *1*(1), 12–47.

Markides, C. (2011, March). Crossing the Chasm: How to Convert Relevant Research Into Managerially Useful Research. *The Journal of Applied Behavioral Science*, *47*(1), 121–134. doi:10.1177/0021886310388162

Markides, C. (2015). Research on Business Models: Challenges and Opportunities. *Advances in Strategic Management*, *33*, 133–147. doi:10.1108/S0742-332220150000033004

Maurer, P. (2017). *It's not just N.G.O.s tackling humanitarian crises: Banks have a role to*. World Economic Forum. Retrieved from https://www.weforum.org/agenda/2017/05/humanitarian-impact-bonds-icrc-red-cross/

Maxwell, P. (2020). Artificial intelligence is the future of warfare (just not in the way you think). Modern War Institute.

Ma, Z., Xu, R., & Dong, X. (2015). World oil prices and agricultural commodity prices: The evidence from China. *Agricultural Economics*, *61*(12), 564–576. doi:10.17221/6/2015-AGRICECON

McFarlane, I. (2016). Agricultural commodity prices and oil prices: Mutual causation. *Outlook on Agriculture*, *45*(2), 87–93. doi:10.1177/0030727016649809

Mcmahon, S., Tintori, G., Perez Fernandez, M., Alessandrini, A., Goujon, A., Ghio, D., Petroliagkis, T., Conte, A., Minora, U., & Kalantaryan, S. (2021). Population exposure and migrations linked to climate change in Africa. EUR 30881 EN, Publications Office of the European Union. doi:,JRC126594 doi:10.2760/4151

Medcof, J. W., & Lee, T. (2017). The effects of the chief technology officer and firm and industry R&D intensity on organizational performance: CTO and firm and industry R&D on organizational performance. *R & D Management*, *47*(5), 767–781. doi:10.1111/radm.12275

Mees, W. (2017). *Security by Design in an Enterprise Architecture Framework*. NATO.

Mehran, M., & Reza, M. A. (2011). Comparative Investigation of the Relation of R&D Expenditures to Economic Growth in a Group of the Less Developed Countries and OECD Countries. *Journal of Social and Development Sciences*, *2*(4), 188–195. doi:10.22610/jsds.v2i4.668

Mehrara, M., Seijani, S., & Karsalari, A. R. (2017). Determinants of high-tech export in developing countries based on bayesian model averaging. *Zbornik Radova Ekonomskog Fakulteta u Rijeci*, *35*(1), 199–215.

Menteşe, S. (2017). Çevresel Sürdürülebilirlik Açısından Toprak, Su Ve Hava Kirliliği: Teorik Bir İnceleme. *Journal of International Social Research*, *10*(53), 381–389. doi:10.17719/jisr.20175334127

Mercan, M., Gocer, I., Bulut, S., & Dam, M. (2013). The effect of openness on economic growth for BRIC-T countries: Panel data analysis. *Eurasian Journal of Business and Economics, 6*(11), 1-14.

Mercan, B., Göktaş, D., & Gömleksiz, M. (2011). AR-GE Faaliyetleri ve Girişimcilerin İnovasyon Üzerindeki Etkileri: Patent Verileri Üzerinde Bir Uygulama. *PARADOKS Ekonomi Sosyoloji ve Politika Dergisi*, *7*(2), 27–44.

MiningK. (n.d.). *Çevre Politikasi*. Retrieved from https://www.kozametal.com.tr/sorumluluklarimiz/cevre-politikasi /

Ministry of Industry and Technology. (2019). *İllerin ve Bölgelerin Sosyo-Ekonomik Gelişmişlik Sıralaması Araştırması Sege-2017.* https://www.sanayi.gov.tr/merkez-birimi/b94224510b7b/sege/2017-il/date:30.04.2021

Ministry of Industry and Technology. (2021). *Yatırım Teşvik Uygulamaları.* https://www.sanayi.gov.tr/destek-ve-tesvikler/yatirim-tesvik-sistemleri/md0103011615/

Ministry of Industry and Technology. (2021). *Yatırım Teşvik Verisi (01.01.2001-31.03.2021).* https://sanayi.gov.tr/istatistikler/yatirim-istatistikleri/mi1304021615/

Ministry of Industry and Technology. (2021). *Yatırımlarda Devlet Yardımları Hakkında Karar.* https://www.sanayi.gov.tr/mevzuat/diger/mc0403018201/date:30.04.2021

Miori, V., & Russo, D. (2014). Domotic Evolution towards the IoT. *28th International Conference on Advanced Information Networking and Applications Workshops.* 10.1109/WAINA.2014.128

MOD. (2020). *MOD Science and Technology Strategy 2020.* Government UK.

Mondal & Rehena. (2019). IoT Based Intelligent Agriculture Field Monitoring System. *Second International Conference on Advanced Computational and Communication Paradigms (ICACCP-2019).* https://zdocs.pub/doc/contoh-artikel-d6w2xzyw9w68

Montobbio, F., & Rampa, F. (2005). The impact of technology and structural change on export performance in nine developing countries. *World Development, 33*(4), 527–547. doi:10.1016/j.worlddev.2005.01.001

Moraes, J., & Luna, I. (2018). *Dynamic and determinants of high technology exports in Latin America and the Caribbean: a network and a panel data analysis.* III Encontro Nacional de Economia Industrial e Inovação. doi:10.5151/enei2018-26

Morgan, F., Boudreaux, B., Lohn, A., Ashby, M., Curriden, Ch., Klima, K., & Grossman, D. (2020). *Military Applications of Artificial Intelligence-Ethical Concerns in an Uncertain World.* RAND Corporation.

Mosca, F., & Civera, C. (2017). The Evolution of CSR: An Integrated Approach, Symphonya. *Emerging Issues in Management,* (1), 16–35.

Mouloudj, K., Bouarar, A. C., & Fechit, H. (2020). The impact of COVID-19 pandemic on food security. *Les Cahiers du CREAD, 36*(3), 159–184.

Muller, T. (2021). *Why the Corona Virus Crisis Is a Unique and Once in a Lifetime Opportunity for Destinations and the Tourism Industry.* https://voyagesafriq.com/2020/03/23/why-the-corona-virus-crisis-is-a-unique-and-once-in-a-lifetime-opportunity-for-destinations-and-the-tourism-industry/

Nafi, N., Ahmed, S. K., Gregory, M. A., & Datta, M. (2016). A survey of smart grid architectures, applications, benefits and standardization. *Journal of Network and Computer Applications, 76,* 23–36. doi:10.1016/j.jnca.2016.10.003

Nair, M., Pradhan, R. P., & Arvin, M. B. (2020). Endogenous dynamics between R&D, ICT and economic growth: Empirical evidence from the OECD countries. *Technology in Society, 62,* 101315. doi:10.1016/j.techsoc.2020.101315

Naresh & Munaswamy. (2019, January). Smart Agriculture System using IoT Technology. *International Journal of Recent Technology and Engineering, 7*(5). https://www.ijrte.org/wp-content/uploads/papers/v7i5/E1987017519.pdf

National Security. (2021, September). *Thoughtco.com.* Retrieved January 31, 2022, from https://www.thoughtco.com/national-security-definition-and-examples-5197450

Nazlioglu, S. (2011). World oil and agricultural commodity prices: Evidence from nonlinear causality. *Energy Policy, 39*(5), 2935–2943. doi:10.1016/j.enpol.2011.03.001

Nazlioglu, S., Gormus, N. A., & Soytas, U. (2016). Oil prices and real estate investment trusts (REITs): Gradual-shift causality and volatility transmission analysis. *Energy Economics*, *60*, 168–175. doi:10.1016/j.eneco.2016.09.009

Nazlioglu, S., & Soytas, U. (2011). World oil prices and agricultural commodity prices: Evidence from an emerging market. *Energy Economics*, *33*(3), 488–496. doi:10.1016/j.eneco.2010.11.012

Nazlioglu, S., & Soytas, U. (2012). Oil price, agricultural commodity prices, and the dollar: A panel cointegration and causality analysis. *Energy Economics*, *34*(4), 1098–1104. doi:10.1016/j.eneco.2011.09.008

Ng, C. C. & Ramasamy, C. (2018). Augmented Reality Marketing in Malaysia- Future Scenarios. *Social Sciences*, *7*(11).

Nguyen, T. T., Pham, T. A. T., & Tram, H. T. X. (2020). Role of information and communication technologies and innovation in driving carbon emissions and economic growth in selected G-20 countries. *Journal of Environmental Management*, *1*(261), 110162. doi:10.1016/j.jenvman.2020.110162 PMID:32148259

Norouzi, N. (2020). 4E Analysis and design of a combined cycle with a geothermal condensing system in Iranian Moghan diesel power Plant. *International Journal of Air-Conditioning and Refrigeration*, *28*(03), 2050022. doi:10.1142/S2010132520500224

Norouzi, N. (2021). The Pahlev Reliability Index: A measurement for the resilience of power generation technologies versus climate change. *Nuclear Engineering and Technology*, *53*(5), 1658–1663. doi:10.1016/j.net.2020.10.013

Norouzi, N., & Fani, M. (2020). Exergetic design and analysis of an SMR reactor nuclear tetrageneration (combined water, heat, power, and chemicals generation) with designed PCM energy storage and a CO2 gas turbine inner cycle. *Nuclear Engineering and Technology*.

NSCAI. (2020). *Final Report National Security Commission on Artificial Intelligence*. NSC.

Ntuli, H., Inglesi-Lotz, R., Chang, T., & Pouris, A. (2015). A Does Research Output Cause Economic Growth or Vice Versa? Evidence from 34 OECD Countries. *Journal of the Association for Information Science and Technology*, *66*(8), 1709–1716. doi:10.1002/asi.23285

Oláh, J., Aburumman, N., Popp, J., Khan, M. A., Haddad, H., & Kitukutha, N. (2020). Impact of Industry 4.0 on environmental sustainability. *Sustainability*, *12*(11), 4674. doi:10.3390u12114674

Olaoye, I. J., Ayinde, O. E., Ajewole, O. O., & Adebisi, L. O. (2021). The role of R&D (R&D) expenditure and governance on economic growth in selected African countries. *African Journal of Science, Technology, Innovation and Development*, *13*(6), 663–670. doi:10.1080/20421338.2020.1799300

Önce, S., Onay, A., & Yeşilçelebi, G. (2015). Kurumsal Sürdürülebilirlik Raporlaması ve Türkiye'deki Durum. *Journal of Economics, Finance and Accounting*, *2*(2), 230-252.

Oppenheimer, T. (2003). *The Flickering Mind: The False Promise of Technology in the Classroom and How Learning Can Be Saved*. Random House.

Otuoze, A. O., Mustafa, M. W., & Lariks, R. M. (2018). Smart grids security challenges: Classification by sources of threats. *Journal of Electrical Systems and Information Technology*, *5*(3), 468–483. doi:10.1016/j.jesit.2018.01.001

Our World in Data. (2021). *Country-by-country data on confirmed cases*. https://ourworldindata.org/covid-cases

Özdamar, K. (2018). *Paket Programlar ile İstatistiksel Veri Analizi Cilt 2*. Nisan Kitabevi.

Pala, A. (2019). Innovation and economic growth in developing countries: Empirical implication of swamy's random coefficient model (RCM). *Procedia Computer Science*, *158*, 1122–1130. doi:10.1016/j.procs.2019.09.252

Panagea, I. S., Tsanis, I. K., & Koutroulis, A. G. (2017). Climate change impact on photovoltaic energy output: the case of Greece. In *Climate Change and the Future of Sustainability* (pp. 85–106). Apple Academic Press.

Pandey, R. K., & Misra, M. (2016, December). Cyber security threats—smart grid infrastructure. In *2016 National Power Systems Conference (NPSC)* (pp. 1-6). IEEE.

Park, Y., Meng, F., & Baloch, M. A. (2018). The effect of ICT, financial development, growth, and trade openness on CO 2 emissions: An empirical analysis. *Environmental Science and Pollution Research International*, *25*(30), 30708–30719. doi:10.100711356-018-3108-6 PMID:30178410

Pathaka, Uddina, Abedina, Anderssonb, Mustafac, & Shahad. (2019, September 13). *IoT Based Smart System To Support Agricultural Parameters: A Case Study*. ScienceDirect. https://www.sciencedirect.com/science/article/pii/S1877050919310087

Patt, A., Pfenninger, S., & Lilliestam, J. (2013). Vulnerability of solar energy infrastructure and output to climate change. *Climatic Change*, *121*(1), 93–102. doi:10.100710584-013-0887-0

Pece, M. A., Ecaterina, O. S. O., & Salisteanu, F. (2015). Innovation and Economic Growth: An Empirical Analysis for CEE Countries. *Procedia Economics and Finance*, *26*, 461–467. doi:10.1016/S2212-5671(15)00874-6

Pérez, C. (2009). *Technological revolutions and techno-economic paradigms*. TOC (No. 20). TUT Working Paper.

Pesaran, M. H. (2004). *General diagnostic tests for cross section dependence in panels* (CESifo Working Paper No. 1229). Academic Press.

Pesaran, M. H. (2004). General Diagnostic Tests for Cross Section Dependence in Panels. *CESifo Working Paper Series*, 1229.

Pesaran, M. H. (2004). *General diagnostic tests for cross section dependence in panels*. CESifo Working Papers 1229. Retrieved from https://www.cesifo.org/en/publikationen/2004/working-paper/general-diagnostic-tests-cross-section-dependence-panels doi:10.17863/CAM.5113

Pesaran, M. H. (2004). General diagnostic tests for cross section dependence in panels. *CESifo Working Papers, 1233*, 255–260.

Pesaran, M. H. (2007). A simple panel unit root test in the presence of cross-section dependence. *Journal of Applied Econometrics*, *22*(2), 265–312. doi:10.1002/jae.951

Pesaran, M. H., Ullah, A., & Yamagata, T. (2008). A bias-adjusted LM test of error cross-section independence. *The Econometrics Journal*, *11*(1), 105–127. doi:10.1111/j.1368-423X.2007.00227.x

Pesaran, M. H., & Yamagata, T. (2008). Testing slope homogeneity in large panels. *Journal of Econometrics*, *142*(1), 50–93. doi:10.1016/j.jeconom.2007.05.010

Pesaran, M., Shin, Y., & Smith, R. P. (1999). Pooled Mean Group Estimation of Dynamic Heterogeneous Panels. *Journal of the American Statistical Association*, *94*(446), 621–634. doi:10.1080/01621459.1999.10474156

Peterson, S. (2011). *Why it Worked: Critical Success Factors of a Financial Reform Project in Africa*. Faculty Research Working Paper Series. Harvard Kennedy School.

Petkim. (n.d.). *Çevre*. Retrieved from https://www.petkim.com.tr/Sayfa/1/12/KURUMSAL-SURDURULEBILIRLIK-CEVRE.aspx

Petrariu, I. R., Bumbac, R., & Ciobanu, R. (2013). Innovation: A path to competitiveness and economic growth. The case of CEE countries. *Theoretical and Applied Economics*, *20*(3), 15–26.

Petruzzelli, M. A., Ardito, L., & Savino, T. (2018). Maturity of knowledge inputs and innovation value: The moderating effect of firm age and size. *Journal of Business Research*, *86*, 190–201. doi:10.1016/j.jbusres.2018.02.009

Phillips, P. C., Shi, S., & Yu, J. (2015). Testing for multiple bubbles: Historical episodes of exuberance and collapse in the S&P 500. *International Economic Review*, *56*(4), 1043–1078. doi:10.1111/iere.12132

Plotkina, D., Dinsmore, J., & Racat, M. (2021). Improving service brand personality with augmented reality marketing. *Journal of Services Marketing*. https://www.emerald.com/insight/content/doi/10.1108/JSM-12-2020-0519/full/html#abstract

Podesta, J. (2019). *The Climate Crisis Migration and Refugees*. Policy brief commissioned for the 16th annual Brookings Blum Roundtable 2020 and beyond: Maintaining a bipartisan narrative on U.S. global development. Retrieved from https://www.brookings.edu/research/the-climate-crisis-migration-and-refugees/

Pradhan, R. P., Arvin, M. B., Bahmani, S., & Bennett, S. E. (2017). The ınnovation-growth link in OECD countries: Could other macroeconomic variables matter? *Technology in Society*, *51*, 113–123. doi:10.1016/j.techsoc.2017.08.003

Pradhan, R. P., Arvin, M. B., Hall, J. H., & Nair, M. (2016). Innovation, financial development and economic growth in eurozone countries. *Applied Economics Letters*, *23*(16), 11411144. doi:10.1080/13504851.2016.1139668

Pratap, K., & Predovich, B. (2020). *Magic Quadrant for IT Risk Management*. Gartner Inc.

Quang Phu, T., & Thi Yen Thao, H. (2017). Enterprise Risk Management Implementation: The Critical Success Factors For Vietnamese Construction Companies. *Journal of Multidisciplinary Engineering Science Studies*.

Radas, S., Anić, I. D., Tafro, A., & Wagner, V. (2015). The Effects of Public Support Schemes on Small And Medium Enterprises. *Technovation*, *38*, 15–30. doi:10.1016/j.technovation.2014.08.002

Radoglou-Grammatikis, P. I., & Sarigiannidis, P. G. (2019). Securing the smart grid: A comprehensive compilation of intrusion detection and prevention systems. *IEEE Access: Practical Innovations, Open Solutions*, *7*, 46595–46620. doi:10.1109/ACCESS.2019.2909807

Raghutla, C. (2020). The effect of trade openness on economic growth: Some empirical evidence from emerging market economies. *Journal of Public Affairs*, *20*(3), e2081.

Raheem, I. D., Tiwari, A. K., & Balsalobre-Lorente, D. (2020). The role of ICT and financial development in CO 2 emissions and economic growth. *Environmental Science and Pollution Research International*, *27*(2), 1912–1922. doi:10.100711356-019-06590-0 PMID:31760620

Ramada, P. (2013). How much did allegedly rigged interest rate (Libor) cost? Academic Press.

Ramos-Villagrasa, P. J., Barrada, J. R., Fernández-del-Río, E., & Koopmans, L. (2019). Assessing Job Performance Using Brief Self-report Scales: The Case of the Individual Work Performance Questionnaire. *Journal of Work and Organizational Psychology*, *35*(3), 195–205. doi:10.5093/jwop2019a21

Rauschnabel, P. A., Felix, R., & Hinsch, C. (2019). Augmented reality marketing: How mobile AR-apps can improve brands through inspiration. *Journal of Retailing and Consumer Services*, *49*, 43–53. doi:10.1016/j.jretconser.2019.03.004

Ravanetti, A. (2016). *Switzerland Bank on Fintech with Lighter Regulations*. Crowd Valley. https://news.crowdvalley.com/news/switzerland-bank-on-fintech-with-lighter-regulations

Rawal, V., & Verma, A. (2020). Agricultural Supply Chains during the COVID-19 Lockdown. *SSER Monograph*, *20*(1), 1–26.

Ray, P. P. (2017). Internet of things for smart agriculture: Technologies, practices and future direction. *Journal of Ambient Intelligence and Smart Environments*, *9*(4), 395–420. doi:10.3233/AIS-170440

Reboredo, J. C. (2012). Do food and oil prices co-move? *Energy Policy*, *49*, 456–467. doi:10.1016/j.enpol.2012.06.035

Refaat, S. S., Abu-Rub, H., & Mohamed, A. (2016, December). Big data, better energy management and control decisions for distribution systems in smart grid. In *2016 IEEE International Conference on Big Data (Big Data)* (pp. 3115-3120). IEEE.

Rejeb, A., Rejeb, K., & Treibimaier, H. (2021). How augmented reality impacts retail marketing: A state-of-the-art review from a consumer perspective. *Journal of Strategic Marketing*, 1–31. doi:10.1080/0965254X.2021.1972439

ReportA. I. (2020). Retrieved from https://www.akbankinvestorrelations.com/tr/images/pdf/2020-akbank-entegre-raporu.pdf

Rezitis, A. N. (2015). The relationship between agricultural commodity prices, crude oil prices and US dollar exchange rates: A panel VAR approach and causality analysis. *International Review of Applied Economics*, *29*(3), 403–434. doi:10.1080/02692171.2014.1001325

Rigaud, K. K., de Sherbinin, A., Jones, B., Bergmann, J., Clement, V., Ober, K., Schewe, J., Adamo, S., McCusker, B., Heuser, S., & Midgley, A. (2018). *Groundswell: Preparing for Internal Climate Migration.* World Bank. Retrieved from https://openknowledge.worldbank.org/handle/10986/29461

Ritchie, B. W., & Jiang, Y. (2019). A review of research on tourism risk, crisis and disaster management: Launching the Annals of Tourism Research curated collection on tourism risk, crisis and disaster management. *Annals of Tourism Research, Elsevier*, *79*(C), 102812. doi:10.1016/j.annals.2019.102812

Rockman, I. F. (2004). *Integrating Information Literacy into the Higher Education Curriculum: Practical Models for Transformation*. Jossey-Bass.

Romer, P. (1994). The origins of endogenous growth. *The Journal of Economic Perspectives*, *1*(1), 3–22. doi:10.1257/jep.8.1.3

Rutherford, M. (2001). Association Institutional Economics: Then and Now. *The Journal of Economic Perspectives*, *15*(3), 173-194.

Rutherford, M. (1998). Veblen's Evolutionary Programme: A Promise Unfulfilled. *Cambridge Journal of Economics*, *22*(4), 463–477. doi:10.1093/oxfordjournals.cje.a013729

Sadaf, A., Newby, T. J., & Ertmer, P. A. (2012). Exploring factors that predict preservice teachers' intentions to use web 2.0 technologies using decomposed theory of planned behavior. *Journal of Research on Technology in Education*, *45*(2), 171–195. doi:10.1080/15391523.2012.10782602

Sağlam, Y., Egelí, H. A., & Egeli, P. (2017). Gelişmiş ve gelişmekte olan ülkelerde Ar&Ge harcamaları ve ekonomik büyüme arasındaki ilişki: Panel veri analizi. *Sosyoekonomi*, *25*(1), 149–165.

Şahbaz, A., & Tanyeri, M. (2018). Küçük ve Orta Büyüklükteki İşletmelerde İnovasyona Yönelik Tutumlar ve İnovasyon Engelleri: Çanakkale İlinde Kobi'ler Üzerine Bir Araştırma. *ÇOMÜ Uluslararası Sosyal Bilimler Dergisi*, *3*(2), 233-263. doi:10.31454/usb.476867

Sailor, D. J., Hu, T., Li, X., & Rosen, J. N. (2000). A neural network approach to local downscaling of GCM output for assessing wind power implications of climate change. *Renewable Energy*, *19*(3), 359–378. doi:10.1016/S0960-1481(99)00056-7

Saiz-Rubio, V., & Rovira-Más, F. (2020, February 3). From Smart Farming Towards Agriculture 5.0: A Review On Crop Data Management. *MDPI*. https://www.mdpi.com/2073-4395/10/2/207/

Salahuddin, M., Alam, K., & Ozturk, I. (2016). The effects of Internet usage and economic growth on CO2 emissions in OECD countries: A panel investigation. *Renewable & Sustainable Energy Reviews*, *62*, 1226–1235. doi:10.1016/j.rser.2016.04.018

Saleem, A., & Sial, M. H. (2015). Exports-Growth Nexus in Pakistan Cointegration and Causality Analysis. *Pakistan Economic and Social Review*, *53*(1), 17–46.

Samimi, A. J., & Alerasoul, S. M. (2009). R&D and economic growth: New Evidence from some developing countries. *Australian Journal of Basic and Applied Sciences*, *3*(4), 3464–3469.

Samimi, A. J., & Alerasoul, S. M. (2009). R&D and Economic Growth: New Evidence from Some Developing Countries. *Australian Journal of Basic and Applied Sciences*, *3*(4), 3464–3469.

Sandu, S., & Ciocanel, N. (2014). Impact of R&D and innovation on high-tech export. *Procedia Economics and Finance*, *15*(1), 80–90. doi:10.1016/S2212-5671(14)00450-X

Saputro, N., Akkaya, K., & Uludag, S. (2012). A survey of routing protocols for smart grid communications. *Computer Networks*, *56*(11), 2741–2771. doi:10.1016/j.comnet.2012.03.027

Sarabpreet, S., & Rajesh, K. (2012). Ambient Air Temperature Effect on Power Plant Performance. *International Journal of Engineering Science and Technology*, *4*(8).

Sarıdoğan, H. Ö. (2021). Vergi Teşviklerinin İnovasyon Üzerindeki Etkisinin Panel Sur Yöntemi ile Analizi. *Abant Sosyal Bilimler Dergisi*, *21*(2), 221–241. doi:10.11616/basbed.vi.857270

Sart, G. (2020). Bireysel Girişimcilik Eğilimi Ölçeğinin Geliştirilmesi: Geçerlik ve Güvenirlik Çalışması. *International Journal of Applied Economic and Finance Studies*, *1*(5), 58–72.

Sart, G., Sezgin, F. H., & Demir, N. (2018). Mobbingin Mesleki Tükenmişlik Algısı Üzerine Etkileri: Kadın Akademisyenler Örneği. *Beykoz Akademi Dergisi*, *6*(1), 118–135. doi:10.14514/BYK.m.21478082.2018.6/1.117-135

Sasa. (n.d.). Retrieved from https://www.sasa.com.tr/kurumsal/surdurulebilirlik/cevre-yonetimi

Satrovic, E. (2018). Economic output and high-technology export: Panel causality analysis. *International Journal of Economic Studies*, *4*(3), 55–63.

Scharre, P., & Riikonen, A. (2020). Defense Technology Strategy. Center for a New American Security.

Scherer, R., Tondeur, J., Siddiq, F., & Baran, E. (2018). The importance of attitudes toward technology for pre-service teachers' technological, pedagogical, and content knowledge: Comparing structural equation modeling approaches. *Computers in Human Behavior*, *80*, 67–80. doi:10.1016/j.chb.2017.11.003

Schimmelp Fennig, D. (2017, November). *Farm Profits and Adoption of Precision Agriculture*. https://www.ers.usda.gov/webdocs/publications/80326/

Schmidt, A., & Kløverpris, N. H. (2009). *Environmental impacts from digital solutions as an alternative to conventional paper-based solutions final report*. FORCE Technology, Applied Environmental Assessment. http://seeds4green.net/sites/default/files/e-Boks_LCA.pdf

Schmiedbaur, M., & Lauwerier, S. (2020). Rebuilding trust in air-traveling in times of a global pandemic. *Star*. Retrieved from: https://star.global/posts/air-travel-experience

Scholz, J., & Duffy, K. (2018). We are at home: How augmented reality reshapes mobile marketing and consumer-brand relationships. *Journal of Retailing and Consumer Services, 44*, 11–23. doi:10.1016/j.jretconser.2018.05.004

Scholz, J., & Smith, A. N. (2015). Augmented reality: Designing immersive experiences that maximize consumer engagement. *Business Horizons, 59*(2), 149–161. doi:10.1016/j.bushor.2015.10.003

Schumpeter, J. A. (1947). The creative response in economic history. *The Journal of Economic History, 7*(2), 149–159. doi:10.1017/S0022050700054279

ScienceDirect. (2003, August 28). *A real-time grading method of apples based on features extracted from defects*. https://www.sciencedirect.com/science/article/abs/pii/S0260877403001894?via%3Dihub

Scott, N., Laws, E., & Prideaux, B. (2008). Tourism crises and marketing recovery strategies. *Journal of Travel & Tourism Marketing, 23*(2–4), 1–13. doi:10.1300/J073v23n02_01

Seçilmiş, N., & Konu, A. (2019). OECD Ülkelerinde Ar-Ge Teşvikleri ve İnovasyon İlişkisi Üzerine Ampirik Bir İnceleme. *Kahramanmaraş Sütçü İmam Üniversitesi Sosyal Bilimler Dergisi, 16*(2), 686–702. doi:10.33437/ksusbd.533175

Selenko, E., Mäkikangas, A., Mauno, S., & Kinnunen, U. (2013). How does job insecurity relate to self-reported job performance? Analysing curvilinear associations in a longitudinal sample. *Journal of Occupational and Organizational Psychology, 86*(4), 522–542. doi:10.1111/joop.12020

Şenalp, M. G. (2007). Dünden Bugüne Kurumsal İktisat. In *Kurumsal İktisat içinde* (pp. 45–92). İmge Kitabevi.

Şenocak, B., & Mohan, Y. B. (2018). İşletmelerde Çevresel Sürdürülebilirlik Bilinci Ve Yeşil İşletmecilik Uygulamalari İle İşletme Başarisi Arasindaki İlişki. *Süleyman Demirel Üniversitesi İktisadi ve İdari Bilimler Fakültesi Dergisi, 23*(1), 161–183.

Sertić, M. B., Vučković, V., & Perić, B. Š. (2015). Determinants of manufacturing industry exports in European Union Member States: A panel data analysis. *Economic Research-Ekonomska Istraživanja, 28*(1), 384–397. doi:10.1080/1331677X.2015.1043781

Seyoum, B. (2005). Determinants of levels of high technology exports an empirical investigation. *Journal of Competitiveness Studies, 13*(1), 64–79.

Sezgin, F. H. (2016). Bayesci Faktör Analizi ve Maslach Tükenmişlik Envanteri Uygulaması. *International Conference on Scientific Cooperation for the Future in the Social Sciences (USAK),* 1283-1296.

Shahin, M. A., Tollner, E. W., McClendon, R. W., & Arabnia, H. R. (2002). *Apple Classification Based On Surface Bruises Using Image Processing And Neural Networks - PubAg*. https://pubag.nal.usda.gov/catalog/815360

Sharma, R., Mahela, O. P., & Agarwal, S. (2018) Detection of power system faults in distribution system using stockwell transform. *Proceedings of the IEEE International Students' Conference on Electrical, Electronics and Computer Science (SCEECS).*

Shawkat Ali, A. B. M., & Azad, S. (2013). Demand forecasting in smart grid. *Green Energy and Technology, 132*, 135–150.

Shayanewako, V. B. (2018). The relationship between trade openness and economic growth: The case of BRICS countries. *Journal of Global Economics, 6*(2), 6–10. doi:10.4172/2375-4389.1000289

Shen, X., Lin, B., & Wu, W. (2019). R&D Efforts, Total Factor Productivity, and the Energy Intensity in China. *Emerging Markets Finance & Trade, 55*(11), 2566–2588. doi:10.1080/1540496X.2019.1579709

Shruthi, M. S., & Ramani, D. (2021). Statistical analysis of impact of COVID 19 on India commodity markets. *Materials Today: Proceedings, 37*, 2306–2311. doi:10.1016/j.matpr.2020.07.729 PMID:32837924

Shumpeter, J. (1911). *The Theory of Economic Development: An Inquiry into Profits*. Capital, Credit, Interest, and the Business Cycle.

Shumpeter, J. (1942). *Capitalism, socialism and democracy*.

Siche, R. (2020). What is the impact of COVID-19 disease on agriculture? *Scientia Agropecuaria, 11*(1), 3–6. doi:10.17268ci.agropecu.2020.01.00

Sigler, T. H., & Pearson, C. M. (2000). Creating an empowering culture: Examining the relationship between organizational culture and perceptions of empowerment. *Journal of Quality Management, 5*(1), 27–52. doi:10.1016/S1084-8568(00)00011-0

Silaghi, M. I. P., Alexa, D., Jude, C., & Litan, C. (2014). Do business and public sector R&D expenditures contribute to economic growth in Central and Eastern European Countries? A dynamic panel estimation. *Economic Modelling, 36*, 108–119. doi:10.1016/j.econmod.2013.08.035

Şimşek, M., & Yazıcı, R. (2004). İhracat Teşviklerinin Etkinliğini Ölçmeye Yönelik Bir Analiz: Bilecik Ve Eskişehir Örneği. *Osmangazi Üniversitesi Sosyal Bilimler Dergisi, 5*(2), 121–140.

Skousen, M. (2009). *İktisadi Düşünce Tarihi: Modern İktisadın İnşası. Adres Yayınları, 6.*

Smashapp. (2011). *Starbucks Cup Magic*. YouTube. https://www.youtube.com/watch?v=n7dEshkTri4

Soft Expert. (2018). *Enterprise Asset Management*. https://www.softexpert.com/solucao/enterprise-asset-management-eam/

Solomon, J., & Maroun, W. (2012). *Integrated Reporting: The Influence of King III on Social, Ethical and Environmental Reporting*. The Association of Chartered Certified Accountants (ACCA).

Solow, R. M. (1956). A contribution to the theory of economic growth. *The Quarterly Journal of Economics, 70*(1), 65–94. doi:10.2307/1884513

SOLVOTEK. (2017). *Selimiye Camii, Edirne 3D lazer tarama (nokta bulutu animasyonu).* YouTube. Retrieved from https://www.youtube.com/watch?v=b9OltaxADgU

Song, X., & Taamouti, A. (2020). Measuring Granger Causality in Quantiles. *Journal of Business & Economic Statistics, 39*(4), 1–42. doi:10.1080/07350015.2020.1739531

Srivastava, Sharma, Jaiswal, & Raj. (2020, July). A Research Paper On Smart Agriculture Using IoT. *International Research Journal of Engineering and Technology, 7*(7). https://www.irjet.net/archives/V7/i7/IRJET-V7I7479.pdf

Stergiou, C., & Siganos, D. (2015). *Neural Networks*. https://www.doc.ic.ac.uk/~nd/surprise_96/journal/vol4/cs11/report.html

Stewart, M. G. (2020). *Climate Change and National Security: Balancing the Costs and Benefits*. CATO Institute. Retrieved from https://www.cato.org/publications/climate-change-national-security-balancing-costs-benefits

Stock, J. H., & Watson, M. W. (1996). Evidence on structural instability in macroeconomic time series relations. *Journal of Business & Economic Statistics, 14*(1), 11–30.

Streltsov, E. S., Rozhin, A. A., Vosiev, S. S., & Kosnikov, S. N. (2021). The economic potential of the brics countries as a challenge to modern world realities. *Propósitos y Representaciones, 9*(SPE3), 1143.

STS. (2018). *Enterprise asset management*. STS. http://www.stsolutions-global.com/enterprise-asset-management.html

Stupples, B., Sazonov, A., & Woolley, S. (2019). UBS Whistle-Blower Hunts Trillions Hidden in Treasure Isles. Bloomberg-Economics. *Bloomberg*. Reviewed in November 2019 https://www.bloomberg.com/news/articles/2019-07-26/ubs-whistle-blower-hunts-trillions-hidden-in-treasure-islands

Stupples, B., Sazonov, A., & Woolley, S. (2019). UBS Whistle-Blower Hunts Trillions Hidden in Treasure Isles. Bloomberg-Economics. *Bloomberg*. Reviewed in November 2019 https://www.bloomberg.com/news/chapters/2019-07-26/ubs-whistle-blower-hunts-trillions-hidden-in-treasure-islands

Su, C. W., Wang, X. Q., Tao, R., & Oana-Ramona, L. (2019). Do oil prices drive agricultural commodity prices? Further evidence in a global bio-energy context. *Energy*, *172*, 691–701. doi:10.1016/j.energy.2019.02.028

Süklüm, N. (2020). Kurumsal Sosyal Sorumluluk, Yeşil Muhasebe Ve Yeşil Denetim İlişkisine Kavramsal Bir Bakış. *Bilecik Şeyh Edebali Üniversitesi Sosyal Bilimler Dergisi, 100*, 151-163. doi:10.33905/bseusbed.752576

Sung, E. C. (2021). The effects of augmented reality mobile app advertising: Viral marketing via shared social experience. *Journal of Business Research*, *122*, 75–87. doi:10.1016/j.jbusres.2020.08.034

Sung, J., & Cho, K. (2012). User experiences with augmented reality advertising applications: Focusing on perceived values and telepresence based on the experiential learning theory. *Human Centric Technology and Service in Smart Space*, *182*, 9–15. doi:10.1007/978-94-007-5086-9_2

Sun, H., Mohsin, M., Alharthi, M., & Abbas, Q. (2020). Measuring environmental sustainability performance of South Asia. *Journal of Cleaner Production*, *251*, 119519. doi:10.1016/j.jclepro.2019.119519

Sun, Y., Mirza, N., Qadeer, A., & Hsueh, H. P. (2021). Connectedness between oil and agricultural commodity prices during tranquil and volatile period. Is crude oil a victim indeed? *Resources Policy*, *72*, 102131. Advance online publication. doi:10.1016/j.resourpol.2021.102131

Surty, M., Yasseen, Y., & And Padia, N. (2018). Trends in integrated reporting: A stateowned company analysis. *Southern African Business Review*, *22*(1), 1–22. doi:10.25159/1998-8125/3841

Sustainable Tourism for Development Guidebook. (2013). *UNWTO*. Retrieved from https://www.e-unwto.org/doi/pdf/10.18111/9789284415496

Sylwester, K. (2001). R&D and economic growth. *Knowledge, Technology & Policy*, *13*(4), 71–84. doi:10.1007/BF02693991

Takalo, T., Tanayama, T., & Toivanen, O. (2013). Estimating the Benefits of Targeted R&D Subsidies. *The Review of Economics and Statistics*, *95*(1), 255–272. doi:10.1162/REST_a_00280

Taleb, N. (2012). Antifragile: Things that gain from disorder. Academic Press.

Talebi, S., & Norouzi, N. (2020). Entropy and exergy analysis and optimization of the VVER nuclear power plant with a capacity of 1000 MW using the firefly optimization algorithm. *Nuclear Engineering and Technology*, *52*(12), 2928–2938. doi:10.1016/j.net.2020.05.011

Taleb, N. (2012). *Antifragile: Things that gain from disorder*. Library of Congress Cataloguing-in-Publication Data. Nassim Nicholas Taleb.

Tebaldi, E. (2011). The Determinants of High tech Exports. A Panel Data Analysis. *Atlantic Economic Journal*, *39*(4), 349–353. doi:10.100711293-011-9288-9

Teodora, M. I., & Marinela, S. R. (2011). An Investigation of Longrun Relationship Between Economic Growth, Investment and Export in Romania. *Annals of Faculty of Economics*, *1*(1), 316–321.

The Open Group. (2011a). *The TOGAF Framework*. The Open Group.

The Open Group. (2011b). *Security Architecture and the ADM*. The Open Group. https://pubs.opengroup.org/architecture/togaf91-doc/arch/chap21.html

The Uniform Law Commissioners. (2015). *Electronic Transactions Act Summary*. The Uniform Law Commissioners.

Thomas, P., Reji, A. G., Mathew, A., & Aswin, D. (2020). Stand alone distribution feeder inter area fault location identification system for Indian utility. In *Proceedings of the 2020 IEEE 5th International Conference on Computing Communication and Automation (ICCCA)* (vol. 30–31, pp. 258–262). 10.1109/ICCCA49541.2020.9250916

Thompson, R. (2009). *Tax policy and the Globalisation of R&D*. The Australian National University Working Papers in Trade and Development, Working Paper No. 2009/03.

Thuriaux-Alemán, B., Eagar, R., & Johansson, A. (2013). Getting a better return on your innovation investment - Results of the 8th Arthur D. Little global innovation excellence study. Technology and Innovation Management, 1-24.

Tidy, J. (n.d.). Sephora+ModiFace Launch The World's First 3D Augmented Reality Mirror in Milan. *PRWeb*. Retrieved from http://www.prweb.com/pdfdownload/11881669.pdf

Tiwari, D. (2017). *Architecture Development Method*. The Open Group. https://pubs.opengroup.org/architecture/togaf9-doc/arch/chap05.html

Toda, H. Y., & Yamamoto, T. (1995). Statistical inference in vector autoregressions with possibly integrated processes. *Journal of Econometrics*, *66*(1-2), 225–250. doi:10.1016/0304-4076(94)01616-8

Toffel, M. W., & Horvath, A. (2004). Environmental Implications Of Wireless Technologies: News Delivery and Business Meetings. *Environmental Science & Technology*, *38*(11), 2961–2970. doi:10.1021/es035035o PMID:15224723

Tondeur, J., Pareja-Roblin, N., van Braak, J., Voogt, J., & Prestridge, S. (2017a). Preparing beginning teachers for technology integration in education: Ready for take-off? *Technology, Pedagogy and Education*, *26*(2), 157–177. doi:10.1080/1475939X.2016.1193556

Tonta, Y. (1999). Bilgi Toplumu ve Bilgi Teknolojisi. *Türk Kütüphaneciliği*, *13*(4), 363-375. http://www.tk.org.tr/index.php/TK/article/view/910/904

Trad, A. (2021a). *The Business Transformation Framework and Enterprise Architecture Framework for Managers in Business Innovation: The Alignment of Enterprise Asset Management and Enterprise Architecture Methodologies*. IGI Global. doi:10.4018/978-1-5225-8229-8.ch001

Trad, A. (2021a). The Security Management Concept (SMC). *STF Conference*. Turkey.

Trad, A. (2021b). *The Business Transformation Framework and Enterprise Architecture Framework: Organisational Asset Management in the Lebanese Context*. IGI Global. doi:10.4018/978-1-7998-4459-4.ch030

Trad, A., & Kalpić, D. (2020a). *Using Applied Mathematical Models for Business Transformation*. IGI Global. doi:10.4018/978-1-7998-1009-4

Trad, A., & Kalpić, D. (2020b). *An Applied Mathematical Model for Business Transformation and Enterprise Architecture-The Holistic Global Security Management System (HGSMS)*. IGI Global.

Trad, A., & Kalpić, D. (2021a). *Business Transformation and Enterprise Architecture: The Holistic Project Asset Management Concept (HPAMC)*. IGI Global.

Tragesser, M. (2022). *January Southern Border Encounters Increased by 321 Percent from Trump's Final Full Year*. Retrieved from https://www.immigrationreform.com/2022/02/17/border-data-hardly-good-news-immigrationreform-com/

Tran, K., & Nguyen, P. V. (2020). Corporate Social Responsibility: Findings from the Vietnamese Paint Industry. *Sustainability, 12*(3), 1044. doi:10.3390u12031044

Troster, V. (2018). Testing for Granger-causality in quantiles. *Econometric Reviews, 37*(8), 850–866. doi:10.1080/07474938.2016.1172400

Troster, V., Shahbaz, M., & Uddin, G. S. (2018). Renewable energy, oil prices, and economic activity: A Granger-causality in quantiles analysis. *Energy Economics, 70*, 440–452. doi:10.1016/j.eneco.2018.01.029

Tsaurai, K., & Chimbo, B. (2019). The impact of information and communication technology on carbon emissions in emerging markets. *International Journal of Energy Economics and Policy, 9*(4), 320–326. doi:10.32479/ijeep.7677

Tuna, K., Kayacan, E., & Bektaş, H. (2015). The relationship between research & development expenditures and economic growth: The case of Turkey. *Procedia: Social and Behavioral Sciences, 195*, 501–507. doi:10.1016/j.sbspro.2015.06.255

Tüpraş Çevresel Sürdürülebilirlik Raporu. (n.d.). https://www.tupras.com.tr/

Turedi, S. (2013). Bilgi ve iletişim teknolojilerinin ekonomik büyümeye etkisi: Gelişmiş ve gelişmekte olan ülkeler için panel veri analizi. *Gümüşhane Üniversitesi Sosyal Bilimler Elektronik Dergisi, 4*(7), 298–322.

Türedi, S. (2016). The relationship between R&D expenditures, patent applications and growth: A dynamic panel causality analysis for OECD countries. *Anadolu University Journal of Social Sciences, 16*(1), 39–48.

Türkiye, C. (2012). *Mercedes Benz'den araç aksesuarları için artırılmış gerçeklik uygulaması*. Retrieved from https://www.campaigntr.com/mercedes-benzden-arac-aksesuarlari-icin-artirilmis-gerceklik-uygulamasi/

Tüylüoğlu, Ş., & Saraç, Ş. (2012). Gelişmiş ve Gelişmekte olan Ülkelerde İnovasyonun Belirleyicileri: Ampirik Bir Analiz. *Eskişehir Osmangazi Üniversitesi İİBF Dergisi, 7*(1), 39–74.

U.S. Energy Information Administration. (2021). *Petroleum & Other Liquids*. https://www.eia.gov/petroleum/data.php

Ulucak, R., & Khan, S. U. D. (2020). Does information and communication technology affect CO2 mitigation under the pathway of sustainable development during the mode of globalization? *Sustainable Development, 28*(4), 857–867. doi:10.1002d.2041

UNHCR Global Trends. (2020). *Figures at a Glance*. Retrieved from https://www.unhcr.org/figures-at-a-glance.html

United Nations Office for the Coordination of Humanitarian Affairs. (2019). *Global Humanitarian Overview 2019*. Retrieved from https://www.unocha.org/sites/unocha/files/GHO2019.pdf

Unwin, D. (2013). *Security Architecture-Enterprise Architecture*. Business Aspect.

UNWTO. (2020). *International tourism growth continues to outpace the global economy*. World Tourism Organization. Retrieved from https://www.unwto.org/international-tourism-growth-continues-to-outpace-the-economy

UNWTO. (n.d.). *International tourism and COVID-19*. World Tourism Organization. Retrieved from: https://www.unwto.org/international-tourism-and-covid-19

Uribe, J. M., & Guillen, M. (2020). *Quantile regression for cross-sectional and time series data: Applications in energy markets using R*. Springer Nature. doi:10.1007/978-3-030-44504-1

Usman, M. (2017). Impact of high-tech exports on economic growth: Empirical evidence from pakistan. *Journal on Innovation and Sustainability, 8*(1), 91–105. doi:10.24212/2179-3565.2017v8i1p91-105

Uysal, H. A. (2010). *ICT Development and Economic Growth: An Analysis of Cointegrating and Causal Relationships with Panel Data Approach* (Unpublished Master Thesis). School of Architecture and the Built Environment,Royal Institute of Technology, Stockholm, Sweden.

Van Huis, A., & Oonincx, D. G. (2017). The environmental sustainability of insects as food and feed. A review. *Agronomy for Sustainable Development, 37*(5), 1–14. doi:10.100713593-017-0452-8

Van Laar, E., Van Deursen, A. J. A. M., Van Dijk, J. A. G. M., & Haan, J. (2017). The relation between 21st-century skills and digital skills: A systematic literature review. *Computers in Human Behavior, 72*, 577–588. doi:10.1016/j.chb.2017.03.010

Varshney, D., Roy, D., & Meenakshi, J. V. (2020). Impact of COVID-19 on agricultural markets: Assessing the roles of commodity characteristics, disease caseload and market reforms. *Indian Economic Review, 55*(1), 83–103. doi:10.100741775-020-00095-1 PMID:32863419

Veblen, T. (1909). The Limitations of Marginal Utility. *Journal of Political Economy, 17*(9), 620-636.

Veblen, T. (1899). *The Theory of the Leisure Class: An Economic Study of Institutions*. The Macmillan Company.

Veblen, T. (1919). *The Place of Science in Modern Civilization and Other Essays*. Huebsch.

Veblen, T. (1946). *The Instinct of Workmanship: And the State of the Industrial Arts*. The Viking Press.

Verbič, M., Majcen, B., Ivanova, O., & Čok, M. (2011). R&D and Economic Growth in Slovenia: A Dynamic General Equilibrium Approach with Endogenous Growth. *Panoeconomicus, 1*(1), 67–89. doi:10.2298/PAN1101067V

Viswesvaran, C., & Ones, D. S. (2017). Job performance: Assessment issues in personnel selection. In A. Evers, N. Anderson, & O. Voskuijl (Eds.), *The Blackwell handbook of personnel selection* (pp. 354–375). Wiley. doi:10.1002/9781405164221.ch16

Vogel, A., & Wagner, J. (2010). Higher productivity in importing German manufacturing firms: Self-selection, learning from importing, or both? *Review of World Economics, 145*(4), 641–665. doi:10.100710290-009-0031-4

Voogt, J. M., Fisser, P., Pareja Roblin, N., Tondeur, J., & Van Braak, J. (2013). Technological pedagogical content knowledge - a review of the literature. *Journal of Computer Assisted Learning, 29*(2), 109–121. doi:10.1111/j.1365-2729.2012.00487.x

Vulić, I., Prodanović, R., & Tot, I. (2019). An Example of a Methodology for Developing the Security of a Distributed Business System. In *Advances in Economics, Business and Management Research*, volume 108. *5th IPMA SENET Project Management Conference (SENET 2019)*. Atlantis Press. 10.2991enet-19.2019.34

Waithe, K., Lorde, T., & Francis, B. (2011). Export-led growth: A case study of Mexico. *International Journal of Business. Human Technology, 1*(1), 33–44.

Wang, C.-H., Chiang, Y.-C., & Wang, M.-J. (2015). Evaluation of an augmented reality embedded on-line shopping system. *Procedia Manufacturing, 3*, 5624–5630. doi:10.1016/j.promfg.2015.07.766

Wang, D. H. M., Yu, T. H. K., & Liu, H. Q. (2013). Heterogeneous effect of high-tech industrial R&D spending on economic growth. *Journal of Business Research, 66*(10), 1990–1993. doi:10.1016/j.jbusres.2013.02.023

Wang, J.-C., & Tsai, K.-H. (1998). The Impact of Research and Development Promotion Schemes in the Taiwanese Electronic Component Industry. *R&D Management, 28*(2), 119–124. doi:10.1111/1467-9310.00088

Wang, J., Shao, W., & Kim, J. (2020). Analysis of the impact of COVID-19 on the correlations between crude oil and agricultural futures. *Chaos, Solitons, and Fractals*, *136*, 109896. Advance online publication. doi:10.1016/j.chaos.2020.109896 PMID:32421108

Water Scarcity. (n.d.). *Definitions.net.* Retrieved January 31, 2022, from https://www.definitions.net/definition/Water+scarcity

Werz, M., & Conley, L. (2012). *Climate Change Migration and Conflict: Addressing complex crisis scenarios in the 21st Century.* Center for American Progress Climate Migration Series. Retrieved from https://cdn.americanprogress.org/wp-ent/uploads/issues/2012/01/pdf/climate_migration.pdf?_ga=2.85303775.772595288.1641935207-813556300.1641595164

White House. (2021, October). *Report on the Impact of Climate Change on Migration.* Retrieved from https://www.whitehouse.gov/wp-content/uploads/2021/10/Report-on-the-Impact-of-Climate-Change-on-Migration.pdf

Woehr, D. J. (2008). On the relationship between job performance and ratings of job performance: What do we really know? *Industrial and Organizational Psychology: Perspectives on Science and Practice*, *1*(2), 161–166. doi:10.1111/j.1754-9434.2008.00031.x

Wooldridge, J. M. (2012). *Introductory econometrics: A modern approach.* Cengage Learning.

Wooldridge, J. M. (2010). *Econometric Analysis of Cross Section and Panel Data* (2nd ed.). The MIT Press.

Wooldridge, J. M. (2010). *Econometric analysis of cross section and panel data.* MIT Press.

World Bank. (2021a). *CO2 emissions (metric tons per capita).* https://data.worldbank.org/indicator/EN.ATM.CO2E.PC

World Bank. (2021a). *GDP per capita growth (annual %).* https://data.worldbank.org/indicator/NY.GDP.PCAP.KD.ZG

World Bank. (2021b). *Individuals using the Internet (% of population).* https://data.worldbank.org/indicator/IT.NET.USER.ZS

World Bank. (2021b). *R&D expenditure (% of GDP).* https://data.worldbank.org/indicator/GB.XPD.RSDV.GD.ZS

World Bank. (2021c). *Mobile cellular subscriptions (per 100 people).* https://data.worldbank.org/indicator/IT.CEL.SETS.P2

World Commission on Environment and Development. (1987). *Our Common Future (BrundlandReport).* https://www.are.admin.ch/are/en/home/media/publications/sustainabledevelopment/brundtland-report.html

World Travel and Tourism Council. (n.d.). *'Safe Travels': Global Protocols & Stamp for the New Normal.* Retrieved from https://wttc.org/COVID-19/SafeTravels-Global-Protocols-Stamp

WWF International. (2013). *WWF - Coca-Cola Arctic Home Campaign - Augmented Reality | WWF.* Youtube. Retrieved from https://www.youtube.com/watch?v=h2Jg8ryVk1k&list=RDCMUC5MDIy3yhWDrx0MyDo4QmYg https://www.webtekno.com/sektorel/domestos-sanal-gerceklik-reklami-h7409.html

Xiaohong, C. (2011). *Research on E-Commerce Transaction Cost-Benefit Characteristics and Evaluation Approaches.* Management and Service Science (MASS), *2011 International Conference*, Wuhan. China.

Xu, X. (2009). *Introduction to Smart Grid.* China Electric Power Press.

Yahya, M., Ghosh, S., Kanjilal, K., Dutta, A., & Uddin, G. S. (2020). Evaluation of cross-quantile dependence and causality between non-ferrous metals and clean energy indexes. *Energy*, *202*, 117777. Advance online publication. doi:10.1016/j.energy.2020.117777

Yang, C. H., Huang, C. H., & Hou, T. C. T. (2012). Tax Incentives and R&D Activity: Firm-Level Evidence from Taiwan. *Research Policy*, *41*(9), 1578–1588. doi:10.1016/j.respol.2012.04.006

Yang, F. (2017). The Positive Influence of High-tech Product Export on Economic Growth in Liaoning Province. *Journal of Simulation*, *5*(4), 7–9.

Yaoyuneyong, G., Foster, J., Johnson, E., & Johnson, D. (2016). Augmented reality marketing: Consumer preferences and attitudes toward hypermedia print ads. *Journal of Interactive Advertising*, *16*(1), 16–30. doi:10.1080/15252019.2015.1125316

Yapraklı, S. (2007). *Ticari Ve Finansal Dışa Açıklık ile Ekonomik Büyüme Arasındaki İlişki: Türkiye Üzerine Bir Uygulama. Istanbul University Econometrics and Statistics e-Journal, (5), 67-89.*

Yeşilorman, M., & Firdevs, K. O. Ç. (2014). Bilgi toplumunun teknolojik temelleri üzerine eleştirel bir bakış. *Fırat Üniversitesi Sosyal Bilimler Dergisi*, *24*(1), 117–133. doi:10.18069/fusbed.72486

Yilanci, V., & Bozoklu, Ş. (2014). Price and trade volume relationship in Turkish stock market: A time-varying asymmetric causality analysis. *Ege Academic Review*, *14*(2), 211–220.

Yilanci, V., & Kilci, E. N. (2021). The role of economic policy uncertainty and geopolitical risk in predicting prices of precious metals: Evidence from a time-varying bootstrap causality test. *Resources Policy*, *72*, 102039. Advance online publication. doi:10.1016/j.resourpol.2021.102039

Yildiz, U. (2017). BRICS Ülkeleri ve Türkiye'de Yüksek Teknoloji İhracatı ve Ekonomik Büyüme İlişkisinin Panel Veri Analizi. *Dumlupınar Üniversitesi Sosyal Bilimler Dergisi*, *53*, 26–34.

Yokota, K., & Tomohara, A. (2010). Modeling FDI-Induced Technology Spillovers. *The International Trade Journal*, *24*(1), 5–34. doi:10.1080/08853900903442897

Yücel, M. A. (2021). Çevresel Sürdürülebilirliğin Değerlendirilmesi: Dinamik Mekânsal Panel Veri Yaklaşımı. *Bilgi Sosyal Bilimler Dergisi*, *23*(1), 53-90. Retrieved from https://dergipark.org.tr/en/pub/bilgisosyal/issue/60370/908722

Yuen, S. C. Y., Yaoyuneyong, G., & Johnson, E. (2011). Augmented reality: An overview and five directions for AR in education. *Journal of Educational Technology Development and Exchange*, *4*(1).

Zachariadis, M. (2003). R&D, Innovation, and Technological Progress: A Test of the Schumpeterian Framework without Scale Effects. *The Canadian Journal of Economics. Revue Canadienne d'Economique*, *36*(3), 566–686. doi:10.1111/1540-5982.t01-2-00003

Zachariadis, M. (2004). R&D-induced Growth in the OECD? *Review of Development Economics*, *8*(3), 423–439. doi:10.1111/j.1467-9361.2004.00243.x

Zachary, W., Ryder, J., Hicinbothom, J., & Bracken, K. (1997). The use of executable cognitive models in simulation-based intelligent embedded training. *Proceeding of the Human Factors and Ergonomics Society Annual Meeting*, 41(2), 1118-1122. 10.1177/107118139704100287

Zahonogo, P. (2016). Trade and economic growth in developing countries: Evidence from SubSaharan Africa. *Journal of Africa Trade*, *3*(1-2), 41–56. doi:10.1016/j.joat.2017.02.001

Zaman, K., Khan, H. U. R., Ahmad, M., & Aamir, A. (2018). Research productivity and economic growth: A policy lesson learnt from across the globe. *Indian Economic Review*, *22*(3), 627–641.

Zavaleta, A., & Kaplan, M. A. (2015). The Tragedy of Unaccompanied Child Immigrants to the U.S.-Mexico Border 2014. In Yet More Studies in Rio Grande Valley History (Vol. 13, pp. 249-271). The U.T.B. Regional History Series, The University of Texas at Brownsville. Retrieved from file:///C:/Users/drmka/Desktop/Mitchell%20Kaplan%20PhD%20journal%20articles%20and%20textbook%20chapters%202021)/The%20Tragedy%20of%20Unaccompanied%20Child%20Immigrants%20to%20the%20U.S.-Mexico%20Border%202014.pdf

Zavaleta, A., & Kaplan, M. A. (2018). Immigrant Caging on the Texas-Mexico Border. In *New Studies in Rio Grande Valley History* (Vol. 16, pp. 341-400). The U.T.B. Regional History Series, The University of Texas Rio Grande Valley. Retrieved from https://riograndeguardian.com/zavaleta-kaplan-immigrant-caging-on-the-texas-mexico-border/

Zhang, Y. (2019, September). The Role of Precision Agriculture. Resource. *Resource Magazine, 26*(6), 9-9. https://elibrary.asabe.org/abstract.asp?aid=50990

Zhang, C., & Liu, C. (2015). The impact of ICT industry on CO_2 emissions: A regional analysis in China. *Renewable & Sustainable Energy Reviews*, *44*, 12–19. doi:10.1016/j.rser.2014.12.011

Zhang, D., & Cui, X. (2018). Research on the Open Development and Industrial Security of China's High-tech Industry. *International Trade*, *12*(1), 19–22.

Zhao, X., Hwang, B., & Low, S. (2013). *Exploring Critical Success Factors for Enterprise Risk Management in Chinese Construction Firms*. Academic Press.

Zhou, F., Duh, H. B.-L., & Billinghurst, M. (2008). Trends in augmented reality tracking, interaction and display: A review of ten years of ISMAR. *7th IEEE/ACM International Symposium on Mixed and Augmented Reality (ISMAR).*

Zhou, X., Zhou, D., Wang, Q., & Su, B. (2019). How information and communication technology drives carbon emissions: a sector-level analysis for China. *Energy Economics, 81*(C), 380-392. doi:10.1016/j.eneco.2019.04.014

Zhou, G., & Luo, Z. (2018). Higher education ınput, technological innovation, and economic growth in China. *Sustainability*, *10*(8), 1–15. doi:10.3390u10082615

Zhou, K., Fu, C., & Yang, S. (2016). Big data driven smart energy management: From big data to big insights. *Renewable & Sustainable Energy Reviews*, *56*, 215–225. doi:10.1016/j.rser.2015.11.050

About the Contributors

Yilmaz Bayar awarded the PhD degree in the field of Economics in Istanbul University Institute of Social Sciences in 2012. He worked as an Assistant Professor in the Faculty of Business Administration, Karabuk University during the period September 2012-March 2015 and as an Associate Professor in the Faculty of Economics and Administrative Sciences, Usak University during the period March 2015-October 2020 and now working as a Professor in the Faculty of Economics and Administrative Sciences, Bandirma Onyedi Eylul University, since October 2020.

Mahmut Unsal Sasmaz was awarded the B.A. and M.A. degrees at Usak University and his Ph.D. degree at the Department of Public Finance in Dumlupinar University. He is currently working as an Assistant Professor in the Faculty of Economics and Administrative Sciences in Usak University. His major research interests are financial incentives, fiscal policy and environmental policy.

Omer Faruk Ozturk was born in Afyonkarahisar in 1981. He graduated from the Department of Economics at Erciyes University Faculty of Economics and Administrative Sciences. Completing his master's degree in Economics at Usak University Social Sciences Institute and his Ph.D. degree in the joint Public FInance program of Usak University-Afyon Kocatepe University, the author still serves as a faculty member in the Department of Public Finance at Usak University Faculty of Economics and Administrative Sciences.

* * *

Naib Alakbarov works as an academician at Uşak University/Turkey. After graduating from Dokuz Eylul University in Turkey, he was in Germany for doctoral studies. He mainly make publications in macroeconomic and international economics.

Vildan Ateş is an Assoc. Prof. Dr. in the Management Information Systems Department of Business School at Ankara Yıldırım Beyazıt University in Turkey since March 2017. In 2010, she received her master's degree from the Management Information Systems Department of the Institute of Informatics at Gazi University. She received her Ph.D. degree in 2014 from the same school and the same department. Dr. Ateş worked as an IT Expert at Gazi University from 2009 to 2017. Dr. Ateş is the instructor on undergraduate topics in e-business, production and services management, database management, computer networks and security on graduate topics in management information systems, system analysis and design, qualitative research methods, human computer interaction. Her research interests include information management, IT security and risk management, educational technologies, human computer interaction, and e-commerce. She is married with two children.

Zühre Aydın Yenioğlu received her PhD degree in Management Information Systems from the University of Gazi in 2019. She worked in IT and Energy Transition Department as engineer in the fields of Digital Transformation, IT Project Management, Data Analysis and Database Administrator between 2007-2022. She continues as a lecturer of Database Management Systems and Information Retrieval Systems courses at Yıldırım Beyazıt University, Ankara. She writes and presents widely on issues of database management systems, energy data analysis, energy efficiency, operational research, cybersecurity in critical infrastructures, energy forecasting with machine learning. Aydın Yenioğlu, has been working at Turkey Energy Market Regulatory Authority since 2014.

Esra Doğan received her Bachelor's Degree and PhD in public finance from Ankara University and her Economics master's degree from the University of Essex. She works as an Associate Professor in Eskisehir Osmangazi University Department of Public Finance. She has studies on theoretical and empirical studies on public finance, and is academically interested in geographic information systems, logic and statistics-based empirical studies. She, who has published in national and international journals, has publications on the information society as well as the publications on budget and tax theory.

Yahya Can Dura has completed bachelor education in the field of public finance. He has recieved master's and doctor's degree in the discipline of economics. He has achieved PhD on institutional economics. He is currently working as the vice dean and head of International Trade and Finance department at Istanbul Gelişim University. Yahya Can Dura has academic studies in the fields of planning, local administration financing, institutional economics, economic growth, exports, project planning, public enterprises, development agencies and public administration.

Ummu Saliha Eken İnan received his PhD in Production Management and Marketing from Selcuk University, Institute of Social Sciences. Between 2019-2020, she has worked as a PhD Lecturer in the same school. She has been working as an assistant professor at the Vocational School of Social Sciences since 2020.

Betül Garda awarded the PhD degree in the field of Production Management and Marketing from Selcuk University Social Sciences Institute in 2010. She worked as a lecturer at Selcuk University Social Sciences Vocational School between 1999-2015. She has been working as an Assistant Professor at Selcuk University, Social Sciences Vocational School, in the marketing and advertising department since 2015.

Muhammed Sehid Gorus holds a PhD in economics from Ankara Yıldırım Beyazıt University, Turkey. Currently, he gives lectures as a research assistant in the department of economics at Ankara Yildirim Beyazit University, Turkey. His research interests include energy economics, environmental economics, and applied macroeconomics. He published more than 30 papers/book chapters/books.

Cengizhan Güler is a Research Assistant at Istanbul Gelisim University.

Murat Gündüz graduated from Mugla University, Department of Statistics and Computer Science. He holds a PhD in numerical methods. His main research interests are econometrics and statistical applications. His research interests include Time Series Analysis, Panel Data Analysis, Causality Analysis, Cointegration Analysis, Total Factor Productivity, Financial Development and Financial Globalization. He is an Assoc. Prof. in the Department of Business Administration at Usak University.

Mitchell Alan Kaplan is a certified professional sociological practitioner in New York City. He received his doctorate in Sociology from the City University of New York Graduate Center in 1987. He was also the recipient of a Postdoctoral Research Fellowship from the National Institute on Drug Abuse. Dr. Kaplan has spent the last 33 years of his professional career working as a research scientist and consultant for several non-profit and city government agencies across the social service and public health spectrum. His articles and reviews have been featured in professional journals on substance abuse treatment, vocational rehabilitation, opioid abuse, and chronic pain, healthcare policy, criminal justice reform, global aging, and regional history, as well as academic textbooks, magazines on higher education and cultural healing in the Hispanic community, and in New York newspapers.

Lina Karabetyan completed her undergraduate education in Health Management Department of Faculty of Health Education in University of Marmara. She did master of business administration degree (MBA) in Graduate School of Business of University of Istanbul, and doctor of Administration-Management and Organization in T.R. University of Istanbul Arel. Doctoral thesis is effect of organizational learning, information management and innovation on organizational performance: is an application in service business. There are her scientific publications on management, organization, organizational, behaviour, and information management and innovation fields.

Aysun Karamikli is PhD student at the Institute of Social Sciences, Bandirma Onyedi Eylul University, Turkey. Her main research interests are related to Public Finance, Public Economics, Development Economics, and Environmental Economics.

Onder Ozgur is an Assistant Professor in Economics at Ankara Yıldırım Beyazıt University, Turkey. His research topics include applied macroeconomics, monetary economics, and energy economics.

Mehmet Hilmi Özkaya graduated from İstanbul University, Department of Economics. He was awarded the Phd degree in the field of Economics in Kocaeli University Institute of Social Sciences in 2007. He worked as an Assistant Professor during the period 2010-2016 in the Faculty of Economics and Administrative Sciences Usak University and now working as an Associate Professor in the same University since 2017. His main research interests are international economics and international finance.

Ugur Korkut Pata is a research assistant of economics in the Faculty of Economics and Administrative Sciences at Osmaniye Korkut Ata University in Turkey. He received his Ph.D. degree in 2019 from Karadeniz Technical University in Turkey. His research interests include energy economics, macroeconomics, and econometrics. He has published in a variety of journals indexed in the Web of Science Core Collection such as Ecological Indicators, Energy, Journal of Cleaner Production, Resources Policy, and Renewable Energy.

Funda Hatice Sezgin completed her undergraduate education in Faculty of economics in University of Istanbul. She did master of business administration degree (MBA) in Econometrics of University of Istanbul, and doctor of econometrics in Marmara University. Her research interests are time series analysis, panel data analysis and statistical methods.

Ahmet Tekin received his PhD in public finance from Istanbul University. He works as an Associate Professor in Eskisehir Osmangazi University Department of Public Finance. He has studies on theoretical and empirical studies on public finance, and is academically interested in fiscal law and taxation systems. He, who has published in national and international journals, has publications on the international taxation systems as well as the publications on the national taxation system.

Veli Yılancı is a professor of economics at the Canakkale Onsekiz Mart University, Department of Political Sciences.. His research interests include econometrics applications in environmental economics, energy economics, and tourism demand in developing countries.

Index

www.ingramcontent.com/pod-product-compliance
Lightning Source LLC
LaVergne TN
LVHW060414300926
849162LV00006B/1421